Stalking the U-Boat

New Perspectives on Maritime History and Nautical Archaeology

UNIVERSITY PRESS OF FLORIDA

Florida A&M University, Tallahassee
Florida Atlantic University, Boca Raton
Florida Gulf Coast University, Ft. Myers
Florida International University, Miami
Florida State University, Tallahassee
New College of Florida, Sarasota
University of Central Florida, Orlando
University of Florida, Gainesville
University of North Florida, Jacksonville
University of South Florida, Tampa
University of West Florida, Pensacola

STALKING THE U-BOAT

U.S. Naval Aviation in Europe during World War I

Geoffrey L. Rossano

Foreword by James C. Bradford and Gene Allen Smith

University Press of Florida
Gainesville · Tallahassee · Tampa · Boca Raton
Pensacola · Orlando · Miami · Jacksonville · Ft. Myers · Sarasota

Copyright 2010 by Geoffrey L. Rossano
Published in the United States of America
All rights reserved

First cloth printing, 2010
First paperback printing, 2021

26 25 24 23 22 21   6 5 4 3 2 1

Library of Congress Cataloging-in-Publication Data
Rossano, Geoffrey Louis.
Stalking the U-boat: U.S. naval aviation in Europe during World War I/Geoffrey L. Rossano; foreword by James C. Bradford and Gene Allen Smith.
p. cm.
Includes bibliographical references and index.
ISBN 9780813034881 (cloth : alk. paper) | ISBN 9780813068657 (pbk.)
1. World War, 1914–1918–Naval operations, American. 2. World War, 1914–1918–Aerial operations, American. 3. United States. Navy—History—World War, 1914–1918. 4. United States. Navy—Aviation—History—20th century. 5. Anti-submarine warfare—United States—History—20th century. 6. World War, 1914–1918—Campaigns—Atlantic Ocean. I. Title.
D589.U6R66 2010
940.4'5169–dc22   2010015135

The University Press of Florida is the scholarly publishing agency for the State University System of Florida, comprising Florida A&M University, Florida Atlantic University, Florida Gulf Coast University, Florida International University, Florida State University, New College of Florida, University of Central Florida, University of Florida, University of North Florida, University of South Florida, and University of West Florida.

University Press of Florida
2046 NE Waldo Road
Suite 2100
Gainesville, FL 32609
http://upress.ufl.edu

This book is for my girls:
Joan, Margaret, and Chloe

CONTENTS

List of Illustrations	ix
List of Abbreviations	xi
Foreword	xiii
Preface and Acknowledgments	xvii
Introduction	1
1. The First Aeronautic Detachment	5
2. Progress Report: September 1917–March 1918	43
3. Under the Gun: NAS Dunkirk 1917–1918	55
4. The French Coastal Unit	81
5. Progress Report: March–September 1918	123
6. Spinning the Spider Web: Naval Aviation in England	149
7. The Irish Bases	208
8. On Duty, Off Duty: The Work and Life of the Station	231
9. Gasbags: Development of the Navy LTA Program	261
10. Sunny Italy: Naval Aviation in the Mediterranean	285
11. The Northern Bombing Group	314
12. Till It's Over, Over There: September 1918–April 1919	345
Appendixes	371
Notes	377
Bibliography	409
Index	415

ILLUSTRATIONS

All illustrations appear after page 185.

Maps

1. NAS facilities in France
2. NAS facilities in Great Britain
3. NAS facilities in Italy

Photographs

1. First Aeronautic Detachment ready for departure from Florida
2. First Aeronautic Detachment personnel at Tours
3. LCdr. John Callan at Moutchic
4. On the Beach, Moutchic, October 1917
5. "Main Street," Moutchic, 1918
6. Capt. Hutch I. Cone
7. Launching aircraft at NAS Dunkirk
8. NAS Dunkirk officers and guests
9. NAS Brest assembly and repair facility
10. NAS Le Croisic
11. NAS Arcachon hangars
12. Pigeon lofts at NAS Arcachon
13. NAS L'Aber Vrach during early construction phase
14. Launching an HS-1L flying boat at NAS L'Aber Vrach
15. Ensigns Waters and Dillon aloft at NAS Tréguier
16. Tellier aircraft destroyed during takeoff at NAS Le Croisic
17. LCdr. Kenneth Whiting and NAS Killingholme complement
18. Short patrol bomber at NAS Killingholme
19. Armament of an H-16 flying boat
20. NAS Queenstown under construction
21. Launching an H-16 at NAS Queenstown
22. NAS Castletownbere

23. The American "beach" at Bolsena
24. Training mishap at Bolsena
25. The officers of NAS Porto Corsini
26. Dirigible hangar under construction at NAS Gujan
27. Dirigible AT-13 getting under way at NAS Paimboeuf
28. NAS Moutchic pets
29. NAS Paimboeuf football team
30. Caproni bomber taking off at Milan
31. David Ingalls, summer 1918
32. Northern Bombing Group assembly and repair facility at Eastleigh
33. Seaplane hangars at Pauillac
34. Capt. Thomas Craven and staff at Brest headquarters
35. Sailors at NAS Moutchic lined up for demobilization inspection

ABBREVIATIONS

A&R	Assembly and Repair
AEF	American Expeditionary Force
ASW	Antisubmarine Warfare
AT	Astra-Torres (dirigible)
CM	Chalais Meudon (dirigible)
CMB	Coastal Motor Boat
CNO	Chief of Naval Operations
CO	Commanding Officer
DD	Donnet-Denhaut
FBA	Franco-British Aviation
HD	Hanriot Dupont
HTA	Heavier than Air
KB	Kite Balloon
LTA	Lighter than Air
NAS	Naval Air Station
NBG	Northern Bombing Group
NRFC	Naval Reserve Flying Corps
OIC	Officer in Charge
RAF	Royal Air Force
RFC	Royal Flying Corps
RN	Royal Navy
RNAS	Royal Naval Air Service, Royal Naval Air Station
USNAFFS	United States Naval Aviation Forces Foreign Service
VZ	Vedette Zodiac (dirigible)

FOREWORD

Water is unquestionably the most important natural feature on earth. By volume the world's oceans compose 99 percent of the planet's living space; in fact, the surface of the Pacific Ocean alone is larger than that of the total land bodies. Water is as vital to life as air. Indeed, to test whether the other planets or the moon can sustain life, NASA looks for signs of water. The story of human development is inextricably linked to the oceans, seas, lakes, and rivers that dominate the earth's surface.

The University Press of Florida's series New Perspectives on Maritime History and Nautical Archaeology is devoted to exploring the significance of the earth's water while providing lively and important books that cover the spectrum of maritime history and nautical archaeology broadly defined. The series includes works that focus on the role of canals, rivers, lakes, and oceans in history; on the economic, military, and political use of those waters; and upon the people, communities, and industries that support maritime endeavors. Limited by neither geography nor time, volumes in the series contribute to the overall understanding of maritime history and can be read with profit by both general readers and specialists.

Historians have devoted considerable attention to the history of military and naval aviation, but until the publication of this volume there has been no book-length examination of U.S. Navy aviation during World War I. Geoffrey L. Rossano admirably fills this lacuna with his detailed examination of how the Navy forged an air service between 1917 and 1919.

The foundation upon which the Navy built its air arm was very weak. At the outbreak of war in Europe, the Navy possessed only 54 planes, most of which were technologically obsolete; the first plane had been purchased as early as 1911. The Navy stationed these aircraft at rudimentary airfields, the most important of which was the training facility at Pensacola, Florida, established in 1914. Of the fewer than three hundred pilots and naval personnel holding aviation ratings, many also held other assignments. The Navy Department divided responsibility for aircraft procurement, maintenance, and armaments among several of the semi-autonomous bureaus, none of whose heads reported to the Office of Naval Aeronautics (established in 1914). Advances made by European air forces between the outbreak of war in 1914 and the American entry in 1917 placed the United States even further behind in virtually all aspects of air power. Yet by the end of the war, U.S. naval aviation had been transformed in size, expanded its missions, and laid the basis for growth during the 1920s and 1930s that placed the U.S. Navy in the forefront among the leading maritime air forces of the world.

This transformation forms the basis of Rossano's study, the focus of which is on developments in Europe, because that is where the Navy met and solved the enormous organizational, logistical, personnel, and operational challenges posed by the war. This is not a top-down institutional study but rather one from the multiple perspectives of commanding officers, aviators, and enlisted personnel, not just from the leaders who planned strategy and the pilots who flew the missions. It also focuses on the organizers who got the men and machines across the Atlantic, established the bases—creating American towns in England, France, Ireland, and Italy from which they operated—and developed the logistical system to keep them supplied with all the necessities—food, fuel, arms, and equipment—to sustain operations. Rossano analyses those operations in terms of both doctrine developed and effectiveness.

Rossano also puts a human face on the entire undertaking, describing the boredom of long patrols, the excitement of bombing raids and dogfights, leisure activities on base, and the difficulties encountered working within a tradition-bound navy. Delving into the organization of the civilian bureaucracy as it rapidly expanded in wartime America, he also explains the similar challenges that faced the U.S. Army as it prepared to fight on the Western Front.

Rossano concludes that naval aviation had less impact on either the conduct or outcome of World War I than the reverse. That is, he describes the obstacles that naval aviation faced during the war and how those challenges helped shape the service more so than naval aviation shaped the outcome of the war. Indeed, the war in Europe formed the foundation upon which naval aviation built during the interwar years. The 1921 establishment of the Bureau of Aeronautics, with control of its own personnel, weapons development, and the 1926 establishment of the office of Assistant Secretary of the Navy for Aeronautics, all attest to both the importance achieved by naval aviation during the war and to its future promise. Guided by wartime experiences, the leaders of these organizations deftly guided naval aviation through the 1920s—a decade during which few Americans believed the nation would ever fight another war—and the 1930s—a decade of burdening economic depression—to mould an institution capable of meeting with comparative ease and efficiency the even greater challenges of the two-ocean world war from 1939 to 1945. This book details an important subject, comprehensively researched, thoroughly analyzed, and clearly explained, from which historians, analysts, and current policy makers can surely profit.

James C. Bradford
Gene Allen Smith
Series Editors

PREFACE AND ACKNOWLEDGMENTS

The seeds of this project were planted many years ago. While preparing the World War I correspondence of naval aviator Kenneth MacLeish for publication, I found myself in need of a concise, detailed study of the Navy's aeronautic efforts in Europe in 1917–1919. Every time I requested such a volume, however, I was told it didn't exist. Right then I decided to write the book myself when time became available. My perhaps overly ambitious idea received a great boost from three distinguished historians who kindly took me under their wing: Dean Allard, then director of Naval History at the Naval Historical Center, his eventual successor, William Dudley, and William "Bill" Still. With their enthusiastic support I received a Vice Admiral Hooper research grant from the Center, which underwrote the first stages of the research process. In recent years the Salisbury School in Salisbury, Connecticut, has provided generous additional travel and research funding.

Researching a subject like this is a lengthy and circuitous journey, and my efforts took me to Washington, D.C., Florida, Ireland, London, and Paris. I also enjoyed locating and visiting the long-abandoned sites of the Navy's World War I stations throughout Ireland, England, and France. Professional staff on two continents proved invaluable in tracking down sources. In Europe, special thanks go to librarians and archivists at the Cork and Wexford County (Ireland) Libraries, the National Archives in Kew, England, and the Service Historique de la Marine at Chateau Vergennes, Paris. In the United States the various professionals at the Library of Congress and the Naval History and Heritage Command could not have been more helpful. The same was true at the Emil Buehler Library at the National Naval Aviation Museum in Pensacola. Richard von Doenhoff at the National Archives provided invaluable access and guidance in sorting through the documents held there, greatly assisted by Barry Zerby.

The volume of material documenting the aviation campaign of 1917–1919 is staggering, filling many hundreds of feet of archives shelving, but a few sources proved central to the task. Official records include flight reports, training manuals, blueprints, photographs, headquarters memos, station logs, daily and weekly schedules, inspection reports, and a hundred other types of paperwork familiar to any member of a large, military bureaucracy. The manuscript history of operations in France prepared at the direction of Capt. Thomas Craven in 1919, though containing some errors, is a monumental work. Similarly, Clifford Lord's enormous administrative history of naval aviation 1898–1939 identified the players, gathered the documents, and limned the outlines of organizational and policy efforts. Published and unpublished letters, memoirs, and journals of the participants proved illuminating and inspiring. In addition, visiting the largely abandoned sites of the former Naval Air Stations in Ireland, England, and France provided a perspective not otherwise available. Finally, Reginald Arthur's *Contact!* gathered together biographical and service-related details of the Navy's first 2,000 aviators, an extraordinary achievement.

As the manuscript began to assume shape, several individuals generously read various drafts and offered helpful corrections and advice, including my mentor of many years, Roger Lotchin, Dwight Messimer, Richard Curtis, William Still, Lt. Col. (Dr.) John Abbatiello, and William Trimble. They all offered encouragement and saved me from many gaffes. I appreciate the diligence of the copy editor, Patterson Lamb, who tightened the manuscript and raised questions that needed to be asked. Any remaining errors are my own.

Finally, I would like to thank my girls, Joan, Margaret, and Chloe, who waited patiently while I tapped away at the word processor, wished me bon voyage as I set out on my research trips, and welcomed me home at the end of my journeys. This book is dedicated to them.

INTRODUCTION

With twin Rolls-Royce motors roaring just above his head, Ens. Ashton "Tex" Hawkins from Carlsbad, New Mexico, wrestled his aging H-12 flying boat higher and higher through the impenetrable rain, mist, and fog, clawing his way to a patrol altitude of 10,000 feet. Hawkins, copilot Lt.(jg) George Lawrence from New York City, and the remainder of the flight crew of four departed NAS Killingholme on the banks of the Humber estuary in northeastern England at 10:30 in the evening of August 5, 1918, in search of marauding German zeppelins. About midnight, after a cold, wet climb, they rose above the dense clouds into clear air, somewhere over the North Sea. Completely alone in the dark sky, they cruised for hours, sometimes mistaking distant, winking stars for engine exhausts and small, scudding clouds for enemy airships. On and on they flew in the darkness, the powerful motors thundering in the silent heavens, but without any accurate idea of their position. Primitive navigational aids offered little help. Eventually, the rising sun illuminated an unbroken expanse of brilliant white clouds stretching everywhere to the horizon. By now running low on fuel, Hawkins began a blind descent toward the North Sea, emerging from the clouds only 200 feet above the forbidding gray water. Still hampered by fog, he headed west until the stone breakwater at Tynemouth loomed out of the mist. The young pilot quickly set the flying boat down with its tanks almost dry, 150 miles from his home station, after an all-night patrol covering over 400 miles. All things considered, it had been a successful mission. Though they failed to find any zeppelins, Hawkins and his crew suffered no mechanical breakdowns, avoided a forced landing at sea, and returned safely home, wet, cold, and tired. Not all of their compatriots would be so lucky.[1]

Patrols like this, and hundreds more, formed the heart of a military innovation destined to remake the face of warfare. Conceived in home waters as far back as 1910, modern naval aviation endured its protracted birth "Over There." In the cold, foggy expanse of the North Sea, English Channel, and Bay of Biscay, aeronautic pioneers built a new branch of the Navy one patrol, one adventure, one mishap at a time. Between the declaration of war in April 1917 and the Armistice just 19 months later, naval aviation literally invented itself, despite initial headquarters apathy, virtually nonexistent planning, technological backwardness, and crippling equipment and manpower shortages. Reluctantly shifting course as the war progressed, the U.S. Navy Department marshaled resources for the emerging combat arm by initiating massive training and building programs in the United States; negotiating contracts for thousands of aircraft, engines, and necessary equipment; and ultimately dispatching hundreds of pilots, nearly 20,000 bluejackets, and 500 warplanes to Europe.

Long before training and construction programs yielded tangible results, Navy flyers jumped into a fight for which they were completely unprepared. In fact, when Congress declared war, naval aviation scarcely existed. Looking back from the early 1920s, W. Atlee Edwards, who served during the war as aide for aviation under Adm. William S. Sims, the commander of United States Naval Forces Operating in European Waters, recalled, "An inventory of our efforts . . . showed that we had practically nothing in the way of material and very little in personnel." He added, "We were not only unprepared, but we had very little idea how to prepare for aerial warfare." The entire "force," if it could be so termed, consisted of a few dozen pilots, 54 obsolescent aircraft, a single dirigible that couldn't fly, and 200 aviation ratings, more or less, generally concentrated at a single training station in Pensacola, Florida.[2] Three years of forced-draft growth and exponential technological advances in the war zone had left the United States standing at the starting line. In some ways the Navy attempted to do the virtually unthinkable, create a revolutionary new combat arm thousands of miles from home under daunting conditions while in the midst of war. Despite the country's massive industrial base, its manufacturing sector seemed incapable of providing modern aircraft, motors, or equipment. Virtually everything would have to be done from scratch, and immediately. And the need was desperate. Germany's unrestricted submarine campaign brought America into the conflict and it would be the Navy's task to defeat it. Nearly 3,000,000 tons of shipping losses between February and June 1917 harshly underscored the deadly seriousness of the task. Indeed, if the U-boat campaign proceeded unchecked, England might be driven from the fight. This, combined with the collapse of Russia and the exhaustion of France, would spell certain German victory.

The challenge of projecting military power overseas proved daunting. Within a few months, however, the Department committed itself to establishing an extensive series of bases, schools, and supply facilities along the coast of Europe, an undertaking that required a massive construction program, allocation of tens of thousands of men, shipment of enormous quantities of supplies and building materials, and manufacture of thousands of aircraft, engines, and all the sophisticated technological equipment that went with them. All this needed to be accomplished while the United States attempted to supply its allies *and* dispatch an army of 2,000,000 men to the Western Front.

Factors exacerbating the challenge were legion. Attempting to coordinate the efforts of fractious Bureaus in Washington and headquarters in Europe ruffled feathers on both sides of the Atlantic. Germany's 1918 spring offensive disrupted all planned shipping schedules for men and supplies. Command rivalries and resentments at the highest levels affected the program, while attempting to make technological breakthroughs in the crucible of war vexed everyone from designers of motors and aircraft to frontline mechanics who had to maintain them and pilots whose lives depended on them. Conflicts with the Army over missions and allocation of scarce aviation resources often raged unchecked.

The massive construction program, frequently carried out at inhospitable locations in countries without necessary resources, encountered conflicting customs, attitudes, and priorities. This required the Navy to erect entire autonomous towns and villages three thousand miles from home, complete with water systems, electrical plants, communications gear, and sanitary facilities. The dungarees gangs also built theaters, published newspapers, performed in jazz bands, and played baseball as if each match were the final game of the World Series. Everywhere they went, Americans tried to recreate a small piece of the United States.

The process began with dispatch of the First Aeronautic Detachment to Europe in May 1917, a tiny force of 122 untrained personnel under the dynamic leadership of Lt. Kenneth Whiting. His inspections and negotiations with the French government laid the basis for almost everything that followed in that country. Commander Hutch Cone's arrival in the war zone in late September propelled the effort into a new phase, expanding activities to Ireland and northern England. John Callan's foray into Italy extended naval aviation's sphere of operations to the Adriatic Sea. By November 1918, 27 stations were operating or would be in a matter of weeks, and aviation strength stood at more than 1,150 officers, 18,300 bluejackets, 400 aircraft, 50 kite balloons, and 3 dirigibles. Four squadrons of Marine aviators complemented this aggregation. Eventually, the aeronautic force grew to become one of the largest overseas naval contingents. Navy pilots amassed more than 1,000,000 miles of combat patrols and training flights in the war zone. They stalked the famous North Sea "Spider Web" patrol routes, attacked U-boats, escorted convoys, and joined in dogfights and bombing raids over the Western Front. More than 120 aviation officers and men lost their lives while on foreign service.

Yet even with this enormous effort, it is unlikely that naval aviation significantly altered the duration or outcome of the war. Fighting ended before the full weight of the military buildup could be unleashed. Navy pilots sank no submarines nor did they destroy U-boat facilities through aerial bombardment. Instead, aviation forces cooperated with escort vessels, deterred some attacks on merchant ships and troop transports, and definitely saved lives and cargoes, though these achievements fall into the category of significant but not quantifiable. What is undoubtedly true is that these efforts created the vision, hard-knocks experience, founding myths, trained cadre, and high profile that underlay the emergence of modern naval aviation.

1

THE FIRST AERONAUTIC DETACHMENT

Naval aviation took a first tentative step toward its wartime mission in Europe in September 1908 when the Department of the Navy assigned an officer to observe acceptance trials of a Wright Brothers aircraft being purchased by the U.S. Army. In September 1910 Capt. Washington Chambers, assistant to the Aide for Material, was designated to handle all correspondence and questions related to aviation. Other events quickly followed. During the next few months Curtiss pilot Eugene Ely executed takeoffs and landings from specially fitted warships at Hampton Roads, Virginia, and San Francisco. A handful of junior officers—Theodore Ellyson, John Rodgers, John Towers—began flight instruction at Wright and Curtiss schools, the trailblazers for all who followed. In 1911 the U.S. Navy ordered its first fragile aircraft and established an aviation camp at Greenbury Point (Annapolis), Maryland. By 1912 nine aviators had begun or completed flight training. During the winter of 1913 the flyers relocated to Guanatanamo Bay to coordinate activities with the fleet. The following winter U.S. Marine elements of the aviation force relocated to Culebra, Puerto Rico, for exercises, while a Navy unit of 9 officers, 23 men, and 7 aircraft cruised to Pensacola aboard *Mississippi* to establish a flying school. Only two months later in April 1914 two aviation detachments aboard *Birmingham* and *Mississippi* hurried to Mexican waters to participate in operations at Tampico and Vera Cruz. Later that summer, war broke out in Europe, leading to new levels of activity. Three officers—John Towers, Bernard Smith, and Victor Herbster—were assigned as aviation assistants to the naval attachés at London, Paris, and Berlin, respectively. That fall the first Naval Aeronautical Station was established at Pensacola, with organized classes commencing the following year.

While the period between the outbreak of war in Europe in summer 1914 and America's entrance into the conflict in April 1917 is sometimes characterized as backward and shortsighted, the Navy did make progress in many areas of aviation. Aircraft were launched from warships by catapult, and several vessels were equipped with these devices. The Department ordered its first dirigible and first kite balloons, and in February 1917 an additional 14 airships of an improved design. The first group of enlisted men began receiving flight training. New aircraft were tested and purchased. The Naval Appropriations of 1916 allocated $3,500,000 for aviation and authorized a Naval Flying Corps and a Naval Reserve Flying Corps. The latter provided the organization in which several thousand aviators would serve in the war soon to come. Various boards developed plans for expanded aeronautic activity. Still, developments on the home front could not possibly keep pace with those occurring overseas, and the Navy remained woefully unprepared to take on the great challenge it would soon face. When war was declared, naval aviation forces totaled 48 officers (34 aviators), 239 enlisted men, 54 aircraft, 1 airship, 3 balloons, and 1 air station.

After months of escalating tensions and acrimonious debate the United States entered the cauldron of the Great War on April 6, 1917. The arrival in Washington of British and French military missions a few weeks later did much to focus attention on the daunting challenges confronting the nation. Defeating the German submarine menace, casus belli for President Woodrow Wilson's decision to enter the conflict, stood atop the list. England's population faced the very real possibility of starvation, while the French army was bled nearly white. It would soon be necessary to transport vast quantities of men and equipment to Europe right through the enemy's deadly U-boat gauntlet. Allied coastal aviation stations and antisubmarine patrols had thus far proven incapable of deterring submarine attacks. Clearly, German submarines must be driven away from Allied ports and coasts at all costs. Many hoped the Navy's infant aviation arm would play a significant role in this endeavor.

Secretary of the Navy Josephus Daniels, who first flew at the Annapolis aviation camp in May 1913, began the process of projecting aeronautic forces overseas on April 20, 1917, by cabling Adm. William Sims in London, soon to be designated commander of Naval Forces Operating in European Waters. Daniels requested immediate and full information concerning British naval aviation, including descriptions of aircraft types employed and tactics that had proven most successful over water, on coastal patrol, and searching for submarines. The British Air Ministry prepared a memo for the American Naval Attaché that he forwarded to Washington on May 23 emphasizing four areas: manufacturing motors and airplanes, and instructing pilots and mechanics. To speed the process, the British suggested that certain motors be licensed for production in America but stressed that new orders must not conflict with existing contracts. Pilots required some form of intermediate education, as it would be bad policy to jump directly from basic training aircraft into high-powered combat machines. Instead, the British believed the United States might provide preliminary training of British pilots in exchange for advanced preparation of Yankee aviators in England. Engine fitters could also be trained abroad.[1]

At least by Navy Department lights, the British seemed ambiguous about their requirements. On June 22, Daniels notified Sims that they had failed to indicate preferences in the area of naval air support and directed the admiral to make further inquiries. Sims replied July 3 that the Royal Navy desired seaplane carriers, seaplane tenders, 100 kite balloon units, powerful aircraft engines, trained pilots/mechanics, and one complete squadron of large seaplanes, but they showed little interest in independent American bases or organized units of Navy personnel. As yet, Sims added, he had not received word from Paris, and the small size of his London staff precluded securing such information. For French needs, Daniels instead drew on a communication from the French naval attaché in Washington. In addition, Marine Corps Capt. Bernard "Barney" Smith, Assistant Naval Attaché (aviation) in Paris, would be heading home shortly with information.[2]

Running parallel to and separate from discussions in London, the French Ministry of Marine requested dispatch of American personnel to aid their antisubmarine campaign. Shortly thereafter Chief of Naval Operations (CNO) William Benson determined to send 100 men to France for training, to be known as the First Aeronautic Detachment. Benson placed Lt. Kenneth Whiting in command of the group, with instructions to gather sufficient sailors and supplies as quickly as possible. The unit necessarily consisted of inexperienced men, with the primary mission of providing a visible token of the nation's military commitment. Whiting would exercise administrative control of the unit but operate under French command. Other officers directed to join the group included Lt. Grattan C. Dichman, Lt.(jg) Godfrey deC. Chevalier, Lt.(jg) Virgil Griffin, Paymaster Omar Conger, Assistant Paymaster Frederick Michel, and Assistant Surgeon Arthur Sinton. The detachment would travel to Europe aboard two colliers, *Jupiter* and *Neptune*.[3]

In choosing Whiting, the Navy Department selected one of its most aggressive and energetic officers. Born in Stockbridge, Massachusetts, in 1881, he graduated from the United States Naval Academy and served in the Atlantic Fleet and then with the Asiatic Squadron. Following promotion to ensign he became executive officer of *Supply*, a station ship at Guam. Never in one place very long, he soon joined *Rainbow*, the flagship of the Philippine Squadron. While in the Philippines he embellished his reputation as a "hard-drinking mischief-maker." At this point, 1908, Whiting's career took a dramatic mid-course correction. *Porpoise* and *Shark,* the Navy's newest submarines, were on their way to Asia, with Whiting assigned to ready the boats for commissioning. Two months later he assumed command of *Porpoise* and a string of similar assignments followed. One story claims that he had himself launched from a torpedo tube to test its feasibility as an escape technique. An observer called Whiting a "fire-eating, impulsive, dare-devil" who participated in every dangerous naval enterprise he could reach.

Returning to home waters he served aboard *Cleveland* and then commanded *Tarpon,* a newer undersea craft. In 1911 he oversaw commissioning of *Seal* (later *G-1*), the Navy's largest and most modern submarine. While aboard *G-1* he took her to a depth of 256 feet, then a world record. Whiting departed submarine service in 1914 and joined the infant naval flying arm, being ordered to Ohio where he received flight training from Wilbur Wright. Later that fall he reported to the Naval Aeronautical Station at Pensacola. During the next two years he continued his flight training and then assumed command of the Aviation Detachment aboard *Seattle*. He also helped equip three cruisers with airplane catapults. Many believed Whiting flew "for the pure, wholesome hell of it." At the outbreak of war in April 1917 he received his fateful orders to assemble a naval aviation unit for service in Europe. A flyer who served under Whiting later in the war recalled that the lieutenant was a natural leader of men, "not very tall, perhaps 5'9", of athletic build, compact and strong." He walked with a spring in his step, moving purposefully, and with his "keen eye" ruled with "a strong hand in a velvet glove."[4]

Several pioneering aviators joined Whiting in this important overseas assignment. Lieutenant Grattan Dichman was born in New York in 1885 and graduated from Annapolis in 1907 where he excelled in fencing. Service aboard several battleships and cruisers followed. He reported for duty at Pensacola in 1915. After reaching France in June 1917 he attended military flight school at Tours and the naval aviation school at St. Raphael, receiving brevets at both. During the war he commanded facilities at Brest and Moutchic before transferring to destroyer duty in September 1918. Lieutenant(jg) Virgil Griffin, nicknamed "Squash," hailed from Montgomery, Alabama. He passed through the Pensacola training program, received his French naval brevet at St. Raphael in the summer of 1917, and later served at the Paris headquarters and the Royal Naval Air Station (RNAS), Great Yarmouth, England. Griffin commanded Naval Air Station (NAS) St. Trojan from March 1918 to the end of the war.

Lieutenant(jg) Godfrey DeC. Chevalier hailed from Providence, Rhode Island. A 1910 graduate of the Naval Academy, where he excelled at track, he later served aboard *New Hampshire* and *Petrel*. Chevalier reported for duty at the Navy's first flying camps at Annapolis in December 1912 and Guantanamo in January 1913. He joined the aviation detachment aboard *Birmingham* at Tampico the next year; he later reported for duty in Pensacola and acted as instructor at the Burgess Company in Marblehead, Massachusetts. While on board *North Carolina* in 1916 he became the first pilot launched from a permanent catapult.

At the time Whiting commenced his European mission in early May, he possessed vague written guidance from Rear Adm. Leigh Palmer, chief of the Bureau of Navigation "in connection with aeronautics at such places in France as may be necessary in connection with the oral instructions you have received." He had orders to keep the Naval Attaché in Paris "advised of your whereabouts." Before leaving Washington, Whiting also obtained a letter of introduction to Commander de Blanpré, the French naval attaché in Washington. This communication described the need to train detachment members as "air pilots," with the specific request that they all "be qualified as water flyers." Whiting was to exercise command over the unit and be responsible for discipline. Orders to the group would emanate from him, though it would operate under "the commander of the French force" to which it was assigned. Duties might include "patrols, sea scouting, expeditions, etc." The American lieutenant also received authorization to conclude an agreement with French authorities by which the "exact official status of the Detachment may be fixed and confusion avoided." Whiting's attempts to extract more specific information from his superiors proved unsuccessful; he was told that if he wanted to get to the war zone quickly, he should leave before someone changed or revoked his orders. The vagueness of Whiting's instructions likely reflected a Department notion that the French would use the small detachment as they best thought fit, not that the young lieutenant should develop policy, establish separate bases, or negotiate other agreements. Little did they know![5]

While Whiting could call on a few seasoned officers, the bulk of his force consisted of young men brand new to the service. Enlisting in Baltimore just before the declaration of war, for example, were George Manley, John Ganster, James O'Brien, Charles Boylan, and Charles "Haze" Hammann. The Baltimore contingent soon found themselves outfitted in bell-bottom trousers, blouses with wide collars, and big black neckerchiefs. Others tried to join up but fell afoul of rigid physical and written examinations. Another eager recruit typical of First Aeronautic Detachment volunteers was Irving Sheely of Albany, New York, whose exploits from March 1917 until November 1918 encompassed the entire history of naval aviation in World War I. Young Sheely enlisted in Schenectady, New York, where he "passed the severest exam possible." He reached Pensacola on April 2 after a three-day train trip. His initial schedule in the last prewar days had him rising at 7 A.M., breakfast at 7:30, muster at 8, and military drill until 9, with the rest of the day off. He eagerly anticipated beginning instruction in copper building, machine building, and woodworking. Sheely found the flying school at Pensacola "a pretty little place," with bright green trees and grass and plenty of birds and seagulls, everybody sea bathing when off duty. He had never seen so many airplanes. "By gory," he exclaimed, "but those airplanes are flying around all the time." In similar fashion, Joseph Cline enlisted in the Navy as Landsman for Quartermaster, with pay of $17.60 per month; he arrived at Pensacola shortly thereafter but found no real program under way. He later claimed he received no training in these disorganized days and never sat in an airplane. Instead, Cline spent his time wandering through the hangars.[6]

The pace of activity quickened after Congress declared war. George Manley and his mates started the day with morning chow, then an hour of close order drill, followed by study of airplane motors at the motor repair shop, then another hour of drill and then dinner, with the evenings free. The sailors found their uniforms the key to a social life. As Sheely informed his family, "We can't get out in civilian clothes but can go anywhere in uniform." Pensacola was home to many varied activities and new bluejackets soon grew accustomed to the frenetic activity. In early May the now blasé enlisted man observed, "How about it? I've just blotted this [letter] and it looks like the big zeppelin air ship we have here [DN-1] so I'll leave it. My but it's a whooper [sic]. I don't pay attention to aeroplanes anymore, they're too common."[7]

By then (May 9) orders had come down to assemble the First Aeronautic Detachment. Recruit Cline related how their commander, LCdr. Robert Cabaniss, lined the men up and asked for volunteers for service aboard colliers *Neptune* and *Jupiter*, with no further explanation. Many seemed reluctant to commit themselves, but finally some stepped forward, not knowing fully what they were getting into. By 11 P.M. the following evening they were loaded aboard a train, heading north. Their route took them through Montgomery, Alabama, then Atlanta, Georgia. By May 13 they were in the Blue Ridge Mountains of Virginia, enjoying "dandy weather for traveling." Due to shipping shortages, the group divided approximately in half, with one portion scheduled to sail from Baltimore/Norfolk aboard *Neptune* and the other from

New York/Hoboken on *Jupiter*. Eventually, the addition of commissary stewards, yeomen, ships' cooks, messmen, officers' servants, and others raised the overall total to 122 enlisted men. The vast majority consisted of landsmen for quartermaster, landsmen for machinist mate, and machinist mates 2c. Sheely's contingent reached Baltimore May 14 and proceeded directly to *Neptune*, then taking on supplies at the B&O Railroad grain elevator terminal at Locust Point. Officers Whiting, Griffin, Chevalier, Conger, Sinton, and Michel accompanied them. Lieutenant Dichman commanded the New York contingent aboard *Jupiter*.[8]

The last days in port introduced landlubbers to a more authentic nautical experience. They had to stand watch on the starboard deck every other night from 2 A.M. to 4 A.M. Sheely didn't mind the duty but did resent getting up at all hours and "the wild way they call you." Even a ship in port required maintenance. Seamen had to chip rust, paint, and swab decks all day and sleep in a hammock at night. They received only half a pail of fresh water each day to do all their washing. "Wash your clothes, then wash your feet, then take a bath. Then wash your face and finish with washing your teeth or vice versa all in the same water. How does that appeal to you?" Sailors remained unaware of their final destination, but morale was high and the spirit of adventure strong. "It's a pretty big boat," Sheely wrote enthusiastically, "but I'm hanged if I can say for sure where she is going. In fact I don't care for I am in for four years and I might as well see all I can while the seeing is good." James O'Brien and the rest of the detachment spent part of each day practicing infantry tactics, along with bayonet and rifle excercises.[9]

Work at the Baltimore docks included loading rails, wheat, flour, and a few rifles; laboring around the grain elevator proved very disagreeable. *Neptune* shifted temporarily to another wharf to reposition cargo, and then cruised down Chesapeake Bay to Norfolk on May 22 and 23 to take on remaining stores, passed through Hampton Roads, and spotted some of the Atlantic fleet. Two days later *Neptune* sailed for Europe. The *Jupiter* detachment, 59 strong, reported aboard in Hoboken on May 17 and departed New York Harbor on May 23. For the Atlantic crossing, a pair of destroyers accompanied each collier. Endeavoring to save fuel, the larger vessels attempted to tow the small warships with heavy lines, but the cables parted and the plan was abandoned. Instead, the little destroyers refueled twice from the mother ships during the crossing.[10]

The voyage lasted nearly two weeks. *Neptune* passed through Hampton Roads about 1:30 in the afternoon. The men began learning semaphore signaling the following day. Officers taught international Morse code and everyone practiced manning the lifeboats. Aviation volunteers watched with interest as the *Neptune's* gun crew took target practice. By May 27 the vessel started rolling. The ship's complement celebrated Decoration Day with a "dandy dinner, fried chicken, cranberry sauce and everything." The following day seasickness hit. Then came stormy weather and the ship pitched wildly. During the tempest, waves broke over the rail and smashed two lifeboats secured in the well deck. Trying to eat, sailors found their food sliding into their laps. James O'Brien claimed "tables and chairs flew around the mess hall . . . forced to stand up to eat, the ship was rolling so heavy." The following day a lookout sighted a suspicious object, causing the captain to initiate a high-speed, two-hour run to the south. When *Perkins* steamed alongside to take on oil, water, and supplies, the rolling sea caused the ships to scrape against each other, tearing away parts of the destroyer's bridge, breaking her forward shrouds, denting her stacks, and flattening a ventilator. Many sailors ate their meals on deck and slept "tied to a post." As the collier and her escorts approached Europe, men received orders to wear life preservers and sleep in their clothes. *Neptune* made contact with French patrol boats June 6 and docked safely at St. Nazaire two days later. When the detachment disembarked they found, not surprisingly, that they could not converse with the locals. That didn't stop them from changing some of their money into francs at the YMCA and sampling refreshments at several local cafes.[11]

The remainder of the detachment aboard *Jupiter* encountered similar conditions during their crossing, and after missing a scheduled rendezvous on June 2 met a French destroyer the following day. While still at sea, the ship experienced a possible submarine attack June 4 about 60 miles from the mouth of the Gironde River, with a reported pair of torpedoes passing first ahead and then astern of the ship. Lieutenant Dichman later recalled somewhat skeptically, "Personally, I think it was a porpoise." With lookouts doubled, the vessel commenced zigzagging. That evening the ship entered the Gironde and reached Pauillac (Trompeloup) the following day where Austrian prisoners off-loaded cargo. For a short while the men stayed in the French receiving ship. They shifted to the naval barracks at Bordeaux on June 9 and remained there 12 days, waiting for assignments, subsisting on local rations, and complaining all the while, a pattern repeated again and again in the months to come. Portions were limited, with little or no coffee or tea, and "red wine was not particularly appreciated."[12]

Immediately after *Neptune* docked at St. Nazaire, Whiting reported to LCdr. William N. Sayles, the naval attaché, who hurried down from Paris to greet the new arrivals. Sayles had been attaché since 1914 and spoke fluent

French. Until August, he provided Whiting's principal conduit to the Navy Department in Washington, though Admiral Sims eventually chafed under this arrangement, wishing to exercise more direct control over the young officer's activities. Not until creation of an official aviation office in Paris and the arrival of Cdr. Hutchinson "Hutch" Cone in September, however, did Sims achieve the organizational authority he desired.[13]

While *Jupiter* men idled in Bordeaux, the *Neptune* contingent, led by Whiting, disembarked on June 10 and traveled by truck to the railroad station where they soon piled aboard a train, 10 men to a compartment. Their route took them through Orleans on the way to Brest, and some sailors brought along a supply of alcohol to make the journey more pleasant. James O'Brien's group managed to finish off a bottle of Benedictine but lost their cognac when Whiting instituted a surprise search. Later that same night the Americans reached Brest, met by Lt. de Vaisseau Darien per orders of the Ministry of Marine. Officers rode to their hotel accommodations in an automobile flying the American flag, while enlisted personnel occupied temporary quarters on the site of the future Brest Naval Air Station where they enjoyed a meal "with an abundance of wine." All basked in the "warm and enthusiastic reception from the crowds of people in the streets." One sailor recalled how local men and pretty French women "strewed flowers in our path and stuck roses in the muzzles of our rifles as we marched." Sailors received liberty the first day and evening, along with their pay in the form of $20 gold pieces, part of a cache of $30,000 in bullion brought by Paymaster Conger. Bluejacket George Sprague and others went out on the town that night, drinking champagne at 80 cents a bottle.[14]

Few members of the First Aeronautic Detachment had ever been to Europe and they were much taken with the sights. Irving Sheely told his family the French people were very patriotic, and a man without a uniform "is of little or no account, especially in social life. . . . It's certainly surprising what three years of war will do to a large country like France." The young American spotted thousands of mothers and widows dressed in black. "There seems to be a pall over the population . . . there is not much gay life going on, no theaters, dances, or athletics." Navy men found living conditions rather different from those at home. The French normally served two meals per day, at 10 A.M. and 4:30 P.M., hardly Navy practice. The Americans claimed the grub was lousy, often only black coffee and war bread. "Sometimes the bread is sour and the coffee is strong enough to poison any ordinary man."[15]

Whiting, accompanied by Capt. de Vaisseau Lefebvre, quickly undertook a round of official calls to various local military figures. Out of those initial meetings came a decision to move his men to the aviation station at Camaret (Centre d'Aviation Maritime de Brest-Camaret), a small fishing town about 15 miles away on the opposite side of Brest harbor. Led by Lieutenant Griffin, 64 men shifted their base first to the Naval Torpedo Boat Station (Brest) June 11 and then to Camaret aboard two French destroyers. O'Brien called the voyage "a beautiful ride past forts . . . zigzagged through minefields that guard the harbor of Brest." The bluejackets found quarters in an unoccupied hotel, with officers boarded nearby. They conducted a modest ceremony June 15, raising the Stars and Stripes over the building and yard. Enlisted men assisted at the station cleaning airplanes and overhauling motors and continuing to complain about the grub. The crash of a patrol aircraft, arrival of a dozen torpedoed Yankee seamen, and occasional submarine alerts enlivened their short time here. A few sailors began working on their French.[16]

Even as *Neptune*'s enlisted contingent migrated around Brest Harbor, Whiting and Paymaster Conger, along with Captain Smith, departed for Paris on June 12 to confer with the Ministry of Marine regarding disposition of American personnel. They arrived the following day and initiated another round of calls, to the United States Ambassador, Attaché Sayles, Adm. Marie-Jean-Lucien Lacaze, French Minister of Marine, and several high-ranking military officials. Operating virtually independently of command oversight, Whiting then commenced negotiations with Admiral de Bon, head of the French naval staff, and Commander Cazenave, chief of the Naval Air Service. Capitaine de Fregate De Laborde, the officer in charge of seaplanes, acted as liaison with Whiting and his men. It soon became apparent, however, that a serious misunderstanding existed. Whiting informed his hosts that French officials who had visited Washington earlier in the spring had suggested that untrained student pilots and mechanics would be welcomed and could be instructed quickly in France. Somewhat taken aback, authorities in Paris expressed their gratitude but noted that the First Aeronautic Detachment, with 65 students, 38 untrained mechanics, and various other personnel, appeared completely unbalanced. They explained that every plane and pilot required more than 10 additional men in support, including a cadre of observers proficient in dropping bombs, firing machine guns, and discharging other important duties. At least 14 sailors designated as pilots, they suggested, should be trained as observers instead. Finally, they listed additional essential personnel, such as fabric workers, joiners, chauffeurs, motorboat coxswains, and engineers.[17]

Initial negotiations focused on training inexperienced recruits as rapidly as possible. French methods for teaching naval pilots actually began with land flying, believing it a faster, safer method that saved materiel and provided dual instruction applicable to certain types of bombing missions. Their widely scattered schools graduated 900 pilots per month; but no school had a capacity for more than 100 students, and they operated under army control. Accommodating Americans thus required additional negotiations with the War Ministry, while Whiting's insistence that his men be kept together as a unit meant shifting French students to other schools. Naval officials suggested sending Whiting's pilots to Tours to take the shortened course being offered their own flyers. They also proposed that after completing work there, "pilot-ensigns" be assigned to Lac Hourtin, a seaplane school near Bordeaux and the likely site of a future American facility. French monitors would assist until new Navy pilots could instruct their own comrades. Potential *chasse* (pursuit) pilots would attend yet another school for advanced training. Alternatively, mechanics would proceed first to St. Raphael on the Mediterranean coast and then to Hourtin. Accordingly, after two weeks at Camaret, 25 *Neptune* men commanded by Lieutenant Griffin journeyed south to St. Raphael. Reinforcing the notion that an army—and a navy—travels on its stomach, this group included a commissary steward, two messmen, and a mess attendant. The entire *Jupiter* contingent at Bordeaux, under Lieutenant Dichman, along with officers Sinton, Chevalier, and Michel, entrained for Tours on June 22 where, a few days later, the remaining men from *Neptune*, led by Lieutenant Chevalier, joined them.

With work under way at Tours and St. Raphael, Whiting continued his Paris discussions on broader matters, beyond the parameters of his vague instructions. French officials proposed that the Americans who had just landed in Europe form the nucleus to operate three coastal patrol stations and a flight school, augmented by additional forces dispatched from the United States. Whiting was eager for the Navy to enter the fight, and broad outlines of a plan quickly emerged. A station at Le Croisic near the mouth of the Loire River would protect the approaches to St. Nazaire and offered a convenient site from which to attack U-boats operating around Belle Isle and Ile d'Yeu. A second base at St. Trojan near the Gironde River would guard the route to Bordeaux. These two ports seemed likely debarkation points for the anticipated stream of American troop and supply convoys. The choice of Dunkirk as the site of a third station seemed more problematic. No American convoys traversed this region. Rather, the location offered an opportunity to enter the fight directly by attacking German submarines operating out of Bruges, Ostende, and Zeebrugge on the Belgian coast. Lac Hourtin, in southwestern

France, site of an existing primary seaplane school, could accommodate a new American training center. All this dovetailed with the ministry's ambitious plan to increase patrol activity in 1917 and 1918.[18]

Proposed stations required complements of 16 working seaplanes, with 8 in reserve, along with 16–20 pilots, as well as other officers and numerous ratings, for a total of approximately 200 personnel. The flying school would begin with 200 men but soon expand to 400. To build and equip each base cost approximately $1 million. Whiting and his hosts agreed that Americans would staff the new stations, though the French promised to lend men as necessary. They would also carry out construction work in the following sequence: Hourtin-Dunkirk-Le Croisic-St. Trojan. While the ministry pledged to provide some building materials, severe shortages of labor and supplies often rendered this assurance moot. Additional American equipment would be required, including tools, flying clothes, hangars and housing materials, vehicles, and airplane motors, placing a greater burden on strained shipping resources. Negotiators optimistically predicted that new stations might be ready in September, by which time Navy personnel would have completed their courses of instruction. In fact, none of these timetables proved attainable.[19]

Tentative arrangements sketched out thus far, and those destined to follow, laid the foundation for much of the U.S. Navy's wartime aviation program. Yet their scope and direction resulted largely from happenstance. Unlike the British, the French lobbied promptly and aggressively for their program. With Whiting fortuitously in Paris, not London, they seized the opportunity to shape American decisions. Whiting himself possessed almost unbounded energy and operated without direct supervision. Neither he nor those back in Washington understood the Allies' conflicting needs and desires. Whiting's work thus took place without any real knowledge of larger strategic or logistical concerns or familiarity with the situation in England. All this tilted the balance toward a Franco-centric policy of greater dimensions than the situation probably warranted. Following the war, W. Atlee Edwards, Sims's aide in London, observed: "It is probable that had their establishment [American stations in France] been the subject of a conference between the Allies and ourselves, part of this force would have been diverted to England or to Ireland . . . therefore the concentration of our naval air effort on the French coast was sound, but in excess of that which was justified by the exigencies of war."[20]

With a basic four-station plan in place, further discussions ensued, by which it was "practically agreed" that additional stations should operate at Brest, L'Aber Vrach, Tréguier, Ile Tudy, Fromentine, and elsewhere. Proposals also emerged to establish American seaplane bases in the Mediterranean near Malta and at Tripoli. Admiral de Bon outlined the program in a July 6 letter to the naval attaché in Washington. He wanted 12 stations manned by Americans, with 16 airplanes each, to be operating by May 1, 1918. Under this arrangement, the United States would manufacture motors and airplanes, recruit and train personnel, and supply necessary construction materials, as well as motor boats and automobiles. de Bon suggested that Captain Smith act as liaison between the U.S. Navy and the French in Washington.[21] Despite the breadth and magnitude of Whiting's conversations, however, Admiral Sims remained completely unaware of this work. He did not even know the First Aeronautic Detachment had reached France or that its commander seemed to be committing the United States to an expansive program of bases and, by implication, determining Navy strategy and tactics for combating the submarine menace. Sims first learned of Whiting's activities at a meeting with the Board of Admiralty, which pointedly inquired why America was secretly concentrating a large air force in France when, from the Royal Navy's perspective, the most vital area was the English shipping routes. Somewhat chagrined, Sims confessed ignorance, agreed that protecting Britain's coast should be the most important objective, and promised to investigate.[22]

Back in France, unaware of any disquiet in London, the peripatetic Whiting forged ahead. Having outlined the rudiments of a program, the eager French arranged an inspection tour of proposed sites. A party consisting of De Laborde, Whiting, Smith, and Conger departed Paris for Dunkirk on June 18, arriving at the beleaguered city the following day. The historic port had endured continuous bombardment for years, and damage caused by large bombers and a huge German naval gun mounted several miles up the coast was instantly visible. The harbor itself appeared narrow and crowded with destroyers, monitors, submarines, and other vessels, studded by a forest of ships' masts, poles, gantries, and towers, all significant impediments to aviation. Whiting commenced his visit with the obligatory round of introductory meetings, then conducted a detailed inspection of a French seaplane base (Centre d'Aviation Maritime de Dunkerque) situated on the eastern side of the harbor just behind the city walls. Equipment consisted of 24 aircraft, including Sopwith scouts, which the American officer described as slow, structurally inadequate, and unseaworthy, having a tendency to flip over when drifting backward. A mix of flying boats performed patrol duties, including Franco-British Aviation (FBA), Tellier, and Donnet-Denhaut (DD) types. At the time, the flat-bottomed FBA was the most popular in French service. The DD was of similar design but somewhat smaller, while the Tellier appeared constructed like a real boat, very strongly made and quite seaworthy.[23]

The following morning the group called on Capt. Charles Lambe of the Royal Navy, commander of Royal Naval Air Service (RNAS) units in the region, at his headquarters on the shore just east of Dunkirk. He offered a cordial reception and thorough overview of the situation. Lambe also showed his visitors detailed aerial reconnaissance photographs of the nearby Belgian coast, including gun emplacements, hangars, aerodromes, and naval vessels and installations, especially those at Zeebrugge. The British also maintained a seaplane base inside Dunkirk harbor, a little south of the French station and adjacent to the dockyard, called by Whiting "compact, snug, neat, and comfortable." It contained three hangars and an assortment of huts. Enlisted men slept as if aboard ship, in hammocks slung from billet hooks above fixed mess tables. Heavily constructed bombproofs provided some protection against attack. Morale at the base appeared at low ebb. Six French planes had been lost on one day in April. Allied scouts virtually abandoned the air between Zeebrugge and the Dover-Dunkirk barrage. The enemy had a new, heavily armed seaplane now acting as "cock of the walk." The very day Whiting reached Dunkirk, RNAS units dispatched two Sopwith fighters and a Short bomber, but encountered a flight of enemy scouts, with disastrous results. The Germans shot down the first Sopwith, killing the pilot, and then downed the bomber, with the loss of the observer. The second Sopwith, riddled with gunfire, made an emergency landing at sea, where a French destroyer rescued the pilot. The English then launched a small motor torpedo boat raid against Zeebrugge, but lost a vessel in the process.

Whiting next turned his attention to the proposed site for the American station. Situated where the inner harbor channel joined the bight, just west of the dockyard, the area stood atop a stone seawall from which aircraft could be lowered to the water, thus limiting the impact of the harbor's great rise and fall of tide, but creating a bottleneck that slowed operations. Existing facilities proved minimal—just a small stone building and a railroad connection, but sufficient space existed to erect hangars, barracks, workshops, and storage huts. Satisfied that a usable site had been selected, Whiting moved on to inspect the massive French and British reserve depots at St. Pol, a short distance west of the city; he canceled one final visit to the nearby Handley Page bomber base at Couderkerque due to lack of time.

Whiting's party returned to Paris on June 21 where they spent the next few days meeting with officials and discussing in more detail disposition of personnel and commencement of work at Dunkirk. With those arrangements in hand, Whiting and Conger departed Paris on June 23 for an extended inspection trip along the southwestern coast, reaching Tours the following morning.

They visited the army flying field (Ecole d'Aviation Militaire de Tours), rendezvousing with Dichman and Chevalier and their enlisted charges. Whiting described the school as of modest size but generally complete, with a large main field, three auxiliary fields, a dozen wooden hangars, and scores of Caudron, Farman, and Nieuport training aircraft. He found his men well quartered and fed, but officers' inadequate bath and toilet facilities required them to board in town. From Tours, the American party journeyed to La Rochelle where they met up with Capitaine De Laborde for a visit to the air station at La Pallice, thence onward by automobile to Fromentine to inspect the site for a possible seaplane base.[24]

In a later report, Whiting carefully enumerated the advantages and disadvantages of this and all other prospective locations. The next stop, Sables d'Olonne, proved a disappointment, with its very small harbor and lack of space along the seawall. Returning to La Rochelle, Whiting and Conger briefly revisited La Pallice, and then continued ahead to Rochefort to inspect a dirigible station, concluding that such craft might best be employed convoying vessels along the coast. The following morning brought an automobile journey to Marennes and an intensive inspection of the coast aboard a 60-foot patrol vedette (motor launch) in search of a site for a base to protect the mouth of the Gironde River. A location on Ile d'Oléron, about three miles south of St. Trojan on the Straits of Maumusson, seemed to offer many advantages. Disembarking, Whiting visited an aerodrome at Verdun before proceeding to Lac Hourtin, suggested site for the American flying school. Though he deemed the location excellent, the presence of an existing naval school threatened overcrowded conditions, and Whiting determined the neighboring lake to the south, Lacanau, offered better prospects. Weather conditions seemed amenable, few houses dotted the shore, and high bluffs to the west promised safe target practice. After spending a night in Bordeaux, Whiting and Conger traveled to Arcachon and then to the gunnery school at Cazaux. "Barney" Smith, by now having returned to the United States, had been through the Cazaux program. Another night in Bordeaux and Whiting visited Pauillac on the Gironde River, 25 miles downstream and the site selected for a major American base. He quickly appreciated that it was well situated to receive and distribute supplies as well as assemble seaplanes shipped from the United States. Returning to Bordeaux, Whiting pushed on to St. Nazaire, and the important site at Le Croisic. In his estimation, Le Croisic appeared superior to Fromentine and should be constructed first. Whiting also learned that the French were nearing completion of a small dirigible station nearby at Paimboeuf.[25]

With this stage of his work completed, Whiting returned to St. Nazaire before visiting Tours one more time. Traveling overnight, he reached Paris on the morning of July 4. Paymaster Conger remained at Tours until July 7, continuing negotiations regarding establishment of bases and initiating construction. He then rejoined Whiting. A conference held at the Ministry of Marine the following day included Maj. Raynal Bolling, Lt. Warren Child, and Constructor George Westervelt of the Bolling Commission, along with Whiting and Conger and several important French officers who used the meeting to brief the visitors about the availability of aircraft for proposed naval aviation operations, possible employment of American workers in local factories, or establishment of an American manufacturing facility in Europe, preferably near a Navy base. Other discussions outlined France's 50-base expansion plan for the remainder of 1917 and all of 1918. This, they believed, constituted the minimum number necessary to force enemy submarines away from harbor entrances and into deeper water. Not confident they could complete such an ambitious program, however, the French again called on the U.S. Navy to build and operate 12 of the stations.[26]

How, when, and how often Kenneth Whiting and the others of his unit communicated with the Navy Department in these early days remains unclear, and only scattered documentary evidence survives. Paymaster Omar Conger wrote a lengthy report for Rear Adm. Samuel McGowan, chief of the Bureau of Supplies and Accounts, on June 18, outlining conditions in Europe, including a very brief summary of the proposed aeronautic program. Lieutenant Whiting's first cable to Secretary Daniels dispatched July 7 reported considerable progress and asked for permission to proceed with the initial four-base proposal. He followed with a major report July 20 that enlarged the envisioned program to 15 bases, including dirigible and kite balloon stations. A variety of additional conduits existed. Whiting's orders required him to keep Attaché Sayles informed of his whereabouts and activities, and Sayles relayed much information back to Washington. Sayles greeted Whiting the moment he stepped on French soil, and his cable supporting the three-base, one-school proposal indicates that he remained fully abreast of events. So did information Sayles dispatched outlining the movement of First Aeronautic Detachment personnel to various French schools and facilities. The attaché also forwarded requests that specific officers be posted to France, including Earl Winfield "Win" Spencer, Albert "Putty" Read, William Corry, and Harold "Cueless" Bartlett. Sayles urged that Paymaster Conger be retained in France, as his detachment would mean "handicap and setbacks." Captain Smith, Sayles's longtime aide, also provided useful information. He maintained close contact with Whiting, Sayles, and the French; inspected several Allied stations with Whiting; and personally delivered a proposal for establishing multiple coastal bases when he returned to the United States at the beginning of the summer.[27]

Finally, Capt. Richard Jackson, sent from Washington at the request of the French, arrived at the beginning of the summer to become senior naval officer in Paris and serve as Sims's envoy at the Ministry of Marine. Sims instructed Jackson to act in a liaison capacity only—as his staff spokesman. Jackson took a very different tack, however, seeing himself as the Department's representative regarding plans and operations. He also attempted to exert authority over the evolving organizational process and establishment of bases and aviation in France. In an early July cable to the Bureau of Navigation, Jackson claimed, "Orders Vice Admiral Sims direct me as Senior Officer Ashore and representative of Navy Department to take charge of naval aviation France." Such assertions, as well as Jackson's practice of providing information and commentary to Secretary Daniels and Admiral Benson back in Washington, acting outside the chain of command, soon got him into hot water. He also clashed with Sayles, who questioned his authority but was told the attaché's activities should be concentrated in the area of intelligence only and would now come under Jackson's "command."

Though the tangled Jackson-Sayles-Sims relationship affected all areas of naval activity, it impacted Whiting's initiatives directly. As early as July 12 Jackson informed his superiors of the four-base proposal and requested that 800 to 1,000 additional men be dispatched within the next two months for training related to duty at these bases. He followed up July 20 by identifying supply and construction difficulties facing the aviation effort, acute local shortages of skilled labor, and complete exhaustion paralyzing the French. Jackson called for portable (prefabricated) buildings and hangars to be shipped from the United States. He also echoed Sayles's call for Read, Corry, Bartlett, and Spencer. The Department responded by ordering Jackson not to commit to any program without authorization.[28]

At the beginning of August, Whiting, Westervelt, and Child returned to Dunkirk for further inspections and to assess progress at the American site. They again met with Captain Lambe and visited outlying aerodromes, a wireless tracking station, and the enormous aircraft depot at St. Pol. Whiting also discovered that the British had abandoned seaplanes for scouting and fighting and relied instead on land-based Sopwith Camels, but without any flotation gear, a practice, he believed, that "must sooner or later result in loss of pilots." In passing, Whiting, made several observations that ultimately proved a portent of things to come, including the "heavy rain falling almost incessantly," and a noontime bombing raid on the town. He called the damage "slight"—15 people were killed and 75 injured, "mostly Chinese." Whiting learned that work at the American site had progressed very slowly, but he received assurances that the job would be completed by September 1. Whiting also inspected a derelict German mine-laying U-boat, UC-61, something of great interest to the former submariner.

With Whiting back in Paris and his dispatch of initial recommendations to Washington, the nascent aviation effort moved into a new phase, proceeding on at least four parallel fronts: further development of organization and planning, pilot training at Tours, mechanics/observers instruction at St. Raphael, and creation of an American flying school at Lacanau-Moutchic. As pilots and observers pursued activities across the breadth of France, Whiting spent a busy summer organizing the campaign from his new office at 23 Rue de la Paix in Paris and composing a stream of weighty reports. At the same time, the unit was transformed from the temporary First Aeronautic Detachment into the more permanent United States Naval Aviation Forces-Foreign Service (USNAFFS).[29]

Whiting prepared four lengthy memos covering nearly the entire spectrum of naval aviation activities in France and adjacent waters. He based his information and conclusions on his own travels and research, data gleaned from other members of the First Aviation Detachment, and numerous interviews with military officials. Taken together, his reports represented the most comprehensive analysis of the military situation available to planners in Europe and Washington and underlay many important decisions impacting development of the Navy's antisubmarine program in the following 15 months.

In his weighty July 20 report to the Secretary of the Navy, Whiting claimed that seaplanes offered the best available offensive and defensive weapon against submarines (a critical decision, and one later rejected). He had thus entered into a provisional agreement to operate stations at Dunkirk, Lacanau, Le Croisic, and St. Trojan. Whiting urgently recommended the Department also back the expanded 12-base program advanced by the French government. Additional American stations should be established at Brest, L'Aber Vrach, Tréguier (guarding the Brest approaches), Ile Tudy and Fromentine (near St. Nazaire), and Arcachon (near Bordeaux). He envisioned airship stations at Brest, Paimboeuf, Rochefort, La Rochelle, and Arcachon. Planning at this stage suggested complements of 24 flying boats and 650 officers/men at Brest, Fromentine, Arcachon, and St. Trojan. Remaining stations would support 18 smaller seaplanes and 250 officers/men. Dunkirk alone would operate fighting scouts, along with patrol/bombing craft. A dearth of suitable aircraft in the United States necessitated contracting with French companies for seaplanes so work at the stations and the school at Lacanau-Moutchic might begin as soon as possible. Whiting requested that 800 men be dispatched to Europe immediately, including radio operators, blacksmiths, carpenters, coxswains, cooks, bakers, messmen, hospital corpsmen, and yeomen. He also recommended establishment of bases in the Mediterranean, but his superiors flatly rejected the notion, saying the United States was not at war with Austria-Hungary.

Whiting's report, possibly the single most important document in the development of the overseas aviation program, also contained suggestions concerning base organization, likening it to a ship (gunboat), incorporating a commanding officer, four to six flying officers, medical officer, and supply officer. The number and type of airplanes required appeared in a separate report, though he added he was even then attempting to acquire "such seaplanes as are available." Virtually everything else would necessarily come from the United States, including boats, trucks, autos, motorcycles, tools, gasoline, pumps, and generators. Whiting emphasized that the submarine threat required decisive measures. He concluded by urging approval of his actions to date and all tentative plans for the future. The Department of the Navy accepted the initial roster of four air stations on August 8. After consulting with Westervelt, Child, and others, headquarters authorized establishment of 11 additional stations on September 16.[30]

Whiting dispatched a second lengthy cable August 4 detailing previous Allied efforts and fundamental needs for future action. This represented a response to the Department's earlier request for information concerning the "present manner and extent of the use of naval aircraft of Great Britain and France, and types of aircraft used," as well as data on the "results obtained by allies . . . and the importance which may be given this branch of naval effort." Whiting described the great value of naval aircraft, circumscribed only by shortages of personnel and material. Most important were antisubmarine, patrol, and escort missions, ability to locate and destroy U-boats and mines, and capacity to bomb submarine bases. He also discussed how use of kite balloons would make destroyers and transports more effective. Secondary aviation activities might include working with the fleet, scouting over the North Sea, and attacking zeppelins and other enemy aircraft. Such work had already attained major significance. In June 1917, alone, he reported, British seaplanes and airplanes had covered 65,000 miles and British airships 50,000 miles more. French naval aircraft in June accumulated 3,900 hours flying over water.

Whiting recommended "Large America" flying boats for patrol and reconnaissance work, a British modification of the Curtiss H-12 type. Dirigibles were best employed for long patrols and kite balloons for scouting in conjunction with surface craft. Whiting claimed no ship had been attacked while escorted by a dirigible. Although he had not visited London, Whiting discussed possible aviation efforts there, suggesting that America assume responsibility for specific sectors along the British coast. He also listed principal objectives of naval aviation efforts: preventing egress of submarines from Belgian bases; protecting transports and commercial vessels in the waters between Brest and Spain; destroying mine-laying U-boats in the Bay of Biscay; and protecting the shores in the Mediterranean Sea. The ambitious program envisioned 12 seaplane and 2 dirigible stations in France, along with a total complement of 3,000 men (a significant underestimate). Since Whiting had not yet received a response to his July 20 report he repeated calls for establishment of bases at Moutchic, Arcachon, Brest, Dunkirk, Ile Tudy, La Pallice, Le Croisic, and St. Trojan. Whiting also renewed suggestions for outposts at Cette and Antibes to protect Nice and Toulon and the Corsica-La Provence route.[31]

The vastly energetic Whiting sent a third major planning memo to Washington on August 26, reiterating earlier points and further expanding the range of aviation possibilities, by far his most visionary, offensive-minded statement. Titled "Information and Suggestions for the Use of Seaplanes," it described existing needs, usages, and potential of seaplane warfare, and called the bombing campaign from Dunkirk "indispensable." Also indispensable were patrol and escort activities against enemy submarines operating west of Calais. Whiting advocated a similar effort in the Mediterranean. He recommended that ships carrying seaplanes operate westward in the Atlantic Ocean and thought it possible to bomb German bases using large seaplane carriers. He also advocated establishing 24 air stations to control the English Channel, with 12 on each shore.

This latest report covered a wide range of tactical and strategic concerns. Whiting discussed enemy submarines at sea and in coastal waters; their use of torpedoes, guns, and mines; and ways to respond to each. He reviewed the scale, defenses, and operations of the German establishment in Belgium as well as the issue of control of the air and efforts to combat enemy air superiority. Whiting called for offensive attacks against U-boats transiting to and from bases. He suggested use of radio intercepts to find submarines and described the lack of success employing land machines over water. Bases in Ireland and the Bay of Biscay could keep U-boats submerged for up to 100 miles off shore; larger aircraft could drive them even farther from the coasts, perhaps as much as 150 miles. Given the limited capabilities of current submarines, this alone would greatly alter the balance in the desperate struggle. Whiting even advocated construction/conversion of Great Lakes–type rail carriers to carry seaplanes for use against submarines in deep water, a concept endorsed by Sims (the conceptual ancestor of the escort carrier of World War II). He also proposed employing seaplanes against the fortifications at Heligoland, 500 bombers and fighters performing fire control, reconnaissance, and bombardment missions, hitting places artillery could not go. He even advocated seizing bases in neutral Holland or Denmark.[32]

The Navy's man on the ground submitted a final memo on September 16 near the end of his tenure as leader of the FAD outlining priorities in the areas of policy, personnel, and materiel. Whiting urged the Department to *decide* whether to conduct operations in England and the scale they might assume. He contended it was necessary to determine whether an offensive against German land bases should be mounted and estimated that six to nine months would be required to gather and train the proper force. Whiting recommended that training in the United States be pushed with vigor, as each proposed station in France required 30 pilots, 45 observers, and 50 mechanics, for a total of 360 pilots, 540 observers, and 600 mechanics, and "this is just the bare beginning." In all, he estimated that the Navy needed 1,875 men trained specifically for aviation and 3,000 nonflying, enlisted ratings, along with replacements at the rate of 5 percent per month. With Moutchic only a finishing school, facilities at home must carry out preliminary flight instruction.

Furthermore, the Department should assemble a corps of men to operate an overseas assembly and repair facility. According to Whiting, the Navy would probably have to supply personnel to French bases, as their own manpower was limited in number and very poor in quality. The country couldn't even fill its own army's demands, let alone its navy's. Whiting described shortages of material as real and acute. In his opinion, the United States must furnish France with raw and finished materials and increase drastically the output of planes and engines. "Every boat or engine they [U.S. companies] make can be used." He estimated aircraft needs at the various stations at 1,000 per year. In total, Whiting's summer missives outlined an aviation program that dwarfed anything ever envisioned in Washington. His superiors must have shaken their heads and wondered what they had unleashed.[33]

Though Whiting displayed great energy and initiative, the question of who actually commanded in Paris during those early days remained unanswered. Bernard Smith returned to the United States early in the summer. Attaché Sayles possessed no operational brief. Whiting, only a lieutenant himself, led a "token" force of seven officers and 122 men but lacked authority to create or command anything larger. Far away in London, others kept Sims informed of events. Into the breach stepped the ambitious Captain Jackson. As early as July 11, Lt. John Callan, recently landed in Europe, attended a meeting in which Jackson explained he had just come over to "superintend aviation." And he fully intended to take control. Jackson's communications to Benson-Daniels-Sims over the next several weeks, largely based on material gathered by Whiting, exhibited an air of authority as if he were, in fact, directing events. A cable to Sims on August 4 discussing proposed bases (including one at Cette on Corsica, and another at Antibes near Nice) underlay the admiral's own report to Benson endorsing Whiting's four-base proposal. Ten days later Jackson announced that he had opened a headquarters for aviation adjacent to the Ministry of Marine, with a communications office in the ministry. "Here will be established my headquarters" and those of the officers in immediate charge of seaplanes and dirigibles. Jackson's "headquarters" would also encompass the senior supply officer for aviation. He requested specific officers to be assigned to him, including Frank McCrary for dirigibles, Warren Child for motors, and George Westervelt for constructor. Sims forwarded Washington's general approval of this arrangement to Paris on August 21, but as events soon showed, the admiral had no intention of placing Jackson in control of that office.[34]

In fact, Sims already had his eye on exactly the man he wanted, Cdr. Hutchinson I. "Hutch" Cone, then serving as Marine Superintendent at the Panama Canal. Cone first approached Sims, his old ally in the gunnery controversy of the early 1900s, on May 29, congratulating him on his recent promotion and pleading, "For God's sakes get me over there with you in some capacity as soon as possible." Cone sought a destroyer command and had written to Admirals Benson and Palmer without success. Sims replied that he would like nothing better than have Cone working for him but feared he could not convince the Navy to turn him loose. Nonetheless, he would ask. The officer Sims wanted had already compiled an outstanding record and was destined to accomplish much more. Born in Brooklyn in 1871, the lean, sandy-haired Cone had graduated from the Naval Academy in 1894 and had served as assistant engineer aboard *Baltimore* at the Battle of Manila Bay. His intimate and longtime friends called him "Reddy." Still a junior officer, he led the torpedo boat destroyer flotilla of the Great White Fleet while aboard *Whipple*. With the temporary rank of rear admiral he had served as chief of the Bureau of Steam Engineering from 1909 until 1913, and in 1915 was appointed Marine Superintendent at the Panama Canal. The former chief engineer was known for his progressiveness and trenchant wit, a man who did not to hesitate in making his own decisions or pressing for action from higher authorities. In 1916 many aviation pioneers in the Department called for Cone to replace Mark Bristol as director of the Office of Naval Aeronautics when Bristol returned to sea duty.[35]

By midsummer it was obvious that the aviation program in Europe, while not yet finalized, had mushroomed into a major initiative. Sims "complained" to Benson that aeronautic work in Europe was too fragmented. He had Westervelt and Child (of the Bolling Commission) advising on materiel, and the naval attaché office exercised a similar responsibility. Furthermore, Whiting was too junior, while Jackson, the latter's superior in Paris who tried to take control of affairs in France, had fallen afoul of Sims. As early as August 3 the admiral urged that a senior and experienced officer be designated to take charge. Two weeks later Westervelt suggested that Sims appoint a staff officer with the rank of captain for this job. Sims informed Washington on August 21 that he wanted an officer of wide administrative experience, not necessarily an aviator, and specifically requested Cone for the post. He declared the new effort "requires a rapidly developing personnel and material establishment of such proportions that a comprehensive organization should be developed immediately . . . the responsibilities of the head of this organization will be so great that an officer of wide administrative experience will be required." Benson granted Sims's appeal and an ecstatic Cone soon sailed for Europe.[36]

At least one officer did not get the message, and that was Jackson, who wanted Cone placed subordinate to him. Completely misreading what was unfolding, Jackson, in a letter in early September to Capt. Nathan C. Twining, Sims's chief of staff, expressed pleasure that Cone was on his way, saying, "He will be able to combine the jobs of engineering officer and construction officer that were needed here in the organization." Jackson continued by commending Whiting as first rate as an inspector and dealing with practical work in flying and who should continue with personnel issues. There was no doubt in Jackson's mind that he would head the entire organization. Sims, by contrast, intended to elevate Cone to a status similar to that enjoyed by Rear Adm. William Fletcher, then commanding the flotilla of antisubmarine yachts based at Brest, and Rear Adm. Henry B. Wilson, in charge of U.S. Patrol Forces based on Gibraltar.[37]

The situation came to a head at the end of the summer. Lieutenant Commander J. F. Daniels visited Paris on September 12 and met with Jackson, Conger, and Whiting. Daniels candidly reported that Whiting had gathered much of the information Jackson sent directly to Washington, bypassing Sims. Whiting gave the impression that "his style was being cramped by Jackson," who would not endorse recommendations for officers he (Whiting) wanted. Instead, the head of the First Aeronautic Detachment was forced to "sit in a two-by-four room at the Ministry of Marine and decode messages, etc., etc." Conger, through Daniels, also complained, saying he wished to concentrate on supply issues but Jackson wanted him to do communications. Further, Jackson penned long personal letters to Benson, Sims's bete noir. He defended himself by claiming that the aviation base program was in such a muddle he was forced to exercise control. Ultimately, Sims charged Jackson with exceeding his role and both Capt. William Pratt in the CNO's office and Sims asked that he be transferred. Instead, in a January 1918 reorganization of naval forces in France, Sayles became intelligence officer on Admiral Wilson's staff in Brest and Jackson assumed the role of naval attaché, a post he filled until the end of the war.[38]

News of Cone's appointment coincided with departmental approval of Whiting's entire 15-station program. When Cone reached England on September 27 Sims welcomed his friend saying, "You cannot possibly imagine how glad I am to have you over here. . . . You have got what must inevitably develop into a very big job and you are the man above all others that I would have selected to carry this out in an efficient manner." Sims also ordered Whiting and Conger to meet with him in London. This was the first time Whiting reported to Sims in person. The very junior Whiting, now a lieutenant commander, formally relinquished command of United States Aeronautical Detachment #1 on October 24, announcing that the unit ceased to exist from that date, bringing the opening phase of the naval aviation effort in Europe to a close.[39]

Even as staffs and departments on both sides of the Atlantic debated the future structure of naval aviation, training of inexperienced Americans commenced. Enlisted men who had been designated pilots entrained for Tours, a preliminary flight school 125 miles southwest of Paris. During the trip the men wore dress blues, sat up all night packed eight to a railcar compartment, and received loaves of potato bread and red wine for rations. Lieutenant Dichman met the travelers at 3 A.M. They boarded trucks and drove to a barracks occupied by Senegalese troops. French officers rousted the sleeping Africans from their beds and the sailors moved in. A predawn snack of coffee, chocolate, cheese, and bread eased some of the residual discomfort from the long trip. According to George Moseley, former All-American end at Yale and now a member of the French Foreign Legion, the camp stood about three miles north of the city. German prisoners of war did much of the heavy labor putting up hangars and other buildings. "They are a husky bunch, well fed and very contented," Moseley observed. At the flying field, female mechanics greased the aircraft, oiled the motors, and pumped gas. They also cleaned around the hangars. He was surprised to see that "they wear overalls and go about their business just like men." James O'Brien noted the presence of many "Singalese [sic]" mechanics in the shops. Americans found a school staffed by eight instructor-pilots, along with barracks, sickbay, officers' quarters, and severely inadequate (by U.S. standards) facilities for bathing and toilets. The French reserved one entire wooden barracks for enlisted flyers, about 50, as well as a mess hall. Petty officers occupied a separate building, with one sleeping in the enlisted men's barracks each night. Others undergoing training at Tours included French student pilots, some American Expeditionary Force (AEF) men, and a few Americans serving in the Foreign Legion, perhaps 100 in all.[40]

In addition to enlisted personnel of the First Aeronautic Detachment, the only other aviators available for duty in Europe in 1917 were members of volunteer college groups, which had begun training before or just after the declaration of war, such as the Harvard Unit at Hampton Roads and the Second Yale Unit at Buffalo, New York. By far the most important was the First Yale Unit, organized in 1916 by F. Trubee Davison, the son of New York financier Henry P. Davison. This group of college men, totaling nearly 30 members, began instruction in 1916 at Port Washington, New York. They enlisted en masse in late March 1917, departed Yale, and with financing provided by private donations and training directed by the Navy's Lt. Eddie McDonnell, spent the next four months working in Palm Beach and Huntington, New York. Unit members began taking their flight tests in July and received commissions; the first of the group, Artemus "Di" Gates and Robert Lovett, were dispatched to Europe in August. Others quickly followed, including Al Sturtevant, John Vorys, David Ingalls, Ken Smith, Sam Walker, Reginald Coombe, Henry Landon, Kenneth MacLeish, and many more. During the months that followed they occupied every post from station commander and chief pilot to staff officer, bombing group wing commander, and frontline pilot in the skies above Flanders. Two members of the unit were killed in combat and a third died in an accident while on duty at Dunkirk. Another became the Navy's only wartime "Ace."[41]

Upon reaching France, Gates and Lovett traveled to Tours for further flight instruction. While there they lived and messed in officers' quarters, separate from the First Aeronautic Detachment. Gates reported, "We can't speak French and they can't speak English, so you can imagine the Babylon jabber at the table." Moseley claimed the facilities included a fine canteen with clean oilcloths and white china plates and glasses. Barracks were big and airy and bedding consisted of two cotton mattresses and a cotton pillow, sheets, a blanket, and a quilt. "This must be heaven!" He enjoyed the food: "good meat, vegetables, and potatoes served on separate plates, all steaming hot." On Independence Day, fueled with cash disbursed by Paymaster Conger, sailors descended on the cafes, enjoyed their share of the local Vouvray wine, and missed 10:00 o'clock curfew by more than three hours. A barracks inspection by Lieutenants Dichman and Chevalier identified the tardy bluejackets, including Joseph Cline and James O'Brien, who received disciplinary action in the form of extra duties.[42]

Training commenced almost immediately. The program at Tours did not offer ground school or any theory of flight. Rather, cadets arose at 4:00 A.M. and wolfed down a quick snack, formed into squads, and marched to the chief pilot's office where huge trucks awaited. There were often too many students to fly at the main field, although it was a mile-and-a-half square, so some drove out to satellite fields. After the morning's work, the men breakfasted at 10:45 A.M. or so, then slept until 3:00 P.M. when they attended lectures. At 4:00 or 4:30 P.M. after another meal they went back to the flying fields, not returning until 9:00 in the evening. Divided into groups of 8 or 10 students, each unit shared a single leather flying coat, one pair of goggles, and one distinctively tiered crash helmet. Simple instrumentation in their Caudron G-3 aircraft powered by 80–100 hp Anzani or 60–80 hp Le Rhone motors included an oil gauge, altimeter, and tachometer. Trainees sat in front, with the monitor, who spoke little English, perched behind, giving commands by pushing the student's helmet or tapping his shoulders. He also carried a piece of cardboard with mistakes written in both French and English. Student Cline's monitor earned a fine record in combat but proved very excitable around his young charges. He yelled and screamed, jumped up and down, and threw his hat or cane on the ground. The flyers all carried good luck talismans, little yarn dolls named *Nannette* and *Rattatin*, or sweethearts' stockings wrapped around their heads. When the entire contingent received Fourth of July liberty, many traveled to Tours to buy stockings.

To take off, a student revved the motor while his classmates held the wings. When they let go, the plane shot ahead and upward. After reaching a height of

500 feet the fledgling cut the motor and glided back to earth, landing without aid of brakes. Instructors referred to the crack-ups as "landing like an omelet." Moseley found Caudrons easy to fly, with the monitor or teacher available to correct any mistakes. Landing was the hardest part and took a little longer to learn. Some novices considered it a safe machine. "It is surprising how many things you can do and not get hurt," Moseley opined. One plane hit the top of a tree, broke off a branch as big around as a man's wrist, and kept flying. Another plane went into a wing slip, crashed into the ground, and broke into two pieces, but the pilot escaped unscathed. According to Lieutenant Dichman, "The men seemed to learn the game quickly" and made their initial solo attempts after three or four hours of dual instruction. Chief Boatswain's Mate Marchand went first; only three or four men failed to solo. Dichman and Chevalier took the army brevet, while Dr. Sinton learned to speak French.[43]

Despite assertions of safety, the reality proved rather different. In late June at an altitude of 600 feet Thomas Barrett and his instructor, M. Robery, fell into a nosedive and crashed; both died in the fiery wreck. Rain marred Barrett's early morning funeral, drenching the honor guard of companions outfitted in dress blues and leggings. A few weeks later K. H. Tuttle sideslipped his aircraft, crashed, and broke his jaw, but flew again two days later, his fractured bone wired in place. George Manley died in a midair collision August 21. A board of inquiry determined that while in flight his aircraft sliced the tail off a passing Caudron piloted by instructor Sgt. Jacques Bisson. The Frenchman quickly cut his engine and went into a "dead leaf" glide, landing alongside the barracks, suffering a broken leg and internal injuries. Manley's machine nosedived from a height of 100–200 feet and fell into a vegetable garden just beyond the road. The gas tank crushed him upon impact and he died in the hospital, never regaining consciousness. Still another death occurred at the end of July when Harold Halstead succumbed to encephalitis. During the entire war at least 37 members of the FAD became pilots; 24 were designated Naval Aviators; 14 died in flying accidents.[44]

The rash of accidents at Tours and other flying schools attended by American personnel, and while on duty at various stations, reflected rapidly evolving but still primitive aircraft and engine technology and the enormous pressure to turn out trained aviators in the least possible time. Neither FAD members nor pilots drawn from the First Yale Unit, attended a proper ground school. Their machines were prone to structural failure and mechanical breakdown. Safety equipment was inadequate or nonexistent. Many harbors utilized by American forces were constricted and experienced fierce tides. Safety yielded to expediency. The inevitable results in flight school where the equipment was relatively simple and slow was occasionally tragic. When pilots were confronted by faster, more powerful, less stable machines at places like Ayr in Scotland or at Dunkirk, the death toll rose rapidly. If they survived the risks and completed basic training, students took a series of flight tests to demonstrate proficiency, performing high and low spiral descents, followed by "petit voyages," cross-country flights of 30 to 40 miles' duration. An altitude test required novices to climb to a height of 8,000 feet and remain there for more than an hour. They finished with two long, cross-country triangular courses. Lieutenant Dichman reported that the men made anywhere from 34 to 75 flights during their training, lasting up to one hour each, though most were of much shorter duration. J. D. Jernigan completed his two-month instruction stint with 17 hours of flight time. A few were released for "inaptitude" and assigned other duties. In mid-August the first group of sailors transferred to Hourtin near Bordeaux and the Bay of Biscay to master flying boats. By mid-September all First Detachment personnel had completed their work at Tours.[45]

Ranking as one of its most experienced pilots, the Navy placed Lt. Godfrey Chevalier in charge of the proposed combat unit at Dunkirk. So he might develop proper training routines and command a fighting squadron, Chevalier completed the entire French flight program. He began work on Caudrons at Tours, then Bleriot "Penguins" and Nieuports at Avord, more advanced work at Pau, and finally aerial gunnery at Cazaux. He passed through these courses rapidly and received "excellent" reports throughout. George Moseley, who later flew at Dunkirk, encountered Chevalier during the training regimen at Avord, recalling, "Stuff (Dumaresq Spencer) and I had another surprise day before yesterday when Chevalier came into camp. He is training here so that he will be able to drive one of the fast little seaplanes the Navy intends to use. . . . He is a fine fellow, full of pep and fire." A bit later the Yalie added, "Poor old Chevy, he was sorry to see us go and believe me we were sorry to leave him. He is a peach." After temporary duty in Paris, Chevalier assumed command at NAS Dunkirk November 10.[46]

While a contingent from the First Aeronautic Detachment practiced at Tours, men assigned as observers and mechanics attended the school at St. Raphael, Capitaine Chauvin commanding, on the Mediterranean Riviera coast near Nice. After two weeks at Camaret, Lieutenant Griffin and approximately 25 *Neptune* men entrained for St. Raphael. They traveled south, via Paris, through "wonderful country." In St. Raphael the sailors met up with Chief Gunners Mate O'Connor and 25 other bluejackets from *Jupiter* who arrived the previous day. Upon reaching the coast they set about exploring the city, dictionaries in hand, trying to chat up the local girls. Actual instruction commenced June 25. During three sequential, three-week courses, Americans studied gasoline motors and airplane assembly taught by English-speaking French instructors. Those designated observer-trainees also received instruction in bombing and machine guns. During this period many experienced food shortages; at one point three-quarters were on the sick list. Lieutenant(jg) Albert Stevens arrived as medical officer in July and added fresh vegetables and sugar to the men's diet, which seemed to clear things up.[47]

The sequence of instruction for mechanics/observers began with motor erecting, assembly, and timing, including work on Hispano-Suizas, Salmsons, and Clergets. The V-8/12 engines like those in the Hispano-Suiza and later Liberty were characterized by opposing, angled banks of cylnders mounted above a straight crankcase. Radial engines such as the Salmson had an odd number of stationary cylinders (often nine) arrayed in a circle. Rotary motors like the Clerget, Gnome, and Le Rhone also had their cylinders arranged in a circle around the crankcase, which was bolted to the aircraft frame, while the propeller was bolted to the engine case (cylinders), which spun, generating enormous torque in the direction of the spin, a potentially deadly characteristic.

Lieutenant Griffin taught principles of aircraft. Then the men helped assemble seaplanes. All the while they took careful notes, filling notebooks with charts and specifications. In late July sailors began the observer course, which included bomb dropping and machine gun practice. They also learned semaphore signaling, wireless radio operating, and Morse code. Actual flying commenced at the end of the month, first in Donnet-Denhaut and then FBA flying boats. The men celebrated their baptismal flights with an evening banquet. One called it "a wonderful day's experience." "I had my first jump," he reported. "I sat in the machine beside the pilot and away we went." They soared out above sea, back over the mountains, and after gaining an altitude of 2,100 feet started to spiral down. The same trainee also discussed aerial bombing. "It's just the same as shooting at a target," he claimed. "You look over the sight, keep your machine horizontal in flight, draw a fine bead, pull the spring, and the bomb falls. . . . It doesn't have to drop exactly on the sub but as near as possible. If it is within 50 feet it will destroy a submarine or sink it."

Despite wartime pressures, instruction moved at a leisurely Gallic pace. Training flights occurred in the early morning before heat and wind made conditions problematic. This allowed ample time for sightseeing and other activities. Holidays like Fourth of July or Bastille Day brought extended liberty and outings to Frejus, Nice, or Cannes, where a few Americans met a group of Canadian nurses with whom they enjoyed picnics and swimming parties. When not relaxing, the men took care of business, washing clothes, writing letters, getting barbered, and complaining about the food, condemning a constant diet of stew, war bread, and beans. Irving Sheely groused, "We only get two meals a day . . . and these are so rotten that I sometimes do without." Americans also fed their souls. A retired minister led YMCA Sunday School meetings, and Sheely opined, "It was fine and I enjoyed it immensely. He surely give [sic] us a good talk."

The young men's high spirits, notwithstanding, they couldn't help but be sobered by the continual carnage. Diarists recorded a litany of disasters, both large and small. A French pilot crashed July 3 and broke his arm, his machine a total wreck. Three days later a plane fell from a height of 200 feet, seriously injuring the pilot, "probably will die." Another wreck occurred the following day, broken arms and broken wings. Yet another machine fell July 12, the pilot killed instantly. "Our fellows helped dig him out of the wreckage." Writing home in August, Sheely reported that "another of our fellows has been killed." He and a French pilot collided in the air. The Frenchman landed safely but the American crashed and fractured his skull. The navy men reported the deaths of several Frenchmen during their sojourn on the Riviera, with one judging, "I think it is due mostly to carelessness."[48]

In late August, after two months' instruction, followed by a battery of examinations, the mechanic-observer program at St. Raphael ended and the enlisted contingent set off for Moutchic-Lacanau near the Bay of Biscay, site of the United States' infant naval aviation school. There they found a tent encampment hugging the shore of an almost deserted lake overseen by a thin, intense officer named John Lansing Callan. An important addition to the Navy's nascent aviation program occurred when Callan transferred ashore from *Seattle* and reported to Whiting in Paris. He expected to take charge of the ship's 12 experienced aviation ratings, but the vessel departed St. Nazaire without disembarking the men. Instead, Callan went to Tours, Hourtin, and then Moutchic-Lacanau to oversee the proposed school there.[49]

Callan, known since childhood as "Lanny," was born in Cohoes, New York, in 1886, son of a prominent local real estate broker. He attended the Curtiss flight school at Hammondsport in 1911 where he met several aviation pioneers, including William Doherty and Beckwith Havens. He also watched the Navy conduct its experiments with the Curtiss Triad seaplane. Upon graduation he became an assistant instructor in both land and hydroplanes and later participated in the famous Eugene Ely flights at Norfolk. After several years' service for Curtiss, including duty aboard *Mississippi* working with John Towers and *North Carolina* with Kenneth Whiting, as well as a busy stint with the Italian Navy, Callan enlisted in the U.S. Navy in February 1917. He soon developed into one of the service's most accomplished "advance men," repeatedly assigned the task of getting a new station up and running, first at Moutchic, then Le Croisic, Ile Tudy, and finally in Italy. A slight, wiry man with a neatly trimmed mustache, Callan wore stylish, tightly fitted uniforms, and after a career lasting more than three decades, retired in 1948 with the rank of rear admiral.[50]

Callan arrived in Paris July 11, checked in at the Hotel Meurice, and met with Kenneth Whiting, Attaché Sayles, and Captain Jackson. The following day he arranged his accounts with Paymaster Conger and set off for St. Nazaire, with further instructions to visit Le Croisic, and then establish a training school at Moutchic. Callan's initial impressions of the situation were pessimistic, claiming Germany held control of the air over the English Channel, the French army was "all in," and the British would sue for peace if the U-boats were not checked. Callan reached St. Nazaire two days later and met with Lieutenant Commander Vaschalde of the French naval flying service, with whom he motored to Le Croisic, calling their driver the wildest he had ever known. Callan finalized plans to establish the Navy station there on two small islands near the center of town. Callan then returned to St. Nazaire and proceeded to Nantes and Rochefort, accompanied by an officer from a sunken ship, who recounted decent treatment at the hands of a U-boat commander who allowed him to keep the instruments that were his private property.

At Rochefort, Callan viewed the dirigible station and discussed plans for the school at Lacanau, then proceeded to Bordeaux. The next day, July 16, he motored to Lacanau and toured the lake from a slow motorboat. Lacanau lay four miles from the ocean, one-half mile from Moutchic railroad station, and approximately 30 miles from Bordeaux. Only a rough road around the lake and a few houses offered evidence of human habitation. Dense pine forests covered the dunes almost to the water's edge. A later commentator called it a "wilderness of pine and sand." Following earlier discussions with Whiting, the French Navy negotiated a construction contract with a local builder, the same contractor responsible for work at future NAS Arcachon and St. Trojan. Ultimately, severe shortages of civilian labor, materials, and rolling stock required Navy labor to perform most tasks. Some planned projects remained uncompleted 15 months later. On his first visit Callan inspected grounds for the camp and possible houses for officers. He believed considerable timber clearing needed to be done and a new road built. He also drew up initial plans, examined the road to Moutchic village, and returned to Bordeaux.[51]

Back in the city, Callan confessed that he loafed until the end of the month, playing tennis, sea-bathing, attending the theater, and having dinner with English and French women. Not everything was relaxation, however, as he became embroiled in a controversy concerning the price of the land for the school. The French demanded $30,000 for the site; Callan valued the plot at only $5,000. The American consul in Bordeaux suggested an offer of $6,000, urging, "We need to be stern." The pace of activity accelerated July 31 when three enlisted men arrived, and the following day Callan hired two mule teams and two extra men and commenced unloading supplies in the rain. Workers began felling trees and clearing the site. The French surveyor inspected Moutchic while bluejackets finished their tasks. Callan then traveled over to Pauillac, seeking suitable ground for an aircraft assembly facility, and selected a location next to the new Navy station. He followed this with a visit to Cazaux where the French maintained both flight and aerial gunnery schools. Then it was back to Moutchic with the chief engineer of the French Navy where he acquired a small villa, "Tours de Pins," to serve as temporary quarters and began redrawing plans for the school, all the while pelted with continuous rain.[52]

Actual work began August 13 when Callan's small crew put up a kitchen tent and the following day erected the first canvas shelter on "Camp Street," a task performed in a downpour so heavy "you couldn't see 100 yards." At that moment the contractor arrived and assumed control of construction. This allowed Callan to visit the French school at Lac Hourtin to arrange instruction for a detail of Americans scheduled to arrive in the next few weeks. The commandant, a veteran of the Dardanelles campaign, presided over a rather primitive facility, with just three propellers available for seven aircraft and most men sleeping in flying boat packing crates. The Moutchic project received a significant boost at the end of August when Lieutenant Griffin and 54 enlisted First Detachment mechanics and observers arrived from St. Raphael. Early in September Lieutenant Dichman and 11 student pilots from Tours reached camp. During the next several weeks, as initial construction proceeded, Moutchic evolved into something of a transit center. A parade of officers and enlisted men passed through the raw station on their way to and from various French training facilities. An initial party departed for Cazaux for the gunnery course and returned three weeks later, quickly replaced by 12 more. Several officers transited on their way to Hourtin, while Lt. William

Corry and 11 enlisted pilots entrained for St Raphael. Dichman and seven additional men returned from St. Raphael October 21.[53]

Moutchic received its first important visitor September 20 when Admiral Sims toured the site. Two days later the men erected a Bessaneau hangar near the water's edge. Bessaneau hangars were modest, temporary structures with timber frames, covered with canvas, named after their manufacturer. Shortly thereafter the first FBA flying boats arrived in crates after being held at the railroad station for two weeks. Ensign Robert Lovett and an enlisted crew assembled the first of the FBAs. He made the school's initial flight September 27. At the same time men began taking courses in navigation, gunnery, signaling, airplane structure, engines, and Navy regulations. During these early weeks, life at Moutchic remained rustic at best. Sailors fished for perch and slept in hammocks. They pressed FBA shipping boxes into service as mess halls.

All during the fall and into the early winter, many lived in tents or makeshift bunkhouses. According to one sailor their lives seemed like "camp life I've done in the north woods." They cooked their meals over a fire on the ground, slept in tents, bathed in the lake, and washed their own clothes. Spare time was devoted to baseball, football, writing letters, reading, sometimes sewing. "We go to bed with the chickens," he wrote. "Guess I won't know how to live in civil life after this or how it will feel to wear a collar again." On occasion, sailors received overnight liberty in Bordeaux where they strolled around town or rode the streetcars for the equivalent of one cent. Officers enjoyed relative comfort and boarded at a small hotel on the coast, "commuting" to Moutchic each day by truck. Mostly college men from affluent families, they found accommodations a bit primitive—no heat, no bathtubs, and only candles for light. Hardly any of the Americans spoke French, and few of the staff spoke English. Even getting a drink of water posed a challenge. Local residents seemed unfamiliar with the custom. On the other hand, their hosts provided copious quantities of local red wine.[54]

Despite unsettled conditions, progress continued. Work on two more FBAs commenced and construction gangs erected a second hangar, and then a third. Additional personnel just landed from the United States entered camp. A few "ambulance men" joined the detachment, as did several of the "Yale" flyers. By mid-October eight aircraft were assembled or under construction. The station roster counted 126 men, with 12 more at Cazaux, 26 at St. Raphael, and 19 at Lac Hourtin. Sailors began erecting a YMCA building (with a barber shop). Others utilized a simple darkroom for photography. The swelling complement also required expansion of mess facilities. Observer/Mechanic Sheely wrote,

"Busy all day changing mess hall, making it bigger for boys who arrived from Brest and Pensacola." By autumn the weather turned raw and damp. Some bluejackets made stoves for their tents out of discarded tin cans. Callan borrowed blankets from the French for his uncomfortable sailors. For a time only pinecones and sticks gathered in the surrounding forest provided fuel. Between October 8 and 14 heavy wind and rain greatly impeded aeronautic activity, with virtually no flying attempted. At one point Sheely noted that the sun had finally come out after 14 days of rain. Water had come in through the tent fly and soaked everything, including clothes and bunk. The arrival of cool weather only made things worse: "Mornings very cold now, rather tough crawling out in the A.M."

In order to speed preparation of naval aviators, at least while organizing and equipping the school at Moutchic, several dozen observers and pilots trained at the French aerial gunnery school at Cazaux near Bordeaux and the seaplane school on Lac Hourtin, officially the Ecole d'Aviation Maritime de Hourtin (L'Ecole de Pilotage de Hourtin). John Callan led an initial contingent of 12 observers to Cazaux 40 miles to the south. The setting there closely resembled that at Moutchic, a lakeside location, "nothing but soft, white sand with scrub pines growing almost everywhere . . . the water was never really rough." Directed by Commandant Marzac, the regimen at Cazaux seemed busy and rapid. Trainees commenced target shooting using .22 and .303 carbines, then blasted skeet with shotguns, followed by machine guns. They also rode in gliders and motorboats, the general idea being to accustom them to aiming and firing while experiencing many different types of motion. Then they went aloft in a Farman airplane and fired at targets on the ground. Next they progressed to flying in an airplane and shooting at a balloon with a .303 carbine. After a week they graduated to firing a machine gun aloft.

One aspect of training recalled by virtually all was shooting at "Maggie's drawers," a cloth target towed behind another airplane. In only a short period, future observers became proficient in the use and maintenance of Lewis and Vickers machine guns. They took examinations in shooting deflection and learned how to fix breech jams while in the air. At the end of three weeks new gunners ascended to an altitude of 4,000 feet in a Caudron, the first land machine they had been in. One enlisted man reported, "They tow a sausage shape bag around with an airplane and we shoot at it from another airplane. Sounds like a lot of Bluff, don't it?" By late September this first class of Americans finished work and returned to Moutchic, quickly replaced by a dozen more.[55]

A swelling cadre of American student-pilots in need of up-to-date flight instruction began reaching France in late summer, especially men of the

First Yale Unit. For their education the French government set aside places at Lac Hourtin for preliminary seaplane training and at St. Raphael for more advanced work. In mid-September Robert Lovett and Artemus "Di" Gates, having already passed through Tours, transited Moutchic on their way to Lac Hourtin, 12 miles away, where they joined a small contingent of enlisted pilots recently arrived from Tours already training in FBA flying boats. The widely used machines exhibited the dangerous handling characteristics imparted by the rotary action of their 130 hp Clerget motor. Kenneth MacLeish, later claimed, "I'm not crazy about them . . . they do queer little tricks due to the gyroscopic action of the rotary motor and the controls aren't very sensitive." A left-hand turn might put the plane into a spin, while the aircraft's flat bottom resulted in jarring landings unless set down tail first. MacLeish opined, "I never flew a rottener contraption in my life."[56] Di Gates described Lac Hourtin as a little larger than Lake Worth (Palm Beach) and expected to be there just a week, then proceed to the Mediterranean for rough water flying. The school stood "in some large pine woods on the side of a hill beside a beautiful lake. Life (was) very primitive, like camping in the Adirondacks or Maine." Students slept in small tents with no chairs or lights except small candles. No flying took place on Saturday afternoon or Sunday. Instead, everyone spent his time swimming and keeping cool. At one point Gates reported being startled when a large French dirigible returning from an ocean patrol flew overhead at an altitude of only 200 feet. "I first thought it was a zeppelin," he admitted sheepishly.

The school gathered together a great assortment of humanity. Gates noticed a group of French sailors playing leapfrog, while nearby several Annamites (Vietnamese) "played some weird tunes," and not far away American bluejackets played baseball. Close by stood a camp holding German POWs. The Annamites and Germans did the heavy labor. "The Germans seem perfectly peaceful," Gates reported, "but we still sleep with revolvers beside our cots." John Vorys, one more of the Yale contingent, dismissively described Hourtin as a "temporary sort of a place" with canvas hangars and log huts, the lake a puddle among sand dunes, the dunes held in place by pine trees, wild boars, and wild Moroccans. He and other Americans ate in the officers' mess. The system of instruction appeared haphazard to him. All the teachers were enlisted men. First, someone fixed up an FBA a little so it could fly. Then they flew until the weather turned bad, the machine crashed, or the instructor felt tired. In that way it took three weeks to fly four hours and solo. Vorys called it a "ham school." Chip McIlwaine dined at the French mess and felt quite at home. He detected very little system in the instruction, however, and his hosts never talked about flying. Instead, they discussed women, boar hunting in the nearby piney woods, women, the commandant's boat, and women.

Henry Landon, one of McIlwaine's classmates, detected a different attitude, with instructors hurrying to turn out pilots, and rough landings the order of the day. After a jarring descent the plane taxied to shore where the teacher ordered a mechanic to look it over. He usually climbed in, took off, and brought it back, saying everything was O.K. Captain Thomas Craven later explained that the French considered FBA instruction complete after seven hours. Bluejacket J. D. Jernigan's training lasted only five hours. The entire American detachment, both officers and enlisted pilots, finished work during the fall after four to eight weeks at Hourtin.[57]

After preliminary training at Lac Hourtin, several American pilots journeyed to St. Raphael for further work, the same facility utilized by enlisted mechanic-observers in July and August. This detachment included members of the original First Aeronautic Detachment trained at Tours, such as Joseph Cline and Jernigan, as well as several Yale Unit officers. Here they received more advanced instruction in flying boats as well as gunnery and seaplane bombing. Upon completing coursework, two became instructors at Moutchic. Many others went on to active duty stations such as NAS Le Croisic, Ile Tudy, and St. Trojan. After the flying school at Moutchic became fully operational, no further pilots trained at St. Raphael. Later, a dozen enlisted men journeyed to Issoudun for instruction in pursuit planes and then went to England and Scotland for Royal Flying Corps (RFC) training before being assigned combat duties at Dunkirk.

Neophyte aviators found the Mediterranean environment as congenial as the observers had. Di Gates wrote enthusiastically, "Talk about winter at Palm Beach! I started my winter season on the Riviera. Have put on whites and hope to discard my blues." John Vorys moved into the Hotel de la Plage where he rendezvoused with Gates, Lt. William Corry, and Dr. Sinton. Reflecting the local custom, a French officer from the school lived openly with his mistress. The young American had seen the same thing at Hourtin. At first, large numbers of French pilots and then the mistral delayed training, and Vorys took advantage of the idleness to read guide books, rent a bicycle, and tour the sights. Idyllic or not, however, there was work to do. At the beginning of October, Gates described the program, flying FBAs with rotary and Hispano motors, then moving on to DDs and Telliers. He found the French water brevet even easier than their land brevet. He also offered a running commentary on events and conditions, including the ferocious mistral that prevented flying, and required the men to sit around and wait for the wind to die down. Gates sat through many lectures (in French) but couldn't understand them. He also spotted a "large number of [black] troops here, 40,000 from French West Africa, [who] always wear big heavy overcoats, even on hot days." According to the young man from Iowa, they delighted in bringing back German heads as souvenirs. A few weeks later Gates spotted a dirigible that he thought was a French airship but it turned out to be a German zeppelin. Though pursued, the off-course marauder began to climb and escaped in the darkness.

Enemy zeppelins were not the only things going astray. When Joseph Cline reached St. Raphael he learned to fly FBAs, DDs, Telliers, and Salmsons. One day while soaring over Monte Carlo his engine cut out and he landed five miles from shore. Unable to restart the motor, he drifted toward the Italian border. Luckily, a French patrol boat spotted him and towed his plane into harbor. Cline spent a very pleasant evening at the Hotel des Anglais, then serving as a convalescent home for Allied officers. Of course, the parade of crashes was witnessed by First Detachment observers during the summer. Gates reported September 23, "saw a smashup Saturday. Arrived to see them pull the badly injured pilot out of the wreck and a dead pilot." A month later he described a further mishap. "Had another smash Friday, French pilot in an FBA was soloing. . . . It went into a sideslip on a turn, the boat turned over several times on the way down, threw him out 30' above the water, hurt but saved." Those who completed the course successfully received their French brevet, what Yale Unit member John Vorys called "a large fancy diploma with a naked lady on it." There was also occasion to ponder less weighty subjects. In his spare time John Farwell "concocted" a new design for winter uniforms he considered "distinctly classy," a combination of blue britches, puttees, and blue coats. Farwell felt these would be more "regulation looking than Marine Corps forest green atrocities."[58]

Back near the Bay of Biscay, operations at Moutchic assumed a more organized aspect. Grattan Dichman relieved John Callan on October 22. The school staff then consisted of Dichman as commanding officer, with Callan serving temporarily as executive officer. Under them Robert Lovett oversaw operations, Frederick Michel managed pay and supply, and Albert Stevens acted as medical officer. Ensign Herman Jorgenson became executive officer when Callan departed. Flying classes commenced October 24 following installation of dual controls in some of the FBAs. Workers erected a flagpole October 29 and the following day the station held morning colors for the first time. The day after that a newly installed ship's gong began striking the hours. Many more flying officers entered camp and the last students returned from Hourtin. Several pilots and observers departed Moutchic to begin operations at NAS Le Croisic, America's first patrol base; among them were Yalies Ken Smith, Reginald Coombe, Sam Walker, and 13 enlisted personnel. In early November additional flyers packed their gear and headed to acrobatic school. Diarist Irving Sheely, who received word November 9 that he had been ordered to Dunkirk, noted, "Maybe I wasn't surprised." With the change of command, commencement of regular training, and departure of personnel for their first duty stations, the First Aeronautic Detachment phase at Moutchic ended.[59]

* * *

Naval aviation activities in Europe began with a handful of junior officers and 120 untrained enlisted men. During his few months of largely unsupervised activity, Kenneth Whiting provided extraordinary drive, initiative, and leadership. Almost single-handedly he created a framework for future aviation efforts in France. Whiting arranged training for a critical nucleus of pilots and mechanics, selected sites for a dozen patrol stations, outlined needs and priorities for the aeronautic campaign to come, and negotiated a series of agreements with the French. With these actions he set the agenda, and Washington reacted to his initiative, not the other way around.

With hindsight, some of Whiting's actions were likely misguided, due to his own limited experience and extraordinary zeal. The decision to operate a patrol station at Dunkirk, for example, proved unwise, as did his overreliance on seaplanes, while the size of the American establishment in France eventually exceeded the true needs of the Navy. As Turnbull and Lord later observed, "It is safe to say that had conferences been held at the level of the high command before Whiting acted, bases in England and Ireland would have been chosen ahead of any facilities in France for supporting aerial operations against U-boats."[60]

For many months the United States depended on French facilities and equipment to carry out its program, especially schools at Tours, St. Raphael, Hourtin, and Cazaux. By early November, however, this early phase had ended. The American school at Moutchic was up and running. New leadership and direction arrived in the person of Hutch Cone. The first station at Le Croisic was ready to begin patrols. The work of the First Aeronautic Detachment was done.

2

PROGRESS REPORT

September 1917–March 1918

Hutch Cone's arrival in Britain in September 1917 initiated a thorough overhaul of naval aviation efforts. He conferred with Sims, Whiting, Conger, and others, reviewed existing correspondence, met repeatedly with the Admiralty, and undertook a forced-draft tour of potential station sites in Ireland and England. Cone then crossed over to France and relieved Whiting October 24, assuming command of United States Naval Aviation Forces in Foreign Service with headquarters in Paris. He first occupied existing offices at 23 Rue de la Paix, but in mid-November secured larger quarters at Hotel d'Iena, 4 Place d'Iena. The Navy took over the entire 90-room structure, with plans to utilize excess space to accommodate the headquarters Marine guard and enlisted staff.[1] During the next year Cone shouldered primary responsibility for developing naval aviation in the war zone, notably assisted by gunnery expert Capt. Thomas T. Craven, director of the Operations Division. In London Lt. Paul H. Bastedo of the Material Section temporarily directed aviation matters, replaced in November by Lt. Walter Atlee Edwards. Cone referred to the latter as "young Edwards" brought up from the Queenstown destroyers. A memo prepared by Sims's chief of staff, Capt. Nathan C. Twining, defined Cone's role as commander of all naval aviation forces in France and Britain, primarily responsible in areas of policy, operations, personnel, and materiel. Twining noted, "The Admiral desires to give Cdr. Cone a perfectly free hand to carry out his ideas." The aviation section in London would be Cone's direct representative, he noted, and urged all officers to maintain the closest contact with the British.

Cone set to work enlarging and reorganizing his headquarters and within a few weeks seemed to have matters well in hand. In his first staff plan he decided to "organize the outfit in two distinct parts," one operational and the other handling business affairs. Cone placed Operations under Cdr. Frank Mc-Crary, a Lighter-than-Air (LTA) expert, leaving Whiting in charge of heavier-than-air matters.² Paymaster Conger headed the Material Section. Civil Engineer Ernest Brownell took control of Public Works (Construction), having been rushed to Paris at Cone's urgent request. Brownell was "well thought of by all the aviation crowd" who had worked with him at Pensacola. Cone described Civil Engineer A. W. K. Billings, Brownell's assistant, as a man of "very high reputation." Lieutenant Commander Benjamin Briscoe assumed leadership of the newly established Assembly and Repair section, while Surgeon H. H. Lane directed medical affairs. Cone also secured the services of two junior officers. Lieutenant Harry Guggenheim became business aide, while Lt. Norman Van der Veer came on board as military aide, both to run the details of the office. The new commander called the pair his office youngsters. Van Der Veer was well known in the fleet as editor of the *Bluejacket Manual*. The presence of these two young officers allowed the commander to "circulate around the French stations and visit England when it becomes necessary."³

At the end of the year Cone updated his organization, creating a tripartite staff, including a new Intelligence and Planning Division overseen first by Lt. Virgil Griffin and then Cdr. Henry Dinger. Operations Division staff now included director McCrary (soon to be replaced by Craven), assisted by Callan (Schools), Van Der Veer (Personnel), and the as yet unnamed head of the Repair Section, as well as commanders of the various schools and stations. The Administrative Division headed by Guggenheim, included sections for Public Works, Supplies, Repair Base, and Secretariat. Surgeon Lane remained in charge of medical affairs. A new Executive Committee to coordinate office efforts consisted of Cone, the three division heads, and Ensign Fearing.⁴ Following reorganization, the original First Aeronautic Detachment officers who had served in Europe since June 1917 went on to fill a variety of posts. After a time in Paris, Whiting visited England to study seaplane conditions and then sailed home to organize the great Killingholme-lighter project.⁵ He returned in May 1918 to command NAS Killingholme, a position he held until the end of the war. Grattan Dichman directed the aviation school at Moutchic, later commanded NAS Brest, and ultimately returned to destroyer service. Godfrey Chevalier became commanding officer at NAS Dunkirk and then the Northern Bombing Group assembly and repair base at Eastleigh. Virgil Griffin served for a while on the Paris staff before spending several weeks at RNAS Yarmouth, and finally assuming command of NAS St. Trojan. Omar Conger, an unsung hero, oversaw the supply effort, until superseded by Captain Bonnafon of the Paymaster Corps late in the war. Surgeon Arthur Sinton, carried out numerous inspections at Tours, Moutchic, and Pauillac.

Cone's (and Sims's) insistent calls for additional officers to fill out the growing staff did not always sit well with the Navy Department, which experienced identical needs on a much greater scale. Unfulfilled requests for the services of the controversial Cdr. Henry Mustin proved particularly problematic. Cone also pressed for regular Navy flyers (especially those recommended by McCrary) to command the stations. He wished them dispatched to Europe sooner rather than later so they might have time "to get wise to the game." At the time Cone exuded reasonableness from every pore, saying, "If for any reason you (Irwin) or the Department sees fit to deny my request (for officers) I don't question your wisdom in the slightest and realize that you need able officers there as well as I do over here." Captain Noble Irwin, in overall command of aviation, and others in the Department let him know, however, that they considered his demands unrealistic. Though expressing "no kicks about the way you fellows over there are treating us," Cone eventually lost patience, responding shortly after New Year's. "You fellows think I am overexcited about getting officers over here," he flared, but there were numerous holes in tables of organization, "together with the fact that we have some 1,500 men with a couple of Ensigns looking out for them, disciplining them, etc., you will realize I am really short-handed." Cone's "pet scheme" of exchanging staff officers between Washington and Paris came to naught. These personnel issues remained a sore point until the end of the war, and after.[6]

Throughout autumn and early winter Cone continued perfecting his organization and filling administrative slots as fast as he could. He informed Sims on November 5 of a pressing need for civil engineers to oversee construction of bases, medical officers, an office manager, technical officers, and a Marine Corps detachment of 60 men and an officer who might act as a permanent Navy Provost Marshal in Paris. More supply men were required as well, while a desperate shortage of trained aviation mechanics hindered rapid progress. Cone and his staff set right to work acquiring aircraft and equipment for aviation stations under construction and by November 27 had placed orders for 17 Telliers, 44 Donnet Denhauts, 10 Hanriot-Duponts, and 5 dirigibles, along with 200 motors and materiel to complete 4 stations—bombs, radios, guns, gas tanks, and trucks at an estimated cost of $6 million. Eventually the Navy contracted for 140 aircraft in France. These plans, however, proved wildly optimistic. By December only 23 aircraft had been received, with 18 more ready to be shipped. Unrealistic delivery schedules, shortages of material, labor troubles, and rising demands from the French army and navy all combined to delay equipping American stations.[7]

Cone seemed to direct his attention in a dozen directions at once. In mid-

November he penned a lengthy missive to Irwin outlining plans to establish an aviation assembly and repair facility at Pauillac, describing the need for hundreds of tents to shelter growing numbers of personnel, and reporting on the painfully slow progress of local contractors. Cone discovered that many green recruits arriving in Europe managed to lose most of their clothing on the way over and supply officers were scrounging surplus garments from whatever naval vessels reached the French coast. The new commander stressed his efforts at cooperating with AEF aviation leaders, particularly Col. Raynal Bolling, whom Cone described as "a perfectly fine man in every way." Paymaster Conger now served on a joint committee controlling purchases in France, with plans under way to establish a small (three members) committee of Army and Navy officers to represent the Aircraft Production Board. Cone claimed, "Rest assured that we are working in perfect harmony." A similar report to Sims highlighted rapidly expanding manpower needs as station personnel allowances spiraled upward. Cone now calculated that manning the 15 proposed facilities required 870 officers and 8,454 men, considerably higher than earlier estimates.[8]

Of course, selecting personnel was not without its pitfalls. In early spring 1918, Edwards in London notified Cone, "I am really quite delighted to have such an excellent excuse to detach Ens. (Tree) from this office as he, unfortunately, appears entirely too young and inexperienced to tackle the job I had outlined for him." It seems the young ensign's diplomat father requested his son's posting, which caused some flap at Cone's level. Two weeks later Edwards wrote, "Ens. (Wilcox), although a conscientious, hard-working officer, is absolutely unqualified for the position to which I had assigned him in this office. Very briefly his trouble is that he is stupid to a remarkable degree and has not been able to grasp the job in any degree."[9]

Naval aviation's priorities in the last quarter of 1917, particularly as refined by Hutch Cone, encompassed creating a formal command structure; finalizing selection of station sites in France, Ireland, and England; commencing training at Moutchic; placing students/mechanics wherever appropriate; opening the first bases; and beginning construction of others. During the winter these goals expanded to include initiating serious construction at more bases, transporting large numbers of personnel to Europe, building up the assembly and repair facility at Pauillac, accelerating training programs, enlarging the command organization, and commencing operations at Dunkirk and Bolsena. To some degree, all of these goals were met.[10]

Promoted to captain in December, Cone shivered in his office next to an open coal fire grate and solidified his aviation staff by issuing Organizational

Memo III on January 29, 1918, which provided a template for all office development to follow. The Intelligence and Planning Division collected information concerning aircraft and equipment from varied sources and continuously monitored the airplane situation. The all-important Operations Division, now led by Thomas Craven and assisted by Frank McCrary (soon to be detached for duty in Ireland) and Robert Lovett, controlled the heart of the aviation mission, training and manning the fighting stations and conducting war operations. Most recently commanding officer of *Sacramento* at Gibraltar, Craven was an acknowledged gunnery expert, who had earlier professed ignorance of the entire field of aviation. Cone reassured him by saying that he, too, knew little about flying. Individual station commanders reported directly to Craven, who exercised day-to-day authority, while Cone tended to larger planning, program, interservice and inter-Allied affairs, and overall command responsibilities. The Administrative Division headed by Guggenheim organized the major work of building and supplying new bases, negotiating contracts and overseeing construction, as well as directing purchase and shipping of equipment. Omar Conger, who came over in June 1917 with the First Aeronautic Detachment, played a central role, as did Ernest Brownell and Benjamin Briscoe. A question also arose about how to deal with Edwards, Sims's aide in London. He had done much good work overseeing aviation efforts there, but his junior rank made it difficult for him to lead an enlarged office. Rather than replace Edwards with a more senior officer, Cone and Sims decided to leave him in charge directing personnel junior to him. The Killingholme project evolved into a separate command under Kenneth Whiting.[11]

Cone instituted his final reorganization March 1, 1918, incorporating slight modifications to the January 29 scheme, but retaining the three-division format of Intelligence and Planning, Operations, and Administration. Dinger continued to head the Intelligence and Planning Division. Craven's Operations Division, assisted by Lovett, exercised "direct charge of the operation of all air stations and schools." The Administration Division, directed by Guggenheim, had "charge of all business and industrial activities," and oversaw Supply, Public Works, Repair Base (Pauillac), and Secretarial Sections. A new Medical Department, headed by Surgeon Lane, reported directly to Cone. An Executive Committee, including Cone and his division heads, facilitated coordination of the organization. The growing headquarters required ever more office space and progressively occupied greater portions of the Hotel d'Iena site.[12]

In addition to the officers and enlisted ratings swelling the ranks of headquarters staff, the Navy also employed a variety of civilians, both in Paris and elsewhere. Knowledgeable men from a wide range of specialties from construction and engineering to business and transportation were engaged to provide needed expertise. Several were enrolled into active service. The Navy generally hired civilian women to augment the clerical workforce rather than dispatch "Yeomanettes" overseas. By mid-1918 these civilian hires could be found in Paris, Pauillac, Brest, and London. In June 1918, for example, Misses Hilda Golby, Gertrude Watt, and Janet Wilson were ordered from Paris to Pauillac for duty, followed shortly thereafter by Mlle. Suzanne Dolbeau. A group photograph of Captain Craven's staff at Brest near the end of the war reveals a similar sprinkling of female staff. Such employees, however, were not found at the operating air stations or construction sites.[13]

With a sizable organization in place, Cone instituted frequent meetings of the headquarters Executive Committee to discuss equipment, operations, transportation, training, personnel, reports on trips and inspections, cooperation with the Army, liaison with the Allies, and any of a hundred other concerns. After September 1, 1918, the conferences convened in London. These meetings mirrored those held in Washington by Captain Irwin, who gathered representatives of Navy Bureaus that controlled portions of the aeronautic effort. Officers returning from assignment in Europe briefed this group, as did liaison personnel from the RAF.[14] Attempting to move construction along, Cone in early December dispatched an inspection committee to view existing and proposed bases/sites, part of the process for finalizing the coastal station program. The group included McCrary from Operations, Surgeon Lane, and Civil Engineers Brownell and Billings. They began work December 1 at Brest and finished at Moutchic 10 days later, submitting their report December 17. This detailed document contained the name and location of each site, identified possible landing and get away fields, and described tides and currents, transportation, communication, construction requirements, piers and runways, gas storage, available/necessary equipment, sanitary conditions, water facilities, and French commitments/arrangements. An important conference held with the Ministry of Marine in early January 1918 further solidified details for establishment and operation of American stations.[15]

Even as officers in France developed detailed guidelines for future action, Sims's newly established Planning Section in London came to general agreement on aviation priorities for coming months, particularly those related to activity in Flanders and over the North Sea. The greatest efforts would be made toward destroying enemy submarine bases in Belgium by utilizing land-based bombing squadrons, aided by *chasse* and photographic reconnaissance units. The Killingholme-lighter project would go ahead as planned, while operations in Italy should proceed as well. The planned network of patrol stations on the French coast should be built as envisioned, as well as dirigible and kite balloon bases, but with the latter's equipment halved. Pauillac would serve as principal assembly and repair facility in Europe, with Queenstown in Ireland functioning as a sub-base with two-thirds the equipment allocated to Pauillac.

At the end of the winter John Callan, then serving as head of the School Section in the Operations Division, compiled a statistical analysis of instruction efforts completed thus far. By early March a total of 180 pilots had trained at numerous European sites, including 81 officers and 99 ratings. Many enlisted aviators later received commissions. Facilities at Moutchic now provided instruction in both flying boats and pontoon scouts. Other training locations included Tours, Lac Hourtin, St. Raphael, Felixstowe, Pau, Avord, Issoudun, Gosport, Turnberry, Ayr, a variety of Royal Naval Air Service (RNAS) patrol stations, Lake Bolsena, and Cranwell. In fact, at this point the number of pilots exceeded available aircraft. Enlisted observer personnel also attended several overseas schools, including St. Raphael and Cazaux. Others attended schools at Cranwell and Eastchurch/Leysdown in England. A total of 91 observers completed their courses by early March, 89 of them enlisted men. Additional bluejackets and a few officers worked at French factories to study construction and maintenance of motors and aircraft.[16]

Creating a headquarters organization, laying out a plan for bases, allocating men and equipment, even training personnel, offered one set of challenges, but the real-world task of commencing war operations proved another thing indeed, and in this area the process moved more slowly. In early November, officers and bluejackets reached Le Croisic and initiated limited patrols a few days later. Additional personnel occupied a partially completed station at Ile Tudy and began flight operations February 28, 1918. During the winter, men, aircraft, and supplies flowed into Dunkirk, with training/test flights under way by February. American personnel reached the dirigible station at Paimboeuf on November 11 and took control of the site on March 1. They made their first flight under Navy command March 3.

Also during fall and winter the Navy resolved the issue of choosing a site for a central European aviation assembly, repair, and distribution center, selecting Pauillac on the Gironde River near Bordeaux. While Paris served initially as principal supply center, it eventually gave way to Pauillac as more American-manufactured equipment arrived. Planning for the new facility began in October with appointment of Benjamin Briscoe to head the Assembly and Repair Section at headquarters, with responsibility for designing, constructing, and equipping the base. A contract let in the United States called for a steel frame building measuring 260 feet × 560 feet, with materials to be delivered to the Philadelphia Navy Yard within 60–90 days. The Navy evaluated thousands of men in the United States and selected 550 for duty in France. The base officially opened December 1, 1917, but did not become operational for many months and was completed only in November 1918.

For most of World War I naval aviation's greatest activity lay not in the area of military operations but in the field of construction. The Navy Department struggled mightily to build a system of overseas bases, supply and repair facilities, and communication and transportation networks virtually from scratch in widely separated foreign countries located thousands of miles from home. Work began at places like Le Croisic, Moutchic, and Dunkirk in the late summer and fall of 1917. During the winter, advance parties of enlisted personnel descended on the coasts of France and Ireland to expand building activity. Drafts of construction workers reached the future sites of NAS Brest, St. Trojan, and Tréguier in January 1918 and Fromentine in February. In late February, Cone made an inspection trip along the coast and found things "in as prosperous a condition as one could wish under the circumstances." Work at Queenstown in Ireland began under Admiralty auspices in December 1917, with the first U.S. Navy complement arriving the following February. Site work, grading, and construction commenced at Wexford, Whiddy Island, and Lough Foyle in December and January by gangs of 100–200 Irish laborers employed by local contractors fulfilling cost-plus contracts. Bluejackets began reaching these sites in February and March.

Despite elaborate plans and strenuous exertions, site work proceeded more slowly than headquarters wished and many stations remained uncompleted until the following summer or fall. Creating a system of bases from scratch posed a massive logistical challenge. The slowness of French contractors who lacked men, materials, and transportation severely impacted progress. Moroccan and Algerian labor often proved ineffective and there were never enough hardworking, disciplined German POWs to go around. Time-consuming local construction methods utilizing masonry, plaster, and tile/slate further slowed the program. Delays in shipping American enlisted men and extreme difficulty acquiring materials and tools from the United States on a timely basis proved crippling. In time, a few innovations helped accelerate matters. To supply sufficient barracks and office space, for example, the Navy developed a simple, mass-produced temporary building. Special crews harvested timber in the Bordeaux district and milled it at a Navy sawmill. They erected a small factory in Pauillac to manufacture prefabricated wooden structures that could be transported by three trucks and erected in four hours. Other building components were shipped from the United States. Finally, the relatively slow trickle of aviation personnel into Europe in the fall of 1917 quickened as the months passed, and by January 1 the number of enlisted men had risen to 1,200. The pace accelerated further in the winter and by early March more than 4,300 bluejackets were at work in France, Ireland, England, and Italy. At Pauillac alone 1,500 sailors gathered, with nearly 400 at Le Croisic and Moutchic. By November 1918 the number approached 20,000.

Naval aviation in Europe did not operate in a vacuum; rather, it navigated through the Department's stormy sea of conflicting priorities, previous controversies, and competing personalities. Nowhere was this truer than in the tense relationship between Chief of Naval Operations William S. Benson and Vice-Admiral William S. Sims, commander of the United States Naval Forces Operating in European Waters. Their disagreements over disposition of America's destroyer flotilla, center of gravity for the war effort, Sims's Anglophilia, Benson's Anglophobia, proper strategy for combating the U-boat threat, analysis of the aggressiveness of the Royal Navy, and overall integrity of the United States fleet were well known. Misunderstandings and almost continual back-channel gossip inevitably involved more than the two principals.

Discord over naval policy impacted development of aviation programs. Benson's prewar skepticism regarding aeronautics did not endear him to the flying contingent in Europe. Upon assuming the position of Chief of Naval Operations in 1916 he had "succeeded in reducing the aviation programs to near impotence," with direction of the effort in turmoil. It required much time and considerable effort by Capt. Noble Irwin and Cdr. John Towers to turn the situation around. Ironically, Benson eventually showed himself to be a hesitant, but important, supporter of certain aviation initiatives, reluctantly backing the largest and most expensive programs such as Whiting's entire bases initiative, the Killingholme lighter project, and the Northern Bombing Group (NBG) bombing campaign, all of which reflected the Navy's aggressive attitude toward battling German forces.[17] Benson sailed to Europe as part of the House Mission October 30, 1917, reaching Plymouth November 7. One result of his activities there was support for creation of a planning section at London headquarters, eventually assigning Captains Frank Schofield and Dudley Knox, and Cdr. Harry Yarnell. This group played a significant role in defining aviation strategy in coming months. Underlining his support for aggressive action against the submarine threat, the CNO also endorsed a plan to operate a substantial aviation station at Killingholme on the North Sea and assemble necessary men, specialty lighters, and large flying boats to undertake long-distance bombardment of enemy U-boat facilities.

While in France, Benson met with Cone to discuss aviation affairs and visited Pauillac, where he observed "great zeal, earnestness, and intelligence on the part of both officers and men." Returning to Washington, he increased Cone's requests for single and twin-engine flying boats and ordered Irwin to speed development of patrol stations along the French coast. Nonetheless, the CNO continued to oppose aviation's institutional ambitions, as did the Bureau chiefs. In postwar letters, Craven, who replaced Irwin as Director of Naval Aviation in May 1919, discussed the gloomy situation with Cdr. DeWitt Ramsey, saying, "Aviation looks sick in the Navy Department just at present. . . . I have been on the point of throwing up the sponge a couple of times, but have resolved to stick it out until the new CNO comes along who may have a different view [from Benson's]." Benson's retirement in October merited another pointed comment from Craven. "There were quite a few dry eyes around here in the Aviation section when he relinquished the chair of office. There was a slight buck-up noticeable at once."[18]

If Sims had problems with Benson, relations with Rear Adm. Henry B. Wilson, commander of naval forces in France after October 1917, did not fare much better. Shortly after reorganizing the command structure in France in January 1918, Sims complained to Benson. Alluding to old Navy controversies, he claimed that Wilson had been a member of the "conservative party" when Sims experienced difficulties caused by efforts to improve fleet target practice and probably retained some prejudices from that time. Wilson, according to Sims, personally disliked Cone and had recently been overheard to say he was "one of the most dangerous men in the service." But the real bone of contention lay in the tangled relationship between Wilson, as commander of naval forces in France, and Cone, head of naval aviation, who reported directly to Sims. This controversy lasted for many months and generated a lengthy, acrimonious correspondence. It was eventually agreed that Cone would command until the construction phase ended, at which time operational control would transfer to Wilson, something that occurred September 1, 1918.

Squabbles among Sims, Cone, and Wilson paled, however, compared to events unfolding on the Western Front. The great German offensive in the spring of 1918 threatened to disrupt important aviation activity set in motion the previous winter. Enemy advances caused the French to plan evacuation of government offices and move industrial works southward. Paris itself came under direct attack from long-range artillery. The most immediate threat to aviation facilities existed at Dunkirk, only a few miles from the front. Coincident with the German assault on the Western Front, attacks on Dunkirk spiked sharply, with increased air raids, artillery bombardment, and destroyer sorties. Cone visited the exposed outpost March 27 to discuss the situation with Commanding Officer Chevalier, giving him instructions to assist the Allies in any way possible, including helping rebuild their aerodromes further behind the lines. Several American pilots and observers rushed to fill slots in beleaguered British squadrons and flew multiple missions in the next three weeks.

At the station, accurate information came at a premium. Recently arrived pilot Dave Ingalls told his mother in late March, "The German advance and British retreat is greatly disturbing everyone. . . . We know very little of what is going on. I wish I could look a week ahead or so." As the assault continued, the Allies developed contingency plans to evacuate. As ordnance officer, Kenneth MacLeish inventoried materiel so emergency transport might be arranged. George Moseley reported that nonflying personnel would leave by destroyer (shades of 1940!). Officers at other coastal stations distributed weapons to bluejackets and commenced drilling for any emergency. On a larger scale, Sims ordered a tally made of naval forces that could be sent to the front to perform transport or auxiliary duty with Allied forces. To make men available, he ordered construction at American bases halted temporarily. Wilson's staff identified 7,000 personnel of all types, with as many as 2,000 from naval aviation. Ultimately General Foch and Admiral de Bon politely declined the American offer, saying circumstances did not call for Navy assistance.[19]

Artillery bombardment of Paris began March 23, inflicting extensive damage and heavy casualties. Some observers, however, remained rather blasé about the experience. In mid-April Cone told his friend Sims, "Things seem to be going along here (Paris) in a normal way, aside from an occasional shot from the big gun which has ceased to cause any excitement in this old town." Continued advances by German troops, however, caused naval headquarters whose staff numbered approximately 220 to develop plans to evacuate Paris and relocate to Pauillac. Orders went out for 1 officer and 30 drivers to proceed from Pauillac to Brest where a shipment of trucks had recently arrived. They were to organize a convoy, each vehicle loaded with gasoline drums, drawing fuel from NAS Brest, Guipavas, and L'Aber Vrach, if necessary, along with lubricating oil and grease. The convoy, carrying four days' rations, should proceed by the shortest route to Orleans. Transportation in Paris, including trucks, cars, and ambulances, would haul staff, food, supplies, and files out of the city. They would drive to Orleans, rendezvous with the trucks from

Brest, and then push on to Bordeaux. The crisis came in June when Sims informed Benson the French Navy was removing their archives from Paris, as well as certain war manufactures. But the lines held along the Marne River and Cone's evacuation plan was never implemented.[20]

* * *

Frustrations and delays aside, naval aviation made considerable progress in the late fall and winter of 1917–1918. Hutch Cone and his aides established a capable and efficient headquarters organization. Construction in widely dispersed locales commenced. New programs in Ireland, England, and Italy emerged. Limited combat operations began at Le Croisic, Ile Tudy, Killingholme, and elsewhere. The powerful German drive caused great excitement, but exercised little lasting effect on aviation programs. With better weather in the offing, the United States was about to enter the fray.

3

UNDER THE GUN

NAS Dunkirk 1917–1918

From the moment the first ratings arrived on a blustery autumn day in 1917 until equipment, aircraft, and personnel hurriedly relocated to Belgium a year later, the naval air station at Dunkirk was under the gun. Established to combat U-boat operations in the North Sea and English Channel and bomb German facilities in Flanders, the base stood on the northeastern coast of France, astride the Channel approaches, just a few miles behind the front lines. With its proximity to determined and skilled enemy forces, Dunkirk endured continuous attack from the air, raids from the sea, and long-range bombardment from large-caliber artillery. The exposed station also battled atrocious weather, a crowded harbor, inexperience, and serious shortages of equipment and aircraft. Nonetheless, personnel carried out the most extensive combat operations against enemy aircraft, submarines, and shore installations undertaken by any American naval air station in World War I. This included activities originated there and those undertaken by aviators, observers, and mechanics temporarily attached to neighboring English and French squadrons.[1]

The story of NAS Dunkirk actually began in June 1917, shortly after Kenneth Whiting reached France. While bluejackets took up temporary quarters, Whiting hurried ahead to Paris before embarking on a tour of possible sites for future American stations. He headed first to Dunkirk, focal point for offensive work against German submarines based at Ostend, Bruges, and Zeebrugge. His thorough inspection, combined with extensive discussions with Allied officers, convinced him the United States should operate a station there. After returning to Paris, Whiting participated in several conferences in which his hosts agreed to provide initial materiel and labor to begin construction at several sites, though Navy men and supplies would be required to complete the work. While other proposed coastal stations such as Ile Tudy, St. Trojan, and Le Croisic received careful analysis regarding topography, logistics, and strategic placement, Dunkirk did not, an omission that exerted a far-reaching impact on its operations.[2]

During the summer the French employed local contractors, Moroccan laborers, and a few soldiers to level the ground. Work commenced July 20 but proceeded very slowly, belying the original promise to complete the project by September 1. With France straining every sinew in the war effort, meeting the needs of newly arrived Americans often proved beyond their capacity. Contractors completed the first barracks September 2, and the first Bessenau hangar October 5. By the time Ens. C. R. Johnson arrived October 10 to oversee operations, six dirt-floored barracks were up, with work on a seventh under way. A crane for raising and lowering aircraft was on its way from England. The nascent station still lacked facilities for cooking, and a shortage of masons left latrine construction with little hope of completion except by American forces. Later in the month work began on a galley and washroom and installation of electric lights, but progress continued to lag. Excavation for a bombproof dugout began October 13 but foundered due to lack of materials for walls and roof. Nor was building activity immune from the war. That same day a small bomb struck a hangar, part of the nearly continuous raids that rattled the city. Nearly all French forces quartered below the port fortifications, but little (and relatively safe) space remained for the Americans. The local commander urgently requested heavy searchlights to counteract night attacks.[3]

Several unassembled aircraft arrived in late October and early November, the first for the embryonic base, including five Donnet-Denhaut (DD) flying boats and two Hanriot-Dupont (HD) seaplanes. The Royal Naval Air Service promised to supply stores, oil, lubricants, and other miscellaneous materiel. A draft of 52 seamen reached Dunkirk November 4, the first installment of an envisioned complement of 200 ratings. Lacking suitable places to eat and sleep, the bluejackets bivouacked in an old city building, obtaining blankets and mattresses from the French and eating at a local restaurant. Godfrey DeC. Chevalier soon joined the men, assuming command November 10, accompanied by Asst. Paymaster Thomas Stockhausen as Supply Officer. Chevalier, at that time perhaps the best-trained flyer in the Navy, had just completed the entire French instruction regimen for pursuit pilots. At Dunkirk the Americans operated under command of the Commandant de Patrouille and Admiral at Dunkirk, who in turn reported to a British admiral at Dover.

Construction continued into November and December, with special attention given to assembling aircraft and excavating dugouts, the latter activity absolutely crucial. Shortly after the first Americans arrived, enemy destroyers attacked, firing more than 250 shells against the harbor works and fortress, and damaging a British monitor. Land batteries and naval forces answered the assault. Air raids occurred almost daily. A headquarters report in mid-November described nearly complete destruction of the RNAS station by bombs and gunfire, and Whiting observed a few weeks later, "The bombing of Dunkirk has become a very serious question and until now no reliable means have been found to stop the German bombing planes that operate at night." He noted, however, that the quantity of bombs dropped on Ostend, Bruges, and Zeebrugge greatly exceeded the number hitting Dunkirk "so that if the Germans can stand it, I guess we must." Amidst destruction, the Navy men sat down November 29 to a Thanksgiving dinner of hardtack, coffee, and "canned bill," even as the warning siren "Mournful Mary" wailed.[4]

Machinist Mate Alonzo Hildreth, recently arrived in Dunkirk, provided a personal view of the continuous bombardment. "The only danger is from falling pieces of bursting shells," he noted. "Our camp is called the bulls-eye because the guns are all centered over here." Two days later he added, "It looks as if it had been a beautiful city in peacetime, but the parks and buildings are all torn up from bombs and shells." A few days before Christmas he recorded, "... worst raid yet; French seaplane set on fire, 3 or 4 hangars burnt, we went over to help put it out, and it was raining steel all the time from the guns." Official sources documented how "nightly raids by enemy aeroplanes rendered construction and assembly work difficult. Work is progressing as well as can be expected, however, under the circumstances. All personnel are obliged to live in dugouts as protection from enemy bombs."[5]

Attacks notwithstanding, slow progress continued. By early December a third hangar had been erected. Chevalier recorded assembly of four Donnet-Denhaut and five Hanriot Dupont aircraft, and a total of six DDs and nine HDs a week later, despite almost continuous bombing. In addition to assigned duties, enlisted men often aided British or French forces during emergencies. By early January, 129 ratings had reached Dunkirk, 91 housed on the station with the remainder quartered in the city. French artificers aided in several areas, including construction, electrical wiring, and painting, while a party of a dozen Moroccans continued leveling ground. A newly completed bombproof accommodated 160 men. Chevalier voiced one complaint, however, his inability to secure dependable officers' servants.[6]

Onset of winter weather limited flying activities along the Channel, and the lure of fighting aerodromes and nearby front lines became irresistible.

Both officers and bluejackets utilized free time, especially Sundays, to explore the strange, dangerous, new environment. A few visited local flying fields and inspected aircraft there, including huge Handley Page bombers. Alonzo Hildreth used his Sunday half-day off to see "a little town near the lines; they say it is not torn up near as bad as this city." Two weeks later (also a Sunday) he "lingered" in bed until 7:30 A.M. then went sightseeing and "took in an English movie shown here in town for men in the service. The pictures were all American, had a Charlie Chaplin comic." The Christmas holiday brought mixed reactions. "Doesn't seem like Xmas Eve to me," he lamented December 24. "Most of the boys are singing and making all the noise they can." The following day felt just like "any other day, snowing by spells, had a fairly good dinner, no work." Station officers also used free time to explore and socialize. Di Gates, recently arrived from Paris and St. Raphael, spent one Sunday visiting the front, passing several villages "practically wiped off the map." Shells screeched overhead. He stopped on the way back at an Army evacuation hospital, had dinner with some American doctors, and a few nurses, "one of whom was the best girl I've seen since I've been in France—All anxious to find cause to visit hospital again." On New Year's Eve, Gates enjoyed dinner with British officers and attended a concert given by enlisted men where he watched "several comedians among the mechanics." At midnight everyone went out in the snow and danced around a large fire. On New Year's Day the men and officers joined hands and sang.[7]

Visiting Marine Corps officer and pioneer aviator Alfred Cunningham had little to celebrate. Conducting a tour of flying establishments and the front lines, he reached Dunkirk on Christmas Day, sick and in pain. He immediately sent for the American doctor (Stevens?) who was "away on a drunk with the French officers" but soon arrived, diagnosed a kidney stone, bad cold, and rheumatism combined. The doctor "gave me some dope and put me to sleep. This was a Merry Xmas." The doctor returned the following day and ordered his patient to stay in bed. Cunningham expected a visit from an unnamed officer, but recorded, "XX (Chevalier?) has not shown up and no-one knows where he is. HE is liable to be away drunk for several days." When Cunningham awoke the next day XX came to visit. "He had been on a tear with French and British officers." The flyer got out of bed, dressed, and drove to "his" station that appeared "too crowded and in a bad location." The Marine found 17 aircraft, but none flying. During the next few days he visited St. Pol aerodrome, inspected intelligence photos, toured the French and British seaplane bases, and then the RNAS bombing field (Couderquerke) to observe Handley

Page machines in action. He described the bitter cold, artillery exchanges, and general level of misery and destruction. Cunningham called Dunkirk a "sad, deserted place . . . scarcely a whole pane of glass in the city . . . hard to find a building which has not been scarred or damaged by bombs." The American officer experienced a "weird feeling walking through the city without a single light or sign of life in it."⁸

By New Year's 1918, seven DDs and ten HDs were assembled, although actual flight operations seemed far in the future. Laborers completed a gasoline storage tank, but no sooner did they finish than a bomb exploded nearby, burying the fuel under several feet of earth and masonry. Official raising of the colors took place January 1, 1918, and Machinist Mate Hildreth recorded, "Old Glory went up over our camp for the first time, and it looks for sure as if we mean business. It's on a 75-foot pole and can be seen all over the city." Hutch Cone visited the base in mid-January and Di Gates called him "a very good, level-headed, common sense man." Gates also liked Chevalier, "Chevy," who he described as a "Peach." The former Yale gridiron star found the officers' mess a congenial one. The paymaster (Stockhausen) was a "reserved old Penn grad." Doctor Albert Stevens, from Yale and Oxford and a Rhodes scholar, had taught Gates at the Hotchkiss School in Lakeville, Connecticut. Gates noted thankfully, "There hasn't been a favorable night for a raid since two days before Christmas."⁹

As part of its antisubmarine activities, NAS Dunkirk operated two types of aircraft: lumbering Donnet-Denhaut flying boat bomber/patrol machines and small Hanriot Dupont pontoon scouts to provide protection. Since training at Tours, St. Raphael, Hourtin, or Moutchic did not offer instruction in this type of craft, small numbers of potential pilots attended British aerial combat schools at Gosport, Turnberry, and Ayr. The contingent consisted of both enlisted pilots from Tours/Issoudun and some Yale men from the United States. In order to secure additional experienced aviators, the Navy also enrolled veterans from the Lafayette Flying Corps, such as Willis Haviland, William C. Van Fleet, Charles Bassett, and George Moseley who trained at Tours, Avord, and Pau and served with French escadrilles. In early December Moseley mused, "We are thinking of joining the Navy again . . . and be sent to Dunkirk, where we will be in an escadrille under Chevalier." Moseley had met Chevalier the previous summer, observing, "When he sets out to accomplish something, nothing stands in his way." By early February the transfer process was complete and Moseley reported, "I went over to the Navy shortly after I arrived in Paris. They grabbed hold of me, took me upstairs, shoved the notice of my French release under my nose, and told me to go downstairs and take my physical exam." The new officers, already experienced land pilots, proceeded to Moutchic for a course in hydro-aeroplanes before being posted to Dunkirk in February and March.[10]

Atrocious weather, equipment shortages, and a severe deficiency of experienced pilots delayed commencement of flight operations that winter but did little to stop enemy air raids. During the evening of January 14 a German assault destroyed seven airplanes and a large wooden hangar at the nearby French base, while also damaging a storehouse and pay office at the American site. Three days later another bombing raid tore out one end of the mess hall and damaged the Petty Officers' quarters. Yet another attack January 25 blew out the windows in the commanding officer's office. Di Gates described this activity as "some nice warm parties lately." A few nights earlier the Germans began their raid at 6:30 P.M. and continued until 2:30 A.M. Gates got into bed and stayed there, even after long-range artillery began shelling the city. "Being a fatalist," he assumed "No dugout could stand the shock of that thing." He was unimpressed when he saw his first "Gotha" bomber, exhibited in the town square, "far below my expectations, no refinement."[11]

Despite the gloom of winter and constant attacks, organizational pieces began coming together. In mid-January Vickers machine guns, bombing sights, and turrets arrived and pilots Gates and Virgil Griffin initiated test flights of a few assembled aircraft. Gates and Chevalier carried out further Donnet-Denhaut flights later in the month, each lasting anywhere from 5 to 55 minutes. Gates, who did the bulk of the flying, continued the tests into early February. More pilots reported for duty, including Willis B. Haviland, Charles Bassett, and Ralph Loomis, all Lafayette Flying Corps veterans, as well as a few enlisted aviators back from training in England. Their presence allowed tests of HD pursuit planes to begin. A more adventurous trial occurred February 19 when a single DD commanded by Gates and two HDs flown by Haviland and Bassett crossed the Channel to Dover. Attempting a return leg, Bassett's balky Hanriot twice landed in the freezing, choppy water, the second time capsizing due to damaged pontoons. Gates rescued the downed flyer, with the swamped plane towed into Dover and disassembled, a complete loss. Due to bad weather, however, the group did not return to Dunkirk until February 21. The following day a large draft of flight personnel reached the base, including five more enlisted pilots and eight enlisted observers. In addition to initiating flights, more mundane activities demanded attention. Measles arrived January 15 and medical personnel quarantined the station. Particularly sick men transferred to a Navy hospital at Brest and the quarantine ended five days later. Chevalier held deck courts for 10 seamen absent without authority, while at the end of the month Marine and Navy officers visited Dunkirk to explain War Risk Insurance and Family Allowances to the men.

NAS Dunkirk suffered its first fatalities a month later when a DD piloted by Ens. Curtis Read, a Yale Unit aviator, and his observer, Edward Eichelberger, crashed into the water just off Dunkirk, wrecking the aircraft and killing both men. The young flyer, one of four brothers serving in naval aviation, had been haunted by premonitions of death. In his diary he wrote, "Expect orders for the front any day . . . feeling of fatalism . . . would be a climax if I should have the privilege of making the greatest sacrifice . . . have the feeling there is absolutely no other way out." Only two days after reporting to the station, Read took off on a practice flight February 26 and seemed to handle the plane well, but at 10:20 A.M. fell in a fatal nosedive. The station launch quickly reached the wreck. Read was barely alive, but Eichelberger was missing. Read died in a military hospital less than hour later. The event made an enormous impression on everyone who saw it. Diarist Hildreth, one of the rescuers, wrote, "Well, everything seemed to go wrong today. Ensign Read was killed, also one of his observers. Read was lying on a piece of the tail when we got there. He died shortly after we got him to camp. The observer couldn't be found. . . . Read just came here for duty on the 24th. His first flight here. Also had three planes hit the seawall and bust up."[12]

The pace of operations increased markedly in March, as did the level of German offensive activity. Early in the month aircraft mechanics installed guns, turrets, and bombing gear. Station personnel now included 3 naval aviators, 7 student aviators, 7 observers, 42 aviation mechanics, and 5 aviation mechanic students. Everyone sensed a major offensive coming. Attacks on the exposed base were relentless. Then on the evening of March 12 the Germans came out in force. Two air raids rained down destruction, one at 9:30 P.M. and a second at 4:30 A.M. Artillery bombardment complemented the air strikes. Enemy warships sortied. According to Hildreth, "Fritz lost five of his raiding ships and the fight lasted into the morning; the English lost one destroyer; Fritz also lost four Gothas. They [German bombers] were met by some fighting scouts just after daybreak." Di Gates described the mood in Dunkirk as the expected German spring offensive neared. Excitement was plentiful, as was danger from continuous crashes. At noon one day a Belgian officer came to lunch, but just as he sat down, a dispatch rider hurried in with news his post was under attack.[13]

Daily reports documented the general work of the station on the eve of battle. Personnel carried out limited patrols. An HD piloted by Bassett landed off Calais March 18 with motor trouble and an allied destroyer towed him into harbor. That same day Bassett carried out an antisubmarine patrol with a French squadron. Two days later Haviland's HD landed at sea with motor trouble, while a DD with Ens. Edward DeCernea at the controls struck the harbor seawall and damaged a wing. The number of aircraft available each day, nominally 11 DDs and 5 HDs, never approached those levels and fluctuated widely, rarely more than two or three of each type, contingent on repairs and inventories of spare parts. Some planes lacked propellers. There was danger ashore as well. Stray machine gun bullets fired from the armory accidentally wounded an enlisted man in his barracks. The observer was cleaning the gun when it discharged. A bullet punched through the barracks wall and injured the unsuspecting sailor while he stood before a mirror combing his hair. More personnel reached Dunkirk, bringing the total to 10 aviators and 16 student aviators. They included both college-educated reserve officers and enlisted veterans of the First Aeronautic Detachment arriving at their first combat assignments.[14]

Ironically, despite danger and heightened tension, some new arrivals waxed positive about life at Dunkirk, due in part to the fact they lived away from the station in a "fine villa right on the shores of the sea." Dave Ingalls called it an "old French mansion," complete with stoves to keep warm, a piano, even a phonograph, "but no decent records." Young officers also had Navy stewards to cosset them, keep quarters clean, and serve meals, "in short, nothing more or less than our valets." The broad beach right outside their door provided plenty of room to play baseball, football, "and about every other game." A baseball match drew hordes of citizens who cheered both sides enthusiastically. Of course, each time the warning sirens wailed, the game came to a sudden stop. George Moseley, another recent arrival, praised the food, "real American meals," with plenty of oatmeal, sugar, and white bread. Occasionally they headed into Dunkirk or Calais for a restaurant meal, "China plates, plenty of knives, forks, spoons, even napkins." Within just a few days, however, this "idyllic" life came to an explosive end.[15]

In the early morning of March 21, 1918, Major General Erich Ludendorff unleashed his powerful spring offensive, the "Kaiserschlact," against British forces in Flanders. The long-awaited blow fell along the old Somme front between Arras and Laon. Utilizing "Hutier" tactics proven effective in Russia and Italy, intensively trained shock troops, aided by a short, sharp artillery and gas barrage, overran Allied strong points and broke into open territory. Within two weeks the Germans advanced as much as 40 miles along a 70-mile front. With only a confused picture of events under way, the American outpost grew uneasy. Alonzo Hildreth, now a four-month Dunkirk veteran, noted, "Well, we are still under fire, and we have reports of hard fighting on a 50-mile front at and near Cambrai. Although we are getting all kinds of rumors, don't know how many of them are true." A second German thrust in early April brought advancing enemy formations within 30 miles of the station. Many feared the Channel ports and installations might be abandoned, and Gen. Douglas Haig, British commander-in-chief, issued his famous "backs to the wall" order forbidding any further retreat.[16]

Allied aerodromes along the English Channel were among the most active and exposed during the desperate battles of March and April, and the seaplane station at Dunkirk was no exception. Located just a half-hour's flying time from enemy submarine pens and naval installations at Bruges, Ostend, and Zeebrugge, and perched astride the Flanders battlefields, Dunkirk suffered nightly bombing raids, destroyer assaults, and heavy shelling. Many of the buildings that somehow survived earlier attacks now succumbed to new hammer blows. Most of the men waited patiently, enduring the incessant shelling by retreating to their underground bombproofs. Di gates recalled, "for last 26–27 hours shelling all around from big gun up the line, about every 40 minutes, impatient with their shots, scatter them everywhere." The next day a beleaguered Hildreth reported, "Fritz is still throwing big shells at us, one hit last night at 9:15 within 100 feet of barracks, rock and brick came through the wall while we were all sleeping." Observer Irving Sheely added, "We are so close to the lines that the guns sound like the constant roar of thunder." Continuous shelling meant a marked loss of sleep as men spent long hours in cramped, uncomfortable dugouts.[17]

Many watched the battle like spectators at a sporting event. Kenneth MacLeish, recently arrived from training in England and Scotland, told his fiancée, "It's the most gorgeous sight I've ever seen. The English are evidently bombing the daylights out of the Huns because you can see the Hun star shells and flaming onions bursting over the lines." George Moseley sensed "the guttural roar of the guns makes the air seem to throb constantly with a low rhythmic measure." He called night raids "a picturesque affair and at the same time very spooky." First came the zoom-zoom of the big German planes, then the blood-chilling sound of the air raid siren. "The guns begin banging away, then stop, then three or four tremendous explosions. Soon searchlights go on, firing on destroyers off shore." Hildreth recorded a visit to the front, explaining, "Sure had some trip. . . . We were in sight of the line and guess, in fact, that we were about a mile from the front trenches for a long time last night. . . . Could see the flames of the guns."[18]

During the same period the station hosted a short visit from the commander of American naval aviation forces. On his way back from London to Paris, Hutch Cone stopped at Dunkirk on March 27 and carefully reviewed the situation with Chevalier, Captain Lambe, and Captain De Laborde. Cone instructed Chevalier to help the British reerect their aerodromes well back of the lines and assist in any other way with personnel or such material as he had on the ground. Fears the Germans might overrun British lines caused the Navy to prepare evacuation plans. Moseley noted, "If the Boche should break through and we should have to evacuate, we will probably either go to England or south along the French coast." The aviators would load as much ammunition as they could carry in their machine guns and "empty them into the close German formations as they advance. . . . They are getting gas masks and steel helmets for us—funny things for aviators." About a dozen American nurses worked nearby and Moseley and his mates went to see them, reassuring the women they would look out for their safety. A few days later Gates described extensive evacuation plans but noted that the situation looked more encouraging. In the end, British lines held and exhausted German columns called off their attacks. No evacuation took place, but it had been a close run thing.[19]

As Germany's spring offensive surged forward, Britain mobilized every available aviation unit to cover retreating troops, obtain crucial intelligence, and harass enemy concentrations. Casualties mounted alarmingly. In late March, Chevalier offered some of his men to the beleaguered RNAS forces stationed at nearby Bergues aerodrome. Dave Ingalls recorded in his diary, "Ken (MacLeish), Havilland, Shorty (Smith), and I are to go to . . . No. 13 Squadron tomorrow. This means action all right." Others at the station also looked forward to possible combat duty. MacLeish wrote excitedly, "At last I am going to get some action. . . . I will be right in the middle of the greatest battle the world has ever known." By the end of March, Haviland, MacLeish, Ingalls, and Smith reached No. 13 Squadron flying Sopwith Camels. Di Gates accompanied them to join No. 17 Squadron employing DH-4 day bombers. Bob Lovett remained on duty with No. 7 Squadron operating Handley Page bombers from the field at Coudekerque. Several observers found themselves at No. 2 Squadron flying reconnaissance missions, also in DH-4s. Enlisted men like Machinist Hildreth joined the battle too. At least eight mechanics served at a British repair facility near the Handley Page field. American personnel, many of them young college frat boys on the most terrifying, exhilarating lark of their lives, found their new comrades an admirable and congenial lot. According to Gates, "We all have temporary jobs with British squadrons and are enjoying it immensely." Lovett called them "the bravest lot he had ever seen." RNAS flyers, including many Canadian and Irish pilots, enjoyed youthful pranks. Evening raids on neighboring messes were common.[20]

The Royal Flying Corps and Royal Naval Air Servce merged April 1 to form the Royal Air Force (RAF), with former naval squadrons renumbered by adding 200 to their original designation. Thus No. 13 Squadron, RNAS, became No. 213 Squadron, RAF. The Royal Navy bitterly contested this move and young flyers at Bergues quickly initiated their own battle. Pilots from No. 13/213 Squadron raided No. 2/202 Squadron mess, and after smashing every chair, window, and picture, and consuming all their liquor, moved on to No. 17/217 Squadron to repeat the assault, but worse. In the fray they knocked over a red-hot stove. When it was set aright someone crawled on the roof and dropped a smoke bomb down the chimney, nearly blinding everybody. After being ejected, No. 13/213 raiders returned to their barracks, pushing some compatriots into a nearby canal. Mayhem continued into the wee hours as inebriated aviators unleashed fire extinguishers and even an automatic pistol.[21]

Despite such hijinks, life in an RAF squadron was deadly serious and within days the erstwhile Dunkirk flyers began conducting war patrols in one of the hottest sectors on the front. An exhilarated David Ingalls in a new Camel joined five British pilots on a late afternoon mission. After rising more than three miles above the battlefield, he swooped down to 6,000 feet, "doing half rolls and having a great time." When the air pump in his gas tank failed, he opted for gravity feed instead. After pressure returned he raced over Ypres and then 70 miles beyond the front lines. Working at altitudes they rarely experienced, American aviators suffered a variety of discomforts, including weakness, headaches, ringing ears, and nausea from oxygen deprivation and drastic changes in air pressure. Irving Sheely's reconnaissance work frequently took him to 20,000 feet, an activity only possible with electrically heated flight suits and bottled oxygen. On one mission he froze his nose and lips so badly the skin turned brown and peeled off.[22]

Experience was a great teacher. David Ingalls found heading out over the Flanders landscape in a thin leather coat and no tunic, one pair of shoes, and light gloves a major mistake. Ken MacLeish's first ascent into frigid realms resulted in a frozen compass and oil gauge. As he noted, "Ask someone how cold it has to be to freeze castor oil." Other flights led to frostbitten fingers, despite wearing silk gloves, covered by rubber gloves and a pair of fur-lined, fur-covered flying gauntlets. Discomforts notwithstanding, what the men observed awed them. MacLeish called early morning patrols "the most marvelous things in the world." Rising above ground mists and entering sunlight before the rays reached earth was exquisite. "You look down and it seems like night," he exclaimed, "and yet the morning is shining on you in all its glory."[23]

Though American personnel participated in a wide range of missions, their efforts centered around the campaign to destroy the U-boat complex at Bruges, Ostend, and Zeebrugge just up the coast in Belgium. Their targets included extensive concrete submarine pens in Bruges and the heavily fortified mole at Zeebrugge, a massive, 1.67 mile-long structure. The entire edifice supported a roadway and railroad siding, with submarines, destroyers, and other naval craft berthed alongside. Defenses at Ostend, though less concentrated, were still formidable. Deep canals connected Ostend and Zeebrugge to Bruges (eight miles inland) and its heavily defended facilities. Several dozen submarines and destroyers sheltered at these sites. Destroyers and other craft, heavy artillery batteries in coastal dunes, a thicket of antiaircraft weapons, and several squadrons of land-based aircraft and seaplanes protected the installations.

Germany maintained two principal seaplane bases along the Belgian coast, one at the mole in Zeebrugge and the other at Bassin de Chasse at Ostend. Land-based squadrons augmented enemy air power. Seaplanes typically flew in formations of five aircraft, patrolling at an altitude of 1,000 feet. After sighting an Allied intruder they dropped to 50–100 feet and closed up tight. These aircraft, both monoplanes and biplanes, performed several functions. They defended the coast against incursions and shielded destroyers maneuvering off the coast to protect returning submarines. Enemy scouts also carried out reconnaissance missions against British operations in the English Channel as well as sorties against Allied ships and planes. Seaplane units commanded by Friedrich Christiansen stimulated awe and fear among Allied flyers at Dunkirk and elsewhere in the North Sea and Channel approaches. After a career as a shipmaster, he joined the Aviatik firm and learned to fly. Christiansen received his pilot license in March 1914 and remained with the company as a teacher. At the outbreak of war he was 35 years old, ancient for a combat pilot. In January 1915 Christiansen transferred to Zeebrugge, where he remained until the Armistice. During that period he tallied as many as 27 victories, and in September 1917 became commander of seaplanes in Flanders. In December he received the Pour le Merite, the famous Blue Max. By then Christiansen had already participated in 440 raids and amassed 1,164 flying hours. On one of these missions in February 1917 his formation shot down Yale Unit member Al Sturtevant's Felixstowe-based flying boat.[24]

Shifting sandbars criss-crossed the seabed from Ostend and Zeebrugge to Dover, and U-boats could submerge but not run underwater. Vessels entered or departed their lair at high tide, whether day or night, escorted by destroyers and aircraft. Navigation at night proved hazardous, though Hutch Cone noted in May, "It may not be easy for submarines to get out of Bruges, Zeebrugge, and Ostend at night, but they do it constantly and are going in and out at high tide, they try to get through the Calais barrage before day." Recognizing the futility of trying to intercept submarines at sea, British forces carried out bombing raids against Bruges-Ostend-Zeebrugge in hopes of disrupting operations. Vice-Admiral Sir Roger Keyes who took command of Dover Patrol in late December 1917 opted for an even more aggressive approach. Keyes developed a daring plan to take three old cruisers and scuttle them in the mouths of the Bruges canals, thus eliminating the town as a resupply base. Zeebrugge, defended by the fortified mole, would be attacked from the sea to allow blockships to reach the canal. Keyes assembled a large naval and amphibious force, to be aided by aviation missions. He aborted the first sortie on the night of April 11–12 when a wind shift rendered a protective smokescreen ineffective. Commanders called off a second foray two nights later due to inclement weather. On the evening of April 22–23 a third attempt went ahead as planned. Total British casualties in this desperate assault approached 700 killed, wounded, and captured. A simultaneous attack at Ostend failed, as did a second attempt May 9.

In support of this raid, RAF squadrons, bolstered with American flyers, observers, and mechanics, carried out a series of related missions. A flight of specially equipped Camels from No. 213 Squadron set off April 10 to attack Zeebrugge mole from an altitude of only 400 feet or 500 feet. Ken MacLeish joined the group, his first combat mission. After experiencing heavy antiaircraft fire, he failed to locate his target and instead dropped a single 50-pound bomb on hangars at Ostend seaplane base. Two days later Di Gates raced off on a "mysterious stunt." RAF records indicate his mission was an attack by seven DH-4 bombers from No. 217 Squadron against the mole and seaplane base at Zeebrugge. One aircraft returned to the aerodrome minutes after departing with armed bombs still attached. An observer recalled, "I stopped up my ears and ducked, but he got away with it." In addition to heavy antiaircraft fire, this daylight raid encountered swarms of enemy Albatros D-V scouts from Jagdstaffel 1 and 2.

That same day, observer Irving Sheely made his first flight over enemy territory, a photographic reconnaissance mission with No. 202 Squadron. After climbing in his DH-4 to 18,000 feet Sheely proceeded to the objective unmolested. It wasn't until he turned toward home after nearly two hours of flying that the excitement started. Antiaircraft fire burst all around. Soon German aircraft attacked. When the enemy opened fire, Sheely also swung into action. "For the first time in my life," he admitted, "I was aiming to kill a man." The aerial battle lasted over 20 minutes, and shortly after landing safely Sheely counted 20 bullet holes and 2 shrapnel punctures in his plane, "one of the bullets passing within three inches of my hide." The Navy flyers' stint with the RAF lasted about three weeks, and with the sound of battle and roar of motors still ringing in their ears, they returned to Dunkirk to resume antisubmarine patrols, but without enthusiasm. Di Gates told a friend at home, "They [pilots] will certainly hate like poison to go back and I don't blame them one bit." Nonetheless, they had performed a wide range of duties and participated in one of the most dramatic events of the war. With a mixture of pride and relief, a man like Robert Lovett could exult at the end of his time with British forces, "I have at last been through it. I feel a different man altogether."[25]

The return of flight personnel in late April coincided with a shift in American antisubmarine tactics. Frustrated by their inability to intercept U-boats at sea, the Navy formalized plans to create a Northern Bombing Group employing land-based aircraft to mount direct attacks against submarine bases in Belgium. Captain David C. Hanrahan, a nonflying veteran of destroyer service, assumed command of the project, which included a dozen proposed squadrons of both day and night bombers. Right from the beginning it loomed as a much larger operation than the seaplane base at Dunkirk and rapidly pushed efforts there offstage. Word of the project quickly reached the port city and pilots and others speculated about possible roles in the new venture. Since Robert Lovett was both a moving force in organizing the NBG and a close friend of many Dunkirk pilots, they were clued in from the start. By early May, George Moseley felt caught "on the horns of a dilemma"—whether to remain at the station with Chevalier, Gates, and others, or seek a place in the new squadrons. Ultimately, he decided to leave Dunkirk where there seemed little chance of affecting the outcome of the war. Ken MacLeish made the same decision because "We'll never see any action on these seaplanes. I expect to leave for training in southern France in the next few days." By midmonth, Ingalls, MacLeish, and several other Dunkirk pilots had been accepted into the new program, what Moseley called "a very big and expensive undertaking, the biggest thing that naval aviation has done yet."[26]

As long as Dunkirk's best flyers served with the RAF in April, antisubmarine patrols remained on hold, with only five missions conducted that month. With their return and subsequent departure of selected personnel for NBG training, daily operations settled into a new routine that persisted until the fall. From May onward the station carried out regular antisubmarine patrols as weather and available equipment permitted. During this period several new aircraft arrived to replace those destroyed in German raids or lost in a seemingly endless parade of mishaps and crashes. The string of serious accidents that began in February continued for the next six months. In the spring of 1918 there were eleven flying mishaps in which planes were totally destroyed, with four more men killed. In fact, no other station in Europe experienced the aerial carnage that Dunkirk did. While fighting a north wind on April 6, George Moseley attempted to take off from the narrow, congested harbor. Just as he left the water a gust lifted his right wing, forcing the left pontoon into the water, causing his aircraft to slew left, directly toward a British destroyer. Moseley tried to turn away, but his controls failed to respond. He then attempted to "jump" over the vessel's wireless apparatus, but hit something, nosed downward, tried to pull out, and crashed onto the deck of the ship. Moseley knew nothing more till he awoke in the hospital.[27]

Simple inexperience and lack of familiarity with equipment constituted another contributing factor to the accidents bedeviling operations. Poor weather, disruptions and confusion precipitated by the German offensive, and limited numbers of serviceable aircraft made sufficient practice virtually impossible. Quartermaster John Ganster, who perished in May, logged only 35 minutes of flight time during his six weeks at the station. In fact, he did not make a single flight in his first three weeks in Dunkirk. Instead, duties consisted of looking after machine guns. He complained, "We are more or less handicapped here by inefficient mechanics, but they all seem to be willing and will soon learn." David Ingalls, a future ace, agreed, noting, "Most everyone blames the machines, which are undoubtedly bad. How anything can ever be accomplished with them is beyond me." Later that month M. J. Chapin suffered a fatal crash near the British coastal motor boat (CMB) station during a practice flight in an HD scout. Two weeks later Herb Lasher's DD went into a spin and crashed, killing observer Edward Smith, and seriously injuring the pilot. Rear observer Thomas Holliday saw what was coming, threw his guns overboard, and braced for impact. When he came to he had a broken leg, but no other injuries. Despite his condition he sent three pigeon messages back to the base, rescued the pilot, and dived underwater for Smith. Though he could touch him, Holliday couldn't pull Smith clear of the wreckage, and his body went down with the front half of the fuselage. The parade of carnage continued on May 18 when John Ganster piloting a DD lost control flying over Dunkirk. His plane crashed onto a roof throwing him from the machine. Seriously injured, he died in a military hospital. An HD piloted by Boatswain O'Connor crash-landed at Hastings the following day, the plane damaged beyond repair. A few days later while starting out a morning patrol in a DD, Djalma Marshburn went into spinning nosedive from 2,000 feet and crashed into the water one mile northeast of Dunkirk. His body was not recovered. And on the last day of May an HD piloted by Harold Elliott crashed into a trawler while taking off. The plane was completely wrecked, though the pilot escaped uninjured.[28]

June saw no let up in the mayhem. On morning patrol June 5, Lawrence DeSonnier's HD made a forced landing 12 miles northeast of the station. His plane later capsized in heavy seas while under tow. Landing in the harbor, an HD piloted by Charles Wardwell "tripped" and turned turtle. The plane sank, although Wardwell escaped uninjured. Tragedy struck again on August 14 when a DD flown by Edward DeCernea, one of Dunkirk's most experienced aviators, crashed offshore during an early evening test flight. He and one of his observers were badly injured, but a French motor launch rescued them. DeCernea sustained a broken back while observer Harry Laven suffered a fractured skull, broken jaw, and broken ankle and later died. A second observer, W. C. Love, escaped unhurt. Not all accidents, however, occurred when aircraft maneuvered in the congested harbor or pilots conducted patrols. One day in late May, Ken MacLeish's mechanic worked on his Hanriot-Dupont scout cleaning the interior, with his upper body wedged inside the fuselage. A light bulb exploded, igniting accumulated gasoline-soaked waste. The unfortunate sailor suffered serious burns on his head and shoulders.[29]

Chasse pilots often painted personal insignia on their planes. Lafayette Flying Corps veteran Moseley placed a blue band and a big red heart on his machine so others could identify him in formation. He reported, "We all have some insignia or sign painted on the machine—one a red, white, and blue band, another a red band, one the cross anchors of the Navy, etc." MacLeish named his aircraft "Priceless Priscilla" and emblazoned it with a pure white tail, dark blue stripe, and a red, white, and blue crest showing gold, crossed anchors, surmounted by an eagle, with his fiancee's name inscribed beneath the shield. Edward Bamrick stenciled a prominent "BAM"—the first three letters of his last name—on his fuselage. Machinist Mate Alonzo Hildreth noted that almost every plane had some good luck charm. One pilot hung a small teddy bear in the cockpit.[30]

Offensive missions mounted in May and thereafter typically consisted of patrols carried out along the coast and in the Dover Straight, usually three to eight planes, a mix of DDs and HDs. The patrols lasted up to two hours and covered search legs of 5 to 20 kilometers. The first patrol went out early in the morning, sometimes before 4:30 A.M.; a second patrol departed in the afternoon, anywhere from 2:00 to 5:00 P.M. George Moseley explained, "Our patrols take us up along the coast then out into in Channel, over close to England near white chalk cliffs (Dover) and then back across to France, takes about two hours. We keep looking but so far no sub has dared to show its face." Observer Sheely often rolled out of his bunk at 3 A.M. to prepare for a mission. On average he flew every other day, complaining, "It is so foggy over the sea that we have to navigate entirely by compass. We carry four pigeons as messengers. . . . It is not yet a week ago since one of these little messengers carried a sad message back to us. It was a call for help, and quick. . . . We arrived at the scene just as the big flying boat was almost gone." Official logbooks documented wretched flying conditions, with frequent references to short flights, early returns, and poor visibility. High winds, dense cloud cover, and rough seas confined aircraft to harbor for as much as a week at a time.

Since U-boats typically ran on the surface at night to recharge batteries, submerging again at dawn, actual sightings proved rare and attacks rarer still. One came August 11 during an early morning flight when a single DD piloted by DeCernea spotted a submarine under way 30 miles northwest of Dunkirk with its conning tower awash. At 5:30 A.M. DeCernea attacked across the bow, with one bomb hitting about 20 feet to port and another 10 feet to starboard. Some oil appeared on the surface. This proved just the beginning of the young New Yorker's one-man campaign to sink the submarine. No sooner did he return to the station than he flew off again in a second machine, raced to the site, and surveyed the oil slick. Finding nothing, DeCernea hurried back to base, climbed aboard his original aircraft, now refueled and rearmed, and set out on a third patrol. He located some French vedettes (motor boats) and notified them of the U-boat's presence via a communications buoy. Later that afternoon DeCernea set out one more time in search of the wounded raider, dropping four more bombs on the growing oil slick. Actions like these earned him quite a reputation among those who witnessed his spectacular landings in tiny Dunkirk harbor. Two days later in an even more dramatic encounter, two DDs and three HDs spotted a large submarine running on the surface at approximately 6:20 A.M. They flew a semicircle around the craft attempting to identify it, while also firing a Very light (signal flare). The suspicious vessel responded by manning its deck gun and firing five shells, with three bursting next to a DD flown by Julian Carson. He returned fire, apparently hitting two of the gun crew. When Carson commenced his bombing run, the U-boat cleared its decks and dived. One bomb struck the spot where the conning tower disappeared beneath the waves. A second landed ahead of the ship. Soon the submarine broke the surface bow first, and just as quickly slipped back by the stern. When Carson's plane returned to the station, crewmen found shrapnel embedded in the forward struts of the right wing.[31]

Sometimes, instead of encountering U-boats American airmen attacked floating mines, deadly explosive eggs laid by specially fitted submarines. Dunkirk-based aircraft also carried out frequent rescues of stranded Allied and American pilots. The events of May 6 were typical. Two DDs lifted off on patrol at 9:30 A.M. At 11:00 a pigeon flew in reporting one of the planes adrift in the open sea. A speedboat went out to retrieve the men and plane, with Di Gates aloft in another DD scouting ahead. Gates found the downed machine at 12:30 P.M., with the speedboat arriving an hour later. By that time an HD scout with David Ingalls at the controls had also been dispatched to look for everyone. Gates's DD and the station launch returned safely, but Ingalls's machine disappeared. The rescue boat set out again, but found nothing, although it searched until dark and did not return until 10:00 P.M. Finally, word arrived that Ingalls had reached Le Havre, 150 miles away. Lost in the mist and running low on fuel he landed at sea near a French schooner which towed him ashore. Ingalls spent the night at Dieppe, and lunched the next day with the American consul and his two daughters. In August a Handley Page bomber ditched in the Channel off Nieuport with a crew including RAF Lieutenant Hitherington and Navy observer C. W. Kennedy. An American DD flown by Gates with only one observer aboard hurried to the site, discovered the aircraft still afloat, and retrieved the exhausted crew who had been clinging to the wreck for nine hours. A month later King George V awarded the Distinguished Flying Cross to Gates for his exploit and Sims recommended him for the Medal of Honor.[32]

One of most spectacular events in the station annals occurred July 7 on a rescue mission gone wrong. Alonzo Hildreth, who survived the ordeal, called it the "Day of Days." During a morning antisubmarine patrol, a flying boat piloted by Edward DeCernea along with observers Chord and McGee, went down in the water about 25 miles out to sea, northwest of Dunkirk. The DD itself had been sent to pick up an HD wrecked earlier that day. Shortly thereafter another DD with a crew of pilot James O'Brien and observers Coash and Seiler, and its Hanriot escorts flown by Franklin Young and Edward Bamrick, spotted the stranded machine and returned to Dunkirk to report. Bamrick's machine sank while landing due to a hole in the pontoon. At 11:40 A.M. the station launch departed in search of the lost aircraft, carrying a crew of five commanded by Asst. Surgeon Albert 'Doc' Stevens, accompanied by observer Coash to act as navigator. A French destroyer raced ahead. Two additional aircraft set off at 12:40 P.M. At 2:00, word arrived that the French warship was towing the downed DD, with pilot and observers aboard, and the motor launch received orders to return to port. The damaged flying boat reached the station at 4:20.

Unfortunately, while returning, the launch experienced compass troubles. As the crew neared the coast they assumed they were west of Dunkirk but had actually blundered into dangerous German waters near Nieuport. Aircraft from No. 217 Squadron quickly scrambled to assist, while the British Commodore notified two CMBs to stand by. At 4:45 P.M. the Americans came under fire from shore batteries. A shell pierced the canopy and Stevens ordered everyone to grab life preservers and enter the water. For a while the boat continued on, making circles, until two direct hits sank it. The sailors began swimming toward shore. A French seaplane plucked Hildreth from the water. Strong tides pushed Bailey and Coash toward Allied lines. Coash, by now exhausted, would have drowned had not two British officers from a battery of siege guns swum 1,000 yards offshore to rescue him. The Dunkirk commander's report of the incident credited French personnel with making a similar rescue of Bailey. Two more Americans, ironically the best swimmers, reached the beach in German territory and were taken prisoner. "Doc" Stevens, still wearing his blue uniform and white cap, emerged from the surf with his arms raised. Charles Tatulinski and John Vogt were last seen on life preservers swimming away from the sinking launch. That same night, having just returned from his encounter with German shore batteries, Hildreth was jolted from a well-deserved sleep by an air raid siren. He immediately raced for a dugout. Two minutes later a bomb landed 20 feet away, destroying his bed. The following day the body of Edward Eichelberger, the observer killed in late February, washed ashore and was buried with full military honors.[33]

Events, both extraordinary and mundane, punctuated the daily routine of patrol, maintenance, and repair. That summer a contingent of enlisted pilots received official discharges from the regular Navy and simultaneously reenrolled as ensigns, USNRF. This group included First Aeronautic Detachment veterans James O'Brien, Erlon Parker, Herbert Lasher, Walter Huddleston, Charles Wardwell, Julius Carson, Lawrence DeSonnier, Harold Elliott, and Franklin Young. The station celebrated the Fourth of July with a track and field competition, baseball game, and swimming meet, as well as a special dinner. That night, enlisted men put on a talent show, capped by the customary air raid. On Bastille Day, a contingent of 50 sailors (lacking rifles, as only a dozen were to be had) marched in the annual parade and Di Gates shared the reviewing stand with the governor-general. A few weeks later Asst. Secretary of the Navy Franklin Roosevelt arrived from England aboard a destroyer to inspect the base. Bombardment by German guns and planes continued throughout the spring, summer, and into the fall. During an April 21 attack a bomb exploded directly in front of Hangar No. 1, wrecking the building, destroying five aircraft, and damaging more. In early July the *New York Times* reported that Dunkirk had already been subjected to 159 bombings. The air over the town grew crowded. In early May a contingent of Army flyers, including Hobey Baker, Cord Meyer, and Seth Low, came to dinner. That night the Germans launched yet another raid, shutting off their motors, gliding toward the target, dropping their "pills," and then restarting the motors to escape. In the process they passed right over the dinner party. Meanwhile a flight of RAF bombers took off and the two forces passed in the dark, unaware of each other's presence.[34]

Cumulative experience led many at Dunkirk to question the utility of the effort or appropriateness of its site, tactics, or equipment. Losses of personnel and materiel proved sobering. British authorities earlier noted, "Dunkirk is a most uncomfortable place to operate from; neither our people or the French think very highly of entrusting much materiel to this sector." As early as May 1918 Hutch Cone intimated that the harbor might be unsuitable for seaplanes, adding, "Large boats and large seaplanes of any type cannot be used from Dunkirk . . . on account of the limited protected water area." In early August, Di Gates, Dunkirk's new commanding officer, prepared two detailed reports for David Hanrahan, commander of the Northern Bombing Group, outlining activities, equipment, and conditions at the base and their perceived shortcomings. He repeated the frequent complaints that the facilities were too congested, the planes too small, slow, and underarmed, and the antisubmarine weapons inadequate. His gloomy assessment did not, however, advocate abandoning the station. Similarly, his call for an improved seaplane represented a continuation of present policy. A great deal of time and struggle had been invested in establishing and operating NAS Dunkirk, and many were reluctant to write off the entire effort. At the same time Bernard Smith, one of aviation's top troubleshooters, described German preparations for extensive operations in the North Sea area and reported the Germans were developing seaplanes that could land on the water and wait, conserving fuel. Smith thought the Curtiss HA, a single-pontoon, bi-place(two-seat) machine under development and nicknamed the "Dunkirk Fighter," would offer a good response. To the veteran aviator, Dunkirk remained important. Antiaircraft defenses should be upgraded and it would soon be possible to retaliate with NBG attacks. Like Gates, Smith believed Dunkirk could be salvaged.[35]

Within days Hanrahan drafted his own recommendations, but with far greater emphasis on the idea of abandoning the site and pursuing its mission by alternative means. Thus far, he noted, 20 machines, 5 pilots, and 2 observers had been lost in crashes. Faster planes such as the proposed Dunkirk Fighter or Hanriot-Dupont bi-place machine would cause even more problems. Further, the Germans could easily destroy the base if it became too effective. The RAF had long ago eliminated their seaplane station, using land-based DH-4s instead. With these, they had enjoyed much success since March, and with success came fewer casualties. Hanrahan believed the Allies would not object if the Navy abandoned its station and urged creation of land-based, antisubmarine units equipped with DH-4 or DH-9 aircraft powered by American-made Liberty motors. When the planes were ready, Dunkirk should close, replaced by new antisubmarine squadrons flying from Northern Bombing Group fields.[36]

Cone responded almost immediately, endorsing Hanrahan's proposal, contacting Edwards in London, and reporting that a conference on the issue had recommended abandonment. He noted, "The subject has been in debate for some time and the situation at Dunkirk has been most unsatisfactory." Sims followed up with a strongly worded cable to Washington, reporting, "Operations covering four months have demonstrated absolute unsuitability of Dunkirk as seaplane base. Manipulation of seaplanes in small and congested harbor extremely hazardous and inventory of our casualties condemn Dunkirk from this point of view.... Strongly suggest DH-4s be substituted for this station, would patrol Belgian coast and Dover Straights [sic]." Sims argued that the "Liberty Fighter" [sic] then in development might be employed at Killingholme or bases with better harbor facilities. Planners in Washington quickly reached a decision. Swayed by Sims's recommendation, the Department authorized abandonment of Dunkirk station September 12. At conferences with the French and British, officials agreed that seaplane operations at Dunkirk would cease "shortly." The station would close, replaced by two antisubmarine squadrons equipped with DH-4s or similar aircraft. Only continuing aircraft shortages and unexpectedly rapid conclusion of the war less than eight weeks later prevented this decision from being implemented.[37]

Despite much hectic activity lasting many months, NAS Dunkirk experienced only limited operational success. Flight logs for the April–October period reveal that only in May did pilots conduct operations on 65 percent of possible dates. The proportion dropped to 50 percent in June, 45 percent in July, 58 percent in August, and just 40 percent in September. Even on active days many patrols were aborted due to mechanical or weather problems or went out with only a partial complement of aircraft. In fact, bouts of severe weather prevented all activity between August 26 and 29, and again from September 8 to 15. As the season advanced, conditions grew even worse. Dunkirk mounted only 15 patrols in September and just 2 the following month. At least one of those sorties almost ended in disaster. On September 23 James O'Brien's DD landed in rough seas with engine trouble. The monitor *Terror* rescued the crew and the station launch attempted to retrieve the wreck, but failed. The launch itself became disabled and needed to be towed in by an Allied destroyer.[38]

Sporadic flying opportunities in the final weeks of the war, coupled with a growing surplus of Navy pilots, caused a few aviators to be reassigned, at least temporarily, to London headquarters.[39] Several served with neighboring Allied units. Some flew with Escadrille St. Pol, a French navy squadron operating SPAD single-seater fighters, while others chose No. 213 Squadron, equipped with Sopwith Camels. For many it seemed like a reunion, having earlier trained or flown with the Allies. In late September George Moseley rejoined his *amis* at Escadrille St. Pol carrying out combat missions in the busy skies over Flanders. He and other Americans billeted at the same field where the legendary Georges Guynemer had flown, his room still unoccupied, his personal calling card tacked to the wall. Moseley described the "great many Huns" in their sector that often maneuvered in packs of 15 or 20 aircraft. Plans called for Navy men to fly several days behind the lines to familiarize themselves with their new aircraft. Moseley spent much of his time rehearsing dogfights with Di Gates. Constant practice was the only thing that made one a good flyer, he noted.

In early October, Moseley and his mates flew along the front lines from Nieuport to Ypres, watching the Allied advance unfold below. "The earth seemed to spurt fire . . . the air was full of pockets and bumps caused by the passing shells so we bounced up and down like a cork in water. . . . the roads behind our lines were alive with men, ammunition, wagons, and supplies moving along in a long steady procession." The medieval city of Ypres appeared "largely wrecked." A gas attack "looked like a huge white cloud or mist, but which grew in volume and density as it reached the German lines. . . . We flew near the long lines of observation balloons and had a good look at the observers sitting up there in their funny baskets." On one emergency mission Moseley "bombed" French troops cut off from supplies with parcels of food.[40]

A seven-plane patrol led by Captain Delasalle October 4, including four Americans—Gates, Beach, Moseley, and Van Fleet—set out on a morning sweep over Ypres salient. At 9:40 A.M. they encountered a mixed pack of 15 German aircraft and raced back across the Allied lines. Then they turned, climbed, and reentered enemy airspace. At 10:00 A.M. Moseley and Van Fleet pulled out of formation with engine trouble and returned to base. Twenty minutes later over Courtrai, skimming just below the clouds at 13,000 feet, Delasalle signaled to dive, having spotted the same Germans as before. As the Allies dived in a V formation, the enemy pounced on Gates's plane. Fred Beach was the last to see him. Two days later Moseley reported, "We were looking for Huns in the Ypres salient, . . . Art Gates did not come back. . . . He was with us when the attack began, after that nobody saw him." Investigators sent in after the enemy retreated discovered Gates's machine. A follow-up party interviewed a peasant boy who saw the American make a rough landing. Thrown from the cockpit, he went back and tried to burn his plane, and then surrendered to two Germans. After taking him prisoner, Gates's captors moved him to Ghent in Belgium and then Karlsruhe and Villengen in Germany. A daring escape attempt failed only a few yards from the Swiss border. Despite the ordeal, Gates survived the war and was finally freed November 26. He crossed over to England, and returned to the United States in early February aboard the battleship *Arkansas*.[41]

A more sobering event occurred just days later. Following a busy spring at Dunkirk, Ken MacLeish spent the summer receiving daylight bombing training at Clermont-Ferrand, followed by a stint at the front with No. 218 Squadron. Then came duty at Pauillac and Eastleigh, two assembly and repair facilities. He flew from Eastleigh to Dunkirk October 13 where he enjoyed an evening with friends in the Northern Bombing Group. The following morning MacLeish made his last patrols. He began with an early test flight. Two hours later, 19 British aircraft, including MacLeish's Camel, took off for a high-altitude bombing attack against retreating German troops near Ardoye in Belgium. All Allied pilots encountered heavy opposition and three failed to return. In the melee, RAF Captain Green and MacLeish destroyed a Fokker biplane, the log reporting the enemy scout last seen "disappearing amongst the houses at Theurout."

Two hours later MacLeish and a dozen others initiated a second sortie along the coast. Two miles north of Dixmude they spotted 11 Fokkers at 8,000 feet and 3 more at 12,000 feet. A wild scramble ensued and several German planes went down in flames. Among the Allied forces, Captain Green, Lieutenant Allen, and MacLeish failed to return, with MacLeish last seen attacking a half-dozen Fokkers. After that there was no further information. For a time some hope remained that he had been taken prisoner, as had Gates just a few days earlier. But the Armistice came and went and still no word. Finally, in December a Belgian farmer solved the mystery when he returned to his wrecked homestead near Leffinghe and discovered the fully dressed body of an American naval aviator. It was MacLeish. He had just turned 24.[42]

Ensign Robert Read assumed command October 9 following Gates's capture, but rapid advances by the Allied armies eliminated all rationale for maintaining a station at Dunkirk. By then, rumors circulated that the Germans were preparing to evacuate Ostend and the rest of the Belgian coast. Vice-Admiral Henry Mayo, Commander of the Atlantic Fleet, inspected the station October 15. That same day Dunkirk received a send-off from the retreating enemy, yet another long-range bombardment, a total of 20 shells over a period of 90 minutes. Dunkirk also battled the influenza epidemic in October, with as much as 90 percent of the base complement affected more or less seriously. The weakened men spent the period of October 21–November 5 taking down hangars, cleaning the grounds, and loading materiel aboard trucks and a barge for possible repositioning northward along the coast.

Arriving soldiers found Ostend a remarkable spectacle. Not much remained after retreating Germans had destroyed what bombing and shelling had not. Local citizens, however, were overjoyed, filling the streets with flags. Frank Lynch, a First Yale member and veteran of extensive service at NAS Killingholme, flew to France October 13 to deliver a DH-4 to the NBG field at La Fresne and then motored on to Dunkirk. As the Germans retreated, he and others from the station drove to Ostend. They arrived at 8:30 P.M. and discovered the market thronged with old men, women, and children. The mayor and other dignitaries greeted the flyers. The next morning they watched the first Belgian forces march into the city to the strains of the overture *La Brabicon*. Later that day they went to the quay to see Allied warships blow up 45 floating mines. The great concussion broke windows in town.

Subsequent capture of Zeebrugge generated orders to cease operations at Dunkirk, dismantle the station, and move necessary material and equipment to the mole at the former enemy stronghold, a significant logistical challenge, carried out entirely by trucks over very bad roads. Operational command shifted from RN/Dover to the French general commanding in Flanders, and finally to the Belgians. Two days later the Navy raised the colors over the old German seaplane base and began clearing and repairing buildings. A small draft of workers arrived November 6, followed by 68 more two days later. One of their first projects was to build a suspension bridge reconnecting the mole to the mainland, spanning the breach made during the British assault in late April.

With the Armistice, American personnel at Zeebrugge returned to Dunkirk. The Navy began withdrawing in December, and by early January the site was abandoned, transferred to the Committee for Relief in Belgium. A final tally counted 31 pilots ordered to duty, 984 hours of total flying time, and 353 test flights. A year-end report documented 46,630 miles flown at the station. Edward DeCernea, Dunkirk's busiest pilot, logged 106 hours aloft, followed by Charles Wardwell and Di Gates with 89 hours each, and Franklin Young with 72. Dunkirk remains a bustling harbor to this day. The seawall that defined the American station survives, but all traces of the facility are gone.[43]

* * *

Finding and attacking submarines with aircraft posed a difficult task in 1917–1918, and the station at Dunkirk operated under the most extreme conditions. It was the only American base to endure continuous bombardment from land, sea, and air. Dunkirk also battled aggressive enemy air forces in significant numbers. The congested harbor offered treacherous conditions, while the base's limited size and extreme range of tide hampered launch and recovery of aircraft. The choice of machines also worked against completion of its mission. Obsolescent Donnet-Denhaut flying boats were severely underpowered as well as mechanically unreliable. Unfortunately, space restrictions precluded replacement with more capable flying boats.

Most handicaps were known but perhaps not fully understood in the summer of 1917, when the Navy agreed to operate an antisubmarine patrol base there. In their eagerness to get into the fight, aid the Allies, and show Yankee determination and ability, they took on a task with very little chance of success. Had they better understood local conditions, they might have chosen an alternative arena in which to compete. In addition, the Navy committed itself to using seaplanes and overwater patrol methods at the very moment the

British turned away from this tactic. Not until a year later would Americans follow suit.

Nonetheless, some good came out the expenditure of time, money, lives, and machines. NAS Dunkirk accounted for just one part of a many-faceted Allied effort to neutralize the U-boat menace, a campaign that included minefields and nets, land-based aircraft, seaplanes, flotillas of antisubmarine vessels, and direct assaults on German facilities. Patrolling aircraft undoubtedly forced U-boats to remain submerged more often than they wished, making transit through the area more difficult and dangerous. While never destructive enough to cripple operations, attacks on submarine bases at Ostend, Bruges, and Zeebrugge complicated the enemy's life. Anything that made U-boats less efficient aided the Allied effort.

4

THE FRENCH COASTAL UNIT

Between the time the tiny First Aeronautic Detachment reached Europe in June 1917 and the Armistice 17 months later, the Navy created a far-flung system of patrol stations on the French coast designed to shield American troop and supply convoys from German U-boats. In many circles this ranked as the most critical challenge facing the United States. Sixteen installations were planned, including eight seaplane stations, four dirigible bases, and three kite balloon facilities covering most of the coast from Tréguier on the northern coast of Brittany to Arcachon and Gujan on the southern shore of the Bay of Biscay. Americans also built a flying school at Moutchic-Lacanau and an enormous supply, assembly, and repair base at Pauillac. The Navy carried out the enormous task virtually from scratch, at inaccessible sites, hindered by inhospitable terrain, inclement weather, labor scarcity, and crippling shortages of tools and construction materials. Nonetheless, by war's end the majority of stations had actively executed their missions. From the first complement of seven officers and 122 enlisted men, the coastal force ultimately grew to more than 850 officers and 6,174 bluejackets.[1]

Kenneth Whiting, who conducted extensive negotiations with civilian and military officials and carried out extended fact-finding tours, established the basic outlines of the Navy effort. After lengthy review, the Department approved his recommendations in August and September 1917, and by the end of the summer work had begun at several sites, including Moutchic, Dunkirk, and Le Croisic. Hutch Cone's arrival in late September and the centralization of command led to further definition of objectives, and by early winter the full parameters of the program were set.[2] Success of the stations rested entirely on securing sufficient aircraft to conduct operations. The Intelligence and Planning Division under Cdr. Henry Dinger investigated several types for possible use. At first Moutchic utilized FBA training machines, Dunkirk and Ile Tudy flew Hanriot-Duponts and Donnet-Denauts, while Le Croisic employed Telliers. In April 1918 the French government announced that production of Telliers and DDs would cease and offered Levy-LePen aircraft with

300 hp Renault motors in their place. The Navy accepted this proffer for NAS St. Trojan and received eight in June. Le Croisic served as clearing-out station for all French machines. Dunkirk utilized Allied equipment until the end of the war. Later in the year U.S.-manufactured aircraft began arriving; HS-1Ls assembled at Pauillac and Brest went to Fromentine, St. Trojan, Moutchic, Arcachon, Ile Tudy, L'Aber Vrach, and Tréguier.

During the winter of 1918 the flow of personnel to Europe began to surge, and the 1,200 enlisted men present January 1 jumped to 4,300 by March 1, along with 257 officers. That same month the Navy issued a revised, comprehensive plan for establishing, manning, and supplying its network of bases. With the exception of Rochefort dirigible station, this program remained in effect for the remainder of the war. Priorities for the next several months included accelerating construction, commencing combat operations wherever possible, speeding the flow of men and equipment, formalizing the anticipated program for 1919, and transforming and relocating the command structure. By summer, however, most bases in France had still received just a fraction of their allotted flying personnel and aircraft, and a few stations had none. Le Croisic possessed 8 aircraft, Dunkirk 12, St. Trojan 9, with much of that a mishmash of inadequate French machines. Three stations—Dunkirk, Ile Tudy, and Le Croisic—carried out active patrols.[3]

During the same period, headquarters conducted extensive discussions to finalize the 1919 program, reaching their conclusions in early July. A total of 16 patrol bases would operate in England, Ireland, France, and Italy, all to be equipped with American-manufactured flying boats, except Dunkirk and Porto Corsini in Italy. Coastal stations at Brest, Fromentine, and Arcachon would fly H-16s, while L'Aber Vrach, Ile Tudy, Le Croisic, St. Trojan, and Tréguier would operate HS-1Ls. Stations supporting 18 patrol craft would be staffed with 54 officers and 327 to 394 enlisted men. Those allotted 24 aircraft would count 66 officers and 366 to 498 men, in all cases with 2 pilots per plane. Combined allotments for dirigible stations totaled 12 airships, 24 pilots, and 975 enlisted men, along with 3 kite balloon stations operating 18 balloons, with 36 pilots, and 324 enlisted men. The booming assembly and repair facility at Pauillac required 100 officers, 20 pilots, and 5,884 bluejackets. Attempting to regularize station procedures, a board of officers headed by Cdr. Louis Maxfield met at Paimboeuf in late June and developed a standard organizational plan calling for 10 officers serving under the commanding officer and his executive officer. These included the squadron commander and engineering officer, as well as those in charge of medical affairs, gunnery, supply, intelligence, navigation, paymaster, and commissary departments.[4]

Coastal stations in France performed both the earliest and longest wartime service. Initial flights at Moutchic commenced in late September 1917, and the first at Le Croisic in mid-November. NAS Brest conducted the last patrol of the war December 13, 1918, escorting President Wilson into harbor there. Coastal stations formed the largest single group of aviation facilities covering the widest range of territory, employing the greatest number of men and machines. French sources claimed that American stations spotted 27 submarines, attacked 25, damaged 12, and probably sank 4. Navy statistics, based on more stringent reporting requirements, identified no confirmed U-boat sinkings, a conclusion borne out by German operational records. Nonetheless, American planes undoubtedly forced submarines to keep their "heads down," directed surface forces toward the enemy, and gathered information allowing convoys to alter course toward safer routes.

Following establishment of Navy stations, not a single U-boat successfully attacked an escorted convoy on the west coast of France and loss of individual vessels practically ceased. In fact, several aviators complained that they had nothing to do. Also, according to the French, American bases were more active, on a day-to-day basis, than their own, which often employed land planes flying only in good weather and not very far off shore. Of the American stations, Le Croisic and Ile Tudy were the busiest with 113,324 and 104,877 sea miles patrolled. Next came Paimbouef with 48,630. All stations combined conducted 5,671 war flights covering 549,078 miles and 16,347 training flights aggregating 242,320 miles.[5]

After much planning, including extended wrangling with Admiral Wilson, aviation reorganized its command structure, effective September 1, 1918. Hutch Cone, formerly Commander, USNAF Foreign Service, relocated to London and joined Sims's staff as Aide for Aviation, superseding Edwards. Direct control of French coastal stations passed to Wilson, with Thomas Craven, who directed the Operations Division under Cone, becoming Aide for Aviation. Commander Albert M. Cohen served as Craven's assistant. Most Paris staff transferred to 13 Rue de Jean Mace, Brest. The new headquarters included sections for operations, personnel, transportation, medical, public works, supply, inspection, and assembly and repair.

At the end of the summer, staff planners analyzed the entire coastal initiative. They found that most bases operated or would carry out missions soon. Submarine activity had declined noticeably and emphasis now shifted to completing rather than expanding the program. Realizing the patrol establishment had grown larger than necessary, the Navy took steps to promote better organization, stressing efficiency and economy by ordering that only essential public works be addressed. Three kite balloon stations neared completion (Brest, La Pallice, La Trinité) and several destroyer/balloon patrols were made from Brest. Recruitment of sufficient personnel continued to be a problem, however, and dirigible stations remained "backward" due to construction delays. Equipment for all stations was modified and simplified. Collaboration with French centers along the coast remained a delicate matter and military leaders made every effort to avoid friction and promote cooperation.[6]

In general, the coastal stations surmounted many of their earlier impediments as evidenced by increasing flight activity. For the week ending September 21 they conducted 576 missions lasting 475 hours, with 52 aircraft and 2 dirigibles in commission, manned by 185 flying officers. The next week recorded 635 flights, and then 728 in the first week of October. Significantly, as late as September 30, each of these stations continued to rely on foreign-manufactured equipment. Nonetheless, enough U.S.-made aircraft were on hand or in the pipeline to permit cancellation of remaining contracts with the French. Total aircraft amounted to 188 U.S.-manufactured planes, 45 French models, 2 dirigibles, and 28 kite balloons. During the same period, surveyors declared 10 DDs and 8 Telliers unfit for service.[7]

Shortages of equipment and personnel, however, remained a problem until the end of war. An analysis prepared just after the Armistice summarized the overall situation. All stations were in commission, or nearly so, with operations generally under way. Availabilty of pilots and ground officers remained an issue, however, and seriously curtailed flight activities. As of October 15 there were present at various coastal stations 269 of 325 necessary ground officers, 24 of 38 dirigible pilots, 34 of 36 kite balloon pilots, and 158 of 396 seaplane pilots. Of this latter group, 119 were actually available for duty. Craven suggested accelerating arrivals from the United States and borrowing personnel from the Northern Bombing Group. He noted, "The youngsters at Le Croisic and Ile Tudy are pretty well fagged out, and should be given a rest."[8]

* * *

The story of the French Coastal Unit was a mosaic of experiences drawn from the many individual stations. According to Chip McIlwaine, a member of the First Yale Unit and for some time senior flying instructor, NAS Moutchic-Lacanau was "by most odds the most important station abroad." Virtually every American seaplane pilot passed through it. Originally intended as a finishing school, it later added primary flight instruction, gunnery, and bombing, along with an extensive ground school program. McIlwaine proudly recalled that he "never saw men or officers work harder at any station," and by the Armistice, Moutchic surpassed any other Allied seaplane facility. Though a French contractor bore responsibility for building the station, shortages of labor and material necessitated that American bluejackets pitch in. Fred Beach, yet another of the ubiquitous First Yale flyers, described how sailors cleared trees, graded land, and raised a village of tents and aircraft packing boxes. He discovered that the enlisted group contained many skilled men who could do almost anything you wanted—carpenters, masons, plasterers, machinists. When Beach left Moutchic in the spring of 1918 the "camp was almost complete in every detail."[9]

After a slow start, activity quickened in late fall 1917. Large drafts of bluejackets began working with the French contractor. German POWs also contributed to the construction effort. Ken MacLeish called German prisoners "very interesting . . . tickled" at the wonderful treatment they received, "worked like slaves, twice as hard as the French." About this time Moutchic began welcoming a stream of important visitors. Admirals Sims and Benson stopped by on December 2, accompanied by their large staffs. Hutch Cone arrived December 19 for a two-day stay. The Navy requested shipment of DDs and Telliers in late November to facilitate bombing instruction so pilots could be posted to NAS Ile Tudy and Tréguier. The Americans then returned the original, cranky FBAs, or at least those not yet wrecked, with most flyers happy to see them go. Replacement machines, however, proved little better. Of 16 DDs received between December 1917 and May 1918, 9 crashed or burned. Two of four Sopwiths obtained during the winter were wrecked.[10]

Lafayette Flying Corps veterans recently transferred to the Navy, George Moseley among them, trained at Moutchic in the winter of 1918. He told his family in late February, "I am now in the gravy." Moseley lived in officers' quarters and found accommodations delightful. "Can you imagine," he wrote enthusiastically, "real white bread, oatmeal with cream, pie, a white table cloth, and napkins . . . beef, pork, and veal (no horse meat!) . . . real American grub once more, lead me to it." Moseley claimed to sleep 10 hours every night. He took initial flight training in a single-seater with pontoons (Sopwith scout), bouncing on his first landing. On the second trip a defective rocker arm flew off and punched a hole in his pontoon, the motor quit, and he came down in the middle of the lake, where the plane began to sink. With the motor coughing violently, he just managed to reach the dock. Two weeks later Moseley passed his naval aviator's exam "and since then have had nothing to do except eat, sleep, be officer of the now and then, and take my little machine up for a joy ride whenever I felt inclined." Winter jaunts required serious attire, however, including fur helmet over knitted helmet, uniform, soft leather vest, silk sweater, big heavy sweater, silk scarf, woolen wristlets under leather gauntlets, fur-lined coat, and fur-lined boots over shoes. At one point, extreme cold froze part of the lake, leading to temporary suspension of operations.[11]

January marked the beginning of bombing and gunnery instruction, under the direction of Lt. Harold "Cueless" Bartlett. Bartlett had served previously at Pensacola, aboard *North Carolina,* and as junior naval aide to President Wilson. Before commencing work at Moutchic, he studied French and British methods exhaustively. Bartlett assumed overall command February 6. Bombing and gunnery courses each lasted two weeks, with 11 pilots and 11 observers in the first class. Pilots received lectures on bombing submarines, getting the correct line, calculating trajectory, determining ground speed, using various sights (including the Wimperis course-setting bomb sight), and leading a target. Students began practicing on the firing range January 18 and dropped the first dummy ordnance the same day. They learned to release their bombs at an altitude of 500 feet and practiced against 56-foot × 6-foot targets placed in the water. Bombing accuracy against submarines was crucial as aircraft carried only a few, modest weapons, with a "kill zone" of barely 30 feet to 50 feet. Serious damage could be inflicted only with a near or direct hit. Given the rudimentary nature of available bombsights, the task proved challenging. The British-designed Wimperis had the reputation of only being "better than nothing at all." The French Michelin sight could not compensate for wind. Students also lacked a means to accurately determine wind direction or velocity. The crew of Curtis Read and James O'Brien, for example, made their first bombing run in early February and missed the target by nearly 300 feet from an altitude of 900 feet. On a later flight O'Brien's flight suit snagged the bomb release, causing the dummy ordnance to hit the northern lakefront. On yet another occasion O'Brien observed that he had "hit the lake," but not the target.[12]

The gunnery regimen developed by Ens. Charles Park, who had studied at the French school at Cazaux, included firing at a floating raft and at an airplane placed on a raft, shooting at the shadow of a plane on the water, firing at airplane and submarine silhouettes on shore, and simulated aerial combat. Observers learned to strip guns in the air and clear blockages and other malfunctions. Until the Moutchic gunnery course was fully implemented, however, the Navy continued sending personnel to Cazaux. Moutchic graduated its first bombing/gunnery class February 19, with eight pilot/observer pairs sent to Dunkirk, and two crews transferred to Le Croisic. In time, Moutchic also supplied personnel to Porto Corsini in Italy and bombing schools at Clermont-Ferrand and Avord as part of the Northern Bombing Group program. Men arriving from schools in the United States necessitated modification of the Moutchic course of instruction. Officer-pilots from Pensacola, for example, reached France with 25 hours flying time in N-9 and R-6 float planes, but none in flying boats. At that time Moutchic's facilities were limited and devoted largely to bombing and gunnery. John Callan suggested that the school acquire dual-control Telliers to instruct those from Pensacola and also pilots arriving from England who had learned to fly Short pontoon scout-bombers. He also recommended that the Department arrange for men to receive primary flying boat training in the United States.[13]

One facet of training remained a constant, however; it was dangerous. An FBA making a spiral too close to the water, crashed December 3, 1917, badly injuring the pilot and killing seaman Claude Baker who was riding contrary to orders. When members of the Second Yale Unit arrived in the winter of 1918, they found the beach littered with wrecked FBAs that had a tendency to spin when turning left due to the torque imparted by their rotary motors. The men responded by making only right turns. Edward DeCernea crashed his machine and capsized, but escaped serious injury. In early April, Lloyd Petty turned downwind on a dummy bomb run at 1,000 feet and went into a spin. Though he recovered, it was too late to pull out and the plane crashed into thick underbrush, killing the pilot. The observer, thrown from the plane, survived. In July, Woldemar Grosscup on a practice flight in a Sopwith S-1 seaplane, went into a nosedive from 1,500 feet and crashed into 10 feet of water. A rescue launch quickly reached the scene, but Grosscup died of multiple injuries. Finally, on August 14, Delosier Davidson was piloting a DD, accompanied by two student gunners whom he was familiarizing with the location of targets; the plane fell into a nosedive and crashed, with all aboard killed.[14]

Occasionally the same sorts of shortages plaguing operations at active duty stations delayed instruction at Moutchic. Fred Beach claimed that lack of equipment held up his training. New planes kept arriving, but not parts to repair old ones. Instead, mechanics scavenged wrecks, restored motors, and rebuilt aircraft. Using hand-fitted French machinery required considerable ingenuity by shop personnel, mixing mismatched crankshafts, cylinders, and pistons. At any given time one-third to one-half of Moutchic's aircraft were under repair. Beach also claimed that Commanding Officer Bartlett knew how to handle his officers well, managing to get the best out of his men and maintaining a good feeling throughout the entire command.[15]

By summer 1918 extensive courses in a variety of subjects had been standardized, with instructors selected from officers trained at the best French and British schools. The Instruction Department offered a one-week ground course (navigation, meteorology, ship silhouettes, theory of bombing, mechanism of bombs, carrier pigeons, signaling), two-week gunnery course (deflection, Lewis gun, cleaning jams, firing on range, firing from air), and two-week bombing course (passages, Batchelor mirror work, dummy bombing, surprise bombing, bombing a towed target resembling a submarine). Through August, Moutchic turned out 104 officer pilots and 103 enlisted pilots. Headquarters also organized an aviation intelligence officer class. On more than one occasion, however, Bartlett complained that information and examples of the best new equipment and inventions were not forwarded to his school.[16]

Moutchic was now an up-and-going concern, with much construction work completed, though many officers continued to live at Lacanau-Ocean four miles away and "commuted" to the base by truck. Improved weather brought intensified efforts. During the summer Moutchic averaged 175 to 350 flights per week, and by September and October 400 to 500 per week, each lasting 20 to 30 minutes. Instruction originally occurred between 4:30 and 10:30 A.M. and then 3:00 and 8:30 P.M., but as many more students arrived lessons were conducted all day long. A new directive encouraged bad weather flying so pilots might know how to deal with such conditions. Until September it remained Navy practice to pair officer pilots and enlisted observers in an effort to increase the number of crews. A policy change in the United States, however, mandated replacement of enlisted observers with officers as more commissioned personnel became available.

August represented a transition month. Lieutenant Commander Robert W. Cabaniss replaced Bartlett, who returned to the United States to provide advice on training needs in France. The 34-year-old Cabaniss had graduated from the U.S. Naval Academy in 1906, passed through the Pensacola program in 1915, and served as the first commanding officer of the Navy detachment at MIT. Like many contemporary aviation officers, he died in a postwar flying accident. Under Cabaniss the program at Moutchic underwent noticeable intensification, along with greater attention to traditional military regulations regarding appearance and etiquette. Coast Guard aviator Eugene Coffin served with Cabaniss at Pensacola and called him a "driver." Moutchic's official record described the change as "strict observance of Navy Regulations and such points as military appearance and etiquette, and correctness in carrying out all formations." Enlisted personnel put it somewhat differently. One observer described the new commanding officer as "full up on regulations and believes in putting them all into practice . . . started week with having hair cut regulation, skipper was first to appear with 1½ inch of upper deck." One lament: you couldn't get a shave "as they are cutting too much wool." Some sailors "lost the lovely locks that once attracted the *mademoiselles* of Bordeaux." On the training side, the Navy decided to abandon French machines as soon as feasible and use American-made HS-1Ls for all bombing and gunnery instruction.[17]

By late September the school was operating at almost full capacity, and at the time of the Armistice Moutchic supported a complement of 23 permanent officers, 34 officers under instruction, and 493 enlisted men, along with 24 aircraft, including 11 HS-1Ls, along with 6 Telliers, 5 Donnet-Denhauts, and 2 Sopwiths. One tabulation documented 10,807 flights, lasting 4,049 hours, covering 242,320 nautical miles, by far the busiest station in Europe. The first draft of 200 impatient men returned home November 24 and the school went out of commission at 9 A.M., December 31, the facility turned over to the French War Ministry. It eventually became a tuberculosis sanitarium and, ultimately, an RV camping site. Though the lakefront beach of the World War I era is now a grass-covered expanse dotted with mature trees, the original concrete bulkhead remains in place. A villa occupied by American officers also survives, though in serious disrepair. On the deserted site numerous foundations are visible, as well as a derelict range of stucco-clad buildings originally housing the administrative offices, storerooms, chief pilot's quarters, YMCA, and enlisted men's barracks. A small monument, no more than five feet tall and surrounded by a chain supported by anchor stanchions, carries the names of eight Americans who died here. It is the only such memorial along the French coast.[18]

During World War I the city and harbor of Brest, France, situated at the western end of the Brittany peninsula, played a vital role in the military affairs of the United States. For the French, Brest had been an important outpost for centuries and one of the country's most important naval complexes. When the First Aeronautic Detachment arrived in June 1917 they spent part of their time quartered here before dispersing to Tours, St. Raphael, and elsewhere. Kenneth Whiting's early discussions included Brest as a possible site for a coastal base. The American Expeditionary Force disembarked many thousands of troops and mountains of supplies and materiel here, while the Navy maintained extensive installations, including a repair base, receiving ship, and supply depot. Destroyers and armed yachts employed in antisubmarine and convoy work berthed here, as did some of the fleet's heavier units from time to time. Brest also served as headquarters for the commander of Navy forces in France, Rear Adm. Henry Wilson.[19]

Whiting inspected a proposed spot for a seaplane station August 12–13 on the northern shore of the inner harbor, just west of the city at Quatre Pompes. Adjacent to the French torpedo destroyer boat base, the plot of ground consisted of quarry refuse and dredge spoil extending 300 feet inland, with 2,000 feet of shoreline. Steep hills to the rear provided some protection from strong winds, while an artificial breakwater created a calm expanse of water on which to maneuver flying boats. Whiting identified this as the only location available within 50 miles of Brest, and a place of vital importance given the level of submarine activity in the area. French authorities offered to erect some hangars and barracks, but most work required American laborers and materiel. Whiting envisioned a permanent staff of over 600 officers and men. Captain Richard Jackson added, "This is the most important point on the coast of France from which a general offensive against the submarine can be carried on and operations should start as soon as possible." Admiral Sims in London endorsed the proposal two days later.[20]

Brest offered certain other advantages. The Navy hoped to reduce the number of transatlantic convoy routes due to the limited number of destroyers available and Brest (vs. Pauillac/Bordeaux) offered greater freight-handling capacity. This was significant because flying boat hulls and wings came packed in huge, railroad-car–size boxes, and plans for an air station soon expanded to include a large assembly and repair facility from which aircraft could be distributed to stations on the northern coast. In time, this operation evolved into the base's primary responsibility. Early proposals envisioned a single, large seaplane hangar measuring nearly 500 feet in length, accommodating as many as 48 aircraft. Ultimately, the Navy erected several standard hangars identical to those constructed at other sites. Eventually a kite balloon facility also operated here, located between the station and the French navy yard.[21]

Local contractors began work on launching slips and hangars at the end of the summer, employing POWs and Moroccan laborers to build roads and foundations. In early October Lt.(jg) George Romulus reported to represent naval aviation and expedite construction contracts signed the previous summer. Drafts of American workers arrived during the winter, and on occasion station personnel assisted unloading equipment and supplies from Army transports. About the same time (January 13), FAD veteran Grattan Dichman assumed command from Romulus. William Corry replaced Dichman on June 6, with Romulus remaining as executive officer.[22] During the winter, grading, road building, and construction of portable barracks commenced, and in

March sailors and local contractors initiated work on more permanent accommodations. Throughout this period and for months afterward, however, the French proved incapable of securing sufficient supplies and laborers.

As early as May 18, Hutch Cone complained to the Ministry of Marine about the failure of the Societe de Construction Economiques to carry out work on a large hangar. According to Cone, the contract, originally signed October 15, 1917, should have been completed by January 14, 1918. The decision to create an assembly and repair facility at Brest made satisfactory progress on this project even more urgent. Apparently the minister never responded to the American's plea, and Cone wrote again July 31, ingenuously suggesting "in some way it [the letters] failed to reach you." Still receiving no satisfaction Cone communicated yet again August 21 requesting cancellation of the contracts, with bluejackets to do the necessary work instead. In part, he blamed the government for diverting scarce lumber to other projects. Despite construction difficulties, several dozen buildings eventually arose at the site, including two large double hangars, built by either local or American labor. The steamer *Bella* hauled materials, though it sometimes took six or seven days to unload the vessel. By the end of the war, bluejackets had erected barracks sufficient to accommodate 1,000 enlisted men, 75 chief petty officers, and 50 officers, two 93-foot × 214-foot wooden hangars (and most of a third), and a 1,000-foot × 120-foot steel kite balloon shed.[23]

Brest's emergence as an assembly site delayed implementation of war patrols, and by late July the influx of HS-1Ls caused considerable congestion. Construction of the first H-16 flying boat began September 24. Brest satisfactorily tested the first HS-2L aircraft October 13. By fall, significant numbers of aircraft had been assembled and ferried to other stations, a total of 15 by October 5. Crews set a goal of five planes per week. Just before the Armistice, two HS-2Ls from Brest flew to the North Sea base at Killingholme, England, a distance of more than 600 miles. In all, the assembly facility delivered 53 HS-lLs and 11 HS-2Ls.[24]

Brest suffered its only fatal accident August 21 when an HS-lL commanded by Ens. Robert Clark crashed, killing him, second pilot Ens. Arthur Boorse, and observer William Redman. Clark attended the Navy's MIT ground school and flew with the RNAS at Westgate, Portland, and Felixstowe before acting as instructor at Brest. The less-experienced Boorse, who had passed through flight school at Moutchic and Clermont-Ferrand but had not yet completed training in HS-1L flying boats, may have been in control at the time of the accident. The crew were out near Pointe du Moulin Blanc, about three miles from the station, making steep banks and spirals in rough air. At a height of

700 feet the plane fell off the wing (slide slip), dived toward the water in a tailspin, and crashed. When rescuers reached the wreckage only Bourse showed signs of life, trapped in the plane, bleeding profusely, but with his head held above water by local fishermen. The Navy crew used a file to cut a restraining pipe, loaded him into a rescue boat, and attempted first aid and resuscitation for two hours, to no avail.[25]

Despite slow construction, by fall 1918 NAS Brest operated with increasing efficiency, especially the repair and assembly unit. HS-1Ls and HS-2Ls undergoing work crowded the hangars and apron Admiral Wilson conducted an extended inspection at that time. Station personnel counted 22 officers, 13 seaplane pilots, 18 kite balloon pilots, and 786 enlisted men. NAS Brest flyers conducted aviation's last "war patrol" December 13 when they escorted President Woodrow Wilson's convoy into the harbor. Thereafter demobilization proceeded swiftly, with the station placed out of commission February 15, 1919, and the land returned to the French Navy. During World War II, occupying German forces constructed a massive, 1,000—foot-long submarine pen on the site. Despite heavy bombing, the enormous concrete structure survived the war relatively unscathed and is utilized by the French Navy to this day.

America's first combat outpost, NAS Le Croisic, stood in a small Breton village on the Baie de Croisic. Two small artificial islands, Les Petit et Grand Joncheres, long used by fishermen to dry their nets, lay a few yards offshore. A seawall sheltered the harbor located 18 miles northeast of St. Nazaire, while the dramatic rise of tide necessitated use of a derrick to launch and retrieve aircraft. For many AEF men, a glimpse of patrol craft from Le Croisic on the horizon offered their first welcoming sight of Europe. Even before the Navy arrived, the French maintained a patrol station (*poste de combat*) on the mainland, a very small operation "carried on in a perfunctory manner," used as an *alerte* post and treated as something of a rest assignment. For their own station the Americans chose to operate from the two small islands near the village, one connected to the mainland by a strong iron bridge. German POWs later built a stout wooden span linking the second island to the first, allowing men, material, and aircraft to move from one to the other. NAS Le Croisic stood practically in "the heart of town" and station activities overflowed to the shore. It was thus less compact and isolated than other American outposts. Throughout the war a great feeling of camaraderie developed with local inhabitants.[26]

Whiting and Capitaine De Laborde visited Le Croisic in July 1917. The American officer inspected the existing post consisting of one hangar and quarters for 20 men and decided to build a station here, but he chose a different spot, the adjacent islets. He judged the existing base not large enough for Navy purposes. Work began July 26 under French supervision, with a small group of German POWs wielding picks and shovels. Not surprisingly, difficulties securing sufficient tools delayed progress. Recently commissioned Ens. Rufus H. Bush, a former chief petty officer with 10 years' experience, reached Le Croisic October 5 and found a few buildings under construction, while a Bessaneau hangar on the mainland housed three DD flying boats. A young flyer who served with Bush later called him "a regular guy and 100 percent." That same day, the first Tellier aircraft arrived in crates. Navy enlisted men bivouacked temporarily in a local hospital. They assisted with road building and helped transfer the existing hangar, planes, and crane to the island. They also began assembling the crated Telliers.[27]

In November a contingent of flyers from Moutchic appeared, including Yale Unit members Kenneth Smith, Henry Landon, Samuel Walker, and Reginald Coombe, along with 2 enlisted pilots and 11 observers. On their way to Le Croisic some of them spent a night in Bordeaux, spotted General Pershing in a restaurant, and enjoyed showing off their new green uniforms. Bluejackets moved from the hospital to the island in early November, pressing empty airplane crates into duty as mess halls. Later, Americans leased a small building on the mainland (a movie hall) for a mess and galley, eventually showing movies from home several nights a week. The Navy also rented houses for officers' quarters and took over other buildings for use as sickbay, dispensary, storehouse, brig, telephone office, and pigeon loft. Several additional drafts of men soon reached Le Croisic, 100 ratings led by Ens. Henry Landon, followed by John Callan and 100 more who had just stepped off a transport in St. Nazaire. Callan assumed temporary command November 3, superseded by Lt. William Corry four days later. A 1910 Annapolis graduate, Corry passed through the original training course at Pensacola and attended several flying schools in France. Following the war he received the Medal of Honor (posthumously) for attempting to rescue a fellow officer from a flame-enveloped aircraft. Enlisted pilot Joseph Cline later said of Corry, "He had always been an inspiration to me and I think he was one of the greatest fellows I ever met," while one of the Yale pilots called Corry "An old Pensacola man. . . . He took charge and things began to hum." The following week experts from the Tellier factory came to inspect aircraft and oversee trial flights. Lieutenants Corry and Griffin (the latter down from headquarters in Paris) made the first attempts, followed by enlisted aviators Cline and Gillespie.[28]

With everything seemingly in order, Le Croisic conducted its initial patrol in the European war zone November 19, just five months after the First Aeronautic Detachment landed in France. This inaugurated flight activity that continued largely uninterrupted until the Armistice, the longest run of service at any American facility in Europe. On this occasion two seaplanes made a tour of their patrol sector. The first war operation occurred next day, a search for floating mines, followed by more familiarization flights. At the commencement of patrol activity the station created an alert section consisting of two planes kept in readiness from dawn to dusk, with bombs attached.[29] During this period submarine warnings arrived at a rate of four or five per day. Early on the morning of November 22 Le Croisic received an alert. Plane handlers readied a Tellier, with Ens. Kenneth Smith chosen to pilot this first attack. He and observer Frank Brady and mechanic Homer Wilkinson, departed at noon, flying south. All crew members lacked experience, and dispatching a single aircraft proved a mistake. Smith later recalled, "Conditions were not ideal to fly, clouds being very low and quite a sea running." Unknown to comrades at Le Croisic, Smith's plane soon made a forced "tail-to-wind" landing with motor trouble in a big running sea. At 2:30 P.M. he sent a pigeon message reporting his course and suspected location. Smith and Brady soon became terribly seasick. Much later they discovered the left gas tank had not been feeding properly, but by then it was too late to fix.

It began to get dark around 4 P.M., and back at Le Croisic the pigeon message had not arrived. At dusk another search plane labored aloft, only to be recalled. Soon the alarm went out all along the coast. At daylight the following morning Corry dispatched three aircraft, but their efforts proved fruitless. After returning to the station they discovered a pigeon message dispatched at 7:30 A.M. containing vague positional information. Three more search planes went out, but two did not return, with one later towed in by a French patrol craft and the other spending a night in the surf on a deserted beach. Still more aircraft, a dirigible, and various vessels joined the search. Finally, on the afternoon of the third day, a telephone message from La Pallice reported that Smith and his men had been rescued.

While aircraft and myriad vessels searched in vain, the young pilot attempted to lift off in rough seas and almost wrecked his machine, breaking the left wing, and opening seams in the hull. The crew slept one at a time, while another bailed and the third perched on the wing to balance the aircraft. Despite their dire predicament, Smith "could not help marveling at the morale of the men." Eventually they set the broken left wing adrift and tried to remove the right one but were too tired and their tools inadequate to loosen the locking nuts. The derelict aircraft took on water and came close to sinking.

Just as darkness began to fall at the end of the third day a French destroyer steamed to their aid. Wilkinson spotted the vessel and "let out a yell," even though it might have been a submarine. The flyers had been without adequate food or protective clothing for 52 hours. Some would-be rescuers suffered their own mishaps. Reginald Coombe set out before daybreak November 23 to look for Smith's downed plane and searched all morning and afternoon. After flying until dark he ran ashore at the nearest sand beach where he and his crew stayed awake until dawn trying to keep the plane from breaking up in the surf.[30]

Smith's ordeal highlighted significant operational shortcomings and inspired several changes to make patrols safer. In the future, aircraft would operate only in pairs, with proper emergency rations and life-saving equipment aboard. (Smith did not have a Very pistol or sea anchor with him.) Three-man crews proved too heavy for underpowered Telliers so the number was reduced to two. Just two weeks later Smith and Brady made another forced landing that caused severe damage to their machine. They drifted onto the beach and sent up distress rockets, then had lunch and dinner at a small hotel and spent the night aboard an American minesweeper. Eventually they disassembled their plane and loaded the pieces onto the vessel, which towed the flying boat hull back to Le Croisic. Reginald Coombe commented on these early mishaps. "The whole thing was, we didn't understand French equipment. . . . We tried to do too much too soon and had a good many bitter and costly experiences."[31]

The new station formally entered service November 27 with a huge ceremony attended by dignitaries and a U.S. Army band. In early December a top-heavy inspection party led by Admiral Benson, Sims, Hutch Cone, and Jackson visited the Navy's first combat station. In time Le Croisic evolved into a sort of Yale Club reunion, with pilots Ken Smith, Sam Walker, Reginald Coombe, Henry Landon, and Bart Reed present. John Farwell, another First Yale veteran, visited in early April. The college boys filled virtually every important post except commanding officer, including executive officer, chief pilot, assistant chief pilot, and ordnance officer. Reginald Coombe reported, "We have all made many mistakes and I can't make just what the CO thinks of reserve officers. . . . The longer we are here the more we realize we are up against it." There were now 8 officers and 299 enlisted men at Le Croisic.[32]

Work continued throughout the winter. Additional drafts of men arrived. More hangars arose, a total of five by late December, and mechanics placed radios aboard aircraft. Most hangars stood on one island, with the launching derrick on the other. Crews hauled the planes back and forth over a recently completed bridge. Flight operations continued to evolve. Henry Landon spotted a "sub" northwest of Belle Isle on December 4 and went to investigate. Circling overhead, he realized it was actually a French vessel. More pilots arrived. On the day after Christmas they began bombing practice with concrete bombs. For the men's entertainment the YMCA leased the theater building in town and installed electric lights, a basketball court, and handball court. They later held church services there too. Inexperience, shortages of equipment, and dreadful weather, however, hampered flight activities. Several planes went down at sea with broken wings and broken crankshafts. The fate of Tellier-73 proved typical. Flying boats T-72 and T-73 set out on a patrol of the Ile d'Yeu sector January 14, 1918. T-73 made a forced landing caused by loss of air pressure in the gas tank. The crew used a hand pump until it broke loose from its supports. One wing tip pontoon filled with water and the left wing buried itself in the waves. A station boat commanded by Sam Walker set out on a rescue mission. After the crew was taken aboard, the abandoned plane sank. An official report concluded that the loss would have been avoided if the pilot had turned back immediately when trouble became apparent.[33]

Only a week later a patrol craft flown by enlisted pilot Thomas Weddell made a forced landing in rough seas. The station launch set off, using Reginald Coombe's hand-drawn chart to locate the site about 25 miles away. Heavy seas broke over the bow and men on board launched signal rockets trying to communicate with the downed flying boat. Hampered by wind, fog, and driving hail it took four hours to reach the stricken aircraft. When he finally located Weddell's plane, launch commander Sam Walker tried to tow it in but it began breaking up. Weddell then attempted to jump into the launch in his heavy flying suit and boots but fell into the ocean. Crewmen hauled him in with boat hooks. Eventually the rescue boat neared shore, spotted a light, and increased speed, only to slam into the rocks, turning on its side, then righting and passing over them, taking on a great deal of water. Crewmen stuffed newspapers and rags into the leaks, managed to restart the drowned engine, and reached Le Croisic harbor where they beached on a sand bar after 12 hours at sea. A fisherman's dory retrieved them at 4 A.M. The following month the station received an airplane equipped with a recoilless rifle. The gun and related equipment weighed 400 lbs. and tests showed that it worked well, but the additional load greatly slowed the flying machine. There is no record it was ever used in combat.[34]

During this period Le Croisic managed only limited communication with the outside world, and one frequent complaint centered on the lack of news about the progress of the war. Reginald Coombe told a friend, "We lead a very narrow life here in this little fishing town; occasionally ships officers, army officers, etc., come up and we mess, but that is the only way to get news." Two months later he added, "You probably know a lot more than we do for we might just as well be on a desert island as far as knowing what is going on around us is concerned." Sometimes, however, local events provided all the excitement necessary. A remarkable mishap occurred March 4 when a plane flown by Joseph Cline set off on an *alerte* mission. Hurrying to get the machine into the water, someone installed the bombs improperly. Just as the aircraft accelerated, "up on the step," the left side weapon detached, hit the water, and exploded, (perhaps) causing the other bomb to detonate as well. This destroyed the motor and threw the entire fuselage aft of the pilot's seat high in the air. Though the plane was cut in two, the men escaped relatively unscathed. Luckily, the crash boat picked them up almost immediately. Chief Pilot Coombe, an eyewitness to the event, called it the "only exciting news in a long time."[35]

As spring approached, the pace of activity quickened and the German offensive in March and April generated excitement at the isolated base. Commanding Officer Corry mustered the men April 2 and described the emergency. Sailors began landing force and small arms instruction. Bayonet exercises commenced, but the newly sharpened skills were never tested. In May, Coombe compiled 53 flying hours, the most at the station. In June Ensign Gillespie counted 47. In late June Lt. William Masek replaced Corry as commanding officer as the station complement rose to 17 officers and pilots and 327 enlisted men. Prior to establishment of the base, frequent U-boat attacks had occurred in the area, especially around Belle Isle, Ile d'Yeu, and on the St. Nazaire routes. After regular patrolling began, however, virtually no enemy vessels appeared. As early as March, Coombe noticed the paucity of submarines and growing boredom of fruitless reconnaissance missions. But the work continued with little variation. In mid-May he complained, "I have to fly at least one patrol a day, 4:30–9:00 am. I suppose it's necessary, but by God it's deadly monotonous. Nothing to look at but sea and clouds and never a sign of a sub." From May through September Le Croisic averaged 20 to 45 flights per week, operating a mixed fleet of DDs, Levy LePens, and Telliers, the number in commission ranging from four to eight, with six being typical. Le Croisic also served as assembly point for flying boats of these types, with finished aircraft ferried to other patrol stations.[36]

Patrol, escort, and related activities, though often monotonous, resulted in continuous mishaps at sea. Summer began with tragedy when Thomas Weddell, who earlier had cheated death in the icy winter waters of the bay, along with observer E. C. Knapp, perished in an accident July 1. As the pilot throttled the motor back to make a hard spiral and landing, the wing collapsed in midair, and the plane crashed, killing both men. A freak misfortune in early September led to the loss of another aircraft when the hardwood side keel anchoring both side and bottom veneer split, causing the machine to sink. Early in the fall Le Croisic received an urgent call (*Allo*) from the dirigible station at Paimboeuf. Though already dark, two pilots and an observer volunteered to go out, and "beach mules" lowered two aircraft, and hooked a third on the crane. As the machines taxied away in the dark, one piled high on a sand bar. The crew lowered another plane and the pair headed out, but by then the U-boat had submerged. The next day seaplane LC#3 made a forced landing and attempted to motor into Ile d'Yeu harbor, about 57 miles from base. With no boat available to tow it back until October 13, the crew anchored their machine in the water for 11 days. They finally returned under tow from a minesweeper, with one crewman perched on the left wing to maintain balance. The minesweeper wake filled the forward cockpit and the nose plowed straight under, washing the observer backward and trapping him beneath the wing. He eventually freed himself, but swam with difficulty due to his bulky clothing. The plane then flopped on its back. Using their whaleboat, the minesweeper crew pulled the capsized aircraft alongside and attempted to hoist it, but steep swells swept away the wings and the rope cut clean through the fuselage, with only the tail brought aboard. A court of inquiry determined the loss could have been prevented if the station had been better equipped with a boat to tow the plane before it became waterlogged.[37]

Admiral Mayo's visit in late October provided the last bit of excitement before the war ended and patrol activity ceased with the Armistice. There were then 24 officers/pilots at Le Croisic and 337 enlisted men present, operating seven Telliers, five Levy LePens, and four DDs, with about half in commission at any moment. The station compiled an impressive record, mounting 1,045 flights of 1,890 hours' duration, covering approximately 113,000 miles over water, making it the second busiest American station in Europe. Demobilization proceeded rapidly and was completed by January 28, 1919. The French Navy then assumed control of the site. Today Le Croisic is a vibrant tourist town and an active fishing port. The islands of Les Petit et Grand Joncheres remain prominent features of the waterfront, though no remnant of the American station survives, save the stone seawall from which aircraft were launched and retrieved during the course of daily operations.

Located a short distance south of Brest near the famed pottery center of Quimper, NAS Ile Tudy received credit (mistakenly) for sinking "Penmarch

Pete," a legendary submarine lurking in the Raz de Sien, a narrow inshore passage used by ships transiting the coast. The French already operated a tiny outpost here and the Navy determined to construct a larger facility to control the channel and respond quickly to *Allos*. Ile Tudy itself was a quiet, picturesque Breton village. The base stood at the end of a low, flat sand spit with the Bay of Biscay to the south. It soon became one of the most important American coastal stations. Kenneth Whiting first inspected the location in mid-August 1917, accompanied by the commandant of the French aviation center at L'Orient. Whiting believed Ile Tudy admirably situated to protect shipping from Brest steaming south or from Bordeaux and St. Nazaire heading north. He praised its strategic location, safe flying conditions, ample space, good transportation links, and abundant fresh food. Whiting recommended that a 15-plane station be established forthwith. John Callan arrived November 30, 1917, accompanied by Asst. Paymaster W. T. Hopkins and a lone seaman. Existing facilities consisted of a single hangar and a small radio station, with a large stone sardine factory serving as barracks. The French had begun alterations to the building, but early reports described very poor conditions. The old factory was damp, with no heat or light, no kerosene, no latrines (used the beach), unsanitary water, and no stove to boil it. Located six miles from the railroad, transport at Ile Tudy depended on two broken down French-owned trucks. An additional 100 bluejackets arrived in early December, led by Ens. Norman Cabot, who relieved Callan. Christmas Day brought liberty for the entire station.[38]

Despite the base's humble condition, the Navy quickly developed plans to expand it by building machine and carpenter shops, stone oil house, garage, and storehouse, as well as making water, sanitary, and electrical improvements. Sailors lacked construction tools, however, and none of the complement spoke French. Pay accounts fell so far in arrears some men had not received wages since leaving the United States. Nonetheless, labor gangs completed most assigned projects by March 1918, whereupon French personnel withdrew. Ironically, the deadly Paris gun that began bombarding the capital in late March solved the issue of clean water. For many years water for the local population came from a spring on a nearby noblewoman's estate. Despite the arrival of hundreds of sailors, the estate manager refused to increase the allocation to the town (and naval air station). Local French officers considered American water consumption extravagant. When Paris came under attack, however, the *marquisse* hurried to her estate and soon gave the Navy control over the spring.[39]

Command at Ile Tudy passed to Lt. Charles "Chick" Sugden, USCG, February

8, 1918. A 1909 Coast Guard Academy graduate, he flew at Pensacola in 1916 and Moutchic in 1917. Promoted to captain, Sugden remained in command at Ile Tudy until the Armistice. Two weeks later the station received its first aircraft, a pair of DD flying boats transferred from Le Croisic. Actual air operations commenced February 28, the initial plane to leave the water piloted by Leo Harvey responding to an *Allo*. Harvey's DD climbed too quickly, stalled at a height of 150 feet, fell into a sideslip, and crashed into the mud, killing both pilot and observer, Andrew Skaggs. Harvey and Skaggs had been members of Whiting's First Aeronautic Detachment. Four officers and 188 men raised the colors March 14 and placed the station into commission. The pace of activity accelerated in the following months, and the station complement eventually grew to 15 officers (8 pilots) and over 360 enlisted men by the Armistice.[40]

Completing necessary facilities remained the highest priority. Work on a new Bessaneau hangar began in late February, followed by a bomb house and more barracks. For grading and repairing roads men hauled sand up from the beach in wheelbarrows, though the material frequently washed away and needed to be continuously replenished. Bluejackets finished two more canvas hangars and began work on a large, timber double hangar measuring 214 feet × 93 feet. The crew used old-fashioned ingenuity, contriving a self-rigged gin pole out of a wooden mast found washed up on the beach. Construction of portable barracks allowed many ratings to leave tents and move into semi-permanent accommodations. With no stone locally accessible for making concrete, sailors collected rock some distance away, hauled it to the site, and broke it up with hammers. They mixed cement by hand. Construction of the apron and concrete runway commenced. This proved to be a massive undertaking with the entire apron covering 80,000 square feet (160 feet × 500 feet), supplemented by a planned runway measuring 20 feet × 1,240 feet. Workers completed 675 feet before the end of the war, allowing aircraft to take off at half tide. Before building a proper runway/launching ramp, "beach mules" maneuvered airplanes across shifting sand on makeshift rails. When American-made HS-1L flying boats supplanted the station's elderly DDs, the men raised the canvas hangars to accommodate the taller planes.

By the end of March, Ile Tudy pilots had carried out 39 flights of 58 hours' duration, including the first two *Allos*. Two daily convoys passed through the Raz de Sein-to-Ile Verte sector and under favorable conditions two station planes provided protection, with a second pair relieving the first whenever possible. Kenneth Smith, member of the First Yale Group and veteran of service at Le Croisic, served as chief pilot, joined by Henry Landon, another Yale flyer. Smith's only complaint related to Executive Officer Ens. John

Lemanski who, amid bursts of anger, often muttered about the college boys, "You couldn't do a thing like that aboard ship." Patrol activity accelerated as more aircraft and pilots arrived. By the end of May 16 flying boats were on hand, with 7 to 12 serviceable at any one time. With warmer weather the number of available flying days rose into the mid- and high teens each month. In April *Allos* increased to 9 and the number of convoys escorted to 19. The figure jumped to 47, 53, and 46 in the next three months, reinforcing the importance of this task. Total sorties varied from 16 to 67 per week, usually in the 40-flight to 50-flight range. August proved the busiest month in the station's history, with 31 *Allo* flights and 71 convoys escorted, 440 flying hours in all, covering 22,770 miles over water. The average flight lasted 1.5 hours at a speed of 55 mph.[41]

Aircraft issues plagued operations throughout the station's history. Until mid-September, Ile Tudy operated obsolescent DD flying boats. Though their Hispano-Suiza motors proved generally reliable, pilots and mechanics experienced numerous problems with radiators, oil systems, carburetors, magnetos, and propellers. In addition, it became ever more difficult to keep the aging aircraft watertight. By fall, Ile Tudy's aged DD's were ready for the bone pile. A special inspection board found 2 of 15 aircraft damaged beyond repair, condemned 6 for further use, and recommended the other 7 be completely overhauled. At the end of the summer, American-made HS-lLs began arriving, along with their own special set of problems. On just a few rare occasions were 50 percent of the aircraft actually available for operations. Often, the station lacked enough working motors for the available planes. A well-maintained Liberty motor lasted 50 hours between overhauls, but those with inadequate light crankshafts and bearings required rebuilding every 25 hours, while mechanics encountered extreme difficulty obtaining replacement propellers and spare parts. Of 13 HS-1L aircraft on station in mid-October, 10 incorporated light crankshafts and bearings. The engineering officer stored these dangerous machines in the hangar and the station depended instead on three HS-1Ls with heavy crankshafts and a few worn-out DDs.[42]

Given its strategic location, the volume of oceangoing traffic passing through its patrol zone, high levels of enemy submarine activity, and (relatively) large numbers of pilots and aircraft available for patrol and convoy work, Ile Tudy compiled a fairly extensive combat record: 16 attacks against suspected U-boats in all. The first strike occurred April 23, 1918, when Ken Smith and Robert Harrell took their aircraft out on convoy duty, joining a southbound group of about 20 ships approximately six miles north of Point Penmarch. In heavy fog they flew to the rear of the convoy on the lookout for stragglers, then circled and came to a parallel course. About 11:45 A.M. they spotted a rapidly moving wake. Smith dived and loosed his two bombs along the presumed U-boat's line of travel. Harrell's plane dropped a phosphorous buoy. In short order Smith rendezvoused with destroyer *Stewart*, which steamed rapidly to the site, joined by French gunboat *Ardente*. The American vessel dropped three depth charges and oil and bubbles rose to the surface. For two weeks afterward a large slick covered the area and the French government credited Smith and observer Williams with destruction of the submarine, awarding them the Croix de Guerre. Four months later Williams received his medal at Moutchic. One observer boasted, "This was no oil and wreckage stuff, but a genuine kill proved exclusively when the French dragged for the hapless submarine and found it lying on the bottom, very dead indeed." In fact, modern evidence shows the submarine survived.[43]

Six weeks later in early July, two more Ile Tudy DDs piloted by Harold Rowen and C. J. Boylan attacked a suspected sub near Point L'Ervilly. The following month three aircraft on two separate patrols responding to an *Allo*, raced to a spot near Point Penmarch, where they glimpsed oil and what they believed to be a periscope. They dropped two bombs and a French trawler began firing as well, followed by more bombs from the circling Americans. Oil, bubbles, and debris floated to the surface. Yet again on August 27, Edwin Pou, son of North Carolina congressman Edward Pou, initiated another attack within two miles of Point Penmarch generating more oil and bubbles. Further inconclusive attacks occurred September 10 and 27. Air assaults continued into the final weeks of the war. Accompanying a southbound convoy on October 22, two of the station's new HS-lLs bombed an oil slick two miles south of Penmarch. That afternoon two planes departed Ile Tudy heading for the spot of the earlier attack. They spied an oil wake and both aircraft bombed it. All the while a French patrol boat listened on underwater gear. Following the attack large quantities of debris surfaced and the underwater noises ceased. Commandant of the French boat *Leger* asserted that the U-boat had been hit and probably destroyed, though there is no corroborating evidence. The same day another aircraft successfully detonated a floating mine. William Sprague and Elbert "Doc" Dent followed this "successful" sortie on October 26 when they dropped six bombs on a suspicious slick, causing large quantities of oil to rise to the surface. Shortly afterward another plane, flown by Rowen, bombed the same spot. The French later asserted that Sprague's initial attack had destroyed the sub.[44]

Noncombat perils of aerial work could be calamitous, even the routine act of heading out on patrol. On one spring mission Henry Landon performed convoy escort duty. While aloft on a clear day in good air, his propeller flew apart. Luckily, Landon managed to set the aircraft down safely. He and his observer then lit cigarettes and waited for help. An American destroyer pulled alongside and hailed them in French. Landon declined aid, saying the station boat would soon get them. But the rescue boat didn't arrive, an offshore breeze came up, and the crew opened emergency rations of hard tack and canned tomatoes. Then they got out a hacksaw, trimmed the remains of the propeller, and started the motor, hoping to taxi toward shore. Against a strengthening breeze they couldn't make headway, and with the motor threatening to break loose, reluctantly shut it down. Two search planes spotted them at 7:30 P.M., circled overhead, and left the scene. Eventually Ken Smith returned, landed nearby, and taxied up until the wings of the two planes touched. The observer climbed into the rescue plane then decided not to leave Landon and jumped back, landing half in the water. Smith circled, took both stranded flyers on board, and returned to Ile Tudy about 9 P.M. The station boat retrieved the derelict aircraft around three the following morning.[45]

Reports of missions aborted due to broken propellers, magneto problems, takeoff and landing mishaps, malfunctioning oil and gas pumps, and generic "motor trouble" filled the station logbook. In May a DD piloted by Harold Elliott attempted to lift off in heavy seas but crashed into a trawler instead, wrecking the aircraft. Returning from a supposedly successful raid October 26, William Sprague's plane went into a flat spiral and crashed, killing the pilot and seriously injuring observer Harry Roptker. The plane quickly caught fire and Francis McDermott battled to extinguish the flames while also swimming beneath the wreckage attempting to rescue the pilot. Headquarters cited him for his "act of distinct bravery." Two days later while flying a newly delivered HS-1L, Edwin Pou attempted to land into the blinding sunset, striking a spar buoy. The wrecked plane burst into flames. Observer John Young, uninjured in the crash, tried unsuccessfully to douse the fire and save Pou. A second observer, John Banks, sustained serious injuries but survived. A French admiral with typical gallic excess claimed that Sprague had been "killed gloriously," as had Pou, who was "fighting for civilization against barbarism."[46]

Overall, NAS Ile Tudy compiled an impressive record, the busiest of all American bases. An inspection carried out in mid-August praised Sugden for the military deportment of his men, who appeared happy, content, and in good spirits. They earned five Croix de Guerre and amassed 2,100 hours and 117,000 miles over water, escorting 6,900 vessels without a loss. Ile Tudy flyers responded to 54 *Allos* and mounted 16 attacks, though it is virtually certain that aerial bombing sank no submarines. Following cessation of hostilities, the Navy quickly dismantled the station and placed it out of commission January 25, 1919. The waterfront site occupied by this busiest of all American stations is now covered by neat vacation cottages and a public beach. Not a single vestige of NAS Ile Tudy is visible.[47]

NAS Tréguier occupied a sloping site on the north Breton coast about four miles from the sea near the junction of the Jaudy and Guindy Rivers where they form the Tréguier River. Ninety miles east of Brest, between the towns of Tréguier and Plougiel, the station guarded the southwestern entrance to the English Channel. The French Ministry of Marine established a small seaplane base here in May 1917, eventually erecting four canvas Bessaneau hangars, a few temporary buildings, and rudimentary aircraft handling facilities, including a crude and incomplete slipway. Activity remained intermittent, however, equipment inadequate, and personnel limited. The station did not carry out extended patrols or convoy work. Nonetheless, it enjoyed a strategic location and the French Navy offered to transfer it to the Americans who would then initiate patrols in the approaches of the English Channel and into the Channel Islands, overlapping with stations at L'Aber Vrach and Cherbourg. Discussions concerning possible American operations out of Tréguier began in late fall 1917 and continued for many months thereafter. In early January Cone announced that the United States envisioned equipping the station with 18 HS-1L aircraft, with the number possibly increasing to 24. Given the limited space available at the current site, he considered construction of a station annex (hangar only) at the mouth of the Tréguier River. Ultimately, the proposal proved unworkable and the Americans dropped the expansion plan. After considerable delay, the Navy assumed control of the facility August 14, 1918, with Lt. Augustus Baldwin, a reserve officer, serving as the first and only commander.[48]

NAS Tréguier faced great operational challenges. Prevailing southwesterly winds meant taking off and landing in crosswinds; the river was smooth but narrow; low tide left rocks and mud exposed and narrowed the channel to only 35 feet, making it difficult to see at dusk or in cloudy conditions. An extreme tide of nearly 30 feet also hampered activities. The incomplete and temporary nature of much previous construction necessitated major enlargement of the site. During the first two weeks approximately 70 bluejackets and a few trucks arrived, later augmented by additional ratings from Pauillac and Guipavas and 6 seaplane pilots. Construction began August 21. The station's location near the end of a narrow gauge railroad made it necessary to send work parties 22 miles away to transfer supplies from the main line, and then offload them onto trucks for the final two-mile trip. Work was completed on a mess hall, galley, and barracks in mid-October. Construction crews raised two new hangars as well and began work on a third. As at many other stations, inadequate transportation, shortages of equipment, supplies, and material, and portable building parts damaged in transit continually delayed progress. The base's water system did not become fully operational until November 17, a week after the Armistice. Tréguier's first aircraft, two HS-1Ls, arrived September 24 and the initial official flight occurred a week later. Eventually eight flying boats reached the site.

Word reached Tréguier October 3 that a French seaplane had gone down in the Channel about 45 miles southwest of Guernsey, and Commanding Officer Baldwin dispatched the captain's barge to search for the plane and flyers. A steady gale blowing for 24 hours whipped up high seas, forcing the small vessel to lumber along at two to three knots. With hatches battened down, men in the engine space became ill from fumes and could revive themselves only by crawling into the forward compartment. At 2:30 P.M. a French destroyer overtook the struggling Americans. The barge headed back to station, returning to Tréguier at 5 P.M., severely battered. A month later the Americans launched another rescue when they learned that a local fishing craft had been dismasted in a storm. Again the captain's barge set out in foul weather, located the vessel, and towed it into port. In fact, Tréguier was better known for its amicable community relations than patrol work. Among many tasks undertaken, the men stored and transported artillery for a coastal fort at Plougrescant, carried French sailors to the destroyer base at Lezardrieux, and transferred 400 wounded German prisoners to a nearby hospital where most were treated by Navy medical staff. They also delivered 10 tons of coal to Belgian refugees at Plestin, hauled concrete and gas for Allied forces, and relocated war orphans and baggage to Lannion and Guingamp, 40 miles away

After much hard work the Navy formally commissioned NAS Tréguier on November 1, 1918, though official transfer to American control did not occur for another week. Many believed the station represented a poor use of the Navy's scarce resources. As early as July 1918, Commander Dinger had advised that taking over and operating the facility was not justified as long as "personnel and material can be used effectively elsewhere." At the time of the Armistice, Tréguier maintained eight patrol aircraft and six pilots but never implemented regular patrols. Station records documented 30 flights between October 5 and November 11 totaling 23 hours and covering 1,400 miles. A final tally counted 16 officers and 266 enlisted ratings. The facility reverted to the French Navy on January 19, 1919. In summary, work at the station began late, never enjoyed a high priority, and never really got into the fight.[49]

Ironically, NAS Tregieur is the only American station on the French coast commemorated with an identifying monument. Though the site soon reverted to cropland, the concrete piers along the river bank that supported the wooden launching ramp remain in place. Bits of debris poke through the grass, line the shore, and occasionally emerge from the hillside field during plowing. An empty aerial depth bomb stands sentinel in the underbrush. Local authorities built a small cement platform with a comfortable bench overlooking the launching site, marked by a rough-hewn stone stele that carries a brass plaque dedicated to the French and Americans who occupied this place. An accompanying historical marker tells the story in words and pictures. The site honors the service of *"Les Ailes du Jaudy,"* the Wings of the Jaudy.

One of the Navy's most inhospitable stations, NAS L'Aber Vrach (Wrac'h), perched on rocky Ile d'Ehre, about 1,000 yards offshore in Vrach harbor, 21 miles north of Brest. A good road and narrow gauge railroad connected it to that critical port. L'Aber Vrach's strategic location, 1.5 miles south of the large Ile Vierge lighthouse marking the southwest entrance of the English Channel, covered an area around Ushant and permitted aircraft to meet aerial patrols sent out from Irish bases. Kenneth Whiting and a group of French officers inspected the site in August 1917. He described the roadstead as protected and the island well situated to mount patrols into the English Channel, though much grading would be required and long runways constructed. Whiting estimated that ample room existed to operate six or eight "Large Americas" (H-12s). By contrast, a later press report called L'Aber Vrach "nothing but a lonely, weather beaten island of rock," the shore lined with boulders, offering treacherous landing in rough weather. After the war Craven recalled, "It would have been difficult to find a more desolate and hopeless task than the first draft found confronting them."[50]

Gunner Carlton A. McKelvey arrived at this remote place in January 1918. McKelvey enlisted in the Navy in 1908 and by 1917 had risen from Chief Radioman to Gunner (Temporary, Radio), a warrant officer rank. Ordered to Europe in December 1917, he underwent an interview at Paris headquarters and then received the L'Aber Vrach assignment. McKelvey traveled to Brest on January 24 and immediately set out for his new post, accompanied by Asst. Civil Engineer C. P. Conrad. They rented quarters at the Hotel Belle Vue and visited the island the next morning in a small fishing boat. The officers found the place barren and uninhabited. They selected a site in the center of the island and returned to the village. Up to this point U-boats operated in the area with impunity, but when a German submarine surfaced nearby on February 16, its officers saw nothing worth shelling.

Conrad soon departed with a promise to send construction equipment as quickly as possible, while McKelvey made arrangements for the first draft of men, essentially commandeering the entire hotel with a room set aside for an office. He used his high school French to good advantage, meeting with the mayor, village priest, and "commodore of the fishing fleet." Hard cider, rather than water, accompanied his first meal. McKelvey's hosts told him the water was polluted, but he later learned there was a surplus of cider. The locals also piled manure next to the village well, which accounted for its special flavor. Manure heaps lay beside their houses as well, a custom throughout the country. Chief Carpenter's Mate Milton DeMitt arrived January 26, along with 37 men, who quickly set up housekeeping. With no electricity, they found their lodgings lit by oil lamps and their rooms by candles taken up each night and then returned by the chambermaid. Two enlisted men helped in the kitchen. Meals were good but meat scarce, except for veal, and they soon began calling one of the waitresses "Mademoiselle Cutlette de Veau." As McKelvey recalled 45 years later, "Everyone got well fed up on veal."

McKelvey's initial attempts to establish his command depended on memory, as no printed regulations or organizational manual existed. A small shipment of tools and foul weather gear arrived from Brest and the first work crews went to the island January 29, ferried over in three fishing boats, though the passengers couldn't understand local crews who spoke only Gaelic (Breton). After work began, a semaphore signalman on the island communicated with the pier on the mainland. For building materials the men walked to a sawmill three miles away to obtain lumber and hauled it back in a two-wheeled horse cart, a type found throughout rural France. The first construction projects included a boat landing and adjacent toolshed. Facing a dramatic tide of 26 feet, building the pier proved a complicated task. One group of men picked rocks, a second carried stones to the shore, and a third used them to erect an eight-foot-wide landing. Shortly thereafter an archaeologist visited the camp, urging preservation of five-foot-high neolithic cairns and soon "Hands Off" signs appeared. After securing a shipment of dynamite, the men began blasting a hill on the south end of the island for additional building material. Eventually, enlisted laborers constructed a stone jetty. Lacking mess facilities, sailors took lunches to the island, with hot coffee sent over at midday.

After the first week, additional officers arrived to handle supply, medical needs, and finances. More bluejackets reached L'Aber Vrach, requiring additional cots in hotel rooms. In late February, a 40-foot launch motored into the harbor, along with material for a 10,000-gallon water tank. By March 1 the crew had pitched tents on the island and most ratings had moved over.

A YMCA tent arrived, along with a secretary who conducted church services and acted as personal assistant to the executive officer. As the weather moderated, the station complement increased to about 100. Several more boats arrived, then a pigeon loft with a keeper and flock. Surprise orders received March 30 to form the island company into a military battalion temporarily interrupted work. The German advance on Paris had the entire country in an uproar and sailors marched with rifles sent from Brest. The emergency ended 10 days later. Bluejackets began building a causeway to the mainland, usable at low tide, with villagers and their carts hired to help with grading and hauling. Women and children did much of the work. Ruins of a nearby monastery provided some stone.

Lieutenant Henry B. Cecil supplanted McKelvey as commanding officer on April 26, occupying the post until the end of the war. McKelvey remained as executive officer until he was replaced by Lt.(jg) Avmar Johnson, at which point he assumed the duties of radio officer. A Tennessean by birth, Cecil trained at Pensacola in 1916. The following year he became Officer in Charge (OIC) of aviation training at Newport News before sailing for France. He assumed command at Pauillac in February 1918 before arriving at L'Aber Vrach in April. Cecil continued his naval career after the war and perished in the *Akron* airship crash in 1933. When he reached the station approximately 180 men labored there, and throughout the spring they worked from "daylight until dark with a spirit that never failed." Late in May officers joined the men on the island, establishing quarters in the small tent village already sprouting. They built a hot bath from a French tub, a coffee heater, and a wine cask. The Navy formally commissioned the station with a flag-raising ceremony June 4.

Materials for hangars and barracks arrived in small shipments from Pauillac aboard the steamers *Bella* and *Mecknes*. The cargoes were unloaded at Brest, to be hauled overland by narrow gauge railroad, then ferried to the island. Hangar material came as rough lumber. Using only hand saws, augers, and simple carpenter tools the men built enormous "bowstring" trusses on the ground and then hoisted them into place, 24 for each hangar, employing brute manpower and a gin pole and tackle. In fact, under the leadership of Chief Boatswain's Mate John Bray, they became quite expert at this process, raising four trusses per day. The same construction gangs managed to erect a 20-foot × 107-foot prefabricated building in only 48 hours. A visitor that summer reported that the men worked hard and appeared to be in the best of health and spirits, with no eight-hour work laws or labor unions to hamper them. Cement and a small mixer secured from the Army allowed workers to build a lengthy runway and pier, as well as hangar floors and an apron measuring 214 feet × 112 feet. A double wire telephone became operational in mid-October. By then facilities included eight barracks, two mess halls, two chief petty officer quarters, two officers' quarters, a wireless station with twin 120-foot masts, and numerous auxiliary structures.[51]

Throughout this period relations with the local population remained good. During a fierce April storm, a rowboat from town crossed the tossing water carrying a woman and desperately ill baby. Some of the sailors waded out in the surf, brought the boat safely to shore, and rushed the child to the sick bay. (The child recovered from its unspecified illness.) Navy medical officers often aided area residents, while churches set aside a day of prayer for the Americans and their doctors. Station personnel raised money for local relief. Stern Bretons attended movies and theatrical performances at the station's "Y" hut; most had never seen a movie or telephone before. The Navy placed a high priority on providing sufficient and proper recreation and leisure for the men, especially at L'Aber Vrach, known as "a lonely post." The YMCA assigned a secretary as early as February and his domain eventually expanded from a tent to a large frame building. The facility included a fireplace, billiard table, and stage with electric footlights.

Mechanical deficiencies and equipment shortages plagued air operations at L'Aber Vrach throughout its history. The first American airplane arrived July 18, an HS-1L assembled at Brest, then flown to the station by Commanding Officer Cecil. That particular plane lacked or experienced problems with its ignition switch, voltage regulator, primer assembly, motor starter assembly, exhaust pipes, bomb carriers, bombsight, and all signal apparatus and could not be placed in commission for five weeks. A report prepared near the end of the war detailed the condition of each flying boat received at L'Aber Vrach between late July and early October. Shortcomings included missing ignition switches, motor starters, bomb carriers, bombsights, signal apparatus, exhaust pipes, and air speed indicators. To ferry aircraft, pilots flew a single plane to L'Aber Vrach, removed its starters, switches, and other necessary parts, then drove back to Brest where they reinstalled equipment into the next flying boat. This inefficient procedure continued until mid-August.[52]

Nonetheless, by September 2 they had ferried 10 aircraft to the base, and ultimately 19. New Liberty motors proved particularly prone to breakdown. Early motors came equipped with "light" crankshafts and three broke in flight September 3–5. Each shaft broke at the same spot, in one case knocking the bottom out of the crankcase and damaging the propeller. The commander's daily report of September 6 recorded, "Flying suspended pending the receipt of heavy types of Liberty motor crank shaft." About the same time the first American-manufactured bombs arrived but proved to be defective, and aircraft could not be armed until fitted with French ordnance October 7. L'Aber Vrach never obtained more than two Aldis signaling lamps, four radio sending sets, or two radio receiving sets. Only by mixing, repairing, and scavenging did mechanics manage to keep two to four aircraft in flying condition. Eventually, as the number of planes and supply of spare parts increased, an average of six to eight flying boats became available for daily operations, with 10 to 13 more under maintenance or repair.[53]

Official patrol flights commenced August 29 and escort duty in early September. L'Aber Vrach was well placed for convoy duty, with one assemblage of 12 to 30 ships in its sector at any time of the day, whether coastal traffic rounding Finisterre or crossing the Channel to Britain. Station aircraft escorted a convoy of 11 freighters toward southwest England on October 18, joining with four patrol boats and a French blimp. A British dirigible relieved them in mid-Channel. The following week the Americans accompanied a convoy all the way to Cornwall, circled over the Lizard, and then flew home. During operations L'Aber Vrach experienced its share of mishaps, at least one of which Commanding Officer Cecil blamed on his inexperienced aviators.[54]

Nolan Kindall departed the station October 3 at 2:50 P.M. in LV-1 to practice squadron maneuvers. At an altitude of 1,000 feet the motor began vibrating strongly and he immediately cut power and landed, where he discovered a hole in the motor crankcase and half a connecting rod bearing lying atop the gas tank. A second flying boat, LV-2, under the command of Oscar Trail, landed nearby, while two more machines circled overhead. When Trail attempted to lift off again his motor stopped after several cylinder water jackets burst. The downed flyers dispatched pigeon messages and in the early evening the station barge hove into sight; it took both aircraft in tow on separate lines, but the planes suffered extensive damage in the churning seas. The barge crew eventually set LV-2 loose and it soon disappeared from sight. Towing LV-1 continued throughout the night, but the following morning the lines parted. Pilot Kindall managed to save his codebook but none of the instruments. The exhausted men returned to the station at 11:00 A.M. Later that day a fishing boat hauled LV-1 into harbor, but extensive searches failed to locate LV-2. Fishermen at Plouescat finally recovered it the following day about 20 miles east of the station, lower wings shattered but hull intact.

In his report to Craven, Cecil sharply criticized Trail (LV-2) for using "very poor judgment" and disregarding instructions by "landing in a rough sea when the crew of LV-1 was not in danger." He charged that young pilots abandoned their machines too quickly, perhaps because "fairly rough seas look very scary to them." In fact, neither craft took on "a drop" of water and there was no excuse for abandoning them. Cecil pledged that in the future he would impress upon his pilots the necessity of staying with their aircraft. The day after the chastised crews returned to the station one of the search planes, LV-11, made a forced landing in 15-foot seas. Pilot Fred Lang misjudged the size of the swell and when his aircraft hit the water, the violent impact damaged the starboard wing and pontoon and "crashed" the hull. Both pilot and observer were shaken and bruised. A French trawler rescued the crew. They also attempted to tow the sinking aircraft, but three lines snapped and it drifted out of sight.[55]

Mishaps aside, plans for close coordination with French forces in the area were in place by fall, and at the end of the war the base complement included 26 pilots, 14 observers, 15 ground officers, and 463 enlisted men, making it one of the Navy's largest stations. Personnel began leaving the site shortly after the Armistice and NAS L'Aber Vrach was completely demobilized by January 22, 1919, with barracks and hangar lumber turned over to the U.S. Army. The island quickly reverted to its barren, prewar condition, and to this day the site is completely covered by gorse, ferns, and brambles. Portions of the original concrete launching ramp survive, however, as well as a few massive hangar truss piers and lengths of the concrete/stone pier. The causeway constructed by local labor emerges at each low tide, making it possible to walk to the island, known today as "La Ile aux Americans," the American Island.

If ever there were an orphan patrol base, it would have been NAS Fromentine. Situated below the Loire estuary in the water-logged coastal province of Vendee, Fromentine perched on a windswept waste of sand at the southern tip of Noirmoutier Island. The island itself, 12 miles long, lay about one-half mile from the mainland. Sheltered water between the island and the shore seemed ideal for aerial operations, though subject to a swift run of tide and the many storms that lashed this area. Roughly in the vicinity of St. Nazaire and Nantes, it still lay 35 miles from the nearest large town. A tiny hamlet (La Fosse) clustered near the camp gates, with the principal village perched on the mainland. Natives observed knowingly, "Fromentine is a lost country." A later judgment determined the site offered the least diversion of any base but proved excellent for operating and health reasons. The first Navy representative, Gunner R. I. McGee, arrived February 4, 1918, followed by additional officers and men in the next few days. After preliminary arrangements were made, construction began soon thereafter. Leased houses in Fromentine village served as temporary barracks, and sailors working on the desolate island ferried across the channel each day on a small steamer.

Groundbreaking occurred February 23 under the guidance of Asst. Civil Engineer G. D. Ellsworth. Hutch Cone visited February 27. A small tent village went up March 6 and the first mess opened three days later. Tables stood in the open and eating posed a real challenge. If it rained the men grabbed their food and raced into the tents. On blustery days they ate with one hand, trying to keep the other warm. A new commanding officer, LCdr. Warren 'Gerry' Child, succeeded Gunner McGee March 10. Born in Utah in 1883, Child served in submarines before transferring to aviation, training at Pensacola, and then on balloons and dirigibles. He joined Constructor George Westervelt as a member of the Bolling Commission. Further drafts of workers reported in March and April. By then the complement of sailors on the island totaled approximately 300. A flock of pigeons also arrived. The first typewritten edition of "Plane Talk," the station's newsletter, appeared and eventually evolved into a printed, weekly, four-page sheet.

Transporting supplies to the remote site proved very difficult. Shipments from Pauillac required one to two weeks to reach Challons, then were transferred to a narrow gauge railroad to Fromentine (15 miles), and moved by hand to the end of a long wharf. Men unloaded material into wheeled carts, to be carried piece by piece onto 40-foot motor sailing launches that crossed about 2,000 feet of open water. Sometimes local French labor, consisting of the very young and very old, who "made a surprising appearance," helped load supplies. On rare occasions, extreme low tide—the normal range exceeded 17 feet—permitted trucks to drive along the bay bottom, but the danger of sinking into soft mud and risking loss of the truck to incoming tides precluded much use of this route. A tramway installed on the island later speeded the task somewhat. Eventually, the coastal steamer *Bella*, running from Pauillac to Fromentine and manned by a Navy crew of 25, eased the problem. A load of concrete arrived in April, with additional deliveries of hangar material in May. These shipments finally permitted construction to proceed at a predictable pace. Navy crews did all of the work, much of it backbreaking. They built and raised huge hangar columns and trusses by hand. Grading the sand dunes proved endlessly tedious, with much of the previous day's progress blown away by strong winds. The next, and final commanding officer, veteran flyer Lt. Wadleigh Capehart, reached Fromentine April 26. Capehart graduated from the Naval Academy in 1910, worked as an instructor at the Burgess aircraft company in 1914, served at Pensacola in 1915, and trained the Second

Yale Unit in Buffalo during the summer and fall of 1917. Lieutenant(jg) A. D. Warwick acted as executive officer.

Fromentine's first eager liberty parties set off in late April. One detachment toured Pornic, a picturesque village about 12 miles away. The following week they visited Les Sables d'Olonne, a beautiful summer resort 35 miles distant. Throughout the summer, men overnighted there, driven by truck. The station also arranged a few trips to Nantes and Ile d'Yeu, with the latter soon discontinued due to fear of submarine shelling. A short visit by Assistant Secretary Franklin Roosevelt in August helped break the daily routine. At the end of the month a party of 13 congressmen inspected the site, accompanied by Hutch Cone, who was making his final tour before taking up new duties in London. Nonetheless, such opportunities proved to be few and far between. Back in May, Capehart wrote, "Hope to find some way to give them [the men] interesting amusement after work and on Sundays, but doubt success as Fromentine is absolutely isolated unless gasoline is used." A September 21 report added, "The situation of this station regarding liberty and recreation for both officers and men is desperate." This, presumably, could lead to "staleness" and a loss of efficiency would ensue.

Community relations ranked high among headquarters' concerns. The death of a young local boy, "Noly," something of a mascot to the station, moved the Americans to buy flowers for his funeral and send an escort of officers and ratings to the sad event. In early September the citizens of Noirmoutier entertained 50 men and officers with an elaborate program and banquet. Other events of note included an outbreak of influenza in July, with 42 cases, but none serious. Five bedraggled crew members of the torpedoed transport *Covington* reached the station in August. Two days later a lifeboat floated in with rations and emergency supplies still intact.[56]

Fromentine's first aircraft arrived in late June—two HS-1L flying boats assembled and flown in from Pauillac. Since the station lacked launching trucks to move the machines from hangars into the water and back, the beach gang anchored them in the bay, a very harmful practice. Though these were flying *boats*, the extreme damp warped wings and propellers, rusted engine parts and fittings, and caused hulls to swell and leak. Eight planes arrived by the end of July, but even in late September just two with reliable, heavy crankshaft Liberty motors were in service. When mechanics overhauled either one, they removed critical parts and reinstalled them in other aircraft. The commanding officer and executive officer directed the Flight Department, which carried out aerial operations, including inspection, testing, launching, and handling of all aircraft. The station's Intelligence Department tracked convoys by means of a map table dotted with small wooden boats and airplanes represented as flags on pins. Preparing for war operations, Fromentine established an alert section charged with responding to all *Allos* within three minutes.

NAS Fromentine provided its initial convoy escort August 17, 1918, though encounters with the enemy were rare. One month later a flight section circled over a spot where destroyers had earlier dropped depth charges. During the same patrol they bombed a suspected submarine 15 miles northwest of Les Sables d'Olonnes. Two HS-1Ls attacked an oil slick south of Ile d'Yeu October 13 and large oil bubbles rose for 15 minutes. Station aircraft carried out a rather different mission October 27, distributing war loan circulars over nearby French villages. Despite limited service, Fromentine enjoyed the distinction of being the first base to carry out its missions in American-built aircraft. Admiral Henry Mayo and a party including Captains Craven, King, Jackson, and others, conducted a final inspection in late October. Patrols ceased with the Armistice two weeks later.[57] Before the war ended, pilots and observers conducted 200 flights lasting 406 hours, escorting 79 convoys through their district. The station's seven original pilots/observers compiled 90 percent of these miles and hours. They also carried out 55 patrol flights of 89 hours' duration and 103 practice/test flights lasting 48 hours, in all weather conditions, covering approximately 29,000 total miles. The final station roster included 31 officers (18 pilots) and 356 enlisted men.

Accomplishments on the construction front were notable as well. Despite shortages and delays, the completed station consisted of two large double hangars, eight barracks, four storehouses, three mess halls, galley and bakeshop, hospital, machine and carpenter shops, radio hut, powerhouse, blacksmith hut, aerographic office, bomb storage, latrines, and YMCA hut. It was one of five bases built entirely by American labor with American materials. After rapid demobilization the station closed January 28, 1919. Ile de Yeu is now home to a bustling vacation community, and most of the former aviation site is covered with beachfront cottages and a huge earthen approach ramp to the modern bridge providing access to the mainland. The entire concrete launching ramp survives, however, as do several hundred feet of seawall and a few vestiges of the station pier. Former hangar floors and apron have reverted to modest enclosures for livestock, though portions of the concrete base show through the grass, as does a small range of hangar truss piers.

Established near the mouth of the Gironde River amid pine-covered sand dunes, NAS St. Trojan boasted a beautiful, quiet setting. Situated on the Straits of La Maumusson separating the southern end of Ile d'Oléron from the mainland, the base was positioned to protect ships running into the Gironde and destined for Pauillac and the port of Bordeaux. St. Trojan was one of four bases to be built and equipped by the French and turned over to the Navy per negotiations carried out by Kenneth Whiting. Delvert and Co. signed a construction contract for 1,200,000 francs ($225,000). Original plans called for 16 patrol aircraft and 20 buildings, including 4 Bessaneau hangars measuring 65 feet × 90 feet or 85 feet × 90 feet, with work to be completed by June 16, 1918. In October, French Lieutenant Darchis and 15 men moved onto the site to prepare it for the contractor's arrival. When Assistant Paymaster J. M. Bregar visited St. Trojan on November 9 to discuss future transportation and material requirements, he found two knock-down barracks, one housing 20 unskilled Algerian laborers, the other Darchis's office, 15 Frenchmen, and some stores. Work had begun repairing the old pier and setting the mess hall foundation. The Algerians cleared trees, graded the ground, and excavated where needed.

Work on the seawall and hangar foundations commenced in January, but completion targets slipped constantly. The contractor encountered serious difficulty obtaining material, especially cement. Significant labor trouble also plagued the project, particularly with the Algerians. Many were sick and their "capacity for work [judged] very small." They seemed willing to strike at the smallest pretext. Their masters responded by denying them food until they returned to work. Efforts to secure more efficient and energetic German POWs came to naught. In time, U.S. enlisted men worked directly for the contractor, hired out at 80 centimes an hour. The first draft of personnel reached St. Trojan at the end of January and boarded in a local hotel, "Le Chateau." After a day to settle in, the Americans commenced digging a well and latrines and grading the site. Further drafts also quartered at the hotel, and each day marched two miles to the station. Building materials began flowing in, with a schooner chartered to make deliveries to the island. Water transport proved critical because of "the almost hopeless condition of the railway transportation." Gunner J. N. Finney assumed command February 3.

First Aeronautic Detachment veteran Virgil Griffin became commanding officer on March 11, a position he held until the Armistice. Transfer of personnel to the station began. Soon more barracks were erected, the terrain graded for hangars and aprons, and 1,200 feet of road opened. The Navy assumed nominal control of the site April 1 and work on hangars using material shipped in from Pauillac commenced May 20. During this same period the Algerians departed in groups, replaced by bluejackets. Manual labor powered most work, with as many as 150 sailors raising the 107-foot hangar trusses.

They completed the hangars by June 20. The Navy took formal control of the site July 14. Though some public works remained uncompleted until November 1918, progress advanced sufficiently that limited flight operations could begin in late June.

The first two seaplanes reaching St. Trojan, cranky Levy-Le Pen flying boats with six-cylinder, 280 hp Renault motors, flew in from NAS Le Croisic June 29. Eight more followed. These had been shipped in parts from the factory to Le Croisic and assembled there, then ferried to St. Trojan. The aircraft were pusher types, with the motor started using an automobile-style crank. This meant they needed to be muscled into the water by the beach crew and started once afloat. Some motors had already been overhauled two or three times. Mechanics experienced great difficulty obtaining spare parts. Nor did aircraft come outfitted with bombing gear. Equipment received from the French had to be adapted from another airplane type. Each flying boat carried four 112-pound bombs, two under each wing. Crew consisted of a pilot, machinist mate, and observer. Pilot and machinist mate sat side by side, with the observer and his bombing sight in the nose. St. Trojan's first convoy escort flights set out July 19 with enlisted pilot G. H. Hasselman and Ens. W. M. Barr at the controls. Thereafter convoy and reconnaissance flights occurred as often as the motor situation permitted, a condition that persisted into August, with work continually hampered by shortages of planes and motors.

Faulty equipment led to serious mishaps. While on convoy duty August 7 a St. Trojan Le Pen piloted by Ens. Howard Sargent made a forced landing when the motor exhaust manifold blew off and struck the whirling propeller, breaking it. Sargent attempted unsuccessfully to beach his aircraft. Instead, a French trawler towed the damaged plane to La Pallice. Upon inspection mechanics discovered hot exhaust gases escaping through the broken manifold had burned the upper wing spar without the pilot's knowledge. Had this continued a few more minutes, the wing would have folded up causing a deadly crash. It seems mufflers supplied with the Le Pens were too thin, and the aluminum sheathing was more danger than help because it concealed the damage.[58]

St. Trojan suffered the largest single loss of life in naval aviation history August 20 when the explosion of two 112-pound bombs destroyed a seaplane while descending the runway. One witness, and almost victim of the blast, 19-year-old mechanic Robert Gilbert of Meridian, Mississippi, was assigned as a crew machinist mate to Levy-Le Pen flying boat ST-14. On the fateful day he was sick and another machinist stood in for him. Up until then it was policy to launch aircraft with the bombs unarmed. While taxiing across the water the observer crawled back and inserted the detonators, occasionally resulting in some being dropped into the harbor. As Gilbert remembered it, "The skipper had gotten disgusted with the number of detonators being lost when the plane was out in the water and had the detonators attached before starting down the ramp." With Gilbert watching from the hangar, the "beach mules" maneuvered the plane down the ramp, but when the dolly hit the water, one of the bombs fell off and exploded. Pilot Edmund Barry, observer/electrician Earl Vath, and six of the handling crew died in the blast. Eighteen others were wounded, several very seriously. An official inquiry blamed defective bomb carrying gear and suspended flying for a week. According to John Farwell, recently arrived to take up his duties as armament officer, neither the French nor the Americans used safety catches. In his opinion, a bomb falling loose from an insecure rack with no safety mechanism caused the tragedy.[59]

The explosion, poor weather, illness, and equipment shortages limited total flying time in August to just 33 hours.[60] At the end of the month the first two HS-1L planes arrived, but without any ordnance gear. About this time the influenza epidemic struck, with St. Trojan one of the hardest hit stations, suffering 6 deaths and 210 men incapacitated to varying degrees. The sickness lasted about three weeks and "at times the station was completely unable to carry on operations." War work in September and after consisted largely of reconnaissance rather than convoy escort. The base could not conduct both missions due to equipment shortages, and leaders deemed reconnaissance the more valuable activity. A single H-16 aircraft delivered September 26 never saw active duty. It lacked bomb gear, the hull leaked, and the steps had to be rebuilt, problems similar to those encountered at other bases. The amount of flying completed throughout this period varied greatly, ranging from 2 to 27 patrols per week. News of the Armistice brought an immediate cessation to operations.

Due to a variety of factors, St. Trojan compiled a rather slim combat record. When the French at Bordeaux reported a submarine September 6, Ens. William Leek set off in pursuit and bombed the site, but the enemy disappeared in the fog. The following day one of the American HS-1Ls caught fire while in flight when a propeller broke and cut the fuel line and it fell from a height of 160 feet. The crew managed to set the craft down safely, jumped clear, and swam ashore. A month later two planes went out on patrol. One made a forced landing in a rain and windstorm and could not be located until the following day, having drifted 32 miles west of Hourtin. The station became noticeably more active in October; flying hours jumped to 149, more than the previous three months combined. There were now 26 officers (12 pilots) and

343 enlisted men present as well as a grab bag of airplanes that included four Levy-Le Pens, six HS-1Ls, one HS-2L, one H-16, and one Paul Schmidt.[61]

St. Trojan dispatched an emergency patrol October 14 to search for a French seaplane. Aircraft piloted by Ensigns Ransom Clark and Henry Stanley proceeded until they encountered a violent thunderstorm and sudden drop in temperature. Clark made a heavy landing, wrecking the hull, while Stanley circled above. As the downed plane began sinking rapidly at the bow, the second sent a radio message and then landed to take the other crew on board. With seas running at 10 feet and buffeted by a 30-knot wind, the stricken flying boat proved largely unmanageable. Only by having the observer run out on a wing to make it drag in the water could the machine be made to turn. About 3:20 P.M. the "sound" aircraft taxied up to the derelict machine from leeward and took off the pilot. The observer jumped into the water and was hauled aboard. Only the tail and three feet of the fuselage of the damaged aircraft remained above water.

Unable to take off in the remaining plane, the flyers released a pair of pigeons and tried to taxi to shore but made barely two miles. Clark and his observer used their bodies to block seawater from entering the cockpits, while the observer of the sound aircraft stood on the wing to make it drag. At 4:30 P.M. a French drifter appeared and the Americans signaled with their Aldis lamp. The vessel set a tow line, with all hands aboard the drifter. At 10:30 P.M. they anchored outside La Pallice and early next morning moored at the French air station where the Americans went ashore. Stanley later wrote of his observer R. C. Quinn, "He must be commended as being exemplary in every way. At no time did he lose his head, nor did he at any time forget his sense of duty, and his work and his judgment . . . were invaluable."[62]

During its entire period of active duty, NAS St. Trojan conducted 246 flights covering 19,500 miles. Demobilization began November 13 when the French contractor received orders to cease work. After removing motors and instruments, personnel torched surviving planes. Six officers and 170 enlisted men returned to the United States November 21. Most remaining men received 10-day leave in Paris during the holiday season where the Salvation Army provided Christmas dinner. The Navy decommissioned St. Trojan station January 19, 1919. A few ratings lingered at the forlorn site until February and then relocated to Pauillac. They sailed home to Hampton Roads February 24 aboard *Mercury,* along with 2,400 soldiers and 350 sailors.[63] NAS St. Trojan survives today as the only substantially intact American World War I naval aviation facility in Europe. After the conflict ended, regional authorities converted the former station into a tuberculosis sanitarium for children.

Today it serves as a sort of "rest home" for the elderly. Though the hangars are gone, the concrete apron, lengthy launching ramp, and most camp structures survive. These include the guardhouse, commanding officer's quarters, infirmary, chief petty officers' barracks, three enlisted men's barracks, latrine, galley, mess hall, chief pilot's quarters, radio shack, machine shops, engine house, administrative offices, and pigeon loft. The remains of the foundation for the radio antenna are visible on a hillside overlooking the beach.

NAS Arcachon, one of the coastal stations scheduled to be built by the French according to agreements reached with Whiting in the summer of 1917, occupied a site amid pine-tree–covered sand dunes, overlooking the Bassin d'Arcachon, on the eastern (inland) shore of Cap Ferret, about three miles from its southern point and lighthouse. In peacetime, this popular resort with a resident population of 8,000, welcomed up to 100,000 tourists annually, the vacation precincts marked by "pagoda-like monstrosities," while the town itself consisted of houses, shops, and hotels constructed of stone, stucco, terra-cotta, and tile. NAS Arcachon formed part of a sprawling aviation complex in the Bordeaux region. A Navy dirigible station later stood on the opposite shore of the Bassin at Gujan-Mestras and the flight school at Mouthic-Lacanau operated a few miles north along the coast, while the French school at Hourtin lay just beyond that. The station escorted coastal shipping from the Gulf of Gascony north to the Gironde River and provided antisubmarine patrols below the Gironde, as far south as the Spanish border, where some believed U-boats resupplied, especially near the port of San Sebastian. Others, however, saw little justification for establishing a station at this site and ultimately recommended it be used for training only, or abandoned, with the material and equipment employed elsewhere.[64]

In late June 1917, Whiting, accompanied by Paymaster Conger and Capitaine De Laborde, visited the area on their coastal tour and chose this spot for a future base. Acting on behalf of the United States, the French Navy negotiated a construction contract, with work to begin in the fall of 1917. Contractor M. Hauret, the same man hired to build the Moutchic instruction center, commenced work November 5. By the end of January approximately one-third of necessary leveling and filling was completed. At first Hauret employed boys, women, and old men, and later Senegalese laborers. American forces arrived in late January, a few officers to make arrangements for those to follow. A work detachment reached Arcachon February 1. Officers quartered at Hotel de France and men bivouacked in a nearby hostelry. At the end of February the sailors transferred to the station site, housed in Army tents.

The first commander, New York native Lt. Leman L. Babbitt, gave way to

Lt. H. G. Puller on April 10, until succeeded May 10 by Ens. J. N. Brown. The station entered official service June 8. Command passed to Lt. Zeno Wicks from Pauillac from June 15 onward. By this time, however, NAS Arcachon enjoyed a very low priority in the larger scheme of things. As early as February 11 Ens. G. A. Smith, a liaison officer at Paris headquarters, described the site as far more useful to the French than the United States because it lay too far south to escort American ships. Construction slowed to a crawl in early March following a strike by Senegalese laborers, material shortages, and discontent of native French workers occasioned by shortages of bread. Virtually nothing useful occurred between April and early July. In fact, a large detachment of U.S. personnel shifted to Pauillac on May 25, leaving only a small guard in place. The men returned a month later and building resumed with the aid of American workers. At the same time, work began on the station hangars.

Known by some as the "hard luck station in France," Arcachon received its first aircraft, HS-1Ls, only in mid-August, and they lacked much necessary equipment. At that time starters were in woefully short supply and being allocated to stations based on proximity to Brest and the mouth of the Loire River. By this time the Army had practically abandoned Bordeaux as a debarkation point so Arcachon stood last in line. Not until early September did any of the planes receive starters; thus patrol work proved impossible. The first fully equipped seaplanes were not ready for war patrols until mid-September. By then the French contractor, aided by American labor, had erected two large, double hangars as well as the slipway, allowing access to the water for eight hours of each tide. Completion of the apron provided storage space for up to 14 aircraft. Many other projects lagged, however, and several buildings remained under construction when orders came November 11 to cease work.[65]

NAS Arcachon became operational September 14, though with only one pilot and observer present, contrary to Navy policy against sending out small seaplanes singly. Some test flights occurred, but spare parts remained scarce and mechanics cannibalized equipment from one group of six planes to keep the other six in flying order. This particular base experienced particular trouble with gasoline feed pumps. Mechanics also experimented with a wide variety of improvements to the controls and cockpit design. By early October enough parts were on hand to equip nine machines, and for a while Arcachon supported an interesting assortment of aircraft and personnel. At the end of September the French station at Lac Cazaux went out of commission and the local commander asked if Arcachon could accommodate two or three seaplanes. Two DDs and crews arrived from Bayonne October 1 and began patrol work that same day, operating under French orders, augmented by a single American HS-1L. Joint patrols continued for about two weeks. Additional flying personnel arrived from Moutchic October 17, supplemented a few days later by pilots and observers from Ile Tudy. Regular patrols commenced October 18 after much necessary modification of planes and equipment, including gas pumps, seating arrangements, compasses, and bombing gear.[66]

At 6 P.M. on the evening of October 22 the station received an *Allo*. Early next morning an alert section of two planes set out in search of the enemy. The machine piloted by Boatswain G. A. Wilson made a forced landing in rough water 45 miles northwest of Cap Ferret. The accompanying plane returned to the station for help. Arcachon did not possess any rescue craft so word went out to other French and American bases along coast. In the meantime Wilson and observer Haizlett could not restart their engine, and by 10 A.M. rough seas had destroyed the aircraft's lower ailerons. The crew pitched equipment overboard to lighten the boat—bombs, machine guns, and instruments—but a storm blew up, forcing the plane even farther seaward. As the seams of the watertight compartment gave way, the craft began to flood. At 3:25 A.M. October 24 the exhausted flyers spotted a light and an exchange of Very flares ensued. Soon a French patrol boat hove into view, picked up the crew, and attempted to tow the plane. They set it adrift soon after, however, and eventually some fishermen picked up the derelict aircraft and carried it into San Sebastian. A court of inquiry identified metallic filings in the gas tank as the culprit as they had clogged the fuel line. They likely originated during welding of the main fuel tanks and from the aluminum piston in the gas pump wearing against a brass bushing. Similar problems had been reported in other planes.[67]

Arcachon also fought its own round in the battle of the light crankshafts. HS-1L #1750 made a forced landing at sea October 24, one of three to suffer that fate in recent weeks. The plane was on convoy duty at 4:20 P.M. when the crankshaft broke, shattering four propeller tips. Fragments penetrated the wing in three places and the hull in four, two below the waterline. Commanding Officer Wicks claimed he had never received notification not to fly these planes. A French patrol craft towed this particular aircraft all night to La Pallice. The following day a severe accident occurred aboard the captain's barge when a lantern set off an explosion in the hold. The powerful blast blew Steven Matthews out the forward compartment through a small deck hatch. Though severely burned, he worked with others to save the boat and extinguish the fire. While engaged he noticed U.S. Army Sgt. Edwards had been knocked unconscious by the explosion and fallen overboard. Matthews rescued him from drowning, placed the soldier in a wherry lying alongside, and paddled him to shore.[68]

Between the first week of October and the Armistice, Arcachon pilots completed 106 flights of 138 hours' duration, covering approximately 8,700 miles. When the war ended, personnel consisted of 27 officers and 312 enlisted men employing 13 HS-1L aircraft to conduct regular patrols. The number actually in commission ranged from two to five, largely resulting from a shortage of heavy crankshafts. The station received orders to cease operations on November 14. Demobilization proceeded quickly, and French authorities assumed control January 7, 1919. Final disposition of the site took many months. Modern-day Cap Ferret is a bustling seashore community, and attractive vacation homes cover the former NAS location. Many stand right on the water, and a rubble seawall of concrete debris from the aviation station protects the shoreline. Remaining open ground serves as a public beach and small sailboat launching area. Among the trees can be found some traces of building foundations, including several hangar truss piers. The spot is identified on tourist maps as "La Plage des Americains," the American beach.

* * *

During the late spring and summer of 1917, Lt. Kenneth Whiting carried out an intensive series of discussions, inspections, and negotiations that ultimately led to establishment of several aviation stations designed to protect the approaches to the ports of Brest, St. Nazaire, and Bordeaux. Stretching from Tréguier in the north to Arcachon in the south, these facilities shielded arriving troopships and supply convoys from enemy U-boats. Largely built from scratch, many stood in remote locations. French contractors performed some work, but bluejackets carried out most construction. They became, in effect, self-contained American towns and villages scattered along the coast of Europe. The first station, Le Croisic, began operating in November 1917, with all able to conduct at least limited duties by autumn 1918. Flight personnel frequently included members of the First Yale Unit and large numbers of pilots and observers who traveled to France in the spring of 1917 as part of the First Aeronautic Detachment. Hindsight suggests that the Navy built more and larger stations than necessary. Nonetheless, the combination of convoy escort, naval patrol, and aerial surveillance largely negated the submarine threat and few, if any, doughboys who landed safely in Europe questioned whether there were too many bases or aircraft.

5

PROGRESS REPORT

March–September 1918

Between March and September 1918 naval aviation in Europe transformed itself from a concept into an operational reality. By the end of summer, final organizational adjustments had been made and command structure realigned to reflect the new combat reality. Eight stations in France conducted war operations. The Northern Bombing Group established several aerodromes and placed dozens of pilots with RAF squadrons to obtain vital experience. David Ingalls, not yet 20 years old, flew his way into history as the Navy's first and only ace. At Killingholme, enormous flying boats conducted extensive patrols across the cold expanse of the North Sea, while aviators at Porto Corsini battled the Austrian air force in the skies above Pola. All four stations in Ireland reached operational status. Flying schools at Moutchic and Lake Bolsena functioned at full capacity, while the accelerating flow of aircraft from Pauillac, Brest, Queenstown, and Eastleigh began to break previous equipment logjams.

In addition to operational issues, planners devoted considerable attention to many collateral concerns, such as possible amalgamation of Army and Navy flying forces, the challenges of establishing productive liaison with the Army and foreign governments, sometimes contentious intradepartmental relations, and the option of expanding the overall program. Throughout the period the entire agenda underwent extensive scrutiny from visiting congressional committees and high-ranking Department officers and officials like Asst. Secretary of the Navy Franklin Roosevelt and C-I-C Atlantic Fleet Henry Mayo.

* * *

During spring and summer 1918, naval aviation made enormous strides toward implementing its wide-ranging operational objectives. By the end of the period most planned stations were performing their wartime missions or were just a few weeks removed from that point. Priorities defined and refined in April and July provided the blueprint. In the spring, headquarters concentrated on accelerating construction efforts at more sites, inaugurating the Northern Bombing Group program, commencing operations at additional stations, and moving the Killingholme initiative to completion. Additional objectives included beginning shipment of American-manufactured aircraft and motors, and focusing on the "1919" program and planned transformation/relocation of the command structure. During the summer, emphasis remained on moving unfinished bases to completion, placing additional stations in operation, implementing command realignment, and beginning NBG missions, shifting the offensive thrust away from the French coast and northward to Flanders and Killingholme.[1]

At Paris headquarters, the Operations Division headed by Thomas Craven oversaw implementation of plans finalized during the preceding winter. Frank McCrary directed affairs in Ireland, while John Callan guided efforts in Italy. The German assault on Paris in the spring of 1918 caused some staff to relocate temporarily to Pauillac, while the Allies politely declined the Navy's offer to use its nonflying personnel on the Western Front. At Moutchic the flying school assumed a more efficient stance, offering comprehensive instruction in bombing, gunnery, aerial navigation, radio work, meteorology, and intelligence. Between April and June alone, 83 pilots completed coursework. Preparation of flight personnel at Army and Allied schools also gained speed. Eighteen pilots and observers received day bombing instruction at the AEF's Clermont-Ferrand training center. After completing their course, three transferred to Dunkirk for work with the British to learn the duties of flight commanders. Others attended RAF day and night bombing schools at Stonehenge, Salisbury Plain, and Boscombe Down, and then joined squadrons near Dunkirk flying Handley Page machines. Ten ensigns trained at Avord-Cher, a French flight school. Many naval officers served with RAF coastal stations in England and Scotland, learning to pilot pontoon scouts and large flying boats. At Lake Bolsena, Italy, several dozen officers and enlisted aviators received seaplane instruction, while other contingents learned to fly Caproni bombers at Malpensa field near Milan.

Better weather and arrival of more building supplies allowed construction at various stations to quicken. The Navy acquired two small coastal steamers, *Mecknes* and *Bella*, to deliver materiel. In late April, Hutch Cone claimed that naval facilities could accommodate 90 HS-1L aircraft and three dirigibles. He predicted the number would increase to 138 HS-1Ls and 68 H-16s by June 1, and then the entire allotted complement of aircraft and six dirigibles by July

1 if necessary iron fittings for hangar construction arrived in a timely manner. Until American-manufactured aircraft reached Europe, however, the Navy remained dependent on French supplies, calling for 19 new seaplanes by April 15, followed by five more by May 1, 38 by May 15, and an additional 43 machines by June 1. The Navy preferred deliveries of Tellier flying boats with 200 hp Hispano-Suiza motors, and only enough DDs to cover any Tellier shortages. In late April, Cone also expressed a desire to purchase 30 Levy-LePen flying boats equipped with Liberty motors. The Navy promised to supply sufficient motors and enough three-veneer plywood to complete 30 aircraft for the Americans and 30 more for the French. Ultimately, the French pledged to supply 17 Telliers and nine DDs, as well as eight Levy-LePens, the latter to be assembled at Le Croisic and then flown to St. Trojan.[2]

The number of personnel at aviation stations rose sharply in this period, topping 10,750 by June 30 against an allotted complement of 19,963. Approximately 250 pilots had reached Europe, with 88 in training and 83 listed as students. At the same time, four bases carried out active patrols—Dunkirk, Le Croisic, Ile Tudy, and Paimboeuf. Seaplane stations had tallied 1,830 flying hours thus far. There were 21 aircraft in commission, along with 40 officer pilots and 36 enlisted flying personnel. Equipment consisted of a mishmash of French aircraft with as yet no American-manufactured airplanes in commission. Operations also began at Killingholme in England and Porto Corsini in Italy. Headquarters finalized projected 1919 complements for existing stations by July 6, a total of 16 stations to be equipped/reequipped with American-made HS-1L and H-16 aircraft and motors (with the exception of Dunkirk, Porto Corsini, and Pescara), a total of 398 planes and 780 pilots. H-16 bases included Arcachon, Brest, Fromentine, Killingholme, Lough Foyle, Queenstown, Wexford, and Widdy Island, while Ile Tudy, L'Aber Vrach, Le Croiosic, St. Trojan, and Tréguier would utilize smaller HS-1Ls. Headquarters planned to maintain 32 aircraft at Dunkirk and 48 at Killingholme, with pilots allocated on the basis of two for each airplane. Larger bases required 66 officers and 366–498 enlisted men, while smaller outposts would support 54 officers and 327–394 ratings.

Other facilities included four dirigible sites at Brest-Guipavas, Arcachon-Gujan, Paimboeuf, and Rochefort (later canceled), slated to receive 12 airships and a total of 975 enlisted men and 24 pilots. Three kite balloon stations at Brest, La Pallice, and La Trinité required 18 balloons, 36 pilots, and 324 men. The reorganized NBG program of eight squadrons, including 40 heavy night bombers and 72 day bombers, called for 292 officers (including 236 pilots) and 2,140 enlisted personnel, while plans for the related assembly and repair facility at Eastleigh mandated a force of 40 officers and 1,960 ratings. Projected manpower levels at NAS Queenstown totaled 35 officers, 10 pilots, and 563 men, while the principal supply and assembly depot at Pauillac required 100 officers, 20 pilots, and 5,884 bluejackets. Finally, headquarters establishments in London, Paris, Brest, Queenstown, NBG, and Rome necessitated 119 officers and 251 enlisted men.

Along with revised complements, headquarters placed increased emphasis on codifying station organization. As early as March, Cone had sent a circular letter to commanding officers defining the duties of intelligence officers at RNAS stations and suggesting similar arrangements for American bases "as seems expedient." The following month the Operations Division submitted a "Memorandum for Organization of Air Stations" containing a proposed scheme to systematize administration. Each station would be led by a commanding officer, seconded by an executive officer. Reporting to them would be the various departments, including Ordnance (armory, magazine, ordnance instruction), Navigation and Intelligence (navigation, intelligence, radios, communications, pigeons, photography, meteorology), Flight (flights, pilots, observers, handling crews), Executive (guard, mail, cadre), Supply (commissary, supply, pay), Repair (aircraft, carpenters, boatswains, transport, repair crews), Medical (hospital, welfare), and Public Works (buildings, grounds, land and water, transport). A desire to standardize management led to a conference held at Paimboeuf in late June, the attendees including station commanders Maxfield, Corry, Sugden, Cecil, Griffin, and Capehart. Their report resulted in a revised organizational plan distributed to station commanders in mid-August.[3]

Transition from organization and construction to active military operations dominated naval aviation throughout the summer of 1918, a goal largely achieved by September 30. By then a half dozen French coastal stations, in addition to Dunkirk, conducted war patrols. Convoy escort duties demanded the greatest efforts, followed by antisubmarine patrols. In northern England, Kenneth Whiting's Killingholme detachment conducted a wide range of daily missions across the North Sea, from convoy escort and antisubmarine patrols to reconnaissance flights over the mine barrage and all-night antizeppelin hunts. All Irish stations became operational in September—the last, Queenstown, on the final day of the month. Under the aggressive leadership of Lafayette Escadrille veteran Willis Haviland, NAS Porto Corsini south of Venice battled Austrian forces over the Adriatic Sea and carried out aerial assaults against the fleet anchorage at Pola. Units of the NBG reached the field in Flanders and served with RAF squadrons while awaiting delivery of their own aircraft. The school at Moutchic operated at full capacity, with officer pilots/observers trained in pairs. Assembly facilities at Pauillac, Brest, Eastleigh, and Queenstown all increased levels of activity, as the supply of American-manufactured aircraft grew rapidly. On September 30, total aircraft at hand for French coastal stations alone included 188 U.S. planes, 45 French, two dirigibles, and 28 kite balloons. Headquarters then canceled contracts for additional French aircraft.[4] Naval aviation effected far-reaching command reorganization September 1 when Cone joined Sims's staff in London as aide for aviation, while the bulk of his Paris headquarters relocated to Brest, where Craven became Wilson's aide for aviation. Craven exercised operational control over all aviation activities in France except Dunkirk and the NBG.

A number of concerns remained, however, frequently preventing complete realization of objectives. The NBG siphoned off personnel, and the number of flying officers at some stations remained well below planned levels. The quantity of aircraft available also posed a problem, as did continuing mechanical shortcomings. Ironically, while stations sometimes lacked aircraft, assembly facilities at Brest and Pauillac experienced acute crowding. In late July, Lt. De-Witt Ramsey at Paris headquarters informed station commanders in France that a recent influx of HS-1Ls at the ports had caused great congestion. The list of defects on newly arrived Liberty motors seemed endless: weak crankshafts and bearings, unsatisfactory hand starters, defective propellers and radiators, unsuitable spark plugs, nonworking gasoline pumps, shortages of radio sets, and many of those not practical for Navy use. Craven was one of several Americans who found operating with French aviation centers along the coast "a delicate matter." The transfer of men, equipment, and money to projects such as Killingholme and NBG led to calls for economy of funds and materiel in France, with construction now restricted to public works necessary for base operations. Young reserve officers also caused some concern. Frank McCrary described men recently separated from civilian life as willing and capable, but with their limited experience, "trivial things caused the few regular officers much annoyance and worry." Sims urged senior officers to show patience and strong support when dealing with inexperienced but enthusiastic personnel.[5]

Transformation of Pauillac/Trompeloup on the banks of the Gironde River from an underused stretch of riverbank into a virtual factory town in less than a year constituted naval aviation's most significant logistical achievement in Europe. Eventually the Navy constructed a complete industrial complex, turning a small derelict village, vineyards, and cow pastures into a throbbing center of activity, with sawmills, sail lofts, railroad sidings, machine shops, assembly and repair factory, hangars, warehouses, hospitals, mess hall, barracks, garages, and a theater. This they accomplished despite simultaneously carrying out four competing tasks: building the base, serving as a supply distribution center for coastal French stations, acting as a receiving/transfer facility for aviation personnel arriving in Europe, and assembling and repairing American-manufactured aircraft and ferrying them to active stations.[6]

The process began early in the war. At the beginning of June 1917 a small commission of French officers and naval attaché Sayles inspected Trompeloup village on the shores of the Gironde, 30 miles downstream from Bordeaux and just north of the town of Pauillac, for possible use as an American base. A modest port facility already existed there, consisting of a wharf, a few warehouses, and auxiliary structures. While most early discussions centered on developing Pauillac as a support facility for patrol vessels,[7] its possible use as a receiving barracks, supply depot, and assembly and repair site for aviation also merited consideration. Whiting visited the place in early summer and discerned its utility for aviation use. He regarded Pauillac/Trompeloup as well placed to receive and distribute supplies to coastal stations, especially Moutchic, as well as to assemble aircraft shipped from the United States. It possessed good rail connections, deep water, adequate space, and amenable climate. While no definite action occurred that summer, the arrival of Hutch Cone in early fall moved things into high gear, and in late October he established the Repair and Assembly Section at Paris headquarters.

By mid-November, Cone had refined his thinking about the issue. He explained to Captain Noble Irwin, then in charge of the aviation desk in the office of the Chief of Naval Operations, "I have practically definitely determined to establish at Pauillac the repair and assembly plant and am now making arrangements to secure the use of sufficient land for our purposes." Cone intended to gather "most of our stores, supplies, spare parts, etc., at the same place," as well as assembling aircraft "when you send them over and fly them to their different stations." Returning disabled machines for repair would be more difficult but could be accomplished with acquisition of a vessel to transport aircraft and distribute supplies. Given the emphasis on aircraft matters, Cone recommended setting aside Pauillac as an aviation center. In fact, he predicted, it "will eventually be the heart of the entire organization."[8]

The first aviation personnel, Ens. Ralph Nourse and Asst. Paymaster Russell Thomas, accompanied by two dozen enlisted men, reached Pauillac on November 27, 1917, temporarily quartering in Building #1, a former laundry. It provided offices, crew quarters, mess hall, and galley. At that time, available acreage at the site remained limited. The new station was placed in commission December 1, with planned facilities to include prefabricated barracks/shops/offices, hangars, and a large steel frame assembly and repair structure, all to be manufactured in the United States. Additional personnel soon arrived, LCdr. A. W. K. Billings, Public Works Officer, along with Civil Engineer O. H. Richardson and Lt.(jg) Hubert Burnham to organize the local construction effort. Despite extreme material shortages, workers began laying railroad track, grading, and preparing sites for barracks and repair shops. The day after Christmas the Americans obtained permission to occupy five buildings of the French quarantine hospital (*lazarette*). The new naval base at Pauillac shifted to control of the air station on New Year's Day 1918, with Nourse as temporary commanding officer. Exactly one month later, Lt. Henry Cecil assumed command, retaining Nourse as his executive officer.[9]

During February the pace of activity accelerated. The Navy acquired more land, and work commenced on a provisions warehouse and foundations for the assembly and repair shops. Materials started arriving from American ports.[10] Work crews averaging 250 bluejackets erected 5 portable barracks, the first of 85 such structures planned or built, along with Warehouses #3, #4, and #5. Assembly and repair activities really got under way in March when LCdr. Benjamin Briscoe and his staff arrived. Initially, they concentrated on road and water transportation to coastal stations and readying the base for the extensive demands of the NBG project. As the scope of the work expanded and increasing numbers of men crowded the site, several issues emerged that bedeviled local efforts for many months—particularly shipping problems. As early as March 1 Briscoe reported, "Confidentially I can say to you that the way some of this material is shipped over here was the most ridiculous thing you ever saw. If there was a chance to ship anything upside-down, it got that way. . . . Apparently the easiest things to load are the first things shipped and parts of several things are much more easily shipped than one complete thing." Maintaining motor transport and small vessels posed challenges as well. Briscoe noted, "For some unaccountable reason, somebody forgot to ship any spare parts for the cars that are here. . . . I have been chasing around among my friends in the Army, pawing over a few junk piles to get some things to keep us running."

Finally, the base's mission kept expanding. "Every day is full of surprises," Briscoe observed. Word came down from Paris that "We now find that we are expected to run a radio repair shop here, and the radio dept. has issued a few orders to us to segregate part of the factory and take in a force for this department." Nonetheless, he maintained his positive approach, claiming staff and men were getting used to the situation. "With all of our troubles," Briscoe claimed with some pride, "we nevertheless, I think, have accomplished a great deal. The Public Works Division has certainly done splendidly here." More important, everyone remained focused on the ultimate objective. "We presume this will also help lick the *bosches* and that's what we're here for—a thing we try never to forget, although sometimes it's more or less difficult to coordinate our heart and our liver." Eventually, headquarters decided to acquire still more land for a flying field to test aircraft destined for NBG squadrons. Work on additional barracks continued. A crew of 300 labored night and day on the seaplane hangars. During June the men completed most steelwork on the assembly and repair building, finished the first double seaplane hangar, and forged ahead with plumbing and sanitation work. Construction efforts crested in July, with more than 1,350 bluejackets at work. The total complement now consisted of 109 officers and 4,593 enlisted men. After this point Pauillac shifted from being a frenzied construction camp into a manufacturing facility.[11]

In the midst of all this activity, the task of assembling aircraft for combat operations began. The first dozen Liberty motors reached Pauillac on April 23 and eight crated HS-1L aircraft on May 25 aboard *Houston*. Engineers carried out the initial test stand motor run on June 6 and the first official flight of an American-manufactured plane in France, an HS-1L flying boat, occurred on June 13 with Lt. Charles Mason at the controls. Within a week deliveries to the school at Moutchic commenced. The first H-16 flying boat arrived June 11 and was assembled and flown by July 8. On the initial test hop, again with Mason in charge, a forced landing caused considerable damage.[12]

Getting the aviation program under way had not been easy. Facilities remained uncompleted, shipment schedules were chaotic, and the command situation demanded attention. For a time, mechanics carried out engine work in converted barracks. In early June, Cone bemoaned, "We are up against it in Pauillac in more than one way, but principally because of the hardest kind of luck in the matter of commandants. Poor old [Cdr. John] Patton has been in hospital for some time, things have slopped along w/o any head, now determined medically unfit." Cone wished to secure Capt. Frank Taylor Evans as Patton's replacement. The logistical situation caused continual anxiety. Material deliveries were delayed for months, followed by a flood of equipment, congesting the docks. Aircraft arrived without starters and Cone confessed, "I am actually ashamed to tell allies the real reason we are not ready with more planes."[13]

Much to everyone's relief, the command vacuum disappeared when Capt. Frank Taylor Evans relieved Patton July 17. In only 10 days Cone observed the difference: "Conditions are steadily improving in our business and especially at Pauillac since the arrival of Taylor Evans." Work on the airfield pushed ahead, with 27 acres put in good shape, and similar progress reported on the assembly and repair complex. Laborers laid thousands of feet of railroad track and built a capacious sawmill. They also began manufacturing prefabricated barracks for use at many stations. By then the Navy had taken over the old village of Trompeloup and razed most existing structures, in part to secure more land to accommodate ever-expanding activities, but also to address imminent sanitary concerns. The remaining population posed a health threat due to their "open latrines, open wells near latrines, great quantities of animal waste, no drainage, large trash piles, and expanses of stagnant water." A small group of German POWs helped clear the site.[14] Construction continued even after the Armistice, including final work on the YMCA theater, sickbay, and power plant. Reserve officers who before the war worked as engineering contractors oversaw this enormous construction effort. A postwar history of the public works effort noted how the Navy was "unusually fortunate in having a fine class of men able to handle almost every phase of construction work." The author lauded the ratings as "the best American type of labor . . . great spirit and willingness under hard conditions and very long hours."

Despite successes on the construction front, aircraft assembly lagged considerably. In late July, Cone expressed disappointment at the small number of airplanes flying due "to short shipments of certain essential parts from home." The situation caused much anguish and recrimination and generated extensive correspondence between headquarters in Europe and Washington, as well as fact-finding visits by FDR, and later Admiral Mayo and the Westervelt Board. Pauillac lacked a foundry to cast missing parts and local manufacture of starters proved a stopgap measure at best. A surviving photograph of the assembly and repair building interior reveals a vast jumble of flying boat hulls, along with ranks of wing sections and other parts.

The experiences of reserve lieutenant Kenneth MacLeish, not a patient man, who served at Pauillac as a test and inspection officer, highlighted some of the frustrations. In one instance a delivery of crated aircraft offloaded at the wharf lay 200 yards from the hangar for which they were destined. They sat there throughout the day and MacLeish complained, "There are about 36 people running the operation and only a couple of men to obey their orders." A few days later the impatient officer attempted to secure a drill. He dispatched a mechanic, who didn't return for an hour. MacLeish then went searching for him, finally locating the enlisted man from the sound of his "violent, but muffled cursing." The bluejacket had been rebuffed at one shop and sent to the stores office where he was forced to fill out several sets of paper. The mechanic then continued on to a supply officer, who interrogated him again. After signing more forms he was directed to a second stores building where he had to wait while someone opened a crate containing the tool. A few more papers, and he set off with the "sacred drill."[15]

Even in the face of bureaucracy and confusion, work proceeded with growing momentum. The first American-manufactured DH-4s were ready by late August. Even the disgruntled MacLeish was enthusiastic: "It sure is a wonder. Talk about power. . . . She seemed very solid. She stunted beautifully too." By November crews had assembled 82 airplanes and overhauled 322 engines. The Navy was then prepared to turn out five aircraft per day and even assume some work for the Army. Test pilots made 446 flights and compiled 244 flying hours. Coastal stations received 72 planes via air routes. Looking back on the Pauillac experience Craven observed, "It is regrettable in view of the time, labor, and lives that were spent on the construction of this station, that it did not attain its maximum possibilities before the conclusion of hostilities." He identified several factors preventing Pauillac from fulfilling its mission as successfully as originally envisioned. The base was started and permitted to grow without careful direction, while the shift in focus toward the NBG initiative worked to the detriment of coastal stations. Craven believed Pauillac to be poorly located for the purpose it served. Communications with distant Paris and Brest suffered. In an effort to speed shipments to Europe, some planes traveled as deck loads aboard vessels headed for Brest. Once landed, they could not be reshipped. French railroads were overtaxed and naval aviation enjoyed little clout with local administrators. More than one officer recalled French control of the Pauillac docks as "very unsatisfactory."[16]

Like many from the United States, Craven found working with the French very trying. Conducting business in Europe did not resemble doing business at home. Rather, "In order to make the slightest progress it would be necessary to conform to customs of the country." Local officials employed the expression *c'est la guerre* to explain why laxity and profiteering flourished. This same attitude sometimes affected American officers, along with the belief that it was necessary to "cut red tape to win the war. This caused inexperienced paymasters to play fast and loose with the rules, . . . and worry about the consequences later." Insistence on "going it alone," to "run our own little entertainment," as Craven put it, also created obstacles. Thus, "partial independence proved expensive in time." The sheer magnitude of trying to coordinate this massive undertaking in wartime, over vast distances, in a foreign country, while combating dozens of competing priorities and organizations strained the system to the maximum. Frequent changes in procedures only added to the difficulties.[17]

The most dramatic event in Pauillac's history occurred on the final day of the war when a workforce from the base raced to fight a fire aboard a Portuguese ammunition ship. Executive Officer Battle assumed personal charge of the firefighting party. A single wooden bulkhead separated the coal bunker where the fire raged from 450 tons of explosives packed in tin containers. American sailors laid fire hoses into the hold, while *Nokomis,* a converted yacht serving with the Patrol Squadron, pulled alongside with three-inch lines. Daring firefighters included the Seaman's Guard, bandsmen, and black stevedores. Two days later Commanding Officer Evans held general muster and read a congratulatory message from Sims commemorating the signing of the Armistice. The Army eventually assumed control of the station for use as a troop embarkation center, with the Navy temporarily occupying some space to accommodate crews retained to man seized German vessels. Today a vast oil storage facility occupies the site of the American station. A few of the original requisitioned buildings survive, while the riverbank is littered with the remains of the wartime wharf. There are no markers identifying Pauillac's former use or the pivotal role it played in American military operations.

A wide range of issues, many not specifically related to the actual task of readying naval aviation for combat missions, occupied headquarters staff throughout the spring and summer months. Liaison with the Allies required serious and delicate coordination, while the vexing issue of amalgamation, creation of an independent or combined Army-Navy aviation force, engendered enormous concern and suspicion. Influential and important visitors frequently toured aviation facilities. Finally, intradepartmental relations occasionally proved troublesome, with strong policy differences flowing from differing perspectives on the home front and in Europe.

Securing cooperation from the Allies and the AEF and facilitating the flow of information, equipment, and advice ranked high on headquarters' list of priorities. The Navy operated in several foreign countries and remained utterly dependent on its hosts for supplies, aircraft, weapons, motors, and construction support. To foster close relations in Paris, London, and eventually Rome, the Navy maintained extensive liaison efforts and detailed numerous personnel for that purpose. The Allies responded by seconding their own officers to serve in American headquarters. Success of these efforts depended as much on tact and personality as they did on intelligence and experience. Central to the entire process was Lt. Walter Atlee Edwards, a native of Philadelphia and 1910 USNA graduate. After serving with the fleet, Edwards spent two years at Pensacola receiving aviation instruction while also assisting in outfitting the destroyer *Ericsson*. Following the outbreak of war he served six months aboard destroyers *Jarvis* and *Cushing* conducting antisubmarine operations out of Queenstown, Ireland, and in the fall of 1917 became aide for aviation on Sims's staff. He held the position for most of the remainder of the war.

Edwards's many duties included acting as liaison officer to the Admiralty. Sims later extolled his work, describing Edwards as "extremely capable," with a gift for "getting along splendidly with our Allies, particularly the British, with whom our intercourse was necessarily extensive, and with whom he was very popular." At the same time LCdr. G. C. Neilson became an aide to Fifth Sea Lord (aviation) Godfrey Paine. These were crucial appointments. Sims commanded all American forces in European waters, while the most aggressive antisubmarine activities occurred in the Flanders-North Sea-Irish theaters, Britain's spheres of operation. Finally, development of very large flying boats remained entirely a British-American venture. Admiral Paine offered to accommodate as many as 30 officers, but Edwards declined, saying he had a small office and 5 would suffice. At least three British officers served at Cone's headquarters in Paris. Spenser Grey, a British bombing expert with lengthy service in the RNAS, worked closely with naval forces, while officers at Dunkirk maintained active coordination with Captain/General Lambe.[18]

Following the war Sims lauded his British counterparts for supplying valuable information to American forces. Though he may have overstated their willingness to disclose *all* secrets, the level of cooperation proved extraordinary nonetheless. From a myriad of sources the Navy obtained RNAS/RAF documents on varied subjects ranging from technical developments to training to hydrophone installations. American personnel such as Robert Lovett, Joseph Eaton, and Charles Fuller forwarded a continuous stream of reports from RNAS stations, while staff members like Henry Dinger, head of the Intelligence and Planning Division in Paris, and Lt. Bernard Donnelly, in charge of the Ordnance Section, conducted lengthy and detailed investigations of British aviation facilities and factories. Much of this information eventually appeared in biweekly reports issued by the Director of Naval Intelligence.

Cross-pollination offered significant benefits but also entailed risks. In discussing placement of an officer in the new RAF Air Ministry, Edwards observed, "I feel confident that being on the spot . . . would be of value and pick up a tremendous amount of material which would be of use to us." That same month Capt. Francis Scarlett, RN, head of the Air Division at the Admiralty, offered to provide a small office next to his where Edwards could spend a few minutes two or three days a week to review papers without red tape. "Capt Scarlett is a fire-eating old fellow," the young American noted, "and is all out to win the war and very keen for us." Access was crucial, but also important was having the right man in the right place, with Edwards dismissing one choice with the damning words, "I am very much afraid that [Wilcox] is not qualified for that job as he does not appear to possess enough pep and initiative."[19]

Similarly, not every British officer assigned to American service worked out well. One, a Wing Commander Bone, proved to be a trial. In early April, Edwards dispatched him to Ireland for a few weeks, and now enjoyed "living in comparative calm. He [Bone] . . . will turn out to be quite all right, as soon as he has thoroughly realized that his appointment was not to command the U. S. Naval Forces Operating in Foreign Waters, but rather to lend a hand as a seaplane expert." But the Bone saga was not quite ended, and two weeks later Edwards reported the officer had been detached for duty in the Aegean. As Edwards informed Hutch Cone, "As you can well imagine, this transfer has afforded me infinite relief, as Bone gradually grew almost unbearable. . . . Being a most egotistical and self-centered man, he failed absolutely to realize what he was here for. This, I hope, ends the chapter of Wing Commander Bone, DSO, RN."[20]

The work of British officers in Washington also caused concern at Navy headquarters in Europe. They worried that messages carried to the United States might diverge from views held on the other side of the pond, particularly their amalgamation agenda. Edwards notified Washington in April that Capt. Gilbert More, RAF, would soon be arriving in Secretary Daniels's office, and perhaps occupying a place in Operations. Instead, LCdr. A. J. Stone at the Bureau of Ordnance decided to place a desk in his own office and keep an eye on More. And with good reason; not long afterward Edwards received a letter from More that left him spluttering. "I am writing this confidentially," More began, "and I am quite certain that if you had seen what has been going on over here [D.C.], you would realize the great importance it is to us to get the very best man we can appointed in Capt Irwin's place." Edwards immediately reported this bombshell to Cone. In similar fashion, Cone confided to Irwin he was amused that the Director of Naval Aviation had interviewed More and Commander Porte about "Cone's Technical Department." According to Cone, Porte had never been to Paris nor visited headquarters there. Of More, he sniped, "I consider [him] little better than a boy on any such matters."[21]

Relations with various French ministries also demanded careful attention, and as early as October 1917 Ens. G. A. Smith assumed duties as liaison officer at the Ministry of Marine, this in addition to the role played by Naval

Attaché Sayles and Richard Jackson, his eventual successor. Ensign G. R. Fearing undertook a similar assignment with AEF aviation. In early winter Smith began work with the Service Technique et Industriel de l'Aeronautique Maritime, one of several Navy officers filling such positions. Smith later acted as liaison officer to the RNAS in Paris. American officers also coordinated with the Sous-Secreteriat d'Etat d'Aeronautique Militaire et Maritime. The French made similar appointments, such as Lt. de Vaisseau Tanzi, who served on Cone's staff (dirigibles). French headquarters strengthened the interactive process by attaching a representative to each American station, following a March 20 request from Cone that such a plan be implemented—men like Ensign Guierre at Dunkirk. In August, French observer/mechanic Boucher joined the Navy complement at NAS Fromentine. At Moutchic, Lt. Henri De Haven, descended from French nobility, and his family offered hospitality to many young pilots. Ensign John Schieffelin described how the genial raconteur wore his red kepi "at a jaunty angle, sported a neat mustache, and possessed a merry disposition."[22]

Fostering cooperation with the Air Service presented a greater challenge, and relations in Europe frequently veered toward the confrontational. With the Army and Navy both pursuing enormous aviation programs at home and abroad, the danger of self-defeating competition for scarce resources was one to be avoided. To foster cooperation, Paymaster Conger became a member of the AEF Purchasing Board. Cone also kept in close touch with Col. Raynal Bolling. In November 1917 the two officers suggested creating a joint Army-Navy committee in Paris to represent the Aircraft Production Board, with Bolling serving as chairman and the Navy holding two seats. Sims received notice November 10 that the plan had been accepted in Washington and turned final negotiations over to Cone. Eventually, however, the Navy commander grew uneasy about the possibility of being disadvantaged in his dealings with the larger Army. Ultimately Gen. Benjamin Foulois, the new head of AEF aviation forces, validated his fears. American Expeditionary Force commander John Pershing approved a six-man board for the committee, but Foulois insisted that the Army hold four seats and that he (Foulois), not Pershing, review the committee's decisions and thereby, in effect, veto Navy programs. On February 2 a thoroughly disgusted Cone suggested dissolving the group. Foulois accepted the move and so informed Pershing on March 2. But the committee did not disband and struggled on for two more months, with relations deteriorating further due to Army objections to the emerging Navy Northern Bombing Group proposal.

In late May, Cone reviewed the subject of cooperation with the allies and the U.S. Army. His observations represented a rebuttal of Pershing's charges that the Navy failed to collaborate, describing the AEF commander as misinformed (by Foulois and Maj. Fiorello LaGuardia, no doubt). In fact, Cone said, a liaison office with the Army had been established back in November 1917. But the Army did not respond in kind. Cone even submitted some correspondence beforehand for comment but the Air Service failed to reciprocate. The wrangling that later erupted over the NBG program strained relations to the breaking point.[23]

One issue hovering over everything, the possible amalgamation (consolidation) of aviation forces, was exacerbated by Army opposition to various naval programs and pressure exerted by creation of the Royal Air Force. As early as January 1918, Navy planners had expressed great wariness about the concept and having anything to do with the seemingly chaotic and uncooperative AEF program. Cone described apparent discord in the Paris offices of Army aviation, suggesting the Navy stay out of it. When Cone arrived in Europe, Col. Raynal C. Bolling (in private life a U.S. Steel attorney and not imbued with the Army/Navy rivalry) was in charge and the Navy worked closely with him. "We were working splendidly together," he recalled. Things turned south, in Cone's view, with the arrival of Gen. Benjamin Foulois, "a young officer with little experience handling large affairs."[24] One or two pleasant interviews held promise, but intense friction soon developed within the Army organization, particularly between Billy Mitchell and his adherents, and Foulois and the headquarters staff. Many reserve officers voiced discontent quite openly all over Paris. There was also a lot of talk going around about a single air service combining the forces of the Army and the Navy as was being done in England. Initially, Cone thought this might actually be a good idea, "the correct organization," but strongly advised against participating in such a scheme because "it would result in our becoming a very small part of a large concern greatly confused and unable to produce anything near the desired results." Aviation aide Edwards carped, "Unfortunately, I must confess that I do not hold the aviation office of the U. S. Army in London in very high esteem as they apparently have no organization and the majority of their business is being done for them by a civilian employee." For his part, Sims hoped the Army "would come to their senses and get down to business," but until then "keep out of the row."

Noise about consolidation, amalgamation, and independence emanated from several quarters, however, not just discontented Army officers. Naval reserve officers at Paris headquarters received alarmist letters from their friends at home containing bitter complaints about the Bureau system, "ridiculously small" appropriations from Congress, how naval aviation would never progress until there was a separate corps like the Marines, and kicking against what Cone called "old customs and a lot of rigmarole." Both Cone and Sims had seen such communications and though they didn't think there was much to it, "just the ordinary growl," it would be good to let Irwin know about complaints to "keep him informed of the criticism that comes from the other side."[25]

The related issues of aviation consolidation and independence developed very differently for the Army and Navy. In the Army the battle raged between those who advocated retaining the Air Service as an integral part of the land forces, and those like Mitchell, Foulois, Fiorello LaGuardia, and Asst. Secretary Benedict Crowell, who urged creation of an independent Air Force. Conversely, the Navy debate flared between those who desired to create a separate Bureau of Aeronautics and those who wished to retain aviation within the Office of Operations, with portions of the program distributed among existing Bureaus. Virtually everyone in the Navy believed in keeping the air arm as part of the fleet.

Despite the real war raging at the front, the amalgamation conflict would not go away, and the Navy's bombing initiative, the NBG, only exacerbated tensions. That spring, Edwards met with an AEF officer who revealed that aviation would soon be separated from its parent and reorganized as the Army Air Service. The whole matter "recently assumed an air of resentment over what he called Navy 'butting in' on the Army's job," namely, NBG squadrons, and also how the Navy had "pinched" 800 Liberty motors. A few weeks later Cone met with Gen. Mason Patrick, the new chief of the Air Service sent by Pershing to discuss the advisability of combining air activities under one head. The Army suggested placing naval aviation in the Dunkirk area (NBG) under a single leader, who would control all operations on the Western Front, but Cone rebuffed the suggestion, explaining that the Flanders bombing initiative constituted part of the Navy's larger antisubmarine campaign, cooperating with forces afloat, and any change would have to be made by the Supreme Council.[26]

Further down the ranks, reaction to unification proposals was more direct. Kenneth MacLeish, then under instruction at Clermont-Ferrand, fulminated, "If army-navy aviation are consolidated, all of us will get out of aviation . . . the Navy gets horribly rooked. . . . I'll get out all together, go home and then get drafted." Two months later the outspoken flyer responded to yet another consolidation rumor, spluttering, "I'm going to land in Holland. . . . I consider this the greatest piece of plain ordinary dirty work the US ever saw. They even have the English working for it." Antagonists fought the amalgamation campaign on the home front too. Relying on his many sources, Edwards learned in May that the British Air Ministry planned to send a commission to Washington to "make certain representations to the President" that a Joint Council of Army and Navy members should control aviation affairs. One RAF leader, Gen. Sefton Brancker, offered solace, observing that amalgamation of naval aviation with the less efficient Army organization made little sense. The English general, on his way to Washington, promised to emphasize the Army's shortcomings and the Navy's efforts to promote cooperation.[27]

The amalgamation controversy bubbled throughout the summer. The RAF, created April 1, 1918, played a central role in the controversy and, in Navy eyes, offered a perfect example of what not to do. General Scarlett, Edwards's confidant, called amalgamation of the two services "only temporary and that it would never last." Edwards suggested that the Navy use Scarlett as ammunition in Washington "with a view to killing any proposed amalgamation" by sending the disgruntled soldier as a liaison officer, "as he is so violently opposed to any amalgamation." Cone threw his own influence into the debate, warning Irwin that amalgamation in England meant army squadrons would get the best men and before the war was over the United States would have to assume all RNAS duties. "In this connection," he cautioned, "anyone who is advocating the amalgamation of the two services had better inquire as to the results in England . . . , because these results have been most disastrous, and especially so to Navy interests."[28]

Armed with testimony like this, Edwards, Cone, and others feared the machinations of both Army officers and the infant RAF. In mid-August, Brigadier-Gen. Guy Livingstone, RAF (Deputy Master General of Personnel), traveled to Washington. Edwards advocated preemptive action, cabling the Department that if Livingstone attempted to influence anyone "he [would] be discounted." Only a day later Edwards was banging away at his typewriter again, warning Cone of the many visits by high-ranking RAF officials, perhaps with the intention of influencing "our people at home towards amalgamation." In fact, a virtual parade of British personnel descended on Washington throughout the spring and summer of 1918, where they occupied offices at the Navy Department and sat in on Irwin's weekly conferences.[29]

Others besides junior staffers (like Edwards) entered the debate. Cone sent a strongly worded letter to Irwin, and indirectly to CNO Benson, calling consolidation a "fatal mistake" by creating another War Department when it was already "hard enough to keep army, navy, and marines 'hitched up.'" On the other hand, Cone believed that neither the Army nor Navy should be responsible for production of aircraft (directly challenging the Bureau system and concept of the Naval Aircraft Factory), "and I think the sooner you get your organization lined up around this, the sooner we will receive material over here with which to work." Sims proved equally negative. In late August he called creation of the RAF a complete failure from the naval operational standpoint and claimed the Admiralty desired to reestablish the RNAS. He also opposed joint production agreements between the War and Navy Departments if they contributed to combining the air services. Two weeks later Sims again urged his superiors to oppose unification of flight activities. His opinions also appeared in various American newspapers. The Armistice a few months later did not end this controversy; rather, it stoked the flames into a violent conflict that lasted for years.[30]

At least one other controversy separated participants on both sides of the Atlantic, the question of promotions. Both Sims and Cone wished to hurry advancement for many junior officers taking on greatly enhanced responsibilities in the war zone or displaying outstanding gallantry in combat. This objective collided directly with the Navy's long tradition of very slow promotion and Congress's reluctance to speed the process. Sims grew so frustrated that he urged Secretary Daniels to give his personal attention to the matter. The admiral claimed that young men were making the Navy proud, risking their lives every time they flew, and dying at the rate of one a day. They also brought fresh enthusiasm to the struggle, yet their treatment at the hands of the Department inevitably affected morale. Sims had recommended several junior officers for promotion from ensign to lieutenant(jg), with their names going to a board, which entailed great delay. He urged that others be advanced based on specific acts of gallantry. Instead, Sims sought authority to make immediate promotions. He also hoped to commission older men with special skills, yet regulations required that they first enlist and then pass regular examinations. Such a process was not appropriate for a 50-year-old man. The admiral realized that officers in the United States wished to fill many of these slots, but staff in London and Paris did not know them and they were usually unsuitable for the specific tasks envisioned.[31]

Sims's proposals faced a torrent of opposition, however. Admiral Leigh Palmer, chief of the Bureau of Navigation, reported that he had indeed put recommended names forward for promotion, but the word in Washington was that there would be "no jumps from Ensign to LCdr." Instead, young officers would have to wait for a while and work up one grade at a time. Palmer promised that Irwin would send a final list and promote as many as possible. He asked Cone to understand how hard it was to get any reserve officer, admitting, "there has been an uphill condition we have been working against since the beginning of the war and there has been the strongest opposition to give anyone a promotion no matter how deserving he may be." But Sims did not cease advocating for his youthful charges. At the end of August he again urged the Department to move swiftly on recommendations made four months earlier. Sims grew so exercised on this topic that he returned to it again and again, both in comments on the Westervelt Board report and in his postwar testimony before Congress.[32]

The promotion imbroglio also interfered with the understandable desires of officers in the United States to receive overseas assignment and get into the action. A stream of messages from stateside personnel documented their frustration. In late August 1918, for example, Marine Capt. David Brewster contacted friend DeWitt Ramsey, a member of the "Old Pensacola tribe," at Paris Headquarters, complaining, "We are still here mooning away and a few more months will see us up in the trees with the squirrels. Inactivity breeds the worst sort of despondent behavior and what good is despondent behavior, I ask you like a friend?" Another of Ramsey's old buddies, R. D. Kirkpatrick in the Office of Naval Operations, lamented, "I envy all of you birds over there. This is certainly a hell of a life and all of us here are on the verge of mutiny." Like many officers stationed in Washington, Kirkpatrick confessed, "I get awfully discouraged at times because it looks as though I will never get away from this swivel chair job. . . . I want to get to the other side of the pond." Fitzpatrick had appealed to Irwin, but "he has religiously turned me down," and now hoped a direct request from Paris might earn him a billet there.[33]

Throughout the war a parade of high-ranking officers and civilian officials toured naval facilities. Both Sims and Cone repeatedly urged their compatriots in Washington to cross the pond and observe conditions in Europe, believing such familiarity would bring Department representatives over to the Sims/Cone view of matters. As early as September 1917, C-I-C Atlantic Fleet Henry Mayo headed to Europe, followed by CNO Benson in November and December. Equally important were tours by influential congressmen. During the summer of 1918 the powerful House Committee on Naval Affairs, led by chairman Lemuel Padgett, sailed for Europe aboard the battleship *Arkansas*.

If there were any group Sims, Cone, and others in the naval establishment needed to impress, this was it. Arriving safely in London, the congressmen attended a dinner in their honor arranged by Sims and they enjoyed the hospitality of the British Admiralty. They visited naval headquarters where they raised many questions about the aviation situation and, according to Edwards, "seemed fixated on Liberty Motors rather than the larger view." While Congressmen Padgett, Riordan, and Butler tarried in London, others in the party visited the large aviation station at Aghada/Queenstown in Ireland.

France was next on the itinerary. Edwards alerted Cone, "At Capt. Twining's request, I am going to drive Cong. Sherley to Dover on Saturday morning. He will go to Calais and then proceed by car to Paris. I understand that the Admiral attaches great importance to this gentleman and is very anxious to have us show him every courtesy." Cone spent much time and energy escorting lawmakers and later reported, obviously pleased with the effort, "Just got back from trip along the coast with Congressional Committee. Our tour of the coast air stations proved to be very satisfactory in every particular and I am quite sure that the entire membership of the committee are sincere in their enthusiastic praise of the manner in which we pulled it off."[34]

Of even greater significance was the July-August visit of Assistant Secretary Roosevelt, one of naval aviation's most ardent supporters and a staunch foe of the entrenched Bureau system. A nasty squabble over equipment deficiencies and shipping delays precipitated his trip. All plans and programs under way or envisioned in Europe ultimately depended on timely arrival of trained personnel and reliable, effective equipment—aircraft, motors, instruments—from the United States. But thus far, this had not happened. In fact, failure of both American manufacturers and the Navy to satisfy equipment needs of the European stations had become something of a scandal and source of increasingly critical comment on both sides of the Atlantic. At least part of the problem rested on the inability of the independent Bureaus to coordinate their procurement programs.

Supply and equipment issues ignited a rancorous fight between Cone and the Department. The commander in Paris urged the Bureaus to dispatch their own experts to inspect European designs and thus improve American construction. For the most part, however, the experts did not come. Cone also moved to disseminate technical information from Paris and London, alarming Bureaus well aware of his disapproval of the Navy's divided system of accountability. As former head of the Bureau of Steam Engineering, Cone knew well whereof he spoke. Of course, he denied any malign motives, such as attempting to subvert the system, but that's exactly what he was trying to do. Cone told Irwin, "I am entirely out of accord with you on the whole question of your organization for producing the latest type of aeroplane," but urged the Director to reassure the Bureaus that even though he (Cone) didn't believe in their organization, he would loyally support the Department. Cone finished by urging Irwin to come to Europe, which would convince him of the need for a new system.

Word of the troubles affecting equipment transported to Europe began circulating almost immediately through assembly depots, front-line stations, and headquarters. One problem related to confusion in shipping and packing. Simply put, materiel arrived at the wrong ports, and packing crates often contained incorrect items or lacked necessary parts and equipment. Aircraft hulls and wings were shipped but without starters, bombing gear, propellers, or batteries. Materiel that did reach Europe frequently came broken or incorrectly assembled. Flying boat hulls were damaged. Control wires were the wrong length. Aileron hinges were out of line. Rudders often lacked proper clearance. Many wing panels and struts were warped. Much of the motor equipment was faulty. Workers needed to disassemble and repack 75 percent of water pumps. Crews completely disassembled and rebuilt virtually all Liberty motors, at an expenditure of 200 or more man-hours each. Without access to sufficient French or British equipment and cut off from suppliers at home, aviation mechanics turned to other solutions. Lacking starters, the support ship *Prometheus* manufactured them from scratch. It took six weeks to make the first, but eventually workers learned to turn out one a day.[35]

Complaints, official and otherwise, reached a crescendo in midsummer. As early as July 8, Cone lamented to Irwin, "We are up against it at Pauillac," with management and organizational issues exacerbated first by late arrival of material and then a sudden glut. In early August, Cone protested more forcefully: "I am very much exercised on the subjects of shipments from home in the case of complete seaplanes. . . . It is incomprehensible to me how there could be such discrepancies in shipping, but the bald fact stares us in the face that we have, at this writing, 126 HS-1L seaplanes and 37 H-16 seaplanes on this side and are able actually to fly only five HS-1L seaplanes, and not one offensively, because of lack of equipment." Cone deemed the situation critical, made the Navy look ridiculous, and disarmed any argument against a separate aviation service. Sims weighed in August 21 with a no-holds-barred analysis prepared for Secretary Daniels. He observed, "We have completed almost all necessary construction [of stations], but are prevented from participating in the war offensively due to the serious confusion in which Naval Aviation shipments arrive in Europe." He listed dozens of categories of missing equipment, everything from bombsights to fire extinguishers. The propeller situation was a disaster, which "caused us great embarrassment." Even more significant, Liberty motors almost invariably required overhauling. All of this meant the United States was "falling behind our estimated entry into the war from the standpoint of naval aviation."[36]

In fairness, many of these difficulties were literally inevitable. The quantity, variety, and complexity of shipments abroad was staggering, encompassing everything from the exotic to the mundane. Loaded aboard warships, transports, colliers, passenger liners, mine carriers, or just about anything else that could float, supplies included woodworking and machine tools, welding equipment, ladders, cement, lumber, roofing, trucks, automobiles, motorcycles, bake ovens, stoves, oil, gasoline, paint, sheet asbestos, boilers, electric motors and generators, heating equipment, radios, nuts and bolts, and a thousand other items. Beyond the logistical difficulties of gathering and transporting vast quantities of materiel to myriad foreign destinations, bringing complex, innovative machinery to the battlefield posed additional challenges. Development of the Liberty motor, for example, upon which so many aviation projects depended, involved a frustrating "shakedown" process by which a complex machine was readied for mass production. Originally designed to generate 330 horsepower, improvements increased motor output to 375 and then 440 horsepower, requiring nearly all jigs and tools be changed, as well as modifications in metallurgical specifications and at forging plants. The latter gave rise to the problem of "light" crankshafts that so crippled flying operations in late summer and early fall. Transportation and fuel shortages further slowed shipments. These issues, whether related to motors, equipment, or aircraft, resulted from the decision/necessity of sending unassembled airplanes to Europe, many still requiring significant modification. Had they first been assembled, tested, and flown in the United States, most of these problems could have been avoided. In fact, Sims made just this suggestion to Irwin in mid-August. The Director's weekly meeting examined the admiral's proposal but rejected it in favor of more spot checks at various factories.[37]

In July, the Department dispatched Asst. Secretary Franklin Roosevelt to Europe to inspect naval facilities and investigate complaints about construction contracts, shipping delays, and condition of equipment sent abroad. He made the transatlantic voyage aboard the destroyer *Dyer* loaded for bear, reaching Portsmouth, England, on July 21. Thereafter he held numerous conferences with British officials, inspected American facilities at Queenstown, and met with King George V. Roosevelt crossed over to Dunkirk aboard a British destroyer. Upon landing he observed the conditions hampering aviation activities, "not a whole house left in the place," and recommended the Navy not expand operations there. From Dunkirk, FDR moved on to St. Inglevert and met Robert Lovett, writing of the future secretary of defense, "seems an awfully nice boy." Roosevelt's party proceeded to Paris and another round of high-level conferences. Edwards had already alerted Cone that the visitors were "very keen about aviation and will, no doubt, want to see all our stations." After spending a few days at the front visiting troops and touring the battlefield at Verdun (against the wishes of Naval Attaché Jackson), Roosevelt continued on to Rome and more conferences before returning to France where he conducted an extensive inspection of aviation facilities.[38]

FDR traveled widely and worked energetically, exhibiting his trademark enthusiasm. He visited Pauillac and had dinner with 3,000 sailors in the new mess hall. He also flew above the Gironde River in one of the station's seaplanes. At Paimboeuf he hitched a ride aboard dirigible AT-1. Roosevelt's inspections prompted an indignant cable to Secretary Daniels. He noted that so many planes had arrived that ports were congested, but only eight aircraft were ready to fly. Inspection of equipment in the United States had been lax or not done at all. Wings had to be completely rebuilt. Each engine required 200 hours to overhaul. There were only eight starters available, no bombsights, no spare parts. Questions directed to the Department seldom generated timely responses. Roosevelt urged Daniels to order drastic action, calling current conditions nothing less than scandalous.

The future president desired to shake things up, something not likely to endear him to much of the brass in Washington, especially as he sided so obviously with the "suspect" Sims-Cone crowd. Roosevelt identified aviation as the Navy's greatest flaw overseas, but did not blame Cone, who had "cut red tape and surmounted obstacles in masterly fashion." Rather, it was the Department's "unsound system . . . , which I have verbally and in writing protested against to you [Daniels] on many occasions." Roosevelt castigated indistinct and indefinite relations between the office of aviation and Department mandarins and lack of authority to follow up with the Bureaus. He called aviation "the child of a half dozen parents," and further charged unless the Navy cleared up the mess it would strengthen those trying to take aviation away from the fleet (the amalgamation bugaboo). Roosevelt did more than complain. He urged that a "man of business" be placed in charge of naval aviation armed with authority over the Bureaus and called for creation of a Bureau of Distribution and an Inspection Department with real teeth. All aircraft should be assembled and test flown before being sent abroad. Roosevelt's report confirmed all the complaints voiced in Europe during the past few months and ultimately led to creation of an official board headed by Cdr. George Westervelt to investigate further and propose solutions.[39]

Roosevelt returned to New York in late September, seriously ill with influenza and double pneumonia, and spent several weeks recuperating before returning to his duties in Washington. During that period he drafted a report containing a description of his recent activities and suggestions for administrative overhaul. He pushed his ideas at a weekly meeting of the Council in the Department, but ran into staunch opposition from Bureau chiefs. They said the Navy already possessed plans to spare, and conditions at Pauillac had improved since Roosevelt's visit. Officials in Washington claimed that machines assembled for use at coastal stations in the United States performed well, requiring only 20–30 hours of work to prepare. Attempting to deflect criticism, they charged sabotage of motors must be taking place after inspection, said defects were so negligible as to be easily remedied, missing parts were already on the way, and "faulty' gas pumps would work by simply changing the pitch of the propellers.

By the spring of 1918 the Navy's aviation program had assumed definitive form. Nonetheless, planners considered many modifications, usually at the behest of the Allies. In late April, Cone informed Irwin that the British repeatedly urged him to build or man additional stations along the English Channel, Scotland, or Ireland, including a dirigible station at Peterhead, Scotland, and another in the southwest. Cone consistently rejected expansion, saying the United States had as much on its plate as it could handle. Other proposals envisioned stations at Kingston on the Irish Sea and on the northwest and western coast of Ireland. All were rebuffed. The Admiralty suggested that the Navy assume control of stations at Gibraltar and Alexandria. Three weeks later Sims said no, the United States had other irons in the fire. In the Mediterranean Britain, France, and Italy called for American facilities at widely dispersed locations such as Sardinia, Nice, Corfu, the Gulf of Taranto, and the North African Coast. These ventures would have required many hundreds of aircraft and thousands of men. Despite reluctance, headquarters did entertain a few suggestions. With British manpower shortages escalating, discussions commenced in midsummer that might have led to the Navy operating bases on the southwest coast of England, including Tresco in the Scilly Isles, Newland near Land's End, Cattewater near Plymouth, and Prawle Point in Devonshire. Both Edwards and Twining endorsed the proposal, which would have created an unbroken line to patrol stations from Lough Foyle to Arcachon, but the war ended long before any substantive action occurred.[40]

Whether entertaining expanded responsibilities or not, since January the early, limited aviation program had evolved into a far-flung enterprise, with new stations planned or building in Ireland, England, and Italy. In June, Cone formally recommended relinquishing his post in Paris and relocating to London. From there he could maintain close contact with Sims, supervise the overall aviation effort, plan for the future, supply materiel and personnel, and disseminate technical information. Sims was already on record that when construction ended, control of operations in France would shift to Wilson at Brest. Separate officers would command each theater. Craven would assume control of the French stations. Frank McCrary would direct Irish facilities. Kenneth Whiting would command at Killingholme under the British admiral in charge of East Coast defenses, while David Hanrahan's NBG squadrons, along with NAS Dunkirk, would report to the British vice-admiral at Dover. In Italy, attaché Charles Train would exercise overall authority, with John Callan directing operations.

Word of proposed changes circulated rapidly. Sims tentatively approved reorganization and forwarded detailed plans to Washington. The move to London reflected, at least in part, the center of gravity of aviation efforts shifting from western France to Britain and Flanders. At the end of July, Cone informed headquarters staff that changes were imminent, and Sims announced on August 22 that the Operations Division would report to Wilson September 1. As planned, Cone relocated to London, eventually amassing a staff of 50 officers and appropriate clerical support. Craven moved to 13 Rue Jean Mace in Brest and assumed the role of aide for aviation to Wilson, with Cdr. Albert Cohen as second in command. From this venue Craven exercised direct control over operations in Brittany and the Bay of Biscay. This allowed closer contact with French bases and better coordination between aviation and other naval activities. Craven noted, however, that Brest was not Paris, but rather a "seaside bog . . . a miserable place," beset by mud and constant rain, where it was impossible to get either exercise or a bath. He also found communications "wretched," the mail slow and irregular, and the telephones "almost impossible."[41]

* * *

Spring and summer 1918 was a period of rapid change for naval aviation as the organization implemented plans initially developed the previous fall and winter. For many, the process seemed to unfold maddeningly slowly, but the difficulties encountered and surmounted had been daunting. Pauillac developed into the central facility for the entire aviation effort. Ensuring efficient liaison with Army and Allied commands required patience and continuous effort. The amalgamation controversy diverted energy and attention from more immediate challenges, as did various disagreements between headquarters in London, Paris, and Washington. With its people, equipment, and organization finally in place, however, naval aviation stood ready to enter the fight over a front stretching a thousand miles from Lough Foyle, Ireland, to Porto Corsini, Italy.

6

SPINNING THE SPIDER WEB

Naval Aviation in England

While naval aviation activities commenced in France immediately after the arrival of Kenneth Whiting and the First Aeronautic Detachment, similar operations in England lagged by many months. This disparity resulted from several factors. The French Ministry of Marine lobbied aggressively for American aid while the Admiralty did not. Based in Paris, Whiting focused almost exclusively on matters there and helped commit the Department to a Francocentric program. In contrast, the RNAS was a far more formidable force than the Aviation Maritime, with a better developed program of bases, equipment, training facilities, and missions, and thus saw less need of assistance in the form of actual American stations.

Despite its sizable aviation efforts in France, the American Navy looked principally toward Britain for guidance. During the war Britain constructed an enormous number of air stations, depots, training establishments, and experimental sites. Its technical advances dwarfed those of other nations. The Admiralty supported extensive activities to combat the submarine menace, protect the homeland from aerial attack, and provide eyes for the fleet, utilizing dirigibles, kite balloons, land planes, seaplanes, and the world's most advanced flying boats. The vast reach of the Royal Naval Air Service stretched from Scotland to France, the Mediterranean, Greece, Egypt, Africa, and Iraq. The Royal Navy worked to marry aircraft to the fleet, deploying seaplane carriers, balloon ships, lighters, warships carrying scouting machines, and by 1918 conducting experiments with aircraft carriers.

For some time it remained unclear what role the U.S. Navy might perform in Britain. Not until Hutch Cone reached London in late September did naval aviation establish a substantial presence there. Nonetheless, several noteworthy initiatives eventually emerged. That the two forces spoke nearly the same language and Anglophile Sims established his headquarters in London, rather than Paris, inevitably strengthened these ties. Scores of American pilots, observers, mechanics, and others trained at British schools like Cranwell, Ayr, Felixstowe, Eastchurch, Turnberry, Roehampton, Gosport, and Salisbury. Equally significant, large numbers of personnel served at RNAS and RAF stations in Britain, carrying out extensive wartime missions ranging from patrols, to convoy duties, to zeppelin hunts. At many bases they performed a substantial percentage of the work. Finally, in 1918 the Navy took control of Killingholme station near Hull and transformed it into the single largest American patrol base in Europe.

* * *

Obtaining advanced training for flight personnel constituted a priority in the winter of 1917–1918. Urgent demands for skilled *chasse* pilots to defend lumbering patrol bombers at NAS Dunkirk constituted one crucial need. Planners tried to meet this shortage by enlisting American flyers originally taught by the French and currently serving with the Lafayette Flying Corps. Others would be drawn from the First Aeronautic Detachment and the First Yale Unit. In late fall 1917, negotiations with the Admiralty resulted in an agreement whereby a score of such men would be sent to England and Scotland and instructed at the best Royal Flying Corps schools—Gosport, Turnberry, and Ayr. The process commenced when headquarters selected Yale Unit members Lovett, Gates, and Ingalls for "acrobatic work," detaching them from duty in France and ordering them to London. Contrary to expectations, upon arrival Lovett learned that he would head to the RNAS station at Felixstowe while Gates was sidetracked for other duties. Instead, Kenneth MacLeish and Edward "Shorty" Smith, also Yale pilots, joined Ingalls, with all three assigned to the RFC aerodrome at Gosport near Southampton on the English Channel. After short layovers in London the trio rode down to the coast to commence instruction in AVRO trainers.[1]

The School of Special Flying at Gosport began as something of an experiment founded in 1917 under the direction of Lt. Col. Robert Smith-Barry, RFC, a veteran officer of forceful personality and strong views. According to a detailed report compiled by MacLeish, Smith-Barry "wrote repeated letters to the War Department," arguing that it was a waste of time to train men at front-line squadrons. Given a chance to establish his own school, Smith-Barry handpicked the staff. His methods emphasized complex aerial maneuvers, acrobatics, and forced landings, and focused on increasing student confidence. There was little or no red tape. As long as a man did his work, no questions were asked. According to the Americans, instructors were a fine bunch of men, very good flyers, and many pupils were officers who had served at the front for a year or two, and now, for the first time, were really learning how to fly.²

Initial work at Gosport lasted only a few days due to the Christmas holidays, and the Americans returned to London and a joyous reunion with a gaggle of naval aviators. They returned south on December 27, and as the only students present enjoyed the undivided attention of their instructors. Taking advantage of fleeting good weather, Ingalls and the others went flying on New Year's Day. They made rapid progress in their basic Avro trainers and within a week soloed in Sopwith Camels, one of the most dangerous aircraft on the Western Front. Mounting a powerful rotary engine generating a spin-inducing torque, the Camel earned a dreaded reputation as a pilot killer. Ingalls reported, "The machine handles so lightly that anything can be done and it is so easy that you simply couldn't fly straight if you wanted to. But very foolishly I did a lot, six or seven, tailspins at a terrible rate. I felt rotten for two or three hours afterward."

Fair weather breaks were few and far between, however, and dreadful conditions often interfered with training. Ingalls told his father, "The weather has been rotten. Wind, clouds, snow, and worst of all, fog." MacLeish echoed those thoughts, "Rain and hail have lost their fascination. Snow is quite the thing to fly in." In mid-January conditions grew so bad that Gosport temporarily suspended instruction. The Yalies returned to London where they stayed at the American Officers Club, attended the theater, and reported to Sims and Cone who urged them to finish their work quickly. In the following weeks students resumed training in a program punctuated by dramatic flights and near disasters. On more than one occasion they fought mock battles in the skies above southern England. At other times they took cross-country jaunts testing their endurance, ingenuity, and navigational skills.³

The rapid pace of instruction and abominable weather caused frequent mishaps. In early January "Shorty" Smith nearly died when a loose seatbelt caught the stick and he lost control of his Avro while looping at 2,500 feet. That same day Ingalls flew into a maze of telephone lines but managed to land his damaged plane. Two weeks later MacLeish smashed the propeller and undercarriage of his Camel while stunting with an instructor. Nonetheless, increased confidence brought aerial hijinks. The young ensigns enjoyed "buzzing" less-experienced pilots, the "Huns," or looping within a few hundred feet of the ground. They also loved "bush-bouncing," racing along just above the ground, then hopping over houses, trees, and startled farmers and their animals. Returning to the aerodrome they sometimes landed just a few feet from the hangars. Madcap flying, however, did not divert the Americans from their true purpose. During his weeks at Gosport MacLeish made careful notes about British flight instruction methods, hoping to use the information to improve the Navy system. After passing through the course, he recommended that all flight training begin with land machines and that instructors be chosen on the basis of interest in their pupils, flying proficiency, ability to effectively impart knowledge, and satisfaction with their jobs. MacLeish compiled an even more detailed account of the RFC aerial gunnery courses at Turnberry and Ayr in Scotland. He forwarded his reports to headquarters in Paris and Washington. Bob Lovett believed that MacLeish's outline of training for single-seaters in gunnery and acrobatics was his greatest contribution to the service.[4]

In early February, Ingalls, MacLeish, and Smith finished work at Gosport, and after attending a farewell dance hosted by aerodrome officers, traveled to the RFC gunnery school at Turnberry where they met up with a dozen enlisted First Aeronautic Detachment pilots trained by the AEF at Issoudun. These men had first reported to the Army facility in December 1917 and received instruction flying the Morane Parasol and a series of Nieuport *chasse* machines. Flight time averaged 20–25 hours per student and included tests for spirals, *vrilles*, wing slips, *renversements*, and formation flying. They departed for Scotland in mid-February.[5]

Overlooking the Firth of Clyde southwest of Glasgow, Turnberry offered instruction in the use, mechanics, and maintenance of automatic weapons. Lectures and demonstrations filled the days, with evenings devoted to copying notes and studying. The Americans boarded at a hotel overlooking the golf links. Rather than the older, more experienced pilots training at Gosport, Turnberry was geared toward inexperienced cadets. Trainees spent their days "sitting on hard wooden benches in sorts of classrooms, studying twice as hard as [I] ever did in school." Instruction began at 8:45 A.M. and continued until 12:00 noon, followed by a short break and then more work until teatime at 4:45. Lectures lasted from 5:30 until 6:45, followed by dinner and then hours copying notes. MacLeish called the pamphlets "really libraries," and claimed he got to bed just in time to wake up for breakfast. Very little flying occurred; the nature of the course and perpetual drizzle precluded active operations. When not studying or seeking shelter, the young officers played bridge, what David Ingalls named "England's national game."[6]

After a few weeks at Turnberry, Navy pilots moved on to the nearby School of Aerial Fighting at Ayr. Students at this finishing school included aviators from England, Ireland, Canada, Australia, and South Africa, the small Navy contingent, and dozens of Air Service flyers like Elliot White Springs and

George Vaughn. American mechanics also trained here. Work commenced with a detailed gunnery course, beginning with elementary instruction on the firing range studying both aiming and stoppages, including how to test rounds and ammunition belts. They learned how to fire bullets in tight groups by shooting short bursts. Cadets used both wooden models and paper silhouettes of planes to practice deflection and angles. All cadets stripped and cleaned their guns after each session. An enclosed shed contained a mockup of a plane used to teach the workings of synchronization gears. Eventually they fired at surprise targets from a range of 200 yards while seated in a movable fuselage running along a track. Noncommissioned officers acted as range instructors and their word was law.

Advanced work in the air initially utilized two-seaters from which flyers practiced correcting stoppages, firing at a raft in the water, and then aiming with a camera gun. Soon they moved on to front-line warplanes, mostly Camels and SE-5s. They engaged in aerial battles with students or instructors and employed camera guns to determine the winner. Individual encounters quickly gave way to contour chasing and group operations, mimicking tactics employed at the front. In early March, 50 aircraft from the station carried out a mock raid on the nearby coastal town of Troon. Straining to graduate pilots as quickly as possible, the RFC rushed men through the course, with the inevitable result that scores were injured or killed in training mishaps. Ingalls told of an airplane that pancaked on top of a hangar, with the nose embedded in the roof, what he called "the stupidest and funniest thing I ever saw. The poor nut." Training ended in early March and naval aviators received travel orders for London, and then onward to Paris, and finally Dunkirk where active patrol operations were about to begin.[7]

At Ayr, tensions surfaced between enlisted and commissioned Navy pilots. MacLeish called the FAD veterans the "Hard Guys" and the "Roughnecks." He claimed they refused to perform required drill, sported "non-reg" Sam Browne belts, and scoffed that they'd wear whatever they damn well pleased. He also mocked their flying ability. Ingalls concurred. Corroborating the Yalies' jaundiced views, enlisted pilots did experience some difficulty at Ayr. At least two, Harry C. Velie and Frederick Hough, both Chicago natives, died in accidents. Several more later perished in crashes at Dunkirk. Aviation Aide Edwards notified Hutch Cone that enlisted flyers at Ayr often failed to conduct themselves properly. He initially prepared a letter for the British commanding officer over Sims's signature but withdrew it; he decided to send a personal representative and obtain fitness reports on the men. In this case, unlike a similar situation at Roehampton balloon school, the Navy opted for personal discussions rather than official reports. Such actions and comments, however, said as much about the officers as it did about the enlisted pilots. The American Navy had a well-ingrained class system, in this case exacerbated by the cultural and social divide between the affluent and socially prominent "Ivy League" pilots and the noncommissioned flyers. At least one of the latter remarked about this gulf, especially the disparity the two groups exhibited in spending money.[8]

Even as the Navy selected pilots for advanced flight training, it also identified observers to attend British schools. Many were veterans of the First Aeronautic Detachment who had already trained at St. Raphael and Moutchic. Several labored at Dunkirk, building dugouts and enduring German attacks. In late November they received word to head to Paris for new orders. One of these men (a total of 15), Irving Sheely, left a diary and letters describing his experiences. He left Dunkirk November 23 and spent a few days in Paris sightseeing, taking in a show, and enjoying a good, hot bath. By November 28 he was in London, and two days later arrived at RNAS Cranwell.[9] The school occupied a site about 32 miles north of London in Lincolnshire, just west of "the Wash," lashed by frigid, damp winds sweeping in off the North Sea. Heavy fog often made aviation impossible and men remained in the barracks, reading, studying, or nursing frequent colds. Their English hosts welcomed them warmly, however, conducting a gala dinner that included songs, speeches, and toasts to King George V and President Wilson. Sheely happily described accommodations at Cranwell as O.K. "The food is fine and plenty of it." Being able to converse in English offered another important benefit. Work began almost immediately with a course in bomb dropping and the use, operation, and repair of Lewis machine guns. Other lessons included the study of ammunition and high explosives. After a few days the observers initiated training flights, and on a clear day the sights from the cockpit proved inspiring, with beautiful countryside spread all about below. As was often the case, the work could be very dangerous. One of the training machines crashed and "the pilot was burned to a crisp."

The stay at Cranwell proved to be a short one, and in mid-December the men moved on to Eastchurch on the Isle of Sheppey, east of London near the mouth of the River Thames. The British ran the school "by the book" and Americans found the routine of quick-step marching and exaggerated arm-swinging objectionable. Sheely complained, "English had an idea we had joined the English Navy and tried to make us drill their way. Nothing doing." Once again work commenced immediately with more practice on the Lewis gun, including live firing, followed by flying exercises aboard the fragile-looking BE 2c, formerly a front-line aircraft but now long retired to training use. Trainees practiced a series of bomb-dropping exercises, attempting to hit targets from altitudes ranging from 500 feet to 3,000 feet. They also dropped incendiary bombs and then turned to midair machine gun firing. Marine Captain Alfred Cunningham toured the facility on New Year's Day and called it "a very large, interesting, and well managed school." He shared lunch with the commandant, Captain Steele, who had been captured by the Germans but escaped and made his way back to England. Cunningham spent the day studying instruction methods while experiencing "the coldest kind of cold . . . goes right through you like a knife."[10]

At the end of the month the base suspended operations for Christmas and the Americans received leave in London and Kent. By December 27, however, they were back on the Isle of Sheppey, only to be relocated to Leysdown, about two miles from Eastchurch, for more intensive gunnery work. On some occasions observers climbed out of the cockpit in midair to free up their weapons, a particularly hair-raising experience. They often participated in exciting flights, looping, stalls, sideslips, and spinning. Trainees also continued refining their bombing skills. Weather permitting, they went aloft three to five times each day, dropping both small bombs and larger 50 kg (112 lb) models. In a letter home Sheely observed, "By Gosh but that big one sure made a jar. This is the kind we use on submarines so you can imagine what they are like." When not working, the men wrote letters, washed laundry, and watched movies. A few traveled to Chatham and Sheerness to buy crab medicine for those suffering from the "French itch."

Formal work on the observer course commenced in early January, with special emphasis on navigation, wireless telegraph, semaphore, and visual lamp signaling, the latter a difficult task, trying to read Morse code in midair. Sheely found it "rather a hard proposition . . . coming with much difficulty." They also practiced sending Morse code, signaling with flashlights, ship spotting, and use of aviation cameras. In late January the Americans learned to operate the Hythe camera gun, a specially fitted Lewis machine gun reengineered to capture single-frame photographs each time the "gunner" pulled the trigger. During this same period "Gotha raids" on London caused quite a bit of excitement. Assaults by large German bombers first occurred in daylight, and later at night. The Isle of Sheppey lay under the flight path of the raiders and men in camp could recognize the distinct droning of their Mercedes engines. Antiaircraft fire flared on the horizon, and on a few occasions shrapnel came raining down nearby.[11]

By late February the work was done, the course was completed, and the

Americans received their RNAS gilt observers insignia, a hollow "O" flanked by a slim pair of wings. The Navy later disallowed wearing the award, saying there was then no Aerial Observer rating, much to the disgust of the men who had earned their wings. The commanding officer at Eastchurch complimented departing Yanks enthusiastically, especially their generally high caliber and ability to assimilate difficult subjects. He recommended that all but two be promoted to the next higher grade. The sailors then transferred to London, crossed the Channel to Paris, and returned to Dunkirk from whence they had departed three months earlier. Most believed the shooting war would soon begin.[12]

In early fall 1917, additional aviation personnel began arriving in England, either from France or the United States, but they found no American aircraft or stations to accommodate them. Conversely, Britain possessed sufficient planes and bases but a growing shortage of pilots and ratings. A mutually agreeable plan soon emerged to send small groups of neophyte pilots to RNAS stations to gain valuable experience while providing critical manpower. Some compiled extensive reports on activities and procedures, information sorely needed by American forces. Still others conducted inspection trips to British bases, training establishments, and factories. Felixstowe, located in Harwich harbor and the heart of British seaplane/flying boat operations, quickly became a principal destination. The Belgian coast lay just 90 miles away across the North Sea, with Terschelling Island and the nearby Bight of Heligoland 180 miles distant. Halfway to the Hook of Holland, 50 miles out, floated the North Hinder lightship. Enemy submarines often ran on surface, including both commerce destroyers and mine layers. Harwich served as the most important naval base on the east coast of England, and all activities that were centered there, including the air station, fell under the command of RAdm. George Cuthbert Cayley, who proved friendly to the Americans. Lieutenant Commander O. H. K. Maguire, called "Number One" and a stickler for naval style and manners, commanded at Felixstowe air station. He kept hours with a big bell, divided the staff into watches, and referred to the gravel parade ground as the "quarterdeck." When personnel departed the station they "went ashore." The complement included 60 officers (30 flyers) and 1,400 men accommodated in endless rows of huts. Three enormous 200-foot × 300-foot sheds sheltered aircraft, and a tall iron fence surrounded the base.

In addition to Felixstowe's patrol and combat operations, Cdr. John C. Porte labored there doing experimental/development work on large flying boats. He designed his original boat while associated with Curtiss at Hammondsport, New York, in 1914. Some of these reached Britain in 1915 but performed poorly. In 1916 Curtiss built new aircraft to Porte's specifications. Porte also developed several flying boats at Felixstowe, including the F2A, F3, and F5. His final effort, known as the "Porte Superbaby" or "Felixstowe Fury," was a monster triplane weighing 15 tons, with a 127-foot wingspan, and five motors generating 1,800 hp. Ultimately, it proved too big and slow for regular service. Instead, Felixstowe pilots flew the smaller F2As with a 96-foot wingspan, 42-foot hull, and twin Rolls Royce 345 hp motors. Four machine guns, four bomb attachment points, and a crew of four completed the aircraft's outfit.[13]

Still-green Americans visiting Felixstowe during the fall and winter expressed amazement at what they saw and bemusement with unfamiliar English ways. David Ingalls, the Navy's future "Ace," and still just 18 years old, made a brief visit in early October 1917, shortly after landing in England. The large number of pilots impressed him, as did shipshape hangars, surrounded by dugouts and bombproofs for protection against German air raids. The "Superbaby" awed Ingalls, the "most gigantic machine I ever saw carrying six men—two pilots." Ingalls also inspected the regular machines (H-12s and F2As), "somewhat smaller with two motors, three men, four guns, but still three or four times as big as our F-boats." Felixstowe also operated Short seaplanes and one land plane, the Sopwith Pup, which he described as "a peach of a land machine, little and just the first land fighting machine I had ever seen." Fellow Yale man Reginald Coombe accompanied Ingalls on this early inspection trip and came away similarly impressed with the "Superbaby" and the "Pup," noting how the British had "practically given up on pontoon machines" and used huge flying boats instead.[14]

Though Ingalls and Coombe quickly moved on to further duties in France, other Americans began assembling for longer stays at Felixstowe. Ensigns John Vorys and Al Sturtevant, two more Yale veterans, reached England in early December. Kenneth Whiting, about to return to Washington, greeted them with the following instructions. "Your mission," he said, "is to be diplomatic as well as military. We expect you to learn all you can; you are the first officers to be attached to British service for active duty; how well you get on will affect those who come later." Lieutenant Carl Hull soon joined them ("to observe administration of the station"), as did Ensigns Nugent Fallon and Philip Page. Many British officers received the Americans with open arms. Major Douglas Hallam, commander of the War Flight, noted, "They were splendid chaps. Keen on flying, and could not be kept out of the air." While the station's old-timers viewed patrolling as a hard and exacting business, the Americans saw it "as novel and entertaining sport." The Yanks seemed fascinated by their new surroundings. John Vorys reacted immediately to the station customs and drills. The entire ship's company, he recalled, mustered on the "quarterdeck" each morning and noon, "a marvelous piece of smartness," the effect heightened by attendance of a bagpipers' band, which also marched the men to mess. He later added, "These Britishers don't seem to mind the cold, they don't even heat their houses except with coal grates, which are pretty to look at through the white vapor of your breath. . . . Anyhow, we have to bundle up like Eskimos."[15]

Inexperienced Navy pilots assigned to Felixstowe underwent a short training course before commencing combat operations. They began in H-4 flying boats called "Small Americas," stepped up to H-12s known as "Large Americas," and then moved on to F boats, typically soloing after four hours of instruction. The men also attended informal ground school where they studied navigation, machine guns, and bombing. Thirty-two-year-old Ensign Phillip Page of Boston, a prewar exhibition flyer for Burgess and Curtiss, became the Navy's first casualty December 17, 1917, when he died in a crash during a test hop. The veteran flyer lifted off from the water about 2:35 in the afternoon, made a circuit of the bay, and then landed, handling the machine well. He quickly took off again and flew steadily into the wind for about 200–300 yards, rising to a height of perhaps 25 feet. Suddenly, he "hoicked" the machine, banked sharply to the left, then turned 180 degrees and fell from the top of the "hoick," tail to the wind, in a sideslipping dive into the water from 40 or 50 feet. Extensive damage suggested either his seat backrest gave way or the port engine failed. Writing two days later, Kenneth MacLeish reported, "He was flying one of those 'Americas' down where Al (Sturtevant), John (Vorys), and Bob (Lovett) are. He stalled the machine on his first solo; bad luck wasn't it. He was an awfully nice chap. They haven't found his body yet." The ever-sardonic John Vorys later observed, "Just staying in the air was quite a feat in our day."[16]

When not flying, young officers enjoyed an active social life, especially compared with those "marooned" at isolated outposts along the French coast. The Americans, as many as 21 at one time, lived in a rented manor house about a mile from the station and commuted by automobile. Tea was served at 5:00 P.M., while the officers' mess, enlivened by special song nights and parties, observed many formalities, including dressing for dinner. On occasion, young officers attended meals with Admiral Cayley aboard the station ship HMS *Ganges*, the former 1863 ironclad HMS *Minotaur*, followed by card playing. Others enjoyed the hospitality of the nearby Depot Battalion mess. The battalion consisted of men wounded at the front and then sent home to act as instructors. One American noted that in the group of about 40, "there was scarcely a single whole man present." Nonetheless, a jolly time unfolded, with the regimental band playing and then a legless pianist banging out popular tunes. The party did not break up until one A.M.[17]

Not every interaction between Americans and their British hosts proved sunny, however. Ensign John Schieffelin, recently arrived from Moutchic, encountered occasional "infuriating snide remarks to the effect that we were latecomers to the war and it was about time for us to show up." Even more galling were wardroom comments that Phillip Page's recent death resulted from deliberately attempting "a reckless stunt." At northerly Killingholme, Harold Wilcox, a law school graduate, complained about the constant discordant bugle calls, and especially the treatment of the Royal Navy's enlisted men. In February he claimed, "The ratings are servile and humble.... They have 1,500 where 500 could do the work. The officers treat them like hogs.... God help England if these are a sample of her officers." A few days later he unleashed a few more barbs, claiming officers lolled around the wardroom drinking and talking about uniforms, never read newspapers, and thus had no idea of the progress of the war.[18]

In frequent letters to family and friends, as well as reports sent to London, young Americans provided detailed descriptions of operations at Felixstowe. A patrol system of searching for submarines introduced in 1917, known as the "Spider web," centered on the North Hinder light ship anchored in the North Sea midway between Britain and Holland and covered 4,000 square miles. The web appeared on charts as an octagonal figure 60 miles in diameter, with its radiating arms measuring 30 miles each. Three sets of circumferential lines at distances of 10, 20, and 30 miles out from the center completed the pattern. Pilots proceeded along prearranged sequences of spokes and circumferentials. In five hours, one aircraft could search one-quarter of the area. Experience showed that an altitude of 1,000 feet offered pilots the best view. Patrols generally consisted of two or three H-12 or F2A flying boats cruising in a "V" formation for protection against enemy scouts. In some cases Commander Porte dispatched aircraft to provoke action, believing the machines could defend themselves. He recommended fitting out specially armed aircraft mounting 11 machine guns and carrying a crew of six. Others believed this tactic quite ineffective, saying that turning flying boats into fortresses impaired their antisubmarine effectiveness. Better, they argued, to conduct escort flights from Dunkirk.[19]

F2A flying boats incorporated slightly vee'd bottoms with a hydroplane step and carried 6.5 hours of fuel for cruising at 60 knots, and a top speed of

80 mph. Twenty men were required to roll these planes out of the hangars. The aircraft carried four machine guns and four 100-pound bombs with delay fuses that detonated 2.5 seconds after hitting the water, 60 feet to 80 feet below the surface. The flight crew consisted of a first pilot, second pilot, wireless operator, and engineer. The first pilot took off and landed, flew over hunting grounds, and while in the air sat in a small padded arm chair on the right side of a central cockpit covered by a transparent wheelhouse. Unlike those stationed in open cockpits, he did not wear goggles. Instrumentation included compass, air speed indicator, altimeter, bubble level, inclinometer, oil pressure gauges, and rpm counters, with gas switches and throttle control levers close at hand. An upright wooden yoke carried an 18-inch steering wheel. A strong rubber "bungey" attached to the control yoke could be adjusted to compensate for tail- or nose-heaviness. As the pilot worked the steering rudder with foot controls, the second pilot (who acted as gunner, bombardier, navigator, and relief pilot) stood beside him, but if a submarine were sighted he ducked forward into an open nose cockpit containing machine guns, bombsight, and bomb release levers. He also guided the pilot when the commander lost sight of the target. The wireless operator faced forward on the right-hand side of the cockpit, just behind the first pilot, monitoring the wireless telegraph, sending/receiving messages, firing the recognition signal if a submarine appeared below, and manning one of the guns when under attack. The engineer occupied a separate cockpit amidships, surrounded by fuel tanks, a maze of pipes, and innumerable gadgets. Two wind-driven pumps forced gasoline from the main tank into a small tank on top of the wing, and then to the motors by gravity. The engineer also acted as lookout for the aft quadrant and operated a machine gun if necessary.

Supplies carried aboard included leather coats and pants, binoculars, emergency rations, sea anchors, Red Cross boxes, "bungey" cords, tool kits, pigeons in baskets, revolvers, and cameras and film. A small instruction book mandated a broad range of procedures and techniques. Pilots were ordered to commence watch-keeping once airborne and report all buoys, lightships, and wrecks. No one should automatically assume he had actually seen what he thought he had seen and should be prepared to give the aircraft's position at any moment. An officer made a small pencil mark on a chart recording the aircraft's track every 15 miles and noted every change, with the appropriate time. If the airplane seemed likely to crash, efforts must be made to save everything possible—pigeons, rations, Very lights, Red Cross outfits.[20]

Escorting the "Beef Trip," or neutral Dutch traffic, constituted a principal responsibility of Felixstowe station, usually two or three convoys per month carrying beer and beef between England and the Hook of Holland. Convoys steamed at 11 knots and took 10 or 12 hours to cross the North Sea. Aggregations of 10 to 15 cargo vessels set off in the early morning hours, accompanied by warships from Harwich. At the Hook of Holland another group of merchantmen waited to be convoyed back to England. Aircraft patrolled the route the night before, searching for U-boats and mines, and provided aerial escort during the actual voyage. Airplanes set out in relays, each pair of scouts providing five or six hours of coverage. Such work called for very careful navigation. Enemy vessels usually waited in advance of convoys so planes flew great loops 5 to 15 miles ahead looking for mines and submarines.[21]

Perhaps the most significant visit by an American naval aviator to Felixstowe occurred in December 1917 when Robert Lovett, quickly emerging as one of Hutch Cone's top troubleshooters, arrived with orders to observe and learn everything possible about seaplane activities. Fellow Yale Unit veteran Vorys wrote, "Bob came along . . . found out how the wheels of the station ran around, armed with notebook and pencil and diplomatic questions. . . . Received and sent big confidential letters to Captain Hutch-eye Cone and Admiral Sims." Lovett's January 2 report proved to be one of the most important such documents compiled during the war for what it said about the current state of operations at the epicenter of British naval aviation. The Royal Navy, after all, not the French, provided the model by which Americans guided their own efforts. Lovett's basic report ran to 18 densely packed pages and included several of his own hand-drawn diagrams, covering the widest range of topics from equipment to operations and instruction.[22]

He began by noting that the station possessed three constituent parts, the "War Flight," "School Flight," and experimental station. The "War Flight" employed large flying boats of the F2A, F2C, F3, and F5 types, all known for superior lifting capacity and great cruising radius. Conversely, older flat-bottomed H-12s had been virtually abandoned. Attempts to run combat operations, flight instruction, and experimental work in the same place at the same time had proved impractical, requiring separate staffs and machine shops. The young lieutenant filled several pages with accurate data describing the instrumentation and performance of major British flying boat types and their Rolls Royce motors. He praised the V-hull, two-step construction that permitted takeoffs and landings in sea conditions that excluded flat-bottomed boats. Lovett also identified two design problems to be avoided in American aircraft: lack of longitudinal watertight bulkheads between the fins and the main hull, and weak tail construction of wood and canvas. He seemed most intrigued with the aft sliding trap doors in the hull ("the finest bit of design . . . a remarkably clever device") that permitted Lewis machine guns to be swung clear of the tail allowing the engineer to cover the aircraft's defensive blind spot, with fire converging a mere seven yards astern of the rudder. Finally, Lovett urged that plans and specifications for H-16 and HS-1L aircraft then under development in the United States be forwarded to Britain for scrutiny by Felixstowe experts to identify necessary modifications, warning that the H-16, based on the F2A boat, did not incorporate modifications already built into the updated F2C type. Lovett cautioned, "I believe we might profit considerably by having any alterations done in the United States prior to shipment." Had this advice been followed, many difficulties encountered with these aircraft in 1918 might have been avoided.

Lovett departed, voluminous notes in hand, in late December, about the time American pilots commenced actual combat duty. Vorys and Sturtevant made their first war flights in January on spider patrol. In early February the station observed increasing aggressiveness by German pilots, flying offshore in small, fast seaplanes. Some feared trouble, believing British H-12s and F2As to be hopelessly outclassed in speed and maneuverability. Nonetheless, Al Sturtevant set out February 15 as second pilot in an old H-12 with a crew consisting of First Pilot Purys, engineer S. J. Holerdge, and wireless operator A. H. Stevensen. A second plane piloted by a South African named Faux accompanied them. The aircraft lifted off at dawn, flying ahead of a Dutch convoy. About halfway across the North Sea, at an altitude of 1,200 feet, with heavy clouds just overhead, a cluster of hostile fighters jumped them. Reports of the numbers vary. Captain Friedrich Christiansen out of Zeebrugge led the enemy squadron. One airplane, Faux's, broke off and turned back toward Felixstowe. The Germans attacked the other, chasing it southward toward the Belgian shore. Near Ostend the bullet-riddled flying boat burst into flames and fell into the sea and subsequent searches for the aircraft and men proved fruitless. The Germans later reported seeing the downed plane in rough water, with three men standing on the wings. Presumably they drowned. Sturtevant's death in combat quickly circulated among naval aviation circles, especially the Yale group of which he had been a prominent member.[23]

Despite danger and foul winter weather, combat operations continued. A group of three flying boats, including Ens. Nugent Fallon serving as second pilot in an H-12, successfully engaged five enemy seaplanes near North Hinder light March 12, shooting down two and killing the observer in a third. All personnel returned safely. One week later a long-distance patrol off the German coast came under attack by enemy warplanes. Ensign Stephen Potter, a member of the Second Yale Unit, downed one of them, the first naval aviator credited with an aerial victory. Potter's triumph proved short-lived, however. Acting as second pilot, he set out from Felixstowe on a two-plane patrol April 25, heading due east. Six miles southwest of North Hinder light ship, seven enemy fighters jumped Potter and his mates. The RAF flying boats huddled together for some time, until Potter's aircraft fell behind. The second flying boat slowed, allowing the gap to close. Potter's plane then turned to port, exposing itself broadside to two Germans immediately behind. Riddled with machine gun fire, the "Large America" burst into flames, descended, seemingly under control, and crashed on its port wing tip. The wreckage burned on the surface for a while and then slipped beneath the waves. Potter's body was never recovered. A final letter, written nine days before his fatal mission, predicted, "If you receive this you will know that I have done my duty the best of my ability. Be sure I am wonderfully glad that I could give up my life so usefully."[24]

Aircraft from Felixstowe and Great Yarmouth carried out a particularly dramatic sortie on June 18, a long-range reconnaissance along the Dutch coast. Ensign Kenneth Keyes participated in the action and later submitted a lengthy report to Admiral Sims. In fair weather, light winds, and a ceiling of 10,000 feet, three flying boats departed at noon, heading northeast to Yarmouth where they rendezvoused with two more warplanes. Royal Air Force Captain Leckie then assumed leadership of the formation. The squadron headed east and sighted the Haarks lightship around 2:30 P.M., about the same time they spotted a fleet of Dutch fishing smacks. Ten minutes later Keyes and his compatriots spied the Dutch coast, shifting direction to the northeast following the shoreline of Texel and Vlieland Islands, and then finally Terschelling Island. The squadron then headed west, but turned back when Leckie's aircraft made a forced landing with a broken gas feed line.

The situation changed dramatically when five German scouts appeared. Keyes's crew prepared for action, including Captain Barker, the pilot, and Lieutenant Galvayne, second pilot. Keyes occupied the forward cockpit with one machine gun and 400 rounds of ammunition. The British aircraft turned toward the enemy who soon veered away, with the allies in hot pursuit, struggling to protect the flying boat bobbing in the water. After a short pursuit Keyes's aircraft and the others turned back, only to be approached a second time by the enemy scouts. Again the Allies gave chase. This gambit unfolded two more times, but on the last maneuver Keyes spotted 10 additional enemy aircraft racing at wave-top level, soon joined by five more. The outnumbered flying boats closed up into battle formation and headed directly at the Germans. As soon as the aircraft came within range shooting broke out in all directions. As many as a dozen machines surrounded Keyes's plane and he described incessant firing, the air blue with tracer smoke. The American ensign worked his machine gun, firing at hostile planes on his port side at a distance of 200 yards. When he turned to look back toward the cockpit he noticed Galvayne slumped over, grievously wounded by a bullet in the head.

The fight continued, with Keyes's plane racing east, eventually cut off from the sheltering formation and surrounded by seven enemy scouts. They then turned toward the southwest and engaged in a running fight for 10 miles, finally driving the Germans away, only to discover the port engine misfiring and the gas line broken. Keyes removed Galvayne's body from the second pilot's chair, cleaned away some of the blood, and took the seat himself. At 5:45 P.M. Keyes's plane set down near Vlieland for a few minutes. When they took off they spotted two British planes, joined them, and laid course for Great Yarmouth, landing there shortly after 7:00 P.M. Galvayne lay dead, with the flying boat "more or less riddled" by gunfire. Of the remaining Felixstowe-based flying boats, one was last seen taxiing toward shore near Vlieland, while Ens. Joseph Eaton's boat landed in the water between Texel and Vlieland.[25]

Though Felixstowe acted as principal center of British flying boat activities and hosted the largest number of Americans, pilots served at many different stations in the winter and spring of 1918. With a major expansion of antisubmarine activities under way, the RNAS/RAF grew hard-pressed to allocate sufficient aircrews, and Navy assistance proved timely and beneficial. As early as Christmas 1917 a significant number of pilots were assigned to train in England, eventually totaling more than 80, distributed among a variety of stations, including Cattewater (Devon), Calshot (Isle of Wight), Dundee (Scotland), Fishguard (Wales), Killingholme (Yorkshire), Great Yarmouth (Norfolk), and Westgate (Kent), as well as a few at Portland and the Isle of Grain. Ensign John McNamara, still weeks shy of his 20th birthday, served for a time at RNAS Portland and on March 25 initiated the first attack by a Navy aviator on an enemy submarine. Admiral Sims later reported the strike as "apparently successful," and Secretary of the Navy Daniels commended McNamara for his "valiant and earnest efforts on this particular occasion." On the same day, Ens. Paul Ives also attacked a U-boat, but his bombs failed to explode.[26]

Joseph Eaton and George Compo were among seven Americans assigned to RNAS Cattewater. Located across the harbor from the ancient city of Plymouth, RNAS Cattewater housed 40 officers and 700 enlisted men, many of them trainees. Eaton and Compo began their tour of duty inauspiciously. After reaching a small rail station, the pair clamored aboard the only taxi available, an overworked Model T. With heavy rain beating on their heads and the hilly Devon countryside to traverse, they dismounted several times to push the car. Upon arrival, now fully drenched and spattered with mud, Eaton and Compo repaired to their new accommodations, small rooms measuring barely 6 feet × 9 feet and containing a single bed and chair, along with a washstand with china bowl and pitcher. Just then a valet walked in, "our man" as they called him, who quickly attended to their clothes and other personal needs.

The Americans reached Cattewater on February 8, soloed for the first time five days later, and continued to make practice flights almost every day thereafter. The station operated Short 184 seaplanes, powered by 12-cylinder Sunbeam motors with twin ignition systems for each side. The engine ran at 2,000 rpm, while four magnetos, set on a little shelf at the rear of the machinery turned over at 3,000 rpm. Out on patrol, the magnetos often broke apart and pieces flew back into the cockpit. Pilots prayed at least one of the two on each side worked because the plane could not fly on six cylinders. Eaton described the aircraft as very stable, "quite seaworthy when necessary," with a cruising radius of six hours, but the unsatisfactory motors greatly impaired the efficiency of this and other stations. He noted, "Forced landings accompanied by damage to the machines by towing, occur too often." The Americans joined the regular patrol roster on February 24 when Eaton made his first sortie, lasting 3.5 hours and cruising well out to sea. Compo carried out a convoy escort mission, accompanying 13 merchantmen and 7 small warships. The two-man Short crews navigated with charts, compasses, and watches, deriving wind speed and direction based on conditions at the time of takeoff. When not aloft on missions, they devoted much of their time to studying patrol methods, signals, and coding, and charting coastal regions.[27]

Far to the north on the Firth of Tay, about 10 miles north-west of St. Andrews, stood RNAS Dundee, a patrol station responsible for surveilling the broadest expanse of the North Sea. Renowned for its fierce weather, RNAS Dundee hosted several Yankee aviators in the winter and early spring of 1918, including Ens. Charles Fuller, a member of the Harvard group who trained at Hampton Roads in the summer of 1917. He described Dundee as "compactly arranged," with two hangars on the river Tay and plenty of taxiing room for aircraft after leaving the slips. Unlike hangars at American stations, Dundee's were constructed of corrugated iron lined with asbestos. Machines could be launched via the slipway or with a crane. In a March 5 report, Fuller offered detailed descriptions of the aircraft attached to the station. Flying machines included Short pontoon bombers and a few scouts. Bombs were stored in the hangar sheltering the ready machines, those slated to go out on patrol. A large parade ground in the center of the station provided space to conduct daily drill, while a tall iron fence and barbed wire separated the base from the city of Dundee.

Consistently bad Scottish weather permitted very little aerial activity, and the process of integrating American aviators into the official flight schedule progressed very slowly. By early March, no Navy flyer had yet been out on patrol, though Fuller expressed appreciation for the treatment the Yanks received. While the men secured some instruction in bomb sighting and wireless telegraphy, until the weather allowed real work (i.e., flying) Fuller believed such lessons had little value. Shortages of equipment, especially fur-lined flight suits, also restricted activity. In the week ending March 11, Americans at Dundee made just three flights. One was made by Ens. Russell Hyde, who piloted a Hamble "Baby," which suffered a broken propeller while taxiing into the slipway. Navy aviators discovered both the Hamble and Sopwith Scout to be unsatisfactory war machines, too light to be used in any but perfect weather. Their Clerget rotary motors proved so undependable "that a sea patrol [was] dangerous." With so few flying hours, Fuller and others spent their "free" time studying wireless and Aldis lamp signaling and working on motors. In fact, the Americans at Dundee carried out only limited flight activities, and in April, Aviation Aide Edwards requested that Fuller be assigned to headquarters. He arrived in London in May where he remained until the end of the war. Apparently he found his aviation duties unnerving and many years later his widow recalled, "It left him with a horror of aeroplanes for the rest of his life."[28]

RNAS Great Yarmouth, due east of Norwich on the North Sea coast, hosted at least seven Americans in 1918, including Ens. Donald "Doc" Alvord, a preenlistment graduate of the Curtiss schools at Buffalo and Newport News. He served there from February to June, when he requested a transfer to the nascent Northern Bombing Group. Headquarters sent him to Ireland instead. The large aviation complex at Great Yarmouth supported more than 100 aircraft. Like most aviators flying North Sea patrols, pilots encountered dreadful weather that often prevented offensive activity. Others fell victim to the harsh environment and temperamental equipment. Ensign George T. Roe flying an F2A on a long-range patrol in the Borkum area made a forced landing May 30, 1918, about one mile from the Dutch coast. His last message reported, "On the water, attacked by three Huns." German aircraft drove off an accompanying British plane. They captured Roe, a 25-year-old Boston native, along with other members of his flight crew, and held him at Landschut

POW camp for the duration of the war. Following the Armistice and repatriation he continued his career in naval aviation but died in a plane crash at NAS North Island in 1921. Other Americans at Great Yarmouth included Ens. Myron Hofer who supplied weekly reports to headquarters.[29]

In May and June the Navy detached most aviators piloting Short seaplanes at various coastal stations for further training at Felixstowe in "Large America" flying boats to ready them for assignment to Killingholme and elsewhere. In late June, Cone received word that the first group of eight had been ordered to Lough Foyle in northern Ireland. Nine others remained at Felixstowe, two of them acting as instructors. They expected to graduate by mid-July, moving on to either Killingholme or another Irish station.[30]

Beyond training pilots and enlisted personnel in everything from flying and bombing to gunnery, aerography, wireless telegraphy, and aerial photography, the British Admiralty and War Department hosted a steady stream of Navy visitors at their depots, stations, training establishments, and factories. These tours, carried out by a variety of specially trained officers, proved invaluable in keeping American aviation abreast of the latest developments in the field. Important visitors included Cdr. Henry Dinger, head of the Intelligence and Planning Division at Paris headquarters, Marine Capt. Bernard Smith, one of the Navy's top troubleshooters, and Lt. B. P. Donnelly, in charge of the Ordnance Section in Dinger's office. Donnelly's inspection, carried out in January 1918, included visits to more than a dozen sites, including RNAS stations at Calshot, Crystal Palace, Felixstowe, and Eastchurch, a supply depot at White City, the RFC flight school at Hythe, Enfield and Vickers armament factories, and Fairey Aeroplane Works in Middlesex. Befitting his position as head of the Ordnance Section, he focused his examination on recent developments in the fields of armament and tactics. Later that year Dinger and Smith spent two weeks touring British sites. Dinger departed England July 11 and crossed over to Dunkirk aboard a destroyer. A few days later he prepared a lengthy report for Cone summarizing his recent actions and presenting suggestions for future naval aviation activities around Europe and recommendations in specific areas. These included using dirigibles in coordination with submarine hunting units, employing listening devices in airships and seaplanes, amalgamation, and production of Handley Page bombers. That so much of his analysis represented either an extension of British programs or specific reactions to them (e.g., amalgamation controversy) speaks volumes about the importance of Anglo-American interaction in the field of naval aviation.[31]

Even before Hutch Cone reached Europe in September 1917, Admiralty officials planned an inspection trip for him, including stops at a seaplane school, their largest seaplane station, a dirigible and balloon facility, and experimental aircraft field. Following his tour, which lasted about a week, Cone announced that the United States desired to help and asked what could be done to assist. The Admiralty believed that operating air stations in Ireland and coordinating with activities of American destroyers already stationed there made the most sense. Further inspections then took place, out of which evolved the naval aviation program in Ireland. By contrast, creation of American stations in England received much lower priority. Ultimately, the Navy established just one operational base, Killingholme, on the northeastern coast near the North Sea, for the purpose of conducting long-range bombing raids against German targets.[32]

NAS Killingholme stood on the west bank of the Humber River, just above the estuary, and two miles below the small city of Hull, a virtually unknown site before the war noted only for its cold and mud. In 1912 the Royal Navy erected a large oil storage depot there and two years later the RFC established an adjacent flying field accommodating four aircraft. Killingholme also lay under the flight path of attacking zeppelins. By July 1916 an active RNAS station had been developed, at least in part to counter the airship threat. A few large hangars were built and in November 1916 Squadron Cdr. C. R. Finch-Noyes assumed control. At the time Killingholme supported a complement of approximately 200 men and an assortment of FBA, Sopwith Baby, and Short 184 aircraft, soon supplemented by Curtiss H-4 "Small America" and H-12 "Large America" flying boats. Operational drawbacks included the dangerous tide in the river, frequent high winds, and recurrent rain and fog. The following year the scope of operations expanded greatly to include antisubmarine patrols and flight instruction for seaplane pilots. Overall personnel increased to 900 officers and men, operating as many as 100 aircraft.[33]

The origins of NAS Killingholme traced back to the late summer of 1917 when Kenneth Whiting drafted a report for Sims discussing the possibility of a large-scale bombing campaign against German naval facilities like Heligoland and Wilhelmshaven. He said Allied forces might capture sites in Holland or Denmark for a base or, perhaps, convert 15 to 20 large (500-foot) vessels into seaplane ships, each carrying 30 planes. Chief of Naval Operations Benson, however, quickly ruled out the use of seaplane carriers. Nonetheless, the prospect of attacking the German fleet directly in its lair proved tempting to the American administration. In October the Admiralty proposed a plan to build a fleet of 80 lighters, to be towed by destroyers, which would carry large flying boats to within 50 miles of Cuxhaven, Kiel, or Wilhelmshaven. The aircraft would be offloaded at sea, attack their targets, and then fly home.

Such a lighter had already been suggested at Felixstowe. In late September 1916, Commander Porte broached the idea of a specialty craft and over time an ingenious design evolved. These would be substantial vessels, 58 feet in length, sufficient to carry flying boats weighing up to five tons. Constructed of steel, they would incorporate an airtight trimming tank in the stern that could be flooded by means of high-capacity pumps and emptied with compressed air. By lowering the stern, flying boats would be launched or retrieved through use of a trolley/cradle and winch. Aircraft would then take off from the water. The shape of the hull and a special bridle allowed destroyers to tow lighters at speeds up to 30 knots. The first sea trials occurred in June–September 1917 and met designers' expectations fully.[34] The Admiralty planned to build 50 craft capable of accommodating H-12, F2, F3, and F5-type flying boats. They asked the Navy to operate a complementary base supporting 30 additional lighters and 40 planes (both American built) on the east coast of England, with preparations to be completed March 15, 1918. The British suggested that the United States manufacture flying boats from F2A plans but incorporating new Liberty motors. They also agreed to hand over 15 hulls and 75 wing sets then under construction at the large Curtiss plant at Buffalo in upstate New York that could be used for testing and training. Discussion of the plan during a conference in October 1917 led Cone and Whiting to inspect RNAS Killingholme to assess its suitability for the project.

Nothing definite resulted at first, but when Benson visited London in November he approved the general plan and sent word to Washington to begin construction of necessary flying boats at once. His directives also led to large numbers of pilots in France and the United States being sent to British stations for training. When ready, the aviators, joined by a large contingent of enlisted personnel, would assume control at Killingholme. Such plans represented a decisive shift away from defensive activity along the Brittany and Bay of Biscay coasts to a more offensive strategy based in England and Flanders. Despite his general enthusiasm for schemes like this, Whiting compiled an extensive list of reasons he believed the plans to be unrealistic. Nonetheless, the Department selected him to head the American portion of the venture and soon ordered him back to the United States to hurry things along. Whiting quickly scheduled visits to the Admiralty and then Felixstowe to gather information before returning to Washington where he received assurances from Benson the project would receive top priority.[35]

Choosing and then manufacturing aircraft for the proposed station caused inevitable delays. One possibility, the proposed Curtiss H-16 flying boat, represented a much-improved version of the Curtiss H-12 or "Large America," then used at several English stations (in heavily modified form) as the F2A. Curtiss redesigned the H-16 to utilize new Liberty motors, to be manufactured at its Buffalo plant and the Naval Aircraft Factory then under construction in Philadelphia. It measured 46 feet in length, with a 96-foot wingspan. Two 400 hp Liberty motors provided power, generating a top speed of 95 mph. The plane remained aloft for four hours at maximum speed or up to nine hours at cruising speed. With an empty weight of 7,400 pounds and loaded weight of 10,900 pounds, the H-16 carried a crew of four, radio equipment, four or five machine guns, and two 230-pound depth bombs. Meanwhile, the British-designed F-5 flying boat, culmination of the Felixstowe series, offered a more capable alternative. During 1917, Porte's team redesigned the H-16 hull to better withstand rough waters of the North Sea and allow quicker takeoffs. Somewhat larger than the H-16, the F-5 was also much heavier. The plane possessed greater endurance than the H-16, carried more armament, and had twice the bomb load.

Ultimately, the Navy Department opted for the H-16, on which work was further advanced, fearing significant delays if the F-5 were adopted. Curtiss completed its first H-16s in mid-February and shipped them to Hampton Roads for evaluation. Early flights revealed many mechanical deficiencies. In fact, the initial example sank and needed to be refloated. Problems emerged with the tail, instrumentation, bombing equipment, fuel system, and machine gun mounts. A Naval Aircraft Factory version flew at Philadelphia March 27. The Navy decided to ship completed Curtiss products to Europe "as is," with necessary modifications done overseas. Naval Aircraft Factory versions incorporated requisite changes before being shipped. Work on the lighters also moved ahead. The Department dispatched orders for steel plate in December, with materials forwarded to the Hull Division at the New York Navy Yard in early January. Some shipments, however, encountered heavy rail congestion and the last steel did not arrive until mid-March. Government shipbuilding crews manufactured the vessels.[36]

Gathering up necessary personnel for the Killingholme initiative required careful coordination. A nucleus of pilots already served Europe, with many dispatched to British bases for further training and to gain war experience. Back in the United States intensive instruction commenced for additional pilots, radio operators, and engineers. Forty crews attended the RAF school at Forth Worth, Texas, in the winter of 1917–1918. Others trained at the Packard factory in Detroit (Liberty motors), Savage Arms Works (machine guns), Delco (radios), and the Philadelphia Navy Yard. Still others traveled to New

York to learn about the lighters. From Texas and elsewhere pilots moved on to Hampton Roads to study large flying boats.

Aviators began arriving in northern England during the winter. At the time Royal Navy veteran Cdr. F. W. Bowhill directed affairs at Killingholme. The first Navy pilot, Ens. Francis Allen, just turned 20, reached the station February 9. Others followed, and they quickly worked into the daily routine. An initial draft of 57 enlisted personnel sailed for England in late February, soon reinforced by 300 more. Ensign Harold Wilcox called the first group of ratings to reach Killingholme "a splendid crowd." Ensign William Peterson arrived about March 1 and took temporary command of the detachment, relieved in April by Lt. Carl Hull. He remained in charge until Whiting landed in late May. A March 30 Department report cited extensive preparations under way to receive personnel and material on their way. Special mechanics had been ordered up from Felixstowe to modify H-16s, and local contractors received instructions about the nature and quantity of food needed by the Americans. Work on additional slipways proceeded as well. Recent arrivals had a lot to say about their new home. Ensign Wilcox found the weather cold and damp, but enjoyed unlimited sugar and food, in contrast with conditions in London. The mess enjoyed tea at 5:00 P.M. and dinner at 7:30. Wilcox thought the station a "beautifully run organization," with lots of machines and mechanics and good discipline. He made special note of the 10 hangars, 2 slipways, and a 10-knot tide in the river, as well as the great variety of aircraft including H-12s, F2As, Shorts, Sopwith Schneiders and Pups, Hamble Babies, and Maurice Farmans.[37]

Pilots assigned to Killingholme began war service flying Short floatplanes, noted for their enormous wingspan and ungainliness while afloat. Ensign George Rumill, a 23-year-old native of Mt. Desert, Maine, made the first American patrol February 19. The growing size of the operation impressed many observers. Lieutenant Commander Kenneth McAlpin, recently appointed medical officer at the station, informed a friend, "This station (Killingholme) is a dandy, mighty glad to be here . . . size surprised me, you could take all we had in Virginia and at the old station (Palm Beach) in front of the buildings and then that again before you were as crowded as we used to be." Ensign George Lawrence sailed to Europe aboard *Baltic* and landed at Liverpool in early June. After "a long, dreary trip across England," he reached Killingholme. Lawrence seemed much impressed with the camouflage, searchlights, and general warlike look. It was "much bigger than we expected, well organized."[38]

From February to July, Killingholme pilots conducted 321 patrols and the Americans carried out 171 of them, accounting for 596 of 1,095 total flying hours. Daily activity typically included two to five Short patrols and one or two F2A missions. Short patrols generally covered 150 to 250 miles, while the longest F2A patrol in April tallied 334 miles over water. Submarine sightings were rare. On one of the spring missions Ensigns James Phelan, pilot, and Knight Owen, observer, underwent a harrowing ordeal. They departed the station May 14 at 5:35 A.M. in a Short seaplane in poor visibility and high wind, and after two hours made a forced landing out in the North Sea. Carrying neither water nor emergency rations (but they did have 30 cigarettes), they dispatched a pigeon message. Several times they tried to restart the motor, but without success. A flying boat from the station passed overhead but did not see them.

The following day the tail pontoon began leaking. Since the plane had a reputation for flipping over on its back and floating upside down, they abandoned the cockpit, crawled out on the wing, and attempted to head the machine toward land, hoping to utilize wind and current. They worked at this for four days with little success. Phelan and Owen tried to drink radiator water but found it too rusty. A thunderstorm on the afternoon of the fourth day provided some relief, but also carried away the rudder and caused them to be blown farther away from shore. Almost as quickly, the violence of the storm gave way to dead calm, sun and heat, and great thirst. On the morning of the sixth day the beleaguered crew spotted a vessel in the distance, the British destroyer *Retriever*, which they attracted with Very lights. At the time of rescue they were 90 miles out at sea and had drifted 180 miles. The station log observed, "It was considered nothing short of miraculous that they had survived. If the sea had been at all rough during any of the five days they drifted the Short floatplane would undoubtedly been smashed and the men would have disappeared without a trace." The men received two weeks' leave to recuperate.[39]

A few days later Ens. George Shaw and observer Schuyler Page also cheated death in one of the station's Shorts. They set off at 2:35 P.M. into a 27-knot wind and high seas, quickly losing sight of land. They first headed north, and then west, striking land at 4:15 P.M., but farther north than expected. They changed course, flying into the wind, but made little progress. Off Flamborough Head their balky motor lost power, forcing them to land in 5-foot to 7-foot waves. Rough seas might have smashed the aircraft, but a nearby lighthouse keeper spotted them and called a patrol boat. Still, it was a close thing. Within 15 minutes their floatplane's fuselage broke off aft of the rear seat and they were within moments of sinking. Five patrol boats gathered around the stricken airmen and carried them to safety, but proved unable to retrieve the aircraft.[40]

In addition to work with Short floatplanes, Americans also began carrying out varied missions in British H-12 and F2A flying boats. An F Boat piloted by RAF Lieutenant Robinson and Ensign George Hodges (second pilot) departed May 30 at 8:30 A.M. with orders to drive back a zeppelin cruising over the North Sea. They sighted the enemy airship at 11:20 and started climbing. The Germans spotted the approaching aircraft at an altitude of 2,000 feet and proceeded to drop 15 bombs to aid its own climb and perhaps hit the flying boat. By 12:00 Robinson and Hodges had ascended to 7,500 feet but the zeppelin climbed faster and floated 4,000 feet above its pursuers. In frustration the allies opened fire with their two forward machine guns, but the range proved too great, the guns jammed, and they broke off pursuit and returned to Killingholme at 3:30 in the afternoon after a flight of seven hours. During the same month more than 20 pilots flew missions from the station, the number increasing to approximately 30 as the Navy readied to assume control. These flights included both short test hops and training exercises and lengthy patrols lasting up to 7 hours, as many as 175 hours per week. About a half-dozen planes were available for war work, with an average of three utilized on a daily basis.[41]

While Americans flying over the North Sea battled weather and the Germans, back in the United States Whiting labored in the Office of Naval Operations. After numerous delays producing/testing/shipping planes and lighters, enough supplies and miscellaneous gear were amassed to begin operations. Whiting and a mountain of equipment, including 23 crated H-16s and 8 lighters, along with 8 officers and 150 men, departed for Europe May 18 aboard *Jason*. Three destroyers accompanied the ship on its voyage. During the last 40-mile leg of the trip into the Humber, an H-12 "Large America" flown by Lieutenant Hull and Ens. Ashton "Tex" Hawkins convoyed Whiting and his critical cargo, the first All-American flying boat patrol from the station. *Jason* reached the Immingham Docks May 30. Transporting the enormous airplane crates to the new station via narrow gauge railroad required that all signal posts and lines be moved.[42]

Whiting's arrival initiated a month-long transition to Navy control, but not without some confusion. No flights or squadrons existed yet, with only eight Navy pilots trained for big boat flying, and just five with real experience. Ensign Lawrence noticed that though the Royal Navy remained in charge, Americans reported to Whiting, which led to considerable friction. The Yanks did not like taking orders from the British and vice versa. It also proved difficult to get bluejackets to follow advice from their hosts, what Lawrence called "too much of a know-it-all attitude." He admitted that the British were excellent workmen and certainly knew their jobs but wasted much time at afternoon tea and other extracurricular activity.[43]

After two weeks of the Whiting touch the situation started looking different. Flyer John Schieffelin later remarked, "It was great to be under his hand, and I mean *great!*" With experienced aviators LCdr. Bruce G. Leighton serving as executive officer and Tom Murphy as squadron commander, things began running smoothly. Initially, Whiting arranged the American force into two divisions. The Flight Division consisted of two squadrons, further organized into flights, with a beach gang to handle machines, an armorers gang, a machine shop gang, a carpenters gang, and a boat gang to run the launches. Squadrons contained four flights, each with a flight commander, and five planes. Every machine carried a four-man crew—pilot, second pilot/observer, engineer, and radio operator, and each flight incorporated a spare engineer, wing men, and general workers. Whiting also created intelligence and photo departments, meteorological bureau, and radio and electric units. The other division consisted of guards, mess cooks, attendants, yeoman, general stores, transportation, and medical departments, and a large construction gang of 600 men. The Navy took over operations July 1 and assumed formal control July 20. Many Americans looked back fondly on their service with the British and Bowhill's leadership, later writing, "In spite of our joy at serving again under the 'Stars and Stripes,' it was with a feeling of great regret that we saw Commander Bowhill depart."[44]

By that time NAS Killingholme had grown to enormous proportions. The Navy complement counted 67 officers and 902 enlisted men and the station extended across 135 acres of low-lying riverside ground. Eight hangars had been built, including the gigantic #6, a 10-bay structure that was 800 feet in length and 220 feet deep and covered nearly four acres. The concrete apron blanketed 10 acres of the shoreline. Two 800-foot slipways constructed of stout planks and piles driven into the riverbed carried aircraft from the concrete apron, across the wide Humber mud flats, and down to the water. A city of brick and frame huts stood at the southern edge of the station, replacing a vast assemblage of cold, damp tents. The very rough, swampy flying field, only partially usable, and definitely not at night, lay well back from the river, reflecting Killingholme's origins as an RFC aerodrome.[45]

An American crew assembled the first H-16 in early July, but a test flight revealed defective propellers and radiators, delaying the next ascent for three weeks. During the initial H-16 patrol mounted July 28, a propeller cracked and both radiators leaked, postponing any further missions until new propellers arrived in mid-August. Radiator problems continued to plague operations and available equipment proved completely unsuitable, causing many forced landings at sea. One pilot noted, "The H-16s flew faster, climbed faster, and broke down a lot sooner than did the British flying boats." This led to instructions (temporary) forbidding H-16 crews to fly beyond sight of land. Numerous mechanical problems undoubtedly resulted from hurried production and inadequate testing in the United States caused by the rush to put the Killingholme plan into operation. Because American-built H-16s proved unreliable, Whiting arranged with the British to retain six 320 hp Shorts and nine F2As, the former for coastal patrol work and the latter for long-range reconnaissance. Some sense of equipment woes facing air stations in World War I can be gleaned from a "Daily Return of Machines and Engines" compiled August 18. All aircraft listed had been obtained from the British; none of the H-16s brought by Whiting were yet ready for service. Only 7 of 22 machines were rated fit for flying.[46]

Compounding equipment issues, the need to train pilots consumed many man-hours that might otherwise have been devoted to patrol duties. In the beginning there were very few pilots with significant experience flying large aircraft. Until more pilots arrived from Hampton Roads, a few Felixstowe veterans did most of the flying. Lieutenant Farrell, the gunnery officer, established a machine gun school, with practice every day. Men also received lessons in use of bombsights and the bombs themselves, as well as lectures on aerial navigation, radio, and signal practices. The most important learning came at sea. Semi-experienced pilots often combined training and war work, practicing landings while flying up and down the river, to and from patrol.

War work encompassed several categories, including convoy escort, submarine search, long-distance reconnaissance, special patrols against attacking planes/craft, and patrols over the North Sea mine barrage. The daily flight duty officer stood a 24-hour watch over the "beach" and hangars, with an officer under him in charge of the gang responsible for getting flying boats "overside," a big job requiring 20–30 men for each machine. The flight duty officer received orders for the next day's missions from the squadron commander the night before. He turned out flight crew and beach personnel in the predawn hours, gave pilots their instructions, and then saw flights away safely and on time. During the day he directed all operations on the beach and in the hangars and rounded up additional pilots/crews for emergency patrols. Morning flights usually got away at daybreak and lasted five to eight hours. Often, aircraft went out singly to a point 60–70 miles off the coast and stalked the spider web, hoping to catch a submarine on the surface. Killingholme also maintained an alert section, two boat crews near an airplane at all times, prepared to be in the air within 15 minutes.

Successfully mounting daily missions posed a complex challenge, dependent on smooth coordination of many men and departments. The confused events of September 12 illustrate how difficult it could be to make everything mesh. Night orders had been issued at 7:00 P.M. the previous evening and the Flight Duty Officer received the following day's orders about 9:30 P.M. Instructions were left at the guard house to call the chief of the boat crews at 4:30 A.M., but he was actually summoned at 3:45. A call to the coxswain of the boat crews also scheduled for 4:30 actually went out at 3:15. The bosun in charge of the first section of the beach handling detail received his wake-up call at 4:05 rather than 3:45. The bosun leading the second section was not called at all. When a much-perturbed executive officer, Bruce Leighton, reached "the beach" at 4:50 he found two H-16s and a Short in proper position. Further orders had been left for the pilot of the first plane, Ens. Theodore Grosvenor, to be called at 4:00, but by 5:00 he had not appeared and the Flight Duty Officer found him having breakfast. The chastened pilot reached the hangars at 5:20, got into his gear, and then discovered the pigeons carried on each mission had been placed in the wrong aircraft. Grosvenor's H-16 finally left the slipway a little before 6:00 A.M. Leighton felt the aircraft should have launched at least a half hour earlier and blamed the delay on the pilot.

Similarly, the first Short did not depart until 6:00 A.M., something Leighton again blamed on the pilot, Ens. Malcolm Stevenson. The flyer arrived on the beach at 5:15 with the plane in position and the motor running, but when he went to get his gear he did not have the correct key for his locker. Difficulties multiplied because just one section of the beach gang had been called and the slow departure of the first H-16 blocked the only usable slipway. A second H-16 scheduled to leave at 6:15 A.M. (Ens. Kenneth Hodges) also faced delays because the armorers had not loaded emergency rations and other gear, and the storeroom was locked. Ensign Ellis Butchart assigned to cover the intelligence office did not show up, later explaining he had not been called. Leighton noted this was the third time such a thing had happened. When a standby H-16 was readied, Leighton discovered the first pilot, Ens. Knight Owen, had "gone ashore," left the station without permission. Yet even with these delays, the station carried out its full range of missions that day. Grosvenor's H-16 performed convoy duty in poor visibility and low clouds, traveling 350 miles. Stevenson's Short also carried out convoy duty but made a forced landing at sea with engine trouble and required a tow back to base. The second H-16 piloted by Hodges completed a 425-mile convoy mission. The second Short failed to take off due to engine trouble, but a replacement fulfilled its assignment. Finally, the reserve H-16, with pilot Owen now located, conducted a special submarine patrol over a distance of 300 miles.[47]

Despite shortages of serviceable aircraft and trained pilots, the summer of 1918 proved particularly busy at Killingholme, with numerous submarine sightings, a dozen attacks, and several encounters with marauding zeppelins. Aircraft occasionally caught U-boats on the surface but more often spotted them by their wakes and leaking oil patches. Intelligence officers covered their war charts with the presumed tracks of enemy vessels. On July 9 an H-12 flown by John Schlieffelin, with Ens. John Staub serving as second pilot, sighted an oil patch. They circled overhead, dropped two bombs, then signaled nearby destroyers with Very lights. British convoy escorts dropped depth charges causing air bubbles to appear and the oil patch to spread widely. The Admiralty classified the attack as having "probably seriously damaged" the submarine. Ten days later Schlieffelin and second pilot Ens. Roger Cutler went out again. Whiting briefed them personally, using a large blackboard marked with red chalk. Setting out an hour before dawn, Schieffelin and his crew roared off in their flat-bottomed H-12 through a stiff northeast gale. While 25 miles northeast of Whitby he a spotted a U-boat and the submarine made an emergency dive; Schlieffelin's bomb exploded nearby just as the conning tower slipped beneath the waves. The vessel nosed down quickly, the screws almost breaking the surface, but just as quickly disappeared. Later that day the same U-boat attacked a convoy, until forced to the surface by depth charging, whereupon a destroyer rammed and sank the submarine. Sims later recommended Schlieffelin be awarded the Distinguished Service Medal for these exploits, saying, "This officer was at all times an example of courageous loyalty."[48]

"Tex" Hawkins offered an interesting analysis of antisubmarine operations in this period. He claimed that British aircraft patrolled constantly with the idea of forcing U-boats to stay submerged. Under this scenario sighting and attacking a submarine became simply a matter of luck. Hawkins called such work drudgery, causing a loss of efficiency and enthusiasm. He described the Navy policy as trying to surprise U-boats in a specific area, a strategy pursued by Whiting, an old sub commander, who put himself in the place of the enemy captain and tried to outwit him. He tracked each vessel the Intelligence Division identified, studied shipping channels and water depths, and then sent patrols out hunting in the targeted sector.[49]

But even with the best intelligence and tactics, pursuing submarines often proved fruitless. Mist, clouds, rough water, and a host of other factors made identifying stealthy enemy vessels extremely difficult. George Lawrence and George Hodges flying an F2A on July 13 "sighted" a submarine wake and bombed it, causing oil spots and air bubbles to rise to the surface. They directed destroyers to the area who continued the attack with depth charges. A few days later, however, the Admiralty determined, "It is doubtful whether a submarine was in the vicinity at the time." The following month three H-16s launched at 8:35 A.M. (McNamara), 11:50 A.M. (Ives), and 4:00 P.M. (Hawkins) all attacked a suspected submarine. In each case it turned out to be "a sunken ship . . . an uncharted wreck which looked like a submerged submarine from the air." In early November the British sent a communication to Killingholme listing the location of all known wrecks, in part to prevent such mistaken attacks. In similar fashion, on September 21 pilots Paul Ives and George Compo chased a disguised enemy "cruiser" for five hours, not returning to base until 10:35 P.M. It was actually a British merchant ship.[50]

Zeppelin hunting offered a dramatic break from monotonous antisubmarine patrols. German airships patrolled Dogger Bank that summer and Whiting wanted a crack at them. "Tex" Hawkins, with previous night-flying experience, and second pilot George Lawrence embarked on their momentous, though fruitless, overnight mission August 5. Whiting also ordered three planes out August 10, but only one managed to lift off, an F2A piloted by RAF Capt. T. C. Pattinson and George Lawrence, which departed at 1:25 P.M. Three hours later while 50 miles off the Dutch coast they climbed through clouds at 6,000 feet and spotted a zeppelin perhaps 20 miles away. They raced toward the airship through the top layer of clouds and eventually emerged two to three miles away, just beneath it. They then dove back toward the clouds seeking cover, but the Germans must have seen them for the zeppelin began a rapid ascent, quickly shooting upward to 9,000 feet. Realizing further pursuit would be fruitless and having reached their fuel limit, Pattinson and Lawrence dropped down to sea level and headed home.

By then they had entered the enemy's Borkum patrol area, 50 miles from Heligoland, near the mouth of the Elbe River. As they skimmed over a fleet of Dutch luggers on Dogger Bank with German craft hidden among them, a lively fusillade of pom-pom fire erupted. The flying boat returned fire, with neither side suffering any damage. Racing on through a light mist they came upon a British light cruiser but did not make the proper signal in time and drew fire again. The flying boat, at that point just 10 feet above the water, finally identified itself by raising its wings to display its markings. They flew three more hours and sighted the coast 30 miles from the mouth of the Humber. Now cruising along peacefully, they were startled when a 'zeppelin' loomed into view just ahead. It fact, it was a British airship. As they approached to get a better look they determined it was either the R-33 or R-34. Pattinson landed at 9:30 P.M. by means of flares after a dramatic patrol lasting almost 10 hours and covering over 500 miles. Later that evening a frantic fire call jolted the station from its sleep. Two machines were ablaze in the central hangar. Mechanics had filled the aircraft with gas, and armorers were inspecting it with lighted lanterns. This ignited vapors that settled in the hull bottom. Frantically working to save the entire complex, crewmen attached ropes to the aircraft and pulled them out of the hangar. One burning plane, an H-16 readied for early morning patrol, was armed with machine gun ammunition and two 230-pound bombs. A member of the armament crew realized the danger, ran in to the plane and pulled a release wire, dropping the enormous bomb on his shoulder. He carried it out through the fire and then went back for the other, suffering severe burns in the process. Pilot Lawrence called it "one of the bravest things I have ever seen."[51]

Apart from war patrols and zeppelin hunts, Killingholme personnel spent much of August and September readying balky H-16s for service, with only partial success. Instead, the station used F2As with Rolls Royce power plants for all long flights. More than one aviator praised the "ever reliable Rolls Royce motors." Navy pilots liked the F2As and some of those obtained from the British were of the most recent type. Even after H-16s began patrol work, F2As performed all long reconnaissance missions, anything more than 50 miles at sea. Eventually they wore out or crashed and only three remained operable in October, carefully reserved for emergencies. Working the bugs out of the H-16s, especially their motors, took time. Many aircraft crashed or suffered damages inflicted by pickup boats, slipway mishaps, the fast tide, or fire. George Lawrence called the design and construction of Liberty motors excellent, but the accessories awful, with 100 little annoyances and some major problems. Radiators "practically fell to pieces" on flights more than 30 miles long. They had faulty oiling systems and soft cranking gears that sheared off easily.

According to George Lawrence, H-16 boats arriving from the United States were totally unfit for war service and had to be practically rebuilt inside, including shifting fuel tanks, constructing gun mounts, installing bomb gear, and adjusting controls. Nearly every machine exhibited a curious twist that made it tail heavy and wing heavy, imparting a tendency to turn left. Crews worked on this problem for months but never fully corrected it. Well into

September only a half-dozen planes were operable. New radiators did not arrive until October 1 and were not installed on all planes for two weeks. At the peak of activity in October the average number in service rose to 15. Flight mishaps continued to plague operations. An early morning patrol mounted October 11, with Ens. Stanley Curran in command, departed at 6:15 A.M. About fifteen minutes later one of the motors stopped and Curran lost control of the machine, which went into a fatal spin and crashed into the river near Immingham. Curran managed to reach the surface where a Royal Navy picket boat rescued him. The impact threw second pilot Charles Tyson from the wreck and his body could not be recovered. Trapped in the wreckage, engineer Bennet Sergai and radio operator Robert Richardson drowned.[52]

Despite all these setbacks, progress was made. The number of war flights increased from 25 in August to 36 in September and 46 in October, while the frequency of emergency landings at sea diminished, decreasing from 11 in September to just 6 in October. On several days in October, H-16s carried out all or nearly all daily missions. Special reconnaissance flights often ventured successfully 225 miles out to sea. During the autumn, aircraft and crews averaged over 100 hours of flying per week, and sometimes exceeded 200 hours. In fact, they compiled the highest number of hours and escorted the most ships (6,000+) of any station in England. Toward the end of the war, American pilots provided protection for British minelayers based at Immingham, just down river from Killingholme. They might have accomplished even more but for severe weather in September when hardly a day passed without rain, fog, and high winds. On October 20 while on convoy escort duty, aircraft piloted by Harold Wilcox and Benjamin "Benny" Lee missed each other by only 50 feet in the mist. When Ens. Raymond Atwood ferried Lt. Harry Guggenheim up to Whitby in mid-October the wind registered 53 knots. Ironically, fog and rain constituted the best weather for U-boat hunting and the worst for flying.[53]

Admiral Mayo and his staff visited October 2, part of his grand inspection tour. He described operations as well planned and executed. The intelligence section had shown itself to be particularly efficient. Killingholme's location for antisubmarine work seemed excellent. Mayo found living quarters and mess halls untidy, something only partly accountable to muddy conditions. He called the personnel adequate and competent, but generally "green." Aircraft material received thus far had proven unsatisfactory, particularly radiators and propellers. Flying boats exhibited weak bottoms, weak covering on the tails, improperly designed steps, and shortages of instruments, lights, radio apparatus, the latest bombsights, and engine spare parts.[54]

And what of the great lighter project, original justification for the entire effort at Killingholme? Toward the end of February 1918, naval forces from Harwich mounted an exercise in the North Sea. Destroyers towed lighters into position. Rough water and high winds caused crews to spread oil on the water to calm the waves. The first airplane slipped easily into the water but buried its nose, and oil soon covered the windscreen, pilots' goggles, and compass. The plane then attempted to take off with no visibility, bouncing 14 times before becoming airborne. The flight crew assumed they would attack Germany, but sealed orders sent the formation back to the coast 40 miles from Felixstowe, then home. It turned out to be just a practice route along the spider web. The first actual sortie occurred on March 19, a mission near the enemy coast, which resulted in the downing of an attacking seaplane.[55]

Several other operations involving American aviators followed. On the morning of May 17 crews at Felixstowe placed three F2As aboard their lighters. Personnel boarded at 3 P.M., and an hour later destroyers commenced towing the craft northeastward toward Denmark, slicing through the night at 20–25 knots. At 4:40 the following morning, crews "sank" the lighters and launched flying boats in smooth seas and light breezes. RAF Captain Clayton and Lieutenant Pattinson piloted the first machine. U. S. Navy aviators Ashton Hawkins and Joseph Eaton commanded the second, while John Schlieffelin and "Benny" Lee took charge of the third. Once airborne, they chased a zeppelin for 20 minutes but soon headed to Blaavand Point, then turned southward toward Haaks light off the Dutch coast, thence across the North Sea to Great Yarmouth and Felixstowe, returning at 12:35 P.M., having flown 475 miles in 7.5 hours. Though the allies encountered no enemy aircraft or experienced any mechanical difficulties, the problem of wind drift presented a major challenge. Five days later a flight of three aircraft returning to Felixstowe fetched up at Killingholme instead due to changing winds.[56]

Work continued throughout the spring and summer, but with little to show for it. In one exercise in late June, three Felixstowe F2As were winched aboard lighters at 4 P.M. to carry out maneuvers with the fleet. At 2 A.M. the flying boats slid into the water and started their motors. Sea conditions seemed favorable, with no choppiness and little wind. A long swell, however, made takeoff difficult, causing serious damage to one craft and total loss of a second. The third plane, piloted by Ens. John McNamara, left the water at 3:25 A.M., circled, and proceeded on alone, searching for British coastal motorboats. He found them 30 minutes later and guided the small craft back to the fleet. Further orders directed McNamara to return to base, but one-half hour later while circling a drifter his inside motor seized and the aircraft sideslipped badly, crashing while making a stall landing. The F2A sank quickly to the upper wing. Ten minutes later a whaleboat from the drifter picked up the crew and the skipper rammed the plane three times attempting to sink it. A destroyer also rammed the wreck, finally sinking it.[57]

Even with some limited success, by July the British decided to terminate the lighter-bombing initiative, and in early August Sims notified Cone of their intentions. "Operations with towing lighters," he noted, "have not proved very satisfactory." Weather conditions could not be forecast accurately, resulting in three or four failures for every successful action. Antiaircraft defenses had improved considerably, and flying boats were vulnerable to attack. By contrast, land-based bombers, capable of self-defense, had been developed for either day or night action. "Accordingly," he reported, "the Admiralty do not now contemplate long distance bombing operations in any large scale with seaplanes from towed lighters" and had diverted some of their equipment from Felixstowe to northern bases to act as temporary accommodations for "Large Americas" used for reconnaissance and attacks on enemy mine sweepers and light forces. The American commander suggested Killingholme's lighters be retained for that purpose and personnel trained accordingly. A few days later Edwards told Cone, "I believe that conditions have so altered in the North Sea since the time the Killingholme project was conceived that there is absolutely no use attempting to operate lighters in that area." He concluded, "I cannot see any possible chance of our utilizing seaplanes or flying boats for this purpose."[58] Nonetheless, sporadic experiments at Killingholme continued. But as the weeks passed, the likelihood of attacking Kiel in 1918 grew more remote. As late as October some proposed putting the original bombing plan into action, but bad weather and rough seas made experiments impossible. Planes would have been wrecked on takeoff. Efforts to secure scarce American destroyers for these experiments also failed. Nonetheless, NAS Killingholme planners kept trying and might have attempted a raid had not the Armistice intervened.

Just before the war ended rumors swept through the Navy that Germany might attempt some sort of last-ditch action, such as making a mass attack with the High Seas Fleet or unleashing a final spasm of U-boat assaults. Accordingly, headquarters strengthened aviation activities in the North Sea. Operating under the direction of No. 18 Group, RAF, Killingholme received numerous directives regarding possible operations. In late October, Whiting learned that the station might be called upon to conduct reconnaissance missions and he should hold aircraft ready. Ten days later came word Killingholme should mount at least two flights per week, three machines per flight, to extend as far as South Dogger Bank light ship. The station should also hold a flight of three flying boats ready to carry out whatever special work the Admiralty required. As late as November 7 planners contemplated increasing activities over the North Sea, adding new bombers, conducting additional patrols, and dispatching more flying boats to Dundee.[59]

As part of the defensive buildup, the Navy diverted pilots from the Northern Bombing Group and coastal stations in France to northern England. In late October, headquarters also ordered several F2A's from Killingholme detached for service at RAF Dundee. Three aircraft, piloted by Lt.(jg) Paul Ives and Ensigns Ashton Hawkins and "Benny" Lee, departed mid-morning October 28. The first to lift off, piloted by 24-year-old Lee, circled overhead waiting for the others but soon fell off on the port wing into a right-handed spin, recovered slightly, and at 12:45 P.M. crashed into the river at high speed, erupting into flames. Small vessels raced to the wreck. Both Ives and Hawkins quickly landed their aircraft and taxied toward the downed plane. At the crash site radio operator Harris survived the fall, grabbed unconscious engineer Raymond Fisher, and placed his body across some wreckage, then headed toward second pilot Ens. Joshua Garrison.

As Harris turned back toward Fisher, floating debris sank and the engineer disappeared. Meanwhile, second pilots Lt.(jg) Richard McCann and Ens. George Hodges from the would-be rescue aircraft, stripped off their gear and jumped into the water. McCann "made a long dive and came up among the wreckage which was blazing slightly. . . . Just at this moment the whole area burst suddenly into flame." He searched for Lee and Fisher, making repeated dives into the wreckage. Hodges also dived from his flying boat and swam under the burning machine, emerging in a pool of flaming gasoline. He located Garrison and carried him to the rescue boat, keeping the injured man underwater intermittently and protecting him with his own body, thus sustaining severe burns himself. According to Ives, "To his (Hodges) promptness and presence of mind and absolute disregard to himself Ens. Garrison unquestionably owes his life." Garrison's injuries proved severe and caused partial paralysis of his legs. Harris survived with only a slight bruise on his face to mark the ordeal. Lee's body was never recovered. The very next day the Navy remounted the mission, dispatching three aircraft northward toward Dundee. They departed about noon, with the air thick and bumpy. John Schieffelin's plane made a forced landing at South Shields. Harold Wilcox "got lost back of Holy Island; landed at Whitby to remove pigeon," and finally arrived in fog at

Dundee at about 4:00 p.m. On November 1 the Americans departed the Firth of Tay, circled over the assembled warships, and dipped their wings, before heading back south.[60]

During this period of heightened tension Navy aircraft conducted several long-range flights. An eight-hour patrol October 30 commanded by Kenneth Hodges flew 200 miles offshore in a 35-knot wind, and still had 1.5 hours of gasoline left at the end. A second mission that day, a nine-hour convoy exercise flown by Lt. Stanley Kennedy, carried a full military load and 280 gallons of gasoline. When the excitement of late October ebbed away, however, many looked with resignation at the prospect of spending a miserable winter on the coast. Then, suddenly, it was over. The entire station complement, marching to airs played by the Killingholme band, assembled in front of the hangars to hear notice of the Armistice read and soon most personnel headed home. Within 10 days 1,000 ratings and 60 officers, led by Commander Leighton, returned to the United States aboard *Leviathan*. The flag was taken down January 6, 1919, and remaining officers and men departed a few days later.[61]

Though NAS Killingholme never carried out the great lighter project, it still compiled a substantial war record. At the time of the Armistice the contingent included 91 officers and 1,324 enlisted men, the largest naval air station in Europe. More than 60 officer-pilots served there, the most at any American facility. Whiting heaped particular praise on Bruce Leighton, his executive officer, who did "did practically all of the work of organizing the station, conducted all of the practical part of starting operations, assisted in the assembling and training of the personnel, and the assembly of material in the United States." Whiting also singled out pilots Rumill and Ives for their extraordinary contributions and the work of Intelligence Officer Dennis. The final scorecard tallied 233 patrols, 968 flying hours, and 57,647 miles of sea patrol. Aircraft convoyed 6,243 ships, experienced 35 forced landings at sea, and recorded 10 attacks on enemy submarines, 4 with "results." Two officers and seven enlisted men died in accidents.

Today the shoreside site throbs with maritime activity. Oceangoing ferries and automobile transport vessels dock here regularly. The former hangar apron has been repaved and is covered with cars and trucks awaiting shipment. None of the station structures survive, however, and work crews demolished the old brick-lined, Royal Navy oil storage tanks only a few years ago. No markers identify the site's historical importance. A walk along the riverbank, however, soon reveals the substantial sloping remains of a derelict aircraft launching ramp, extending far out into the muddy water of the Humber. Several hundred feet further on can be found a few eroded stubs of the pilings that once supported a second ramp.

* * *

By any measure the Americans and their British allies crafted a fruitful relationship in the realm of naval aviation. Royal Flying Corps and RNAS schools trained scores of pilots and observers when the need for such instruction was greatest. These aviators went on to perform vital service at many Navy facilities. The British also provided vast quantities of data, technological cooperation, and operational guidance. In many ways the Navy's aviation arm patterned itself on that of its British hosts. In return, the United States provided sorely needed personnel to their ally during the winter and spring of 1918. At Killingholme the Navy established its largest station, working in coordination with the Royal Navy and Royal Air Force in their efforts to combat the German fleet on the watery front lines of the North Sea.

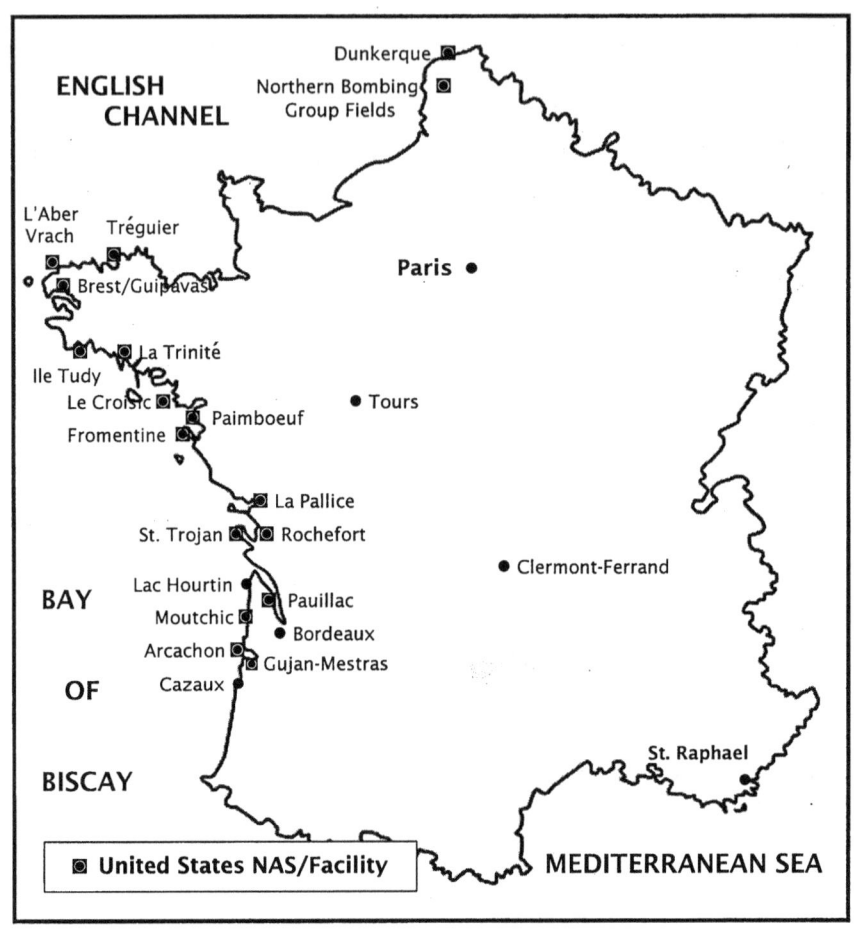

Map 1. United States Naval Aviation Stations/Facilities: France

Map 2. United States Naval Aviation Stations/Facilities: Great Britain

Map 3. United States Naval Aviation Stations/Facilities: Italy

Figure 1. Part of the First Aeronautic Detachment, ready to depart on their long journey from Florida to France in May 1918. Most of the men in this group had been in the Navy for less than six weeks. Courtesy of National Archives.

Figure 2. A portion of the First Aeronautic Detachment posing in front of their barracks at Tours in France in the summer of 1917. Courtesy of National Archives.

Figure 3. LCdr. John "Lanny" Callan, first commanding officer at Moutchic, was one of the Navy's most important "advance men." He stands here beneath the dense pines that covered the Moutchic site and had to be felled by hand before construction could begin. Courtesy of John Callan Collection, Naval History and Heritage Command.

Figure 4. Bluejackets hauling a Franco-British Aviation (FBA) training aircraft along "the beach" at Moutchic in October 1917. Pilots found the FBA to be a cranky, dangerous machine. Courtesy of John Callan Collection, Naval History and Heritage Command.

Figure 5. "Main Street" at Moutchic in 1918. At its height the school accommodated more than 500 officers and enlisted men. The range of buildings on the right survives to this day, though in derelict condition. Courtesy of National Archives.

Figure 6. Captain Hutch I. Cone, known to his close friends as "Reddy," was the commander of naval aviation in Europe in World War I; from a c. 1912 photograph. Courtesy of Naval History and Heritage Command.

Figure 7. Launching a Hanriot-Dupont scout over the side at Dunkirk, 1918. The congested harbor was a major factor in several fatal accidents. Courtesy of Naval History and Heritage Command.

Figure 8. The officers at NAS Dunkirk and their Allied guests. Dr. Albert Stevens is kneeling center. Lt. Artemus "Di" Gates of the First Yale Unit is standing, third from the right. Ens. Eddie DeCernea of the Second Yale Unit stands second from the right. Courtesy of National Archives.

Figure 9. Aircraft lined up at the assembly and repair facility at NAS Brest in October 1918. The facility was just getting up to speed at this time. An HS-2L flying boat is positioned in the foreground. Courtesy of National Archives

Figure 10. A 1918 view of NAS Le Croisic, the first American patrol base placed in operation, taken from the nearby shore. The small hut in the foreground was used to store detonators. Courtesy of Naval History and Heritage Command.

Figure 11. These huge double hangars and the wooden launching slip at NAS Arcachon give some sense of the scale of construction necessary to implement the Navy's antisubmarine campaign. Virtually all work was done by hand. Courtesy of National Archives.

Figure 12. The pigeon lofts at NAS Arcachon. Each patrol station kept a flock of carrier pigeons that often carried important messages from flyers downed at sea. Courtesy of National Archives.

Figure 13. The barren island of L'Aber Vrach and the Navy tent village that sprang up in the spring of 1918 during the early construction period at this station. After the war the island returned to its earlier desolate state. Courtesy of National Archives.

Figure 14. Launching an HS-1L flying boat from NAS L'Aber Vrach, November 1918. Movie footage shot by the Army Signal Corps shows the crew riding the launching truck down the ramp like a kid's wagon. Courtesy of National Archives.

Figure 15. Ensigns Waters and Dillon aloft in an HS-1L flying boat at NAS Tréguier in the autumn of 1918. The station was operational for only a few weeks. Courtesy of Naval History and Heritage Command.

Figure 16. The wreckage of pilot Joseph Cline's Tellier flying boat at NAS Le Croisic. While Cline was taxiing to takeoff on March 4, 1918, a bomb fell loose and exploded, breaking the aircraft in half. Miraculously, both pilot and observer escaped without serious injury. Courtesy of Naval History and Heritage Command.

Figure 17. LCdr. Kenneth Whiting and his command at NAS Killingholme, situated on the banks of the Humber River in northeastern England. Killingholme was the largest combat station operated by naval aviation during World War I. Courtesy of National Archives.

Figure 18. A Short 320 patrol bomber at NAS Killingholme. The eccentric position of the radiator made it difficult for the pilot to see. The Short had an unfortunate tendency to flip over on its back. American pilots operated these aircraft from February 1918 until the end of the war. Courtesy of National Archives.

Figure 19. The armament aboard an H-16 flying boat, consisting of multiple .30 caliber Lewis machine guns, including those accessed through sliding doors installed in the fuselage. Courtesy of National Archives.

Figure 20. NAS Queenstown in Ireland under construction in late summer 1918. Much of the work was carried out by civilian Irish laborers. An H-16 flying boat lies at anchor in the harbor in the left background. Courtesy of Naval History and Heritage Command.

Figure 21. Launching an H-16 flying boat at NAS Queenstown. This chore required a crew of 20 or 30 "beach mules." The massive concrete ramp survives to this day and is used to launch and retrieve sailing vessels. Courtesy of Naval History and Heritage Command.

Figure 22. An aerial view of NAS Castletownbere, the Navy's only kite balloon station in Ireland. Clearly visibly are the canvas balloon sheds, fuel oil storage tanks, and a baseball diamond. Only the fuel oil containment structure remains today. Courtesy of Naval History and Heritage Command.

Figure 23. The American "beach" at the Bolsena training facility, located about 60 miles north of Rome. The Navy operated a flying school here from February to November 1918, under the direction of William "Bull" Atwater. Courtesy of Lawrence Sheely.

Figure 24. A typical mishap at the Bolsena flying school. Such accidents were common. Courtesy of Lawrence Sheely.

Figure 25. The officers of NAS Porto Corsini in a formal group portrait. Commanding Officer Willis Haviland, a veteran of the Lafayette Escadrille, is seated center in the fur-trimmed overcoat. A fighter, not an administrator, he had several run-ins with his superior, LCdr. John Callan. Courtesy of Naval History and Heritage Command.

Figure 26. A massive dirigible hangar under construction at NAS Gujan, near Arcachon, France. Most of these hangars were built with hand tools and strong backs. This station was never completed. Courtesy National Archives.

Figure 27. The dirigible AT-13 about to get under way at NAS Paimboeuf, the sole American airship station to conduct wartime patrols. AT-13 was the only Navy dirigible to be attacked by an enemy submarine. Courtesy of National Archives.

Figure 28. Pets could be found at all air stations, everything from birds to bears. This trash cart at Moutchic was pulled by a favorite donkey, along with some furry passengers. Courtesy of National Archives.

Figure 29. Athletics played a major role in the off-duty lives of station personnel and were much encouraged by commanders. Baseball and boxing were the most popular sports, but the men enjoyed many others as well. The NAS Paimboeuf football squad posed for this photograph in the fall of 1918. Courtesy of National Archives.

Figure 30. A Caproni Ca. 5 bomber taking off at Milan, Italy. These aircraft powered by poorly manufactured Fiat motors provided nothing but headaches for the Navy's Northern Bombing Group and were responsible for the deaths of several aviators. Courtesy of Naval History and Heritage Command.

Left: Figure 31. David Ingalls of the First Yale Unit served with the No. 213 Squadron, RAF, from August to early October 1918. During those weeks he downed at least six aircraft and balloons, winning the accolade "Ace." This informal view, taken in that period, shows the nineteen-year-old "Crock" Ingalls with his trademark pipe and rumpled tunic. Courtesy Ingalls Foundation.

Below: Figure 32. An aerial view of a portion of the Northern Bombing Group's sprawling assembly and repair facility at Eastleigh, England. By November 1918, approximately 2,000 officers and men labored here preparing aircraft for use on the Western Front. Courtesy of National Archives.

Figure 33. The Navy's supply base at Pauillac, France, on the banks of the Gironde River, grew into a bustling factory town. The large hangars pictured here accommodated flying boats being readied for duty at patrol stations along the coast. Today nothing remains except a bit of rubble piled along the riverbank. Courtesy of National Archives.

Figure 34. For much of 1918, Capt. Thomas Craven, seated center, directed the Operations Division at aviation headquarters in Paris. In September he and his staff, shown here, relocated to Brest where he served as Adm. Henry Wilson's aide for aviation. Craven found Brest a dismal place after having spent the previous seven months in Paris. Courtesy of National Archives.

Figure 35. Bluejackets at Moutchic lined up with their bedrolls and seabags awaiting demobilization inspection in late December 1918. From here it was off to Pauillac and home. Courtesy of National Archives.

7

THE IRISH BASES

*You've heard about the men who fought
And broke the Kaiser's line!
You've heard about destroyers
Shielding ships from sub and mine;*

*But who has heard in poem or prose,
in sermon or oration,
a single word to praise the work
Of "IRISH AVIATION"?*

In the early years of World War I the lengthy Irish coast constituted an enormous gap in Britain's aerial antisubmarine defenses. Shortages of aircraft and pilots and Sinn Fein agitation dissuaded the Royal Navy from establishing patrol stations, despite vast quantities of shipping passing along these shores. Losses proved heavy, the most infamous being the sinking of the *Lusitania* in May 1915. A program to erect dirigible stations eventually resulted, but only in December 1916 did the Admiralty create an antisubmarine division in Ireland to coordinate all antisubmarine warfare (ASW) efforts and devise new strategies to combat the underwater enemy. This group soon developed the concepts of destroyer hunting patrols, aerial surveillance along the coast, and convoys. Implementing air patrols required construction of bases, however, and in early 1917 surveyors began identifying sites for seaplane and kite balloon stations. Shortly after Congress declared war in April 1917, American destroyers sailed to Queenstown (now Cobh) where they operated under Adm. Lewis Bayly, RN, Commander-in-Chief, Coast of Ireland. In the following months additional fleet units arrived, and by September the Queenstown-based American armada contained dozens of vessels and the destroyer tender *Melville*, Admiral Sims's titular flagship. In fact, Queenstown quickly mushroomed into the largest Navy outpost in Europe.[1] As early as midsummer 1917, Sims recognized the value of antisubmarine aviation patrols. A communication to Washington on August 3 tallied hundreds of thousands of over-water miles flown by French and British aircraft. He also described various types of bombing, patrol, and convoy duties. "In establishing the work to be done around the British coast," Sims recommended that the Navy follow his earlier suggestion of July 3 in which he identified the Admiralty's need for seaplane carriers, seaplane tenders, kite balloons, seaplane squadrons, powerful engines, trained pilots, and mechanics. Such units as the United States provided should be used to take over specific sectors and would be of "great importance to the limits of available construction and training facilities." American observers believed such a policy was necessary because the Royal Navy could not adequately patrol the coasts, nor had operating stations yet been established in Ireland or Scotland. In April alone, U-boats sank 100 ships in those waters.[2]

The Navy responded slowly, however, particularly compared to developments in France, and throughout the summer no officer on Sims's staff assumed direct control of aviation affairs. Hutch Cone's arrival in late September changed that. He met with Whiting and Conger and then in October sat down with Commodore Godfrey Paine, the Admiralty's newly created Fifth Sea Lord (aviation). During their meeting Cone expressed a desire to cooperate with the British and asked for suggestions. As American destroyers already patrolled the south coast of Ireland, Paine recommended that the Navy operate seaplane and kite balloon stations planned there. The same proposition had been made to Adm. Henry Mayo during his recent September visit. Paine's plan also included one station on the northern Irish coast (Lough Foyle) and another on the west coast of Scotland (Sleat Sound), each to be equipped with "Large America" flying boats. Cone endorsed the overall concept, if proper sites could be found, and suggested an inspection tour to include himself, Whiting, and a few others. The Admiralty detailed three officers, headed by LCdr. F. R. E. Davis, a construction expert, to accompany the Americans. It turned out to be a very comprehensive tour. The party departed London on October 8 and visited Queenstown, Whiddy Island, Lough Foyle, Berehaven, Waterford, and Wexford in Ireland and then crossed back to Sleat Sound/Arisaig and Stranraer in Scotland. In Scotland, the Navy party also inspected the RFC gunnery school at Turnberry and an operating seaplane base at Dundee, finally returning to London on October 21.

At a conference held upon his return (his third conference in as many weeks) Cone agreed to establish stations at Lough Foyle in the north of Ireland, and Queenstown, Whiddy Island, and Wexford, in the south. Lough Foyle commanded the North Channel approach to the Irish Sea and would work in conjunction with RNAS seaplane bases on the west coast of Scotland, while Wexford's coverage extended over the St. George (southern) Channel. Whiddy Island would protect ships coming in from the Atlantic along the southern Irish coast. Queenstown, homeport to American destroyers, would serve as an aircraft assembly/repair facility and also conduct patrols across the Irish Sea. Cone initially rejected a balloon station in the north as the United States deployed no destroyers there and said no to Sleat Sound in Scotland due to its inaccessibility and awful weather. The Admiralty announced that they could not provide buildings at American sites but agreed to help construct foundations and slipways. The allies set July 1, 1918, as the target date to begin patrol operations. Sims recommended these bases to Chief of Naval Operations Benson on October 22 and the Department authorized him to proceed a week later.

Following Cone's inspection trip and ensuing conferences, Lieutenant Commander Davis traveled to the United States carrying plans and lists, and for the next 10 or 11 months preparation and construction dominated aviation efforts. By November additional arrangements were finalized to build two balloon stations, the first at Castletownbere behind Bere Island, near the mouth of Bantry Bay for use in cooperation with U.S. destroyers. The second would be located at Rathmullen on Lough Swilly, a few miles west of Lough Foyle, manned by the Royal Navy until American vessels began operating in northern waters.[3] Kite balloons were large sausage-shaped gasbags inflated ashore, transferred to a warship, and towed along at sea at a height of several hundred feet. Used for spotting and scouting, they could be flown for days, except when winds were very high. An observer suspended beneath a balloon could see 25 miles or more ahead, much farther than from the bridge of a destroyer. These LTA craft did not need large bases but did require proximity to destroyer facilities. In fact, the Navy never assumed control of the Lough Swilly site. The United States later argued against Castletownbere as well, pushing for Queenstown instead, but the Admiralty insisted that work had advanced too far to be abandoned.

These facilities—four air stations and one kite balloon base—constituted the final Irish program, though on occasion other initiatives generated discussion. At one point the Admiralty pressed for a base at Kingston near Dublin. They also proposed operations by land machines, obsolescent DH-6s, off the northeastern coast, going so far as to offer 30 aircraft and all necessary materials. The scheme would have required 50 officers and 500 enlisted men, however, and Cone rejected it as beyond U.S. capabilities. The question of substations and mobile stations, particularly on the west coast, also arose, a plan whereby three to six planes might moor temporarily in a harbor, with a mother ship providing quarters and a depot. Additional suggestions envisioned kite balloons being carried with convoys along the entire Atlantic route, with a repair/refit base at each end of the route. The British even asked the Navy to operate bases on Ireland's west coast to help stem the flow of arms to Sinn Fein forces but the United States emphatically refused.[4]

Naval aviation's first formal presence in Ireland appeared at New Year's when Asst. Paymaster E. D. Foster, Civil Engineers E. H. Brownell and A. L. Stitt, and Asst. Surgeon E. H. Lorentzen began an inspection tour of proposed sites. They landed at Dublin on December 30, 1917, soon leased a large, partially derelict storehouse/warehouse on Sir Rogerson's Quay, and in the next few weeks investigated means and availability of transportation. A construction draft of 169 men disembarked in early January, followed by additional supply officers and paymasters who dispersed to the various bases. Most were young, inexperienced officers, and shortages of qualified enlisted personnel made the situation more difficult. Coincidentally, Cone submitted a summary estimate of the proposed Irish establishment, calling for 24 H-16-type aircraft at both Whiddy Island and Queenstown, along with 58 officers and 498 enlisted men, and 18 H-16 types at Wexford and Lough Foyle, each facility supporting 45 officers and 394 enlisted men, as well as two kite balloon stations manned by a total of 4 officers and 277 men.[5]

In common with Navy programs elsewhere in Europe, the Irish effort endured frustrating mix-ups in shipping, with incomplete or incorrect items often sent to the wrong destination. It became necessary to break open each shipping box to inspect its contents, slowing progress immensely. Orders from aviation headquarters in Paris, however, demanded that nothing should be left undone to secure necessary supplies, regardless of cost or paperwork. As a consequence, nearly all requests came marked urgent, requiring immediate delivery. Looking back on the difficulties they confronted, one officer recalled, "There have been many times when the outlook has seemed discouraging . . . but in spite of many difficulties, and undoubtedly some mistakes and shortcomings, it is hoped and believed that those connected with the supply work for the air stations in Ireland can feel that their labor has not been all in vain."[6]

Almost from the beginning the Navy organized its Irish stations as a single unit under one officer, the first being Lt. Carl Hull, followed by LCdr. Paul J. Peyton. Commander Francis B. McCrary, who previously headed the LTA program in France, took command on February 14, a position he held until the end of the war. McCrary later described station sites as well chosen, but Civil Engineer D. Graham Copeland remained unconvinced. British criteria for locating stations included a broad expanse of sheltered water, suitable foreshore, level ground, road and rail access, and convenience for operations and communication with senior naval officers. Such sites might be adequate when measured by strictly military considerations, he observed, but the British failed to address concerns of medical officers, construction issues, supplies of labor and materiel, adequate drinking water, or the suitability of the ground. According to Copeland, by the Admiralty's own standards, only Wexford came close. Queenstown required excavation of 50,000 cubic yards of fill and construction of 2,100 feet of seawall. Barracks stood one-half mile away atop a 300-foot ridge.[7]

Transforming ambitious plans into practical reality thus posed a daunting task. Simply moving construction materials and equipment proved a major burden. Shifting supplies to a railhead by truck badly cut up poor Irish roads. McCrary believed that "the greatest handicap was the lack of water transportation, which was not rectified until the last month of war, private boats rented but in very bad condition." Even Queenstown headquarters experienced difficulties due to insufficient numbers of lighters and motorboats. Similarly, Lough Foyle waited endlessly for material and equipment from Londonderry only 10 miles away. Delays obtaining equipment and spare parts directly impacted wartime operations. In Wexford, for example, the date for commencing combat patrols slipped by at least a month due to shortages of propellers, starting cranks, and radio equipment. Shifting strategic priorities during the lengthy buildup phase, usually linked to changing parameters of enemy submarine activity, also impacted construction efforts. Irish weather imposed a further burden. McCrary later recalled, "Weather was a handicap which could not be overcome." At Whiddy Island, low ceilings, rain, even gales prevented flight operations on 78 of 134 calendar days between July 1 and November 11, 1918. Maximum winds of 78 mph lashed the station on October 7. Queenstown recorded "more or less continual rainfall." The same damp affected equipment at Berehaven, shortening the working life of balloons.[8]

Unease with the local political situation pervaded American thinking. Washington recommended that Irish stations be commanded by line officers of the regular Navy, leaders with experience handling men and capable of using discretion in the event of internal disorder. From London, Edwards suggested the Queenstown flotilla as a possible source of such men. Local labor strife and fear of Sinn Fein agitation impacted many building projects. Trouble began in March 1918 and extended into the autumn months. In late April, McCrary reported that construction lagged due to the number of contract laborers quitting. Every worker at Castletownbere resigned, along with 130 at Whiddy Island, and 75 at Queenstown. Whiddy Island projects fell months behind schedule due to the "mere handful" of men available. The commander replaced the entire contract labor force at Lough Foyle in early June 1918, while a separate strike broke out at Wexford caused by Sinn Fein agitators. A short stoppage hit Dublin when the Navy attempted to unload *Long Beach*, and more trouble seemed likely.[9]

General inexperience impaired efficiency. At the outbreak of the war not a single officer or enlisted man in the Navy had ever constructed, commanded, or operated a combat station. Green pilots possessed limited knowledge of seamanship and navigation, and "a patrol when at sea or landing on the water, caused the Commanding Officer [McCrary] a great deal of unrest." Bases carried out almost as many training flights as patrols, and second pilots frequently received instruction while on actual missions. Some practiced landings only after completing a war patrol. Individual sites suffered intermittently from not having experienced commanders, with three started by acting radio gunners. A few officers proved unsuitable for independent command, either failing to cultivate the goodwill of local inhabitants or not maintaining military control over their stations. Radio personnel trained at Harvard University seemed "absolutely unfamiliar with the delicate and intricate seaplane equipment" and needed to be taught British methods. Very few had ever been in a seaplane and many became airsick. Similarly, lack of familiarity of paymasters and supply officers with military procedures caused confusion. At the end of March, McCrary described the deplorable condition of enlisted men's wage accounts, which "causes a spirit of discontent by not getting the pay to which they are entitled."

Despite bad weather, political unrest, and inexperienced personnel, significant construction activity commenced in late winter, following initial British work on foundations and slipways. By the time McCrary reported for duty February 14, a force of eight officers and 200 men labored at Queenstown, with small pioneer parties sent to outlying sites and quartered in the nearest towns. A few aviation supplies arrived aboard *Lake Michigan* on March 28, and still more in April. Under the direction of civil engineers, workers eventually completed all sites at about the same time, after approximately six months' labor. The Navy commissioned its stations in the following order: Queenstown, February 22; Castletownbere, April 29; Wexford, May 2; Lough Foyle, July 1; and Whiddy Island, July 4.

Most stations stood ready to receive warplanes one or two months before actual deliveries commenced due to delays completing Queenstown's assembly and repair facility. Nonetheless, McCrary lauded engineers' efforts, calling nonarrival of supplies the greatest impediment. The kite balloon station at Castletownbere never did much active work due to a shortage of destroyers. As preparations neared completion, headquarters ordered the base closed up and personnel/equipment relocated to Brest, France. The Navy later restaffed and reequipped Castletownbere with one balloon to operate in conjunction with *HMS Flying Fox* between July 14 and August 14. In the fall the base supplied balloons for sorties undertaken by battleships *Utah, Oklahoma,* and *Nevada* operating out of Bantry Bay.[10]

The Irish stations served under a single officer who answered to two different commanders, one for internal administration and the other for military operations. As Commander, U.S. Naval Air Stations (USNAS), Ireland, McCrary reported directly to Commander, U.S. Naval Aviation Forces Foreign Service (USNAFFS)(Hutch Cone) until September 1, and thereafter to the Force Commander (Sims). By contrast, Adm. Lewis Bayly, British Commander-in-Chief, Coast of Ireland, directed military operations, with McCrary, serving on his staff. In response, McCrary maintained two separate headquarters. One, at Aghada House, accommodated aides for administration, personnel, communication, supplies and transport, public works, and medical affairs. McCrary occupied a separate office adjacent to Bayly's in Queenstown, with responsibility for military operations of American bases. He spent much time shuttling between these sites or away on long inspection trips. As his subordinates became more experienced, McCrary assumed a more general, supervisory role.[11]

Navy engineers designed the Irish bases on the same template, with poured concrete forming the base for hangars, apron, ramp, and shorefront slipways. Most buildings were prefabricated of wood and erected to the rear of the hangars. A nearby "mansion house" occasionally provided officers' quarters. Individual stations adopted the organizational model of RNAS Felixstowe, but adapted to American ratings, with the flight department divided into three flights. Planners envisioned stations mounting three patrols per day: 6 A.M.–10 A.M., 10 A.M.–2 P.M., and 2 P.M.–6 P.M., with at least six planes operating at any one time, two planes per patrol, though no base ever reached this level of activity. Official instructions advised pilots to undertake no more than four hours' flying each day. No one anticipated any combat.[12]

Three southern stations—Queenstown, Wexford, and Whiddy Bay—functioned as a unit directed from McCrary's headquarters near Admiralty House. The outpost at Lough Foyle operated under direction of the Royal Navy at Buncrana, not Queenstown, but nonetheless forwarded information to McCrary's offices. Most flying performed at the northern site consisted of point-to-point convoy escort. The other stations carried out patrol work, usually overlapping with British aircraft from bases in England and Wales. After some trial and error, defined procedures evolved for planning and executing missions. Each evening before 8:00 P.M. the Air Operations office in Queenstown received notices from outlying stations of the number of aircraft available for duty the following day. General orders then went out describing necessary special convoy work, escort duty, or patrols. Operations staff disseminated information on submarine locations. Enemy U-boats might be sighted by ships or planes, or detected with land-based radio direction finders. Radio direction usually intercepted U-boats at night when they ran on the surface to recharge their batteries. Operations tabulated reports on a chart using color-coded thumbtacks. Information transmitted to outlying stations included a submarine's first sighting, speed, course, and probable location at dawn.

Station intelligence officers received more specific directions around midnight (or later). They then drew up detailed flight orders, most for missions of four- to five- hours' duration. Aircraft began tuning up about one-half hour before dawn, and lifted off at daybreak. This system was fully in place October 1. Flying boats on patrol informed the station of their positions every 20–30 minutes by wireless telegraph (if available). In the event of an emergency or landing at sea they dispatched messenger pigeons. Daylight alerts initiated a frantic scramble to process information, disseminate it, and then launch aerial strikes. Under ideal circumstances, the Admiralty received reports of visual contacts within 10 minutes, and in 10 minutes more forwarded the information to Operations. From there, data, including the intruder's location, course, and speed, could be routed to individual stations. A plane on standby took off shortly thereafter hoping to intercept the enemy vessel.[13]

The sinking of *RMS Leinster* by German submarine UB-123 in October 1918 underscored the importance of these operations. On the evening of October 9, one of the few operational airships at Malahide station was wrecked, leaving *Leinster* to sail unescorted the following day on its voyage from Kingston, Ireland, to Holyhead, Wales. She carried 687 passengers and 70 crewmen when the torpedoes struck, killing and injuring more than 500; among them was Hutch Cone. He survived the first blast and was helping women into the boats when a second torpedo hit. Before being rescued the badly injured Cone kept himself afloat for hours by clinging to debris in the water.

After an extended construction period, American stations all became operational within a few weeks of each other: Lough Foyle, September 3; Wexford, September 18; Whiddy Island, September 25; and Queenstown, September 30. Difficulties acquiring aircraft and equipment greatly slowed this process, including confusion concerning shipment of planes. H-16 flying boats were scheduled initially to reach Queenstown in early July. Rumors soon circulated that five were going to Lough Foyle (true), then 10 to Queenstown, then others to Glasgow lashed to the deck of a mine carrier. At the time no one in Queenstown had any real experience working on Liberty motors or H-16s.[14] Further questions arose when sufficient propellers and starting cranks failed to arrive. Radio direction equipment became available only in late October. Eventually, 43 aircraft reached Ireland—38 at Queenstown and 5 at Lough Foyle. Queenstown personnel assembled planes and ferried them to outlying stations. The longest hop, from Wexford to Lough Foyle, exceeded 300 miles. Of the aircraft reaching Ireland, 15 were not assembled and later sent home. Mechanics cannibalized one of these for spare parts. Twenty-eight actually flew; nine were wrecked. Queenstown workers dismantled the surviving 19 after the Armistice and returned them to the United States.

Despite rarely having more than two or three aircraft in commission at any location, the Irish stations recorded 761 flying hours and almost 48,000 patrol miles. At no time did aviators enjoy favorable weather conditions. Navy personnel bombed seven (suspected) submarines, including one preparing to attack a convoy. Following the Armistice the largest number of bluejackets sailed home in December 1918. A few skeleton crews remained to maintain the sites. The stations themselves would be cleared and land ceded to its owners unless required by British military forces. The Navy vacated Lough Foyle and Whiddy Island by the end of January, and Wexford in mid-February, 1918. NAS Queenstown remained open until April 10, 1919.[15]

* * *

Situated at Aghada at the southeastern end of Cork harbor, 4 miles by water and 20 miles by road from Queenstown, NAS Queenstown was well positioned for sub hunting. A four-hour patrol covered most of the area where enemy U-boats previously were most active. Queenstown also served as an assembly and repair facility for Irish bases and as a training site for all pilots in H-16 flying boats. Initially envisioned as a 24-seaplane station with a complement of 60 officers and 498 enlisted men, establishment of an aircraft assembly site increased its planned size to 75 officers and 2,300 men. Actual personnel strength reached 48 officers and 1,398 men on November 1, 1918, including a construction gang of 340 bluejackets. Despite certain operational advantages, NAS Queenstown suffered from poor ground transportation links to the city, which is on an island, as well as to the rest of Ireland. Instead, the station depended on lighters, with these always in short supply. Terrain and tide necessitated construction of a very long slipway. For one hour before and after low tide, crews could neither launch nor retrieve planes. They compensated by launching aircraft early and then mooring them to a buoy. If the temperature rose high enough some men stripped to their skivvies when maneuvering flying boats into deep water.

Work commenced December 15, 1917, under Irish contractor T. J. Moran and Co. Before the Americans arrived, local workers poured concrete for hangar foundations, apron, seawall, and lengthy slipway. When an initial draft of officers and men appeared in early February they settled in at "Timbertown," a former British army camp of minimally adequate facilities. Located about one-half mile from the shore, Timbertown's three dozen rude, wooden barracks perched well above the future station site and the men lost much time shuttling back and forth for meals. Further, it proved difficult for officers to maintain supervision over ratings while in camp. The Navy later erected additional enlisted barracks directly adjacent to Timbertown, at a place nicknamed "Tintown."[16]

The actual station site required an enormous amount of excavation and concrete work though workmen possessed no proper tools or equipment. This included relocating a coastal path and carving away a portion of the shoreside hill to accommodate buildings and aviation activities. Undaunted, the Navy mounted an extensive search for machinery and eventually located "an immense antiquated steam shovel" in an old gravel pit, 2 miles from a road and 26 miles from a railroad. The Navy leased the rusting shovel and bluejackets broke it down and hauled it by truck to Aghada, where they eventually got it working again. Armed with this ancient iron beast, the men did all the digging at the assembly and repair site before turning to the hangar area. The station also ordered a concrete mixer from London, but it took months to arrive and more time still for its wheels to be delivered. A British-installed water system proved inadequate, and base personnel eventually tapped five springs over a mile away.

Americans took formal control at Aghada on February 22, under command of LCdr. Paul Peyton, a 31-year-old native of Hazelhurst, Mississippi, and a veteran of the Pensacola program. They acquired a mansion house, Aghada Hall, for station officers' accommodations and Sabroan Cottage for headquarters officers. Contractors built the initial double hangar, with the second and third erected by bluejackets in less time than it took to raise the first. In some cases the men used wooden planks recycled from airplane packing crates to fashion hangar trusses. Until September 1, civilians and enlisted men labored in tandem. Thereafter, American sailors did all the work. Concern over relations with local citizens, especially fear of Sinn Fein troublemakers, affected leave policy and other issues. Everyone received warnings to keep their eyes and ears open. Regulations barred visitors from the base after 9 P.M. and excluded them entirely from buildings. The watchwords were "Trust No One!" Sailors wore dungarees during the day, and then regulation blues or whites as prescribed. They received liberty in Queenstown on both weekday evenings and weekends. But there was no liberty granted in Cork due to perceived political unrest there and several scuffles with local toughs. Each day the Navy dispatched a shore patrol to keep order in town.[17]

The first eight H-16 aircraft in huge packing crates arrived in late June aboard *Cuyama*. Ten more followed July 24 on *Kanawha*. The base received 38 planes in all. After reaching Queenstown, crews loaded the crates aboard lighters and moved them across the harbor. Sailors beached the lighters next to the slipway and then employed a gin pole to hoist the enormous boxes onto shore. These were huge flying machines, weighing 7,500 pounds empty and almost 11,000 pounds fully loaded for war service. The complicated task of assembling the aircraft, making modifications, and testing all systems took many weeks. Shortages of starting cranks, of all things, caused additional delays. An initial test flight lasting 10 minutes occurred August 3, with Ens. Joseph Lancto at the controls. A native of Chateaugay, New York, Lancto had served previously at RNAS stations Calshot, Newhaven, and Felixstowe. Another early flight resulted in a crash only 30 seconds after takeoff due to crossed aileron wires. Mechanical problems led to the loss of at least four aircraft in September and October. Two planes foundered while landing in very rough seas. Others fell victim to defective crankshafts, a common problem with Liberty motors.

Despite accidents, aviation activity increased throughout the fall. Total flying to August 31 counted 25 test hops lasting 13 hours. Air operations in September expanded to 34 test flights and 1 patrol (September 30), with half the days suitable for flying. In October, activity increased further to 50 test flights and 47 patrols lasting 138 hours. The end of the war in early November reduced operations that month to 25 test flights and 17 patrols. Throughout this period Ensigns Phillip Gadsden, Joseph Lancto, and Edward Dolececk shouldered the brunt of flying assignments. With only a handful of aircraft available, NAS Queenstown compiled a limited war record, further hindered by the need to train pilots destined for other stations. More seasoned aviators also carried out test flights. Queenstown pilots tested eight machines in September and seven more during October, with most ferried to Wexford and Whiddy Island. All these activities consumed invaluable man-hours.

Mechanical problems plagued operations right to the end. In early November an aircraft landed at sea with a misfiring motor. The pilot alerted a British minesweeper by firing two Very lights and secured a tow back to base.

But there were notable achievements as well. Just before the Armistice, a flying boat carrying five crewmen, two bombs, and extra gasoline conducted a record-breaking patrol lasting 9 hours, 37 minutes. In the final week of the conflict, Queenstown launched 15 patrols covering 3,300 miles, a record for any station, and on November 11 a flying boat laden with six men climbed to an altitude of 10,750 feet in 63 minutes. The Navy conducted no patrols thereafter and all flights ceased 10 days later. Queenstown's wartime record tabulated 155 flights lasting 254 hours, including 64 patrols of 198 hours' duration covering 11,600 miles, and 3 bombing attacks against suspected submarines.[18]

Aghada Hall was destroyed during the "Troubles" that wracked Ireland after World War I, but recent residential construction uncovered the original dressed stone basement walls. Sabroan Cottage was partially destroyed also, but later it was restored and a portion remains in use as a residence. The country lane that workers rerouted across the estate grounds behind the mansion house survives today as the "Yankee Road." "Timbertown" and "Tintown" are long gone. The modern coastal highway, a tennis club, boat storage/launching facility, and contemporary industrial building occupy the actual station site. One enters the tennis club through a pair of pillars commemorating the American base. The entire concrete hardstand/apron remains, as does the lengthy and very substantial seawall. Tennis courts stand on slightly elevated concrete pads that originally formed the floors of large double hangars. A commodious yacht repair building occupies the site of the assembly and repair facility, while the enormous slipway, originally used to maneuver flying boats, is now renowned as one of the finest boat launching ramps in Ireland.

The United States Navy built NAS Wexford at Ferrybank on the River Slaney. Protected from wind and waves, the sheltered anchorage facilitated easy takeoffs and landings. Though the channel to the harbor followed a tortuous route, the sea lay only 2.5 miles away and the station could be reached easily even in heavy mist thanks to the many lighthouses in the immediate vicinity. One of the spots selected by the Admiralty early in 1917, Wexford surveyed an area of heavy submarine activity. U-boats often attacked within a few miles of land and frequently ran on the surface, sometimes sinking three or four vessels per week. The projected 100-mile patrol radius of NAS Wexford reached across the Irish Sea (St. George Channel) to encompass most of the western coast of Wales and into the Bristol Channel, as well as south to Queenstown and north of Dublin. Many considered Wexford the best Irish station, with good rail and highway transportation and adequate local labor and materials. The original projected complement prescribed 36 pilots, 18 aircraft, and 412 officers and men. By war's end, the base counted 5 pilots, 10 flying boats, and 417 officers and men.[19]

A civilian contractor working for the Admiralty commenced preparations in December 1917. Eight sailors led by Gunner Rodgers arrived in late February. His responsibilities included grading, pouring concrete foundations, and excavating/laying out roads. The Navy also occupied two nearby residences, Ely House and Bann Aboo, providing temporary quarters for work crews and later officers. Eventually, young sailors fresh from civilian life performed most construction tasks. Lieutenant Commander Victor D. Herbster took command on March 28. An officer with extensive aviation experience, Herbster had graduated from the Naval Academy in 1908 and had participated in the first flying camp at Annapolis in 1911 and the aviation camp at Guantanamo Bay in 1913. Herbster also served as Assistant Naval Attaché in Berlin in 1914. According to Craven, he was ambitious and aggressive and had strong ideas of what he wanted. With the hoisting of the naval ensign and appropriate ceremonies, NAS Wexford was formally commissioned on May 2, 1918.[20]

Long-feared labor troubles erupted in late spring. Irish carpenters working on the first hangar walked off the job June 11. They returned in the afternoon with a list of demands. Herbster refused to negotiate and told them to send delegates to Queenstown instead. He then erected barriers bolstered by an armed guard to keep strikers away and took control of the road under the Defense of the Realm Act. The following day laborers went on sympathy strike. Herbster believed troublemakers had been imported from Dublin and outlying towns and deeper motives were at work, either Sinn Fein agitation or German espionage. Some workers, he claimed, had been interned previously.[21]

Navy crews took over construction and by pushing very hard soon completed a second hangar. Herbster believed in keeping his men busy and his command shipshape. He placed great emphasis on maintaining strict discipline, "the foundation of efficiency," and ensuring that work parties cleaned up after themselves. By his own words Herbster intended to build the "ideal naval air station. . . . That Wexford managed to excel in the race between the Irish stations," he later recalled, was "a matter of considerable pleasure to me." Sometimes the workday stretched from 5 A.M. until 9 P.M. Herbster was not a complete martinet, however, and an element of his "keep busy" philosophy encouraged athletics, part of a recreational program that included baseball, football, a base orchestra, and a well-organized YMCA. Sundays were always given over to rest, worship, and recreation. In addition, bluejackets received liberty one evening in four. Looking back, sailors expressed great pride in their wartime service. In time, and with much effort, they built warm, comfortable barracks and an attractive mess hall. They extolled the "Wexford Spirit" and good-natured competition between departments and between pilots.

During the influenza epidemic, Herbster imposed extreme precautions. When the scourge hit Dublin, he banned travel there. When it reached towns 14 to 20 miles from the station, he placed those off-limits too. Medical officers made daily inquiries in Wexford, and when the disease arrived they ordered the base under quarantine, cutting communication to a minimum. No one could enter or leave without a special pass. Men received a menthol/oil spray in their noses and throats and swabbed the barracks every day with an antiseptic solution. In a five-week period when local authorities tallied 3,500 cases of influenza, not one occurred at the station.

Flight operations commenced in mid-September when four H-16s arrived from Queenstown but soon encountered numerous obstacles. One aircraft crashed, wrecked beyond repair. Another suffered serious damage being brought onto the "beach." For a time a harbor dredge blocked access to the slipway and flying boats moored in the water, while endless rain meant considerably more work to keep machines flight worthy. Reconciling the dawn start of operations and ever-changing rise and fall of tides meant that crews often worked nearly 18 hours per day. Some men stayed awake up to 48 hours until finally ordered to turn in.

Mirroring the experiences of other Irish stations, motor troubles and lack of spare parts initially hindered patrol activity at Wexford, but in the fall the number of flying hours increased rapidly, from only 58 in September to 166 in October and almost 90 in the first 11 days of November. Planes ferried to and from Queenstown always flew with full armament just in case they spotted something along the route. The first attack against a submarine occurred September 21, damaging the U-boat and preventing it from submerging. The American plane, however, could not radio its position and the enemy vessel limped away on the surface. Wexford pilots spotted and bombed suspicious oil slicks October 11, 13, and 16 with inconclusive results. Despite occasional diversions, many flight personnel found the work monotonous and wearying. Ensign "Mac" McCormick recalled years later, "Patrolling the Irish Channel became rather tedious at times. Those old H-16s were not as comfortable as modern jets. Appropriate first aid was dispensed at the village pub in Wexford."[22]

Only a few vestiges of NAS Wexford remain today. Of the residences occupied during the war, the more modest of the two, Bann Aboo, survives, incorporated into a restaurant/hotel complex. The larger, Ely House, gave way to a hospital of the same name. Brick walls from the original enclosed garden still stand, however, sheltering an assortment of flowering plants. A few hundred yards farther along the shore a modern, low-rise automobile dealership and garage occupy the site of the station's hangars. Across the shore road stands a seawall and, abutting that, the original American slipway, perfectly preserved where it extends into the river.

NAS Whiddy Island, the southwestern-most aviation outpost in Ireland, often called Bantry Bay station, stood on the northeastern end of the island of that name, 16 miles from the sea. It was well situated to protect vessels coming in from the Atlantic Ocean. The site had previously been a farm, protected from night winds and coastal gales by significant hills on all sides. Bantry village on the mainland lay about two miles away across the water. Originally planned to accommodate 24 aircraft, 48 pilots, and 516 officers and men, the final complement counted 3 flying boats, 8 pilots, and 410 personnel. Local contractor, Moran and Co., began work on December 16, 1917. Civil Engineer A. L. Stitt, Asst. Paymaster E. D. Foster, and Asst. Surgeon E. H. Lorentzen inspected the site in early January. Ultimately, Navy crews completed most of the base's facilities. The first detachment arrived March 11/12 under Gunner W. Schuss(e). With no accommodations on the island, they boarded in Bantry. The sailors lost much time in transit and never possessed enough boats to ferry men and supplies.[23]

Widespread discontent over the issue of Irish conscription led to frequent strikes and unrest among local workers. During these weeks Americans erected barracks and other buildings, but no further labor drafts arrived for nearly three months. The original crew worked in bad weather, without rubber coats and boots. They boarded boats returning to Bantry by wading waist deep into the cold water. Not until the end of April was sufficient shelter available to house men on the island. Several attempts to sink wells failed, and eventually three separate water systems evolved. When barracks and water became available the small Navy contingent moved to the island where they dined on "regular American chow" after subsisting on Irish war bread and the limited output of the local market.

Disciplinary issues in Bantry Bay caused McCrary considerable worry in late April and early May. The commander visited the isolated station and found morale among officers so poor he feared he must either court-martial the entire group or replace them with a whole new cadre. As the commanding officer (likely Ens. William Peterson) had done a commendable job with the construction program, McCrary decided to retain him until a career lieutenant commander arrived. He sent most of the others away. Down the Bay at Castletownbere, the district Senior Naval Officer (RN) caused a stir by asking

McCrary's "inexperienced C. O." to provide American trucks and drivers to transport British troops to suppress Sinn Fein disturbances. McCrary approvingly reported how the young officer, Lt.(jg) Carl Shumway, "fortunately had the backbone to refuse such a request."[24]

Work on Hangar #1 commenced May 20 and was finished in early July by the Irish labor force of 110. By contrast, fewer than 60 enlisted Navy workers completed Hangar #2 in 45 days without any woodworking machinery. In fact, little or no equipment ever reached the base, and powered tools did not arrive until after most construction was done. Under such conditions, officers credited their men with "splendid initiative and painstaking care." Workers first moved building materials in farmers' carts and later with a large Packard truck floated to the island aboard a barge. Construction of wireless facilities greatly simplified communication between bases, and operators picked up signals from as far away as the American coast, the Mediterranean, and Moscow. Despite delays, the men raised the Stars and Stripes July 4, officially placing the base in commission under the leadership of LCdr. Paul Peyton. Almost 12 more weeks elapsed, however, before aerial operations commenced.[25]

Whiddy Island suffered just one aviation fatality. While returning from patrol on October 22, H-16/A-1072 crashed at sunset, killing radioman Wilfred Anderson and injuring others in the crew. A Board of Inquiry determined that the accident occurred when it was too dark for pilot Ens. George Owen to read the instruments, but not dark enough for the phosphorous dials to glow. As the plane glided in, the glassy water prevented the crew from gauging their height and the aircraft struck the water at the angle of descent. Just before impact Ens. William Peterson threw up his hands, the emergency signal to level off, and Owen pulled back on the controls, but too late. The hull collapsed fore and aft of the wings, with radio operator Anderson trapped inside.

Two days later two new aircraft arrived, and then two more in November, making a total of five on hand. Of 89.5 possible flying hours, Whiddy Island pilots actually flew 65.5, including 23 hops in October. The average patrol lasted 60 minutes. Station planes suffered only two forced landings. Several times the flight officer dispatched aircraft in response to suspected submarine sightings. On one occasion a flying boat on patrol received a wireless transmission about a Queenstown plane in distress, flew to the downed aircraft, and rendered assistance. Local pilots also escorted five convoys. Foul weather created formidable impediments to flight operations. Between July 1 and November 11, a period of 134 days, rain prevented activity 78 times. Many other days brought very low ceilings or strong winds. Gale-force blasts October 5 tore the roofs off two buildings and two days later wind speed reached 78 miles per hour.

Notices at the end of October predicting that U-boats operating in the Mediterranean might head for the west coast of Ireland temporarily energized the base. Previous to that "practically no hostile subs operated in Irish waters." Whiddy Island lay well outside scheduled convoy routes and thus few submarines ventured into its patrol sector. Some planners had even advocated sending material and personnel to Lough Foyle or Wexford instead. The German scare, however, quickly caused the Navy to develop plans for mobilizing all aircraft in the area to attack this supposed homeward bound flotilla, but no such movement occurred. Then came the Armistice and thereafter demobilization proceeded quickly, with all equipment removed by February 1, 1919. Total cost of the station amounted to $331,475, with the only unresolved claim being a complaint by Robert Kelly of Bantry who asked for £10 from the U.S. Navy for running over his dog with a station automobile.[26]

Modern-day Whiddy Island is accessed by a brightly painted wooden trawler/ferry that lands passengers at a wharf about a mile southwestward from the former station. The most direct way to reach the site is by foot along the shingle shore. From the beach, one of Europe's largest mussel farms is visible. Surviving evidence of the base is extensive, including a substantial collapsing seawall, remains of the sewage/drainage system, small concrete piers to support aviation gas and fuel oil pipes, the enormous slipway sloping down into the bay, and much of the concrete hardstand, now partitioned by stone walls and overrun with vegetation, but still visible.

The U.S. Navy placed a station at Lough Foyle in northern Ireland as part of the Admiralty plan developed in the summer of 1917. At that time German submarines operated in the vicinity and the facility was intended to guard the North Channel entrance to the Irish Sea. NAS Lough Foyle stood 18 miles from open water on the northwestern shore of a lough of that name, on a small promontory known as Leper's Point. Londonderry lay only 10 miles away. Most observers agreed the site possessed a good strategic location but a very bad meteorological one. High winds, thick clouds, and heavy rain never ceased. Strong gusts demolished a recently built garage on June 9. Lough Foyle began with a planned complement of 18 aircraft, 36 pilots, and over 400 other officers and men but actually finished the war with 7 aircraft, 10 pilots, and 440 personnel present. The station operated under the aegis of the Royal Navy commander at Buncrana, Vice Admiral F. S. Miller.[27] Construction commenced in January 1918 with Irish labor, under Admiralty sponsorship. A few American carpenters commanded by Gunner Herbert Mosely reached the site on February 26. More men arrived in mid-March and additional small groups thereafter. The detachment began quartering at the station in late April. Bosun A. G. Raymond assumed temporary command May 13, followed a few days later by Cdr. Henry Cooke. Initially the Navy encountered great difficulty hauling supplies to the site, a problem eased somewhat with the arrival of trucks driven several hundred miles overland from Queenstown. Work unfolded steadily through the spring—new barracks, hangars, and wells—with the lengthy slipway ready May 1.

The Stars and Stripes first flew over the base on May 20, hoisted aloft on the water tower. Craven and McCrary, along with British and American officers, inspected the station two days later. When Irish laborers went on strike in early June demanding higher wages, Navy enlisted personnel took over the work. The United States formally commissioned the base July 1 as Admiral Miller reviewed American personnel. One notable planning error plagued later operations: the finished slipway stood above the water at low tide, preventing crews from launching or retrieving aircraft at certain times of the day. Lieutenant Carl Hull relieved Commander Cooke on July 7, succeeded in August by Lt. Edward McKitterick. Born on an Indian reservation in South Dakota, he passed through the Pensacola program in 1916 and later directed both the Navy's large ground school at MIT and NAS Chatham on Cape Cod. McKitterick retained command at Lough Foyle until the end of the war.

With construction virtually complete, attention turned to flying. The station received a few seaplane parts in early July, and the first aircraft, shipped aboard *Guyana* to Glasgow and then Londonderry, arrived July 20. A second cargo reached Ireland at the end of the month aboard *Kanawa*, a total of five in all. Station crews loaded the machines aboard trucks and transported them to Lough Foyle. Assembly and modifications began immediately, including rebuilding the steps on the hull. Ammunition arrived in early August and the first successful test flight lasting 45 minutes occurred August 21, following an unsuccessful attempt the previous day. A second flight the following morning ended after only 15 minutes due to "continual high winds, hail, and rain, low hanging clouds." Additional test and instruction hops continued through the last 10 days of August, though shortages of parts slowed work.

Isolated Lough Foyle enjoyed widespread renown for its athletic and entertainment activities. The station team played its first baseball game on Decoration Day and celebrated the Fourth of July with sporting events and a dance organized by the base Welfare Committee. Rain interrupted a second field day August 31 and the men hastily arranged movies and dinner instead, followed by a play "Shove Off," an original musical sketch in two scenes written by a station officer and performed entirely by enlisted men. Another YMCA celebration occurred in mid-October, followed by a new play, *Aces Up*, which premiered before a large crowd, including McCrary. One amateur critic wrote, "The play was very well presented, particularly the members of the troupe impersonating female characters." The YMCA did yeoman work at Lough Foyle, encouraging letter writing, showing movies three nights a week, and running a small school teaching arithmetic, geometry, trigonometry, geography, English, and history. Work began on a station newspaper, *The Ash Can Special*. At least one sailor at Lough Foyle, Benjamin Smith, met his future wife, Margaret Jane Gallagher, while on duty. They married in Londonderry and after the war she accompanied him to the United States.

After a bomb-handling lesson provided by an RAF sergeant, war patrols began September 3 with a four-hour mission flown by Ens. Parker Teulon, followed by a second sortie later the same day. Lough Foyle aircraft escorted their first convoy September 9. Operations continued sporadically throughout the month, as poor weather limited aerial operations to just 16 flights. Patrol missions lasted approximately 2.5 hours. A meteorological facility at Malin Head, the most northerly point in Ireland, dispatched weather bulletins every six hours. Lough Foyle also received reports from the Royal Navy at Buncrana in Lough Swilly. Not surprisingly, the station experienced communications difficulties. The Irish phone system was very poor, and wind and storms frequently downed trees or shorted out the lines, interrupting service for days at a time. Telegrams were "as slow as the mails."[28]

October witnessed increased operations, with patrols conducted most days, usually by one or two aircraft, 23 flights totaling 66 hours, double the record of September. An H-16 crashed October 4 near Warren Point light, hitting the water "with great force" at 90 mph but without casualties. Six days later *SS Otranto* carrying army troops collided with another vessel off the coast. Six bedraggled survivors "in a destitute condition" received medical treatment. Three days after that a station aircraft escorted *HMS Leviathon*, despite winds of 50 mph. In the third week of October, instruments at Mallin Head recorded winds of 97 and 99 mph. While escorting a 32-ship convoy on October 19, a flying boat spotted a submarine and launched a seemingly successful strike for which the crew received official commendation. The station's longest flight occurred October 26 lasting six hours. Only the day before Ens. J. S. Thompson landed at sea and called for help by dispatching a messenger pigeon.[29]

November experienced a reversal of momentum as war-related activity quickly wound down. A storm November 4 wrecked one plane and ripped two others from their moorings. The surrender of Turkey and Austria led to an immediate 50 percent reduction in flying operations, while the Armistice brought an end to all such action. Construction ceased a few days later. All told, Lough Foyle conducted 41 war flights lasting 99 hours and covering 6,000 miles, with aerial operations generally restricted by "bad weather, no compasses, low clouds, and heavy seas." The station hosted a peace banquet and dance November 25, and the first draft of 300 men departed for the United States on December 3. Most officers were detached from service December 7 and ordered to Portland, England, for passage home.

Today the former American station is reached by following the shore road eastward from Londonderry, passing through the small village of Muff. About two miles beyond the settlement a small, pasture-covered promontory slopes gently toward the lough shore. The site is generally bare except for a partial screen of low evergreens and a large, open yard covered with salvaged construction materials. Though none of the 1918 buildings survives, much evidence of the air station remains, including the vast concrete hardstand/apron on which hangars and work buildings once stood, derelict portions of the sea wall, bits of the barracks/mess hall drainage system, and most important, the concrete slipway that slopes into the water and once provided the only means of launching and retrieving bulky flying boats.

Castletownbere kite balloon station, the only such Navy facility in Ireland, stood near the mouth of Bantry Bay, close to the Atlantic Ocean. The base occupied a former golf course laid out for Royal Navy officers about three miles from Castletownbere at a sheltered spot behind Bere Island, which also screened shipping from submarines. McCrary called it the "most logical port in Europe" from which to protect shipping sailing to Britain. Lying within 30 miles of Fastnet light and 60–70 miles closer to the principal transatlantic route than Queenstown, Bantry Bay anchorage could accommodate the entire American fleet. One officer quipped, "Doubtless [God] could make a better harbor, but doubtless God did not." As early as April 1917 the Admiralty suggested that Navy destroyer and patrol craft concentrate their operations at Bantry Bay/Berehaven, and the general conception for the station envisioned transferring kite balloons from shore to ships and then towing them to sea at an altitude of approximately 500 feet to 600 feet. From that vantage observers could spot approaching convoys up to 20 miles farther away than from the vessel's bridge. They could also see mines and submarines and could communicate threats via telephone. Like all the Irish stations, the extremely wet climate negatively impacted operations. While sea-influenced modulated temperatures reduced gas losses, high humidity kept hangars constantly damp, shortening the life of the balloons. Fabric work could not be done in such facilities and crews used a storehouse instead.[30]

The Royal Navy promised to build the balloon station and then turn it over to the United States. In addition, the British utilized the same site to construct a fuel oil depot consisting of two large, circular tanks set in an enormous oval concrete retaining structure. The full site layout included six canvas balloon hangars flanking the road running from the coastal highway to the shore, with requisite barracks, storehouses, offices, and workshops neatly arranged on the former golf links. The oil depot lay a few hundred yards away near the water. McCrary visited Castletownbere on April 18, 1918, and recommended that the site be transferred to American control. At that point the facility was "practically completed" and only awaited delivery of winches. When they arrived, the Navy would recall 24 balloon pilots training at Roehampton. Perhaps five destroyers might operate from here. A small party of 2 officers and 18 enlisted men led by Ens. John Gibson assumed control of the base on April 24. Captain Page, RAF, formally transferred the base to American control on April 29 as Ens. Carl Shumway took command. Shumway, a native of Melrose, Massachusetts, had attended Dartmouth College and trained on kite balloons at Akron in 1917. Within days, an additional 8 flight officers, 1 chief petty officer, and 61 enlisted men arrived and British personnel soon departed for Roehampton.[31]

In a small ceremony, the station company raised the national colors on May 2 and quickly went to work placing the facility in operation. They erected additional buildings, set up gas compressors, put gas generators in working order, and inflated the first balloon on May 16. Lieutenant Commander J. H. Dessez assumed temporary command the following day. Actual flying began May 21 when Ensigns Gibson and Noland conducted practice flights in balloons towed by trucks. The following week McCrary inspected the site and requested that headquarters assign a destroyer to coordinate with the base. None were available, however, and despite original plans Castletownbere never worked with American destroyers. Even without a warship at hand, by mid-June Berehaven had received 18 American-made and 12 British balloons. Sims visited on June 24 and witnessed several exhibition flights. Nonetheless, lack of destroyers and growing convoy operations along the coast of France soon precipitated a decision to shift men and equipment from Castletownbere to the balloon station then under development at Brest. Only three officer-pilots and approximately three dozen enlisted men remained behind as site caretakers. Dessez turned the seemingly abandoned station back to Shumway.[32]

The situation changed yet again on July 14 when *HMS Flying Fox* sailed into Bantry Bay to carry out experimental work. Ratings placed a balloon aboard on July 17, along with nine officers and men. The following morning they took a short trip down Bantry Bay, with a second flight the day after. *Flying Fox* cruised to Queenstown on July 27, with Ensigns Shumway and Charles Reed alternating as pilots. During the voyage a few enlisted men also ascended as observers. The patrol lasted all of one day and most of the next. Ensigns Reed and Harry McIntyre participated in further patrols July 29 and 30. Exercises with the Royal Navy continued into early August, when one mission ended tragically. Three ensigns reported aboard August 11 and the following day the ship set out at dawn with Reed riding aloft as pilot. As the crew hauled the gas bag down on the 13th, it took a sudden nosedive over the port quarter. Reed was thrown from the basket while wearing his harness and parachute. The balloon and gear slipped under the stern, but the vessel could not reverse. Read's body was never recovered.

Ensign Carleton Eldridge succeeded Shumway as base commander on August 19, but he and all personnel relocated to Queenstown only two weeks later under quarantine for spinal meningitis. The future of the base remained in doubt. Many believed it lay too far to the west and proposed building a new facility at Queenstown. Instead, following quarantine, Castletownbere was reinforced yet again with the return of 9 officers and 72 men from Brest. Admiral Mayo and McCrary inspected the site on September 11 and two days later Ens. J. C. Roseborough assumed command. Work on the gas plant resumed, with test flights conducted within 10 days. Revised plans called for a complement of 6 balloons, 12 pilots, and 116 officers and men.[33]

Evolving plans to station three American dreadnoughts in Ireland precipitated renewed activity at Castletownbere. At the end of July, Sims informed Admiral Bayly that the Department contemplated sending three warships of the *Pennsylvania* class to Bantry Bay, with the mission of protecting Allied convoys should German battle cruisers break out from the North Sea. Sims wished to know whether existing antisubmarine nets could provide adequate security. Bayly gave assurances a few days later. The Department then selected *Utah*, *Nevada*, and *Oklahoma* for Irish duty, and the latter two with escorts arrived August 23. *Utah* crossed the Atlantic a few weeks later. Castletownbere station was scheduled to supply emergency balloon personnel to the warships when called on. In fact, the dreadnoughts had been practicing aerial operations for some time. Before heading overseas they conducted exercises off Hampton Roads, and between July 14 and 26 launched balloons nearly every day, transferring craft from sub chasers to the larger ships. The squadron operated out of Bantry Bay throughout the fall. Station personnel transferred a balloon to *Utah* on September 20 and in the first week of October placed them aboard *Nevada* and *Oklahoma*. During a severe hailstorm October 4, lightning struck *Utah*'s balloon and it fell into the harbor in flames at 1:30 A.M. The dreadnoughts departed on a three-day cruise October 13, convoying some troop transports and taking three emergency pilots from the station in addition to their own personnel. On the first night out lightning again struck *Utah*'s balloon. A sudden squall carried away *Oklahoma*'s gas bag. *Nevada* lost its balloon but later recovered it.[34]

At the very end of the war plans resurfaced to shift operations to Queenstown and coordinate with destroyers based there, but the conflict ended before any decision could be reached. After the Armistice, military activities quickly ceased, with most personnel withdrawn immediately. A skeleton crew manned the site until February 14, 1919, when they handed it back to the British as No. 17 Balloon Base. The RAF evacuated the base in August 1919, placing it on "care and maintenance" status until July 1920. Despite the Irish Civil War, the Royal Navy retained control of the facility until World War II. Recreating the site's original use, the Castletownbere Golf Club has been active here since the 1980s. Though little evidence of the balloon station remains, a small concrete jetty used for operations in World War I survives, while the golf clubhouse and parking lot stand next to the substantial bulk of the fuel containment structure, which today shelters tennis courts and a miniature golf course.

* * *

An outline of the U.S. aviation program in Ireland emerged as early as October 1917, but actual combat operations did not commence until nearly a year later. The Navy's ambitious efforts encountered enormous challenges from weather, labor, equipment, supplies, shipping, transportation, and inexperience. Limited infrastructure throughout the island only exacerbated the situation. At no time did the program enjoy the same priority accorded efforts at Killingholme, the Northern Bombing Group, or even many of the French coastal stations. Undeterred, officers and men worked very hard, cooperated well with the British, and exhibited great spirit and high morale. Significantly, only the Irish program depended entirely upon American-manufactured aircraft and motors. Unfortunately, both the huge H-16 flying boat and Liberty motor required extensive debugging before they could fully contribute to the antisubmarine campaign, and by then the war was over.

8

ON DUTY, OFF DUTY

The Work and Life of the Station

The two-dozen seaplane patrol and bombing stations established along the coasts of France, Ireland, England, and Italy constituted the iron fist of naval aviation's antisubmarine campaign. Though differing widely in terms of geography, weather, size, and equipment, they shared many features, including physical layout and operational procedures. Organized much like individual warships of the fleet, stations were typically isolated and self-contained, yet closely linked in a larger scheme designed to protect American convoys and Allied merchant ships and hunt U-boats to extinction. Naval aviation stations resembled discrete factory villages but with a more destructive purpose. These military communities, however, lived two separate lives and exhibited two personalities. When "On Duty," almost every action focused on antisubmarine missions and the work and duties that made those missions possible. This included the Navy's highly structured approach to time, work, order, rank, and discipline. Being "Off Duty," and everyone knew exactly when that was, encompassed the officers' and bluejackets' other lives, their leisure time, recreation, athletics, pets, leave, and liberty. One world covered the hangars, launching ramps, armories, shops, and offices. The other included the barracks, mess hall, YMCA hut, makeshift theater, boxing ring, baseball diamond, nearby attractions, and distant metropolises. The two worlds often intersected but never surrendered their essential distinctness.

Antisubmarine missions offered the raison d'etre of the naval aviation station and necessitated regular reconnaissance, convoy escort, and antimine patrols, interspersed with specific *alerte/allo* and rescue operations. All were designed to complement each other and work in coordination with the fleet of surface vessels—destroyers, sub chasers, minesweepers, drifters, and trawlers. For the most part, flying personnel performed their duties in comparative safety. Only at Dunkirk and Porto Corsini did aviators face the risk of combat, although on at least one occasion a surfaced U-boat attacked a dirigible from NAS Paimboeuf and another bracketed a DD flying boat from Dunkirk with shrapnel. Conversely, all personnel, no matter what station they flew from, faced extreme danger from equipment failure at sea or malfunctioning ordnance. In fact, the aviators' war often seemed less directed against the Germans and more against fog, waves, low clouds, physical discomfort, and numbing boredom.

Contemporary U-boats, though mechanically unsophisticated compared to their successors, nonetheless represented cutting-edge technology in their day and posed a lethal threat to warships and merchant vessels alike. Armed with torpedoes with an effective range of up to 10,000 yards and capable of maximum surfaced speeds of 14–17 knots, large submarines traveled as far as 10,000 miles without refueling. Underwater some dashed at seven to nine knots for very short periods or crept along at two or three knots for several hours. They preferred to maneuver for attack on the surface, however, only submerging for the final run. Early in the conflict it took as long as 2.5 minutes for a large boat to drop beneath the waves, but by 1918 oceangoing versions plunged out of sight in about a minute. Smaller coastal versions could dive in 30 seconds. Safe depths exceeded 150 feet. Manned by a crew of 30 to 50 officers and ratings, their greatest advantages were stealth and invisibility, offset by limited underwater endurance, relative fragility, a need to resurface every day to recharge batteries and ventilate the boat, and a complete inability to attack or navigate once totally submerged.

Given these realities, naval aviation's greatest contribution to the antisubmarine war was not sinking U-boats, as it was almost impossible to locate and attack a surfaced vessel successfully before it slipped underwater. Further, most ordnance carried by aircraft proved incapable of destroying a submarine unless it landed virtually on top of the enemy, though bombs could damage sensitive equipment or cause oil leaks, allowing marauding surface vessels to mount depth charge attacks. Rather, aircraft forced submarines to dive when spotted, effectively blinding them, thus granting warships and cargo vessels safe transit through the area. There was an inverse statistical correlation between submarine activity and aerial surveillance, most noticeably at night when aircraft did not venture out and U-boats ran on the surface, and during rough and foggy weather. German commanders commented frequently on the impact of Allied aviation efforts and the ways they necessarily altered U-boat tactics and operational procedures. Aerial patrols also played a useful role detecting floating mines left by UC-class mine-laying submarines, many of which operated out of bases along the Belgian coast.[1]

Antisubmarine aircraft used during the conflict came with their own quirks and shortcomings. Many were mechanically unreliable and underpowered, with limited ordnance-carrying capabilities. The enormous weight of a wooden flying boat hull, as compared to the canvas-covered fuselage of a land aircraft, as well as the tremendous quantity of fuel required for long-range patrols, meant that only small bomb loads could be carried. Principal types employed by the Navy during 1917–1918 included Donnet-Denhaut, Tellier, and Levy-LePen flying boats acquired from the French; Short seaplane bombers and Felixstowe flying boats at RNAS/RAF stations; and HS-1Ls and H-16s manufactured in the United States. Such aircraft typically cruised at speeds of 55 to 75 miles per hour for anywhere from two to five or six hours, though several longer flights occurred. Crew members communicated with the base, ships, and other aircraft with a variety of devices, all with limitations, including wireless telegraph, messenger pigeons, phosphorous and message buoys, Very flares, and Aldis lamps. Armament consisted of .30 caliber machine guns for defense against other aircraft, although at least one attack on a surfaced submarine occurred. Short seaplanes carried just one gun, while the largest flying boats mounted four or five. The French, American, and British navies all experimented with placing cannon aboard aircraft, and at least one Tellier flying boat at NAS Le Croisic was armed with a recoilless rifle.

Depth bombs weighing anywhere from 100 to 230 pounds constituted the chief antisubmarine weapons. The 112-pound example possessed an estimated kill zone with a 30-foot radius and the 230-pound model a somewhat larger 42-foot radius. Over time, smaller bombs came to be seen as ineffective and fell out of favor; they were used only on aircraft that could not accommodate larger weapons, especially French machines. Late in the war a few British stations began utilizing a 500-pound bomb with a supposed lethal zone of a 51-foot radius. A delayed action fuse detonated the bombs at a predetermined depth of 60 to 80 feet below the surface.[2] A mixture of TNT and ammonium nitrate known as amatol typically provided explosive power. Fuses consisted of a detonator utilizing fulminate of mercury set off by a spring-activated firing pin. The small explosion, in turn, detonated a relay of several blocks of Tetryl (TNMA = trinitromethylaniline), which then set off the entire weapon. British bomb makers created delay fuses by incorporating an additional restraining celluloid disc, a capsule of acetone, and a secondary firing pin. When the detonator in the nose of the bomb hit the water, the secondary firing pin ruptured the acetone-containing capsule and the corrosive liquid quickly dissolved the celluloid restraining disc, thus releasing the primary firing pin and detonating the bomb. Some French ordnance had the unfortunate habit of exploding upon impact, defeating the purpose of using a delay fuse. Station personnel stored bombs and detonators in separate buildings, well apart from each other, gasoline tanks, and the other structures. Excessive moisture in the magazine sometimes caused the ammonium nitrate to absorb water, even to the point of oozing liquid through the fuse hole, though this was not considered dangerous due to the great stability of the amatol mixture.[3]

Allied aircraft employed varied bomb-dropping apparatuses during the war. A report written by Lieutenant Donnelly in late January 1918 described several utilized by the RNAS, but noted "none . . . are giving entire satisfaction." The constant "working" of the aircraft structure frequently interfered with their operation. Bomb-carrying devices also posed challenges. Malfunctions experienced on a Handley Page mission executed in March 1918 forced Lt. Eddie McDonnell to leave his assigned position to release jammed bombs with a sharp kick. A balky bomb carrier at NAS St. Trojan in August 1918 caused a blast on the launching ramp that killed eight sailors. A similar explosion at NAS Le Croisic the previously March ripped a taxiing flying boat in half. To avoid further accidents, aircrews on Le Pen flying boats carried out patrols with the bombs' safety engaged at all times. A special mechanism tripped the safety and armed the bomb only "when dropping for a war shot." During the war the Allies devised numerous bombsights. American forces operating in England most frequently utilized the Wimperis Mark II-A model, supplanted by the Wimperis Mark I Course-Setting Sight. After adjusting for altitude and airspeed, the bombardier aimed it like a rifle. Without a stabilizer, however, movements of the airplane in flight affected the Mark I's accuracy, although it could compensate a little for wind. According to Ensign Fuller at Dundee, "Not much faith is put in bomb sights here, and a practical eye is considered of more use."[4]

Despite many advances, mechanical and structural problems plagued aerial operations throughout the war. Neither the state of technology nor contemporary manufacturing methods produced many reliable motors. Power plants and their electrical systems used at sea suffered from exposure to salt and the extended strain of lifting huge flying boat hulls aloft. Forced landings caused by damaged radiators, broken propellers, substandard magnetos, defective exhaust systems, and faulty crankshafts posed an ever-present danger. The pounding of the waves whether planes were taking off, landing, or taxiing at sea stressed every seam and connection. Flying boat hulls, complicated examples of the boatbuilder's craft, tended to leak, especially if stored outside or in the water, and required constant care by skilled carpenters. The British found that these airplanes enjoyed an active service life of only six months. Floatplane pontoons leaked constantly, collapsed during rough landings, and if filled with water might cause the airplane to flip over on its back, while the engine-radiator-propeller combination in the nose of some machines severely limited visibility. Controlling the largest flying machines while on patrol demanded exhausting effort, which, combined with the thunderous roar of the engines and bone-chilling cold of open cockpits, made for a thoroughly uncomfortable experience.

Reports of aircraft and crews forced down at sea due to unreliable equipment crowd the annals of early naval aviation, beginning with Kenneth Smith's ordeal at Le Croisic in November 1917. The commanding officer's monthly operations report from that base for May 1918 identified 10 forced landings at sea "due to gas tanks breaking loose from supports, magneto trouble, oil pump pressure going down, carburetor trouble, and valve trouble." Other difficulties included one aircraft losing its left wing during a forced landing at sea, while a second seaplane set down during low tide, punching a hole in the hull abaft the after step.[5] Virtually every station experienced problems of this sort. In one particularly harrowing episode American Ens. E. A. Stone and British Sub-lieutenant Moore from RAF Calshot on the Isle of Wight spent 3.5 days clinging to the underside of a capsized Short bomber.

With Stone at the controls they departed June 4, 1918, at 9:00 A.M. on convoy patrol, but their balky Sunbeam motor soon "dropped dead" and they landed in rough seas. Without a radio, the stranded aviators released a pair of pigeons. One returned to the station, but the other perched on a wing. Moore threw his navigation clock at the bird, which then flew away from the wreck but failed to return home. The flyers spent three days holding on for dear life, soaked and battered by waves, with no food or water. Finally, on the evening of the fourth day a trawler approached and effected a rescue. Moore lost six toes to gangrene. Ironically, aircraft and vessels from both sides of the Channel had been searching for them since the first pigeon brought news of their dilemma, but with no success.[6]

Antisubmarine and antimine patrols occurred whenever manpower, weather, and equipment permitted. Along the French coast they were done in a precise way, with charts dividing the patrol area into a series of grids, constructed of boxes 25 miles square, then subdivided into smaller 5-mile squares. Patrols typically extended 50 miles or so out to sea and aircraft transmitted their "exact" positions every half hour, either by radio or pigeon. NAS Le Croisic, one of the busiest American stations, dispatched three sections of two aircraft daily to conduct patrol and convoy work, and occasionally as many as four or five, if equipment and weather conditions permitted.[7] Aircraft patrolling the North Sea often utilized the "Spider Web" system of octagonal grids 60 miles across. Once airborne, crews depended almost entirely on basic eyesight, perhaps aided by binoculars, to detect submarines. Very few enemy vessels were ever spotted, occasionally a periscope wake, and more often oil slicks glistening on the surface that might indicate the presence of a U-boat lying beneath. Over time "open-ended" searches fell out of favor as they rarely resulted in documented contact with enemy ships, replaced by special patrols dispatched to a specific area identified by radio intercepts.

Sheer boredom often constituted flyers' greatest emotion, especially along the western coast of France, where submarine sightings decreased rapidly in 1918. Physical discomfort augmented boredom. As early as March 1918 Reginald Coombe at Le Croisic complained to a friend, "This sea work is getting very monotonous; no subs around here. I believe they're getting fewer and fewer; we plot every one seen on a chart and there are hardly any on it now." In a similar vein Edwin Pou wrote to DeWitt Ramsey at Paris headquarters in October 1918 asking for help "securing a transfer to ANYWHERE from Ile Tudy." After three months on the south coast of Brittany, he was "fed up with everything on or near the station." Pou chafed to get into the action "before the big game is up," claiming the greatest excitement he had "was the hop we had together down here when we came near blowing up that sub-chaser." By contrast, Ens. George Montgomery, who served at Killingholme, Queenstown, and Lough Foyle, didn't complain, recalling, "I remember being able to look downward at waves instead of sideways at bullets."[8]

Physical discomfort accompanied many flights. Open cockpits exposed all crew members to extremes of wind, rain, and cold. No matter how many layers of silk, wool, leather, and fur aviators donned, hour after hour aloft left them stiff or numb. Kenneth MacLeish reported that early spring missions high over Flanders froze the alcohol and castor oil in his instruments. Other aviators suffered extensive frostbite. Sitting near the roaring engines induced further discomfort. According to Coombe, "In these damn machines you sit right under the motor and the noise is terrible; after a two-hour flight you have a hell of a headache and don't feel like doing a damn thing for the rest of the day." Castor oil exhaust fumes from some motors caused serious intestinal distress. Heavy controls on larger flying boats induced considerable fatigue in the pilots who wrestled the yoke for many hours. Oxygen deprivation and resulting "muddle-headedness" also afflicted flight crews operating for long periods at high altitudes.[9]

Despite the monotony and discomfort, the chance of unexpected action remained an ever-present possibility. Pilots' instructions advised them to attack into the wind to lessen the chance of their quarry hearing its pursuer and, if possible, with the sun behind the aircraft. Bombing runs should commence immediately after sighting to reduce the U-boat's chances of submerging. Aggressive tactics urging pilots to "bomb first and ask questions later" occasionally caused embarrassing results. In October 1918 while on patrol from Le Croisic, Ens. Robert Whitehouse spotted "a commotion" northwest of Belle Isle. He approached as rapidly as possible, circled the disturbance, and dropped two bombs, one of which detonated. Later he learned the "commotion" had been caused by the explosions of long-range shells fired from French shore batteries. To avoid the chance of "friendly fire" incidents, American stations received charts and data indicating the areas in which British submarines might be training or operating, as well as various signals by which to identify and contact likely Allied vessels.[10]

Over time, convoy duty constituted an increasing proportion of aviators' efforts. In fact, this proved to be the single most important activity performed by naval aviation during the war. Aircraft greatly augmented visibility of the antisubmarine forces, and U-boats maneuvering on the surface could be detected easily, denying the enemy his chief advantage—surprise. Large flying boats (or dirigibles) with great loiter time and relatively low speed met individual convoys well offshore, whether traversing coastal routes or arriving from the United States. NAS Killingholme on the northeast coast of England safely shepherded more than 6,000 vessels between ports. Stations such as Ile Tudy and Le Croisic specialized in convoy escort work. Aerial escort tactics in French waters achieved tremendous success. When first picking up a convoy, flying boats circled over it, flying low enough to be clearly identified. One aircraft remained around the mass of ships while the other flew ahead, scouring the ocean for submarines and mines by zigzagging broadly before returning, repeating the maneuver as often and as long as possible. Before departing, the aerial guardians circled one more time. Aircraft communicated with ships by means of message buoys, phosphorous buoys, and Very pistols. If launching an attack against a suspected submarine, the airplane dropped a phosphorous buoy to alert patrol boats working in the same area.[11]

At most stations, one or two aircraft constituted an "Alert" section, ready to take off almost immediately in response to suspicious sightings. The *Allo* might come via radio, pigeon, or telephone. In addition to aircraft aloft, stations maintained a motor launch ready to respond to accidents or mechanical breakdowns. According to one chronicler, at NAS Ile Tudy "hardly a week would go by that *Allos* were not received." In March the commanding officer noted, "It has been the aim of this station to have at least two machines ready to take to the air at short notice." The Alert section answered two *Allos* that month, and both times seaplanes took off within 15 minutes. On March 14 flyers reached the designated area "six minutes after receiving the warning." During the spring, submarine alerts arrived at American bases at the rate of dozens per week, and several triggered aggressive, though usually unproductive, responses. Le Croisic received a submarine report at 1:00 P.M., May 18, and two seaplanes set out within 15 minutes, followed by two more a half-hour later, and still two more an hour after that. The warplanes searched for five hours, only ceasing due to darkness and an approaching thunderstorm. When news of a U-boat cruising the Bay of Auderne reached Ile Tudy July 5, two seaplanes hastily responded. Discovering a suspicious wake, one plane marked the spot with a phosphorous buoy and then both aircraft attacked, dropping their bombs in advance of the wake. One did not explode. Several minutes later the water erupted, probably from the delayed detonation of unexploded ordnance.[12]

Given the hazards of early flight, station personnel conducted numerous search and rescue missions. This might be accomplished by sending out scouting aircraft that could land beside a downed flying boat and retrieve the marooned crew, or dispatching a motor launch, often in very rough seas. The men at Dunkirk frequently assisted in searches for British and French flyers as well as their own crews. Sailors at Ile Tudy came to the rescue of French crews from Camaret and L'Orient. If possible, they towed downed planes back to the station. In August 1918, Di Gates and his observer rescued the crew of a British Handley Page that had ditched off the coast at Nieuport and clung to the floating wreck for nine hours. Another rescue mission mounted at Dunkirk in early July resulted in the loss of the motor launch to enemy fire, capture of the station doctor and two sailors, and death by drowning of another crewman.

The general unreliability of the complex weapons systems known as World War I flying boats made so many rescues necessary. Though several flyers died in crashes, those who set their machines down safely in the water survived. Miraculously, not a single American aviator was "lost at sea." In all cases, stricken craft managed to stay afloat, sometimes for several days, long enough for help to arrive. This was due at least partially to the fact that aircraft patrolled relatively close to shore (as did German submarines), and warships, cargo vessels, and fishing boats literally infested the waters, despite the U-boat threat. Due to the undependable nature of contemporary aircraft, general instructions disseminated in August 1918 permitted large flying boats to venture forth singly, but decreed that smaller machines go out only in pairs. If one encountered trouble, the other should turn back. Orders forbade pilots to undertake flights outside their assigned sectors. Before each flight the pilot should inspect his aircraft carefully: motor, structure, ordnance, accessories. At least four pigeons should be taken on patrol and, if necessary, released in pairs to lessen the threat of hawk attacks.[13] Commander Herbster at NAS Wexford offered additional advice. He demanded frequent weather reports throughout the day, coupled with careful and redundant inspection of aircraft by the pilot, chief pilot, machinist mates, and engineering officer. Preflight tune-up began early to discover any faults. Herbster required accurate and detailed orders from the intelligence officer, coupled with an absolute prohibition of stunt flying.

By the spring of 1918 a combination of research and firsthand experience led headquarters to codify the types of skills necessary for crews to carry out their assigned operations. In addition to basic flying proficiency and boat handling, HS-1L and H-16 pilots studied aerial navigation, bombing, gunnery, and recognition of ships and submarines. Enlisted observers, engineers, and radio operators necessarily honed their skills in radio telegraphy and telephony, bombing, aerial gunnery, and engine mechanics. Those flying two-place day bombers and observation aircraft practiced formation flying, station keeping, and high altitude bombing. Dirigible pilots studied aerostatics, meteorology, aerial navigation, low altitude bombing, ship recognition, map reading, and airship rigging. Lighter-than-air crew members mastered a range of duties, including radio telegraphy, visual signaling, airship rigging, engine mechanics, ship and seaplane recognition, and directional and altitude piloting, as well as the care and use of 47 mm and 75 mm rapid-fire cannon.[14]

Flight operations at most stations typically began early, well before dawn, with preparations initiated the previous afternoon. At Fromentine, the engineering officer notified the Flight Department of aircraft available for use for the following day, usually around 4:30 P.M. The Flight Department then informed pilots, observers, and beach and hangar gangs of the scheduled departure times the following morning, which planes would be used, and other necessary details. The position of the convoy to be escorted and weather conditions governed the time of departures. *Allo* planes were to be kept warm throughout the day and ready to depart within three minutes. At northerly Killingholme, the first morning flight often lifted off by 5:00 A.M., or even earlier. The station log even recorded a July 9 antisubmarine patrol setting out at 4:15 A.M., and another August 10 at 4:00 A.M.

Effectiveness of the missions depended directly on the quality of intelligence available. In France, a Franco-American office in Brest, in liaison with district commanders along the coast, directed all shipping movements.

Notices of proposed/scheduled convoys reached stations the previous day by encrypted telegram. When the Navy began patrolling, Craven deemed the system unsatisfactory, calling it indirect and very slow. At first there were no intelligence officers to gather, digest, and distribute information; those tasks typically fell to the chief pilot. By the end of the war, however, trained officers served at each station whose duties included keeping track of confidential charts and the position and movement of aircraft, mines, and submarines in the area, issuing patrol orders to pilots, ascertaining the number of available aircraft, and monitoring shipping in the patrol area. They also digested and distributed intelligence reports collected at the station, acted as liaisons with other bases, and learned how to identify friendly submarines.[15]

NAS Wexford's Intelligence Department offered a model for many stations. Operations centered on a plotting room containing chart boards, material cabinets, drawing table, safe, and necessary furniture. A large grid chart occupied one wall, on which different colored threads marked daily patrols. A piece of paper pushed along a string indicated each aircraft's current position. Small flags denoted the location of U-boats, allied vessels, and allied submarines. The unit performed many tasks: coding and decoding all messages to and from aircraft, other stations, or headquarters at Queenstown; adding daily recognition and identification codes/signals to patrol orders; preparing charts and courses for pilots, corrected by the latest weather forecasts from the meteorological office; developing wind deflection cards and discs; tracking submarines, and providing the latest data on enemy activity. To maintain rapid communication between the radio hut, intelligence office, and commanding officer (via his yeoman), the crew installed an intrastation telephone line.[16]

Before each patrol at Lough Foyle, the intelligence officer briefed pilots, giving them a blueprint chart to trace their course. They were to maintain contact via radio and pigeons. Radios were effective up to 40 miles. Each station operated a radio sending and receiving unit, consisting of two tall masts supporting antennae wires and nearby radio hut. American facilities in Ireland and England employed British equipment, while those in France made use of radios manufactured there. Short seaplanes operated at most English coastal stations carried sending dynamos powered by batteries or wind-driven propellers to transmit and receive messages through 300 feet of dangling aerial wire. At L'Aber Vrach, flying boats utilized antennae constructed of 150 feet of silicon bronze stranded wire with lead weights at the end, wound on a reel inside the hull. When airborne, the wire was let out through a tube and trailed astern. When ready to land, the radio operator reeled in the antenna and placed a watertight cap over the opening. Dirigibles used similar reel-type antennae. Radios remained a problem until the end of the war. As of October 22, 1918, aviation forces in Europe possessed 50 operating airplane transmitters of French and British types. Units from the United States for H-16 aircraft were too heavy. Lighter units were in transit for two months or more. Intercom telephone sets had not yet proved practicable. Orders from the British for radio sets were still incomplete. Shortly before the end of the war several aircraft carried out experiments using telephones, allowing efficient pilot-to-pilot communication, but only over short distances.[17]

As communications equipment did not function when an airplane floated in the water and often failed while airborne, the role of messenger pigeons, *pigeons voyageurs*, proved crucial. Each station maintained a flock and they lived on special diets of dried rice, peas, corn, flax seed, and other grains, most of it shipped from the United States. Handlers trained the birds by first letting them grow familiar with their new surroundings, and after a week or two taking them short distances away from the station and releasing them for a quick flight home. Over time the pigeons returned from ever-greater distances, up to 70 miles. The birds went on patrols for further training, carried aloft in small (wicker) boxes. Pigeons proved very reliable and played crucial roles in several rescues. Messages written on small pieces of tissue paper were placed in an aluminum capsule attached to the bird's leg. In at least one case the disoriented crew of a flying boat turned a bird loose and followed it home. Aviator John Schieffelin recounted the story of a pigeon that saved the crew of a British F2A operating out of Great Yarmouth. The plucky bird carried a message from the aircraft downed at sea 100 miles back to the station and then died on the launching slipway. Following rescue, station officers stuffed the animal and placed it under a glass dome. A brass plate carried the epitaph, "A very gallant Gentleman," and visitors saluted the plucky animal whenever they entered or departed the mess hall.[18]

Setting a pigeon loose from a floating plane entailed no risk, but starting a bird while in flight posed a challenge. The handler began by holding the wings firmly against its body, standing up in the cockpit, leaning as far over the side as safely possible, and then throwing the pigeon clear, downward and outward, to lessen the risk of being hit by the aircraft or propeller. Flight crew and pigeon handlers were cautioned never to feed the birds before a mission or they might not return to base. Though several birds were lost to hawks, most made it home. During the war Le Croisic received at least 70 pigeon messages, while Ile Tudy received 49, Paimboeuf 35, and Dunkirk 24. At Pauillac, 78 birds delivered 698 messages in one month. One drawback—the birds did not fly at night or in heavy fog.

While comparatively few aviators died directly from encounters with the enemy, the work proved very dangerous nonetheless. Porto Corsini lost three pilots/observers in crashes. Additional training deaths occurred at Bolsena, Dunkirk, Moutchic, and Felixstowe. Phillip Page died at Felixstowe in December 1917 during an orientation flight. At the Moutchic school Ensigns Lloyd Petty and Woldemar Crosscup were killed in crashes. Ensigns Robert Clark and Arthur Bourne and observer William Morse all died at Brest harbor in August in the crash of an HS-1L. Whiddy Island's only operational fatality occurred in October 1918 when the crew of a returning H-16 became disoriented and crashed at sunset. Nor was danger restricted to flight personnel. Much of a handling crew at St. Trojan perished while launching a Levy-LePen aircraft when a bomb dropped from its rack and exploded, killing eight. Mechanic George Killeen died in a work-related accident at Porto Corsini when a blowtorch exploded in the machine shop. At Paimboeuf, seaman N. H. Lamport walked around a dirigible engine nacelle during a test run and was struck by the propeller.

All the effort and expense of creating a system of antisubmarine bases would have been for naught without sufficient quantities of modern aircraft capable of carrying out the missions necessary to defeat the underwater menace. Given the limited capacity and experience of domestic airplane manufacturers in April 1917, it was virtually assured that America would be forced to rely on foreign-built aircraft for a year or more. At the outbreak of war the Navy placed orders for several hundred training aircraft, including Curtiss N-9s, R-6s, and F boats. With instructional needs in the United States addressed, it became necessary to determine naval aviation's war role and from whence combat aircraft could be secured. At first it was not even certain that the nation would manufacture and send combat airplanes abroad. Nonetheless, by October the Navy had committed to building and operating a substantial collection of patrol bases and schools stretching from northern England and Ireland to southwest France. This led to the purchase of scores of European aircraft and construction of many hundreds more in the United States. Aircraft such as the large H-16 and its smaller cousin, the HS-1L were expensive. Financial data supplied to Sims indicated that a fully equipped H-16 cost approximately $38,500, including $18,000 for the hull and wings, $15,750 for the power plant, $2,800 for the ordnance, $1,500 for the radio, and $500 for instruments. The smaller HS-1L also carried a hefty price tag, more than $19,000, including $8,000 for the hull and wings, $7,870 for the power plant, $1,400 for necessary ordnance, $1,500 for the radio, and $300 for instruments. Spare parts and replacement engines, of course, cost extra.

By any measure, these were complex machines, at the outer edge of contemporary technology, and none more so than the Curtiss flying boats employed in Europe and American coastal waters in 1918. Unlike patrols and bombing raids carried out by land-based war planes, overwater antisubmarine missions required naval aircraft that were both aerodynamically efficient and highly seaworthy, able to withstand rough seas and repeated pounding on takeoffs and landings. This demanded a strong, stiff, but relatively light hull-fuselage. Such complicated aircraft required special care. Maintenance crews were admonished NEVER to leave a flying boat hull resting on its bare side bilge and keel. Rather, they should always be chocked. Further, hulls required periodical washing with fresh water to prevent shrinkage, while all metal fittings should be greased for protection from the harsh ocean environment. Finally, most flying boats were designed for patrol only, with pilots warned not to execute steep banks or acrobatics "of any kind without incurring unnecessary danger."[19]

America's overseas stations—the facilities from which aircraft operated, missions were mounted, and where officers and enlisted personnel lived—occupied diverse sites. They included the narrow canal bank at Porto Corsini, a wide estuary at Killingholme, and remote islands at L'Aber Vrach and Bantry Bay, as well as sand dunes at Arcachon, a twisting river at Tréguier, bustling harbors in Dunkirk and Brest, tiny man-made islands at Le Croisic, and even a golf course at Castletownbere. Station complements normally varied from 200 to 400 men, though a few bases such as Killingholme, Pauillac, and Queenstown grew considerably larger.

Stations necessarily occupied sites near the water's edge and typically employed lengthy concrete slipways to maneuver huge flying boats into the water. Many survive to this day. Along rivers and canals, as at Porto Corsini, Tréguier, and Killingholme, stout wooden ramps resting on concrete piers or pilings driven deep into the river silt served the same purpose. Killingholme's two "runways" extended 800 feet out over the Humber mudflats to deep water. At Dunkirk and Le Croisic, both of which experienced enormous ranges of tide, cranes hoisted aircraft from the water and set them atop stone seawalls. Running along the water's edge and extending well inland lay a vast concrete apron or hardstand on which hangars stood and aircraft maneuvered, usually bounded by a protective poured-concrete seawall. At Killingholme, the largest of the American outposts, the hardstand measured 1,000 feet in length.

Airplane and dirigible hangars, the largest and most visible station structures, came in several varieties. The Navy used the canvas-covered Bessaneau type on sites taken over from the French, such as LeCroisic. Typically measuring 65 feet or 85 feet × 91 feet, they could accommodate only the smallest patrol craft, such as Telliers and Donnet-Denhauts. At Porto Corsini and Pescara, the Italian government erected large masonry buildings. One reconstructed triple hangar complex in Porto Corsini remains in use to this day as a warehouse. Killingholme possessed an enormous, metal-sided, 800-foot × 220-foot, 10-bay hangar unmatched at any other station. Most American bases utilized a standardized hangar type constructed of wood, the roofs supported by enormous latticed bow trusses. They incorporated a clear opening 24-feet high and measured 107 feet wide and 93 feet deep. Often doubled, they easily accommodated several of the Navy's largest flying boats. At least one pair remained standing at Wexford until the 1970s. Dirigible stations, located some distance from the sea, required special structures even larger than this, possessing a clear width of at least 70 feet, height of 80 feet, and length of 600 feet, with massive and elaborate doorways and windbreaks. A fair-sized balloon station needed space to accommodate three inflated and three deflated balloons, and construction crews erected rectangular steel-frame sheds with a clear span of 30–40 feet, height of 30–40 feet, and depth of 100 feet. Castletownbere possessed six canvas-covered sheds. Special crews at Pauillac constructed a huge steel-frame assembly shop measuring 250 feet × 600 feet and four standard doubled hangars.

Each base contained a wide assortment of structures, rapidly evolving into small towns. Though not every station utilized exactly the same building types, larger ones exhibited a certain uniformity, particularly those built to the standard Navy plan; wooden or Bessaneau hangars, barracks, mess hall/galley, latrines and wash facilities (many of these discharged directly into the bay/river/harbor), a radio shack and antenna for communicating with aircraft, magazine, administrative offices, power plant, medical buildings (dispensary, ward, open rooms), machine shops, a brig, detonator storage building, carpentry shops, and store and supply buildings, all covering several acres of ground. Many of the buildings at Killingholme and Eastleigh were made of English brick. French-built barracks, shops, and offices, especially those in the south of the country, came whitewashed with tile roofs and decorative gable trim. In Italy, local masons employed concrete block and stucco. Stations built by bluejacket labor utilized "portable" wood-frame structures manufactured at Pauillac or in the United States. Most stations laid out firing ranges and stored detonators, bombs, ammunition, and gasoline in widely separated facilities.

As aviation's focus shifted from construction to combat, Hutch Cone moved to reorganize the command structure, regularize operations at disparate bases, and require uniformity of procedures and expectations. Toward this end he distributed an organizational outline to commanding officers at all naval air stations on August 15, 1918, to "be put into effect at once so far as practicable." The comprehensive directive derived from the work of a conference of station commanders held at Paimboeuf in June. In many ways it followed the Station Order Book compiled by Squadron Commander C. R. Finch-Noyes at RNAS Killingholme the previous year. That document covered all aspects of station routine, including personnel duties, record keeping, communication, schedules, inspections, stores, and more. It even prescribed the proper load of ordnance and ammunition carried on patrols.[20]

First and foremost, the new report outlined the duties of the various officers and departments, including the commanding officer, executive officer, chief pilot, paymaster, medical officer, and those in charge of engineering, ordnance, intelligence, supply, aerographics, radio, transportation, and public works. The commanding officer, always called "Captain" no matter what his rank, bore ultimate responsibility for all personnel and activity. His authority mirrored that of a ship captain and he provided the link to higher command, as well as the local community and Allied officials in the district in which his station operated. He was charged with promoting efficiency and meeting construction and operational goals established by his superiors. As chief executive he coordinated the work of station departments and when practical held daily conferences with all department heads. The captain made regularly scheduled, comprehensive inspections of personnel, facilities, and equipment. The commanding officer reviewed correspondence going to/from headquarters and prepared dozens of required reports, including fitness reports on his officers. As the ultimate source of authority, he bore responsibility for discipline and presided over captain's mast and summary courts-martial. He oversaw station morale, established leave policy and daily work schedules, monitored health and safety, directed boards of inquiry, and made recommendations for decorations. The commanding officer often participated in athletic competitions, hosted major celebrations, and attended station entertainments.[21]

Commanding officers generated mountains of memos, reports, cables, letters, and other materials documenting events and conditions at their bases, but only rarely did they reveal personal attitudes concerning leadership of men and military organizations. Much of what we "know" is gleaned from occasional observations or asides drawn from Board of Inquiry reports, disciplinary proceedings, or postwar reminiscences. Commander Victor Herbster at NAS Wexford, proved the exception. In a *History of U. S. Naval Station Wexford, Ireland*, he provided a detailed analysis of a commander's responsibilities and the impact he should have on the tone, morale, and efficiency of his officers and men. One of the Navy's pioneer aviators, Herbster believed in discipline and work as the keys to successful leadership and "the foundation of efficiency." By his own words he intended to build the "ideal naval air station." Most Wexford sailors were new to the service. If he did not maintain strict discipline, Herbster believed, progress would be delayed and "by the time of operation the station would be in chaos." For this reason he organized his command "practically the same as a ship's organization" and inculcated Navy ideas, Navy ideals, and Navy traditions from the start. Herbster kept his men busy and his station shipshape, ensuring that work parties cleaned up after themselves. Reflecting the pride and prejudices of a line officer, Herbster argued that if a civil engineer were in charge during the construction phase, "great difficulty would have been experienced by the Officers and Commanding Officer upon taking charge."

Centralization and coordination of effort were paramount, with just one motto guiding everyone's actions: "RESULTS COUNT." With labor in short supply, "every man on the station was a valuable asset and every hour of work possible had to be secured out of each and every man." Herbster ordered the executive officer to compile a daily distribution sheet of assignments for department heads who, in turn, prepared their own sheets for chief petty officers and ratings. In this way the commander fixed responsibility for work, with no chance given for excuses. Men and officers learned to "take pride in what they did. . . . They learned that being busy was being happy; they realized that he who excelled was rewarded." Herbster expressed great satisfaction in the progress of his men and station. As each new draft of ratings arrived, it was "swallowed up and became part of the cog wheel." He worked to develop an intense spirit of competition to spur sailors' efforts, one department versus another, Wexford against other Irish stations, all of Ireland against France. Describing competition against cross-Channel stations, Herbster crowed, "Ireland has beaten France so badly as to practically make it no contest at all."

Herbster demanded much of his men and officers and in return did everything possible for their well-being. His aggressive and remarkably successful response to the threat posed by the influenza epidemic offered just one example. Herbster wrote at great length concerning the health, comfort, and contentment of his charges, what he defined as the "mental attitude of the crew and officers." He believed these factors more directly affected efficiency of the station than any others. Toward this end, the medical officer maintained "an eagle eye" on sanitary conditions. He and the officer of the day inspected the food for every meal. Barracks were kept clean and shipshape all day long and living spaces made as "homelike" as possible, supplemented by the attractive YMCA facility. The commanding officer also exhibited an enlightened attitude toward his men's health, urging them to report to the sick bay for treatment rather than feel if they did they would be considered slackers. Given the heavy demands on the men during the week, Herbster insisted that their time off be their own. Regardless of the press of work, "Sunday was given over as a day of rest, recreation, and worship." Only aeronautic crews labored. Though required to conduct Sunday inspections, Herbster performed this duty "to interfere the least possible with the plans of the men."[22]

In addition to the captain, several staff officers worked to ensure that each station carried out its assigned missions competently and efficiently. The executive officer, normally a nonflying position, policed the base; compiled and forwarded all reports; oversaw internal discipline; monitored the comfort, welfare, and education of personnel; bore responsibility for fire drills and firefighting; handled the mail; inspected the food; organized examination boards; and assigned new ratings to specific departments. Many kept an index file of personnel, noting their occupations in civilian life and service experience. An officer of the day served a 24-hour stint and assisted the executive officer in carrying out the daily routine, fire drills, and firefighting. Other duties included ensuring that barracks, washrooms, and heads were kept shipshape; writing the daily log; inspecting the mess for cleanliness; seeing that the men turned out promptly for reveille and turned in after taps; investigating reports of misconduct; determining that sufficient drinking water was available; and supervising the movements of liberty parties.

Kenneth Whiting at Killingholme called for a flying officer, designated the squadron commander, to direct the Operations Department; he was to be the next most senior officer to the commanding officer and assume control of the station if his superior were called away. Such an officer should not be hampered with any administrative details that were not "intimately connected and vital to the operations." He exercised immediate control over flying crews, gunners gang, hangar crews, boat crews, aerographer, intelligence, communication, and photography. Bruce Leighton filled this role admirably. At other stations the chief pilot typically performed these functions, directing the flight department, with responsibility for operation of all aircraft and organization of squadrons and flights.

Upon receiving information from the intelligence officer, the chief pilot wrote specific flight orders for daily patrols and ensured that individual flight records and daily flight reports were submitted after completion of every mission. The chief pilot also served as chief inspector. He informed the engineering officer of the condition of the planes, regulated the time and order of flights, and directed movement of aircraft. Handling crews (the "beach party") maneuvered the machines in and out of the hangars and up and down the slipways. The engineering officer, working closely with the chief pilot, oversaw maintenance and repair of all power-driven machinery, shop and power plants, and machine tools. This duty extended to repairs of mechanical equipment, radios, instruments, armament, and most important, aircraft. The station's various machinists, carpenters, and artificers reported to this officer.

Without accurate information, aviation stations literally "flew blind," and a skilled intelligence officer was essential to carrying out daily missions. Headquarters believed such officers must possess a good general education; some military training; general knowledge of navigation principles; and the ability to handle paperwork, collect and tabulate information, and sum up and draw conclusions quickly. Those whose previous civilian occupations might have prepared them included businessmen and lawyers, technical salesmen, and men with experience managing industrial work. The intelligence officer, "virtually a confidential aide to the Commanding Officer," performed multifaceted duties. He secured and dispensed information on operating aircraft, maintained charts displaying the disposition of enemy vessels, prepared daily station compilations of statistical data, and oversaw signal equipment. He also furnished outgoing flights with necessary charts, information, signaling devices, and confidential patrol orders carried in a weighted bag. The communications, radio, photography, and aerographic officers reported to the intelligence officer. The radio officer directed the entire radio plant, radio compass, and all erected installations, and also tested often-unreliable radios to ensure they were in working order. His qualifications included general knowledge of all signaling methods, coding, and decoding; excellent knowledge of gas engines, storage batteries, operation and installation of wireless telephone sets; and the ability to send and receive 30 words per minute by radio telegraph.

Station officers performed a range of duties; many were pilots who wore two or more hats. The ordnance officer directed the care, preservation, and maintenance of bombs and rockets; managed the magazine; and provided weapons instruction, serving as gunnery officer. An additional duty included oversight of the station guard. Such a position required actual experience in the care, repair, and use of machine guns and small arms and methods of handling ammunition and bombs. The possible recruiting pool included gunners, ex-gunners, or reserve officers with the necessary arms experience and the ability to act as bombing instructors. The supply officer, a member of the

Paymaster Corps, handled routine station business, ensured prompt delivery of stores, requisitioned necessary materials, and maintained bookkeeping records. One commander noted, "Nothing is more necessary to a station than a live-wire Supply Department." Quoting the old proverb "God helps those who help themselves," supply officers scoured every source for as long as it took to acquire "it," whatever "it" was.

The station medical officer, a critical position during the great influenza epidemic, kept health records and made reports. He remained on duty whenever aircraft operated, while also supervising base sanitation and providing medical care as appropriate. This included the barracks, mess hall/galley, and latrines. Regulations required doctors to be on hand in case of accidents, either at the landing or aboard the rescue launch. This requirement led to the capture of Dr. Albert Stevens near Dunkirk in July 1918. The transportation officer exercised authority over transport and took control of supplies while in transit. Qualifying experience included handling men and the care of motor vehicles, as well as the ability to unload stores. Repair officers might include ex-railroad machinists, men who operated or managed automobile and gas engine repair shops, or Navy officers with mechanical experience and a general knowledge of aircraft. Finally, the public works officer, often a civil engineer, directed all construction, maintenance, and inspection of buildings, magazines, water systems, hoists, and other aspects of the station's infrastructure. Hutch Cone's mid-August circular also suggested appointment of an athletics officer to oversee and promote that important aspect of station life.[23]

The senior officers and hundreds of aviators who formed the heart of the Navy's overseas aeronautic campaign traveled many different routes to their European rendezvous. Principal commanders were all Annapolis graduates who had compiled extended service at sea, including action in the Spanish-American War and with the Great White Fleet, but were not aviators. This group included Hutch Cone (CO USNAFFS), Thomas Craven (HQ), Henry Dinger (HQ), Bayard Bulmer (Eastleigh), David Hanrahan (NBG), and Frank Taylor Evans (Pauillac). Nonflying supply, paymaster corps, medical, and civil engineering officers such as Omar Conger also played key roles in the enormous construction, financial, and logistical effort necessary to implement and sustain the naval aviation program.

A few pioneer flyers assumed positions of great responsibility, such as Kenneth Whiting, leader of the First Aeronautic Detachment and later NAS Killingholme, and Frank McCrary, head of naval aviation activities in Ireland. Command of most patrol bases, whether in Ireland, England, or France, went to younger officers, principally Naval Academy graduates, who began flying as early as 1911–1912, and formed the heart of this pioneering venture. Included in this group were Victor Herbster (Wexford), Godfrey Chevalier (Dunkirk), Wadleigh Capehart (Fromentine), William Corry (Le Croisic), Grattan Dichman (Moutchic), Virgil Griffin (St. Trojan), and several others. Of the handful of Coast Guard officers trained at Pensacola, Charles Sugden eventually commanded NAS Ile Tudy. Other pioneering airmen who did not usually command stations but nonetheless held important positions within the aviation hierarchy included Edward McDonnell, Tom Murphy, Bernard Smith, Bruce Leighton, and DeWitt Ramsey. As a group they ranged in age from 26 to 35. Beyond this cluster, however, virtually no Annapolis graduates served as aviators in Europe, based on the Department's decision to retain such officers for duties with the fleet.

Instead, the Navy drew on disparate groups to fill its aviation ranks, both at home and abroad. Several civilian flyers who spent years spreading the gospel of aeronautics joined the service as war erupted. The most prominent included John Callan, who commanded several European stations in their infancy and ultimately directed aviation efforts in Italy. He was joined there by William "Bull" Atwater, who led the American detachment at Lake Bolsena. Another group of early flyers counted a few enlisted men who reported to Pensacola for flight training in 1916. Several went on to serve in Europe, such as Clarence Hawkins who became chief pilot at NAS St. Trojan (after commissioning). A few other bluejackets took their flight training after the outbreak of war, such as Rufus Bush and William Miller. Men like these typically possessed great experience as petty officers or mechanics and proved invaluable in a branch of the Navy where such expertise was in short supply. Lawrence DeSonier, at 30 a rather old trainee who had enlisted in 1910, was eventually assigned to flight duty at Dunkirk.

Recently enrolled enlisted personnel formed the vast bulk of the First Aeronautic Detachment dispatched to Europe in May 1917. This group, more than 100 in all, joined the Navy just before or after the outbreak of war, typically as landsman for quartermaster or landsman for machinist mate. First Aeronautic Detachment enlistees included auto mechanics, newspaper reporters, draftsmen, and toolmakers. Ordered to Pensacola, they received the most rudimentary instruction before sailing to France. Once ashore, they underwent training as pilots or observers, first with the French and later at RFC/RAF or American facilities, and eventually supplied a large percentage of flight personnel at several stations, including Le Croisic, St. Trojan, and

Dunkirk. Many were later commissioned. One FAD member, Charles "Haze" Hammann, received the Medal of Honor for his exploits at Porto Corsini.

Several men who became Navy flyers first served with the Allies, particularly with the French Foreign Legion. Conspicuous among this group was Willis Haviland, who later commanded NAS Porto Corsini. He was joined there by Kimberly Stuart who fought in the French Army at Verdun. His awards included the Navy Cross, the Croix de Guerre, and the Italian War Cross. In fact, a surprisingly large body of men trained and served with the French before joining the Navy, nearly two dozen in all. Many later had active careers over the lines and stalking enemy submarines. Still another group of young Americans performed dangerous duty prior to enrolling in naval aviation driving ambulances in the battle zone, often for the American Field Service but occasionally for the French Army. One more body of men who made a substantial contribution to the naval aviation effort in Europe consisted of those who joined up at Brest or Paris in France and then trained at Moutchic or Lake Bolsena, thus bypassing newly created ground schools back in the United States.

Far and away the largest number of aviators serving in Europe were young men associated with America's colleges, particularly institutions in the Ivy League. The Naval Appropriation Act for fiscal 1917 authorized formation of a Naval Flying Corps (never actually established) and six classes of personnel constituting a Naval Reserve Force. Of these, Class 5 was to form a Naval Reserve Flying Corps (NRFC). Under this scheme, thousands of college men, some as young as 17 and others in their 30s, enlisted in the Navy, most commonly with the rank of seaman 2c. From the enlistment office they were assigned to ground school, typically at MIT or Dunwoody Institute. Upon completion they shifted to Pensacola or Miami for preliminary flight training. If successful, they were certified as proficient in heavier than air flight (HTA) and following examination, commissioned as ensigns. Many then received gunnery training in Texas and large flying boat instruction at Hampton Roads before sailing for Europe.

Some college volunteers belonged to units organized before the war, such as the famous First Yale Unit. Others coalesced just after the fighting began, including a sizable group from Princeton, who trained with the RFC in Toronto in the summer of 1917; a similar group of Harvard men who learned their craft at Hampton Roads, Virginia; and the Second Yale Unit, which received instruction at Buffalo, New York. These early pilots did not attend formal ground school. Once tested, commissioned, and ordered overseas, the "college boys" filled virtually every available position, from station commander to executive officer, chief pilot, and on down. In addition to volunteers from Yale, Princeton, and Harvard, their peer schools in the Ivy League supplied scores of recruits. Other colleges from around the nation also sent forth a flood of volunteers. Even the New England Conservatory of Music supplied a few recruits.

The vast majority of aviation officers serving in Europe were young men only a few months removed from college or civilian life. A few, among them Hoosier Ens. William Jackson and Lt.(jg) Alexander McCormick, learned to fly before they learned to drive an automobile. To better acquaint the youngsters with their new responsibilities, freshly commissioned ensigns arriving from the United States in 1918 took a course of instruction on how to be officers. The orientation stressed the importance of handling enlisted personnel and cultivating the proper spirit. Some degree of self-training would be necessary. Officers should lead by example; avoid criticizing superiors; and show good manners, coolness, and control. In dealing with subordinates, officers should know the men thoroughly and interest them in their work. Praise always yielded better results than censure, but if necessary, it should never be public. Suggestions should be welcomed. Smartness and cleanliness were essential. In the tradition of all military units, petty officers were to be seen as invaluable assets. New officers were admonished to look out for the comfort of their men, stimulate competition, and guard their charges from petty annoyances.[24]

Bluejackets performed most work at the station. Actual distribution of enlisted personnel to various departments varied widely, based on the type of aircraft flown, level of flight activity, and progress of construction. NAS St. Trojan began active operations in August 1918 with a complement divided into eight departments, and the variety of specialties was extensive. Dirigible station NAS Guipavas' ratings included seamen, carpenters mates, machinist mates, quartermasters, electricians, firemen, ships cooks, mess attendants, ships fitters, yeomen, coppersmiths, blacksmiths, pharmacist's mates, boatswain's mates, storekeepers, hospital apprentices, and painters, as well as a coxswain, gunner's mate, plumber, warrant officers cook, and chief commissary steward. All carried photographic I.D. cards

The station complement offered a varied cast, with its own pecking order. According to some tongue-in-cheek observers, specific ratings exhibited distinctive traits and personalities. At Eastleigh, near the English Channel, boatswain's mates possessed voices like foghorns and an aching desire to put men on report. A ship's cook always got enough to eat, and the best, but was often accused of poisoning the ship's company. Machinists mates were rough and ready with an enormous capacity for spirits—not the heavenly kind. Storekeeper was a political rating held by former city councilmen, lobbyists, and broken down Republicans. A chief special mechanic received the pay of a senator, possessed the knowledge of a Schwab, and strutted about with the air of a duke. Seamen went around without a single care in the world, free and happy-go-lucky, possessing an intense hatred of work and the knack of getting the pretty girls in town. Finally, there was "Landsman for Something," with undiscovered genius and ability just cropping out. He could convince everyone of his extraordinary abilities except the examining board.[25]

The proficiency of specialist aviation ratings directly affected a station's success. Paris headquarters suggested that riggers be trained in the assembly of machines at either the Naval Aircraft Factory or the Curtiss Company. Ideally, carpenters, both quartermasters and carpenter's mates, came from the ranks of experienced cabinet and furniture makers. For machinist's mates the Navy should rely on men trained at the Packard, Pierce-Arrow, Stearns, and Crane-Simplex factories, as well as the nation's industrial teaching institutions. Fabric men could be drawn from the most qualified sailmaker's mates with the ability to recover wings by all methods, sew by hand and machine, and patch fabric on wings. Experienced acetylene welders made the best coppersmiths, with responsibilities including sheathing propellers and baffling gasoline tanks. In the spring of 1918, armorers were in short supply and the Navy depended on instruction provided by the British. Headquarters recommended additional armorers be trained in the United States in the care and upkeep of machine guns, mounting and synchronizing of gears, mounting bomb racks, and armament and care of bombs.[26]

One group generally missing from the ranks of naval aviation overseas was women. While many observers remarked on the presence of female staff at French, Italian, and British installations and factories, the American force was largely devoid of females, except for a few civilian clerical employees at the major headquarters sites. The Navy's "Yeomanettes," roughly the equivalent of the Royal Navy's WRNS, were not assigned duty overseas. There were, nonetheless, thousands of American women doing war work overseas— nurses, YMCA girls, ambulance drivers, Red Cross entertainers, first-aid workers, Salvation Army "Doughnut Girls." Both aviation officers and enlisted men took every opportunity to meet them and spend time together. Another group rarely encountered among overseas aviation forces were the Navy's African American sailors. The rigidly segregated institution provided few opportunities for Black enlistees, and African American flyers or skilled ratings were unheard of. Nonetheless, a few blacks were employed as cooks, stewards, messmen, and stevedores. When George Moseley reached Dunkirk in late March 1918 he described officers' quarters as a villa near the shore, where "three American Negroes keep the place neat and clean, serve our meals, and in short, are nothing more or less than our valets." A group of Black stevedores helped extinguish a potentially catastrophic fire aboard an ammunition ship docked at Pauillac in November 1918.[27]

No matter what the day or duty, the clock ruled sailors' lives. Life at NAS La Trinité began with reveille at 5:30 A.M. The men at Queenstown might stay in bed until the advanced hour of 6:30 A.M. Standardized printed daily schedules, however, failed to reveal the intricate ballet of station activities. A "typical" day at Lough Foyle began with all hands turning to at 6:00 A.M., followed by barracks cleanup and swab down and then inspection. At 6:45 the men washed up and cleaned mess gear, while also welcoming the return of overnight liberty parties. They ate breakfast at 7:00 and mustered a half-hour later, followed by morning colors. Sick call commenced at 8:30. Throughout the morning a seemingly endless series of drills and inspections proceeded—firefighting equipment inspection, boat drill, inspection of mess cooks and servants, Seamen's Guard drill, inspection of provisions, station inspection by the executive officer.

Midday meal break came at 11:30, with dinner served at noon, followed by first mail call. The men mustered at their barracks at 1:00 P.M. and resumed work. Cleanup of shops, hangars, beach, and slipway began at 4:30 and the workday ended at 5:00. Daily liberty parties mustered for inspection at 6:30 and "went ashore" (departed the station). At 8:00 heads of departments reported; at the same time the executive officer, captain of the yard, and officer of the day carried out their individual inspections. Many enlisted men used this period for recreation, relaxation, or study. Evening colors sounded at sunset. Lights and fires were extinguished at 9:00, with tattoo at 9:55 and taps five minutes later. The officer of the day performed further inspections at 10:00, 12:00, and 2:30 A.M. The station posted a guard throughout the day and night on a four-hour rotation. In addition to the busy daily routine, the commanding officer mandated a series of weekly activities and reviews. On Mondays, Wednesdays, and Fridays men aired their bedding. Tuesday's duties included testing firefighting apparatus, followed by fire drill on Wednesdays. The station carried out tests of sewerage and sanitary systems on Thursdays. On Fridays the sailors enjoyed a field day. The captain conducted station inspection on Saturdays, followed by review of the men on Sundays.[28]

On occasion, visits by dignitaries punctuated the daily routine, officers such as Admirals Benson, Sims, and Mayo, and Captains Hutch Cone and Noble Irwin, or officials like Franklin Roosevelt, Assistant Secretary of the Navy, or members of Congress. Alonzo Hildreth, the enlisted diarist at Dunkirk, noted July 31, "Today was a big day, or rather we had a big man [FDR] with us, but only for a very few minutes. Just before he got here a German picture machine came over." During their lengthy inspection tours, both Roosevelt and Mayo took meals with the men and attended some of their entertainments. FDR's visit to Pauillac caused one correspondent to report, "His visit proved an appreciated break in the routine life of the camp, such affairs being as rare as the proverbial hen's molars down this way." Not long after, members of the congressional Naval Affairs committee arrived, along with several high-ranking officers. The distinguished group ate dinner with "the dungaree complement," followed by an "inspiring" address from Chairman Padgett who received "rousing applause."

Bluejackets seemed to accept the regimen with good nature and postwar reports almost uniformly complimented their efforts and spirit. No less an officer than LCdr. Benjamin Briscoe, head of the headquarters Assembly and Repair section and the man overseeing construction at Pauillac, lauded the men. In early March 1918 he informed Noble Irwin, "It is marvelous to see how quickly these Navy boys can do things. I look out of the office window in the morning and see a vacant spot. If I happen to look out in the afternoon, it may have a building on it. This happens time and time again."[29] A wag at L'Aber Vrach described the situation a bit more light-heartedly. "We don't have to show we are workers," he opined; "we admit it; each day seems to work wonders at this station. With the buzz of the seaplanes above and the clang of picks, shovels, and hangars below, and the dashing hither and yon of our officers and chiefs after the crafty gobs who are slyly sneaking in every available corner to snatch a smoke."

Despite the grousing typical of military life, most men at naval air stations enjoyed amenities not available to their counterparts aboard ship. Aviation facilities (except NBG aerodromes) occupied fixed locations, with relatively permanent accommodations, and the Navy exerted considerable efforts to provide adequate clothing, barracks, mess halls, latrines and washing spaces, and entertainment opportunities. Nowhere was this more apparent than in the area of food. This was undoubtedly the best-fed group of servicemen the nation had yet sent to war. George Moseley, after flying with the French, transferred to the U.S. Navy, which sent him to Dunkirk. There he lauded "real American meals," oatmeal, sugar, and white bread, and plenty of them. The Navy maintained large freezer facilities at Pauillac from which it distributed meat to the stations and supplied American flour to local bakeries to make fresh bread. According to commanding officer Carlton McKelvey, food at L'Aber Vrach was always excellent, partially due to the site's location near Brest, a principal Army/Navy supply depot. He believed good food contributed to high morale at the isolated station and sailors agreed. When the new mess hall opened, the crew sat down to silverware, vinegar, salt, and pepper containers, "noiseless soup spoons . . . steam-heated ice cream freezers . . . hand-crocheted water bottles . . . and grooved knives so the peas don't slip." Students at Bolsena cheered when "American" food arrived. Their Italian cooks learned "the mysteries of oatmeal and the profound morning kick of American coffee." The men deemed it only fair, as they had done their bit for the war effort by learning to "juggle macaroni."

The widespread presence of pets, a time-honored Navy tradition, supplied another morale booster. L'Aber Vrach enjoyed Buster, a 30-pound shorthaired dog given by the French. The lively animal loved to fly, and whenever an engine started up he trotted over to the aircraft and begged to go. While in flight, Buster stood on the seat with his paws on the edge of the cockpit, looking all around at the sky and water. The Bolsena school kept three dogs named "America," "France," and "Italy." Officers at Le Croisic kept a German shepherd, while Charles Hammann at Porto Corsini had a small canine companion, as did Kenneth MacLeish at Calais. Marine Lieutenant Samuel Richards of the NBG kept a pet dog, "Camouflage," at the field, a gift of some Belgian troops. Local goats also proved popular. The camp mascot at Moutchic often rode around the station perched on the back of a trash-hauling donkey.

The question of recreation and liberty loomed large in the considerations of naval planners. Whether to boost morale, provide rewards for hard work, or keep the men occupied and away from temptation, headquarters took pains to provide officers and enlisted personnel with entertainment, publications, sheet music, athletic competition, and sufficient liberty. In an effort to promote these activities aviation headquarters issued its first Recreation Bulletin May 11, 1918. Several pages long, it included news and gossip about sports teams, visits, poetry, humor, doggerel, cartoons, and entertainment. Killingholme, Eastleigh, and Wexford produced yearbooks, while many stations printed small newspapers, like Paimboeuf's *Gas Valve*, Pauillac's *Pilot*, Fromentine's *Plane Talk*, Lough Foyle's *Ash Can*, and Porto Corsini's *Leading Edge*. A few stations, such as isolated Arcachon, were known as hard-luck posts.

With a population composed of energetic young men, air stations in Europe enjoyed vigorous athletic competition, everything from baseball and football to boxing, track and field, and swimming meets. Commander Bayard Bulmer, commanding officer at Eastleigh, observed, "Give me a boy who likes sports! HE will be far superior in mind and body and more valuable to his country than the man of the common enemy to health giving activities." Wexford commanding officer Herbster became an outspoken champion of the value of competition. In early May, William Corry, the commanding officer at NAS Le Croisic, called baseball the favored sport, with "everyone taking the greatest interest in the old National pastime." Tennis also enjoyed great popularity, with sufficient courts available to accommodate both officers and enlisted men. The arrival of summer promised to make swimming the "first sport," with fine beaches near the station and several talented swimmers among the personnel. An aerial photograph of the kite balloon station at Castletownbere in Ireland reveals hangars on one side of the station, barracks and offices on the other, and a very prominent baseball diamond right in the center.[30]

Headquarters in London, Paris, and Brest supported morale-boosting activities, and each base received at least $75 per quarter for equipment. The station orders manual prepared at Paimboeuf in the summer of 1918 specifically advised commanding officers to encourage athletic activities and appoint an officer to oversee the process. On occasion, however, the rage for sports elicited cautionary admonition. At one point Hutch Cone wrote each commanding officer reminding them construction and other work must be pushed at all costs, even if this meant some restrictions on the amount of athletics and entertainment. Lieutenant Leman Babbitt at Gujan received a specific rebuke for permitting men to play baseball during working hours. He defended himself by denying that his station was "an athletic and entertainment camp." A few weeks later the editor of the Recreation Bulletin, no doubt with official sanction, reassured everyone, "Any intention of frowning on athletics is disclaimed."[31]

Frequent "smokers" provided the venue for raucous celebrations. This popular form of entertainment interspersed skits, music, vaudeville, and boxing. One of the most memorable occurred in early August when Moutchic hosted "another of its famous smokers," with both French citizens and Pauillac bluejackets invited to participate. The grand celebration included a good boxing match, "some darn good musical numbers, and very clever vaudeville sketches." Pauillac reciprocated the following night with a big-time match between their own "Fighting Fitzpatrick" and Moutchic's famed Eddie Nugent. The Moutchic contingent, smelling victory, arrived at 8 P.M. and the bell for the first round sounded at 10. In fact, it was not much of a contest, with Nugent emerging victorious in the second round. The winners spent the next half-hour collecting their loot and set off at 11:30, escorting the "Duke of Moutchic" back to camp.

In addition to athletics, movies, music, and theatrical performances enjoyed enormous popularity, often bringing a bit of home to young men serving an ocean away from familiar surroundings. Paimboeuf screened silent films every Wednesday and Saturday, while Killingholme offered movies three times a week. Station complements contained many musical performers, and virtually every station formed at least one band. Killingholme called its ensemble the "Killingholme Koncert Krowd." Fromentine's band introduced the great "Madelon" to much acclaim, followed by the entire company rising to sing the "Star Spangled Banner" and the "Marseillaise." At the time, jazz was sweeping America, and so too at aviation stations. Fromentine audiences loved "raggy pieces." One listener described a concert as "the realest American thing we have seen in France and it made us homesick. We lacked only our best girl beside us to have the picture perfect." Even at Bolsena a band of local musicians, sailors of the Italian Navy, offered concerts each Sunday evening, playing the latest American music and trying to qualify as a jazz band. Minstrel shows and vaudeville skits entertained enthusiastic crowds. According to one reviewer, a performance at Le Croisic in early May "made the house rock as though Huns were dropping noise pills." Station commander Corry acted as interlocutor. Visits by celebrities such as all-star pitcher Grover Cleveland Alexander and Elsie Janis, "The Sweetheart of the A.E.F.," always drew large crowds. John Schieffelin called her performances "absolutely smashing, as always." National holidays entailed elaborate celebrations.

Virtually every station welcomed the ministrations of the YMCA. The "Y" offered a wide range of activities and amenities, including religious services. The men at Lough Foyle, after working all day, spent some of their free evening time building the "Y" hut, raising nine trusses and metal roofing in just a few hours. In many places the "Y" organized classes in arithmetic, algebra, geometry, English, history, and French. Sailors often carried small, pocket-sized dictionaries and primers. Instructors sometimes promised their charges would be able to *parlais* soon, but it didn't always work out that way. One observer remarked that some men could be hung for their interpretation of *Francais*.

No matter what the frequency of scripted leisure activities, everyone looked forward to liberty, time away from the physical and disciplinary confines of the station. Daily schedules usually included after-hours or Sunday liberty in nearby cities and towns for up to half the complement, and then overnight liberty for up to one-quarter of the men each weekend. To keep the lads in line and away from certain types of women, most stations established a patrol force to make sure excursions didn't get out of hand. NAS Gujan, for example, organized a 12-man patrol to monitor events in neighboring towns, with 6 sailors on duty one week and the other 6 the next. Of course, the folks back home wanted to know what their boys did on these visits. According to one clever scribe, sailors told their parents that when they went to town they stopped at the YMCA for a nice chat with the chaplain, read copies of the *Literary Digest*, went to the movies, took long healthy walks, and then returned to camp to retire at an early hour. But *actually*, the swabbies rode to town on the trolley, flirted with the conductoress, met some friends for a drink, made a date with the barmaid, threatened to lick anyone they met, grabbed the last car to camp, and arrived home "by a shave."[32]

Time away from the station occasionally gave rise to disciplinary issues, and abuses of alcohol and liberty regulations constituted the largest category of infractions. The Navy system included captain's mast and deck courts, nonjudicial procedures, for relatively minor offenses such as drinking or overstaying leave. Typical punishments included loss of pay or liberty privileges, disrating, or confinement to barracks. As an alternative, sailors could request summary court-martial, a judicial hearing conducted by a group of station officers. More grave offenses such as rape and murder, meriting hard prison time, were usually referred to a general court-martial, with a panel of officers assembled for the proceeding. The most serious general court-martial could result in the death penalty, though only with the permission of the president of the United States.

Other infractions seemed more ephemeral, even good-natured. While on the rail journey from Brest to Bordeaux a group of aviation ratings stopped for lunch at a trackside facility. After the meal, the ensign in charge of the detail demanded 50 cents from each man, saying many eating articles had disappeared, apparently as souvenirs, and rather than spend time searching for them, he would assess a "fine" to pay the restaurant. During Bastille Day celebrations at Pauillac in July 1918, Lt. Charles Mason "held citizens of Bordeaux spellbound while he dexterously piloted his HS-1L over the city in dangerous proximity to house tops, steeples, telegraph poles, and other various obstacles to aerial navigation." Fred Michel from the supply department, went along for the ride and came away impressed with the machine and its performance, as well as the "nonchalance of the pilot, and it is unofficially reported that he has expressed his desire to make subsequent trips to Bordeaux by more conventional and less sensational routes." Commanders received reminders that stunt flying was strictly forbidden.[33]

One grim fact of life exerted a debilitating, and frequently fatal, effect on the sailors—the specter of disease. Far more men died of influenza and pneumonia than combat with enemy aircraft, flying accidents, bombing raids, or work mishaps. At one point, Pauillac admitted 300 cases to the hospital, with 400 more personnel confined to barracks. The NBG counted 493 infections and nearly 20 men died at Eastleigh from this scourge. When influenza visited Gujan station, the CO and several men "owed their lives to the "constant and untiring efforts of Lt. Dr. E. D. Hardin." The "average" case of influenza debilitated a man for five days, if it did not lead to complications like pneumonia. In many places the disease seriously affected operations. NAS St. Trojan became incapacitated for several weeks in September, suffering seven deaths. In the prevaccine era, mumps, measles, and meningitis also posed serious risks. A draft of 100 aviation ratings aboard *Rochambeau* experienced an outbreak of mumps that sent 3 men to the Army hospital and kept the rest quarantined for a month in a YMCA building. The station medical officer placed NAS Dunkirk under quarantine for one week in January 1918 due to measles, while a case of spinal meningitis caused the entire complement at Castletownbere to be relocated to Queenstown for quarantine. Other health dangers included scabies and venereal disease. The former, known as "the French Itch," tormented sailors throughout Europe.[34]

* * *

Under the best of circumstances, naval aviation stations formed tightly knit, efficient, almost organic entities focused on carrying out assigned tasks as safely as possible. Discipline flowed from the top down, but leaders decreed that the concerns and morale of all should be valued. Every man had his specific role, job, and responsibility, with stations guided by the principle of a place for every thing and every thing in its place, and all thought and action directed toward carrying out the essential mission—Get the Subs!

No matter what their station or duty, young aviation personnel exuded "American-ness" from every pore. They were energetic, high-spirited, and keen to "get on with it." They walked with a swagger, spoke with their peculiar slang, and bounced to the newest jazz tunes. Though fascinated by the places and things they saw and the people they met, officers and enlisted men everywhere attempted to recreate versions of home, with their own food, sports, movies, publications, music, and entertainment. And no one had any doubt—it was the greatest adventure of their lives.

9

GASBAGS

Development of the Navy LTA Program

When the United States entered World War I the Navy had barely taken its first steps in the realm of lighter-than-air aviation (LTA). Total inventory included one soon-to-be grounded dirigible, one floating dirigible hangar, one kite balloon, and one free balloon. During the next 19 months, however, interest in this new field increased exponentially, with numerous bases established in Europe, the United States, and elsewhere, and substantial purchases of modern airships. But while American involvement in LTA activities before 1917 had been limited, such was not the case in Europe where major combatants had made significant commitments of money, manpower, and materiel.

Several categories of "gasbags" had evolved. The rigid airship, of which the zeppelin was the most famous, was constructed around a lightweight metal skeleton and was the largest example of its type. Nonrigid airships, similar in shape but smaller, lacked internal skeletons. The British eventually nicknamed this variety "blimps." Both types were also termed dirigibles interchangeably and were powered by one or more motors. Kite balloons were nonrigid gasbags, without motors, roughly cylindrical in shape, with a basket suspended beneath. They were towed at sea or tethered if used on land. Free balloons, spherical in shape, functioned in a similar fashion. By 1917, airships performed many tasks, from scouting and observation to bombardment. Hydrogen-filled airships offered excellent visibility and great staying power, offset by slow speed, high danger of fire, and significant infrastructure requirements. Kite balloons towed behind vessels also served many uses. Observers could spot torpedo wakes, identify U-boats at long distances, and deceive the enemy as to convoys' true direction.

The Unites States was not unaware of these developments. Captain Mark Bristol, head of the prewar Office of Aeronautics, helped fuel initial interest in LTA matters, while pioneering aviators Victor Herbster, Holden Richardson, and Frank McCrary drew up specifications for the Navy's first airship (DN-1).

A few months later the Department ordered a free balloon and kite balloon from Goodyear. The contract included a provision for training two officers, and soon McCrary and Lt. Louis Maxfield reported to Akron, Ohio, for instruction. Work also proceeded on a more capable airship type known as the B class. The Navy ordered 16 of them in March 1917, procuring examples from several manufacturers. While working on B-class airships, Goodyear erected a hangar and test facilities at Akron and proposed a pilot training program. Instruction began in June. Both Goodyear and the military supplied instructors. Maxfield became OIC, with Warren Child and Frederick Culbert on staff. Maxfield's pet dog, "Lanny," photographed in an officer's hat, offered some comic relief. Work progressed rapidly, and in September, Maxfield reported that the Naval Air Detachment at Akron had 11 qualified LTA pilots and requested that they be designated Naval Aviator (Dirigible).[1]

At least one event in Europe during these months exerted considerable influence on naval thinking concerning the use of kite balloons and other LTA craft. In June and July 1917, the Royal Navy conducted operations in the North Sea to intercept submarines. On July 11 a group of five destroyers with three kite balloons set out on patrol. An observer lofted above *HMS Patriot* spotted U-69 at a distance of 28 miles. The destroyer raced ahead at a speed of 25 knots, but while the ship was still six miles distant the enemy submerged, only to surface about four miles away. British vessels opened fire and dropped depth charges; a tremendous underwater explosion followed. Thick brown oil bubbled to the surface, the slick ultimately spreading as far as the eye could see. This action seemed to validate the balloons' combat possibilities.[2]

Kenneth Whiting's extensive tours in France included discussions concerning possible LTA facilities, but the Navy's direct involvement began in August 1917 when Lt. Zachary Lansdowne and Lt.(jg) Ralph Kiely sailed to England for dirigible training. They attended school at RNAS Cranwell and graduated in November. At the same time, McCrary and Maxfield joined the fledgling aeronautic detachment in Paris and participated in conversations with French authorities. An October 1 conference yielded a tentative agreement to establish several stations (provisionally Paimboeuf, Gujan, Rochefort, and Guipavas), confirmed the following day in a letter from Hutch Cone to the Minister of Marine. Selection of sites mirrored the rationale for seaplane base location, protection of convoy routes to Brest, Bordeaux, and St. Nazaire. Plans for Paimboeuf and Gujan unfolded first, followed in November by further discussions concerning Guipavas (near Brest) and Rochefort. At the same time, preliminary talks commenced about establishing two or more kite balloon facilities, including one at Brest, another near St. Nazaire, and possibly a third at Pauillac.[3]

Accordingly, two dirigible pilots, Maxfield and Culbert, would learn to operate coastal airships, with an additional 40 American bluejackets instructed in their care and upkeep. As soon as pilots and mechanics completed training, they would be posted to Paimboeuf with the goal of assuming control of the station. The French agreed to leave a few of their own people in place until the Navy could operate on its own. The Americans would train future detachments, with additional stations established as material and manpower became available. The French pledged to transfer hangars, premises, workshops, and material, and complete work currently under way. The United States would also assume control of airships AT-1 and VZ-3. Substitution of American personnel for French at Paimboeuf would occur "progressively." About this time McCrary became head of the LTA effort in Cone's office.[4]

Culbert reported for duty November 10, followed by an enlisted detachment. Later that month additional LTA pilots reached France. This first contingent was part of the initial Akron class and included eight ensigns. The neophytes traveled to Europe aboard *St. Louis,* and after reporting to the American consul at Liverpool, checked in with Sims and the naval attaché in London, Cone and the naval attaché in Paris, and then the French commandant and senior naval officer at Rochefort, as well as the Commandant of Patrol at St. Nazaire. The ensigns dined in the French mess, under orders to speak only French so as to improve their language skills. Their first meal included escargot.

In early December, Culbert and three new arrivals began training. Maxfield reached Paimboeuf January 4, 1918, and assumed command of the American unit. Despite signs of progress, many in LTA circles became disillusioned. Cone, for example, recommended that airships be used for convoy work only and characterized the prospect of offensive operations against submarines as "doubtful." Dirigibles lacked sufficient speed and appeared too vulnerable to the vagaries of weather. McCrary's opinions also grew increasingly negative. A report to Cone and Sims analyzed the relative value of dirigibles and echoed British opinion that seaplanes had proven superior for antisubmarine operations. Better, they said, to acquire more "Large America" flying boats than additional airships. According to pilots interviewed by McCrary, the dirigibles' field of usefulness was very limited. Any money spent building equipment and training men for airship work "is more or less a loss of time." McCrary also revealed that Maxfield, after two months with the French, had made an unofficial request to be transferred to a seaplane base. McCrary himself soon left LTA operations to command air stations in Ireland. Ultimately, despite concerns, work on the airship program continued, with construction carried out at Paimboeuf, Guipavas, and Gujan.[5]

To equip its stations, the Navy conducted extended discussions about acquiring airships and even investigated the possibility of purchasing Italian examples. Original plans contemplated employing dirigibles shipped from the United States (B-class airships), but these proposals were dropped by December 1917. McCrary then asked French sources whether additional airships could be obtained in Europe, citing a need for at least eight to equip proposed Navy stations. Headquarters staff soon examined Astra Torres (AT) and Zodiac (VZ) dirigibles. They discovered that the French had the greatest experience with craft of 9,000–10,000 m^3 capacity of the Astra and Chalais Meudon (CM) types. Under favorable conditions, large dirigibles could remain aloft for 20–24 hours, and carried 1,200 pounds of bombs and a 47 mm or 75 mm cannon.

Such airships operated 35 percent of days in the winter and 75 percent the rest of the year. They could also ascend to safe heights if attacked, more easily carry radio equipment than aircraft, and patrol as much as 100–150 miles offshore, much farther than seaplanes. There were some suggestions that the Navy might assist production of the Chalais Meudon type in the United States, hoping either B. F. Goodrich or U.S. Rubber would take on the project. Further negotiations included a proposal to retain the Astra-Torres (AT-1) then operating at Paimboeuf, purchase the airship *Capitaine Caussin*, order two VZ types and two larger CM examples. Additional discussions followed, largely linked to the ability of French companies to produce necessary craft. These discussions ultimately resulted in firm orders for the AT-1, *Capitaine Caussin*, two VZ models, and two CM type dirigibles, all to be completed by July. In April, Omar Conger, working through the General Purchasing Board, placed orders for additional airships of the AT, ZD, and VZ types, to be delivered between August and November.[6] During spring and summer, airships based at Paimboeuf carried out several successful patrols, and much of the earlier LTA gloom dissipated. Maxfield, who previously wished to leave dirigible service, suggested on August 17 that an assembly and repair facility be established at Paimboeuf, with new patrol stations constructed in the Penmarch area of France and on the south coast of England. The Anglo-American conference of September 17 recommended that the United States take over additional dirigible stations in Britain.[7]

One problem unique to LTA operations was "sludge" and what to do with it.

The chemical process that generated hydrogen consumed enormous quantities of raw materials. In a closed apparatus, technicians combined water, ferrosilicon (an alloy of iron and silicon), and caustic soda. The resulting reaction released hydrogen and produced large quantities of a toxic alkaline sludge, ferrosilicate. Stations typically discharged this noisome material into the nearest body of water where it poisoned fish stock and oyster beds. According to Craven, "Disposal of sludge became a matter of importance as well as annoyance to almost all of the LTA stations." Engineers developed a separating tank to facilitate disposal, but few were actually installed. NAS Guipavas made arrangements to truck sludge from the station tank to the sea, with solid waste buried on site. At La Trinité, crew members pumped waste across a peninsula into another arm of the bay to spare a shellfishing ground. NAS Brest dumped its sludge in the harbor.[8]

Operating mammoth airships posed many challenges. The gasbags were enormous, as much as 300 feet in length; hydrogen-generating, compressing, storage, and delivery systems were complicated and prone to breakdown; the fuel was outrageously dangerous; and the dirigible fabric envelopes were fragile. Inflated machines required constant attention, with extreme care paid to fire prevention and firefighting techniques. Among the extensive list of regulations: no smoking, naked lights, or gasoline stored inside the hangars; no fires; no skylarking; no testing of spark plugs; and for men working above the airships, all tools must be attached to their belts with lanyards. Prior to each flight all controls and valves received careful examination. Before the ship left the hangar, mechanics ran the motors for 10 minutes. When starting a motor, a member of the ground crew stood nearby with a Pyrene fire extinguisher. Any spilled gasoline should be caught in a bucket or drip pan. If any fell on the hangar floor, handlers moved the ship away before starting the engine. Whenever testing motors, crew members set all movable objects to one side, away from the violent prop wash, and made mooring lines fast. Safety lines placed around the nacelle kept personnel from walking into the deadly propellers.[9]

Before a dirigible left the hangar, the commanding officer checked to ensure that proper equipment was stowed aboard, including international alphabet flags, flashlights, code book, maps and charts, log book, extra water for radiators, binoculars, and life preservers. Prior to flights, designated officers studied air currents around the field. Maneuvering the enormous vessels out of the hangar required the combined strength and careful coordination of the large ground crew, especially if the wind were blowing with any force. Mammoth windbreaks flanking the doors aided the process. Lines attached to the envelope controlled the ship's movements. While maneuvering, officers demanded complete silence and strict attention so that verbal commands and visual signals could be obeyed in a timely fashion. American officers established this procedure in direct contrast to the French method in which the handling officer never ceased talking and each of the handling crew carried on conversations with his neighbor.

The process began by discharging a small quantity of water ballast while the airship was still in the hangar, allowing the ship to rise slightly, with the ascent limited by men pulling on the maneuvering ropes to the command of "Hold Her!" An officer walked toward the door ahead of the airship inspecting for any possible obstructions, while the crew slowly marched the vessel forward and then out onto the field. The handling officer stood in front of the nacelle, with a bugler behind him, and the airship crew climbed aboard. They then removed the maneuvering lines, except for those carried aboard while in flight. Men on the ground doubled on the remaining lines, holding the ship in place. A bluejacket with a pyrene extinguisher approached the nacelle and the process of restarting the motors commenced. When the commander believed all machinery was working properly, he signaled the handling officer, who held both arms upward, signaling the bugler to blow a long blast. The line holders then released their grip, and those near the nacelle shoved it upward, keeping clear of the propellers. As soon as the ship began ascending, the commanding officer checked maneuvering lines and beneath the nacelle to ensure that no water ballast had leaked and no ground crew member was carried aloft. If something were wrong he immediately maneuvered the craft for landing. Otherwise the commander circled the station to see if the recall signal had been hoisted. With the airship safely away, the handling officer ordered the maneuvering lines gathered up and placed on the part of the field where the airship would probably make its landing. While in flight, the ship's commanding officer kept a log and a record of all messages sent and received. The radio officer remained on constant watch. In the event that crewmen abandoned the ship over the water, they stripped off their "flying combinations" and boots and donned life preservers.

Bringing the dirigible safely back to earth and into the hangar presented even greater challenges than launching, requiring experienced officers and crews. Immediately after sighting a returning dirigible, the handling officer, cognizant of atmospheric conditions, assembled personnel and selected the best landing position. He detailed men to the lines and ordered all necessary signals displayed. A broad arrow laid on the ground provided guidance to the gasbag pilots. The airship then maneuvered over the assembled ground crew and dropped its own lines, to be taken by the men, who gently hauled the vessel downward. In some cases a taut drag line was also employed. The engineering officer shut down the motor and the ground crew slowly maneuvered the airship back to the hangar. Practice showed that having a portion of the flight crew dismount from the nacelle, assigning sufficient handlers to support the nacelle, and then turning the ship so the wind would "sail" it toward the hangar relieved serious strain on men and maneuvering line patches. If the dirigible broke away, the call went out for rescue trucks, and if the motors could not be restarted, the station dispatched a rescue party.

The work of launching and retrieving dirigibles continued at Paimboeuf and then Guipavas throughout the summer and fall. By late October, naval forces possessed 12 dirigibles, either flying or under order or repair. AT-13 and the small VZ-7 operated at Paimboeuf, while VZ-13 remained in Paris waiting to be flown to the coast. The rest were under construction and scheduled for later delivery. Two other airships used at Paimboeuf, VZ-3 and AT-1, had been returned to the French earlier or shipped to the United States, respectively.[10] When the shooting finally stopped, Paimboeuf was the only operating American airship station. Since March, pilots and crews had completed nearly 50,000 miles of ocean patrols and convoy duties, one of the largest aggregate totals for any station. An airship from Paimboeuf also enjoyed the distinction of being the only American LTA vessel attacked by a submarine. NAS Guipavas was completed and ready to operate but had no dirigible available for service until November 23. Lack of materials delayed construction at Gujan, and the base remained at least two months from completion. Rochefort, another site selected for an American facility, was ceded back to the French. The Navy disposed of its backlog inventory of airships by completing, testing, and accepting four while canceling contracts for three others.

The Navy's kite balloon program also achieved mixed results. Headquarters received final authorization on February 4, 1918, to proceed with construction of stations at Brest, La Trinité-sur-Mer, and La Pallice. Pilots, enlisted men, and equipment from Castletownbere in Ireland relocated to Brest in July. In late August, Hutch Cone informed Admiral Wilson that coastal stations were rapidly nearing completion and requested information about vessels that would be utilizing balloons. Wilson identified ships drawn from those stationed on the west coast, most likely larger armed yachts like *Aphrodite*. Vessels based at Brest would carry out coastal escort and patrol work, while those operating from the Gironde would meet convoys 400–600 miles offshore.[11] Navy records described all balloon stations as operative at war's end but lacking suitable craft to carry out assigned missions. Several vessels conducted experimental work at Brest, with at least four destroyers attempting balloon operations—*Benham, Ericsson, Winslow,* and *O'Brien. Cushing* was completely ready for work, while *Sigourney, Stringham, Taylor, Fairfax,* and *Bell* possessed winches of inadequate design. Armed yachts *Harvard, Sultana,* and *Rambler* were made available for balloon activity, but only *Harvard* had a winch. The total number of balloons received in France included 12 Goodrich type M and 18 Goodyear type R. All had to be repaired and altered for sea duty. Some were later given to the RAF, one to the AEF, and the rest returned to the United States. The Navy ordered a few small balloons from the French, but none was delivered before fighting ended

Though the Navy did not establish airship stations in the British Isles, scores of officers and enlisted personnel trained at Royal Navy facilities and several served with RNAS/RAF units. While Lansdowne and Kiely received instruction at RNAS Cranwell, the Navy negotiated to obtain two British SS (Submarine Search) airships being built at Wormwood Scrubs, and they were accepted in November 1917 after "excellent trial flights." One operated at Cranwell for the use of American students, with the other crated and shipped to New York. By that date, 30 enlisted personnel had been accepted for instruction at Cranwell (airships) and 15 at RNAS Roehampton (kite balloons). Lansdowne, who inspected the SS airships prior to acceptance, then moved on to RNAS Polgate (Sussex) for further instruction. During the winter months he inspected English stations and in March 1918 returned to the United States. Instruction at Cranwell went well, with 15 airship pilots qualifying in two days and then undertaking solo flights in their own SS-Z-23. Enlisted "general utility" and groundwork students made good progress too and soon completed coursework. Eighteen enlisted men transferred to Paris for assignment to French bases. With work at Cranwell largely completed, the Navy returned the SS-Z-23 airship to British control on February 28, along with a crew of five enlisted men.[12]

In early March, a second, larger contingent of 22 kite balloon officer-pilots landed at Liverpool and traveled to Roehampton, known as No. 1 Balloon Training Depot. Following graduation, they would be distributed to British stations to observe operations from destroyers and then sent to facilities in France and Ireland. Unfortunately, the situation at Roehampton quickly developed into a major embarrassment. After a visit, Atlee Edwards wrote to Hutch Cone describing the poor showing made by students. Edwards met with the station commanding officer "and to my regret was informed that the majority of the 22 KB pilots . . . have apparently shown very little inclination to learn and many of their examination papers were almost ridiculous and insulting to their instructors." The students' tests contained many negative observations by instructors, including failures due to "want of keenness." Fitness reports prepared for Sims by Ens. Fred Stoppel corroborated British charges. He frequently employed terms like "efficient" and "hard-working," but just as often found much to criticize, such as "Efficient but indifferent and does not like the KB branch of the service," or "Will never become a first-rate officer, too indifferent to all things," or "Better fitted for work along mechanical lines."

Though Edwards leveled no specific charges, he made much of the ensigns' generally poor conduct and indifference so marked "as to render them . . . almost objectionable to the British authorities." During his visit he found several sitting around in the afternoon drinking port. Sims's aide apologized to the commanding officer and agreed it would be a mistake to let the men continue studying in England. He decided to send them to McCrary in Ireland instead. "The majority of these men [reserve ensigns] are apparently nothing more or less than thugs and have conducted themselves accordingly." They were not all black sheep, however, and Edwards believed McCrary would be able to sort them out. Of 22 original pilots, McCrary retained one in Ireland and detached another from Roehampton May 5 at the suggestion of the commanding officer for having created "a spirit of discontent and unrest among the rest of the pilots." Eventually all returned to Queenstown, except Ensign Stoppel, who served at headquarters in Paris.[13]

Ironically, the greatest handicap facing the kite balloon program had little to do with balloons or personnel. Rather, the Navy simply did not possess enough destroyers to support active operations. The facility at Castletownbere never worked with American destroyers and only for a limited time with a single Royal Navy ship. Similarly, no escort vessels ever coordinated with balloon stations at La Trinité and La Pallice. The same destroyer shortages bedeviling relations between Admirals Sims and Benson kept the kite balloon program from playing an active role in the war against the U-boat.

During 1918, small groups of Navy airship pilots and personnel served at several RNAS/RAF bases. Before being sent to NAS Paimboeuf, Ens. Thomas McCracken performed antisubmarine and convoy duty at RNAS East Fortune in Scotland. In March, Ensigns Piper, Scroggs, and Learned, each with about 15 hours' flight experience, reported to RNAS Capel. A coastal airship station situated just east of Folkstone, Capel's dirigibles carried out patrols in the Dieppe-Calais-Boulogne sector. The Americans made their first flights on March 9, Piper's a 45-minute orientation cruise. The same day, Learned embarked on a two-hour patrol to Dungeness and back. For the rest of the month they executed numerous missions, instructional flights, and active patrols lasting anywhere from 5 to 13 hours. On March 18, Scroggs took the controls for an hour. The following day Piper spotted oil rising from the seabed and summoned a trawler. Three days later he sighted a mine and called a destroyer to dispose of it. Learned's airship bombed a "periscope" March 24 but later discovered it was actually a wreck. On another flight his airship got lost in the fog for four hours. Piper made his last flight on March 26, noting, "Took Major Latimer for a joy ride."

While at Capel, young officers carefully observed station practices. Discipline was strict and strictly applied. Officers should set an example for the men, especially in the area of dress, as "any slovenliness is strongly deprecated." Dinner dress required formal blues, stiff collars, and white shirts, with pink shirts forbidden. Ratings were expected to show all marks of respect to officers. Seamen returning late to the station must be warned that anything said could be used against them. Airship captains should hold themselves personally responsible for the efficiency of their ships in all areas except the engines. While on patrol, pilots should maintain a good lookout, remain within the patrol limits, render assistance to airplanes or surface craft in distress, keep careful watch on the weather, maintain contact with the station by wireless, and *never miss the opportunity of bombing enemy submarines!*[14]

Later that spring a select group of Navy personnel served at RAF Howden, a dirigible station in East Yorkshire, not far from Killingholme. Apparently they impressed the commanding officer, and in early April 1918 he wrote to Sims saying that if a substation were established, he would like to give it to the four American men training at his station. The officer judged Ens. Philip Barnes quite capable of taking command of the unit. No such Navy stations operated in England per Department policy, however, and most personnel later transferred to bases in France. The British did, however, set up a "mooring out" station at Crowthorpe in East Yorkshire, with Barnes in command. Robert Piper and Norman Learned from RNAS Capel soon joined him. In ensuing weeks Barnes and his fellow Americans compiled an enviable record. In late May Barnes piloted airship SS-Z-23 on a patrol lasting almost 26 hours covering a sector from Whitby to Spurn and amassed nearly 143 hours of flying time for the month. Ensign Harrison Goodspeed piloted SS-Z-38 for 62 hours in May. By late June the nine-man contingent had compiled 1,882 hours aloft, led by Ens. Joseph Homer with 301 hours, followed by Barnes with 254. RAF Superintendent of Airships S. M. Maitland praised the excellent work, saying that Barnes commanded the mooring out station very efficiently and to the parent base's entire satisfaction. Still other Americans, such as Ens.

Max Baehr, served at RNAS East Fortune, about 20 miles east of Edinburgh. After receiving training there he later transferred to NAS Paimboeuf.[15]

* * *

Legions of Doughboys and vast quantities of supplies scheduled to disembark at St. Nazaire near the mouth of the Loire River demanded aggressive antisubmarine measures. Construction of a lighter-than-air station to undertake long-distance patrol and convoy duties constituted an important element of the proposed defensive scheme. As early as June 1917, Kenneth Whiting's inspection party visited a small, partially completed French facility located at Paimboeuf, a coastal village that was once the seaport for the historic city of Nantes. Whiting's examination led to the unfinished outpost being designated one of the sites to be operated by U.S. forces as soon as sufficiently trained men and appropriate equipment became available. Not until fall, however, did movement toward this objective begin. A Navy presence at Paimboeuf commenced when Frederic Culbert reported for duty on November 10, followed by 3 more officers and 17 seamen a few weeks later. For a time they lived in quarters at a neighboring French base. Lacking a typewriter, Culbert kept Cone informed with a series of handwritten reports. In early December he and three other pilots obtained permission to receive flight instruction from their hosts, Americans "doubling" with the French, following them through the daily routine and flying as observers on each mission.[16]

Culbert temporarily assumed command of the detachment December 28 until Maxfield arrived from Rochefort January 4. Maxfield then initiated formal instruction in aeronautics, arithmetic, chemistry, gunnery, signals, and French. Over the next two months, additional personnel reached Paimboeuf, including men from Rochefort and Moutchic, gradually supplanting the French contingent. By March 1, the day the Americans assumed control, the total complement counted 12 officers and 205 enlisted men. Maxfield commanded, with Culbert as executive officer. Flight operations actually began January 30 when dirigible AT-1 flew in from Rochefort, partially manned by a Navy crew. During the next few weeks, station hands practiced moving the airship in and out of the hangar. A second dirigible, VZ-3, arrived from Guipavas on February 3. AT-1, named by the crew "*Captain Cone*," made its first flight under American command on March 3. The Navy acquired VZ-3 on March 20 and conducted the first patrol with that vessel the following day.[17]

At the time of transfer the base barely functioned. Craven later remarked, "When the U S Naval Air Station at Paimboeuf was taken over from the French the equipment was very primitive," and included a steel skeleton, canvas-covered hangar, and very limited electric light supplied by a gas-powered generator. A dynamite factory and chlorine gas plant stood nearby. He described the site as "devoid of comforts," but work to improve the station began immediately, including a new hangar, along with roads, drainage, and enclosed sewer to replace the noisome open trench utilized by the French. A lack of supplies, however, limited progress, as workmen labored with simple hand tools. Several factors combined to prolong building efforts, including uncertain deliveries, bad weather, and competing demands of an augmented French program. Finally, the necessity to conduct flight operations, even as construction and training inched ahead, proved a significant impediment.[18]

Conditions improved in April when a large cargo of lumber and bolts arrived aboard *Bella*, permitting crews to begin fabricating hangar trusses and barracks frames. May brought further grading and excavation of hangar piers, along with a new well and additional building supplies. By May 10 all the men bunked in new or adequate barracks, and work on a YMCA hut began. By month's end the first two concrete hangar piers were in, with all mixing and pouring done by hand. Late spring witnessed accelerated progress—more barracks, assembly of the first huge hangar trusses, scores of new men, four additional railroad cars of lumber, and a powered concrete mixer. By the end of July a new mess hall, three barracks, galley, dispensary annex, and cold storage house were finished and several hangar trusses erected. A 900-loaf bake oven, more barracks, another mess hall, and warehouse followed, despite the fact that most available labor raced to complete the hangar. Similar work continued right up to cessation of hostilities.

In mid-April airship AT-1 temporarily ceased service for installation of a new hydrogen bag, a project requiring six weeks to complete. The following week VZ-3 departed for Rochefort, thus creating space in the hangar for another vessel, *Capitaine Caussin*, which arrived from Paris on April 18 with an American crew aboard. The new craft immediately encountered difficulty, however. On a patrol mounted April 25 with Maxfield and Culbert at the controls, a gas valve failed to close and the vessel deflated while in flight, eventually plunging into the sea. During the descent, Chief Machinist's Mate Cobb removed detonators from bombs on board and the ordnance was dropped into the sea. Two crew members, clad in heavy fur flying suits, nicknamed "teddy bears," went into the water. One, Gunner's Mate Alley, cried out, "Oh, these teddy bears. I can't swim." He and Quartermaster Elliot would have drowned but for the heroic work of Maxfield and Culbert, who immediately jumped into the icy sea and kept the men afloat until they could be rescued. Meanwhile, *Capitaine Caussin*, with an American and French officer still aboard, drifted onto the beach, later to be dismantled, packed on trucks, and hauled back to Paimboeuf. Another potential disaster occurred June 5 when a fire erupted in Usine (Factory) #3 in town, threatening to detonate the whole gunpowder complex. Station personnel helped extinguish the blaze.[19]

Increasing experience, better weather, and more equipment quickened the pace of flight operations. VZ-3 returned from Rochefort on May 1. Aviators successfully tested a submarine listening device on June 9 aboard the refitted AT-1. The same airship under the command of Culbert carried out a patrol in commendable fashion on June 18 in conditions that would have grounded seaplanes. The vessel departed at 2:30 A.M. Culbert's orders directed him to rendezvous with American troop ships as well as other convoys passing through the patrol area. Without specific route information, however, AT-1 cruised aimlessly for some time. Lookouts eventually spotted aircraft from other stations and the pilots followed them to a rendezvous point, all the time under worsening flight conditions. Late in the morning, with the wind still rising, Culbert received orders to return to Paimboeuf, but could barely make headway.

After encountering repeated mechanical trouble, the airship finally reached the station. A drag line parted during the hauling down process, however, and Culbert restarted his engines, ascended several hundred feet, and unspooled his radio aerial to explain the type of landing he intended. Heavy wind and rain delayed another attempt. Culbert then rigged an emergency drag line, reeled in the aerial, and headed back to the station at 10 mph and a height of 150 feet. A sharp gust of wind over the field forced the nose-heavy airship toward the ground, but the altitude pilot quickly compensated, thus avoiding a crash landing atop a nearby peasant's cottage. A motor stoppage resulted in another near crash, but the senior flight mechanic soon restored power. Barely missing the hangar and making just 5 mph against the wind, Culbert maneuvered his ship into position and dropped lines, holding the dirigible steady by varying the speed of the motors. With wind measuring 32 mph, the ground crew showed considerable dexterity in finally bringing the ungainly machine to rest.[20]

Culbert also piloted the airship during a record-setting, 25.5-hour flight completed June 27–28, the longest by an airship of this kind. The vessel departed at 7:40 A.M., conducted active operations well into the evening, and then throttled down to spend the night aloft. Culbert rendezvoused with a southbound convoy at two o'clock in the morning and stayed with it until motor trouble forced a return to Paimboeuf at 9:23 A.M.[21] During the same period VZ-3 and VZ-7, the latter flown in from Paris on June 8, completed patrols of nine hours' duration—also records for the Vedette type. Despite difficulties maintaining sufficient airships in service, American flyers continued to compile notable records. In July, Ens. Alfred Gardner and his crew completed 17 flights aboard VZ-7 totaling almost 165 hours. The following month they flew an additional 71 hours, eventually tripling the French record for this type of ship. In July and August, repeated attempts to inflate *Capitaine Caussin* proved unsuccessful due to defective fabric. A new airship, AT-13, reached Paimboeuf from Paris on August 30, replacing AT-1, now deemed unfit for patrol work, relegated to instructional use, and eventually deflated and shipped to the United States. In late September the Navy withdrew VZ-3 from patrol service and returned it to the French.

Several officers were encouraged anew about the possibilities that airships offered, in direct contrast to the pervading gloom in January. District Commander Magruder advised Admiral Wilson that Paimboeuf dirigibles could meet convoys 120 miles at sea and accompany them to an "envelope" of airplanes 60 miles offshore. About the same time, Maxfield claimed that dirigibles could make 24- to 40-hour patrols, carry bombs, a crew of 10, and a heavy gun, travel at 10 mph to 50 mph, look out for downed flyers, signal by radio and several other methods, reach a convoy faster than a towed kite balloon, and loiter and wait for a convoy for hours. A German submarine tested these assertions October 1 when it turned the tables on its tormentors by actually attacking AT-13. The airship departed Paimboeuf at 7:15 A.M. to patrol the northern sector, picking up a southbound convoy from Brest late in the morning. After shepherding the ships to port, the Americans flew on to intercept the La Pallice-Quiberon convoy, which they met around dusk. Circling the ships, the crew observed a suspicious object about five miles away and headed toward it. The object turned out to be a U-Boat that immediately opened fire, filling the air with shrapnel from at least 14 shells. The dirigible turned back toward the convoy and finally returned to base at 8:40 P.M. after an eventful patrol of more than 13 hours. Follow-up searches for the submarine, lasting nearly a month, discovered nothing.[22]

After the *Capitaine Caussin* had been out of service for nearly six months, station personnel successfully reinflated it in early October, only to see the ship transferred to Guipavas two weeks later. A replacement, VZ-13, arrived October 25 and flew regularly until November 5 when it crashed into a tree while returning from patrol after dark. Nonetheless, this period proved very successful, with one vessel, AT-13, undertaking patrols on 20 of 21 flying days and amassing over 200 hours in the air, a record exceeded only by a single French station in the Mediterranean. During the same four-week span, long-serving commanding officer Maxfield departed Paimboeuf for inspection duty in Italy and the United States, replaced as station commander by the equally long serving Culbert. Admiral Mayo visited at the end of October and Noble Irwin toured the site on November 2. By the time the war ended a few days later, the station had completed 257 flights covering 48,630 miles. The 30 officers and 477 ratings cared for airships P-3 (VZ-7), P-4 (AT-13), and P-5 (VZ-13).

Active patrol work ceased with the Armistice and a huge Thanksgiving celebration marked a fitting close of operations. Soldiers from the 309th Engineers joined the festivities, along with Red Cross nurses, YMCA girls, and local citizens from miles around. Teams from Le Croisic arrived to compete in a football game and cross-country meet. Army pilots performed stunt flying and parachute jumps. The crowd enjoyed boxing matches, movies, a band concert, and vaudeville performances. Everyone then sat down to a feast of chicken soup, roast chicken, spiced ham, potatoes, peas, asparagus, mince pie, pumpkin pie, and chocolate cake. That evening the men burned the Kaiser's effigy, watched fireworks, and dreamed about going home. With the war ended, crews deflated two VZ airships for shipment to the United States. AT-13, a larger craft, remained in commission for another month, and flew to Guipavas on December 13, where it helped escort President Woodrow Wilson's arriving convoy. Three days later, with official duties completed, AT-13 returned to Paimboeuf to be deflated and removed from service.[23]

Discussions then commenced to return Paimboeuf (as well as Tréguier and Le Croisic) to the French Navy as quickly as possible. American authorities hoped they might take control of United States property at the base and liquidate it for the Navy. Craven, who made the request, failed to receive a timely response, however, and on January 8, 1919, issued a not-so-veiled threat. Without an agreement, the United States would be unable to liquidate the stations and be forced to remain indefinitely. This missive brought more positive results and a Franco-American commission quickly reached an agreement, though not without quibbling over the exact terms of restitution and compensation. The United States completed demobilization on January 26, 1919, and the site reverted to the French Navy.[24]

Navy planners conceived NAS Guipavas as part of a defensive complex protecting the approaches to Brest, for the AEF one of the most important ports in Europe. Situated at the western end of the Brittany peninsula, seven miles from Brest, Guipavas immediately adjoined an existing French dirigible station. The French allowed the Americans to use their landing field, thus avoiding extensive clearing and grading. Assistant Civil Engineer C. P. Conrad and

French officers selected the location during the winter of 1918. Despite its seeming importance, construction, organization, and equipping proceeded rather slowly, and no active wartime operations occurred. The first American on site, Ens. Glenn Round (Pay Corps) visited in late January. Soon joined by Lieutenant Conrad, the two men looked out over a sea of mud and turnip fields. Work did not begin until mid-March when the first labor draft arrived, along with a pair of trucks. They lived temporarily with residents of the town and later pitched tents. During the next few weeks, workers cleaned up the site and welcomed Lt.(jg) Edward D. Andrews (Medical Corps) as the new senior officer present. Late in March a convoy of men, trucks, and construction tools from Pauillac rolled in and building finally commenced. The next few weeks saw a steady influx of personnel and equipment, with smaller contingents arriving sporadically into May and June.[25]

Significant events in the early history of the base included assumption of command April 12 by Lt. John F. Maloney and erection of the first enormous hangar truss June 23. Thereafter progress continued at the rate of approximately one truss per day unless interrupted by material shortages. This was an enormous project; a single 600-foot hangar required scores of giant trusses and 144 concrete truss piers, with nearly all work done with hand tools and strong backs. Construction soon began on a second hangar, with the gas-generating equipment positioned between the two buildings. Five barracks for enlisted men were completed, with one used as a mess hall. Maloney now commanded 5 additional officers and 242 enlisted men. Work surged when several additional officers and 200 seamen reached Guipavas, including a party detailed for temporary duty from *Carola*. All personnel moved into barracks in mid-September, and by October 1 the new water system was in place, the hydrogen plant was in working order, and one huge hangar door was erected. As construction neared completion many ratings departed for other duties. In mid-September, for example, a large Guipavas contingent helped build a telephone line connecting the coastal air stations. In October a group of 18 transferred to the Mediterranean mine base at Bizerte in Tunisia, followed by 40 men who were shifted to NAS Tréguier.

The first pilots arrived September 25, and airship *Capitaine Caussin* flew in from Paimboeuf on October 18, commanded by a French officer but with a Navy crew. The ship resided temporarily at the adjacent French base because the American facility remained uncompleted. A group of 45 experienced sailors from Paimboeuf soon appeared as well. Zachary Lansdowne, recently returned from the United States, replaced Maloney on October 30, with the latter sent to command a station in Ireland. The same day Lt.(jg)

Delano assumed command of *Capitaine Caussin*. Orders to cease work arrived November 11. At the time, the station complement included 15 officers and 396 men, including 4 pilots. Deactivation commenced almost immediately, with 200 ratings returning to New York City on November 15. Officers began departing a few days later. Remaining sailors rushed to complete the dirigible hangars.

Finally, at 10:45 A.M. November 23, Commandant Sales transferred *Caussin* to the Navy, though it remained housed in the French hangar. A Guipavas crew piloted *Caussin* December 13 when it escorted the *George Washington* with President Wilson aboard. Cameramen aboard the airship took moving pictures of the event, the last official flight of an American dirigible in Europe. The following day seamen began deflating *Caussin*. The Navy evacuated Guipavas January 13, 1919, and transferred the site back to the French, who agreed to pay 465,600 francs ($80,000) for the hangars and hydrogen plant. Shortly thereafter they abandoned the station. One of the American hangars was destroyed in a storm around 1930, but the second survived at least until the end of the decade. During World War II the *Luftwaffe* utilized the field. Today Brest-Guipavas airport occupies the site. Several utility hangars, the home of the Aero Club de Finisterre, and their taxiing/parking area are located where the U.S. hangars once stood. Indeed, they may be sitting on the original hangar floors. All other traces of the Navy station have been obliterated.

Plagued by severe shortages of men and material, NAS Gujan, situated on the flat, sandy shore of Bassin d'Arcachon west of Bordeaux, never progressed past the construction stage. At least two months' additional work beyond the Armistice would have been necessary to complete the station. Navy planners intended to operate dirigible patrols over the Bay of Biscay south of the Gironde River escorting coastal vessels in the Gironde-Bayonne sector and hunting for neutral vessels supposedly supplying German submarines. The same construction priorities that marooned nearby NAS Arcachon, however, affected Gujan as well. The first small draft of men arrived February 2 and obtained quarters in a sardine factory in the village of Mestras. The station, occupied by three officers and eight enlisted men, Gunner J. H. Cowan in command, was commissioned February 3, 1918, and by July 1 personnel had increased to 146 men, and at the end of the war to 252. During the spring, Lt. Leman Babbitt replaced Gowan. Very little, however, could be accomplished between February and mid-July due to the usual pattern of limited supplies, equipment, and personnel. Between late May and late June, nearly the entire station complement was detached to work at Pauillac. A later report called it a period of "comparative idleness," and it sometimes proved difficult to maintain morale. In an effort to keep his men motivated, Babbitt allowed them to play or watch baseball during the week, even during working hours when there was no specific assignment. Somehow word got back to headquarters in Paris and the young officer received a rebuke from Hutch Cone. Definitely stung, he responded in late May by justifying this activity as a reward for working on Saturdays and unloading railroad cars on overtime. Babbitt insisted that his base was definitely not an "athletic and entertainment camp."[26]

When the crew at Pauillac returned in late June, real construction began. They commenced pouring foundations and fashioning huge trusses, all with hand tools, a process that continued into October and November. Before the Armistice, the men assembled and raised 19 lofty trusses in 28 working days, never with more than 53 laborers available. Babbitt tried to keep his men interested in their tasks by detailing officers to give lectures on dirigible aviation. When the war ended there were three pilots at the station, but no airship. The Navy placed the base out of commission on January 15, 1919, and the AEF took control of the barracks and lumber on site. In his lengthy inspection report, Admiral Mayo ascribed failure to complete the station to difficulties transporting material and use of personnel for other projects with higher priority.[27]

Early on, Navy planners selected Rochefort, site of an existing French LTA facility, as a location for a dirigible station. By December 1917 a small draft of American sailors from Le Croisic and Pauillac quartered there in a local Red Cross hospital. They were to receive instruction in the handling of Astra-Torres dirigibles. Foul winter weather prevented frequent flights, but the men assembled a Vedette airship and then suspended the car. Sailors spent their days working and studying and attending French classes at night. Eventually a new gas bag for AT-4 arrived but could not be inflated due to limited hangar space. Bluejackets also helped fill a Vedette Zodiac (VZ) dirigible. Navy officers, Maxfield among them, participated in several short hops, including some bomb-dropping exercises, but no enlisted men had a chance to fly. He departed Rochefort January 4, 1918, to assume command at Paimboeuf. Another officer transferred to Paris for instruction at the Astra Company. Additional progress at Rochefort proved slow. Engineers surveyed land for possible acquisition and sketched out base plans, but little of substance occurred. In fact, during the winter a proposal that the site be abandoned and operations at Paimboeuf augmented received careful scrutiny. During the German push of March-June 1918 the French transferred some of their own LTA material from Paris to Rochefort, with the recommendation that Navy personnel and equipment relocate to Paimboeuf. Though a few Americans continued to perform temporary duty, headquarters shelved plans to develop an airship station at the end of the summer.[28]

The kite balloon program on the coast of France experienced the same sorts of delays that bedeviled similar efforts in Ireland. Work began at NAS Brest in October 1917, with the intention of creating a seaplane patrol base, and considerable construction toward that goal occurred. Brest's mission later expanded to include an assembly and repair facility for aircraft shipped from the United States. As convoy activity increased, headquarters decided to place a significant contingent of destroyers there and establish a kite balloon station to operate with them. The actual layout of the facility underwent continuous evolution in the winter and spring, with simultaneous proposals to use the existing French hangar, expand the structure, or build one or two new balloon shelters. Similarly, suggested locations of various barracks, offices, and the all-import hydrogen generating plant received frequent review.[29]

An initial detachment of personnel and equipment, totaling 2 officers, 40 men, and 12 balloons, reached Brest July 4, 1918, after crossing the English Channel from Castletownbere. One week later the Navy flew the first American-made balloon, a Goodrich type "M," hauled behind a French trawler. With little space or support facilities yet available at NAS Brest, officials devised arrangements with the adjacent French station to provide storage space, a hangar for sheltering one inflated balloon, sufficient gas for operations, and use of certain winches. At the same time a large contingent of Queenstown destroyers relocated to Brest; several participated in LTA operations in the following months. Before American vessels could be used, however, modifications were required, including installation of specialized equipment for towing and shortening some ships' mainmasts to prevent snagging tethering cables. The crews, with the help of repair ships *Prometheus* and *Bridgeport*, completed most of this work.[30]

Cushing put to sea July 20 on the first all-American LTA patrol, conducting several test haulings and transfers. The vessel set out again August 1 on a five-day patrol. Getting under way in early evening to rendezvous with an incoming convoy, *Cushing* sent an observer aloft just before 8 P.M., but soon retrieved him on account of poor visibility. In light breezes and smooth seas, balloon and equipment seemed to function well and the gasbag remained aloft overnight at an altitude of approximately 800 feet. Operations commenced next morning before sunrise. With the wind rising, however, and the vessel rolling badly, it took 30 minutes to bring the observer back aboard. The crew's inexperience added to the difficulties, as did a major outbreak of seasickness. Commanding officer W. W. Puleston noted, "All of them suffering; some suffered worse than others." Despite these impediments, observers serving in shifts remained aloft until 4:45 P.M. At midday the captain also went aloft and came away convinced "of the advantages of the balloon for observation purposes."

Weather conditions continued to deteriorate, however; it became increasingly hazardous to "top off" the balloon, and there was "considerable trouble and a certain amount of danger in getting the observer from the basket to the deck." Unable to inflate properly, the unwieldy balloon began nosediving. About 1:30 P.M. the following day a lookout spotted a suspicious object on the horizon and *Cushing* gave chase at 25 knots. The now seriously underinflated balloon "took two violent nose dives" and actually hit the water. Only by ringing up full speed ahead could the crew coax the stricken craft aloft. Weary handlers then managed to haul the balloon down, get an observer aboard, and begin reinflating. With proper pressure restored, the balloon floated serenely aloft, though telephone connections and some guy ropes were torn away. Sea conditions remained awful on August 4 when the destroyer rendezvoused with the incoming convoy. Wind gusted to Force 7, again hampering inflation, with the craft "nose diving and yawing so excessively that it was impossible to secure the home." At the same time the suspended basket actually dipped into the sea, threatening the observer with drowning. Unable to get back aboard the ship by the conventional method, a Jacob's ladder, he dived into the water to be hauled aboard with a line. *Cushing* returned to port the following day, having kept its wounded charge aloft only through the use of balloonettes.

Nonetheless, skipper Puleston termed the experiment a success, observing, "It is eminently practicable to operate the kite balloon at sea," adding, "the kite balloon has great possibilities, both for observation and fire control." He believed beneficial changes in the equipment could be made easily, and more training would further improve efficiency. Puleston recommended that destroyer crewmen handle balloon duties, reducing strain on available berthing space and lessening the risk of having personnel incapacitated by seasickness. Otherwise, before going to sea, balloon personnel should undergo "two or three cruises on destroyers to get over their seasickness." Finally, Puleston wondered if trained balloon pilots were needed at all, suggesting that any officer/quartermaster combination could handle the duties. If a tow wire parted, basket occupants had few choices anyway, the most likely being a parachute jump. Contrary to some balloonists' claims, he believed it would be impossible to navigate an untethered craft.

No sooner did *Cushing* return than *Ericsson* departed on a short, seven-hour cruise, though with some difficulty. Its balloon had just been out on a 36-hour patrol and returned only the night before, seriously deflated. The crew planned to haul it to the French hangar and gas up there but was instead ordered to meet an incoming convoy. Within minutes of putting out to sea the balloon started losing hydrogen, but the situation seemed to stabilize, and two observers went aloft. Both experienced difficulties. Nonetheless, Ensign Mickey spotted the incoming convoy a full two hours before men on the bridge sighted it. The successful cruise almost turned to disaster after *Ericsson* returned to harbor. Moored alongside *Prometheus*, the crew began hauling the balloon, with pilot yet aboard. While the balloon was still 400 feet in the air, a wind gust caught the gasbag and hurled it into a nearly fatal nosedive. Luckily, the busy harbor was clear of shipping; otherwise, pilot and balloon might have smashed into one of the vessels normally anchored there.

Events proceeded more smoothly for *Ericsson* on another patrol begun August 14. In a cruise lasting 100 hours, balloonists conducted 60 hours of observation duties. One week later *Ericsson* put to sea yet again, leading a small group of vessels out of port. Three days later *Ericsson* turned its charges loose and moved to intercept an incoming convoy. At one point the observer spotted the incoming convoy 35 miles away. With calm seas, the group reached port safely August 25. Nonetheless, commanding officer M. J. Aster remained unconvinced. Despite the patrol's success, Aster believed balloons could not operate in foul weather while still permitting the mother ship to remain an effective part of the escort screen, asserting, "Time will be lost, the ship consequently out of formation for hours."[31]

As experiments proceeded during the summer and early fall, construction crews worked rapidly to improve facilities, erecting a hangar and laying a high-capacity gas line from the French generating plant to the American site. Activities shifted to the Navy location on October 19. Throughout the period, sailors conducted numerous tests of the most efficient suspension systems, along with several parachute jumps. In September, in a moderate breaking sea *O'Brien* carried out balloon operations. Attempting to switch observers caused the apparatus and two observers to drag in the water. The ship stopped; the men managed to free themselves and swam in rough water until the destroyer plucked them from the ocean. By war's end, five destroyers had been modified to carry out balloon operations, with three armed yachts slated for conversion. Brest station's 786 personnel included 18 balloon pilots, led by Chief Kite Balloon Pilot Ens. Robert Blakely. Shortly after the Armistice the Navy conducted further experiments aboard *Benham*, this time utilizing an improved steam winch and assessing the aerodynamic qualities of the type "R" balloon. During a short cruise the crews effected nine successful transfers of pilots and observers. Unpredictable autumn weather cooperated and ample open deck space on *Benham* proved beneficial. While the winch performed satisfactorily, the balloon itself revealed significant deficiencies owing largely "to its very noticeable and annoying fore and aft motion of the basket." Active operations soon ceased and demobilization proceeded rapidly thereafter. The United States decommissioned the base on February 15, with the site subsequently returned to the French. The host government purchased the American facilities for 692,570 francs ($120,000). Major installations of the modern French Navy now cover the former balloon station site.[32]

The Navy established a second balloon station at Trinité-sur-Mer, known as NAS La Trinité, to supply patrol vessels covering a sector extending from Quiberon Bay to La Pallice. It stood in a picturesque fishing village on an inlet of Morbihan Bay, near the famous neolithic mounds and monoliths of Carnac. Planners expected La Trinité to work in concert with destroyers/patrol craft by taking on balloons at a transfer buoy near the shore and returning them when their patrols ended. The shallow harbor restricted potential operations, however, as did limited maneuvering space and an absence of mooring buoys. Local authorities concluded initial arrangements for establishing this base on March 14, 1918. Lieutenant(jg) R. D. Patterson arrived that same day and the first draft of bluejackets 10 days later. The Navy leased five summer villas to accommodate its men and made provisions with a local bakery to supply bread made from American flour. Water from local wells proved undrinkable; instead, the Navy tapped into the city water supply. Gunner C. M. Johnson assumed command April 10, but work fell behind schedule. Some excitement occurred April 25 when airship *Capitaine Caussin* made a forced "landing" in Quiberon Bay. Station personnel picked up the dirigible's officers and crew. They also salvaged the envelope and nacelle and returned them by truck the following day.[33]

In early April approximately 30 Bulgarian POWs arrived to perform unskilled labor. Work began on a seawall. Men equipped with borrowed wheelbarrows, shovels, picks, and two sledgehammers started building a road to the site. They carried sand for roads in large dishpans secured from mess equipment. Actual construction materials arrived April 29. Machinery from Paris to produce hydrogen reached the station in late April, but without a compressor. In fact, the compressor from the United States never arrived, and without it bottles could not be charged, which meant balloons could not go to sea. The gas works remained unfinished until October 1. Seventy-five additional Bulgarian POWs appeared July 1 and work on hangar foundations commenced. Four weeks later La Trinité received the parts for a steel balloon hangar from Pauillac, with the structure erected by September 1.

Lieutenant Commander Gardiner from the office of the District Commander at L'Orient inspected the station in mid-August. He found much construction completed, but berthing facilities remained inadequate, with six men per room. The situation seemed acceptable with windows left open but not otherwise. Metal balloon shed parts lay on the ground without nuts and bolts to put them together. Gardiner also observed that the men showed considerable make-do spirit and their leaders demonstrated "ingenuity and resourcefulness." Workers fashioned piping for a water distribution system from discarded boiler tubes welded together and galvanized. They constructed office and mess furniture from rough timber used previously as drying shelves in a nearby brickyard. Tin cans became electric bells and buzzers. Wheels from a hydrogen machine, rough timbers, and scrap iron became a large trailer truck.

The base reported ready for operations October 1, with one pilot present for duty. The first balloon arrived October 18 and a second three weeks later but with no vessels assigned to tow them. In fact, only shallow-draft craft, like small subchasers, could be employed. Despite having little chance to participate in active operations, the men performed several practice flights. Some suggested that La Trinité's gasbags might be used for patrol work or that they could cooperate with local minesweepers or daily convoys between Brest and Quiberon Bay and La Pallice. In fact, La Trinité seemed to be a station in search of a mission. Everyone eagerly anticipated evening leave in town, though the influenza epidemic later restricted this practice. And they awaited news of cessation of hostilities. At the Armistice, 70 men returned to the United States almost immediately, while the remainder lingered until the Navy demobilized the station in January 1919. After February 5, 1919, the hangar passed to Army control.[34]

Work on a third balloon facility at La Pallice, adjacent to the city of La Rochelle, started late and remained uncompleted at the Armistice. The Navy established it to cooperate with patrol vessels working between La Pallice, La Rochelle, and Bayonne near the Spanish border. The proposed site began as a wheat field. Local officials requisitioned the plot but delayed construction until June 23, 1918, to permit farmers to harvest their crops. American personnel arrived May 5, led by Asst. Paymaster Douglas Barnes, later superseded by

Gunner L. J. Peiffer. Lieutenant(jg) J. H. Dashiell assumed command June 17. Additional drafts followed and the station complement totaled 225 officers and men at the close of hostilities.[35]

Serious work commenced in late June, though hampered by delays in receipt of supplies. The first public works consisted of barracks, dispensary, mess hall and galley, garages, oil house, administration building, storehouse, armory, latrines/sewers, and canteen. Other projects begun but not finished included hangars, a water system, hydrogen plant, and sludge pit. La Pallice always remained a low priority facility, located in an out-of-the-way spot and begun rather late in the game. The most excitement in the station's short history came August 27 when sailors fought a blaze in a stockpile of sodium nitrate stored right on the main street, saving much of the town from burning to the ground. A postwar history considered the station operational at the Armistice, with three Goodyear "O" type balloons on hand and construction of the hydrogen works under way. The Navy never commissioned NAS La Pallice and evacuated the site January 5, 1919, transferring the facility to the Army.

* * *

Most Navy LTA activities in Europe during World War I failed to reach full operational status. Only Paimboeuf carried out extensive patrols. Efforts at other sites—Guipavas, Gujan, Brest, La Trinité, La Pallice—foundered on the shoals of insufficient manpower and inadequate equipment, enormous construction challenges, vessel shortages, and competing priorities. Experiments and actual missions seemed to raise as many questions as they answered about the effectiveness of airships and balloons. The ambivalence of many within the military hierarchy and poor strategic siting of some facilities compounded the challenges. Even had the war lasted another six months, LTA assets would have played only a minor role in the larger antisubmarine campaign.

10

SUNNY ITALY

Naval Aviation in the Mediterranean

In November 1917 the Italian government, communicating through its naval attaché in Washington, requested the United States to furnish personnel for aerial bases to be established along the Adriatic coast, with the objective of attacking Austrian forces at Pola. The Italians offered to instruct and equip 50 American flyers for this initiative. The proposal followed by a few weeks the catastrophic defeat at Caporetto. The Department informed Sims of the proposal on November 21. Chief of Naval Operations Benson believed the program would engender both moral and military support, saying, "We desire to give every aid possible." Sims referred the matter to Hutch Cone, who then ordered John Callan to visit Italy and investigate. Callan, at that time commanding the new NAS Ile Tudy, hurried to Rome and met with Cdr. Charles Train, naval attaché there. Callan seemed eminently suited for the assignment having spent much time in Italy as a Curtiss agent and having flown for the Italian navy as an instructor and patrol pilot.[1] The Cohoes, New York, native had a long and intimate association with Italian aeronautics. While employed by Curtiss he met Capt. Ludovici De Filippi, who later played a critical role in the Navy's Mediterranean operations. Following the outbreak of war in Europe Callan sailed to Italy as a Curtiss sales representative. In January 1915 authorities there requested "Signor" Callan oversee establishment of their first naval aeronautics school at Taranto. Curtiss granted permission and in February "Lanny" became chief instructor and assistant to the commandant of the school. After extensive military service in Italy, he returned to the United States and joined the Navy.

Callan reached Rome on December 19, 1917, and initiated discussions with Capitano de Vascello De Filippi, now head of Italian naval aviation. In fact, Callan knew virtually all Italian naval aviation officers and enjoyed excellent relations with them. Throughout the following year De Filippi remained the Americans' chief contact. He impressed Callan as a "very active, energetic, well informed officer, much overworked due to lack of proper staff."[2] Callan and De Filippi soon discovered, however, that a serious misunderstanding existed. Local military authorities had requested 50 *trained* pilots to help alleviate a shortage of flying officers, but the message reached the United States as an *offer to train* 50 pilots. The Navy also assumed that those men might then be used in France or elsewhere. In contrast, the Italians believed they would receive the services of any pilots they instructed. So anxious were they to secure American involvement in the Mediterranean theater, however, that after learning of the mix-up they decided to proceed anyway, even before the Navy officially accepted the overall proposal. De Filippi informed Callan that a training facility would be constructed at Lake Bolsena, 60 miles north of Rome.

At Bolsena, gentle hills surrounded a large, circular lake approximately eight miles across. Local people were said to be very loyal, of the poorer farming class, with "no socialism fostered in this district." De Filippi described Bolsena as a town of 1,500–2,000 residents with some aviation school buildings already under construction, including 12 small wooden barracks, while a large apartment in town would accommodate a mess and club. For training, the government promised to furnish airplanes, gas, oil, barracks, and officers' quarters, while the Navy supplied the mess, to be run by a local caterer. Americans should bring luxuries like coffee, chocolate, jam, and sugar, however, as they were virtually unavailable in Bolsena. According to De Filippi, seven runways and hangar floors already existed. Lieutenant Mario Calderara, who would head the proposed instruction center, inspected the site and claimed the physical plant would be available by early February. He had previously organized/commanded other schools and was an experienced aviator, having participated in glider experiments as early as 1902 and become the Wrights' first local student in 1909. The Americans received assurances that Calderara spoke perfect English and that other English-speaking officers would be present. The Italian complement included 100 sailors, 30 soldiers, and 60 workers, with 4 instructors expected soon. American students would first study FBA flying boats and then graduate to the Macchi L-3 patrol plane; the best pilots would advance to Macchi fighter seaplanes.[3]

In ongoing discussions, De Filippi outlined Italy's ambitious aviation plans for 1918, including 30 seaplane stations, 20 dirigible stations, 4 airplane bases, 2 combined hydro/land bases, and a large land bomber base at Poggio Renatico. His government urged the United States to operate two or three stations (Porto Corsini, Pescara, San Severo), all on the Adriatic coast, saying that Italy suffered shortages of flying personnel but would happily furnish airplanes and equipment. De Filippi promised that food and water supplies were good, railroad connections at the sites adequate, and hangars solidly built and well camouflaged. Porto Corsini, located near Ravenna and currently operated unsuccessfully by army personnel, would be used for bombing the enemy base at Pola. De Filippi also offered a seaplane station at Pescara, promising to rush completion by late March. San Severo would accommodate land machines, up to 80 large Capronis, operated by 30 pilots, 40 observers, 10 executive officers, 40 petty officer-observers, 130 petty officer-pilots, and a total complement of 1,364. Callan (and headquarters) dismissed this proposal, in part due to its enormous size. Further opposition likely flowed from the Navy's reluctance to develop a bombing program in competition with the Army.[4]

While on his winter foray, Callan visited Pescara, a small city located between Brindisi and Venice, and came away favorably impressed. Buildings at the proposed air station were constructed of brick and iron with slate roofs, while a concrete platform and wooden runways angling down to the water fronted well-made hangars. Water for maneuvering aircraft, narrow and shallow, especially in summer, needed dredging, but would serve. The Italians planned to accommodate 3 squadrons of 9 patrol planes each, along with 6 hydro-chasse machines, and 12 small flying boats, a total of 45 aircraft available for patrol and escort duty. Callan later reported that the Navy could have the station by the end of March, the only expense being the men and their mess. Porto Corsini, further north than Pescara and directly across the Adriatic Sea from Pola, had been operating for seven months. A report coincidentally prepared in Washington declared Pola virtually impregnable to land and water attack but suggested air raids might succeed. Callan thought the entire offer of training facilities and active stations so good the Navy should divert men from France, as bases in Italy seemed better prepared for combat duties.[5]

Callan returned to Paris on January 24, 1918, and submitted his findings a few days later. He estimated that each station required administrative officers, 27 bombing pilots, 27 observers, 12 chasse pilots, 34 CPOs, and 331 enlisted men, all coming from the United States. New bases would operate against Austrian strongholds and attack enemy shipping and naval vessels, with *chasse* planes providing protection for slower bombers. Callan believed meeting Italian needs required increased training in America or delaying some work in France; he recommended the latter. In Callan's opinion the enterprise offered a splendid opportunity for offensive action, would boost Navy morale, and increase American prestige among its allies. Train reflected these thoughts exactly in a "Very Secret" cable to Sims on February 11.[6] In addition to his obvious sympathy, Callan's support of Mediterranean operations may have been influenced by an unspoken but keen rivalry with the U.S. Army. At this time AEF aviation programs in Italy were well under way. Two detachments under Major William Ryan and Capt. Fiorello LaGuardia had arrived for basic flight training at Foggia the previous fall. Many of the men later moved on to instruction in Caproni bombers. Ultimately, more than 180 Army personnel trained on Capronis and 80 served at the front. Others attended gunnery school at Fubara, north of Rome. The first class of 25 entered April 24, 1918.[7]

Cone received Callan's recommendations in late January and believed they contained considerable merit. He enthusiastically endorsed them in his own report to Sims. Echoing Callan's language he called the proposed venture the best chance (next to Dunkirk) to get into the fight quickly. Sims gave his approval February 11 and forwarded the idea to Washington where reaction proved decidedly more hesitant. Many viewed any activity in Italy as a diversion from more pressing needs in France and Britain. Benson cabled Sims February 19 with several questions, and again March 15. Where did this proposal fit into the larger scheme developed by Department planners? Could American-built aircraft be utilized? Would land-based machines be more effective? Benson made it clear the United States could not supply any materials or aircraft for this program until late autumn at the earliest and sought reassurance that the proposal actually originated with the Italians and not overenthusiastic naval officers.

Cone certified that the plan was indeed of local origins, ascribing it to shortages of personnel, not material. But even as Washington debated the merits, plans unfolded rapidly in Europe. A conference in Rome at the end of March among De Filippi, Train, and Callan yielded a projected completion date of May 1 for Porto Corsini and July 1 for Pescara. Paymaster Conger, visiting the Navy's Rome office, emphasized the need to reach "definite agreement . . . relative to the method of supply of these stations" before any commitment to man the bases occurred. Callan then recommended that a commission be sent from Paris to negotiate the base question.[8] A group consisting of Callan, Conger, Lafayette Escadrille veteran Lt. Willis Haviland, Ens. Lawrence White, and Lt. Col. Spenser Grey (RAF) traveled to Italy April 23. They visited Rome, Pescara, Venice, Bolsena, and Porto Corsini, where they watched a pilot perform aerial acrobatics. What commission members observed encouraged them to support the proposed plan, though they offered several cautions. Conger suggested establishing a parallel system of supply.

Not to do so would be poor generalship, like having no reserves, a second line of trenches, or emergency transport. Repeat visits by Callan to some sites also raised concerns. He found current quarters and sanitary arrangements "will not be up to the standards we require." Nonetheless, strong support passed up the chain of command and Sims recommended approval, including in his communication Cone's endorsement and a promise that Porto Corsini would be ready May 1 and Pescara a month later. Department approval came in early May.[9]

Well before Washington granted final authorization, plans unfolded to establish aviation headquarters in Rome at 2 Via Di Santa Susanna above the United States embassy. Callan assumed command April 25, with Ens. Walter White serving as executive officer, joined by Asst. Paymaster William Parker as supply officer and Asst. Surgeon Samuel Solhaus as medical officer, assisted by four enlisted men. This small staff spent the next month contacting various Italian departments, establishing liaison, making arrangements for the bases at Porto Corsini and Pescara, and eventually relocating headquarters to 54 Via Vittorio Veneto, a few blocks away. During the same period Cone issued orders to organize a crew at Pauillac for service in Italy, though the "shortage of personnel render[ed] this difficult."[10]

In some ways the evolving command structure lacked clarity. Air stations would operate under the aegis of Callan, who reported directly to Cone, but Train, naval attaché and Callan's nominal superior, retained authority over all personnel attached to Rome headquarters. In fact, Cone asked Train to act as his personal representative. By contrast, the Italian commander at Bolsena and vice-admiral at Venice exercised direct control of training and combat operations. Sorting out the working relationship between veteran regular officer Train and the junior Callan took some time. Callan had filled a variety of posts in France and enjoyed close personal associations with many at Paris headquarters. He maintained similar contacts in Rome based on his years of service in Italy. Thus armed, he showed great initiative and on at least one occasion Cone warned him not to commit to proposals without approval from his superiors. Callan also demanded that information be routed through him, or at least to him, and that he issue travel orders and other instructions, something the more senior Train assumed to be his prerogative. Train wanted Callan's offices to remain where he could keep watch over his "subordinate."[11]

In most cases Cone advised the squabbling officers to work things out among themselves. During the summer Callan took pains to assure Paris, "Our relations with commander Train are satisfactory at the present time."

Callan felt compelled to write again August 20, "We work well together on all subjects concerning aviation activities and never encounter the slightest difficulties." Nonetheless, some discord remained over who could issue which orders and related matters. As late as October, Callan complained about not receiving an important list of questions to be discussed at an upcoming planning conference. The list had been sent to Train in a personal letter from Cone but never shown to Callan. The latter objected, claiming his office was more in touch with the overall situation than Train's.[12]

Of all the Navy's aviation officers, Callan proved most committed to active operations in Italy. Given his close personal associations, long experience in the country, and sympathetic understanding of national priorities, Callan went to great lengths to assure that Americans behaved in a respectful manner and did not take their hosts for granted. A small flap in early May particularly irked him. Lieutenant Harry Guggenheim from Paris visited Bolsena where he offended several officers, particularly Calderara and De Filippi. They claimed that Guggenheim did not show proper courtesies and rudely demanded a pilot's brevet after a single flight. The "brash" young officer also insisted that a car take him to Rome rather than using the train. Calderara said he hoped Guggenheim did not visit Italy again. Callan soothed the waters by referring to Guggenheim's reserve status and lack of familiarity with local customs and courtesies. As early as April, Callan recommended that from a psychological and moral standpoint, "We make a strong impression of efficiency and organization . . . from the moment we arrive." He insisted, "For many reasons we must make a good impression . . . in everything we do here." A memorandum in early May advised that the United States not pursue any policy or objective that did not have "the fullest and most enthusiastic sanctions of the Italian naval authorities," no matter how desirable or urgent it appeared from the American point of view. Callan visibly chafed at the reality that the Italian front remained a sideshow for Navy planners who routinely diverted equipment and pilots to operations in France. In this matter he fought the general attitude that the Mediterranean constituted a military backwater.[13]

Callan's priorities became abundantly apparent in mid-June as he labored to secure pilots for proposed Adriatic bases. Believing all the best men flew for the Northern Bombing Group (NBG), he complained to Bob Lovett, a friend and former roommate in Paris. "I think you people . . . are wrong in what you are doing," he wrote, "that is, taking away from me the pilots whom I picked out to come down here for work. If you don't quit butting in my work down here and taking away good pilots there is going to be trouble and I will be hopping into Paris one of these days and make a big kick." In reality, the NBG project had become the Navy's largest single initiative and Callan was definitely swimming against the tide. When the issue of ferrying Caproni bombers to France emerged during the summer, he adamantly insisted that pilots accept orders and advice from local commanders at the flying field. Callan reported that American flyers "have acted in a very independent manner and have not respected the commanding officer," and ignored advice as to the best time of day to take off. He even charged that one crash "was no doubt caused by [the pilot's] starting at the worst time of day."

There was probably some truth in these accusations. Navy pilots in their private correspondence sometimes referred to their Italian hosts as "wops," evincing general disdain and amusement at their *domani* attitude and contempt for both the Caproni product and the general inefficiency and poverty of the local war effort. In early October Callan dispatched a rather querulous letter to Cone emphasizing the importance of regional operations. Challenging the heavy emphasis on activities in England, France, and Ireland, he charged, "We are not getting entirely all that we should get in Italy to at least operate our one station." There seemed to be ample observers in France but hardly any in Italy, while men who could be employed locally sat idling at Pauillac. Requests for construction crews at Pescara had been turned down, yet plenty of men and material were available in France.[14]

As commanding officer, Callan dealt with a wide variety of issues. One related to the selection of officers for the new stations. The possible appointment of Cdr. Roland Riggs to command Porto Corsini raised several questions. Riggs outranked Callan, who felt it violated protocol for him to give orders to his superior, at one point noting, "I certainly would feel queer giving orders to him, and he naturally would not like receiving orders from a junior." Callan also maintained a long-running disagreement with Willis Haviland, the officer ultimately chosen to command Porto Corsini. A veteran of the Lafayette Escadrille and service at NAS Dunkirk, Haviland preferred to function as chief pilot and combat aviator rather than station executive. Callan complained, "[Haviland] seems to want to show more interest in taking part in active patrol and bombing expeditions than in the study of naval aerial warfare and operations with the Italians." Instead, "He is inclined to want to be a *chasse* pilot." If Haviland did not show more interest in administrative duties, Callan would return him to France and replace him with his old friend from Curtiss days, William "Bull" Atwater. A few weeks later Callan (and Train) complained about Haviland going along as observer over enemy territory, contrary to instructions. The dispute continued after the war. When Haviland came up for retirement promotion to lieutenant commander, Callan weighed in against him, writing, "I have had a great deal of trouble with him owing to his independence and utter disregard of orders. . . . Train had to reprimand him in Rome." Callan also disliked Haviland's attitude toward the Italians, claiming that he caused trouble between Americans and their hosts. "I certainly can never recommend him for promotion at this time or for future work as a commanding officer."[15]

Long before the command structure solidified or a single patrol station opened, training commenced at Lake Bolsena, 60 miles north of Rome. The first detachment of approximately 30 enlisted men and 12 officers arrived February 19, 1918. They found their new home far from finished, with just one Italian officer present, "no seaplanes in station, hangars under construction." Two days later De Filippi and Train placed the station in commission. Calderara offered "sincere cooperation," and everyone attended a reception where the mayor gave a welcoming speech. An FBA flying boat arrived, received a blessing at a local church, and was quickly assembled with the hope training could begin on Washington's Birthday. Instead, the first flight occurred February 23. Initially, Italian teachers presided, later replaced by Americans. Ten more young officers, previously trained in the United States, arrived for instruction March 25. Despite passing through Navy primary school, they required five to six hours' work before soloing in flying boats. At first the school utilized FBAs only but later added Macchi L-3s and a few M-5s. Ground school curriculum included theory of flight, navigation, theory of motors, the *Bluejacket Manual*, and signaling. Ultimately, 73 men completed the course.[16]

Ensign William "Bull" Atwater, a grizzled veteran at 36 and an old comrade of Callan's, became the first and only commanding officer at Bolsena, serving under the Italian head of school. He already possessed a remarkable flying record. A student of both Wright and Curtiss, Atwater had traveled throughout Asia in the prewar years giving demonstration flights and soliciting aircraft orders. Early in the war he joined the Navy and served at the new NAS Hampton Roads. Ordered to Europe, he worked at Moutchic before taking charge of cadets dispatched to Italy. In practice, commanding officer Calderara turned effective control over to Atwater.[17]

Despite a quick beginning, the Bolsena program evolved slowly, due in part to the now familiar shortages of material and limited facilities. Few instructors were available and the "beach" was in poor condition. Students and enlisted men lived in temporary barracks standing along a shaded street running down to the shore. They proved difficult to heat and eventually the Americans purchased oil stoves for them. A commodious house in town served as a club and mess hall for officers and students, while the handful of enlisted men ate at a hotel. The number of nonflying staff remained quite limited, usually eight to ten men, including a medical officer, chauffer, yeoman, and hospital attendant. During succeeding weeks workers completed additional buildings, hangars and shops, and instruction time gradually increased.

Central Italy was no vacation spot in 1918. Low clouds, hail, fog, rain, high winds, and rough water frequently disrupted flight activities. Between March 10 and May 11 bad weather interrupted 49 of 63 possible flying days. Similarly, between July 28 and September 14 weather disrupted instruction 32 times, with nine more days lost to accidents, funerals, gas shortages, and liberty. Additionally, no flying occurred on Sunday mornings per a request from Calderara not to interfere with church services. The FBAs' light construction made rough water landings problematic. Damaged machines with broken pontoons and wires required time-consuming shipment to the factory because Bolsena lacked repair facilities. Severe fuel and lubricant shortages also caused problems. In one instance Atwater and Commander Mancini departed for Rome on March 6 looking for oil and returned the next day with six barrels.[18]

Faulty equipment and inexperienced pilots caused several accidents, some with fatal consequences. Planes occasionally smashed into each other while taxiing across the water. Others collided with station motorboats. Enlisted pilot Clarence Nelson died March 20 while making his first solo flight when his aircraft spiraled nose first into the lake. Divers found the small flying boat four days later but never recovered Nelson's body. In his honor, local officials renamed the road leading from town to the American hangars "Via Nelson." A training machine piloted by Ensign Buffett caught fire July 1 at an altitude of 1,150 feet. He immediately dived toward the water and made a safe landing, whereupon he and his Italian student jumped overboard. They survived, but flames completely destroyed the aircraft. At the end of the month an Italian plane crashed into the lake, killing the observer. Fortuitously, the pilot wore an American life jacket and survived, attended by the Navy medical officer.[19]

By early April the school had settled into a predictable routine, punctuated by incessant delays, though after Callan assumed command in Rome it became easier to secure necessary supplies. The initial agreement required the hosts to furnish instructors, but they proved incapable. Instead, the United States supplied its own teachers and even lent personnel to the Italian "beach." Ensign Mark Walton and cadets Charles Hammann and James Goggins served as the first American teachers. By early spring the school included 3 hangars and 18 planes, with 8 or so available each day. Four men had soloed, with six more waiting "for a good day to be turned loose." Officers arriving directly from the United States found the new situation very challenging. Atwater noted, "It is taking them too long to learn how to fly FBA boats."[20]

By late May the situation had progressed further. Atwater counted 12 naval aviators (commissioned) and 32 student naval aviators (noncommissioned). Of these, 32 had soloed, with 5 more ready to do so. Conditions continued improving as the weather moderated. The week ending May 27 found 11 planes in commission and 205 flights conducted totaling 102 hours. By early June, instruction for the initial detachment was complete, even as the student contingent increased to 48, and then 60 in July. Paris expanded the school's mission, dispatching men for bombing and aerial gunnery training. The latter regimen began slowly, however, and the first aviators ordered to Porto Corsini lacked these basic skills. Parallel discussions debated withdrawing pilots from Bolsena and sending them to Moutchic for bombing and gunnery work. Callan hoped they would then return to Italy to relieve the men at Porto Corsini.[21]

Local citizens and Navy airmen generally enjoyed excellent relations; Italian and American bluejackets sometimes walked arm-in-arm around town. Calderara's house always stood open to visitors, and his wife gave language lessons in the afternoon. Several sailors at the Italian school spoke English, having at one time emigrated to America and then returned home. When the YMCA donated a movie projector, the men stretched a screen between flagpoles in the renamed Piazza di Staiti Uniti, and "townspeople came down in throngs." One movie, made by the Red Cross, showed the station itself. The town also turned over a building that provided modern bathing facilities, a billiard room, and the "latest American ragtime" played on a Victrola provided by the YMCA. Bolsena's citizens gave the school three Roman wolf dog puppy mascots named "America," "France," and "Italy" in order of their size. Diminutive student Wayne Duffet earned the affectionate nickname "Piccoloisimo" (Shorty).[22]

The transfer of men to Porto Corsini, Moutchic, and elsewhere in early August caused a sharp drop in the number of students at Bolsena. That situation changed dramatically on August 24 when a large draft of new student pilots, all enlisted men, arrived, drawn from many stations in France. They got right to work, made their first flights within a day, and completed the ground school course in October. By then 23 men had passed their naval aviator's tests, or nearly so. Atwater, supported by Callan, worked to secure commissions for some of the enlisted men, peppering his superiors with requests—but with little success. In a handwritten note, Lt. Ralph Kiely at Paris headquarters assured Callan that he had sent *another* telegram to the Department asking for authority to enroll enlisted pilots as officers. Instead, Cone received a ruling from Washington ending enrollment of enlisted men as officers. Rather, they would have to first enroll as enlisted men and then seek promotion. The case of James Goggins proved particularly poignant. A member of the First Aeronautic Detachment, he served as an instructor at Bolsena and received high praise for his energy, devotion, and bearing, but he later died in a flying accident at Porto Corsini. Atwater requested that the deceased aviator be commissioned posthumously, but the Department declined to act—with the explanation that a dead man could not take the oath.[23]

Naval planners expected the August draft of cadets to be the last and envisioned closing the school at the end of the fall. Callan recommended strongly that if this occurred Atwater be detailed as commanding officer at the new Pescara base. He also suggested that the Navy delay any public announcement so as not to upset the Italians. Nonetheless, word of the impending closure leaked out. Although flight activity picked up markedly in September, general conditions seemed to deteriorate. Several hangars remained incomplete or inadequate due to slow contractors and shoddy workmanship. There were insufficient dual control FBAs or spare motors. Lacking adequate sanitary facilities, the men bathed in the lake. The kitchens were dirty, and the Italians and their commander cooled visibly toward the Americans as word of the closing spread. The situation worsened in October when the region experienced a severe bout of influenza. There were no stoves to warm food for bedridden men. Leaking barracks meant moving the ill into the commander's quarters. Up to 9 men a day contracted the disease, more than 40 in all, the majority of American personnel. A medical officer referred several cases to facilities in Rome. Flying activities virtually ceased. The siege finally broke October 17 when no new cases were reported.[24]

Ironically, Bolsena hosted the most trainees in the final weeks of the war, 17 naval aviators and 46 students, but foul weather and the Armistice ended operations. Admiral Mayo, on his grand tour of naval facilities in Europe, visited Bolsena on November 8. He made special mention of the program to train pilots for duty at Porto Corsini by practicing landings in a buoy-marked channel only 30 yards wide. He also reported that the detachment was about to be disbanded now that experienced pilots had begun arriving from America. During the same weeks a few surplus Dunkirk pilots reached Bolsena, including James O'Brien and Charles Wardwell. In all, the school sent 12 bombing pilots and 12 *chasse* pilots to Porto Corsini. More than 130 aviators received instruction and 73 completed flight training. This group included 40 ensigns and 95 bluejackets. Pilots and instructors carried out 5,540 flights lasting 2,216 hours.[25]

Porto Corsini, site of the Navy's only operational combat station in Italy, was a small fishing community, 70 miles south of Venice and a few miles downriver from Ravenna. The base stood on a sandy, three-quarter-mile-long triangular spit of land behind town where two canals intersected to form an artificial harbor. The canal used for aviation activities was barely 100 feet wide. Wind blew across at a right angle, while telegraph wires ran parallel to it. Putting their own stamp on local geography, bluejackets renamed this sandy strip "Manhattan" and christened the canals "Hudson River" and "East River." The principal thoroughfare became "Wall Street." The men messed at the "Winter Garden," where they dined on "submarine" chicken, spuds, slumgullion, and java. Sometimes the station went by another appellation, "Goat City," named after the Navy mascot.[26]

Nonetheless, the base occupied a strategic location, well placed to carry out missions against the Austrian stronghold at Pola, 85 miles across the Adriatic. Before being taken over by the United States, Italian Army *Squadriglia* 263a operated here. The base complement included 12 officers, 15 petty officers, and 112 enlisted men equipped with 15 FBA bombers and 7 M-5 *chasse* machines. Though of solid, plastered masonry construction with tile roofs, buildings lacked electric lights and adequate sanitation-bathing facilities. No satisfactory local drinking water was available. Instead, it was brought in by a combination of train, barge, and hand pump. Several torpedo boats, minesweepers, and submarines sheltered in the nearby harbor. Three- and five-inch guns and an antiaircraft artillery battery between the base and Ravenna offered some protection. When the Americans moved onto the station, the Italian navy showed great courtesy, but the army squadron seemed put out. The U.S. Navy considered existing buildings entirely inadequate for its much larger force and opted to enlarge the mess hall and build new barracks, officers' quarters, administration building, sickbay, and more hangars. In addition they installed plumbing, drainage, and electric lights. Nonetheless, the project remained unfinished until after the Armistice. Even provisioning the mess posed a problem. The Italians supplied their men with a tin cup and cutlery only, and no mess hall furniture.[27]

The first detachment from Pauillac commanded by Willis Haviland and consisting of a few officers and 331 enlisted men pulled into Porto Corsini in the early morning hours of July 24 aboard a special train carrying 240 tons of supplies. They commissioned the station later that day. Haviland and his staff found the situation quite unsettled. Enlisted quarters were overcrowded and the latrines could not be used. Surrounded by extensive marshes and swamps, Porto Corsini faced a continual threat from malaria, necessitating careful screening and twice daily doses of quinine. Half the men bivouacked temporarily four miles away at an abandoned seaplane base on the north bank of the canal. In some cases they pressed aircraft packing crates into service as buildings. Nonetheless, the sailors managed to unload supplies and move into their camps by mid-afternoon. Pilots from Bolsena and mechanics trained at Italian seaplane and motor factories soon joined them. Available aircraft included 5 M-8 bombers, 11 Italian FBAs, 1 French FBA, and 10 M-5 chasse machines. More were promised. A few Italian personnel remained to provide continuity. The very night the Americans took up residence they endured a bombing raid carried out by six Austrian aircraft from Pola. Routed from their beds, the men scurried to trenches and dugouts until the assault ended. While most bombs fell harmlessly along the coast, two exploded within 500 yards of the base leaving craters 16 feet wide and 6 feet deep. Antiaircraft fire from nearby batteries rained shrapnel on the camp but caused no damage.[28]

Flight operations began a few days later, and the difficulty of maneuvering aircraft on the narrow, windy canal soon became apparent. The original wooden station hangar housing FBA seaplanes stood at the tip of the island, exposing airplanes to waterborne traffic and dangerous crosscurrents. Base officers soon concluded that new hangars should be placed in a more protected location, several hundred feet up one of the canals. Eventually two large, triple-gabled, brick-and-plaster structures arose on that site. The Americans also discovered they must avoid at all costs a "large and inviting looking inland sea nearby called Valli de Commachio," actually a dark swamp covered by a few inches of water.

The station's daily routine typically began with reveille at 5:30 A.M., followed by breakfast at 7:30, work duty from 8:50 to 11:30 and again from 1:00 to 4:30, supper at 5:30, and taps at 9:05 P.M. "Stanley's Army," the 50-man Seamen's Guard, provided station defense, sometimes mocked with the words, "The night was dark, the mud was deep, Stanley and Guards were fast asleep!" The men produced a camp newspaper first titled *Flypaper* but later renamed *Leading Edge*. Weekly liberty parties of up to 75 sailors visited Ravenna on the "good ship Seagoing," with orders to return by 9 P.M. A YMCA representative organized entertainments and athletic events, including semiweekly movies and smokers (though the crew sometimes pleaded for more up-to-date war films, by far the most popular choice).[29]

As of August 1 the station counted 30 planes in its inventory, a mix of

FBAs, M5s, and M8s, but only 8 in commission. Many required time-consuming shipment to the factory for overhaul. At the end of the month, Haviland informed Callan, "The shortage of machines on this station is very serious." Some lacked propellers. Others had damaged their wings getting out of the narrow canal. Radiators and other equipment were not interchangeable and shops possessed no spare parts to effect repairs. A summary of conditions at Porto Corsini prepared by Ensign Tilburne offered a snapshot of the station that summer. Hangar #1 appeared ready to collapse after damage sustained in a recent air raid. Enlisted men were overcrowded and the new barracks were unfinished. With no electrical system yet installed, men used batteries instead. Sanitary amenities remained virtually nonexistent, Latrines were filthy, bathing facilities were inadequate, and drinking water had to be purified with chloride of lime.[30]

Despite these difficulties, energetic Navy personnel quickly initiated offensive operations. Weather permitting, pilots patrolled north to the mouth of the Po River, then east across the Adriatic Sea, followed by an overwater return leg to Porto Corsini. In their three months of combat activity, aviators carried out many different assignments, including antisubmarine and reconnaissance patrols, photographic and propaganda missions, convoy duty, and SOS and emergency responses. Instructions from headquarters recommended that seaplane patrols be conducted at an altitude of 900 feet, with two or three bombers in formation, escorted by the same number of *chasse* planes. Under orders from the district commander in Venice, Americans also conducted several bombing missions. A flight consisting of one M-8 bomber and four M-5 *chasse* machines set out August 21 to bombard Pola with propaganda material. They reached the target safely but after dropping the leaflets came under "heavy but poorly directed" antiaircraft fire. Five land planes and two seaplanes rose to challenge the intruders. Ensigns Dudley Voorhees and George Ludlow, and Landsman for Quartermaster Charles "Haze" Hammann, all recent graduates of the Bolsena program, led an attack on three Austrian Albatross scouts and later claimed to have shot one of them down. Two more enemy aircraft then joined the fight.

In a wild melee Ludlow's machine suffered heavy damage, caught fire, and spun toward the water. He splashed down three miles west of Pola. Hammann evaded two pursuers and landed beside Ludlow, who opened the photo port, kicked holes in the wings, and abandoned his sinking craft, scrambling aboard Hammann's plane. With no space in the tight cockpit, Ludlow straddled the hull beneath the engine. The rescue plane was now badly overloaded and riddled by machine gun fire. Taking off in three-foot seas, Hammann further damaged the bow of his machine. Airborne, he fired 100 rounds into Ludlow's craft to finish it off, and with the passenger holding on for dear life, the two raced home across the Adriatic Sea. While landing, their airplane flipped over and sustained further heavy damage. Both men suffered serious bruises, but lived to tell about it. Callan recommended that Hammann be awarded the Distinguished Service Cross for his exploits. Eventually he received the Medal of Honor for his spectacular feat. Hammann finished the war in good health but died in the crash of a flying boat at Langley Field. After-action reports described Austrian machines as faster and better climbers than American craft, but less maneuverable and seemingly flown by green pilots. The Hammann-Ludlow exploit also initiated a debate about the advisability of small flying boats engaging in dogfights with land planes.[31]

In response to this American raid, the Austrians mounted a reprisal strike that same evening. They flew in very low, perhaps 600 feet to 750 feet, commencing their bombing runs about 9:55 P.M. At first, antiaircraft gunners thought the planes might be returning or lost Italian aircraft and withheld fire. The attack did limited damage but inflicted no casualties. For protection, attendants evacuated sickbay patients to a bombproof shelter. Based on events that evening, Callan advised Commanding Officer Haviland to shoot down any planes approaching the station without proper recognition signals as was the practice at English flying fields, though the matter needed to be sorted out with the Italians first.[32]

A pattern of raid and counterraid blossomed. In retaliation for the Austrian strike, Commander Valli ordered another attack, the first night flight attempted at the station. On August 22–23, two M-8s piloted by Ens. Russell "Bart" Read and LQM Clarence Knowles departed at 3:45 A.M. and bombed Pola at 5:00 A.M., hammering the searchlights, arsenal, and airplane hangars. Though the attacking aircraft were held in a searchlight for 10 minutes, the Austrian barrage proved ineffective.[33] Further raids followed on August 24 and 29. Five weeks later, six single-seat M-5s lifted off at 7 A.M. for a reconnaissance patrol and to observe naval activity at Pola. They safely completed two circuits above the harbor, despite heavy antiaircraft fire. Five enemy aircraft rose to challenge them, but no combat ensued. When Vice-Admiral Marzolo, naval commander-in-chief at Venice, inspected Porto Corsini on October 14, he lauded the Americans for the "perfect condition of station and planes, and discipline and smartness of men."

Commanding Officer Haviland played a central role in all combat activities. He had served a stint in the Navy between 1907 and 1911, and after the outbreak of World War I enrolled in the American Ambulance Corps, spending 17 months on the Western Front. From there he joined the Lafayette Escadrille. Haviland transferred to naval aviation in early 1918, acted as chief pilot at NAS Dunkirk, and did a short tour flying Sopwith Camels with No. 213 Squadron, RAF, during the German spring offensive. After assuming command at Porto Corsini, he resumed his active role, leading inexperienced men by example. A colorful assortment of figures, stripes, and insignia emblazoned his aircraft. When the Austrians responded to the propaganda leaflet mission against Pola with a "real" bombing raid, Haviland supposedly responded, "To Hell with leaflets, we'll take bombs next time." During nighttime raids he never took cover, strolling through camp instead as if the ordnance raining down were duds.

After the war, naval pilot Al Williams recounted a story, likely told to him by Haviland and perhaps apocryphal, that nonetheless captured the essence of the veteran's style. According to Williams, "Next flight saw the flashily painted ship of Haviland far in advance of his formation. He wasn't patrolling this day but looking for trouble. Without looking around to see if his men were following him, he dived on an Austrian squadron of a dozen single-seaters. . . . His daring but green command arrived on the scene to finish off what the skipper had started. The Austrian formation took to its heels in screaming long dives behind the lines. A staff inspector heard about the exploit and reported it to headquarters in Paris. A court martial was proposed for disobedience of orders but Haviland's original explanation must have touched someone's sense of humor. 'I wasn't leading my men,' he said, 'I was too far ahead of them.'"

Not all danger occurred during combat missions, however. In fact, all American fatalities resulted from accidents, not enemy action. Enlisted pilot James Goggins fell to his death on August 11 in an M-5 plane. A month later mechanic George Killeen died when a blowtorch exploded in the machine shop.[34] While testing a radio September 15, 26-year-old Ens. Louis Bergen and Gunner Thomas Murphy were killed when they crashed their M-8 near Ravenna. Virtually the entire town turned out for their funeral.

Carrying the fight to the enemy constituted the station's raison d'etre, and combat missions continued throughout the final month of the war. Three M-8s, two FBAs, and eight M-5s departed Porto Corsini on October 22 to join forces from Venice in a powerful afternoon attack against Pola. A total of 43 Allied planes conducted the raid, while a line of Italian destroyers provided directional markers at sea. The entire group rendezvoused 15 miles from the target and flew in formation over the harbor. A week later four pilots left Porto Corsini for a reconnaissance mission over Pola to determine whether a *Viribus Unitis*-type battleship had been sunk. Poor visibility caused them to wander off course, with Chief Quartermaster E. M. Smith forced down with a bad motor little more than a mile from the Austrian coast. Ensign Albert Talieferro landed nearby and effected repairs, and both pilots returned safely to base.[35]

Due to shortages of Italian pilots, several American aviators served temporarily at Venice as part of the final drive against the lower Piave region. Haviland, an experienced combat pilot, wanted to join the action. He wrote directly to Commander Valli, saying he had flyers but not enough planes and wished to lead the men himself. Haviland's wish was granted. In combat operations on the Austrian front, Ens. Austin Parker strafed ground troops and Ens. Caleb Coatsworth accompanied a special Caproni mission carrying Gabriel d'Annunzio over the lines. With Haviland's departure from Porto Corsini, 20-year-old Russell "Bart" Read, member of the First Yale Unit and veteran of service at Moutchic, Le Croisic, and Pauillac, assumed temporary command. At the very end of the war he also joined the Americans flying with the Italians.[36]

Following Austria's precipitous exit from the war, operations at Porto Corsini ceased on November 4. Admiral Mayo visited the following week and later wrote, "This station has the distinction of being the most heavily engaged unit of the United States naval forces in Europe." He judged the station in excellent condition, praised the appearance of the men and shipshape condition of their bags and hammocks, and found discipline and morale to be superb. A questionnaire prepared for the admiral highlighted Lieutenant Haviland's strong interest in flying operations, emphasized difficult landing/takeoff conditions, and recounted four night flights made by moonlight without artificial lights. Overall, Mayo credited Callan with intelligent and judicious work, generally supervised and heartily encouraged by Train.[37] All told, Navy pilots operating from Porto Corsini carried out 745 flights lasting 807 hours. There were no battle fatalities. The largest number of aircraft at the station at any one time was 30, though far fewer were in commission on a regular basis. Throughout the summer and fall, planners examined the possibility of using American-made HS-type aircraft. The HS-2L's increased wingspan made it too large to fly from the narrow canal. Callan said he would try HS-1Ls, but a memo prepared by Aviation Aide Edwards's staff argued against such a disposition until at least one aircraft was shipped to Italy for trials. None ever reached Porto Corsini.

After returning from the Venice front, Haviland forwarded a request to Callan from enlisted personnel desiring to be returned to America as a unit, the men having signed a petition to that effect. This came in reaction to recent orders from Sims that 50 percent of the naval aviation complement should return immediately to the United States. Porto Corsini's bluejackets had served and suffered together and now in a show of solidarity wished to go home together. Their petition said, in part, "Our reasons for making this request are that our duties here seem to be nearing an end. We have given the service the best in us and have performed the duty assigned to us faithfully and conscientiously and the consideration that we desire most of all is that we be ordered to return to the United States as a unit."

Callan sent the request to Sims and promised that efforts would be made to keep the men together as much as possible. Apparently the request was approved and the crew all sailed home on the steamer *Giuseppe Verdi*, departing Genoa for New York January 4, 1919.[38]

Providing a secure and convenient site from which to conduct attacks against Austrian naval bases at Zara, Sebenico, Spalato, and Curzola on the Dalmation coast underlay the strategic rationale for establishing an American presence at Pescara, the second of two naval air stations planned in Italy. Located on the north bank of the Pescara River, near its mouth between the towns of Pescara and Castellamare Adriatico, the proposed patrol-bombing base lay 125 miles from Austrian territory. A Navy commission inspected the incomplete air station there in late April 1918. At the time, work on some facilities had already begun, the program being directed by a Lieutenant Provenzani. A silkworm culture industry occupied a substantial building intended for American use, with 10 small hangars either fully or partially completed. The unfinished structures appeared solidly made, of masonry and tile construction, but designed for a small Italian complement. Both electricity and an excellent water supply were available and the government promised to proceed rapidly with all necessary improvements. A report filed three weeks later, however, belied such pledges and indicated that work had not progressed. Cement shortages and limited enthusiasm on the part of native laborers hampered construction. The Americans made many recommendations to local builders and Asst. Paymaster Parker, who carried out an inspection, suggested that sending bluejackets to Pescara would greatly improve local morale. Callan forwarded Parker's request to Paris, asking for engineers and laborers to speed the process, but no Navy workers ever arrived.[39]

At the end of August, "Bull" Atwater visited the site. He discovered that much construction had been completed since the last inspection but considerably more needed to be done. He also witnessed a distinct lack of cooperation between workers and supervisors. Atwater believed that a few chief petty officers and a gang of bluejackets would move things along. Three days later,

Sims informed Washington that due to aircraft shortages and construction delays the base would not be ready until December 1 at the earliest. Frustrating impediments continued right through October. A representative from Callan's office again called for chief petty officers with construction experience who could also speak Italian (not many of those available). Ensign Lawrence White, executive officer at Rome headquarters, gloomily reported October 18: "hardly any progress since last report." Italian authorities hired local civilians, but they were not very efficient workmen. Skilled labor could not be had and harvest season drew others away. The influenza scourge killed five workers and incapacitated others. Just before the end of the war a small detail commanded by Ens. Joseph Green reached Pescara to arrange for the arrival of a large draft of American personnel.[40]

Even if construction had progressed more rapidly, the base still faced extreme obstacles. The Italians proved incapable of supplying promised aircraft in a timely fashion, and local flying conditions were far from ideal. The river current could be very swift, yet the waterway was barely 150 feet wide and just 5 feet deep in summer. Prevailing winds blew crosswise to the stream, making takeoffs and landings treacherous. A 35-foot iron bridge stood only 2,500 feet upstream, presenting yet another obstacle. In fact, Pescara never reached operational status as the pace of construction failed to match optimistic promises made in winter and spring 1918. Nor did the Navy push the work vigorously. Pescara had never possessed a vital strategic rationale and it ranked very low on the list of American priorities.

In addition to training at Bolsena and establishing stations at Porto Corsini and Pescara, the Navy made enormous efforts to secure heavy, multiengine bombers in Italy as part of its 1918 campaign to break the back of the submarine menace along the Belgian coast and eastern English Channel. Attempts to obtain these aircraft for work in Flanders and, more particularly, active consideration of the Caproni type, began in the winter of 1918. In fact, representatives from the Italian firm had offered their planes to Cone the previous year, but problems at the Joint Army-Navy Board in Paris stalled discussions. When the committee dissolved in April, Cone renewed contact, inquiring about 60 planes for use in a possible double offensive in Flanders and the Adriatic. This led the Caproni agent in the United States to speak with Noble Irwin. Sims soon received authorization to seek day and night bombers, whereupon Cone requested approval to place contracts in Italy.[41]

Lieutenant Eddie McDonnell, one of aviation's principal troubleshooters, was first to seriously investigate the availability of heavy bombers. In February 1918, following visits to French airfields where he observed Italian-made aircraft in action, he proceeded south and examined the feasibility of acquiring Capronis for the proposed Northern Bombing Group (NBG). McDonnell inspected several stations, met with Signor Giani Caproni, toured his factory, and made test hops in a three-engine, 450 hp Isotta-Fraschini Caproni. On one flight the plane performed a complete loop, a remarkable feat for such a large machine. These aircraft seemed quite capable—highly maneuverable, with an excellent ceiling of 15,000 feet and a 1,000-pound bomb load, coupled with very reliable engines. McDonnell also spent time with a Caproni squadron at Padua near the front lines, even participating in a raid as forward cockpit gunner.

Back in Milan, McDonnell met again with Signor Caproni to discuss a new airplane then under development, a 600 hp model powered by triple Fiat engines, reputed to have nearly double the bomb-carrying capacity (1,800–2,000 pounds) and a top speed of 105 mph. McDonnell then returned to Flanders and flew several missions with the RNAS in British-made Handley Page aircraft and came away convinced the new Caproni possessed several advantages, including higher ceiling, greater speed, and wider safety factor due to its third engine. On the negative side, the Italian plane appeared less rugged and more vulnerable to attack from the rear. McDonnell forwarded his recommendations to London and Paris and then returned to the United States as Sims's representative to gather material for the nascent Northern Bombing Group.[42]

Many believed the 600 hp Caproni destined for success. Cone claimed, "We can get better aircraft and better delivery from Italy than anyplace else on this side." A decision to use Capronis for the NBG's night bombing missions caused Lt. Col. Spenser Grey, RAF, and Lt.(jg) Harry Guggenheim to visit Rome in early May to negotiate with the Italian government for purchase of 30 aircraft to be delivered in June and July, 80 more in August, 20 in September, and 20 per month thereafter, an arrangement known as the May 10 Agreement. The parties never formally signed the agreement, however, and Commissioner of Aeronautics Eugenio Chiesa made several arbitrary modifications. Even with these, Italy could not fulfill the plan. Callan warned that the Caproni factory would not meet its ambitious delivery schedules since the head of manufacturing had been dismissed for failing to produce a single successful airplane. He further advised that Fiat engines possessed a terrible reputation. Callan's apprehensions turned out to be accurate; the Navy did not obtain its first bomber until July 21 and by mid-September had received only 18 of the 160 originally promised.[43]

Even worse than delays, severe mechanical difficulties plagued the aircraft. Poorly made Fiat engines suffered repeated breakdowns, as the factory possessed neither the machinery nor skill to implement mass production. Problems included badly machined crankshafts, missing gaskets, fire-prone carburetors, inadequate magnetos, and generally shoddy workmanship. Word of the plane's shortcomings soon leaked out. In fact, according to Callan, the 600 hp models "up to date have not proved satisfactory in their trials. In nearly every instance where machines have been sent out for trials, they have met with accidents and the pilots and observers have all been killed." Captain De Filippi also offered a caution, advising that new planes would be allocated first to the Italian army, then Italian navy, and only last to Americans. Furthermore, Chiesa admitted that no deliveries would be made in June. After reviewing projected production figures, Callan stated, "Personally, I doubt that it will be done." Meanwhile, in Flanders NBG commander Hanrahan anxiously awaited news about the planes; he was destined to wait, largely in vain.[44]

While the Navy negotiated to acquire Italian bombers in April and May, the Army also attempted to purchase Capronis. The Bolling Commission ordered several as early as August 1917, but they were never delivered, in part because Italy faced severe shortages of building materials. In January 1918 the Army appointed Capt. Fiorello LaGuardia its representative in Rome from the Joint Army-Navy Board established in November 1917 to eliminate overlapping procurement programs. A first-term congressman from New York City, LaGuardia joined the Air Service in the summer of 1917 and led a detachment of flyers to Italy that fall. He lobbied strenuously to get Army flyers to the front and undertook a local speaking tour to shore up local morale. At first, John Callan assumed he and LaGuardia could work together amicably, as both had a vested interest in expediting pilot training and production of Caproni aircraft. As early as March 27 he reported being able to utilize LaGuardia and other Army representatives as an alternate conduit of information from Commissioner Chiesa. Callan met with LaGuardia a second time in late March, when the New Yorker urged completion of a naval air station on the Adriatic as a spur to Caproni production. Callan observed, "LaGuardia may be a politician, but he is certainly a very influential one here."

At this juncture the Navy offered to supply lumber and other materials for its own orders, but LaGuardia accused the sailors of playing foul since they controlled transatlantic shipping. He immediately launched a lobbying program that proved highly offensive to Train and Cone. Train informed Paris that his efforts "were frustrated and position greatly embarrassed by the actions of Captain LaGuardia," who undercut the attaché by personally interceding with Chiesa. The congressman claimed that Navy representatives had no authority to negotiate, nor could they guarantee shipments. Train fumed, "such underhand work should be taken up and investigated." In fact, LaGuardia played a double game, using the Navy to placate local officials. Since the Army had no plans to employ Capronis south of the Alps, the Italians had little incentive to fill their order. If the Navy conducted combat operations on the Venetian front or elsewhere local authorities might be more amenable to allocating aircraft to Americans.[45]

As the weeks passed with little movement on either production or training front, competition between the services intensified and acerbic charges and countercharges flew. Hutch Cone sensed that trouble was brewing, describing LaGuardia as a "New York Italian politician and member of Congress principally concerned in pushing a large general project looking toward a campaign in Congress." He warned that Navy people in Rome believed LaGuardia used "underhanded methods" to oppose their plan to obtain Capronis. Of course, word of these difficulties quickly got back to AEF headquarters—perhaps carried by LaGuardia himself, who visited Paris in early May and, the Navy believed, spread false reports. Pershing penned a personal letter to Sims describing a "lack of coordination between officers who are handling the U.S. Army and Navy Air Service in Europe." He charged that there were instances when the services had come into competition in obtaining material, creating an unfavorable impression with the Allies that might affect other areas of cooperation. As an aside, Pershing suggested that there should be only one air service. Somewhat taken aback by these charges, Sims wished to respond to the Army chief and solicited Hutch Cone's "immediate" opinion.[46]

Well understanding the meaning of "immediate," Cone dispatched a reply the following day. He had already shown the Admiral's cable to Col. Halsey Dunwoody, Assistant Chief of the Air Service for Supply, who asserted, "perfect coordination between our offices exists" in all technical and supply questions. Cone recalled that when he first arrived in France cooperation at all levels had been very good, but recently "it has been impossible to get in close touch with the Chief of the Air Service [Foulois]," another Navy nemesis. He denied that the services competed for material, stating that everything was obtained through the Franco-American Mission and the Army General Purchasing Board. With regard to the Caproni contretemps, likely the source of Pershing's comments, Cone smelled a rat named LaGuardia. When he received Train's report he purposely kept it from the Army "to avoid rupture."

Cone worried that close cooperation meant letting the War Department handle Navy business, something he did not believe them capable of doing. As to the notion of a single air service, he thought the concept probably valid, "but at present [considered] it impractical and Navy interests would surely suffer severely."[47]

Meanwhile, the Air Service experienced its own internal discord, with General Foulois in particular. As a remedy, Pershing appointed Gen. Mason Patrick as new chief of the Army Air Service in late May, moving Foulois to another assignment. Patrick and Cone then sat down to thrash out various issues. Cone offered to let the Army conduct negotiations for Capronis but objected to LaGuardia's involvement. Patrick stood by his troublesome subordinate but promised the New Yorker "would faithfully care for the Navy's interests." Attempting to put the squabbling behind them, the senior officers drafted a joint memorandum May 31 to the Royal Italian Aeronautical Mission in Paris, announcing that the Army would represent Navy interests in Rome and use their combined efforts to secure raw materials for Italy. Any previous agreements between the Navy and the Italian government remained in force.[48]

Part of the plan to utilize Italian bombers required sending American mechanics and engineers to the Caproni, Fiat, and Isotta-Fraschini factories, and the first detachments reached Milan, Taliedo, and Varese on June 1. Lieutenant(jg) Austin Potter, for example, spent weeks studying at Italian factories and flying fields, where he subsisted on a diet of pasta, goat milk ice cream, and mutton of "uncertain age but unmistakable flavor." A keen observer of the local scene, he described Fiat shops filled with soldiers returned from the front, those with influential friends, a few youths, and bloomer-clad, black-frocked young women. Work hours stretched from 7:00 A.M. to 6:30 P.M., with 1.5 hours off for lunch. Everyone labored on a piecework basis, with maximum earnings of $1.35 per day. Taken aback by Italian methods, Potter decried inadequate inspection of machining and assembly operations. Working drawings never indicated exact tolerances; rather, they contained symbols, squares, circles, and so on indicating "force fit," "tight fit," "easy/sweet fit," and "running fit." To Potter, manufacturing methods sometimes seemed primitive, with much work done by manual labor that would have been performed by precise machine tools in the United States.[49]

While mechanics studied in various factories, 15 pilots led by Lt.(jg) Sam Walker reported to aviation school at Malpensa in early June. The Italians offered their visitors a grand reception. Festivities began with a great celebration in Milan that included a large gathering in front of the cathedral, then speeches, parades, and a performance of *Madame Butterfly* at La Scala, followed by a formal ball. Nonetheless, some new arrivals expressed disappointment. One recorded, "It seems the school is not very well equipped. There is a great deal of breakage and conditions are overcrowded." John Callan felt the hosts overcharged for training, with the price "unjust and way out of proportion for what [we] will probably get."[50]

Malpensa, the largest training facility in Italy, with perhaps 300 officers under instruction, stood 45 minutes north of Milan by electric trolley. Today Milan's international airport covers the site. The field, about three miles square, lay in the stunningly beautiful lake country, and during practice flights students often passed over Lake Maggiore and Lake Como, ascending into the foothills of the Alps. American trainees lived with Italian officers, following the same rules and regulations. Accommodations were clean and comfortable, but the flying schedule seemed unusual by Navy standards. Instruction began at 5:30 A.M. and continued until 10:30. Next, everyone sat down to a large meal, followed by a lengthy nap lasting until late afternoon, when instruction resumed, sometimes until 10 in the evening. All this was designed to avoid the intense midday heat and air turbulence it caused. Sam Walker, group leader and member of the First Yale Unit, became particularly critical of the regimen, remembering how initial enthusiasm for Italian aviation gave way to sharp condemnation of local training methods and a lack of eagerness to fly. Large numbers of accidents seemed one reason.

Caproni instruction encompassed three different aircraft, designed to qualify students as "second pilots," with experience necessary to earn the rank of "first pilot" gained at combat fields and during actual operations. In practice, the Italians omitted lessons on the 300 hp model and utilized the closely related 450 hp type because more were available. The school allocated one machine and instructor to the Navy detachment. Students learned to solo, climbing to 6,000 feet and making a dead stick landing, followed by a few hours of night flying. They carried out landings aided by searchlights. Reginald Coombe, a college classmate of Walker, recalled, "Compared to the British system this seemed like a smattering of things an experienced pilot should be versed in." He found Capronis easy to master but training progressed slowly; instructors seemed in no rush and it proved difficult to accumulate requisite hours. "*Domani* was the word. They seemed to think us a bit crazy for being in such a blazing hurry to get through with it." Nonetheless, by June 22 all Navy pilots but one had soloed. After obtaining their 450 hp model brevet they undertook only two instruction flights in 600 hp Capronis. Their instructor felt one week of good weather provided enough time to finish. After completing their brevets, students were not allowed to fly any more.[51]

The lack of new Caproni deliveries cast a pall over the training program. What was the use of learning to fly the things, after all, if none could be built? Further, the Italians seemed reluctant even to provide accurate and timely information. In mid-June Callan reported, "The delivery of Capronis is a ticklish question and it is going to be quite difficult to find out exactly when we will get machines." Unresolved mechanical problems further slowed production, resulting in very few completed planes, perhaps a total of 30–40 in June, and 40–50 in July, far too few to meet competing expectations of the many military services with aircraft on order. In July the Department ordered Capt. "Barney" Smith to Italy as "troubleshooter" to investigate the issue, but with little immediate impact.[52]

Whether addressing training or production issues, the Navy focused much of its frustration on the person of Fiorello LaGuardia. Attaché Train exhibited particular displeasure, writing that LaGuardia "should never have been returned here." In early June, Callan reported that since the cooperation agreement, he had worked with LaGuardia "and up to the present time we have had no trouble of any sort." Nonetheless, he warned, "The only thing which I saw which might be a mistake was the sending back to Italy of Capt. LaGuardia for this duty as the representative of both forces." For a while, though, events seemed to proceed relatively peacefully, and during the summer the Navy gathered enormous quantities of materiel for this project, including 20,000 gallons of paint and varnish, 80,000 yards of cotton fabric, 120,000 feet of steel cable, 138,000 feet of lumber, and 7,000 square feet of plywood.[53]

While sensible in terms of presenting a united front with Italian authorities, the May 31 Army-Navy arrangement only inflamed suspicions of those on the ground, and cooperation proved short-lived. According to Train, LaGuardia rarely visited Rome and proved nearly impossible to contact. More important, word filtered down that the AEF officer connived at Malpensa for Army aviators to receive priority in training. Callan charged, "LaGuardia was profuse in his denials, but Train doesn't believe him." Sam Walker had a particular bone to pick, reporting, "We found LaGuardia was all for the Army, meanwhile letting the Navy twiddle its thumbs." Callan requested that Walker keep him informed, as "it is very important for us to know whether he is working for us or against us." The Navy approached the ministry and received assurances that the major had been instructed not to interfere. Well aware of the criticism, the embattled congressman attempted to set the record straight in a lengthy communication to General Patrick. LaGuardia claimed that the

Navy acted "so queer and unfair down here," suggesting that Cone must surely be misinformed of conditions in Italy. He concluded, "I need not point out that the Navy's attitude in this matter was anything but fair and just."[54]

Eventually, the arrival of Maj. Robert Glendenning, LaGuardia's replacement, soothed Navy suspicions and restored a healthy measure of interservice amity. Though inexperienced, he proved "a much more satisfactory representative than the former one." Nonetheless, the war of memos continued, even after LaGuardia relinquished his former duties. Callan wrote personally to Cone in Paris, including much of his correspondence with the Army representative, "together with memoranda I made on LaGuardia's answers." In several places Callan included underlinings and special notes for emphasis, "In order that you may see for yourself exactly how he has acted down here and know that he has not represented us in the proper manner or worked for the best interests of the service."[55] Even this did not end the saga. Following the Armistice, the congressman returned to Washington, where he joined the fierce debate over consolidation of the air services with a ferociously anti-Navy viewpoint. In early January 1919, Sims received notice that Congressman La Guardia planned to make an attack in the near future. Navy officials sought ammunition and ordered Sims to gather up all relevant documents, including the correspondence of the naval attaché in Rome (Train) and send them home forthwith.[56]

Of more immediate interest, in late July 1918 a few Caproni bombers finally became available to the Army and Navy, who soon concluded arrangements to transfer them to northern France. The first step in the process, however, involved using American flyers to help transport another group of planes to southern Italy, at least in part to gain experience in long-distance, cross-country flying. A dozen Navy pilots participated in this operation ferrying bombers from the Caproni factory at Taliedo (near Milan) to Gioia delle Colle, a naval air station near Brindisi. The planned route went from Taliedo to Pisa, then Centocelle, Capua, Foggia, and finally Gioia delle Colle, a two-day journey. American aviators usually paired with Italian enlisted pilots familiar with the route, but broken engines or propellers aborted many missions. Four planes failed to reach the final destination due to accidents. Ensign Henry Clayton completed the trip first. He flew to Pisa to refuel, then onward to Rome before heading south. Lieutenant Howard "Tiny" Maxwell remained unconvinced of the efficacy of the entire arrangement. Flying with an Italian officer, he headed south toward Rome but disappeared for two days. Word eventually arrived that an unidentified bomber had landed in the north, 15 minutes' flying time from the enemy lines. Misadventures like this presaged difficulties the Navy encountered when it attempted to ferry its own bombers over the Alps to Flanders.[57]

Throughout summer and fall the command structure, priorities, and scope of operations in Italy continued to evolve. Rome headquarters eventually included 9 officers and 17 enlisted men, a small complement hard-pressed to complete all its assignments, with personnel often working late into the night. An official history of aviation activities in Rome singled out Callan, Lt. Lawrence White (executive officer), son of famed and notorious architect Stanford White, and Lt. William Parker (Supply) for special praise. In addition to oversight of the facility at Lake Bolsena, operations at Porto Corsini, and the faltering construction program at Pescara, the Rome office shouldered additional responsibilities such as arranging purchase of Caproni bombers, monitoring instruction of pilots and observers, obtaining captive balloons and shipping them to the United States, investigating Italian equipment, inspecting local bases, and developing strategies for future military action. The office also oversaw the general welfare of the growing Navy presence in Italy. Many of the force operated in severe malaria districts or were affected by the influenza pandemic, placing great demands on the headquarters medical officer. In October, as plans unfolded for a substantial increase in aviation activities, Train assumed command of the entire effort, a significant increase in authority over his former role as attaché. Callan remained on staff as aide for aviation and began a countrywide inspection tour. He encountered swarms of ravenous mosquitoes wherever he went.[58]

Unfortunately, the Caproni situation generated continued frustration. Repeated conferences with Italian officials took place, but a resolution could never be achieved. Late in August Callan lamented that the Commisario Generale seemed reluctant to allocate any machines to the Americans, with total August production slated for only 47 aircraft. Both Callan and Glendenning remonstrated and came away with assurances the United States would get its "fair share." And so it continued into the fall, with the outlook "not overbright for obtaining machines with good motors in the near future." Callan observed, "It would seem that we are going about in a circle in regard to this work." Instead, Chiesa "practically denies any contract was ever made, except verbally, which we cannot make him hold to." On one matter, at least, the services agreed, the Isotta-Fraschini motor was far superior to the cursed Fiat and should be used on all future deliveries. Sims proved equally gloomy, reporting in mid-September, "Caproni production will be much less than expected." A week later headquarters dispatched a mission headed by Benjamin Briscoe to investigate continuing shortages of materials necessary to manufacture the star-crossed aircraft.[59]

Caproni matters aside, the Navy also explored plans to expand its mission in Italy In response to Sims's July request for proposals to be discussed at a series of upcoming conferences, Callan submitted a lengthy report endorsing an enormous enlargement of the aviation program. He had pushed ideas like these for months. Unaware that the war was already entering its final phase, Callan believed decisive results could be achieved on the Italian front, with Austria the most vulnerable of the Central Powers. With Austria out of the war, Turkey and Bulgaria would be isolated and the Allies could concentrate their might against Germany. To achieve a knockout blow, he endorsed continuous bombardment of enemy naval targets and constant patrols against all fleet units. He called for creation of a Caproni group to operate against Pola, Trieste, and Fiume, and recommended that the United States establish a large seaplane base at Vallona equipped with H-16s to mount attacks every night. For large bombers, Callan urged the Navy to man the station at Ancona, and if Capronis proved to be unavailable, they should utilize U.S.-made Handley Pages instead. New M7 and M9 flyingboats would be employed where appropriate.

Callan's overall plan envisioned operating stations/bases at Porto Corsini, Pescara, Poggio Renatico (80 Capronis), Vallona, and Ancona, though the latter might substitute for Pescara where construction seemed hopelessly delayed. This program required the stupendous total of 932 aircraft, including 120 H-16s, 72 HS-2Ls, 180 M-9s, 240 M-7s, and 320 Capronis or Handley Pages. To accommodate such an enormous force, the Navy should take over two islands in the Gulf of Venice for an assembly and repair facility. Callan's recommendations sparked debate in London and Paris and extensive negotiations with the Italian government, but the war ended before any final determination could be made.[60]

* * *

Public assurances to the contrary, both the Army and Navy regarded Italy and the Mediterranean as a military backwater. Activities there never enjoyed the priority accorded operations on the Western Front. Nonetheless, policy makers viewed minimal commitments as a way to "get into the fight" and shore up an ally's morale, especially after the Caporetto disaster. For the Navy, John Callan, with his long history and strong emotional attachment to the region, functioned as prime mover on all questions relating to involvement in Italy, though shortages of men and material continually plagued projects developed under his aegis. Despite these impediments, the Navy achieved some success in difficult conditions. The school at Bolsena trained scores of pilots, while the outpost at Porto Corsini became one of the Navy's most active stations. Attempts to obtain Caproni airplanes for the Northern Bombing Group proved far less successful, yielding little more than delays, headaches, and several deaths. Relations with Maj. Fiorello LaGuardia offered the perfect paradigm of the failure of military services to cooperate for a common goal. Callan's plan for an enormous bombing program on the Venetian front mirrored NBG efforts in Flanders, but it is unclear how seriously the highest command levels entertained the possibility of implementing it.

11

THE NORTHERN BOMBING GROUP

The Northern Bombing Group, a unit established to destroy German submarine facilities at Bruges-Ostend-Zeebrugge through aerial assault, became the largest naval aviation initiative of World War I. Initially envisioned as employing roughly 6,000 men, it would have utilized hundreds of frontline aircraft, several airfields positioned across a wide swath of Flanders, and a huge assembly and repair base in southern England. The NBG represented the supreme embodiment of the Department's aggressive approach to combating the U-boat menace. To achieve its objective, the Navy would have created six day and six night squadrons to carry out "round the clock" attacks by light and heavy bombers. Ultimately, the Navy established four day and four night squadrons, with naval pilots manning night squadrons and Marine Corps aviators responsible for day operations. Admiral Samuel McGowan, head of the Bureau of Supplies and Accounts, called the entire project "the largest ever undertaken by the Navy to be consummated in anywhere near so short of time." Captain David Hanrahan, a veteran destroyer captain and skipper of the Q-ship *Santee*, directed the group from his headquarters at Autingues, where he operated under the aegis of the British admiral commanding the Dover Patrol. From the start this venture enjoyed support at the highest levels and received priority over other initiatives. Unfortunately, failure to secure sufficient aircraft prevented the unit from ever carrying out its intended mission. The NBG initiative also ignited a nasty confrontation with Army aviators that blighted relations between the air services in Europe and lasted well into the postwar period.[1]

* * *

Bombing the submarine menace out of existence posed a difficult tactical challenge. In the last two years of the war the Flanders U-boat flotilla claimed one-third of all British vessels sunk in home waters. Located close to major shipping lanes, these facilities ranked at the top of Allied strategists' list as targets for destruction. By 1918 German forces had turned the Bruges-

Ostend-Zeebrugge triangle into a virtual fortress. Coastal artillery emplacements studded the coast, while swarms of land and seaplanes defended the skies. In Bruges, concrete submarine pens offered protection against aerial bombardment. Over 200 antiaircraft guns pointed skyward. Batteries of searchlights powered by gasoline generators pierced the night darkness, 30 at Bruges alone. German defenders received about 30 minutes' warning before any attack. Britain sought to overcome these defenses by deploying heavily armed monitors, swarms of destroyers, CMBs, and other small craft—and, after 1917, DH-4 day bombers and huge Handley Page aircraft at night, but with little success. Not one of the U-boat shelters was hit until September 1918, and only three submarines were damaged. Competing demands for aerial support frequently diverted RNAS/RAF bombing units from antisubmarine missions. By contrast, American planners argued that attacks, to be effective, must be massive, focused, and continuous, and they anticipated carrying out such raids by themselves if the war lasted into 1919.[2]

The shift from defensive to offensive tactics reflected many converging factors. Combating the U-boat constituted the Navy's preeminent responsibility, as it had from the opening days of the war. Hunting submarines by seaplane in open waters, however, had achieved little success. Conditions at Dunkirk remained far from optimal. British airmen, who frequently provided guidance, abandoned seaplane patrol and begun using land bombers to attack Belgian ports. French officers endorsed the British approach. After being rebuffed by the U.S. Army, the Marine Corps aggressively sought a role in the Navy's aerial assault scheme. Nonetheless, severe obstacles existed to such an ambitious program. The proposed size of the NBG proved daunting. Competing, even conflicting, operational and tactical concepts flowed from Washington and Paris/London. The Navy possessed no cadre of flyers trained for land aircraft and missions, no related instruction program, and did not have the requisite machines. Finally, a land-based bombing offensive raised the toxic issue of "poaching" on Army missions and competing for scarce equipment. This, in turn, merged with the explosive issue of "amalgamation."

The concept of shifting away from antisubmarine patrols, essentially a defensive posture, toward offensive bombing of U-boats and their support facilities took root early in the winter of 1918. Following his work at Felixstowe, Robert Lovett visited English gunnery and bombing schools and then spent several weeks with the RNAS Intelligence Department, all the time watching, listening, and compiling notes. Increasingly, he viewed random patrols as a waste of time, men, and material. Lovett returned to Paris headquarters in January and prepared a lengthy memo on how to attack the submarine menace directly. He had been thinking of using seaplanes for this activity, as was done at Felixstowe and other RNAS stations, but changed his mind when he met Lt. Col. D. A. Spenser Grey ("the greatest authority on bombing the war produced") at the Allied Air Council at Army Air Headquarters. The colonel, in turn, introduced Lovett to the heads of British night bombing squadrons at Couderkerque near Dunkirk. Lovett soon became convinced that large aircraft flying at night were ideal weapons and told Cone that Grey would be glad to help the Navy. At that time Grey worked with the AEF Air Service and their bombing program, but according to Lovett, the Army suffered from too much politics and too little gray matter.[3]

Lovett's analysis frankly acknowledged the size of the challenge but argued that bombing offered the only way to check the U-boat. As he explained, just a small portion of enemy submarine forces ventured out on patrol at any one time. The majority could be found in their lairs and should be bombed there—but not by seaplanes, which could not be used at night, had limited load-carrying capacity, and were designed solely for patrol duties. Rather, very large Caproni or Handley Page bombers seemed the logical weapons to employ, for the "effectiveness of these machines [could not] be overestimated . . . [as they were] by far the most deadly weapon any of the Allies have yet discovered." In Lovett's estimation, the USNAS ought to concentrate on large bombing planes and he requested permission to visit the front and amass data. Ultimately, he reported to Captain Lambe at Dunkirk and joined No. 7 Squadron, RNAS, of the 5th Wing to collect information relative to establishing similar American squadrons, gain practical experience operating large bombers, and locate the best sites for new stations.

In mid-February Sims's newly established Planning Section weighed into the debate. They identified the U-boat as aviation's biggest challenge and noted that patrol operations were less successful than anticipated. Enemy raiders could, however, be attacked in their bases, the tactic with the greatest potential to inflict severe damage. The Planning Section then called for sustained bombing. This required sufficient force at Felixstowe-Dunkirk to gain control of the air and then employment of huge land planes with a wide operational radius and heavy lift capacity. While the planners did not recommend abandoning seaplane patrols, they believed such activities should play a supplemental role only. Advocating a shift away from seaplanes to land planes raised many thorny issues, however, ranging from conflicts with the Army to abandonment of planned stations and construction of new facilities. Submitted for discussion, the recommendation kicked off a huge controversy. Cone disagreed with some elements and added others. He thought night attacks would be very valuable, expressed a desire to initiate photographic reconnaissance, and called for use of pursuit/*chasse* planes to protect lumbering bombers. He opposed abandoning antisubmarine patrols. Cone further believed that gaining control of the air required far more than fighters; it also necessitated bombing enemy airfields, another touchy subject. Finally, shifting to land bombing would necessitate extensive retraining of seaplane pilots.[4]

Even as Navy planners in Europe debated proposals for a land-based bombing campaign, the General Board in Washington examined the same subject and reached very different conclusions. The Board conducted hearings in January and February and reviewed material submitted to it, including a plan offered by Marine Capt. Alfred Cunningham, along with testimony from LCdr. John Towers and LCdr. Kenneth Whiting. Cunningham had just returned from an inspection trip to Europe. Towers served as assistant director of Naval Aviation in the office of Chief of Naval Operations Benson. Kenneth Whiting was then stationed in Washington organizing men and materials for the planned bombing seaplane base at Killingholme, England. Their opinions clearly impressed Board members. Cunningham, in particular, provided a detailed analysis of the issue and a plan of action. He prepared a lengthy analysis, and his testimony echoed his report conclusions. Cunningham believed operations from Dunkirk offered the best opportunity to curb the submarine attacks. He called conditions there very congested, but there was no better location in the vicinity. In Cunningham's opinion, the British did not execute aerial missions against the submarines in sufficient force to succeed. Instead, they concentrated limited resources on attacking German bases. Thus, if the United States took up the challenge of controlling the air off the coast of Belgium and sinking submarines transiting these waters, the British would be very pleased and likely render whatever assistance was possible.[5]

Towers expanded Cunningham's analysis. U-boats used restricted channels along the shore to pass into the Channel and French coastal waters and concentrated sufficient aircraft to keep the skies clear of opposing planes. Whenever the Allies attempted to alter the balance, the Germans augmented local forces with fighting squadrons transferred in from other locations. "As the matter now stands," Towers reported, "Allied aircraft don't dare go out very far from their bases." He concluded, "We should make every effort to control the air. . . . No matter how many bombing machines we put out if there are no fighting machines to protect them it is a useless sacrifice." Summarized, the testimony of these officers advocated a three-point plan: employ bombing seaplanes based at Dunkirk, attack submarines in transit, and utilize *chasse* machines to gain control of the air and protect bombers. After conducting hearings, the Board sent a "Proposed Letter" to Secretary Daniels February 25 on the topic, "The control of the air in the Dunkerque-Calais region to prevent the passage of Dover Strait by German Submarines." They expressed grave concern about the current submarine situation. If American naval *seaplanes* (emphasis mine) were to achieve success, some change in tactics seemed necessary. Based on the evidence submitted, the Board drew several conclusions, often, it turned out, rather inaccurate or outdated. German submarines transited an area of narrow channels, often on the surface, to avoid shoals and other navigational obstacles (true). They could not risk running this gauntlet at night (only partially true). In good weather aircraft spotted periscope wakes at a distance of five miles (possible, but unlikely). Bombing aircraft had proved effective against submarines (dubious), and the importance of using such machines in restricted areas while operating from a nearby base "is evident" (debatable!).

Board members criticized earlier British efforts to conduct bombing operations against Belgian sites with seaplanes from Dunkirk and the Navy's mistaken efforts to follow their example, calling prospects of success "futile." Instead, the Board believed it imperative to maintain a substantial "number of the best type of fighting aircraft of the land type to cover and protect bombing planes against German counter-attacks." Cunningham claimed that 30 bombing seaplanes would be necessary, while taking control of the air required 200 land planes. The entire operation would be "distinctly naval, and be under naval control, the Navy and Marine Corps providing necessary personnel." The Board considered the entire program so significant that they strongly urged the Navy to assign priority in manpower and material. Their specific recommendations were these: select sites for land and seaplane bases in the Calais-Dunkirk region, to operate 30 seaplanes and 200 fighting machines; use every effort, beginning immediately, to obtain necessary materiel and train required personnel in order to seize control of the air in this region; proceed so as to have operations commence in May; obtain 64 land fighting machines from the Army or contractors, with an eventual goal of 200 or more; give priority to this project "as being of greater importance in the results to be obtained than any other airplane work abroad and at home"; invite the earnest cooperation of the British and French; and, finally, proceed with the underlying thought "that there cannot be too many bombing and fighting machines supplied quickly."[6]

Support for the endeavor derived from many sources. For the Marines, it offered a chance to employ leatherneck aviators in Europe. Both Commandant

George Barnett and Cunningham had been developing their service's aviation arm with the idea of sending a reconnaissance unit to the Western Front. In November and December, Cunningham visited training schools and aviation stations in Europe, even flying missions himself over the lines. He also labored to convince the Army to support his plans for a land squadron, but was told the AEF had no intention of letting flying Marines anywhere near the front lines. It was only at this point, following discussions with naval and Allied officials in the Dunkirk area, that Cunningham developed a new plan to utilize land-based pilots to escort flying boats attacking submarines along the Belgian shore. Whiting's support may have been influenced by the fact he was then in Washington organizing men and material for the Navy's large, planned *seaplane bombing* base at Killingholme. Officials as important as the secretary of the Navy and the chief of Naval Operations backed the concept enthusiastically and mobilized enormous resources to implement it. Meanwhile, the Department remained wary of challenging the Army in the area of land bombing.

Recommendations to utilize Dunkirk-based seaplanes escorted by land-based scouts to bomb submarines while in transit—and coincidentally defeat a large segment of the German air force in the process—ran directly counter to ideas evolving on the other side of the Atlantic, both in American naval aviation circles and at the Admiralty. But officials in Washington, not least of them Admiral Benson, had the bit in their teeth. In a *highly secret* March 7 cable to Sims, Benson conveyed the gist of the Board's recommendations, adding that Daniels had already approved the initiative and training was under way in the United States. He advised Sims to procure aircraft from French or British sources, if possible. Sims should also initiate a search for airfields, particularly places "not easily located by enemy bombers," and establish necessary facilities. The men could live in tents until barracks arrived. All this was designed to commence operations around June 1. Sims and Cone must have been stunned.[7]

Benson's directive set off a frantic period of analysis, discussion, and inter-Allied consultation. In fact, most of those in Europe considered the Board's recommendations out-of-date, unworkable, and strategically misguided. Almost immediately, Cone dispatched troubleshooter Lovett to Dunkirk to solicit Captain Lambe's views. According to Lovett, Lambe considered it nearly impossible to protect slow-moving seaplane-bombers with fast fighting machines. He argued instead for "self-defensive squadrons" carrying out direct assaults against submarine bases, navy yards, and shipbuilding facilities. In fact, Lambe strongly recommended that Americans eliminate seaplanes entirely and utilize squadrons of DH-4 day bombers equipped with air bags. Single-seat fighting machines should be of the Sopwith Camel or SE-5 type.[8]

As early as March 18 Cone informed Sims the General Board's recommendation "was not considered advisable." Rather, he suggested the proposed force of 200 land planes be *diverted* to the purpose of continuous aerial assault on submarine bases by establishing day and night bombardment units. Cone envisioned the aircraft divided into six Handley Page squadrons equipped with 10 bombers each and six DH-4 squadrons of 18 planes each, with an additional 32 high-performance aircraft for patrol/protection. Sims quickly endorsed Cone's observations and reported that Britain could not supply necessary aircraft. Rather, most bombers would have to come from the United States. Sims also initiated tentative site selection. In other words, he proceeded as if the idea of land squadrons would win out, virtually ignoring the seaplane-bomber concept. Cone's staff also solicited the views of the French Ministry of Marine concerning acquisition of (bombing) planes for Dunkirk but learned that Paris could not supply such machines in the near future. The Navy might secure a few *chasse* machines, though aircraft obtained from the French would likely be diverted from supplies promised to the American Army, something the Air Service would resist strenuously. Instead, the Navy would look toward Italy for bombers.[9]

About this time Cone ordered trusted deputy Lovett, along with veteran Eddie McDonnell, to analyze the entire British bombing operation in Flanders and report back to headquarters. This included participating in several combat missions. McDonnell reached Calais first and went on his initial night raid March 20 in one of the heavy RNAS Handley Page bombers. As a member of Flight Lieutenant Allen's crew, he manned the tail cockpit, operating upper and lower machine guns. Their aircraft attacked the Bruges docks from an altitude of 5,800 feet, dropping approximately 1,700 pounds of ordnance. Powerful searchlights guarded the approaches. A heavy antiaircraft barrage rising to an altitude of 10,000 feet consisted "of a countless number of green luminous balls (nicknamed "flaming onions")," joined by large concentrations of shrapnel and high explosives. During the mission one bomb stuck in the rack and McDonnell climbed outboard to knock it loose. Several other hair-raising adventures followed.

Arriving shortly after McDonnell, Lovett reached Dunkirk the evening of March 21, covering the distance from Paris to the coast by motorcycle with sidecar. By March 23 he had joined No. 7 Squadron, RNAS, and participated in another evening assault on the Bruges docks. Four Handley Pages dropped

6,300 pounds of high explosives. Over the next week Lovett joined in eight raids (two turned back), hitting Bruges five times in four days. Bruges, he noted, was considered the most dangerous objective, guarded by 17 searchlights and "highly trained anti-aircraft batteries," the barrage being box-like, with layers of high explosives and shrapnel and an "over-generous supply of green balls." Multiple attacks caused temporary lessening in the intensity of antiaircraft fire as ammunition became exhausted, but it was replenished within a few days. As usual, Lovett provided a detailed, insightful report of his activities, covering a wide range of subjects. He discovered that raids against railroads and along lines of communication encountered less intense but more accurate enemy fire. German searchlights proved far more powerful than those employed by the French and Belgians. With a full load, the Handley Page could barely climb to 7,000–8,000 feet necessitating bombing from a glide just 5,000–6,000 feet above the target, leading to frequent damage from shrapnel and machine gun bullets.

Lovett's own experience and information gathered from British hosts led him to conclude that continuous bombing of a target had proven quite effective. In the last few days of a sustained assault, incendiary bombs should be added to the mix. This would leave bases such as Bruges-Ostend-Zeebrugge "untenable, if not stamped off the map." Over time, defenses grew weaker. Joined with day raids, resistance often grew so feeble that bombing could be accomplished from ever-lower altitudes. Conversely, Lovett concluded that intermittent bombing constituted a distinct danger to attacking forces as such pauses allowed the enemy to improve defenses and gather vast quantities of ammunition. Lovett urged that naval bombing be concentrated on submarine facilities and not "any promiscuous bombing of military targets except in times of great crisis."[10]

During late March and early April, Lovett, McDonnell, Chevalier, and Cone met repeatedly with Allied officers who strongly endorsed the American initiative and criticized Washington's seaplane proposal. Despite these objections, the Department proved reluctant to abandon its initial plans. It continued supporting the seaplane option, perhaps from fear of antagonizing the Army. Early in April the Department acknowledged Britain's concentrated bombing of the Bruges-Ostend-Zeebrugge triangle and not attacking submarines very vigorously; it planned to supply large water machines to American forces for this latter purpose. If Dunkirk proved unsuitable as a water base, operations could be shifted to England. The Department expected to secure 80 Bristol-Liberty aircraft equipped with detachable landing gear, allowing them to alight on water, and these machines would be suitable for both protection and day bombing. Night bombers would be ordered but not available till the fall, eight months away. In addition, Sims should try to acquire the 32 *chasse* planes and the 40 day bombers discussed in Cone's recommendation in Europe.[11]

With the mention of day bombers, the Department had begun straddling the issue of seaplane versus land-based bombing. Cone objected to such half measures and fired back with a series of "definite and detailed" recommendations to establish a powerful bombing force of six day and six night squadrons. Cone also sought authorization to acquire Caproni bombers until aircraft from the United States became available. The program would require 180 officers and 1,764 ratings, hundreds of aircraft, a repair base employing 2,000 personnel, dispensaries to treat 5,000 men, more than 300 vehicles, 16 telephone switchboards, and 7,000 fuel drums. In fact, officers in Europe had been moving ahead on this track, albeit informally, for some time. As early as April 1, Cone decided to send McDonnell to Washington to "supervise and advise" concerning the naval bombing offensive. Sims followed this advisory with a note to Secretary Daniels reporting that McDonnell had been ordered home as Cone's personal representative and would explain proposed activities in detail when he arrived. Rest assured, Sims concluded, McDonnell was fully qualified and should be returned to France as soon as possible. Also during April, Craven, Billings, Briscoe, and Grey visited the Dunkirk area and made tentative selections for NBG airfields. Shortly thereafter, negotiations commenced to acquire five sites, with grading and sodding to begin quickly. David Hanrahan, the "Iron Duke," an experienced destroyer skipper known for his magnetic, overbearing personality, and sparkling Irish humor, took command of the projected new force. Casual observers and intimates called him popular and unpopular, wild, jolly, mild, violent, bad-tempered, a tower of strength, a good organizer, and a stern disciplinarian.[12]

Throughout these busy weeks, NBG plans underwent continual refinement. In mid-April, Cone dropped the notion of employing *chasse* squadrons, accepting the argument that DH-4 day bombers were fast enough and sufficiently armed to protect themselves. Further, manpower estimates for envisioned squadrons now totaled 527 officers and 5,800 enlisted ratings, including 2,000 personnel to staff a large assembly and repair base. Four day bombing squadrons would be allocated to the Marines, with the other two reserved for the Navy (this to replace the Marines' lost role flying escort machines for bombing seaplanes). Planners anticipated "wastage" of 15 percent per month among day squadron aircrews and 10 percent per month for night bombing formations. They expected aircraft losses from combat, accidents, and deterioration to run 50 percent per month in day squadrons and 33 percent per month among night units. Sims forwarded all the information to Washington with his strong endorsement, calling bombing operations "the primary mission of USNAFFS." Briscoe would be returning to the United States shortly to organize the equipment. Simultaneously, Sims informed Wilson at Brest that NBG planning was now well under way. The repair base would be named the Northern Repair Base, with airfields designated U.S. Naval Flying Field A, B, C, and so on. Night bombing squadrons were numbered 1–6 and Day squadrons 7–12. The proposed organizational plan envisioned a headquarters and repair base at St Inglevert; Night Squadrons 1 and 2 at Campagne; Night Squadrons 3 and 4 at Sangatte; Night Squadrons 5 and 6 at La Fresne; all squadrons were to have two flights of five planes each.[13]

In the face of such determined opposition, Benson and his staff reluctantly abandoned seaplane bombing proposals, and on April 30 prepared a memorandum for Secretary Daniels. They explained that after much consideration the General Board plan of late February had been "*extended*" to include day and night bombing squadrons. The War Department agreed that the new plan was, in fact, "purely naval work." Aircraft requirements for the program now totaled 240 day and 120 night bombers, along with 90 JN-4 and 10 Thomas Morse training machines. A Department circular the same day reflected some of the enthusiasm engendered by the Northern Bombing concept, declaring, "These operations were considered the most important yet undertaken" and should take precedence over all other projects. All Bureaus and offices received orders to expedite assembly of personnel and equipment.[14]

With the mission and organizational scheme settled, attention turned to equipping the bombardment venture; acquiring sufficient aircraft for a project as large as the NBG constituted the most serious impediment. As early as March 7, the same day Benson cabled notification of the General Board's original recommendations to Sims, Secretary Daniels wrote Secretary of War Newton Baker requesting the Army to provide 30 Curtiss JN "Jenny" trainers, 10 Thomas Morse trainers, and 80 day bombers, along with spare engines, for offensive operations against submarines during the spring and summer of 1918. After much wrangling, the two services negotiated an agreement that allocated a portion of future Army production for Navy use and fixed a tentative delivery schedule. In reality, combat aircraft never reached Europe in the numbers or on the dates expected. Nor did these agreements address the need for large night bombers, the only aircraft capable of inflicting the level of damage the Navy envisioned. That issue needed to be settled with the Army in France and ultimately inaugurated the protracted and largely unsuccessful effort to secure Caproni bombers in Italy.[15]

While leaders in Washington managed to sort through this issue, reaction from the AEF proved explosive. General Foulois entered a violent protest April 4 against any allocation of motors to the Navy. Cone responded with a strong memo to Sims three days later. The Air Service chief exploded again the following month after the War Department agreed to apportion aircraft to the Navy. Foulois argued that the AEF needed planes for the present emergency. Frontline squadrons experienced high wastage of equipment and he recommended the least possible diversion of aircraft. The War Department acknowledged their aggrieved representative's objections but informed him that no modifications would be made.[16]

Rapid growth of NBG plans and the inevitable pressures exerted on other aviation activities, such as development of bases in Ireland, Italy, and France, raised concerns at the Department and among the Allies, particularly the British. At the end of May, Benson directed Sims to limit expansion of grandiose plans and missions. Rather, the NBG should bomb "enemy naval activities" only and must reduce its size to four day and four night squadrons to lessen equipment demands on the Army. The number of personnel trained for the program should be strictly limited to immediate needs, with these replaced by Marines as conditions permitted. Due to the danger of German infantry overrunning aviation fields near Dunkirk, it was determined (in Washington) that the assembly and repair facility should be relocated across the Channel. Sims passed the "bad news" along to Cone. "Be governed accordingly," he advised. Rather stung by this admonition, Cone defended his original recommendations and actions taken thus far regarding training programs and attempts to secure aircraft. Nor should there be any reduction in training programs as any excess of pilots/crews "can be used by our allies to advantage." Cone's rebuttal, notwithstanding, Benson's orders stood: NBG strength would be reduced by one-third. This meant, of course, that Navy officers and men currently training to operate day bombing aircraft were, in effect, marooned, developing skills for which no need existed any longer.[17]

Apparently some British officials also expressed concern about the scope of Navy activities. Edwards reported that many in London seemed unaware of NBG plans and uninformed of the cutback to eight squadrons, but he wondered how this could be possible. Cone suggested that confusion existed between headquarters in London and RAF commanders in the field and recommended that Sims tell the Admiralty that the NBG would be under the aegis of the British vice-admiral at Dover. He also noted that the French Ministere de la Marine received formal advice of the project April 29, and conversations with the RAF commander of bombing squadrons at Dunkirk and other high-placed officers were ongoing. Nonetheless, the Admiralty, British Air Board, and vice-admiral at Dover now received official notice as well. In addition, Cone visited British General Headquarters on June 27 to brief General Salmond, the general officer commanding the RAF in the field.[18]

An undertaking as large as the NBG, involving a type of flying not originally considered part of the Navy brief, demanded a new instruction regimen to supply pilots and crew. The Department hoped the Air Service might turn over some fields in the United States for this purpose, but Gen. William Kenly and Col. "Hap" Arnold said none could be spared, nor would they allow Marines to train at Army facilities. Edwards then proposed establishing a landing field adjacent to NAS Killingholme and purchasing a few day and night bombers for instructional use. In the end the Navy exploited several venues: the Army field at Clermont-Ferrand, French and British facilities like Avord and Stonehenge, the Caproni school at Malpensa, and the Marine Corps program in the United States.[19]

In May, Paris began gathering personnel for instruction in day bombing. Many came from Dunkirk. Some expected to become flight leaders in the new squadrons. The largest contingent trained at the Air Service school at Clermont-Ferrand. Word of the program and possible personnel shifts started circulating in April, and by mid-May Dunkirk buzzed with rumors. David Ingalls informed a friend in the United States, "I'm feeling good now, as a lot of us are leaving for further training on land machines, two-seaters, rumors has it." About the same time George Moseley predicted, "I think my days in seaplanes are numbered now. They asked for volunteers from the officers on this station to be sent on day bombing machines. They are land machines and carry an observer who protects you from rear attack. He has two machine guns and the pilot also has two." Once begun, the process moved swiftly. Di Gates reported, "Ken [MacLeish], Dave [Ingalls], and some of our good officer pilots including George Moseley are all busy packing up to leave us. They are going down into France to get some training on land machines." Moseley supplied a bit more news, saying, "I did not expect the orders to proceed to the day bombing school to come through as quickly as they did. We received them and they read, 'Proceed immediately.' Chevy [Commanding Officer Chevalier] was broken hearted to see us go." Moseley described the new program as well as he understood it. "I am in Paris on my way to an Army land bombing school at Clermont-Ferrand, situated in the central part of France. . . . We are to train on the French Day bombing machines, the Breguet, a marvelous training machine."[20]

Aviators sent to Clermont-Ferrand included pilots and observers, the idea being to train two-man crews for DH-4 day bombers scheduled to arrive from the United States. Irving Sheely, an enlisted observer, kept family and friends updated on his progress. "I suppose you will be surprised to hear where I am at present," he wrote June 6. "I am at Clermont-Ferrand training on *avions*. . . . Believe me, I'm glad too because I hate those old seaplanes. Also, it's darned tiresome flying over water all the time. Also, I don't fancy a watery grave like four of our number have already gone to." Sheely had a good eye for local detail, noting, "It is a very beautiful place situated in a broad valley surrounded by hills. . . . It's just like a vacation, considering what we went through at Dunkirk, no air raids, no seventeen-inch [sic] shells bursting around us, able to sleep all night unmolested and good grub. . . . Pretty little French girls to go promenading with occasionally. It seems as if life is worth living after all."[21]

Previously the Michelin Company had used the site to test new Breguet bombing machines. After the AEF acquired it in November 1917 they erected more hangars and several auxiliary buildings constructed of white plaster, with dainty pink roofs. When the sailors arrived, however, especially officers, they recoiled at their accommodations. Typically, Army men carried their own bedding, and sailors likewise. But Navy officers expected a bed, pillow, sheets, and an orderly or money to board away from the station. MacLeish described beds made of two-by-fours and a strip of canvas, no blankets, no mattresses, no place to hang his clothes, and in the same room with 17 other men. In fact, Navy men refused to occupy Army quarters. Ingalls, Moseley, and others lived off station until more acceptable berths could be arranged. There they found the food very good, "oatmeal, bacon, eggs, toast; salad, two vegetables for lunch; little French girls wait on us." "We were spoiled at Dunkirk," he admitted. "We miss our boys who used to take care of us."

Mostly combat veterans, the Navy contingent was well prepared for the training regimen. They rolled out of bed at 5:15 A.M., formed up at 5:45, and flew or attended lectures from 6:00 to 10:00. Instruction began again at 4 P.M. and continued until 8, with an hour off for supper. Ken MacLeish observed, "You have to be very hard on the controls of these machines and even then they answer very slowly. They seem to be very heavy and very lazy in the air." One student compared them to three-ton trucks with wings. Realizing the dangers involved and the likelihood that a pilot might be wounded or killed, Moseley told his observer-crewmate he would teach him to land the plane if necessary. Overall, Navy men encountered few difficulties. Moseley and others went through the course "like a breeze." They learned how to bomb like an observer, while the actual observers passed through ground school. Then they flew together in pairs. In the air the observer gave directions when lining up a target by pulling lines attached to the pilot's arms. They also used camera guns, with observers standing in the rear seat. A bomber would go into vertical spiral, with the observer's body parallel to the ground. Pinpoints in the film indicated where bullets would have hit the plane, all done while going through evasive maneuvers. Pilots found it a great strain to fly in tight formation about 30 yards apart.

One officer singled out for praise by his peers at Clermont-Ferrand was Lieutenant MacLeish. According to Fred Beach, a Yale Unit veteran, MacLeish "succeeded in arousing so much enthusiasm and keeping all hands so good humored that we made fast progress, and incidentally broke most of the school records." Beach especially admired the young officer's "tact and industry" and his ability to "maintain friendly relations with the school, despite the fact that at times there was argument and some feelings over questions of leave, etc." Beach also appreciated the enlisted observers whom he rated "as good as, if not better than, some of the officers." Moseley and others wished to obtain commissions for the observers so pilots could "be more free with them and live in same house, talk over work and learn from mistakes."

The entire program lasted only three weeks and by mid-June the Navy men were anxious to move along. Moseley noted, "Nearly every pilot is a college man, a large percentage being Yale men. We are all 'full out' as the English express it and can hardly wait to get underway." In the following week crews took written and oral exams and completed formation flying and bombing exercises as well as 150-mile cross-country excursions. The former gridiron star boasted, "The Navy did itself proud at Clermont-Ferrand, leaving the station with all the records in their possession. . . . We beat the Army in everything from trap shooting, to bombing, making more hits with our bombs and flying in better formation than they did." Their next assignment would be combat duty with various RAF squadrons in the Dunkirk sector.[22]

In addition to personnel sent to Clermont-Ferrand, Navy aviators destined for the NBG received bombing instruction at RAF aerodromes at Stonehenge and Old Sarum on the Salisbury Plain, and Boscombe Down near Bournemouth. Several had also completed a preliminary program in the French bombing school at Avord-Cher. Plans to send an initial group of 10 pilots for night bombing instruction to Stonehenge were finalized in May 1918, but any more would have displaced Britain's own flyers. After that the entire training schedule had no vacancies for the next seven months. In early June, Sims ordered Cone to send 10 more pilots to the No. 1 School of Navigation and Bomb Dropping at Stonehenge for day bombing instruction, an "extremely advanced course." Other arrangements relied on cooperation with the French, including plans (never implemented) to send 18 pilots to Crotoy.[23]

Work at British schools included preliminary training in Avros and DH-9 day bombers, but often proceeded in fits and starts. Many aircraft at Old Sarum, for example, remained out of commission due to almost endless crashes. Bad weather interrupted operations for as much as two weeks. Navy men here were well fed, however, dining in a mess run by the U.S. Army. Their quarters were new but poorly constructed, leaking continuously. Living conditions at Boscombe Down were worse, with food served in the British mess, something that led to complaints reaching as far as London and Paris. Observers rated the DH-6 training machines as "poor and dangerous." At Stonehenge a few Navy pilots studied night bombing in Handley Pages. Still others were ordered to RAF Waddington for a five-week course in DH-9s.[24]

A wide range of commissioned and enlisted personnel, both flying and technical, played crucial roles in forthcoming NBG operations, and plans for their education tapped diverse sources. The original contingent of enlisted observers trained at Cranwell-Eastchurch-Leysdown in the winter of 1918. Later, Sims's London office arranged for 16 officers and 32 ratings to receive eight weeks of ordnance instruction at Uxbridge. Another group of 10 bluejackets took an aerial photography course at RAF Farnborough. Others attended armorers school in Reading and studied aerial navigation and bombing at Stonehenge. Still others learned meteorological skills at RNAS Dundee. Instrument men studied at the Isle of Grain and Felixstowe and later continued on to Technical Training School at Holton Camp.[25]

Competing demands for trained pilots among the various Navy programs—Killingholme, NBG, Italy—occasionally erupted in strident disagreement. Robert Lovett reported a "knock-down war of words" between Captain Twining and Atlee Edwards because Edwards claimed that authorities in the Bureau let Ken Whiting at Killingholme "hog" all the Davison (First Yale) unit. In fact, Edwards cabled a protest to Washington. Whiting, of course, shot back that the only organization getting the "pork" was the Northern Bombing Group. And down in Italy John Callan complained incessantly about the shortage of pilots. Part of the problem resulted from the desire of aviators throughout Europe to leave their monotonous patrolling duties and "get into the action." Ensign Donald Alvord at RNAS Great Yarmouth repeatedly requested transfer to the bombing offensive, but received orders to head for Ireland and later Italy instead.[26]

One additional fly in the ointment, at least as Navy aviators saw it, was the news that Marine Corps flyers would fill day bombing slots. After all the Navy pilots' training, the cutback in squadrons and substitution of leatherneck flyers left the sailors without a role. Of the Clermont contingent, Fred Beach lamented, "We found everything in a mix-up due to the insistence of the Marine Corps that the land flying of the Navy should be done by them. . . . we saw our dreams of a crack naval squadron . . . vanishing into thin air." MacLeish also cursed the leathernecks, calling them small and childish. Later, after service with the RAF, MacLeish changed his mind. When a pilot in his squadron left to take charge of a Marine unit coming up to Calais-Dunkirk, MacLeish called him a "full out" old scout, and a nice fellow to play around with. "If all Marines are his type I don't think I'll mind them very much." Most likely he was referring to Capt. William McIlvain who had been attached to No. 218 Squadron.[27]

Despite many pilots' objections, the original General Board report and subsequent Department approvals assigned day escort/day bombing missions to Marine Corps aviators, and preparing leathernecks for duty on the Western Front became central to the success of the program. Nothing in the Marines' earlier history, however, prepared them for the task. At the beginning of hostilities a small contingent of 5 officers and 30 men at Pensacola formed part of the Navy complement there. Immediately following the outbreak of war they established the Marine Aeronautic Company at the Philadelphia Navy Yard; training on land plans began soon thereafter. By October 12 the organization included 34 officers and 330 men. Commanders then divided the unit into two separate groups, the First Aviation Squadron and the First Marine Aeronautic Company. The latter relocated to Cape May, New Jersey, in October and then to Ponta Delgada, Azores, in January, where they carried out patrols until January 1919.

Meanwhile, the First Aviation Squadron, led by McIlvain, transferred from Philadelphia to the Army flying field at Mineola, New York, in mid-October and then Gerstner Field in Louisiana at the end of December. A small detachment commanded by Capt. Roy Geiger shifted from Philadelphia to Miami in early February 1918. McIlvain's larger unit rejoined Geiger's men on April 1. Approval of the NBG project led to organization of four squadrons—A, B, C, D—and a Headquarters Company. Ultimately, Marine squadrons became the Day Wing/NBG, with Maj. Alfred Cunningham as commanding officer. Squadron commanders were, respectively, Captains Roy Geiger, William McIlvain, and Douglas Roben, and Lt. Russell Presley. Cunningham filled the pilot ranks by scouring the Officers' School at Quantico and enrolling naval reservists, qualified seaplane pilots who wanted to fly in France. In fact, 78 of the 135 Marine pilots who reached Europe began their careers as naval reservists.

The now-named First Marine Aviation Force, consisting of Squadrons A, B, C and Headquarters Company, departed Florida July 13 and sailed from New York five days later. At this point they remained completely unprepared for the war that faced them, having flown only simple training aircraft; they received virtual no gunnery instruction and absolutely no bombing practice. They reached Brest on July 30 and moved up to Dunkirk in the first days of August. Missteps beset their early activities. No plans had been made to receive and transport the men, so Cunningham "requisitioned" a train for the 400-mile journey to Calais. He complained to an officer back in the United States, "We arrived day before yesterday and found no-one here who knew what we were, where we were to go, or what we were to do here.... The trouble is that no-one in Washington [had] enough interest in us to cable when we would arrive and what we were for." A party dispatched to Pauillac to secure flyers' motor transport found they had to wrest vehicles from the Army. Communications with Hanrahan seemed tenuous at best. The final Marine unit, Squadron D, arrived in September and reached La Fresne in Flanders on October 5. Because the NBG lacked aircraft and none of the Marines had wartime experience, they received temporary billets with RAF units where they conducted combat raids and patrols.

Formal reduction in the number of day and night bombing squadrons from 12 to 8 at the end of May initiated reorganization of airfields and unit assignments. Under the consolidated plan, night bombing Squadrons 1 and 2 occupied "Field A" (St. Inglevert), with an adjacent chateau leased as headquarters and officer accommodations. Night Bombing Squadrons 3 and 4 utilized "Field B" (Campagne). "Field C" at Sangatte, near the coast between Calais and Boulogne, was designated a dummy aerodrome. Day Bombing Squadrons 7 and 8 would be stationed at "Field D" at Oye, adjacent to the highway from Gravelines to Calais, while Squadrons 9 and 10 operated from "Field E" at Le Fresne, situated southwest of Ardres. A second dummy aerodrome, "Field F," would be created at Alembon. With establishment of a supply base across the Channel, the Navy concluded an agreement with the RAF to use their Guines depot for all minor repairs. The NBG built facilities in the following order: St Inglevert, then La Fresne, Oye, Campagne #1, Campagne #2, and Autingues.[28]

The Navy eventually derequisitioned the field at Sangatte after the military governor at Calais objected to its proximity to the city. Earlier plans for an aerodrome at Spycker (Spicker) on level ground near Dunkirk were also abandoned. The advance of Allied forces in the early autumn caused the Americans to derequisition the reserve field at Alembon. At the same time it became obvious that the aerodrome at Oye could not be used in wet weather and Hanrahan decided to abandon this site too. Finally, since Night Bombing Squadrons 3 and 4 never organized or carried out missions, the field at Campagne was abandoned, leaving flight activities concentrated at La Fresne and St. Inglevert.[29]

St. Inglevert field, the first established, occupied high ground, about six or seven miles southwest of Calais. An RAF Handley Page unit operated from a nearby station. In fact, the British occupied a portion of the American field, but most remained unused until local farmers harvested their crops. Night Bombing Squadron 1 (less pilots) organized at Pauillac and departed for St. Inglevert on June 20 under the command of Lt. C. R. Johnson, and the initial draft of 150 men arrived July 3 after a 700-mile truck trip. For their first night and many nights thereafter they lived in tents. German forces seemed well informed of developments and flew overhead several times, bombing what they could. Work crews quickly excavated dugouts. Eventually, they erected standard Navy facilities large enough to accommodate 600 men.[30]

Lieutenant Hubert Burnham found his assignment there "very interesting and at times very exciting."[31] A 1905 Naval Academy graduate, he later resigned from the service to become an architect. Burnham rejoined the Navy in November 1917 and sailed for Europe, carrying out construction work, first at Pauillac, then various seaplane stations, and finally at Dunkirk. The old chateau at St. Inglevert occupied by Americans became a rendezvous for Belgian, French, British, and even Portuguese officers from miles around. Burnham enjoyed life at the chateau, set amid beautiful grounds, noting that in such circumstances "the war was not so bad." Enlisted men lived at a more basic level. To prepare Fourth of July dinner they received Navy-issue cans of tomatoes and beans. Attempting to augment their meager fare, a few hiked out into the surrounding countryside looking for food. According to one story, a bluejacket spied a rabbit hutch. Of course, to steal the animals would be a crime, but feed his men he must; so three full-grown rabbits just naturally insisted on following him home. These same rabbits further insisted on jumping into a pot in which the beans and tomatoes were set to boil. Foraging skills like these played a role in completing construction of various NBG flying fields. Placed in charge of planning and building NBG facilities, Burnham relied on requisitioned material shipped to Calais but finished most of the work before the supplies arrived, thanks "to the cooperation of the French and British authorities and the thieving tendencies of our own men."

The NBG established its overall headquarters in a clearing at Autingues (near Ardres), along with a field supply depot and motor transport park. Offices utilized standard, portable structures shipped from Pauillac. Enlisted men lived in tents; permanent quarters were never erected. This created some very uncomfortable conditions when autumn rains came. Crop harvesting and late arrival of building materials delayed preparations at La Fresne, first of the day bombing fields. Hangars there were of the French portable type with canvas on wood frames. Marines who did get in on some raids in the fall occupied the site. Cunningham created his Day Wing headquarters at Oye (Bois-en-Ardres), utilizing standard portable huts for officers and men. By late October hangars stood ready, but there were still no planes. Work at Campagne, the second night bombing field, 4.5 miles south of Calais, also lagged, with quarters for officers in a chateau and enlisted men mostly in tents. Plans for Guines, seven miles south of Calais, called for 360 officers and men.

After months of delays the Italian government turned over a few Capronis to the Army and Navy in the summer of 1918 and they quickly developed plans to deliver them to aerodromes on the Western Front. Insistent demands for bombers in Flanders led to a fateful (and fatal) decision to fly aircraft across the Alps to northern France. The Caproni ferrying program actually constituted NBG's first aerial operation conducted with its own personnel in its own aircraft. This exceedingly dangerous activity came about due to virtually insurmountable difficulties facing either sea-borne or rail transport. Flight operations on the Italy-Flanders route began badly and then got worse. Mixed Army-Navy crews manned the first batch of aircraft, which were tested and accepted by Air Service representatives. Exclusively Navy crews ferried later airplanes. Caproni B-1 flown by an Army pilot crashed at Turin due to unknown causes. Caproni B-2 piloted by an Air Service aviator, with Ens. Alfred Hudson as second pilot, crashed at Sens, France, on July 28, the plane a total wreck. Ensigns Krumm and Nesbit's aircraft crashed at Turin-Mirafiori on August 1. Reginald Coombe's Caproni went down at Taliedo the same day. Another aircraft with an Army crew crashed at Bra, south of Turin, completely destroyed. By this time Eddie McDonnell had returned from the United States, with orders to proceed to Italy, along with additional Navy pilots, and bring more Capronis north. McDonnell joined up with those who had already ferried planes with the Army and others trained at Malpensa.

A few more Capronis began the journey August 7, others August 10, and still more August 14. On the first leg of the trip to Turin-Mirafiori, nearly every plane experienced engine trouble. Jesse Henderson's plane caught fire at 2,000 feet but he kept the situation under control and landed at Turin. Much of the upper wing, nacelle, and rear motor burned. McDonnell lauded the pilot for his actions bringing the flaming aircraft down safely. Two Capronis departed Turin on August 15; one returned when it caught fire. Ensigns Alan Nichols and Hugh Terres lifted off at 5:00 P.M. August 17 but an engine failure at 250 feet led to a crash that killed both pilots and mechanic Orrin Hartle. According to one witness, "The machine was broken into little pieces, utterly demolished, their bodies had been smashed."

During McDonnell's own journey he replaced an engine, radiator, carburetor, and eight magnetos. He also suffered four midair engine failures and made the leg from Dijon to Paris with a broken magneto. Sam Walker got lost on the way to Lyon, ran out of gas, and crash-landed in mountainous terrain southwest of Lyon. His plane catapulted when it hit the ground and "flew into kindling wood." Reginald Coombe's trip proved to be an epic adventure. He departed Malpensa on August 14, traveling easily to Turin, but he did not continue his journey until five days later. He then got lost in the clouds and returned to the field, waiting four more days for clear weather. When Coombe finally took off he nearly crashed because one of his motors failed to rev. After successfully crossing the Alps into France, he reached Lyon three hours after leaving Turin, traveling at a maximum altitude of more than 11,000 feet. A faulty carburetor delayed Coombe's scheduled departure next day. The leg north from Dijon proved very difficult, as he could not locate important geographic features. Coombe finally reached Orly at sunset on August 30, more than two weeks after leaving Milan. In all, Navy pilots, including Oliver Kilmer who had sailed around the world with "The Great White Fleet," attempted to ferry 17 planes to France, but only 8 arrived safely. Five crewmen died. Bitter recriminations followed this disaster. Local aviation officials charged that American pilots were insufficiently trained and Navy mechanics were unfamiliar with the machines. They advised that ferrying operations be discontinued. And what of the NBG squadrons waiting for a large bomber with which to pound enemy submarine facilities? They waited in vain. Except for one mission flown on August 15, the night bombing squadrons mounted no further attacks.[32]

As pilots and observers in the United States, France, Italy, and England finished training, they moved up to the expanding complex of airfields near Calais. Here aviators and ground crew received additional instruction with RAF squadrons, including intelligence, operations, bombing, aerial gunnery, and aerial photography. The mutually beneficial relationship in place since the German assault of March 1918 now expanded many times over. By serving in RAF units, Navy and Marine flyers obtained invaluable combat experience while the British secured desperately needed pilots, aircrews, and other personnel to augment their weary cadres. Most joined the newly formed 82nd Wing of the 5th Group, including No. 214 Squadron flying Handley Page bombers from Couderkerque and No. 218 Squadron operating DH-9 day bombers at Fretnum. Other Americans rejoined their old Dunkirk mates, No. 213 Squadron, equipped with Sopwith Camels, and No. 217 Squadron, employing DH-4 day bombers.

The first four ensign pilots—Taber, Nisbet, Easterwood, and Frothingham—reported for duty to No. 214 Squadron on June 23, usually flying raids over Belgium. When the Germans blasted the squadron out of its base they relocated to the new NBG aerodrome at St. Inglevert. A steady flow of Navy personnel joined No. 214 Squadron and by August 10, 7 pilots and 40 enlisted men worked with the British, a situation that continued until the end of the war. Many had passed through the night bombing course offered at Stonehenge. The crews shouldered the full burden of combat. In late September six Navy officers participated in Handley Page rides as aerial gunners. Lieutenant Mosely Taylor piloted one of the huge warplanes. On the night of October 13/14 Ens. William Gaston's bomber attacked Deynze Junction, dropping nearly a ton of ordnance on the target. The next day the RAF assigned two aircraft almost entirely to U.S. crews. Like so many areas of aviation, this work proved to be extremely hazardous. Lieutenant (jg) Alexander McCormick went on a night mission on September 24. His aircraft landed with motor trouble at 12:30 A.M., and the young officer descended from the rear cockpit and walked forward, only to be struck by the starboard propeller. McCormick died soon after at Calais General Hospital #30 of a fractured skull.[33]

A second significant group of Navy flyers assigned to RAF units consisted of the pilots and observers trained at Clermont-Ferrand. They joined both No. 217 and No. 218 Squadrons operating DH-4 and DH-9 day bombers, often carrying out attacks against the submarine complex at Bruges-Ostend-Zeebrugge, related aerodromes, docks, and ships in the harbors. Typically, aviators participated in three raids before rotating back to U.S. service. No. 218 Squadron flew balky, underpowered DH-9s, barely capable of 85 mph at 13,000 feet without bombs and 75 mph fully loaded. NAS Dunkirk's log of July 8 identified personnel assigned to British service: pilots Ken MacLeish, David Ingalls, and David Judd and their observers Robinson R. Browne, S. L. Huey, and Irving Sheely. Others performing bomber duty included Charles Bassett and

Fred Beach. A 13-plane raid on July 16 against Zeebrugge included MacLeish and Judd. The flight lasted three hours, antiaircraft fire hit six planes, and one failed to return. Irving Sheely, MacLeish's observer, reported, "Anti-aircraft fire is very active when we go over and scrapnel [sic] flies around us rather abundantly. My first bombing trip one of these shells burst just beneath my tail. A piece of scrapnel went through the rudder. . . . You may be sure the old boat rocked a little." Four days later as part of an 11-plane assault, Judd, Ingalls, and MacLeish attacked the mouth of the Ostend canal and shipping gathered there. Armed with small 25-pound Cooper bombs, they targeted salvage ships, dredges, canal locks, and lock gates. According to Sheely, "We drop our bombs and watch them hit, then come on home." Passing over the trenches, he and his peers would "open up our machine guns and pour bullets into the Huns and shake them up a bit."

The pace of activities proved rapid and intense. George Moseley, another of the Navy's displaced day bomber pilots, said his squadron went over the lines every day, sometimes twice, weather permitting, bombing ammunition dumps, factories, railroads, and troops far behind the lines. His first raid began at 7:30 A.M. when aircrews started the bombers' motors. Planes lined up in formation on the ground, 16 planes, each with eight small bombs beneath their wings. The flight leader took off, then a machine on the left, then one on the right. Raiders formed up in the air, climbed to 15,000 feet, and circled over a town, waiting to pick up a flight of escorting British scouts. Soon they crossed enemy lines. "The Archie begins to pop and bark around us," he wrote, "and makes the plane jump from side to side." First the bombers headed out to sea, then turned toward shore, attacking Zeebrugge, attracting more Archie fire. Almost everywhere Americans flew, they encountered intense ground fire. Sometimes the flyers' luck just ran out. In late August a DH-4 from No. 217 Squadron piloted by Ens. Thomas McKinnon, with Yeo. Marlon O'Gorman as observer, crashed at sea two miles north of Dunkirk. Their aircraft had been proceeding uneventfully in a straight line when the propeller flew off. The plane continued on for a bit then banked sharply, stalled, and spun into the water from a height of 400 feet. A British destroyer raced to the site and retrieved the plane and O'Gorman's body, but could not find McKinnon.[34]

Of all the flyers serving with the RAF in the summer of 1918, 19-year-old David "Crock" Ingalls from Cleveland, Ohio, compiled the most extraordinary combat record to emerge as the Navy's only "Ace" of World War I. After training at Clermont-Ferrand, Ingalls joined No. 218 Squadron where he piloted DH-9 day bombers and took part in three raids against German submarine facilities. From there he reunited with the NBG to assist construction of airfields around Calais. Chafing to resume flying, in early August he managed to secure assignment to No. 213 Squadron at Fretnum flying Sopwith Camels, where he soon made Navy history. In only six weeks he participated in some of the largest raids in the war, engaged in numerous bombing and strafing attacks, and destroyed at least six enemy aircraft and balloons, earning the Distinguished Flying Cross, Distinguished Service Cross, and the Legion d'Honneur.[35]

Created to carry out day bombing missions, Marine squadrons began reaching Flanders in early August, their personnel dispatched to the RAF in small numbers for the next two months. McIlvaine, Roben, Geiger, and Presley preceded them, having joined British units for instruction as squadron commanders. Arrival of Marine formations greatly increased the number of Americans serving with British units, and the First Marine Aviation Force instituted continuous assignment of personnel to the RAF pilot pool at Audembert on September 5. The first six joined No. 217 and No. 218 Squadrons. Two days later an additional six aircrew were assigned to No. 218 Squadron. A dozen more soon followed, and this practice continued until the war's end.[36]

The day the Allied offensive in Flanders commenced, September 28, Lt. Chapin Barr with No. 218 Squadron participated in three raids over the lines and received a mortal wound on the last. He managed to return to the field but died soon after. Also that day Lt. Everett Brewer and Sgt. Harry Wershimer flying with the same unit downed an enemy aircraft over Courtemarke in Belgium, though both were wounded. Three days later Lt. Francis Mulcahy, Capt. Robert Lytle, and Lt. Frank Nelms embarked on a very different mission, delivering 2,600 pounds of food and supplies to beleaguered French troops near Stadenburg. They executed missions at an altitude of barely 100 feet despite heavy enemy ground fire.[37] Lieutenant Ralph Talbot carried out a similar assignment on October 8, dropping tins of food to an isolated unit. He called these resupply runs, performed at a height of 50 feet, his "aerial grocery business." Marine pilots first joined British raids utilizing their own aircraft on October 3, including strikes against Westende, Ostende, Nieuport, and Lichtervelde. The next day Marine planes hit Thourot, then Oroye (October 5) and Ardoye (October 8). In this action the crew of Talbot and Robinson brought down at least one enemy aircraft. The arrival of sufficient DH-4s and DH-9s in mid-October allowed Marine squadrons to conduct operations of their own.

Even as American aviators served in British units, the Navy proceeded with plans to establish an assembly and repair (A&R) facility for the Northern Bombing Group. At first slated for St. Inglevert, a small crew arrived there in early July to begin construction of a modest supply distribution base. But a much larger A&R facility was also needed. One site lay approximately 50 miles behind the lines, but the Germans bombed it. This, combined with recurrent fears of an enemy breakthrough, caused the Navy to reevaluate its plans and consider establishing the base in England instead. Conversations initiated by Sims's office further developed the idea. The admiral informed Hutch Cone of the British proposal that the Americans take over a partially completed facility at Eastleigh near Southampton and the Channel coast. Originally North Stoneham Farm and later developed as an acceptance park for the RAF, the site came under British Air Ministry control in mid-June. At the time, large hangars were approximately 90 percent complete, the storehouses 30 percent. There were, supposedly, accommodations for 300 men. Sims suggested that Hanrahan investigate further and make the final decision. A committee including Hanrahan, Briscoe, and Billings inspected Eastleigh on July 4. The site appeared ideal, close to the airfields in France with a nearby car ferry operating to Dieppe, several convenient steamer routes across the Channel, splendid rail facilities along a siding on the main line from Southampton to London, and only 4.5 miles from Southampton docks. Two weeks later the Navy accepted the British offer as of July 20, with Chevalier, then at Dunkirk, named temporary commander. The sprawling site eventually became known as "Base B."[38]

Chevalier and LCdr. Frederick Bolles, a public works officer, reached Eastleigh on July 23, soon followed by a paymaster and medical officer. They discovered an unfinished base literally adrift in a sea of mud, with no appropriate living accommodations. The officers set up temporary headquarters at nearby Junction Hotel and commuted by taxi for the first month. They found themselves in the dubious position of having no supplies on hand, no crew, and a single pocket edition typewriter, yet they were required to construct a massive and critical base. By hook or by crook they obtained 150 tons of cement and 5 carloads of roofing felt. Untrained drafts of men began arriving. Most had been in the service less than six months and feeding and sheltering such numbers posed a major challenge. The Red Cross donated tents to house some of the bluejackets. Nonetheless, Atlee Edwards offered an optimistic view, informing Cone, "Chevalier tells me that everything is coming along very nicely at E and that he is now prepared to receive the first draft of men." Cone, in turn, raved about the progress being made. He informed Irwin back in Washington, "Our plans, which seem to be constantly changing, are now directed towards using Eastleigh for the heavy motor repair work for practically all the activities (including England and Ireland). The plant we have secured is a 'peach' and is going to be of great use to us as a storage place as well as repair plant and flying field."[39]

After only a few weeks, however, the normally ebullient Chevalier offered a more realistic assessment, complaining that he was getting little sleep, struggling to instruct officers and yeomen at their duties, and trying to pull order out of chaos and inexperience. He also attempted to prepare all hands for the avalanche of work he knew was coming while laboring to generate necessary paperwork with that single typewriter. The actual task of creating a functioning base, however, fell to Frederick Bolles, who arrived from St. Inglevert to rush construction. Eventually the Public Works Department assembled a crew of 700 ratings for the massive assignment. They dug miles of trenches, installed pipes and wiring, built a hospital and isolation ward, and erected an enormous brick galley and a steel-frame mess hall to feed 4,000 hungry bluejackets.[40]

But all that took time. The first draft arrived in early August. Workers slapped together a temporary kitchen at the edge of the flying field and prepared their own food until regular cooks disembarked from the United States. Construction crews completed the new kitchen on November 16 and station personnel gathered to cheer as the original makeshift structure was torn down. The medical department endured similar inconveniences, lacking sufficient quarters and equipment. Onset of the influenza epidemic required immediate construction of a large annex to the isolation ward to accommodate hundreds of ill sailors. Nearly 20 died before the plague ran its course. Many officers boarded initially in Southampton and enjoyed the local hospitality, especially that offered by Lord and Lady Swaythling, who became the Americans' unofficial hosts by opening their estate for recreation and receptions. A number of men attended dances scheduled at area hotels. Some entertainment was home grown. American movies played several times a week. Eastleigh had a band, what Ken MacLeish called "the best I've ever heard," part of Sousa's Great Lakes Band. Dave Ingalls, just returned from the front, admired the drum major, "a bearcat." A quartet of sailors provided "the best music I've heard since I left the States." Ingalls even liked the mess, not as good as Dunkirk, but fine nonetheless.[41]

Despite the sheer size of the task, signs of progress multiplied. Commander Bayard Bulmer assumed permanent command on September 21, with Chevalier ordered back to the United States, a decision with which he vehemently disagreed. David Ingalls called the new commanding officer "a perfectly jolly old bird whose 'figger' sort of reminds me of Santa Claus." He claimed that Bulmer helped instill a very nautical atmosphere at the station, "just like living in some doggoned ship . . . decks are swabbed twice a day, get saluted all the time on the way to the office and back . . . maybe good planning for the military, but mighty rough on a civilian like me." An officer of broad experience, Bulmer's previously assignments included time as engineering officer aboard *Florida* and over two years as overseer of new and repair work at the Charlestown Navy Yard. Eventually Bulmer ordered workshops to perform double shifts to make up for shortages of machinery and tools. Apparently the men did a good job as only two planes sent to France were reported out of alignment. The first DH-4 from Eastleigh reached France October 2.[42]

Transforming the disaster-prone Caproni Ca. 5 into a reliable and safe bomber became Eastleigh's most exasperating assignment. Aviation pioneer Gabriele D'Annunzio reportedly said he would not let his men go out in Fiat Capronis. Landing gear often collapsed during forced landings. Following the nightmare of ferrying aircraft from Italy to St. Inglevert and the failure to mount more than one raid, Navy mechanics in the field vainly attempted to make Fiat motors safer and more reliable but proved unable to complete a four-hour running test. Instead, reports concluded that the motors showed "poor workmanship and poor construction" in practically all cases. After much frustration, the Navy removed them from service. Reginald Coombe, Ed McDonnell, and machinist William Miller delivered one of the "cursed" Capronis to Eastleigh in early October. Shop crews stripped down its Fiat motors, remachined some of the parts, reassembled the equipment, and at one point conducted an eight-hour test stand run, proving the problems lay not in design but in poor manufacture. In fact, none of the original Capronis reentered service. Instead, the Navy sought possible alternatives. One proposal was to use replacement Isotta-Fraschini engines to equip later aircraft deliveries and the first of this type (boxed and packed) reached Eastleigh on November 8. Alternatively, plans were developed to obtain Handley Page bombers. Ultimately, the Americans secured promises for 20 of these machines, half to the Army and the other half to the Navy, in exchange for Liberty motors. The first was being tested at the time of the Armistice.[43]

In the final weeks of the war the pace of activity accelerated. Due to the difficulty of obtaining DH-4s from the United States, the Navy arranged to exchange Liberty motors for 54 British DH-9 bombers. In the week ending October 13, workmen disassembled three Fiat motors for spare parts, rebuilt 13 more, assembled 6 Liberty motors, 2 DH-9s, and 1 DH-4. Pilots assigned to the base carried out frequent test flights and ferried several aircraft to Marine squadrons in France, overseen by Captain McIlvain, temporarily assigned to Eastleigh to expedite the process. Still, personnel battled the unfinished condition of their station. Commanding Officer Bulmer reported that the base remained under construction and had completed very little A&R work thus far. It lacked proper and sufficient machine tools. Severe housing shortages interfered with work, and adequate rain gear remained an absolute necessity in the wet climate. When Kenneth MacLeish moved to the station from nearby Southampton Hotel he called the quarters "not fit to live in." Total personnel by then had risen to 1,982 in over 100 different ratings.[44]

Befitting Eastleigh's importance, a parade of senior officers passed through. Admiral Mayo inspected the facility in early October. He rated living accommodations as very poor, with barracks for only half the men. Others bunked in unheated storehouses, hangars, and tents, far from the galley. The galley was a temporary affair and cooking equipment quite poor. No adequate means existed for looking after the men in their leisure hours. Plans under way to alleviate these conditions, however, impressed the admiral, and station officers hoped to have the living situation squared away by November 15. During Noble Irwin's visit his hosts included Bulmer, Chevalier, the previous commanding officer, and David Ingalls, who recalled the director asking "the doggondest little questions imaginable. . . . He must have been an examination instructor at some school or college." Announcement of the Armistice ignited a raucus celebration, with Commanding Officer Bulmer leader his men on a vast "Snake Dance" across the field. Eastleigh survived the Armistice by almost five months and was the last aviation facility in Europe to close. During the winter many men withdrawn from NAS Brest temporarily bivouacked there. The Navy hauled down the flag on April 10, 1919. A small regional airport and extensive athletic fields occupy the site today.[45]

Even as work at Eastleigh began, NBG units across the Channel commenced operations with limited attempts to launch raids utilizing a handful of recently arrived Caproni aircraft. One plane reached St. Inglevert on August 11 where crews set to work modifying or installing new equipment, including bombing gear, landing gear wires, navigational lights, and machine gun mountings. Four days later the aircraft attacked U-boat repair docks at Ostende. The crew consisting of pilot Leslie "Tex" Taber, observer/pilot Charles Fahy, and gunlayer D. C. Hale, completed their mission by dropping 1,050 pounds of bombs and returning safely to base. As it turned out, this was the first and last war mission carried out by Navy Capronis. The following month Caproni B-11, flown by Clyde Palmer and Phillip Frotheringham, landed safely at St. Inglevert at 3:45 P.M., but when the plane turned to enter the hanger it hit a soft spot in the field and listed to port, nose down. Some observers speculated that the landing gear collapsed. Gunning two motors to break free from the mud only caused the tail to rise even higher.

When the nose hit the ground the nacelle broke off, trapping the pilots between the nacelle and the middle gas tank. Observer A. M. Underwood was thrown/jumped from his position in front of the aft motor. Then the propellers hit the ground and broke off, causing the motors to race. At that instant the port motor carburetor backfired and burst into flames, starting a fire that immediately engulfed the entire plane. Underwood raced back into the inferno and managed to turn off one of the motors, but had to be dragged from the front cockpit when the port gas tank exploded. Officers and men grabbed the super-heated frame trying to rip the wings off and reach the doomed pilots, but to no avail. Ironically, Frotheringham, who trained initially as part of the "Princeton" unit in Canada, had a small pet dog named "Caproni" that went on the flight with him, sheltered in Palmer's flight suit. The pup was able leap free of the wreckage. Wing Commander Bob Lovett praised six officers and three enlisted men for their "utmost coolness and contempt of danger." Among those commended was Reginald Coombe, who later wrote, "It was an awful sight to be there and see these two men burn up, but there was absolutely nothing that could be done." Also singled out for praise was Oliver Kilmer, who had only recently ferried one of the treacherous machines over the Alps. But even this event did not end the Caproni carnage. In December while on its way to Paris from St. Inglevert, headed for the AEF school at Issoudun, aircraft B-17 crashed near Abbeville due to—you guessed it—motor troubles.[46]

The dismal failure of the Capronis placed the night bombardment program in jeopardy and initiated a thorough review of the entire NBG effort. Several points stood out. German attacks in spring 1918 greatly delayed the project and triggered removal of the repair base to England. The Navy had reduced the size of the NBG from 12 to 8 squadrons, while the whole affair complicated procurement in Europe and exacerbated relations with the Army. It even threatened the independence of naval aviation. With all this, was it worthwhile to continue? Ultimately, the Navy decided to press ahead. Too much time and effort had been expended to abandon the program now.

As it was impossible to launch night bombing assaults, no further NBG missions occurred until mid-October, by which time Marine squadrons possessed sufficient DH-4 and DH-9 aircraft to conduct all-American raids. Rapid advances by Allied forces in the fall of 1918, however, led to abandonment of the enemy's submarine facilities in Belgium, the primary target for which the NBG had been created. As Hutch Cone had predicted, "If we keep on pushing on the Belgian front we won't have any objectives for Dave Hanrahan to get at by the time he is ready." The group had already been offered to General Pershing, but rejected. The AEF commander said Navy units could be best used where they were. Instead, Marine aviators supported the British infantry advance, attacking railroads, canal locks, and supply and ammunition dumps. Targets in the waning weeks of the war included Thielt, Thourot, Steenbrugge, Eecloo, Ghent, Deynze, Loheren. In all, day bombing units conducted 14 raids.[47]

A mixed Day Squadron 9 force of DH-4s and DH-9As led by Capt. Robert Lytle carried out the NBG's first independent strike on October 14 against the rail yard at Thielt, Belgium, in conjunction with the 5th Group, RAF. At least one communication claimed that the Americans downed an enemy aircraft and drove another earthward out of control. During the action, Ralph Talbot, one of the naval reservists recruited by Cunningham, and another plane became detached from the formation. Twelve enemy scouts jumped them. In the severe fight that followed Talbot's observer, G/Sgt. Robert Robinson, shot down an enemy scout but was himself severely wounded with a bullet through the elbow. To make matters worse, his gun jammed. Working despite agonizing pain, Robinson cleared the blockage with his remaining hand and continued to fight until shot again in the stomach and hip. When Robinson collapsed Talbot attacked the nearest enemy scout and shot him down. With his observer unconscious and his motor failing, Talbot dove toward the ground to escape, skimming over German trenches. Robinson survived the ordeal, his arm saved by the surgeon-general of the Belgian Army, recovered, and outlived the Armistice by 56 years. For this action and their work October 8 with the RAF, both men received the Medal of Honor.[48]

Lieutenants Harvey Norman and Caleb Taylor, also of Day Squadron 9, carried out a raid into enemy territory against a rail yard at Deynze on October 22 as part of a larger formation. They became separated in the fog, were attacked by seven enemy aircraft, and crashed at a spot about 14 miles from Bruges; both died in the wreck. Belgian soldiers recovered their bodies the following day. Just two days after attending funeral services for Norman and Taylor, Ralph Talbot's luck also ran out. Accompanied by Lt. Colgate Darden, Talbot conducted a motor test at La Fresne aerodrome but failed to become airborne on his first run. On the second attempt Talbot barely lifted off and struck a bomb dump embankment at the end of the field, ripping off his undercarriage and causing the plane to flip over. Darden was thrown clear, but Talbot was caught in the wreck that quickly ignited and he died in the flames.[49]

Marine forces pressed their attacks in the last weeks of the war, launching two raids on October 27. During the morning mission, which departed Varssenaere aerodrome at 10:55 A.M., an aircraft crewed by Lieutenants Frank Nelms and John Gibbs ascended to 9,000 feet, but their motor began sputtering. They stayed with the formation, and dropped ordnance on the target, then started losing altitude. Nelms fired a green signal flare to alert his group leader they were washing out. Spotting four German aircraft nearby, and with their ignition missing badly, they glided down and landed at noon in a plowed field in neutral Holland. The Dutch took control of the plane and weapons and interned the officers until the end of the war.[50]

As the German army continued retreating it became necessary to shift NBG squadrons closer to the front. Preparations began October 27 and by the Armistice one of the day units had relocated to Knessalaere, a former German aerodrome, with the other on the move. Two night squadrons with all their equipment except hangars reached Marin Alta. After the Armistice, all returned to their original bases near Dunkirk/Calais. By that time the force in the field counted 250 officers and 2,400 men, with another 220 officers and 2,200 men at Eastleigh. They operated 12 DH-4s (8 in commission) and 17 DH-9s (7 in commission). Three Capronis were "available" for emergency use. In total, NBG personnel and aircraft dropped 78 tons of munitions, most while serving with RAF units, and destroyed four or five enemy planes, losing in turn one plane in combat, with another interned in Holland. Pilots flying with British and French squadrons scored three aerial victories, losing one pilot killed and one captured. Total losses, including Caproni accidents, amounted to five naval officers and four Marines. At least 25 men succumbed to influenza.

Had the war continued into 1919, NBG activities might have expanded greatly, but this is uncertain. What is known is that the concept of both tactical and strategic bombing seems to have gripped several naval thinkers. Everyone talked about it. Original plans envisioned aerial operations on at least 16 days per month delivering 934,000 pounds of ordnance with all squadrons active. Back in August, Harry Guggenheim had submitted a plan to Hutch Cone, arguing that the Navy should bomb submarine bases first, carry out convoy duty second, and conduct patrols third. Bombers should attack ports, dockyards, and naval craft, as well as factories producing naval material. Down in Italy, John Callan championed the use of bombing raids to break civilian morale. At about the same time, Aide for Aviation Edwards recommended increasing NBG aircraft strength by 200 percent. As Lt. Allan Ames wrote home to his friend Trubee Davison, "Get behind the bombing idea as much as you can; big boat work has been very much overrated from what I have seen here. . . . Big boats all right for some work, but our resources in naval aviation could be applied in an infinitely more effective way."[51]

The following month a conference in London endorsed these ideas, calling for four additional NBG squadrons. Many saw this as a prelude to heavier attacks on the German homeland with longer range aircraft, such as the Handley Page 1500. One wonders, however, what reaction the Army Air Service and Generals Mason Patrick and Billy Mitchell would have had if the Navy had continued its build-up of an enormous bombing force and switched over to nonnaval targets? Or, for that matter, how the RAF or Hugh Trenchard's Independent Force would have handled the situation? Would military planners in Europe and the United States have allowed three or four separate bombing forces to exist and compete for men, materiel, and targets? In fact, none of the NBG programs and none of the excited speculation came to fruition, and after the Armistice demobilization proceeded rapidly. Marine personnel headed home aboard the transport *Mercury* in December. The Navy completed the entire process by February 10, 1919.

12

TILL IT'S OVER, OVER THERE

September 1918–April 1919

Aviation planning in the second half of 1918 proceeded with the belief that the war would last at least into 1919 and perhaps beyond. During the process, staff revisited old decisions and advanced new priorities based on the evolving situation at the front, over the ocean, and at factories and training fields in Europe and the United States. Advocates pushed for expanded initiatives, particularly in the area of land-based bombing. Not surprisingly, views held in Washington, Paris, and London frequently differed, often dramatically. To some degree, consultation with the Allies helped focus these efforts. At the same time a series of high-profile investigations led by Asst. Secretary Franklin D. Roosevelt, C-in-C Atlantic Fleet Henry Mayo, and Naval Constructor George Westervelt examined the vexatious issues of defective equipment/aircraft and transportation deficiencies. Finally, in September and October, virtually all American stations under construction for so many months commenced wartime operations, albeit at lower than planned levels. Then, suddenly, just as the tempo of antisubmarine missions accelerated, the war ended, and the Navy hurriedly implemented policies to demobilize, dispose of equipment and bases, and bring the men home. Despite a late start and limited tactical results, naval aviation's wartime growth and achievements laid the foundations for the emergence of a powerful new combat arm, one destined to play a crucial role in the decades ahead.

* * *

While day-to-day concerns at Paris headquarters in mid-1918 revolved around completing the construction of existing bases, assembling aircraft and motors, and carrying out daily missions, formulating plans for the 1919 campaign triggered additional strenuous efforts. At that moment few believed the war would end soon and all eyes focused on redoubling the aviation effort and implementing new strategies. Discussions actually began early in the year and continued on an unofficial basis until midsummer when the process assumed greater urgency. Commander Dinger's Intelligence and Planning Division in Paris, for example, analyzed a wide range of initiatives, including increasing the number of bombers carrying out missions across the North Sea and augmenting operations at Dunkirk or creating a new base north of Dover. The group also discussed establishing a patrol station near Belfast, a convoy station west of Lough Swilly, and another at the Lizard (Cornwall). Proposals for ramping up operations in France included assuming control of French bases at L'Orient and La Pallice, enlarging the station at Le Croisic, and opening a substation on Belle Ile. Other suggestions envisioned a patrol facility at Gibraltar and two in Portugal. None of these proposals advanced beyond the discussion stage, however, as the Navy strained to implement plans originally developed in 1917.

Planning began in earnest later that summer. At the end of July, Hutch Cone cabled his principal commanders seeking suggestions in developing initiatives for the coming year. Their ideas formed the basis for high-level discussions held with the Allies in the next few months. Those polled included Edwards; Maxfield for LTA; Craven, head of operations at Paris headquarters; Callan, in charge of operations in Italy; and McCrary, commander of aviation stations in Ireland. Many earlier suggestions made by the Intelligence and Planning Division resurfaced for more detailed examination. Edwards advocated a greatly expanded aviation campaign, including assuming control of RAF stations near Land's End while also utilizing 30 lighters originally acquired to facilitate the aerial assault on Heligoland to undertake patrols along the west coast of Ireland. The Admiralty, Twining, and Sims's Planning Section agreed; and with a supply base located at Plymouth, this action would create an unbroken perimeter of bases from Lough Foyle in the north of Ireland to Arcachon near the Franco-Spanish border. Edwards also drew attention to the defensive nature of American actions in much of 1918 and recommended more offensive forays, particularly from the east coast of England against German naval bases, and from northeastern Italy against Austrian fleet installations. To carry out the latter mission he called for two new land plane bases in Italy and creation of a Southern Bombing Group, similar to the Northern Bombing Group. Edwards believed offensive activities required a 200 percent increase in NBG strength and 50 percent increases at Porto Corsini and Pescara. He realized that more land-based aviation resurrected the issue of amalgamation. If it did, so be it, for advantages to be derived from such activity more than outweighed the disadvantages.[1]

Lighter-than-air officers identified many of the same issues and endorsed similar strategies. Maxfield called control of North Sea airspace and destruction of submarine facilities by land-based bombers in France and flying boats from England the Navy's number one priority. Not surprisingly, he also endorsed expanded use of LTA vessels to operate with the fleet, protect convoys, and patrol harbor entrances against mine-laying submarines. He further advocated establishment of a new LTA station at Penmarch on the west coast of France and another on the south coast of England. If nothing else, this would facilitate wider cooperation with the British, allowing the Navy to draw on its ally's greater experience and proficiency. Maxfield championed development of a new type of airship, a large vessel of 10,000 m^3 carrying a 75 mm gun, two machine guns, 800 pounds of bombs, and sufficient fuel for 25 hours' cruising. Maxfield now believed dirigibles surpassed both kite balloons and seaplanes in utility, including the ability to operate at night, loiter while waiting for convoys, and utilize underwater listening devices.[2]

In Paris, Craven developed estimates of aircraft, pilots, and personnel required by seaplane, dirigible, and kite balloon stations through the end of September 1918, along with overall program recommendations. He forecast a need for approximately 232 HS-1L machines, as well as 150 H-16s. He also called for 530 more pilots, with 75 additional ground officers and 2,700 enlisted men needed to bring existing stations up to authorized strength. Craven performed a similar analysis for LTA bases, predicting a need for 18 new dirigibles, 70 more pilots, and 38 student pilots. All estimates incorporated a high "wastage" factor. As to the future of the program, Craven offered several observations. He defined the mission of coastal stations as providing escort for ships arriving and departing France, supplying protection to coastal convoys, surveilling littoral waters to find minefields, and controlling the enemy's underwater activities. Bases at Arcachon, Gujan, and Tréguier had yet to prove their usefulness and seemed poorly positioned for the work assigned them. Craven called for completion of all facilities but suggested that a reduction in complement be considered. In fact, Arcachon, Gujan, and Tréguier might prove unnecessary, in which case men and machines should be diverted elsewhere.[3]

From Ireland, McCrary also weighed in. He endorsed the concept of bombing German North Sea bases and resurrected the idea of using towed lighters, with the proviso that "fighting planes" to protect bombing seaplanes operate from the decks of ships. He opposed construction of additional stations in Ireland, noting that small substations of three to six planes could function from protected harbors if required, serviced by a mother ship. McCrary recommended that cross-Atlantic convoys carry at least two kite balloons. Though they might reveal a convoy's position, their tactical value more than outweighed possible negative factors. McCrary also submitted estimates of personnel and equipment necessary to complete and sustain the Navy program in Ireland, including 26 additional staff officers, 18 kite balloons, and 168 H-16s. He outlined an immediate need for 14 balloon pilots and 172 flying boat pilots through November.[4]

John Callan, one of the Navy's most aggressive air power proponents, offered a rich menu of suggestions. He identified the overriding principles governing aviation for the coming year as frequent reconnaissance flights to discover enemy activities and disrupt them with bombing missions, attacks on enemy aerial and naval units and aerial coastal patrols, and defense of convoys and shipping against submarine attack. He focused particularly on the Austrian sector, which he identified as "undoubtedly the most vulnerable front." Presaging Winston Churchill's "soft underbelly" strategy of World War II, Callan predicted that additional pressure on Austria would precipitate collapse of the Hapsburg Empire, thereby isolating Bulgaria and Turkey, fracturing the Central Powers. To carry out the air offensive, Callan called for a massive commitment of 920 additional aircraft. Callan also urged the Navy to assume control of the existing station at Ancona and build a new base at Vallona to assault enemy installations at Cattaro. Callan's shopping list included more personnel and supplies, and perhaps North Sea-type towed lighters to permit long-range reconnaissance missions, to be supplanted by converting a few fast cruisers into seaplane ships.

Like many of his peers, Callan endorsed a major strategic bombing campaign directed at submarine bases, coast defenses, air stations, arsenal and repair bases, fleets, munitions factories, and merchant ships in harbors. He specifically included civilian attitudes as a legitimate target, noting, "the above program would break down the morale of the civil population, driving them from the towns, thus weakening the manufacturing strength and fostering revolt." Italian operations also attracted the comments of Edwards in Sims's office, who claimed that the British wished to be relieved of all aviation work in the area, including the Adriatic mine barrage, allowing them to switch their efforts to the Aegean and eastern Mediterranean. (In fact, the Royal Navy's suggestions were as much about postwar imperial politics as actual war fighting strategy.) Toward this end, Callan made supplemental proposals in early September recommending that Americans occupy two islands in the Gulf of Venice, erect an assembly facility ashore opposite Venice, and operate a base at Ferrara to aid the assault on Pola and Trieste. Use of Ancona, an existing station, would, allow sputtering efforts at Pescara to be abandoned.[5]

Based on these extensive recommendations and further work by staff in London and Paris, planning began for a series of major conferences, a Franco-American meeting August 29, another with the British September 17, and a final gathering with the Italians October 4. The first of these took place in Paris when Cone, Craven, and Captain Schofield from the London Planning Section met with Admiral Salaun, Directeur General de la Guerre Sous-Marine, and the French staff. Cone had initiated a call for such a meeting July 29, citing the fact that American stations along the coast were ready to begin operations. Franco-American discussions yielded several areas of agreement and little controversy. The number of seaplane stations already built, building, or projected satisfied foreseeable needs. Plans for an American dirigible station at Rochefort would be abandoned, but the Navy would purchase the dirigibles ordered for the site. Participants ratified the changing status of Dunkirk from seaplane station to center of Northern Bombing Group activities. They also examined the possibility of basing land planes at Belle Isle but set it aside as impractical. French officials dropped any requests for seaplane hulls but desired motors and building materials, specifically assistance constructing a zeppelin shed.[6]

The London conference promised far-reaching discussions and required extensive preparation. Both sides developed detailed agendas. Britain wished the United States to take over antisubmarine activities, coastal patrol, long-range reconnaissance, and bombing in the Adriatic Sea and Gulf of Taranto, including the Otranto mine barrage. In turn, the RAF would operate from Great Britain, the Mediterranean, and the Aegean. They also advocated use of a squadron on the west coast of Ireland to interdict Sinn Fein munitions drops. In their view, Americans should operate from Dunkirk, the Bay of Biscay, and Killingholme. From Killingholme the Navy could patrol the North Sea minefields. The towed lighter project should be put back on the table. A preliminary agenda prepared for Cone advocated continuous expansion of the bombing campaign against German naval bases, with secondary priority accorded patrol and escort missions. It advocated American control of American units and withdrawal of Navy elements from mixed commands. Emphasis on bombing precluded missions such as patrolling the west coast of Ireland or the North Sea mine barrage. The Irish venture sparked a particularly negative response. "This is particularly a British effort, and we should not mix in it." Harry Guggenheim on Cone's staff urged expansion of NBG efforts from eight to twelve squadrons, and using DH-4s to replace seaplanes at Dunkirk station. He endorsed expanded activities in the Adriatic and direct attacks against German bases at Heligoland, Wilhemshaven, Emden, Bremerhaven, and Cuxhaven.[7]

In London the Navy secured endorsement for many of its proposals. Both sides agreed that the United States would support British plans to shift forces away from the Adriatic toward the Aegean by taking over bombing of Adriatic bases and patrol of sea lanes and minefields. No expansion of efforts would take place in the British Isles except increased patrol of the mine barrage. There would be no American effort on the west coast of Ireland. Continuous bombing of enemy facilities received the highest priority, including an increase in the NBG force to 12 squadrons, including 2 squadrons of DH-4s to carry out work currently performed at NAS Dunkirk. Should the bombing campaign achieve its specific objectives, aerial forces would then be directed against other "naval objectives if practical, or any other objective suitable to the furtherance of the aims of the military forces." Other concepts endorsed support for programs integrating aviation with the fleet and a bombing campaign against Heligoland Bight.[8]

Sims forwarded a summary of the proceedings to Washington on September 25. He called for a quick response, stating that British plans for 1919 depended on American actions. Sims recommended that Irwin come to Europe to participate in the planned conference relating to Anglo-American-Italian activities in the Adriatic and Mediterranean. Cone also urged support for the Anglo-American initiatives. He emphasized the importance of bombing efforts from Flanders, the Adriatic, and then Heligoland Bight. In all cases *long-range, land-based bombers* should be employed. Cone announced "practical abandonment" of antisubmarine patrolling, with escort patrols being substituted—"In other words, following exactly the experience of the surface craft," advocating use of land planes in almost all instances except distant offshore missions. Spotlighting differences between Washington and Europe about the value of seaplanes, Cone stood by land machines without reservation, noting, "I am also certain that if you came over here you would see in no time that we have got to use land machines for naval purposes if we are going to do our maximum against the enemy." He disagreed with Irwin's concerns about possible amalgamation and its affect on the Navy's strategy and operations. "If it is going to have this effect," Cone argued, "we had better form the third service and get on with the war."[9]

The Department accepted many conference suggestions, though some in Washington must have been astounded at the scope of the proposals. Current seaplane operations should continue, with the exception of Dunkirk;

principal augmentation of aviation efforts should be in the area of bombing enemy naval targets, especially submarine bases; plans and production for operations against German bases near Heligoland Bight should commence. In other areas the Department withheld endorsement or called for modifications. The new Adriatic campaign was approved, but only if seaplanes alone were employed. Use of day and night land bombers by Navy squadrons would be approved for the NBG only. Abandonment of the Dunkirk seaplane station and substitution of two DH-4 squadrons operating from NBG fields was not authorized, with further advice that the Navy confer with Pershing about machines necessary for the enlargement of the NBG. The clear message from Washington was "Stay away from land bombers! Use seaplanes! Be wary of treading on Army turf!"[10]

Many points raised at the Italian conference in early October first surfaced at talks on Mediterranean mine-laying held at Malta in early August. Participants there also examined the possibility of creating a Southern Bombing Group. Then followed John Callan's vigorous calls for expanded activity in the Adriatic theater. Headquarters' response to his proposals proved mixed. Early on, Atlee Edwards supported expansion and told Cone that work in Italy should be enlarged. In September, however, he cautioned Callan that the huge Ancona proposal was not deemed wise and the Navy's existing Italian commitments should be carried out first. Cone also expressed reservations, citing the continuing difficulty securing aircraft from the NBG and fearing the Department had little interest in the idea.[11]

Despite this rebuff, when a commission headed by Benjamin Briscoe visited Italy in early October, largely to investigate the festering Caproni issue, Callan won them over to his plan. Briscoe's group, composed principally of assembly and repair officers, inspected several possible sites in the Gulf of Venice. Following submission of their findings to London, a return cable on October 18 authorized exploratory discussions. The Venice initiative called for an extensive construction program, including many hangars, shops, and quarters for 3,000 men. Accommodation for 90 HS-1Ls would be necessary, as well as docking and warehousing facilities, and quarters for 400 men in the assembly crews. Edwards, however, remained wary, believing Austria-Hungary tottered near collapse, while the bombing project would take months to implement. Additional preparations in Italy included meetings between Train and the Ministry of Marine concerning expanded operations in the north Adriatic and plans for Rear Admiral Orsini and Callan to inspect proposed sites.

Eventually word arrived from London that a commission of five officers would visit in early November to examine the plan in detail. Headquarters did not actually approve the great bombing proposal but promised a quick decision following this review. On October 23 Edwards informed Cone (then recuperating from injuries sustained in a torpedo attack), "I have organized quite a little mission to proceed to Italy and report to Capt. Train for the purpose of investigating the feasibility of our going into the Adriatic area." The group included Kenneth Whiting as head of the commission, along with Billings, Mason, Lane, Guggenheim, and Spenser Grey. "They will leave tomorrow night and will, I feel sure," Edwards noted, "establish a certain amount of prestige for us both by their numbers and by their rank."

Anticipating approval of the bombing initiative, officials in Italy took preliminary measures to implement it, including orders to move a hanger into the region and prepare bunks for several hundred men. Train also recommended transferring 90 flying boats to Poveglia, Sacca Sessola, and Malamocca, as well as 40 land planes to Poggio Renatico, "where [the] station is practically completed." Should these movements be approved, he urged dispatch of a civil engineer, an assembly and repair officer, Ensign Metcalfe (who spoke Italian), and the ubiquitous Omar Conger as liaison supply officer, along with sufficient bluejackets, tools, and stores to begin work. Train's recommendations coincided with the dispatch of the Whiting commission, which by early November was on its way to Italy. The sudden collapse of Austria caused them to cut their journey short in Paris. In fact, except for continued operations at French coastal stations, abandonment of the Rochefort initiative, and partial abandonment of NAS Dunkirk, none of the proposals discussed at the French, British, and Italian conferences ever came to fruition.[12]

During these same months Navy officials on both sides of the Atlantic continued to investigate the vexing issues of transport and equipment shortages and deficiencies. In September, Adm. Henry Mayo sailed to Europe to conduct a wide-ranging inspection trip from Ireland to Italy, including aviation stations. In preparation for these visits, Mayo's staff gathered extensive background information. Commanders filled out lengthy questionnaires addressing everything from missions, personnel, equipment, and facilities to communications, training, morale, and command structure. Much of this material then appeared in a lengthy memo/report for Secretary Daniels. Mayo began his tour in Britain, visiting Killingholme on October 2. He noted the now-familiar litany of aircraft defects—unsatisfactory propellers and radiators, weak hulls, improperly designed steps, shortages and damaged instruments and engine parts. Finally, he discovered that only 7 of 49 assigned H-16 flying boats were available for operations. From the North Sea, Mayo moved on to Eastleigh, and then across the Channel. Cone called his time accompanying Mayo "gay and festive. . . . Jackson is as entertaining as ever and the Admiral is fine as silk." By the end of October, Mayo was at Paimboeuf, Fromentine, and Pauillac where he spent two days touring the huge supply facility. Mayo continued on to Italy, visiting the school at Lake Bolsena on November 8 and the combat station at Porto Corsini two days later. All along the way he met with large groups of enlisted personnel, ate in the mess hall, attended smokers and entertainments, and addressed the men.[13]

Mayo drew several conclusions from his visits. Construction far outpaced shipment of equipment, and getting a station operational required perseverance and management of a high order. Among the factors hindering efforts were the necessity of conforming to French practices, delays in procuring sites, and slow arrival of critical personnel. Construction occurred at many separated and isolated locations. Local building material proved scarce at best, while deliveries of supplies from home were problematic. In some cases personnel or material from one station was scavenged to complete other projects. Mayo believed delays and mistakes in shipments of construction and flying equipment caused the greatest difficulties, and once material arrived, often at the wrong port, reshipping it was almost impossible. Lack of competent supervising personnel in the early months and an overdependence on unreliable French contractors imposed additional burdens. Nonetheless, Mayo believed everyone concerned did the best they could under trying circumstances and reflected great credit on themselves.

The fires ignited by Frankin Roosevelt the previous summer also continued to burn. His reports, and the observations of Lemuel Padgett, head of the House Naval Affairs Committee, directly focused the Department's attention on the shipping/equipment issue. At Irwin's weekly meeting on August 21, the group discussed Roosevelt's critical dispatch. Irwin informed Bureau representatives that he had met with Secretary Daniels who described reports from Roosevelt and Padgett. Both Daniels and Irwin agreed the Bureaus must do a better job of following up on these issues. This resulted in the Department's dispatching representatives from Construction and Repair, Steam Engineering, and Supplies and Accounts to Europe to investigate the situation, with Naval Constructor George Westervelt in charge. Cone claimed, "The Bureaus are stirred up" and were sending men "to investigate themselves."[14]

An Annapolis graduate, Westervelt studied engineering at MIT and helped William Boeing found the company that still bears his name. Nicknamed "Scrappy," Westervelt served on the Bolling Commission in the summer of 1917 and thereafter played a critical role in developing the NC program, supervising design and building of the giant transatlantic aircraft. While Westervelt and other Bureau representatives were in transit, Benson instructed Sims to designate them a formal board to prepare a report for Secretary Daniels. Sims then ordered Westervelt, Cdr. Walter Smead, LCdr. N. W. Pickering, and Lt. J. E. Jones to make a thorough investigation of past and present conditions related to supply and shipment of aviation material to Europe. Edwards and his staff prepared hundreds of pages of data for them. After meeting with Cone, the board visited virtually every station in Ireland, England, and France. It seemed that each facility had a litany of grievances. They first traveled to Killingholme and heard about troubles with radiators on H-16 flying boats. Then came a rapid tour of the Irish bases and criticism of the abuse that aircraft suffered in transit from the United States. NAS Brest experienced difficulties with propellers; the next base complained about bombs that failed to explode.[15]

Despite complaints, the Board praised the overall accomplishments of naval aviation but identified transport as the key problem, beset by "almost insurmountable difficulties." Contributing factors included an inadequate and overloaded transportation network, even as the German 1918 offensive monopolized the full facilities of the French system, to the exclusion of Navy needs. Aviation officers exhibited excellent spirit but often lacked experience. The Board found many stations undermanned, and the ranks of pilots and ground officers understaffed. Cone received inadequate information from the United States about who was coming, when, and where. There were never enough trained civil engineers for such a massive building initiative, while underestimation of the challenges caused many delays. Overall, construction was retarded by circumstances that better management could have avoided—building materials sent in illogical sequences, ships' cargoes jumbled together, material delivered to the wrong ports.

Westervelt's group devoted considerable attention to conditions at Pauillac, aviation's principal supply, assembly, and repair facility. Administration there had been poor before the arrival of Capt. Frank Taylor Evans, with little evident coordination between departments, friction, recriminations, and incomplete/absent manifests and shipping lists. The premium placed on speed often led to damaged equipment, while insufficient storage space meant items needing protection from the weather were often left outside. Some materials were simply lost. Evans, the Board observed, straightened out the entire mess. They also offered high praise to enlisted men. In the area of equipment failures, Westervelt's report identified many concerns. Major problems included inadequate crankshafts and valves, while many parts were missing.

Each Liberty motor required 240 man-hours to overhaul before it could be used. Aircraft shipped to Europe often arrived incomplete. Shortages of spare parts at many bases constituted a major hindrance. The NBG's aircraft problems flowed from the failure of the Caproni initiative and the faulty DH-4s supplied by the Army. Training of early mechanics had been deficient.

After digesting the Westervelt report, Sims forwarded it to Washington, along with his observations. While regretting that members of naval aviation forces in Europe were not part of the panel, he called the final account impartial and open-minded. He noted that the Navy had created a massive, new organization from scratch in an energetic, efficient, and expeditious manner. Officers and men did the best possible job despite inadequacies of material and personnel. Sims identified several obstacles, including lack of a definite, prearranged plan for establishing naval aviation in the war zone; great shortages of personnel in the early stages, especially commissioned officers; and the necessity of placing inexperienced and reserve officers in positions of great responsibility. Such men exhibited zeal but possessed very junior rank, and efforts to obtain promotions often failed. A shortage of officers with expertise in the shipping industry affected movement of materials from the United States to Europe. Attracting knowledgeable men from business and enrolling them as reserve officers might have remedied the deficiency. The German offensive exacerbated transportation woes. Concerning provision of adequate numbers of flight officers, insufficient training at home caused a serious diversion of effort in Europe. Sims concluded by praising the work of Hutch Cone.

The subsequent path traced by Westervelt's report proved a tortuous one. Franklin Roosevelt received a copy of the document and Sims's attached notes just before his second trip to Europe (after the Armistice), but it was mislaid. A second copy reached Admiral Benson on February 18, 1919, and was forwarded to Secretary Daniels on March 11. Along the way Capt. Josiah McKean, acting chief of Naval Operations between January and June 1919, inserted praise for the fine efforts of the Department in Washington and Director of Naval Aviation Irwin, asserting that good work and organization at home made accomplishments in foreign waters possible. He justified the Department's performance and excused the lack of prewar planning by saying aviation was so new the Navy never expected to extend its activities to Europe. McKean also explained how many transportation facilities and personnel for aviation had to be diverted for other activities to best accomplish the needs of the naval service, which was "perfectly proper under the circumstances."[16]

The Westervelt report laid bare several disagreements within the Department. The European crowd complained that they were denied necessary staff and received inadequate personnel to carry out the enormous program endorsed by Washington. Nor did officers in Europe obtain promotions as rapidly as those in the United States or to a level commensurate with their enhanced responsibilities. Hutch Cone (and FDR) clearly scorned the turf-protecting Bureau system. Department leaders responded that those abroad simply did not grasp the larger picture or acknowledge competing priorities and (selfishly?) expected their every demand to be instantly satisfied. Nor did those "Over There" sufficiently appreciate the great efforts being made on the home front. Planners in Washington argued that many factors outside Navy control impacted the aviation situation. In some ways this debate echoed earlier controversies over allocation of destroyers and whether it was more important to defend the home fleet or fight the submarine in European waters. Similarly, should a large aviation establishment be constructed along the American coast or all resources be diverted to Ireland, England, France, and Italy? Many of the same issues resurfaced with particular vehemence in postwar congressional hearings.

In early fall, naval aviation suffered a stunning loss when Hutch Cone sustained serious injuries during the sinking of *RMS Leinster*, torpedoed in the Irish Sea en route from Kingston to Hollyhead. The attack provided stark evidence that the U-boat threat, though much diminished, remained very real. Sims immediately placed W. Atlee Edwards, by now promoted to lieutenant commander, in the position of Force Commander's Aide for Aviation. Edwards held the office through the end of the war and demobilization. In the final weeks, much progress occurred toward completing the aviation program previously laid out. As of October 1, more than 650 officers and 15,000 enlisted men had reached Europe, with additional thousands on the way. Nearly 575 aircraft were received from the United States or acquired overseas. Pauillac could now house transient personnel and handle stores, while aviation's overall organization was virtually complete. Almost all stations carried out operations, though shortages of pilots and aircraft persisted, especially in the area of ground officers, kite balloon and dirigible pilots, and seaplane pilots. Improved weather at Moutchic allowed more work there. In LTA operations *Capitaine Caussin* was inflated and flown to Guipavas October 19; VZ-13, taken over from the French, arrived at Paimboeuf on October 25 and made its first convoy patrol the following day.[17]

Weekly operations reports in late October provided a revealing snapshot of aviation activities near the close of the war. During the week ending October

5, coastal stations in France carried out 728 flights totaling 655 hours, with the highest number conducted at Moutchic. A total of 234 seaplanes had arrived, with 53 in commission. NAS Ile Tudy escorted several convoys, as did dirigibles from Paimboeuf. On one of those flights airship VZ-7 suffered a potentially catastrophic engine fire, which, luckily, the crew extinguished immediately. The following week the Irish Unit made 15 patrol/convoy flights. Officers at Berehaven investigated the loss of three kite balloons during operations carried out with battleships *Oklahoma* and *Utah*. During the same period Killingholme personnel conducted numerous patrols but sighted no submarines. Thirteen seaplanes from NAS Porto Corsini participated in a 43-aircraft attack against Pola. All returned safely and "it is proposed to repeat this operation at once." Bolsena utilized 11 aircraft to carry out 171 training flights averaging 20 minutes each. Seaplane operations ceased at Dunkirk, with the station slated for abandonment. Poor weather prevented most night flights by NBG personnel attached to RAF units. Marines of Day Squadron 9 conducted four successful raids, while others flew with No. 217 Squadron, RAF, or awaited placement at the pilot pool at Audembert.[18]

In the war's final days, aviation headquarters reviewed several further proposals for expanded operations. One envisioned cross-Channel patrols from Cape Finisterre in France to Plymouth, and a conference held November 5 considered the idea. The sudden end of the war one week later prevented any further action being taken. Planners also scrutinized an idea to ferry large flying boats such as the F-5 from England to the Mediterranean across mainland France. This resulted in RAF Major A. J. Miley and Navy Lt. DeWitt Ramsey undertaking a lengthy inspection tour between October 17 and November 18. They traced a route to Brest, Île Tudy, Le Croisic, Fromentine, St. Trojan, and Pauillac, as well as several French stations, then turned inland, following various rivers and canals to Toulouse and the Mediterranean; but they ultimately rejected the concept as impractical.[19] Destroyer *Benham* at Brest carried out a successful trip with a Goodyear balloon November 13, employing the Mumford steam winch.

On a less buoyant note, Director of Naval Aviation Irwin toured facilities in Europe in October and November, and many of the disagreements bedeviling relations throughout the war resurfaced. Craven met Irwin at NAS St. Trojan and described him as "not in the best of humors ... he effects a chronic grouch." On a more substantive basis, the two officers disagreed strongly over the necessity of providing additional training to pilots arriving from the United States and of flying armed patrols—in other words, "that flying pure and simple, is the role of aviation, and that other things do not count."

Irwin believed that the overhaul of Liberty motors was unnecessary and "lives lost because of faulty engines are simply the result of the fortunes of war, and should not be attributed to the inadvertances of man," an opinion that shocked Craven. Writing to his patron, Hutch Cone, Craven observed, "He [Irwin] does not understand our point of view at all, so it is hardly worth while discussing the same with him . . . he does not approach things with an open mind . . . he is over antagonistic." The summer's arguments and Congress's response still rankled the aviation chief. "He seems sore over the telegram sent by Mr. Padgett," Craven reported. Someone had leaked information about the disputes concerning "our shortages and deficiencies," and Irwin placed the blame at Cone/Craven's feet. Roosevelt's comments had only made things worse. Apparently, "both telegrams have started something (this is between ourselves and need not be told Irwin)." A few days later Irwin sailed to Ireland to meet with Cone and inspect stations there. After two long discussions, the recuperating officer endorsed Craven's observations. "His [Irwin's] mental attitude is one of finding fault with us." Having escaped death by a whisker, Cone remained somewhat above the fray. "I have arrived at a philosophical state of mind," he observed, "so that I don't give a darn what he thinks or what anybody else thinks, for that matter."[20]

As the fighting wound down, the thoughts of many aviators turned to the future. Planners examined the feasibility of doing minesweeping from dirigibles. Edwards informed Craven that London headquarters wished to test the concept. If successful, the equipment could be used to help clear the North Sea Mine Barrage. Other areas of interest included the newest, largest British aircraft, especially a giant seaplane prototype known as N-4 and the Super Handley Page 1500. Many now believed land planes married to the fleet rather than flying boats to be the wave of the future. Sims called development of the use of aircraft with the fleet "of considerable importance." For the time being, United States battleships had benefited from cooperation with the Royal Navy. Now plans were under way to install experimental launching devices on the turrets of *Texas*. Chevalier received orders to report to the commander of the Ninth Battle Division to familiarize himself with the Grand Fleet's use of airplanes. Shortly after the Armistice, John Callan asked for a similar assignment. Sims reported approvingly how the British had selected "four ships of large size or value" to convert to "aeroplane carriers." Eight or ten other vessels of various sizes were equipped for "housing, carrying, and picking up, but not launching hydroplanes or aeroplanes."[21]

Admiral Mayo emerged from the war as a vigorous supporter of aeronautic programs. In three extensive reports completed after his autumn trip he described British advances in aviation and enthusiastically endorsed the use of aircraft in fleet operations, urging that sufficient equipment be available for reconnaissance, spotting, carrying torpedoes, antisubmarine patrols, and escort duty, whether heavier- or lighter-than-air machines. He also called for substantial numbers of aerodromes, hangars, and bases, construction of kite balloon stations, and sufficient properly trained personnel in America. Mayo believed that airplane carriers should be constructed with speeds equal to the fastest battleships. Finally, he suggested that the sprawling bases at Eastleigh and Pauillac be disassembled and reerected in the United States.[22]

In contrast to the painstakingly slow build-up of naval aviation in Europe, the end of hostilities triggered stunningly rapid demobilization. Austria-Hungary's early departure from the fighting led to almost immediate action to wind down activities in Italy. Sims sent instructions on November 8 that Porto Corsini remain in commission until the Armistice, but all work at Pescara be canceled and no more students sent to Bolsena. The admiral ordered 50 percent of personnel sent home "with all dispatch." Given the limited commitment of American resources in the Mediterranean and the fact that the Navy occupied Italian facilities and utilized local equipment and aircraft, demobilization unfolded rapidly. Porto Corsini was abandoned on December 31, 1918, and personnel withdrew from Bolsena two days later. In a surprising display of generosity the Italian government notified the U.S. Navy that it would cover all costs incurred by the Americans for aeronautic activities performed in the Mediterranean and "therefore no reimbursements will be expected."[23]

The imminent end of combat on the Western Front prompted similar actions. The false Armistice November 8 focused thoughts directly on the process, even before the shooting stopped.[24] In Washington, CNO Benson, with Irwin's concurrence, recommended immediate cessation of shipments of personnel abroad, ending enlistment, canceling airplane and engine contracts, ceasing overseas construction, and terminating shipments of equipment. In London, Sims requested approval of plans developed for the disposition of aircraft materiel in France. Under his proposal, materials, equipment, and stations could be transferred to the U.S. Army, to foreign governments, returned home, or sold to the public. Boards of Inventory and Appraisal would facilitate this process, with inventory lists and valuations submitted to officers in London and Brest who would confer with representatives of Allied governments. Material specifically identified for reshipment to the United States included metalworking and woodworking tools, unpacked aircraft, airplane motors, all airships and balloons, photographic equipment, and radio apparatus. Sims's planners recommended that assembled aircraft be sold, if possible. If not, they should be stripped of useful equipment, leaving hulls and wings to be scrapped.

Committed to documenting aviation's efforts before the forces dispersed, headquarters issued instructions to compile a "detailed history of naval aviation activities in the present war." Aviation Circular #78 called on station commanders to compile histories of their facilities, addressing the issues of organization, construction, personnel, and operations. First Aeronautic Detachment veterans Whiting, Griffin, and Dichman prepared memoirs of their early activities in France. Eventually Craven's office produced both a photographic record of the French Coastal Unit and a massive historical narrative, with additional information compiled on operations in Ireland, England, and Italy.[25] Craven and Hutch Cone, still recuperating at Dublin Castle Hospital, also discussed the need to post officers and observers to the Grand Fleet quickly to gather as much information as possible before the "break up with our Allies." Craven realized, "The practices of peace will close the avenue of information, and secrecy will become the rule as soon as this trouble is over." The Navy also used the immediate post-Armistice period to dispatch officers to Germany to inspect aircraft and facilities there. Sims notified Washington that he had ordered several observers to Germany, including Child, Maxfield, Ramsey, and Hunsaker, a total of 15 in all. These inspection missions continued through the following winter and spring.[26]

The official end of the war triggered rapid action. Recruitment in the United States ceased, with no additional men forwarded to Europe. Shipment of supplies and equipment ended; contracts were summarily canceled. Station commanders received cease orders for aviation activities, with instructions to discontinue patrols and permit only flights deemed indispensable for mine searching, upkeep of machines, and training personnel. The NAS Fromentine log contained a simple final entry: "Hostile flights abandoned this date [November 12] by telegraphic order of Commander, U.S. Naval Forces France, in accordance with terms of armistice signed with Germany, November 11th, 1918, at 5:00 A.M." Lighter-than-air stations began to deflate all kite balloons. Orders also went out to compile complete inventories of equipment and materiel, everything from large aircraft to small quantities of nails and screws. Sims's office ordered evacuation of personnel to begin quickly, with 50 percent returned home with all speed, retaining only enough men to complete demobilization. On November 13 the Department directed Sims to offer the Irish stations to the Air Ministry at a price to be agreed upon. Northern Bombing Group and French coastal station barracks would be offered to the

AEF for use as cantonments for returning troops. Failing that, a similar offer should be made to the Red Cross.[27]

During the next few weeks the complicated process underwent continual refinement, with emphasis on the issues of cost and reimbursement. The American government, and the Navy Department specifically, was unwilling to give anything away and attempted to dispose of equipment and supplies shipped to Europe but not likely to be returned home at full appraised or invoiced price. An inventory of buildings at NAS L'Aber Vrach, for example, appraised the enormous double hangar at $33,600, large "portable" buildings (107 feet × 20 feet) at $3,200 each, and smaller structures at anywhere from $3,000 to $532, roughly $1.50 per square foot, with the entire assemblage worth $94,427, less overseas freight charges of $28,327.[28]

Inevitably, the scope and complexity of the effort made the process "clumsy and costly." On November 22, Sims informed Wilson at Brest, "General demobilization of Naval Aviation Forces, Foreign Service, is hereby authorized to take effect immediately." All woodworking and metalworking tools, airplane motors, seaplane accessories, and ordnance would be returned to the United States, along with photographic gear, aerographic equipment, dirigibles, kite balloons, still-crated aircraft, medical equipment, land and water transportation, and mess gear in good condition when no longer needed. In some cases the Navy employed colliers and mine carriers for this purpose. Under successive directives, crews packed and shipped materiel aggregating 9,600 tons by March 3, including 5,200 tons from Pauillac and 3,200 tons from Dunkirk. The Navy transferred much of its motor transport to the Army and the Committee for Relief in Belgium (CRB). Port officers utilized remaining vehicles to expedite shipment of troops home. At least one mishap marred the process, offering a reminder that not all dangers ceased when the guns fell silent. In late November a crew from Dunkirk returned from Zeebrugge with a truckload of aviation equipment, including two HD seaplanes. While stopped near Blankenberghe to refill their radiator a buried German mine exploded, destroying the cargo of aircraft and seriously injuring several of the eight-man work party.[29]

Demobilization activities carried out at NAS Fromentine paralleled those at other Navy stations. Property returned to the United States included aerographic and photographic apparatus; ordnance; power, construction, and machine tools; and radio equipment. Work crews transported medical supplies to Base Hospital #5 at Brest, while gasoline, oil, and paint went to the U.S. Army aerial gunnery school at St. Jean de Monts. Other material transferred to the Army included portable barracks and storehouses, hangars, provisions, electrical equipment and generators, and telephone and telegraph installations. While the Navy invoiced most kitchen equipment to the Army, they transferred the station bake oven to a local landowner "in lieu of release from all claims." Bombs and ordnance went back to French ammunition depots. Of Fromentine's HS-1L flying boats, bluejackets stripped 10 at the station, with motors and parts returned home. All others were sent to Pauillac for salvage.[30]

Actually disposing of stations, abrogating contracts, and settling damage claims proved more vexing. Both Allies and Americans held certain grievances and often disagreed over the dollars involved. In early December, Sims received instructions to appoint appropriate boards of officers of the Civil Engineering Corps and confer with the AEF when addressing questions of canceling large contracts or terminating leases. After determining the best course to take, forces in Europe should make recommendations to the Department, which would issue specific instructions. Wilson laid out the American proposals to the French Ministry of Marine on December 16. In fact, the Department quickly determined that a senior official must assume direction of the process and dispatched Assistant Secretary Roosevelt, "to have direction over demobilization of Naval material and particularly concluding agreements involving real estate." As preparation for FDR's work, officers in Europe should assemble all necessary data but refrain from entering discussions or offering opinions to their Allied counterparts. Those who had been principals in negotiating the original agreements to lease/acquire land and property were to be retained in Europe and not sent home. This was later extended to include all regular, accounting, and reserve officers whose services could be used aboard German ships. The recent return of Paymaster Omar Conger to the United States inadvertently muddied the situation, there being "so much unfinished business which he alone was in a position to close."[31]

Roosevelt sailed for Europe on New Year's Day 1919, prepared to conduct his mission in an atmosphere of mistrust. One rumor claimed that the French collected rent for the cemeteries where American soldiers lay buried. Roosevelt requested complete information concerning each station, commenting, "I am particularly desirous of knowing steps taken to limit our liability at any point." Benson, serving as naval advisor to the American peace delegation in Paris, scorned French attitudes, charging that they displayed "the worst Yankee points . . . difficult to settle any financial question . . . cannot escape feeling they are trying to force us to leave as much of our equipment as possible, and give it to them." Thomas Craven, who bore immediate responsibility for demobilization in France, called his hosts "notoriously hard to deal with," showing little inclination to relieve the Americans of stations and refusing to allow sale of building materials for fear of glutting the market. He described the "small dickering business" as "extremely distasteful." So, too, the return to "the old-fashioned perplexities of peace administration," particularly dealing with the French Interior Ministry.

Similar conditions prevailed in Britain where authorities wished to charge for use of buildings. If the Royal Air Force or Royal Navy took over a base, they would pay for hangars and improvements. If not, the Navy should remove everything, including concrete floors and slipways. While the Navy did raze structures at most sites, massive concrete works remained in place. They are still there today. Roosevelt completed his report February 5, 1919, but not everyone believed he had aided the process. Some thought his actions subverted the role of the assessment boards. Craven criticized the assistant secretary's method of issuing orders and his failure to follow Navy procedures, noting, "Mr. Roosevelt has come and gone. His only contribution to business interests has been one paymaster (who) may be of assistance, but I do not exactly see how."[32]

Despite disagreements and impediments, demobilization proceeded rapidly. Within two months total personnel in Europe fell by 72 percent. Events might have progressed even more quickly had more transport been available. The Navy hauled down the flag at Moutchic and Porto Corsini on December 31, 1918, and at Bolsena two days later. Photographs taken of station complements lined up with their seabags, ready for a final inspection, still evince the excitement sweeping the ranks. Dunkirk became the first of the French patrol stations vacated, on New Years Day 1919, with the barracks area turned over to the Commission for Relief in Belgium (CRB). The relief organization intended to use acquired buildings and materials to erect temporary shelters but lacked sufficient transport and manpower. The Navy assembled a large working party to assist the relief group, which soon began operating in Lille. Motor transport, bedding, commissary supplies, medicine, barracks, and miscellaneous clothing were also invoiced to the CRB. Additional supplies, tools, and barracks arrived from Pauillac aboard the little steamer *Bella*. Nearby NBG flying fields acquired originally through the British Claims, Hiring, and Requisition Commission were derequisitioned in the same manner, with the commission responsible for any damage claims. Land acquired from the French received similar treatment, with costs to the United States reduced by restoring farmland where possible.

Demobilization of most French facilities proceeded rapidly. La Pallice and Arcachon closed during the first week of the new year, with 10 more stations decommissioned by the end of the month. Pauillac was simply turned over to the AEF. In some cases small caretaker contingents remained for several weeks. Skeleton crews lingered at La Trinité and Brest until early February. Of the dirigibles under contract at the Armistice, four were completed and remaining orders were canceled. Nine airships were transported back to the United States. At some other sites confusion, procrastination, shortages of transport, red tape, and competing French bureaus caused delays. A few facilities went to the French Navy; others were simply abandoned.

The cost of constructing stations in France approximated $3 million, not counting labor and transport. Le Croisic, Moutchic, St. Trojan, Arcachon, and part of Brest were built under local contracts valued at $950,000, while those erected by the Navy cost approximately $2 million. These facilities were sold in turn for $230,000 and $1,550,000. Aviation material liquidated in Europe included $5 million to the U.S. Army, $1,350,000 to the French government, $741,000 to the Committee for Relief in Belgium, $210,000 to the Italian government, $130,000 to the British government, and $656,000 to other Navy departments. Attempts to dispose of flying boats proved unsuccessful. The Navy decided that rather than ship them home and maintain them in storage, it would be better to spend the funds developing other aircraft. After removing valuable equipment and motors, many were simply burned.[33]

Claims for damages and terminated agreements often involved intricate negotiations. These were normally handled through commissions established in Paris and London, known respectively as the Paris Naval Board on Claims and the London Naval Board on Claims, both created by Roosevelt on February 12, 1918. Additional claims were examined in Dublin. Discussions regarding Arcachon and Moutchic in France dragged out over many months. The cost of removing foundations at Gujan was estimated at $13,600, while land there had been leased from more than 100 property owners. In many places trees had been cut down, crops lost, or roads damaged. Farmers demanded that their fields be restored, concrete removed, holes filled, drainage ditches reopened, and stone walls rebuilt. Owners of the St. Inglevert chateau accused the Navy of leaving the property dirty, but the Americans retorted it was cleaner when they departed than when they arrived. Other claims included payment for repairs when a military truck hit a Dunkirk city tramway and reimbursement to a local homeowner for damages incurred when an aircraft crashed into his roof and chimney. One farmer at Guipavas wished to be compensated for damage to his rolled field when the Navy converted it into a baseball diamond. Yet another claim involved a canceled order for manufacture of aviators' underwear. Various French claims continued to be received long after the war ended.³⁴

Demobilization in Great Britain followed the same patterns. The large force at Killingholme abandoned the site January 6, with equipment loaded aboard *Defiance* at the Immingham docks, the same waterfront that had welcomed Kenneth Whiting and *Jason* just seven months earlier. Of the Irish stations, which had cost $2,535,000 to build, isolated Whiddy Island closed on January 29. The others followed shortly thereafter—Berehaven, Wexford, and Lough Foyle by February 22—with stores and equipment returned to the United States through Dublin. Miscellaneous furniture and supplies were sold privately or at auction. NAS Queenstown remained open until April 10, 1919, as did Eastleigh. And when they closed it was truly over, Over There.³⁵

Even as frantic efforts to demobilize proceeded, however, thoughts focused on naval aviation's future. As Craven observed, "We are very much in the dark over here, as to what the future of Naval Aviation is to be in the United States, and know nothing of any plans which may have been evolved." In December 1918 he called on station commanders to offer their frank views on the subject. From Fromentine, Wadleigh Capehart offered a plan to create a Bureau of Naval Aviation (assuming the responsibilities exercised by the Bureaus of Construction and Steam Engineering) and an aeronatics course at Annapolis given to all members of the graduating class. Robert Cabaniss at Moutchic saw aviation as "an integral part of our Navy," conducting a wide range of missions from scouting, spotting, launching torpedoes, bombarding, and fighting. He also called for establishment of "a separate and distinct" U.S. Naval Aviation Corps, bearing the same relation to the Navy as the Marine Corps. At Brest, Henry Cecil called for radical changes, particularly creation of a separate Bureau of Aeronautics, with an officer corps assigned to permanent aviation duty. Finally, Virgil Griffin, who traveled to Europe with the First Aeronautic Detachment and was now closing up the station at St. Trojan, provided a lengthy analysis, particularly the role of the seaplane in forcing submarines to remain submerged in their patrol areas, and the types of aircraft necessary to carry out varied missions. He also offered ideas concerning manufacture of new aircraft types and the staffing of air stations. Views such as these constituted just a small segment of the debate gathering strength within the Department concerning the future of aeronautics.³⁶

In fact, the Navy's wartime experience raised thorny questions that would take years to resolve. What institutional form, for example, should the aeronautic effort take? How would duties be divided with the Army? Were flying boats effective for more than offshore patrolling? Should the Navy design or manufacture its own airplanes? How could aircraft be married to the battleship fleet? What role would aircraft carriers play, both strategically and tactically? What constituted the proper allocation of funds between the various surface, subsurface, and aeronautics components of the fleet?

One other issue generated enormous interest among the aviation establishment in Europe: who would succeed Noble Irwin? In late January, Roosevelt suggested that Craven remain in France until all business there was settled, something Craven opposed based on his two years away from home. Almost immediately, however, he received a telegram announcing that Admiral Benson wished to nominate him to fill Irwin's post. Craven demurred, saying such a job entailed a lengthy tour of shore duty, something prejudicial to his career. He believed that specializing in aviation would "kill his prospects of further advancement in the line of the Navy." Nor did he relish "again taking up the gentle game of running my head into the brick wall which encompasses the narrow lanes of progress in Washington." Despite Craven's objections, Benson nominated him for the post. The following month the two met in Paris for a lengthy discussion. Craven came away reluctant but willing to take on the challenge. "I am not all keen for the job," he told Hutch Cone, but hoped to leave a structure in Washington that would be useful to the service "on which Aviation may build." He recognized that support of senior officers would prove crucial, whereas "alone and unaided I would be powerless." Roosevelt would help, but Craven was forced to admit that after being away so long "I do not know at all what the attitude of the office is with regard to the Navy, let alone Aviation." He would soon find out.[37]

* * *

During nineteen months of war, naval aviation experienced explosive growth, expanding from a tiny complement of 38 aviators to 1,656 trained pilots, with thousands more in various stages of instruction. The total force surpassed 6,700 officers and almost 30,700 ratings, as well as 282 Marine aviation officers and 2,180 enlisted men. As many as 570 aircraft were shipped abroad or acquired overseas. Approximately 1,150 officers and 18,300 enlisted men reached Europe before the Armistice (plus 151 Marine officers, 840 enlisted men) where 38 officers and 86 bluejackets died.[38] The Navy had built 27 stations and facilities, some tiny like the kite balloon outpost at Berehaven, and others sprawling encampments such as the supply and assembly bases at Pauillac and Eastleigh. According to Department statistics, French-based patrol craft escorted 477 convoys (well over 500 if dirigibles are included), flying more than 9,900 hours on patrols. Northern Bombing Group aviators, whether serving with the RAF or in Marine or Navy units, dropped 156,000 pounds of bombs on enemy targets. The single station in Italy at Porti Corsini carried out 745 combat flights. Killingholme personnel conducted 233 patrols, while the Irish stations added 380 more. Shortly after the war, Edwards calculated that naval forces had completed 5,690 war missions and 16,347 training flights, aggregating 549,000 and 242,000 miles, respectively. Adding NBG missions and those at Bolsena, Porto Corsini, and elsewhere, the total likely exceeded 1,000,000 miles.[39]

Construction in Europe had required Herculean efforts. Dungaree-clad crews, often working with simple hand tools, had erected 1,326,000 square feet of barracks space. Lined up end-to-end the buildings would have stretched more than 12 miles. Total volume of all structures could have swallowed 10 Woolworth buildings. Covered storehouses equaled the combined prewar storage space at the New York, Philadelphia, Charleston, and Puget Sound navy yards. Hangars alone covered 40 city blocks, while airplane slipways, laid to a width of 20 feet, would have stretched 3 miles. Laborer erected piers and conducted dredging operations sufficient to berth the superliner *Leviathan*. The quantity of concrete poured equaled one of the pyramids at Giza. Much of it still rests on European soil. Navy ratings established 29 telephone exchanges and strung 1,323 miles of line. They built 28 powerhouses generating enough electricity to power a city of 40,000.

While statistics were relatively easy to compile, the impact of these efforts on the outcome of the war is almost impossible to quantify. In all likelihood naval aviation did not shorten the war in any appreciable way. In fact, the submarine threat was "defeated" before aviation got into the fight. The airmen simply arrived too late, with too little. And when they did enter the fray, their equipment proved too unreliable and their weapons too weak to affect the outcome. As Craven noted during the false Armistice November 8, "It looks as though we would be going strong in a very short time, and, like John Paul Jones, we can say that 'we have not get begun to fight,' when the enemy is preparing to surrender."[40] Nonetheless, aerial efforts in World War I proved decisive, not in determining the outcome of the war but literally by creating Naval Aviation as a concept, a force, and an institution. An entire pantheon of heroes emerged. The war created a dedicated cadre of supporters with a powerful vision for the future. Simply by existing, flyers and their advocates claimed a place at the table. Despite all its difficulties and shortcomings, naval aviation enjoyed enough success to show that it could perform useful, even vital, functions. Newsreels of flying boats patrolling the submarine-infested seas appeared in every theater in America. Aeronautics emerged from the war as a visible presence within the Department and the fleet, and in Congress.

Wartime programs created a substantial infrastructure in the United States, including multiple air stations and a huge inventory of aircraft, as well as thousands of trained flyers and personnel. Initiatives under way or planned at war's end created momentum for future activities. Available technology, though fraught with problems, had advanced exponentially and revealed its possibilities, most visibly in the transatlantic flights of the giant NC flying boats. Primitive aircraft carriers maneuvered with the Grand Fleet and experiments with dive-bombing and aerial torpedoes were under way. In 1922 the same collier *Jupiter* that carried the First Aeronautic Detachment to France became the Navy's first aircraft carrier, the *Langley*. Unbeknown to many, the weapons of Pearl Harbor, Midway, and the "Marianas Turkey Shoot" had been born.

Perhaps more significant, World War I formed the crucible from which emerged the generation of leaders that guided naval aviation through the long decades of the 1920s and 1930s and into the fleet's greatest test in World War II. Most entered the struggle against the Kaiser as very young men. Though many succumbed to the almost continuous series of fatal postwar accidents, those who survived had decades of service still in them with which to work and campaign for their vision. Between 1919 and 1941 these patient and impatient pioneers forged the weapon wielded with such stunning effect a generation later. John Towers, Irwin's right-hand man in 1917–1919, continued his work as a strong voice for aeronautics, ultimately serving as chief of the Bureau of Aeronautics (BuAer) (1939–1942), followed by important commands in the Pacific theater. DeWitt C. "Duke" Ramsey, the young lieutenant who headed the Engineering and Repair section at Paris headquarters, rose to become skipper of the *Saratoga* at the Battle of the Solomons and chief of BuAer (1943–1945). Marine aviator Roy Geiger led the 1st Marine Aircraft Wing at Guadalcanal and finished the war as commander of the Tenth Army at Okinawa. Charles Mason, who stunted his HS-1L over Bordeaux on Bastille Day 1918, commanded *Hornet* at the Battle of Santa Cruz Islands. George Murray skippered *Enterprise* at Midway, while Nolan Kindall conned *Independence* at Okinawa. Marc Mitscher, one of the NC pilots, become one of the Navy's most successful carrier admirals. Other World War I veterans who performed valuable service in their second great conflict included Victor Herbster, Bernard Smith, Kenneth Whiting, Patrick Bellinger, A. C. Read, Eddie McDonnell, Wadleigh Capehart, Virgil Griffin, George Owen, Thomas Murphy, Wiliam Masek, and Frank McCrary.

World War I reserve officers also played significant roles in the continued development of naval aviation. "Ace" David Ingalls served as Assistant Secretary of the Navy for Aeronautics in the Hoover administration and after Pearl Harbor put on his uniform again, filling a series of important administrative posts. Artemus "Di" Gates, one of the first aviators to reach Europe in 1917 and later commanding officer at Dunkirk, returned to government service in 1941 as Assistant Secretary of the Navy for Air, a post he held throughout the war. During those turbulent years he frequently collaborated with fellow Yalie Robert Lovett, now Assistant Secretary of War for Air. Many of the old "Yale Gang" served again, both in uniform and on the civilian side. In fact, hundreds of World War I reserve officers returned to the fleet, a little grayer and less lean but no less patriotic and committed to aviation.

In some ways, naval aviation fought its greatest battle after the shooting stopped. Huge wartime budgets were slashed, contracts canceled, construction projects abandoned, and stations decommissioned. Proposed outlays declined from an estimated $225 million for fiscal 1920 to a much reduced $86 million proposal from Irwin's office, to barely $25 million in the actual appropriation. The majority of officers and enlisted men soon hung up their uniforms. Within the Department, debate raged over the proper organizational structure with which to accommodate aeronautics and the priorities accorded such activities, particularly in an environment that pitted battleship against submarine against aviation for every scarce dollar. Despite a vocal chorus of flying proponents, ranging from Sims, Mayo, and Roosevelt to Towers, Craven, Mustin, Westervelt, Hunsaker, Maxfield, Bellinger and Whiting, many in the command hierarchy remained unconvinced, most obviously outgoing Chief of Naval Operations Benson and Adm. Josiah McKean. Under a reorganization plan implemented by Benson in the summer of 1919, the new Director of Naval Aviation (Craven) watched his role reduced to head of an almost powerless section within the Planning Division in the Office of Naval Operations. The coordinated functions exercised by Irwin's office during the war were now redistributed among the various Bureaus or other sections of the Planning Division.[41]

As if loud calls for retrenchment and internal conflict were not enough, naval aviation also faced a direct and bitter assault from supporters of an independent air force like Asst. Secretary of War Benedict Crowell, Billy Mitchell, and Benjamin Foulois, congressional enemies such as Fiorello LaGuardia, and many newspaper editors. As early as November 22, 1918, an old friend of Craven's at the Bureau of Ordnance claimed that General W. L. Kenly, Director of Military Aeronautics, "was formulating a plan whereby a separate and distinct air force would be formed." Daniels was "standing with the Navy," but "it is all being done in the dark and we can never tell when the blow will fall." Returning from Europe in February 1919, Mitchell bombarded the ship's company with calls to merge army and navy aviation forces. In numerous instances, including postwar testimony before various boards and committees and in published reports, antagonists revisited the old controversies. Furious attacks by Army partisans yielded at least one benefit for naval aviation, however, inspiring the fleet to close ranks around its flyers. After a tortuous journey through the public arena, aided in part by the support of President Harding, Navy Secretary Denby, and Rep. Frederick Hicks, Congress on July 12, 1921, enacted legislation creating the Bureau of Aeronautics within the Navy Department. For naval aviation, whatever controversies lay in the future, there would be no turning back. The aerial battle first launched against the U-boat in April 1917 had been won.[42]

APPENDIX A Station Summary

Station	Flight Operations Commenced	Aircraft on hand 11-11-1918	# Flights	Miles Patrolled	# Officers	# Men	Date Demobilized	Disposition
Brest	8-1-1918	30 Seaplanes	211	7,355	21	814	2-15-1919	To French Navy
Fromentine	8-9-1918	14 Seaplanes	335	38,009	31	372	1-29-1919	Evacuated
Arcachon	10-1-1918	7 Seaplanes	106	8,727	26	318	1-1-1919	Dept. of the Seine
L'Aber Vrach	7-23-1918	19 Seaplanes	355	29,302	41	458	1-22-1919	Evacuated
Ile Tudy	3-7-1918	21 Seaplanes	1,238	104,877	22	363	1-25-1919	Evacuated
Le Croisic	11-18-1917	16 Seaplanes	1,045	113,324	24	337	1-28-1919	To French Navy
St. Trojan	7-3-1918	13 Seaplanes	246	19,533	26	343	1-19-1919	Dept. of the Seine
Tréguier	9-30-1918	8 Seaplanes	30	1,380	16	266	1-19-1919	To French Navy
Dunkerque	3-18-1918	12 Seaplanes	491	45,630	7	205	1-2-1919	To CRB
Paimboeuf	3-5-1918	3 Dirigibles	257	48,630	30	477	1-26-1919	To French Navy
Guipavas	No Ops	1 Dirigible			15	396	1-13-1919	Evacuated
Gujan	No Ops				10	240	1-15-1919	Evacuated
Brest (KB)		22 KBs			see above			
La Trinité		4 KBs			18	59	2-5-1919	Evacuated
La Pallice		4 KBs			5	150	1-5-1919	To U.S. Army
Paullac		81 mixed	372	15,085	133	4,071	2-1-1919	To U.S. Army
Moutchic	9-30-1918	24 Seaplanes	10,807	242,320	57	493	12-31-1918	To French Army
Queenstown	9-3-1918	28 Seaplanes	64	11,568	72	1,426	4-10-1919	
Lough Foyle	9-18-1918	7 Seaplanes	41	6,000	20	432	2-22-1919	
Wexford	9-25-1918	5 Seaplanes	98	19,135	22	405	2-15-1919	
Whiddy Island	5-21-1918	3 Seaplanes	25	3,870	18	400	1-29-1919	
C'townbere	7-25-1918	16 KBs			12	91	2-12-1919	To RAF
Porto Corsini	2-20-1918	17 seaplanes	745		27	360	12-31-1918	To Italian Govt.
Lake Bolsena	2-19-1918	8 Seaplanes	5,540		11	69	1-2-1919	Evacuated
Killingholme	9-24-1918	46 Seaplanes	404	92,797	91	1,324	1-6-1919	To RAF
Eastleigh	7-20-1918	41 Aeroplanes			70	1,928	4-10-1919	Evacuated
NBG		25 Aeroplanes			294	2,154	2-6-1919	Evacuated

KB = Kite Balloon; RAF = Royal Air Force; NBG = Northern Bombing Group; CRB = Committee for Relief in Belgium

APPENDIX B

Principal Aircraft Types Used by Naval Aviation Forces in Europe 1917–1918

L = Length
MWS = Maximum Wing Span
MW = Maximum Weight
MS = Maximum Speed
PP = Powerplant
AR = Armament

FBA (Franco-British Aviation) Type H: A French reconnaissance flying boat used at NAS Porto Corsini. L 33' 2"; MWS 47' 7"; MW 3,218 lbs; MS 90 mph; PP 180 hp Hispano-Suiza; AR one Lewis gun, 440-lbs bombs. Many Americans trained at Moutchic and Lac Hourtin on the earlier FBA Type A powered by a 130 hp Clerget rotary motor.

Donnet-Denhaut 8: A French reconnaissance/bomber flying boat. The Navy acquired 58 of all types. Used at NAS Dunkirk, Ile Tudy, Moutchic. L 35' 5"; MWS 53' 7"; MW 3,860 lbs; MS 72 mph; PP 200 hp Hispano-Suiza; AR two Lewis Guns, two 75-lb bombs.

Levy-LePen HB-2: A French reconnaissance/bomber flying boat, used at NAS St. Trojan and Le Croisic. Navy purchased 12. L 40' 8"; MWS 60' 8"; MW 5,181 lbs; MS 93 mph; PP 280 hp Renault; AR one Lewis gun, four 75-lb bombs.

Tellier T-3: A French reconnaissance/bomber flying boat, introduced 1917. The Navy ordered 33. Used at NAS Le Croisic, Moutchic. L 38' 10"; MWS 51' 2"; MW 3,745 lbs; MS 75 mph; PP 200 hp Hispano-Suiza; AR two 75-lb bombs.

Hanriot-Dupont HD.2: A French single-place pontoon fighter, the seagoing version of the HD.1. Navy ordered 26. Used at NAS Dunkirk. L 19' 8"; WS 28" 6"; MW 1,520 lbs; MS 115 mph; PP 130 hp Clerget; AR two Vickers guns.

Macchi M.5: A speedy, maneuverable, single-seat, flying boat fighter introduced in autumn 1917 and used at Bolsena and NAS Porto Corsini. Developed by Nieuport-Macchi company of Varese. L 26' 2"; MWS 39' ½" MW 2,266 lbs; MS 118 mph; PP 160 hp Isotta-Fraschini; AR two Vickers guns.

Macchi M.8: a relatively small, two-place, reconnaissance/bomber flying boat introduced in 1917, somewhat larger version of M.5. Used at NAS Porto Corsini. L 29' 7"; MWS 45' 5"; MW 3,153 lbs; MS 104 mph; PP 160 hp Isotta-Fraschini; AR one Vickers gun, four 110-lb bombs.

Curtiss HS-1/2L: The Curtiss HS type was a smaller, single-engine patrol flying boat. Used at NAS L'Aber Vrach, Ile Tudy, Tréguier, Arcachon, and elsewhere. L 39'; MWS 74' ½"; MW 6,432 lbs; MS 82.5 mph; PP 360 hp Liberty; AR one Lewis gun, two 230-lb bombs.

Curtiss H-16 : Used at NAS Lough Foyle, Queenstown, Wexford, Whiddy Island, Killingholme. L 46' 1"; MWS 95'; MW 10, 900 lbs; MS 95 mph; PP two 400 Liberty; AR five Lewis guns, 460-lb bombs.

F2A: A British-developed evolution of the Curtiss "America" type flying boat used extensively over the North Sea. Used at NAS Killingholme. L 46' 3"; MWS 95' 7 ½"; MW 10,978 lbs; MS 95 mph; PP two 345 hp Rolls-Royce Eagle VIII; AR four or five machine guns, 460 lb bombs.

Short 320: A two-place reconnaissance/bomber floatplane used at NAS Killingholme. L 49' 5"; MWS 75'; MW 7,014 lbs; MS 72.5 mph; PP 320 hp Sunbeam.

Caproni Ca.5/Ca.44/Ca 600: An Italian, twin-fuselage heavy bomber. The Navy ordered 20. L 41' 2"; MWS 76' 10"; MW 12,350 lbs; MS 103 mph; PP three 200 hp Fiat AR; two machine guns.

DH-4: Reconaissance/day bomber, manufactured in United States, 51 transferred from Army to Navy for use by NBG. L 30' 8"; MWS 43' 4"; MW 3,472 lbs; MS 143 mph; PP 400 hp Liberty; AR four Vickers/Lewis Guns, 460 lb bombs.

D.H. 9a: British reconnaissance/day bomber; 54 transferred from RAF to U.S. Navy for use by NBG. L 30' 3"; MWS 45' 11"; MW 4,645 lbs; MS 123 mph; PP 400 hp Liberty; AR two/three guns, 460–660 lb bombs.

NOTES

ABBREVIATIONS

FDRPLM Franklin D. Roosevelt Presidential Library and Museum (Hyde Park)
IF   David Ingalls and Louise Harkness Ingalls Foundation (Shaker Heights)
LC   Library of Congress (Washington, D.C.)
MCHC   Marine Corps Historical Center (Washington, D. C.)
MHS   Massachusetts Historical Society (Boston)
NA   National Archives (Washington, D.C.)
NAM   Emil Buehler Library, Naval Aviation Museum (Pensacola)
NAUK   National Archives United Kingdom (Kew)
NHHC   Naval History and Heritage Command (Washington, D.C.)
SHM   Service Historique de la Marine (Paris)
YA   Yale University Archives (New Haven)

INTRODUCTION

1. This episode is recounted in Paine, *The First Yale Unit*, II, 306–8.
2. Edwards, "The U. S. Naval Airforce in Action, 1917–1918," 1863–64.

CHAPTER 1. THE FIRST AERONAUTIC DETACHMENT

1. Lord, "The History of Naval Aviation, 1898–1939," 303; also Memorandum, May 23, 1917, box 155, GU, RG 45.
2. Sims to OpNav, July 3, 1917, in Lord, "The History of Naval Aviation, 1898–1939," 305.
3. Lord, "The History of Naval Aviation, 1898–1939," 302; Whiting to Sims, "History of the First Aeronautic Detachment," November 29, 1918, box 910, ZGU, RG 45.
4. Turnbull and Lord, *History of United States Naval Aviation*, 44; Reynolds, *Admiral John H. Towers*, 22–23; *Killingholme Yearbook*, 3–5; Shirley, "Wartime Memoirs of John Jay Schieffelin," 113–14; Still, *Crisis at Sea*, 461.
5. Palmer to Whiting, May 10, 1917, and Palmer to Blanpré, May 12, 1917, both SS/Ga-144, SHM; also Turnbull and Lord, *History of United States Naval Aviation*,119.
6. O'Neal, "First to Fall"; also Whistler, "The Making of a Dunkirk Aviator"; Sheely, ed., *Sailor of the Air,* passim; Cline in Woolbridge, *The Golden Age Remembered*, 5–6.
7. Cline in Woolbridge, *The Golden Age Remembered*, 6; O'Neal, "First to Fall," 39; Sheely, *Sailor of the Air*, 18–19.
8. Cline in Woolbridge, *The Golden Age Remembered*, 6; Whistler, "The Making of a

Dunkirk Aviator," 340–51; Whiting, "First Aeronautic Detachment," box 910, ZGU, RG 45; Detachment members listed in SS/Ga-145, SHM.

9. Sheely, *Sailor of the Air,* 26–28; Whistler, "The Making of a Dunkirk Aviator," 348.

10. Sheely, *Sailor of the Air,* 26; Whiting, "First Aeronautic Detachment"; and Dichman, "Historical Memorandum," December 3, 1918 (written aboard USS *Conyngham*), both box 910, ZGU, RG 45.

11. Whistler, "The Making of a Dunkirk Aviator," 349.

12. Whiting, "First Aeronautic Detachment," Dichman, "Historical Memorandum," and V. C. Griffin, "Memorandum of Duties," c. Dec 1918, all box 910, ZGU, RG 45; Craven, "History of U. S. Naval Aviation, Foreign Service, French Unit 1917–1918," 7–8, box 912, ZGU, RG 45.

13. Still, *Crisis at Sea,* 40.

14. Whiting to Secretary of the Navy, July 20, 1917; Whiting, "First Aeronautic Detachment," and Whiting to Sims, November 29, 1918, all box 910, ZGU, RG 45; Sprague, "Flying Gobs," 14–15; and Whistler, "The Making of a Dunkirk Aviator," 351.

15. Sheely, *Sailor of the Air,* 33–36.

16. Ibid., 31–36; Whistler, "The Making of a Dunkirk Aviator," 350–51.

17. Whiting, "First Aeronautic Detachment," December 2, 1918, box 910, ZGU, RG 45.

18. Ministry of Marine "Circulaire," June 16, 1917, SS/Ga-146, SHM.

19. Lord, "The History of Naval Aviation, 1898–1939," 347–49; Initial work would be arranged by the Travaux Hydraulique, the engineering arm of the Ministry of Marine; see also French Memo of June 15, 1917, box 461, PA, RG 45.

20. Lord, "The History of Naval Aviation, 1898–1939," 350; Edwards, "The U.S. Naval Air Force in Action," 1873–74.

21. Whiting to Sims, "First Aeronautic Detachment," box 910, ZGU, RG 45.

22. Lord, "The History of Naval Aviation, 1898–1939," 55–56.

23. Several descriptions of Whiting's visit exist, including a handwritten draft on stationery of the Hotel Meurice, 228 Rue de Rivoli, box 144, GN, RG 45.

24. The geographic relationship of many of the sites visited by Whiting is depicted on a detailed, hand-drawn map "Le Croisic a Fromentine" that pinpoints important locations like Le Croisic, St. Nazaire, Paimboeuf, Fromentine, and Ile d'Yeu, SS/Ga-144, SHM.

25. Capitaine De Laborde filed his report on the Whiting inspection trip with the Ministry of Marine July 4, 1917, SS/Ga-147, SHM.

26. "Proces Verbal de la Conference tenue au Ministre de la Marine 8 Juillet 1917," SS/Ga-144, SHM. The Bolling Commission, led by Maj. Raynal Bolling, was a group of Army and Navy officers selected by the Aircraft Production Board to visit Europe "to study aircraft design and production facilities," and prepare to purchase aircraft, allocate raw materials, and arrange for training. See Hudson, *Hostile Skies,* 13.

27. Conger to McGowan, June 18, 1917, box 2, Papers as Assistant Secretary of the Navy, 1913–1920, FDRPLM; some materials related to Sayles's activities in box 132, GA-1, RG 45.

28. Jackson to BuNav, July 1917, SS/Ga-144, SHM; Jackson to SecNav and Sims to Benson, August 4, 1917, both in Lord, "The History of Naval Aviation, 1898–1939," 351–52.

29. Whiting to Jackson, August 10, 1917, box 461, PA, RG 45; "Rapport sur la mission a

Brest de Lieutenant de Vaisseau Whiting pour le choix d'un terrain center d'hydroavions," August 17, 1917, SS/Ga-146, SHM.

30. Whiting to SecNav, July 20, 1917, box 910, ZGU, RG 45.

31. Whiting to SecNav, August 4, 1917, ibid.

32. Cable, August 26, 1917, box 461, ibid; Lord, "The History of Naval Aviation, 1898–1939," 369. Sims called for as much aviation as "your constructional and training facilities permit."

33. Whiting to Navy Department, September 16, 1918, box 910, ZGU, RG 45.

34. Jackson's (and Whiting's July 20) cables precipitated a rapid response not to commit to anything without specific authorization. At this point Sims knew enough of what was going on to opine that the proposed French base program was too large; see also Still, *Crisis at Sea*, 50–52.

35. Cone to Sims, May 29, 1917, Sims Papers, LC; Still, *Crisis at Sea*, 41–42; Turnbull and Lord, *History of United States Naval Aviation*, 122.

36. Lord, "The History of Naval Aviation, 1898–1939," 102.

37. Ibid., 372.

38. All Lord, "The History of Naval Aviation, 1898–1939," 371–72; Daniels to Sims, September 28, 1918, Sims Papers, LC; Still, *Crisis at Sea*, 50–52.

39. The Navy Department approved establishment of 11 bases on September 16, 1917; Sims to Cone, September 27, 1917, Sims Papers, LC; Sims to Cone, and Whiting to U. S. Navy Aeronautic Detachment No. 1, both October 24, 1917, both SS/Ga-144, SHM.

40. Cline in Woolbridge, *The Golden Age Remembered*, 7–8; *Extracts from the Letters of George Clark Moseley*, 61; Whistler, "The Making of a Dunkirk Aviator," 352.

41. For the story of the First Yale Unit see Paine, *The First Yale Unit*; Wortman, *The Millionaires' Unit*; and Davison, "The First Yale Unit," 265–69; see also Wellesley Laude-Browne Papers, NAM, and the Davison Papers, YA.

42. O'Neal, "First to Fall," 40; Whiting, "History of the First Aeronautic Detachment"; and Dichman, "Historical Memorandum," both box 910, ZGU, RG 45; *Extracts from the Letters of George Clark Moseley*, 60–64; Whistler, "The Making of a Dunkirk Aviator," 353.

43. Schedule outlined in Manley to Mother, July 18, 1917, in O'Neal, "First to Fall," 40; See Shirley, ed., "Wartime Memoirs," 105; Cline in Woolbridge, *The Golden Age Remembered*, 8–11; Paine, *The First Yale Unit*, II, 5–11; *Extracts from the Letters of George Clark Moseley*, 60–81.

44. Report of Barrett's death, July 8, 1917, SS/Ga-146, SHM; Board of Inquest Report, August 21, 1917, re: death of George Manley, box 910, ZGU, RG 45; Whistler, "The Making of a Dunkirk Aviator," 353. A detailed account of this accident contained in O'Neal's authoritative "First to Fall," 40–45.

45. David Ingalls's papers contain a detailed description of the RFC flight program at Ayr, Scotland, and emphasize the fatal link between limited training and high accident rates, IF; Report by Lieutenant Dichman, October 22, 1917, claimed FAD pilots completed numerous flights in quarter ending September 30; papers related to those released from flight training for various causes, SS/Ga-146, SHM; especially J. D. Jernigan Flight Log, NAM.

46. *Extracts from the Letters of George Clark Moseley*, 56, 60–61.

47. Griffin, "Memorandum of Duties," box 910, ZGU, RG 45.

48. Sheely, *Sailor of the Air*, 41–44, 47–51.

49. Craven, "History of U. S. Naval Aviation, French Unit," 297–313, box 912, ZGU, RG 45; also John Callan "Diary," Callan Papers, LC.

50. Shirley, "John Lansing Callan," 180–185.

51. Historical overview, statistical records, organizational material found in box 962, ZPA and boxes 466–468, PA, RG 45. See also Callan "Diary," Callan Papers, LC.

52. Callan to Whiting, July 26, 1917, discussing price gouging by French for land, ibid. There is some disagreement about whether these three—Reichelt, Stanley, and Gar(d)ner—were with Callan July 16 or arrived two weeks later.

53. Sheely, *Sailor of the Air*, August to October 1917, *passim*. A letter to Paymaster Conger, October 19, 1917, counted 126 men at Moutchic, 12 at Cazaux, 26 at St. Raphael, and 19 at Hourtin; for French reports on FAD activities at Cazaux, Tours, St. Raphael, and Hourtin, see SS/Ga-146, SHM.

54. Sheely, *Sailor of the Air*, 67–69; Rossano, ed., *The Price of Honor*, 45–47; Paine, *The First Yale Unit*, II, 10–11.

55. The spatial and transportation relationship between these various sites is detailed on a hand-drawn map of the Gironde region of August 22, 1918, SS/Ga-149, SHM; Sheely, *Sailor of the Air*, 55–61. A near contemporary description of the French school at Cazaux in Roseler, O'Neal, and Bailey, eds. "The Observer, Part I," 14–16.

56. Rossano, *The Price of Honor*, 45, 47.

57. A later schematic of the facilities at Hourtin, August 22, 1918, in SS/Ga-149, SHM; Rossano, *The Price of Honor*, 45–47; Gates to Mrs. Davison, September 16, 1917, Davison Papers, YA; David Ingalls spent much time at Hourtin playing bridge and trying to keep warm. See Ingalls Diary, October 15–November 13, 1917, IF. Paine, *The First Yale Unit*, II, 13; James O'Brien at Hourtin in Whistler, "The Making of a Dunkirk Aviator," 357; Jernigan Flight Log Book, NAM; also Whiting to BuNav re: flying hours at Hourtin, October 16, 1917, box 155, GU, RG 45.

58. Gates to Davison, September 23 and October 1 and 5, 1917; also Farwell to Davison, November 4, 1917, all Davison Papers, YA; Paine, *The First Yale Unit*, II, 21–23; Cline in Woolbridge, *The Golden Age Remembered*, 12–14; also Jernigan Flight Log Book, NAM; and Arthur, *Contact!* 44.

59. Jorgenson remained executive officer until the end of the war. Undated ms. organizational chart and Dichman to Callan, December 9, 1917, both Callan Papers, LC.

60. Turnbull and Lord, *History of United States Naval Aviation*, 120.

CHAPTER 2. PROGRESS REPORT: SEPTEMBER 1917–MARCH 1918

1. Cone to Irwin, October 6, 1917, box 2, Papers as Assistant Secretary of the Navy, 1913–1920, FDRPLM; Cone to Irwin, November 16, 1917, Cohen Collection, NHHC; Cone lived in the Passy district, sharing quarters with Tom Craven and Bobby Pollock. Craven to Cone, September 12, 1918, Craven Papers, LC.

2. Many years later Mrs. Mary McCrary said of her husband, "He had an innate shyness, and gave credit to many others for accomplishments of his own," quoted in Arthur, *Contact!* 53.

3. Public Works officers detailed from Bureau of Yards and Docks, accompanied by Civil Engineer Billings, in Lord, "The History of Naval Aviation, 1898–1939," 394; Cone, Office Memorandum #1, SS/Ga-144, SHM.

4. Cone, Office Memorandum #2, December 30, 1917, SS/Ga-144, SHM.

5. Lighters were specially designed, towed craft used to ferry and launch large flying boats assigned to carry out long-range bombing/reconnaissance missions.

6. Cone to Irwin, November 16, 1917, and January 3, 1918, in Lord, "The History of Naval Aviation, 1898–1939," 426.

7. Letter to Cone, November 17, 1917, in Craven, "History of U. S. Naval Aviation, French Unit," 42–44, box 912, ZGU, RG 45.

8. Bolling at that time was head of the Joint Army and Navy Aircraft Committee in Paris. The arrival of Benjamin Foulois ended the "perfect harmony"; see Cone to Sims, November 22, 1917, box 132, GA-1, RG 45.

9. Edwards to Cone, April 8 and 22, 1918, box 133, GA-2, RG 45.

10. Progress Report, USNAFFS, March 15, 1918, box 131, GA-1, RG 45.

11. Craven, "History of U. S. Naval Aviation, French Unit," 47–51, box 912, ZGU, RG 45; Cone to Craven, January 4, 1918, Craven Papers, LC; Cone to Irwin, January 22, 1918, in Lord, "The History of Naval Aviation, 1898–1939," 427.

12. Craven, "History of U. S. Naval Aviation, French Unit," 35–51, box 912, ZGU, RG 45; Progress Report, USNAFFS, March 15, 1918, box 131, GA-1, RG 45; Paris Headquarters Log begun November 1917 recorded personnel movement and command actions and decisions, box 131, GA-1, RG 45.

13. Paris Headquarters Log, June 17 and 18, 1918, box 131, GA-1, RG 45.

14. Minutes of Paris/London Executive Committee sessions in box 2, Aviation Section Reports 1918–1919 (Entry 36), RG 72.

15. Before departing they secured site plans of the proposed locations. See Cone to Minister of Marine, November 25, 1917, and January 8, 1918, and McCrary to Minister of Marine, January 9, 1918, all SS/Ga-144, SHM; Weekly Report, January 26, 1918, announces French approval of U.S. stations at Fromentine and L'Aber Vrach, box 132, GA-1, RG 45; Smith to Guggenheim, January 31, 1918, SS/Ga-145, SHM.

16. Callan, Report, March 1, 1918, box 131, GA-1, RG 45.

17. Reynolds, *Admiral John H. Towers*, 106.

18. Klachko and Trask, *Admiral William Shepherd Benson*, 87 ff., 111–112; Lord, "The History of Naval Aviation, 1898–1939," 393; Craven to Ramsey, July 21 and October 1, 1918, box 2, Records of Naval Forces Operating in European Waters, Aviation Section (Entry 34), RG 72.

19. Ingalls to Mother, March 27, 1918, IF; Rossano, *The Price of Honor*, 149; Cable, March 30, 1918, box 156, GU file, RG 45; *Extracts from the Letters of George Clark Moseley*, 160–161.

20. Weekly Reports, March 30 and April 6, 1918, and ff., box 132, GA-1, RG 45; Cone to Sims April 18, 1918, Sims to Benson, June 14, 1918, both Sims Papers, LC.

CHAPTER 3. UNDER THE GUN: NAS DUNKIRK, 1917–1918

1. Dunkirk flyers' primary opponents were pilots from Seeflugstation I based in Zeebrugge and Seeflugstation II at Ostend, operating Friedrichshafen F.33, Brandenburg W.12, and W.29 aircraft.

2. Memo, Chevalier to Cone, February 21, 1918, says that Chevalier accompanied Whiting, box 460, PA, RG 45.

3. "Draft History of U S Naval Aviation in France: June 5, 1917 to November 1, 1918,"

box 910, ZGU; Johnson to Van der Veer, October 12, 1917, box 460, PA, both RG 45. For base layout, "General Outline of U.S.N.A.S. Dunkirk, France," SS/Ga-146, SHM.

4. German document, October 20, 1917, "Part of our torpedo boat forces attacked D. on night of October 18, 1917, fired 250 shells against harbor and fortress, English monitor damaged with three torpedo hits," and Whiting to Cone, December 10, 1917; Weekly Report, November 17, 1917, states that RNAS St. Pol "practically wiped out by German bombs and gunfire," all box 461, PA, RG 45; Dunkirk descriptions in Paine, *The First Yale Unit*, II, 141.

5. These and following quotes from Alonzo Hildreth, "Over There," 56–63; Weekly Report, January 22, 1918, box 461, PA, RG 45.

6. A December 17, 1917, report shows four hangars measuring 20 × 28 meters and one 26 × 28 meters completed, in Dunkirk file, SS/Ga-147, SHM; Chevalier to Cone, December 15, 1917, box 460, and Weekly Report, 19 January 1918, box 461, both PA, RG 45.

7. Hildreth, "Over There," 22–23; Gates to Davison, January 1, 1918, Davison Papers, YA.

8. Cunningham Diary, December 25–29, 1917, Marine Corps Historical Center.

9. Hildreth, "Over There," 60; Gates to Davison, January 18, 1918, Davison Papers, YA.

10. *Extracts from the Letters of George Clark Moseley*, 140.

11. Entries in Hildreth diary ("Over There") for December/January are replete with reports of cold, rain, wind, and snow; Chevalier, Weekly Reports, January 14 and 26, 1918, box 461, PA, RG 45; Gates to Davison, January 27, 1918, Davison Papers, YA.

12. Read quoted in Arthur, *Contact!* 48; Hildreth, "Over There," 61; also Whistler, "The Making of a Dunkirk Aviator," II, 11.

13. Hildreth, "Over There," 61; Gates to Davison, March 18, 1918, Davison Papers, YA.

14. Dunkirk Daily Reports, box 460. Student aviators were enlisted pilots without commissions. They were no more or less experienced than commissioned flyers. Weekly Report of April 20 listed one Boatswain's Mate 1c and four Quartermaster's Mates 1c readying for commissioning exams, box 461, both PA, RG 45.

15. Ingalls to Father, March 22, 1918, IF; *Extracts from the Letters of George Clark Moseley*, 154–57.

16. Hildreth, "Over There," 61; Cone to Base Commanders, March 30, 1918, box 458, PA, RG 45. In Britain, Ens. Harold Wilcox wrote, "England is just about whipped and are stalling all they can until our troops get over.... News from the front worse, and Channel ports threatened. Personnel at Dunkirk ordered to stand by to run," in Knapp, "Flying Boats," 128.

17. Gates to Davison, March 24, 1918, Davison Papers, YA; Sheely, *Sailor of the Air*, 114–17; Hildreth, "Over There," 61. The great "Loegenboom" gun, officially Batterie Pommern, situated 26 miles east of Dunkerque, became operational May 1917. It was located on the edge of the Bois de Leugenboom, hence the name. It fired shells weighing 700–900 kg.

18. *Extracts from the Letters of George Clark Moseley*, 157–66; Rossano, *The Price of Honor*, 156–57; Hildreth, "Over There," 62.

19. *Extracts from the Letters of George Clark Moseley*, 160–61; Gates to Davison, April 19, 1918, Davison Papers, YA.

20. Rossano, *The Price of Honor*, 130–31; Ingalls, Diary, March 28, 1918, IF; Gates to Davison, April 3 and 15, 1918, Davison Papers, YA.

21. Rossano, *The Price of Honor*, 130–31.

22. Sheely, *Sailor of the Air*, 119.

23. Ingalls Diary, March 31–April 20, and Ingalls to Father, April 11 and 20, 1918, all IF; also Rossano, *The Price of Honor*, 132, 139.

24. Abbatiello, *Anti-Submarine Warfare*, 43; Paine, *The First Yale Unit*, II, 109–15; Christiansen, "Battle Flights over the Channel," 230–32.

25. Sheely, *Soldier of the Air*, 116–17; Daily report of April 20 lists Ingalls, Smith, Mac Leish, Gates, Sheely, and Lowry returning from duty with RAF, box 461, PA, RG 45; Gates to Davison, April 19, 1918, Davison Papers, YA; Lovett to Brown, April 19, 1918, from a family collection privately held by Adele (Lovett) Brown.

26. *Extracts from the Letters of George Clark Moseley*, 166–68; Rossano, *The Price of Honor*, 156–57; Weekly Report, May 25, 1918, box 461, PA, RG 45.

27. *Extracts from the Letters of George Clark Moseley*, 157–59; also Paine, *The First Yale Unit*, II, 147.

28. Ganster quoted in Whistler, "The Making of a Dunkirk Aviator," II, 11; Ingalls Diary, May 20, 1918, IF; Rossano, *The Price of Honor*, 155–156; Ganster and Marshburn's deaths described in Whistler, "The Making of a Dunkirk Aviator," II, 11–13. Weekly Report, May 25, box 461, PA, RG 45. The homeowner entered a postwar claim for reimbursement for damages to the house and chimney.

29. "DeCernea had the style and bearing of a medieval knight," Shirley, "Wartime Memoirs of John Jay Schlieffen," 118; (Gates) to Cone, August 15, 1918, box 461, PA, RG 45; Rossano, *The Price of Honor*, 161–62

30. *Extracts from the Letters of George Clark Moseley*, 163; Hildreth, "Over There," 58.

31. This and following incidents from Memo, Read to Hanrahan, November 23, 1918, box 144, GN; Observers Reports August 11, 1918; Intelligence Officer to Gates, August 13, both box 461, PA, all RG 45; Shirley, "Wartime Memoirs of John Jay Schieffelin," 118; unsigned After Action Report, August 13, and Intelligence Officer to Gates, August 14, 1918, both box 461, PA, RG 45; Whistler, "The Making of a Dunkirk Aviator," II, 16.

32. Ingalls, Diary, May 6, 1918, IF; Confidential Bulletin #10, July 15, 1918, box 156, GU; Progress Report, July 15, 1918, box 131, GA-1; Observers Report, August 22, 1918, box 461, PA, all RG 45.

33. Weekly Report, July 20, 1918, and Gates to Cone, July 8 and 10, 1918, both box 461, PA, RG 45; Vogt was later reported captured. A detailed account in Whistler, "The Making of a Dunkirk Aviator," II, 13–14, and Hildreth, "Over There," 62–63.

34. Gates to Davison, July 14, 1918, Davison Papers, YA; Read to Hanrahan, November 23, 1918, box 144, GN, RG 45; Hildreth, "Over There," 63; Whistler, "The Making of a Dunkirk Aviator," II, 13; Rossano, *The Price of Honor*, 156–57.

35. Cone to Sims, May 11, 1918, box 131, GA-1; Gates to Hanrahan, August 5, 1918; Smith to Cone, August 9, 1918, both box 461, PA, all RG 45.

36. Hanrahan to Cone, August 12, 1918, box 461, PA, RG 45.

37. Cone to Edwards, August 13, 1918, and Sims to Cone, August 25, 1918, both ibid. The Department authorized abandonment on September 12, Lord, "The History of Naval Aviation, 1898–1939," 528. Sims possibly confused the Curtiss HA "Dunkirk Fighter" with

the Curtiss CB "Liberty Battler." It might also be a reference to the DH-4, also known as the "Liberty Fighter"; also OpNav to Sims, September 12, 1918, box 446, Dispatches to/from Naval Forces Operating in European Waters (Entry 54), RG 72.

38. Read to Hanrahan, November 23, 1918, box 144, GN, RG 45.

39. Whistler, "The Making of a Dunkirk Aviator," II, 22.

40. *Extracts from the Letters of George Clark Moseley*, 204–16.

41. *Extracts from the Letters of George Clark Moseley*, 210–11; Weekly Reports, October 12 and 25, 1918, and Hanrahan to Sims, October 24 and 26, 1918, box 144, GN; Confidential Bulletin #22, October 19, 1918, box 156, GU, and Intelligence Officer Report, October 25, 1918, box 461, PA, all RG 45; Paine, *The First Yale Unit*, II, 313–49.

42. Hanrahan to Sims, October 24, 1918, box 144, GN, RG 45; Rossano, *The Price of Honor*, 227–32.

43. Lynch in Paine, *The First Yale Unit*, II, 302; the station was officially demobilized on January 1, 1919; "History of U.S. Naval Air Station, Dunkirk," box 961, ZPA, RG 45.

CHAPTER 4. THE FRENCH COASTAL UNIT

1. Jackson to CNO, July 31, 1917, said most urgent need was protection of American transports and commerce, quoted in Still, *Crisis at Sea*, 121. Figures do not include personnel assigned to NAS Dunkirk, Northern Bombing Group, or headquarters.

2. McCrary et al. to Cone, Inspection Report, December 17, 1917, box 131, GA-1, RG 45.

3. Cone (Conger) to OPNAV via Sims, March 26, 1918, ibid.

4. Progress Report, USNAFFS, July 15, 1918, ibid.; Maxfield to Cone, July 2, 1918, box 2, Records of Naval forces Operating in European Waters, Aviation Section (Entry 34), RG 72.

5. Ellington, "Naval Aviation Activities during the World War," 40, box 910, ZGU, RG 45.

6. Quarterly Progress Report, USNAFFS, September 30, 1918, box 131, GA-1, RG 45.

7. Public Works Officer for French coastal stations to Wilson, October 22, 1918; Cone to Minister of Marine, September 6, 1918; Wilson to Smith, September 21, 1918, and Smith to Minister of Marine, September 23, 1918, all SS/Ga-146, SHM.

8. Craven to Cone, September 21, 1918, Craven Papers, LC; Progress Report, October 1, 1918, to November 11, 1918, box 131, GA-1, RG 45.

9. McIlwaine replaced Robert Lovett at Moutchic November 13, 1917. See Paine, *The First Yale Unit*, II, 25–26; "History of U. S. Naval Air Station, Moutchic-Lacanau," box 962, ZPA, RG 45; Craven, "History of U. S. Naval Aviation, French Unit," 297–313, box 912, ZGU, RG 45.

10. Cone to Minister of Marine, December 31, 1917, requested additional Bessaneau hangar; another letter January 28, 1918, discusses construction of a hospital building at Moutchic, both SS/Ga-147, SHM. Moutchic daily/flight reports in boxes 467–468, PA, RG 45; Griffin to Lt. de Vaisseau l'Escaille, November 28, 1917, SS/Ga-147, SHM.

11. *Extracts from the Letters of George Clark Moseley*, 147–54; Shirley, "Wartime Memoirs of John Jay Schieffelin," 103.

12. See "Proposed Bombing Course–Moutchic," box 3, Records of USNAFFS, Belgian Bombing to France, Misc. (Entry 35), RG 72; also "History of School at Moutchic," March 6, 1918, box 468, PA, and "Schedule of Training at U.S. Naval Gunnery and Bomb-

ing School, Moutchic-Lacanau," box 914, ZGU, both RG 45; Whistler, "The Making of a Dunkirk Aviator," I, 359–61.

13. "History of School at Moutchic;" Callan to Cone, February 29, 1918, Callan Papers, LC.

14. Shirley, "Wartime Memoirs of John Jay Schieffelin," 103; see Daily/Weekly Reports, December 1917–August 1918, boxes 467–68, PA, RG 45.

15. Paine, *The First Yale Unit*, I, 23–26.

16. Bartlett to Cone, June 13, 1918, box 467, PA, RG 45.

17. Recreation Bulletin No. 17, September 14, 1918, box 133, GA-2, RG 45.

18. Sitz, *A History of U. S. Naval Aviation*, 25; cost estimated at 842,000 francs ($150,000).

19. Craven, "History of U. S. Naval Aviation, French Unit," 443–454, box 912, ZGU, RG 45 and "U.S. Naval Air Station, Brest," box 961, ZPA, RG 45.

20. "Rapport sur la mission a Brest du Lieutenant de Vaisseau Whiting pour la choix d'un terrain-centre d'hydravions," SS/Ga-146, SHM. Brest also intended site for kite balloon station; Memo, Whiting to SecNav, August 16, 1917, box 460, PA, RG 45.

21. See original French proposals, SS/Ga-146, SHM.

22. Minister of Marine to Commandant Brest, September 3, 1917. Detailed plans depicted on the hand-drawn "Centre d'Aviation Americain de Brest," both SS/Ga-146, SHM; "U.S. Naval Air Station, Brest," box 961, ZPA, RG 45.

23. Cone to Minister of Marine, July 31 and August 21, 28, and 31, 1918, SS/Ga-146, SHM. The Navy requested (June) additional land for a radio tower, SS/Ga-146, SHM. By mid-August station complement included 33 officers and 888 enlisted men.

24. Ramsey to Commanders, French stations, July 22, 1918, box 156, GU; and "U.S. Naval Air Station, Brest," box 961, ZPA, RG 45; Craven, "History of U. S. Naval Aviation, French Unit," Box 912, ZGU, RG 45. At the Armistice there were 74 HS-1Ls, 6 HS-2Ls, and 1 H-16 at Brest; Owers, "The Curtiss HS Flying Boats," I, 184.

25. CO to Cone, August 22, 1918; Sims to Wilson, August 23, 1918; and Court of Inquiry, October 16, 1918, all box 459, PA, RG 45.

26. "History, United States Naval Air Station, LeCroisic, October 1917–January 1919," box 961, ZPA, RG 45; Craven, "History of U. S. Naval Aviation, French Unit," 344–57, box 912, ZGU, RG 45; also hand-drawn "Extract du plan du port du Croisic," SS/Ga-146, SHM.

27. As early as July 7, 1917, the Minister of Marine wrote to the Commandant at L'Orient of an American base to be established at Le Croisic, SS/Ga-146, SHM; "History of U. S. Naval Air Sation Le Croisic," box 961, ZPA, RG 45; Paine, *The First Yale Unit*, II, 33.

28. Coombe to Davison, January 2, 1918, Davison Papers, YA; Cline in Woolbridge, *The Golden Age Remembered*, 19.

29. "History, United States Naval Air Station, LeCroisic, October 1917–January 1919," box 961, ZPA; Weekly Report, NAS LeCroisic, November 27, 1917, box 465, PA, both RG 45.

30. Weekly Report, NAS LeCroisic, November 27, 1917, box 465, PA, RG 45; Paine, *The First Yale Unit*, II, 36–45. Wilkinson and Brady also penned diary entries.

31. Coombe to Davison, January 2, 1918, Davison Papers, YA; Frank Brady, "Memo of Flight December 4, 1917," December 6, 1917, box 465, PA, RG 45.

32. Progress of the station can be followed in Corry to Cone, Weekly Reports, and

Memo, Corry to Cone re: takeover ceremony, November 17, 1917, box 465, PA, RG 45; Coombe to Davison, January 28, 1918, Davison Papers, YA.

33. Landon in Paine, *The First Yale Unit*, II, 49–50; Landon to Corry, December 9, 1917, box 465, PA; Weekly Report, January 19, 1918, box 134, GA-1, both RG 45.

34. Paine, *The First Yale Unit*, II, 55–57; McCrary to Minister of Marine, December 17, 1917, requests permission to observe test firing of a 75-mm gun mounted on a French flying boat, SS/Ga-145, SHM.

35. Coombe to Davison, January 2 and March 23, 1918, Davison Papers, YA; Daily Report, March 4, 1918, box 466, PA, RG 45. Cline in Woolbridge, *The Golden Age Remembered*, 18–19.

36. Coombe to Davison, March 23 and May 18, 1918, Davison Papers, YA.

37. "History of U.S. Naval Air Station Le Croisic," box 961, ZPA, RG 45; daily report, July 1, 1918, and Thomas to Masek, September 10, 1918, Barrett to Commanding Officer, Le Croisic, October 14, 1918, and papers of Court of Inquiry held October 15, 1918, all box 465, PA, RG 45.

38. Ile Tudy file, SS/Ga-146, SHM; "History of the Organization, Construction, and Operation of the U.S.N.A.S. Ile Tudy," box 961, ZPA, RG 45; Whiting to Daniels, August 18, 1917, Callan papers, LC; French orders to commence construction issued November 11, 1917, SS/Ga-146, SHM. One officer called Ile Tudy so small as to be practically inoperative; Still, *Crisis at Sea*, 126.

39. Weekly Reports, December 15 and 29, 1917, and January 5, 1918, box 462, PA, RG 45.

40. "History of the Organization, Construction, and Operation of the U.S.N.A.S. Ile Tudy," box 961, ZPA; Weekly Report, March 23, 1918, says March 15, box 462, PA, both RG 45; Ile Tudy file, SS/Ga-146, SHM.

41. "History of the Organization, Construction, and Operation of the U.S.N.A.S. Ile Tudy," box 961, ZPA, RG 45; Paine, *The First Yale Unit*, II, 59; SS/Ga-146, SHM, tallies 65 convoys, 4 '*Allos*,' 19,000 miles, and 344 hours flight time in May.

42. Board of Inspection to Commanding Officer, September 25, 1918, and Engineering Officer to Craven, October 12, 1918, both box 462, PA, RG 45.

43. Sugden to Cone April 28, 1918, box 462, PA; Recreation Bulletin No. 15, August 17, 1918, box 131, GA-1, both RG 45. The incident is well documented with various official French and American papers reprinted in Paine, *The First Yale Unit*, II, 62–69.

44. All these incidents are documented in Commander's Monthly Reports, April–October 1918, box 461, PA, RG 45.

45. Paine, *The First Yale Unit*, II, 59–62.

46. Naval Forces Communication Office (L'Orient District Office) to Craven, October 26, 1918; Cable, Sims to OPNAV, November 1, 1918; Ashley to CO Brest, November 9, 1918; Whitney to CO Brest, November 6, 1918, all box 156, GU; Order of the Day, October 29, 1918, box 461, PA, both RG 45.

47. Station inspected August 14–15 by Lieutenant Commander Gardiner per orders of District Commander at l'Orient, Memo to same, August 16, 1918, box 461, PA; "History of the Organization, Construction, and Operation of the U.S.N.A.S. Ile Tudy," box 961, ZPA, both RG 45.

48. "U.S. Naval Air Station Tréguier," box 963, ZPA, RG 45. On August 18 the site contained four hangars and barracks space for 130 men. See also Cone to Minister of Marine,

January 9, February 18, March 5, 1918, all SS/Ga-146, SHM. Ens. Robert Waters, Acting Asst. Chief Pilot, documented station activities with his extensive photo collection now at NHHC.

49. Dinger to Cone, July 15, 1918, box 1, Records USNAFFS, Belgian Bombing to France, Misc. (Entry 35), RG 72; "U.S. Naval Air Station Tréguier," box 963, ZPA; see also statistical summary, box 474, PA, both RG 45.

50. Craven, "History of U. S. Naval Aviation, French Unit," 391–403, box 912, ZGU, RG 45; "Proposed RNAS station on Island of Ehre, French Coast," Air 1/658/17/177/592, NAUK; "L'Aber Vrac'h et ses environs," SS/Ga-146, SHM; Whiting to SecNav, August 17, 1917, box 464, PA, RG 45.

51. Carlton McKelvey, "Construction of U.S. Naval Air Station L'Aber Vrach," NHHC; Craven, "History of U. S. Naval Aviation, French Unit," 396, box 912, ZGU, RG 45; Taussig Journal, August 8, 1918, NHHC.

52. Patrols began August 29, 1918; Daily Reports and Monthly Operations Reports, both box 464, PA, RG 45.

53. Daily Reports and Memo, Cecil to Craven, September 6, 1918, ibid.

54. Ms. History "L'Aber Vrach," box 961, ZPA, RG 45. Some flight activities at L'Aber Vrach in the September–November period documented in pilot Joseph Cline's flight log book, NAM.

55. Kindall to Cecil, October 5, 1918; Trail to Cecil, October 5, 1918; Cecil to Craven, October 6, 1918, all box 464, PA, RG 45.

56. Craven, "History of U. S. Naval Aviation, French Unit," 413–424, box 912, ZGU, RG 45; "History, United States Naval Air Station Fromentine," box 961, ZPA; Until quarters were finished officers lived at "Les Peupliers" in Fromentine, Child to Cone, March 16, 1918. Gardiner to District Commandant L'Orient, September 21, 1918, both box 464, PA, both RG 45.

57. "History, United States Naval Air Station Fromentine," box 961, ZPA; see also Station Weekly Report/Letter, March 16– November 11, 1918, box 464, PA, both RG 45.

58. "History of U.S. Naval Air Station, St. Trojan," November 30, 1918, box 963, ZPA, RG 45; decision to establish a station at St. Trojan communicated by Minister of Marine to officers at Rochefort and Gascogne August 23, 1917, SS/Ga-137, SHM; Still, *Crisis at Sea*, 122; Dinger to Griffin, May 24, 1918; Sargent to Griffin, August 7, 1918, and Griffin to Cone, August 13, 1918, all box 473, PA, RG 45.

59. Robert Gilbert Interview, MHS. Earliest reports to Paris HQ reported death of pilot and one enlisted man, later updated to two officers and six enlisted men killed; Griffin to Craven, January 14, 1919, box 474, PA, RG 45; additional casualties included four pigeons placed aboard the aircraft just before the explosion. Paine, *The First Yale Unit*, II, 72.

60. Cone to Wilson, August 21, 1918, box 473, PA, RG 45.

61. "History of U. S. Naval Air Station, St. Trojan," box 963, ZPA, RG 45.

62. Griffin to Craven, October 29, 1918, box 156, GU, RG 45.

63. Station complement included 26 officers and 343 enlisted men; "History of U.S. Naval Air Station, St. Trojan," box 963, ZPA, RG 45; Sitz, *A History of U.S. Naval Aviation*, 24.

64. Dinger to Cone, July 15, 1918, box 1, Records USNAFFS, Belgian Bombing to France, Misc. (Entry 35), RG 72.

65. "U.S. Naval Air Station, Arcachon," box 961, ZPA, RG 45; Craven, "History of U.

S. Naval Aviation, French Unit," 455–68, box 912, ZGU, RG 45; detailed description of Arcachon in Roseler et al., "The Observer," 13–14; construction supplies were delivered at La Teste and carried to the station in flat-bottomed sailing vessels.

66. Daily Reports, October 2–28, 1918; Wicks to Craven, September 14, and October 4, 1918; also Wicks to Cone, October 31, 1918, all in box 458, PA, RG 45.

67. Daily Report, October 23, 1918; Wicks to Craven, October 23, 1918; Wilson to Intelligence Officer (Brown), October 28, 1918; and Haizlett to Brown, October 28, 1918, all ibid.

68. Wolff to Brown, October 28, 1918; Bailey to Brown, October 28, 1918; and Wicks to Craven, October 24, 1918 re: forced landing of HS-1 #1750; also Wicks to District Commander, Rochefort, October 27, 1918, all ibid.

CHAPTER 5. PROGRESS REPORT: MARCH–SEPTEMBER 1918

1. Progress Report, USNAFFS, July 15, 1918, and Progress Report, USNAFFS, September 15, 1918, both box 131, GA-1, RG 45.

2. Until the end of the war Craven called transportation "our *bete noire*." See Craven to Cone, September 21, 1918, Craven Papers, LC; Edwards to Sims, quoting Cone, April 23, 1918, box 133, GA-2, RG 45; Cone to Minister of Marine, April 1 and 20, and May 24, 1918, all SS/Ga-145, SHM. The agreement to transfer 30 Levy-LePens equipped with Liberty motors to the Navy was abrogated in early summer. Cone to Minister, July 12, 1918, SS/Ga-145, SHM.

3. Craven to Maxfield, June 12, 1918, Craven, "History of U. S. Naval Aviation, French Unit," 60, box 912, ZGU, RG 45; Maxfield Board on Organization and Routine, July 2, 1918, box 2, Records of Naval Forces Operating in European Waters, Aviation Section (Entry 34), RG 72.

4. Cone to Minister of Marine, September 6, 1918, SS/Ga-145, SHM, canceling an arrangement whereby a portion of French aircraft production was diverted to naval forces. In this period 10 DDs and 8 Telliers were declared unfit; 1 Levy wrecked beyond repair.

5. McCrary, "Draft History," box 919, ZGU, RG 45.

6. Intelligence Officer to Craven, "History of U.S. Naval Air Station Pauillac," December 23, 1918, 5, and "History of the Activities of the Public Works Department in the development of Pauillac NAS," prepared at Pauillac, December 10, 1918, both box 962, ZPA, RG 45; Craven, "History of U. S. Naval Aviation, French Unit," 317–41, box 912, ZGU, RG 45.

7. In June 1917, the Navy Department ordered retired Cdr. John B. Patton to develop a small patrol/escort support base in the Bordeaux region. Still, *The Crisis at Sea*, 114–15.

8. Cone to Irwin, November 15, 1917, Cohen Collection, NHHC.

9. Cone to Sims, December 12, 1917; Weekly Report, January 5, 1918, both box 134, GA-1, RG 45.

10. Cone to Minister of Marine, February 6, 1918, requesting acquisition of Lazarette de Tromp-Loup, noting, "I cannot emphasize too much the urgency of this request," SS/Ga-147, SHM; Cone to Minister of Marine February 12, 1918, requesting additional land, ibid.

11. Letter, Cone to Minister of Marine, June 3, 1918, SS/Ga-147, SHM; Cable, Briscoe to Irwin, March 1, 1918, in Pauillac File, Cohen Collection, NHHC; Cone to Minister of Marine, April 29, 1918, SS/Ga-147, SHM.

12. First DH-4 flew September 20, 1918, the first HS-2L in October 16. By mid-October

Pauillac had received 96 aircraft, 845 motors, 207 propellers; Brest had received by then 40 aircraft, 40 motors, 253 propellers. Lieutenant Mason acted as head of Pauillac's Inspection and Test department.

13. Cone to Irwin, July 8, 1918, box 470, PA, RG 45.

14. Cone to Sims, July 26, 1918, box 53, Sims Papers, LC; Cone to Minister of Marine, August 5, 1918, SS/Ga-147, SHM.

15. Rossano, *The Price of Honor*, 198–200.

16. Craven, "History of U. S. Naval Aviation, French Unit," 340, box 912, RG 45.

17. Ibid., 137–40.

18. Sims, *The Victory at Sea*, 332; Weekly Report, November 17, 1917, and Edwards to Cone, January 26, 1918, both box 133, GA-2, RG 45; Admiralty to Sims, June 26, 1918, AIR 1/70/15/9/122, NAUK.

19. Scarlett served after January 1918 as head of Air Division at the Admiralty; replaced in early August; Edwards to Cone, April 22, 1918, box 133, GA-2, RG 45.

20. Edwards to Cone, April 8 and 22, 1918, ibid.

21. Edwards to Cone, August 8, 1918, ibid; Cone to Irwin, August 3, 1918, box 156, GU, RG 45.

22. Weekly Reports, November 3, 1917, and January 19, 1918, box 132, GA-1, RG 45. Received letter Sous-Secretaire d'Etat de l'Aeronautique Militaire et Maritime, January 10, 1918, approving Ensign Smith as liaison officer; Cone to Minister of Marine, February 6, 1918, requesting LTA officer, SS/Ga-144, SHM; Cone to Minister of Marine, April 1, 1918, and Cone to Minister of Marine, August 15, 1918, all SS/Ga-146, SHM; Shirley, "Wartime Memoirs" 103.

23. Cone to Sims, May 22, 1918, box 131, GA-1, RG 45.

24. Cone to Irwin, January 22, 1918, box 131, GA-1, RG 45.

25. Ibid.

26. Craven to Cone, May 17, 1918, Craven Papers, LC.

27. Rossano, *The Price of Honor*, 170, 198; Sims to Benson, June 14, 1918, and Edwards to Cone, May 20, 21, and August 12, 1918, all box 133, GA-2, RG 45.

28. Edwards to Cone, August 12, 1918, box 133, GA-2, RTG 45. "This is just a memorandum to you in case you might want some high ranking official to go to Washington with a view to killing any proposed amalgamation"; also Cone to Irwin, July 8, 1918, box 145, GP, RG 45.

29. Edwards to Cone, August 14 and 15, 1918, box 133, GA-2, RG 45. "It looks to me very much as though our Army are making a drive on Washington with a view to amalgamation." See minutes of April 10 and June 12, 1918, meetings, box 1, Aviation Section Reports 1918–1919 (Entry 36), RG 72.

30. Cone to Irwin, August 3 and 17, 1918, September 24, 1918, all box 156, GU, RG 45; Sims to OpNav, August 23, September 8, 1918, box 446, Dispatches to/from Naval Forces Operating in European Waters (Entry 54), RG 72.

31. As did General Pershing, and for precisely the same reasons; Sims to Daniels, August 8, 1918, Sims Papers, LC

32. Edwards to Cone, quoting Admiral Palmer in letter to Twining, box 133, GA-2; Sims to OpNav, August 29, 1918, refers to letter of April 24, 1918, box 156, GU, both RG 45; also Sims to Daniels, August 30, 1918, Sims Papers, LC.

33. Brewster to Ramsey, August 27, 1918, and Fitzpatrick to Ramsey, undated (June?

1918), both box 2, Records of Naval Forces Operating in European Waters, Aviation Section (Entry 34), RG 72.

34. Edwards to Cone, August 1, 3, 15, 1918, box 133, GA-2, and Cone to Sims, August 29, 1918, box 132, GA-1, both RG 45.

35. Lord, "The History of Naval Aviation, 1898–1939," 528–29.

36. Irwin to Cone, July 8, 1918; Cone to Irwin, August 3, 1918; Wilson to Sims, August 10, 1918, all box 156, GU; Sims to Daniels, August 21, 1918, box 155, GU, all RG 45.

37. *Flying Officers of the United States Navy*, 45–46; Sims to OpNav, August 19, 1918, urging all planes be assembled with engines and instruments, motors run at the factory, then knocked down for packing, box 446, Dispatches to/from Naval Forces Operating in European Waters (Entry 54), RG 72.

38. Edwards to Cone, July 24, 1918, box 133, GA-2, RG 45; FDR Tip File, January–August, 1918, boxes 24 and 25, Papers as Assistant Secretary of the Navy, 1913–1920, FDRPLM; FDR's schedule in SS/Ga-143, SHM.

39. August 17, 1918; quoted in Friedel, *Franklin D. Roosevelt: The Apprenticeship*, 365.

40. Lord, "The History of Naval Aviation, 1898–1939," 477–80.

41. Kiely to Callan, July 2, 1918, Callan Papers, LC; Lord, "The History of Naval Aviation, 1898–1939," 535–37. Shift of headquarters led to new regulations regarding "Procurement of aviation material from the French." See Craven to NAS Commanding Officers and District Commander, September 30, 1918, SS/Ga-145, SHM; Craven, "History of U. S. Naval Aviation, French Unit," 80, box 912, ZGU, RG 45; also Craven to Cone, September 12, 17, and 25, 1918, Craven Papers, LC.

CHAPTER 6. SPINNING THE SPIDER WEB: NAVAL AVIATION IN ENGLAND

1. For Ingalls's correspondence, see Ingalls Papers, IF; for MacLeish, see Rossano, *The Price of Honor*, passim; Paine, *The First Yale Unit*, II, 19.

2. MacLeish, "Report on School of Special Flying," March 4, 1918; also his report on gunnery training at Ayr and Turnberry, dated March 16, 1918, both box 1, Records of Naval Aviation Forces, Belgian Bombing to France, Misc. (Entry 35), RG 72; Stratham, *The Gosport Diaries*, 67–93.

3. Ingalls to Father, December 29, 1917, and January 14 and 17, 1918, IF.

4. See, for example, Ingalls to Father, January 3, 1918, IF; MacLeish Reports on Gosport, Turnberry, and Ayr, March 4 and 16, 1918; MacLeish, *Kenneth*.

5. Jernigan Flight Log Book, NAM.

6. Ingalls to Mother, February 7 and to Father, 21, 1918, both IF; Rossano, *The Price of Honor*, 94.

7. Jernigan Flight Log Book for Turnberry and Ayr, NAM; Ingalls, "School of Aerial Fighting (Ayr)," IF.

8. Rossano, *The Price of Honor*, 101, 110; Ingalls to Father, March 4, 1918, IF; Whistler, "The Making of a Dunkirk Flyer," II, 13.

9. Weekly Report, January 22, 1918, box 133, GA-2, RG 45; 15 men sent, their training to be completed about February 1. Sheely, *Sailor of the Air*, 85–91.

10. Additional documents related to training at Cranwell in box 1, Records USNAFFS, Belgian Bombing to France, Misc. (Entry 35), RG 72; see Cunningham Diary, January 1, 1918, MCHC.

11. Cone to Sims, January 12, 1918, re: progress of 15 enlisted men, box 133, GA-2, RG 45.

12. During 1918 other groups of enlisted men trained at English specialty schools. See Weekly Report, August 3, 1918, box 133, GA-2, RG 45.

13. See, for example, the performance reports on a 1916 version of one of the Porte boats powered by three 250-hp Rolls Royce engines, AIR 1/48/15/76, NAUK.

14. Ingalls Diary, October 6, 1917, IF; Coombe to Davison, October 7, 1917, Davison Papers, YA; actually not true. The Short pontoon bomber continued in service until the end of the war.

15. Vorys and Sturtevant in Paine, *The First Yale Unit*, II, 74–82; Hull to Cone, January 14, 1918, box 155, GU, RG 45; Hallam, *The Spider Web*, 186; Vorys to Davison, January 1, 1918, Davison Papers, YA. The Royal Navy, however, disapproved of the Americans' mustaches. Paine, *The First Yale Unit*, II, 82.

16. Shirley, "Wartime Memoirs of John Jay Schieffelin," 106; Rossano, *The Price of Honor*, 69; Vorys quoted in Arthur, *Contact!* 44.

17. Shirley, "Wartime Memoirs of John Jay Schieffelin," 111.

18. Ibid., 105; Knapp, "Flying Boats," 127.

19. As early as May 1917 the Admiralty said "Large America" patrols had proven effective and the enemy was now sending small fighter seaplanes to challenge them. Telegram to Vice Admiral Dover, "R.N.A.S. Aircraft Patrols in Vicinity of North Hinder Light," AIR 1/654/17/122/511, NAUK. On this subject AIR 1/643/17/122/269 and Porte to Admiralty, March 17, 1917, AIR 1/643/17/122/269, both NAUK. Nineteen air-to-air engagements involving Felixstowe/Great Yarmouth flying boats April 1917–August 1918 resulted in loss of eight British flying boats and nine German scouts. Abbatiello, *Anti-Submarine Warfare*, 189.

20. Vorys to Cone, February 2, 1918, box 1, Records of USNAFFS, Belgian Bombing to France, Misc. (Entry 35), RG 72.

21. Felixstowe aircraft began escorting beef trips in spring 1917. Grant, "Aircraft against U-Boats," 824; Paine, *The First Yale Unit*, II, 79–80.

22. Lovett to Cone, January 2, 1918, box 155, GU, RG 45.

23. The Sturtevant story is recounted in many places, including Paine, *The First Yale Unit*, II, 92–95.

24. Treadwell, *The First Naval Air War*, 94–95; Weekly Report, March 12, 1918; Weekly Report, April 27, 1918, box 133, GA-2 file, both RG 45. Another report of Potter's April 25 flight in Weekly Patrol Reports, AIR 1/342/15/226/270, NAUK; letter quoted in Arthur, *Contact!* 68.

25. Sims, *The Victory at Sea*, 324–27.

26. Sims to OpNav, August 29, 1918, box 134, GA-2, RG 45.

27. Joseph Eaton Interview, NHHC. Eaton and Compo to Edwards, February 26, 1918, box 1, Records of USNAFFS, Belgian Bombing to France, Misc. (Entry 35), RG 72.

28. Fuller to Cone, March 5, 1918; Intelligence Report Week Ending March 10, 1918, both ibid; Arthur, *Contact!* 70.

29. Alvord Papers, NAM; Hofer, "Report #8, Work Carried out at RNAS Great Yarmouth, March 2, 1918," box 1, Records of USNAFFS, Belgian Bombing to France, Misc. (Entry 35), RG 72; Arthur, *Contact!* 90; aviation activity at Great Yarmouth tallied in Weekly Patrol Reports, AIR 1/342/15/226/270, NAUK.

30. Sims/Edwards to Cone, June 21, 1918, box 133, GA-2, RG 45.

31. All reports in box 1, Records of USNAFFS, Belgian Bombing to France, Misc. (Entry 35), RG 72; concerning a visit to RAF Calshot, Craven to Cone, May 17, 1918, Craven Papers, LC.

32. An excellent source is Whiting, "History of U.S. Naval Air Station Killinghome," December 14, 1918, and packet of documents for Sims, both box 961, ZPA, RG 45.

33. *Killingholme Yearbook*, 7.

34. Lord, "The History of Naval Aviation, 1898–1939," 392; the story of the British lighters in Goodall, "Lighters," 72–80.

35. Whiting to Sims, "History of U.S. Naval Air Station, Killingholme," box 961, ZPA, RG 45; Lord, "The History of Naval Aviation, 1898–1939," 393.

36. Concerning the Naval Aircraft Factory's H-16s, see Trimble, *Wings for the Navy*, 19–22.

37. Weekly Reports, March 30, April 10 and 18, 1918, box 133, GA-2, RG 45; Knapp, "Flying Boats," 125, 127–28. During a training flight in an H-12 March 9, 1918, Wilcox's plane made a rough/crash landing in which instructor Ellis lost both his legs.

38. Knapp, "Flying Boats," 128; McAlpin to Davison, April 10, 1918, and Lawrence to Davison, undated, both Davison Papers, YA.

39. Full tally of patrol activity at Killingholme in spring 1918 in Weekly Patrol Reports, AIR 1/342/15/226/270, NAUK; Whiting to Cone, "Weekly Report of Flights," June 12, 1918, box 463, PA, and Progress Report USNAFFS, July 15, 1918, box 133, GA-1, both RG 45.

40. NAS Killingholme Station Log, May 20, 1918, NHHC; Shaw to Hull, June 6, 1918, box 463, PA, RG 45.

41. Whiting to Cone, "Report of Special Reconnaissance Patrol," June 12, 1918, and Confidential Bulletin #8, June 29, 1918, both box 463, PA, RG 45; NAS Killingholme Station Log, May 30, 1918, NHHC; "US detachment at Killingholme have taken over Short war flight and it is expected they will take over Large America flight as soon as sufficient pilots trained," from Weekly Report May 25, 1918, box 133, GA-2, RG 45.

42. Weekly Report of Flights, June 12, 1918, box 463, PA, RG 45; Knapp, "Flying Boats," 130.

43. Lawrence to Davison, undated, Davison Papers, YA.

44. "Transfer of Killingholme Air Station to United States Naval Authorities," AIR 1/639/17/122/182, NAUK; Shirley, "Wartime Memoirs of John Jay Schieffelin," 114; Whiting to Cone, "Organization, U.S. Naval Air Station, Killingholme," July 17, 1918, box 463, PA, RG 45. Thomas Murphy also served as a squadron commander. The Killingholme flying organization eventually consisted of six divisions totaling 27 aircraft, in *Killingholme Yearbook*, 7.

45. From Weekly Report, July 27, 1918, box 133, GA-2, RG 45.

46. Shirley, "Wartime Memoirs of John Jay Schieffelin," 11; Killinghome Daily Return, August 18, 1918, Cohen Collection, NHHC.

47. NAS Killingholme Station Log, September 12, 1918, NHHC; Owers, "Killingholme Diary," I, 194–95.

48. Shirley, "Wartime Memoirs of John Jay Schieffelin," 114–16, "Bombings by U. S. Naval Pilots," undated, box 463, PA file; Weekly Report, October 4, 1918, box 133, GA-2;

Whiting to Sims, August 21, 1918, box 156, GU, all RG 45; NAS Killingholme Station Log, July 19, 1918, NHHC; Sims, *The Victory at Sea,* 322.

49. Hawkins, "Seaplane Submarine Patrol, Felixstowe and Killingholme," September 24, 1918, box 463, PA, RG 45.

50. NAS Killingholme, Station Log, July 13 and August 21, 1918, NHHC; Whiting to Sims, August 21, 1918, box 463, PA, RG 45; and Whiting, "History of U.S. Naval Air Station, Killingholme, box 921, ZPA, RG 45.

51. NAS Killingholme, Station Log, August 5 and 10, 1918, NHHC; *Killingholme Yearbook,* 9; "Zeppelin Patrols," undated, box 463, PA, RG 45; Lawrence Memoir, Davison Papers, YA.

52. C. M. Tyson, Patrol Report, September 10, 1918; Whiting to Sims, October 12, 1918, Sims to BuNav, October 13, 1918; Lynch to Whiting, August 14, 1918, and Naval Bulletin #17, September 14, 1918, all box 463, PA, RG 45.

53. Whiting, "History of U.S. Naval Air Station, Killingholme," box 961, ZPA, RG 45; Knapp, "Flying Boats," 132.

54. Mayo to Daniels, October 13, 1918, box 463, PA, RG 45.

55. One account contained in Paine, *The First Yale Unit,* II, 99–100; Joseph Eaton Interview, NHHC.

56. Reconnaissance from Felixstowe, May 18, 1918, box 1, Records of USNAFFS, Belgium Bombing to France, Misc. (Entry 35), RG 72; Shirley, "Wartime Memoirs of John Jay Schieffelin," 111–12.

57. Confidential Bulletin #11, July 20, 1918, box 156, GU, RG 45.

58. Sims to Admiralty re: project July 31, 1918; Admiralty response, August 4; Sims to Cone, August 10, all box 463, PA; Edwards to Cone, June 6; Sims to Cone, August 4; Edwards to Cone, August 7; and Sims to OpNav August 14, 1918, all box 145, GP, all RG 45.

59. Williamson to Whiting, October 23 and November 3 and 7, 1918, box 2, Secret/Confidential Records Naval Forces European Waters (Entry 30), RG 72.

60. Whiting to Sims, October 28, 1918; Cutler to Whiting, October 28, 1918; Ives to Whiting, October 29, 1918; Hawkins to Whiting, November 2, 1918; Hawkins to Whiting (2), November 2, 1918; Freeman to Whiting; November 2, 1918; Whiting to Sims (Leighton Account), November 2, 1918; Sims (Twining) to BuNav, November 25, 1918, all box 155, GU, RG 45; Knapp, "Flying Boats," 132.

61. *Killingholme Yearbook,* 9.

CHAPTER 7. THE IRISH BASES

1. "U.S. Naval Air Station Wexford Souvenir," 3.

2. Lord, "The History of Naval Aviation, 1898–1939," 100, 304–305. Several draft histories (McCrary et al.) offer a broad overview of development of Irish bases/policy; see boxes 910 and 919, ZGU, RG 45; also Edwards, "The U.S. Naval Air Force," 1872.

3. Craven to Cone, May 30, 1918, Craven Papers, LC; McCrary, "Draft History," box 919, ZGU; Edwards to Cone, December 1 and 7, 1917, box 473, PA, both RG 45; Lord, "The History of Naval Aviation, 1898–1939," 388–90; Still, *Crisis at Sea,* 106.

4. Lord, "The History of Naval Aviation, 1898–1939," 150–151; Craven to Cone, March 23, 1918, Craven Papers, LC.

5. Brownell to Cone, January 15, 1918, box 473, PA, RG 45; also "History of Supply Department . . . Ireland," December 28, 1918, box 919, ZGU, RG 45.

6. "History of Supply Department . . . Ireland," December 28, 1918, box 919, ZGU, RG 45.

7. Copeland to McCrary, December 7, 1918; also Copeland, "Lessons Learned from the Construction of United States Naval Air Stations, Ireland," both box 1, Records of Naval Forces Operating in European Waters, Aviation Section (Entry 34), RG 72.

8. McCrary to Cone, March 31 and April 27, 1918, box 473, PA; Memo of October 18, 1918, says Irish operations curtailed by prohibitive weather conditions, box 156, GU, all RG 45.

9. Much trouble and increased Sinn Fein agitation came in reaction to the British extending conscription to Ireland during the spring crisis of 1918. Edwards to Cone, May 10, 1918, copy of dispatch from Washington; June 12, 1918, box 473, PA, RG 45.

10. Cone to Craven, March 16 and 26, 1918, Craven Papers, LC; McCrary, "Draft History USNAS Ireland," box 919, ZGU, and "History of U.S. Naval Air Station Castetownbere," box 961, ZPA, both RG 45.

11. "Organization of HQ office USNAS Ireland," May 15, 1918, box 473, PA, RG 45.

12. McCrary to Cone, June 21, 1918, ibid.

13. Linkins, "Communication and Operations," December 5, 1918, box 919, ZGU, RG 45.

14. McCrary to Cone, July 9, 1918, box 473, PA, RG 45.

15. Sitz, *A History of U.S. Naval Aviation*, 27–28.

16. "History of the U.S. Naval Aviation Base, Queenstown"; McCrary, draft "History USNAS Ireland," box 919, ZGU, both RG 45. The British valued barracks at $1,500 each, American buildings at $2,000. For site plans see box 3, Records of USNAFFS, Belgian Bombing to France, Misc. (Entry 35), RG 72.

17. "Regulations for the U.S. Naval Air Station, Queenstown," undated, box 962, ZPA, RG 45.

18. "History of the U.S. Naval Aviation Base, Queenstown," and "History of Operations (Queenstown)," box 919, ZGU, both RG 45.

19. Herbster, "History of U.S. Naval Air Station Wexford," box 963, ZPA; "History of Operations (Wexford)," box 919, ZGU, both RG 45. See also Tillotson, "U.S. Naval Air Station Wexford Souvenir." Station ground originally occupied by old farmyard.

20. Craven to Cone, May 30, 1918, Craven Papers, LC.

21. Herbster, "History of U.S. Naval Air Station Wexford"; Herbster to McCrary, July 12, 1918, box 474, PA, both RG 45.

22. Tillotson, "U.S. Naval Air Station Wexford Souvenir"; Herbster, "History of U.S. Naval Air Station Wexford"; "History of Operations (Wexford)"; Memo, Intelligence Officer to McCrary, October 28, 1918, box 474, PA, all RG 45; McCormick quoted in Arthur, *Contact!* 253.

23. McCrary to Roosevelt, January 27, 1919, box 961, ZPA, RG 45.

24. McCrary to Cone, Weekly Letter-Operations, May 11, 1918, box 919, ZGU, RG 45.

25. McCrary to Sims, July 4, 1918, Box 475, PA; Townsend to McCrary, Progress Report, undated, box 919, ZGU, both RG 45.

26. Notice, Peyton, October 22, 1918, and Court of Inquiry, October 26, 1918, both

box 474, and Paul J. Peyton, Whiddy Island Weekly Reports for weeks ending November 2 and 9, 1918, box 475, both PA, RG 45; also Dinger to Cone, July 15, 1918, box 1, Records USNAFFS Belgian Bombing to France, Misc. (Entry 35), RG 72.

27. "War Diary and History of USNAS Lough Foyle," box 963, ZPA, RG 45.

28. Wilson, "History of Lough Foyle," ibid; ms. "History Lough Foyle," box 919, ZGU, RG 45.

29. Flight Report, October 22, 1918, box 466, PA, RG 45.

30. Cable to SecNav April 24, 1917; Daniels to Naval Attache, May 3, 1917; Sims to SecNav, May 7, 1917, all box 458, PA; "History of U.S. Naval Air Station Castletownbere," box 963, ZPA, both RG 45.

31. Weekly Report, March 30, 1918, box 133, GA-2, RG 45. These are Edwards's "bad boys"; McCrary to Cone, April 20, 1918, box 473, PA; Sims to McCrary, April 24, 1918, and turnover authorization from Captain Page, RAF, April 29, 1918, both box 458, PA, both RG 45.

32. Shumway to Cone, Weekly Operations Letter, June 10, 1918, box 458, PA, RG 45; Craven to Cone, May 30, 1918, Craven Papers, LC.

33. Telegram, August 14, 1918, box 156, GU, and Sims to Cone, August 10, 1918, box 458, PA, both RG 45.

34. Sims to Cone, August 10, 1918, box 458, PA, RG 45; see also Memo to Cone, October 18, 1918, box 156, GU; also "History of Stations–Castletownbere," box 919, ZGU, both RG 45.

CHAPTER 8. ON DUTY, OFF DUTY: THE WORK AND LIFE OF THE STATION

1. Jon Abbatiello notes trenchantly, "forcing the U-boat down, through the credible threat of air attack and communication with surface vessels, was the true tactical value of aircraft technology in World War One," *Anti-Submarine Warfare*, 38. Fine summary in Dwight Messimer, *Find and Destroy*. The Flanders U-boats were commanded by Korvettenkapitan Bartenbach and divided into two flotillas, 1-U-Flotile Flandern and 2-U-Flotile Flandern.

2. See, for example, Abbatiello, *Anti-Submarine Warfare*, 29–32. The Navy ordered 2,500 100-kg bombs from the French June 3, 1918, SS/Ga-146, SHM.

3. Craven to Commandant of Patrols, Brest, October 24, 1918, SS/Ga-145, SHM. At Le Croisic, confined space meant the armory stood next to the hangars.

4. Craven to Commandant of Patrols, Brest, October 24, 1918, SS/Ga-145, SHM; Donnelly to Cone, January 25, 1918, and Fuller to Cone, March 5, 1918, both box 1, Records of USNAFFS, Belgian Bombing to France, Misc. (Entry 35), RG 72.

5. Monthly Account # 1 (Le Croisic), May 31, 1918, SS/Ga-146, SHM.

6. Perry, *Our Navy in the War*, 224–230.

7. Monthly Account No. 1 (Le Croisic), May 31, 1918, SS/Ga-146, SHM.

8. Coombe to Davison, March 23, 1918, Davison Papers, YA; Pou to Ramsey, October 17, 1918, box 2, Records of Naval Forces Operating in European Waters, Aviation Section (Entry 34), RG 72; Arthur, *Contact!* 112.

9. Coombe to Davison, May 18, 1918, Davison Papers, YA.

10. Hofer, "Report of Work Carried Out at RNAS Great Yarmouth," March 2, 1918, box 1, Records USNAFFS, Belgian Bombing to France, Misc. (Entry 35), RG 72.

11. The effectiveness of this tactic is hinted at by the fact that (according to the British) only 257 of 83,598 vessels traveling in convoy were sunk. No convoy with an aerial escort was attacked until December 1917, in Abbatiello, *Anti-Submarine Warfare*, 106.

12. Monthly Account #1, Ile Tudy (for March), box 463, PA, RG 45; Monthly Account #1 (Le Croisic), May 31, 1918, SS/Ga-146, SHM.

13. Cone to Commanding Officers, August 15, 1918, box 132, GA-1, RG 45.

14. Ramsey to Cone, May 14, 1918, box 2, Records of Naval Forces Operating in European Waters, Aviation Section (Entry 34), RG 72.

15. Craven, "History of U. S. Naval Aviation, French Unit," 217, box 912, ZGU, RG 45; Aviation Circular #70, October 31, 1918, box 132, GA-1, RG 45.

16. Herbster, "History of U.S. Naval Air Station Wexford," box 963, ZPA, RG 45.

17. Shirley, "Wartime Memoirs of John Jay Schieffelin," 115.

18. Pigeon information contained in SS/Ga-146, SHM; Shirley, "Wartime Memoirs of John Jay Schieffelin," 112.

19. Owers, "The Curtiss HS Flying Boats," I, 167; Cone to Minister of Marine, August 12, 1918, SS/Ga-145, SHM. Cone quoted a $38,500 base price, with added freight charges of $60 per ton, or $12,000. OpNav to Sims, August 5, 1918, box 335, Requisitions and Shipping Orders from Air Stations Abroad (Entry 33), RG 72. Construction & Repair Bureau Technical Note of September 1, 1918, quoted in Aviation Section Confidential Bulletin #18, SS/Ga-144, SHM.

20. Cone to Commanding Officers, August 15, 1918, box 132, GA-1, RG 45. Squadron Book, RNAS Killingholme, September 1917, box 2, Secret/Confidential Records of Naval Forces Operating in European Waters (Entry 30), RG 72.

21. According to the order book, the commanding officer was directed to "dine alone, if that is practicable."

22. Herbster, "History of U.S. Naval Air Station Wexford," box 963, ZPA, RG 45.

23. Cone to Navy Department (Operations) (Aviation), June 3, 1918, box 2, Aviation Section Reports (Entry 36) RG 72; Cone to all COs USNAS, August 15, 1918, box 131, GA-1, RG 45.

24. Arthur, *Contact!* 66, 105; "Syllabus of Lectures Given to Officers Under Instruction Upon their Arrival," box 914, ZGU, RG 45.

25. Bludworth, *The Battle of Eastleigh*, 112.

26. Memo, Paris Headquarters, May 14, 1918, and Memo, Cone to Navy Department, June 3, 1918, both box 2, Aviation Section Reports (Entry 36), RG 72.

27. See, for example, Rossano, *The Price of Honor*, 150, 195; *Extracts from the Letters of George Clark Moseley*, 154.

28. For the Lough Foyle schedule, see box 961, ZPA, RG 45.

29. Briscoe to Irwin, March 1, 1918, Cohen Collection, NHHC.

30. Bulmer in Bludworth, *The Battle of Eastleigh*, 102; Corry to Cone, May 10, 1918, box 465, PA, RG 45.

31. Recreation Bulletin No. 4, June 1, 1918, box 131, GA-1, RG 45.

32. Weekly Report No. 25, May 1918, box 461, PA, RG 45.

33. Robert Gilbert Interview, Massachusetts Historical Society; Ramsey to COs French Stations, July 22, 1918, box 156, GU, RG 45.

34. Weekly Reports, December 22, 1917, and January 26, 1918, box 132, GA-1, RG 45.

CHAPTER 9. GASBAGS: DEVELOPMENT OF THE NAVY LIGHTER-THAN-AIR PROGRAM

1. Grossnick, *Kite Balloons to Airships*, provides an excellent overview of the Navy's lighter-than-air activities in the period 1915–1918 and beyond. See also "History of U.S. Naval Aviation in France, June 5, 1917 to November 1, 1918," box 910, ZGU, RG 45; and Abbatiello, *Anti-Submarine Warfare*, 20–21. The B-class airship was superseded in late 1918 by the much-improved C class. Neither flew in Europe.

2. This incident mentioned in Messimer, *Find and Destroy*, 136.

3. Cone to Minister of Marine, October 1, 1917, in "History of U.S. Naval Aviation, French Unit," 24–26, box 912, ZGU, RG 45; and Cone to Minister of Marine, November 13, 1917, SS/Ga-147, SHM.

4. Cone to Minister of Marine, December 14, 1917, ibid; Weekly Report, November 3, 1917, box 132, GA-1, RG 45.

5. Cone to Minister of Marine, November 14, 1917, and Maxfield to Minister of Marine, July 9, 1918, both SS/Ga-147, SHM. McCrary to Navy Department (Operations), and Cone's endorsement, January 24, 1918, box 145, GP file; Weekly Report, January 26, 1918, box 132, GA-1, both RG 45; Lord, "The History of Naval Aviation, 1898–1939," 455.

6. McCrary to Minister of Marine, December 18, 1917, SS/Ga-145, SHM; Progress Report, March 15, 1918, box 131, GA-1, RG 45; Craven to Minister of Marine, February 12, March 7 and 22, 1918, SS/Ga-145, all SHM; Craven, "History of U. S. Naval Aviation, French Unit," 27, box 912, ZGU, RG 45; Weekly Report, April 25, 1918, box 131, GA-1, RG 45; Cone to Minister of Marine, March 1 and April 8, 1918, SS/Ga-147, SHM; a Cone Memo of May 1918 outlined the entire LTA program: two CM types, three AT types, three Zodiac, one CM "*Capitaine Caussin*," and two Vedette Zodiac, SS/Ga-143, SHM; Craven to Cone, March 25, 1918, Craven Papers, LC.

7. Maxfield to Cone, August 17 1918, box 145, GP, RG 45; Lord, "The History of Naval Aviation, 1898–1939," 569.

8. Craven, "History of U.S. Naval Aviation, French Unit," 177–78, box 912, ZGU, RG 45.

9. For maneuvering airships, see Maxfield to Cone, July 2, 1918, box 2, Records of Naval Forces Operating in European Waters, Aviation Section (Entry 34), RG 72; also schematic "Dispositions Prises pour le Campement du C.M. 4 dans L'Avant-Port du Hangar de Montebourg, Le 18 Juin 1918," SS/Ga-149, SHM.

10. Quarterly Report, October 22, 1918, box 131, GA-1, RG 45.

11. Minister of Marine to Commandant de Patrouille Aerienne de la Loire, February 13, 1918, and Cone to Minister, February 9, 1918, both SS/Ga-148, SHM; Cone to Minister of Marine, Letter of confirmation concerning work at La Trinité, March 9, 1918, SS/Ga-147, SHM; Memo, Cone to Wilson, August 26, 1918, box 156, GU, RG 45.

12. Weekly Reports, November 24, December 1 and 8, 1917; January 15 and 22, February 2, and March 2, 1918, box 133, GA-2, RG 45.

13. British kite balloon training was noted for its high standards; see Abbatiello, *Anti-Submarine Warfare*, 44–45; Weekly Report, April 13, 1918, box 133, GA-2, RG 45; Stoppel to Sims, undated (1918), box 1, Records of USNAFFS, Belgian Bombing to France, Misc. (Entry 35), RG 72.

14. Arthur, *Contact!* 503; Piper to Cone (March 1918), box 1, Records of USNAFFS, Belgian Bombing to France, Misc. (Entry 35), RG 72 .

15. Weekly Report, June 22, 1918, box 133, GA-2, RG 45; also Maitland to Sims, June 24, 1918; Barnes to Edwards, May 24, 1918; Barnes to Cone, March 25, 1918, describing activities at Howden, and Baehr, March 26, 1918, all box 1, Records of USNAFFS, Belgian Bombing to France, Misc. (Entry 35), RG 72.

16. Detailed history of the station in "U.S. Naval Air Station, Paimboeuf," and "History of U.S. Naval Air Station, Paimboeuf," both box 910, ZGU; Weekly Report, December 24, 1917; Culberts ms. letters, both box 469, PA, both RG 45.

17. Later obtained VZ-7 on June 8, the AT-13 on August 30, and VZ-13 on October 25. The AT-1 and VZ-3 became unserviceable in September. The former deflated, sent to the United States, the latter returned to the French at Rochefort, leaving three at the station until the Armistice.

18. Craven, "History of U. S. Naval Aviation, French Unit," 475, box 912, ZGU, RG 45.

19. *Capitaine Caussin* operated at Paimboeuf in fall 1917 and was wrecked December 27 on the hangar doors while being walked in by the French ground crew. The ship was sent to Paris for repairs. See Bulletin #2, May 18, 1918, USNAF Operating in European Waters, box 131, GA-1, RG 45.

20. Culbert, "Report of Flight of AT1," June 18, 1918, SS/Ga-147, SHM.

21. Culbert, "Report of Flight of AT1," June 27, 1918, ibid.

22. Magruder to Wilson, July 13, 1918, box 156, GU file, RG 45; Maxfield to Cone, August 17, 1918, in "History of U.S. Naval Aviation in France from June 5th, 1917, to November 1st, 1918," 11, box 910, ZGU, RG 45.

23. Thanksgiving Day "Programme" in box 469, PA, RG 45.

24. Craven to Minister of Marine, January 8 and 28, 1919, SS/Ga-147, SHM.

25. Detailed history of the station in Craven, "History of U.S. Naval Aviation, French Unit," 495–511, box 912, ZGU, RG 45; also "History . . . U.S. Naval Air Station, Guipavas," box 961, ZPA, RG 45.

26. See especially "History of the Naval Air Station, Gujan-Mestras," box 961, ZPA, RG 45; also Craven, "History of U.S. Naval Aviation, French Unit," 512–16, box 912, ZGU, RG 45; Babbitt to Cone, May 22, 1918, box 462, PA, RG 45.

27. From Mayo Report, box 460, PA, RG 45; station visited by flu early May; CO and several men "owe their lives to constant and untiring efforts of Lt. Dr. E. D. Hardin."

28. Weekly Reports, December 24, 1917, and January 4 and 15, 1918, box 131, GA-1, RG 45; Rochefort survey dated January 29, 1918, and Dispatch to Minister of Marine, both SS/Ga-148, SHM; Cone to Minister of Marine, February 14, 1918, SS/Ga-147, SHM; Weekly Report, January 26, 1918, box 131, GA-1, RG 45.

29. Layman, "Rubber Cows," 164–168; Craven, "History of U. S. Naval Aviation, French Unit," 445–54, box 912, ZGU, RG 45; Sims to Cone, November 17, 1917, PP; account of balloon operations in "U.S. Naval Air Station, Brest," box 960, ZPA, both RG 45. See a French map dated December 1, 1917, and two American plans of February 23 and May 24, 1918, in SS/Ga-146, SHM.

30. "U.S. Naval Air Station, Brest," box 960, ZPA, RG 45.

31. Puleston to Wilson, August 7, 1918; Clark to Commanding Officer, August 7, 1918; Aster to Force Commander, August 27, 1918, all box 459, PA, RG 45.

32. Corry to Cone, August 18, 1918; Report of September 21, 1918, both ibid; progressive

evolution of plans for the American KB base traced in detailed schematics prepared November 1917, February 23, 1918, and May 24, 1918, SS/Ga-146, SHM; Quarterly Report, September 30, 1918, box 131, GA-1; Memo, Corry to Commander U.S. Naval Forces in France (Aviation), November 14, 1918, box 460, PA, both RG 45; "U.S. Naval Air Station, Brest," box 960, ZPA, RG 45.

33. Craven, "History of U. S. Naval Aviation, French Unit," 523–30, box 912, ZGU, RG 45; "U.S. Naval Air Station, La Trinité," box 962, ZPA, RG 45. For a layout of the base and its facilities see hand-drawn "Centre de Captifs Americains a la Trinite, Plan d'Ensemble," SS/Ga-147, SHM.

34. Gardiner to District Commander, L'Orient re: La Trinité, August 13, 1918, box 464, PA, RG 45; "U.S. Naval Air Station, La Trinité," box 962, ZPA, RG 45.

35. Craven, "History of U. S. Naval Aviation, French Unit," 517–22, box 912, ZGU, RG 45; "History US Naval Aviation Forces in France June 5, 1917–November 11, 1918," box 910, ZGU, RG 45.

CHAPTER 10. SUNNY ITALY: NAVAL AVIATION IN THE MEDITERRANEAN

1. SecNav/Benson to Sims, November 21, 1917; "Historical Memorandum of U. S. Naval Aviation Forces in Italy/History of Headquarters, USNAF, Rome, Italy," both box 919, ZGU; Cone to Sims, January 31, 1918, box 963, ZPA, all RG 45; Shirley, "John Lansing Callan," 183.

2. Notes on Conference at Italian Ministry of Marine, April 23, 1918, Callan Papers, LC.

3. Callan to Cone, January 26, 1918, ibid.

4. Lord, "The History of Naval Aviation, 1898–1939," 422–23.

5. Callan to Cone, December 21 and 29, 1917, box 145, GP; Callan to Cone, January 26, 1918, in "USN Aviation in Foreign Service," box 919, ZGU, both RG 45.

6. Cone to Sims, January 31, 1918, box 919, ZGU, RG 45; Cable from Sims to OPNAV, February 9, 1918, ibid; Callan to Train, January 5, 1918, Callan Papers, LC; actual report dated January 31. Train, to Sims, February 11, 1918, box 963, ZPA, RG 45.

7. Hudson, *Hostile Skies*, 242–49; Melville, "Piloti Americani in Italia," 229–43.

8. Cable Operations-Aviation to Sims, box 963, ZPA, RG 45; Conger to Paris HQ, April 9, 1918; Callan for Cone, April 11, 1918, both Callan Papers, LC.

9. Cone to Sims, Benson to Sims, March 16, 1918; Cable, Sims to Rome May 10, 1918, all cables box 919, ZGU, RG 45; Conger to Train, May 24, 1918, Callan Papers, LC.

10. Cable, Cone to Sims, late April 1918, box 919, ZGU, RG 45.

11. Memo Governing Operations of USNAFFS in Italy, May 15, 1918, and Cone to Callan, same date, both ibid. Cone to Callan, June 8, 1918, Callan Papers, LC; Shirley, "John Lansing Callan" 185.

12. Callan to Cone, May 28, 1918; Cone to Callan, May 29, 1918, Callan to Cone, August 6 and 20, 1918, all Callan Papers, LC.

13. Callan to Cone, May 11 and 21, 1918, both ibid.

14. Callan to Lovett, June 15, 1918; Callan to Cone, August 13 and October 4, 1918, all ibid.

15. Callan to Cone, May 15, August 6 and 20, and November 26, 1918, Callan Papers, LC. Haviland retired as a lieutenant commander in 1925.

16. Typewritten list of men/officers dated March 27, 1918, ibid. Bolsena Daily Reports, February 19, 21 and 23, 1918; Weekly Report, 10 April, 1918, all box 459, PA, RG 45.

17. Yale Unit member Curtis Read trained with Atwater in Virginia. Meeting him in Europe in January 1918 he remarked, "Old Bill Atwater is as funny and cheerful as ever and is lots of fun." Paine, *The First Yale Unit*, II, 27. Sitz, *A History of United States Naval Aviation*, 34.

18. Bolsena Daily Reports March 3, 16, and April 4, 1918, box 459, PA, RG 45.

19. Bolsena Daily Reports, March 20 and July 30; Callan to Atwater, August 8, 1918, both ibid.

20. Atwater to Callan, April 10, 1918, Callan Papers, LC.

21. Bolsena Weekly Reports, May 12 and 27 and June 2, 1918, box 459, PA, RG 45.

22. Callan to Haviland July 2, 1918, Callan Papers, LC; Arthur, *Contact!* 118.

23. Atwater to Callan August 14, 1918; Kiely to Atwater, August 17, 1918; Callan to Kiely, August 26, 1918; Cone to Callan, August 15, 1918, all Callan Papers, LC.

24. Fearing to Callan, July 22, 1918, and Callan to Fearing, August 6, 1918, both Callan Papers, LC; Atwater to Cone, September 11, 1918, box 459, PA, RG 45; Atwater to Callan, October 13, 1918, and Callan to Admiral Orsini, October 14, 1918, both Callan Papers, LC; Daily Reports, October 9–17, 1918, box 459, PA, RG 45.

25. Sitz, *A History of United States Naval Aviation*, 29–30; Whistler, "The Making of a Dunkirk Flyer," II, 22; Bolsena Weekly Report, November 3, 1918, box 459, PA, RG 45.

26. Overview in Sitz, *A History of United States Naval Aviation*, 30–31; see *The Leading Edge*, the station newspaper, especially the Christmas issue, box 916, ZGU, RG 45.

27. Parker/White to Callan, June 3, 1918, box 963, ZPA, RG 45; full description in Callan to Cone, May 5, 1918, Callan Papers, LC. De Filippi said the United States should supply this; Callan to Conger noted, June 18, 1918, Callan Papers, LC.

28. "Historical Memorandum of U.S. Naval Aviation Forces in Italy" box 919, ZGU, RG 45, contains two different totals on two separate pages. White to Callan July 13, 1918; see also Train to Sims, July 27, 1918; Tilburne to Callan, September 7, 1918, and Parker to Callan, June 3, 1918, "Report on raid against Porto Corsini," July 25, 1918, and Haviland to Callan, 26 July 1918, all box 963, ZPA, RG 45.

29. White to Callan, October 13, 1918, box 963, ZPA, RG 45.

30. Haviland to Callan, August 27, 1918, and Tilburne to Callan, September 7, 1918. Colors hoisted officially August 1, 1918; Memo, Callan to Haviland, October 25, 1918, all ibid.

31. Haviland, Operations Report, August 21, 1918; Callan to Cone, August 27, 1918; Report, Haviland to Callan, August 27, 1918, all ibid.

32. Report of Intelligence Officer, August 21, 1918, and Callan to Havilland, August 29, 1918, both box 963, ZPA, RG 45.

33. Haviland to Callan, August 23, 1918, ibid.

34. Letter of condolence from Callan to Mrs. Mary Killeen, October 11, 1918, Callan Papers, LC.

35. Memo for Ensign Leighton November 6, 1918, ibid; for flight of November 2, see Operations Report, November 3, 1918, box 930, ZPA, RG 45.

36. Mostly instruction and practice flights; Letter, Haviland to Commander Valli, October 17, 1918, box 963, ZPA, RG 45.

37. Mayo to SecNav, November 12, 1918, box 156, GU file and box 960, PA, both RG 45.

38. Memo from Enlisted Personnel to Commander Naval Forces Italy via Porto Corsini Commanding Officer, and Memo, Callan to Haviland, November 20, 1918, both box 963, ZPA, RG 45; Sims to Benson, December 31, 1918, box 13, Papers as Assistant Secretary of the Navy, 1913–1920, FDRPLM; Callan to Haviland, December 4, 1918, ibid. The ship sailed January 4, with men from Porto Corsini and Bolsena, including 15 officers.

39. Callan to Cone, May 5, 1918, Callan Papers, LC; Parker to Callan, May 26, 1918, "Report upon seaplane station at Pescara," and Callan to Cone, May 28, 1918, both box 459, PA, RG 45.

40. Atwater to Callan, September 2, 1918; Sims to OpNav, September 5, 1918; Report on NAS Pescara, Ens. Lawrewnce White, October 18, 1918, all ibid.

41. Aircraft procured in France would come at the expense of the Army, in Lord, "The History of Naval Aviation, 1898–1939," 467; Shirley, "Capt. LaGuardia," 125–26; Craven to Cone, March 23, 1918, Craven Papers, LC.

42. Aircraft designated the Ca. 5; McDonnell's story in Paine, *The First Yale Unit*, II, 214–16.

43. Cone to Irwin, May 29, 1918, Callan Papers, LC. Irwin's Weekly Conference May 18, agreed to send material to build 60 Capronis, would consider material for 60 additional, box 364, Aviation Section Reports 1918–1919 (entry 36), RG 72; and Lord, "The History of Naval Aviation, 1898–1939," 252.

44. Paine, *The First Yale Unit*, II, 216; Callan to Cone, June 11, 1918; Lovett to Callan, June 7, 1918, both Callan Papers, LC; Weekly Reports June 15 and July 20, 1918, box 963, ZPA, RG 45.

45. Callan to Cone, March 27 and 28, 1918, both Callan papers, LC.

46. Cone to Irwin, May 29, 1918, Callan Papers, LC; Letter of May 11, 1918, to Commissario Generale, Italian Aeronautics, Rome; Cables, May 1 and 15, 1918, both box 910, ZGU, RG 45.

47. Cable, May 16, 1918, box 910, ZGU, RG 45.

48. Shirley, "Capt. LaGuardia," 131–32.

49. Bludworth, *The Battle of Eastleigh*, 96–98.

50. A second contingent of 15 aviators reached the field in October but instruction ended with the Armistice. Lovett to Callan on their imminent departure from France, June 7, 1918, Callan Papers, LC; Callan to Lovett June 15, 1918, ibid.

51. Walker and Coombe in Paine, *The First Yale Unit*, II, 218–21.

52. Callan to Lovett, June 15, 1918; Callan to Cone, July 16, 1918, both Callan Papers, LC. Arthur, *Contact!* 5.

53. Mason Patrick/Hutch Cone to Royal Italian Aeronautical Mission, Paris, May 31, 1918, Callan Papers, LC; material listed in box 335, Requisitions/Shipping Orders from Air Squadrons Abroad (Entry 33), RG 72; Callan to Cone, June 11, 1918, Callan Papers, LC.

54. Walker to Callan, June 29, 1918; Callan to Walker, July 5, 1918; Callan to Cone, July 16, 1918; La Guardia to Patrick, July 21, 1918, allCallan Papers, LC; also Shirley, "Capt. LaGuardia," 134–36.

55. Callan to Cone, July 12, 1918, Callan Papers, LC.

56. Dispatch, OpNav to Sims, January 6, 1919, box 2, Aviation Section Reports 1918–1919 (Entry 36), RG 72.

57. Confidential Bulletin #12, July 27, 1918, and Cable, Coombe to Callan, July 28,

1918, both box 156, GU, RG 45; Paine, *The First Yale Unit*, II, 223–23; Arthur, *Contact!* 98, 125.

58. Callan Diary, passim, Callan Papers, LC.

59. Callan to Cone, August 20, September 27, Cone to Craven, September 24, and October 4, 1918, all Callan Papers, LC; Sims to OpNav, September 19 and 27, 1918, box 446, Dispatches to/from Naval Forces Operating in European Waters (Entry 54), RG 72.

60. Paine, *The First Yale Unit*, II, 221–222; Callan to Cone, August 14 and 15, 1918; Callan to Sims, September 6, 1918, all Callan Papers, LC.

CHAPTER 11. THE NORTHERN BOMBING GROUP

1. Detailed summary in Craven, "History of U. S. Naval Aviation, French Unit," 51–58, box 912, ZGU, RG 45; Bludworth, *The Battle of Eastleigh*, 86.

2. AIR 1/72/15/9/138, NAUK; Abbatiello, *Anti-Submarine Warfare in World War I*, 58–81.

3. Some of Lovett's activities described in Paine, *The First Yale Unit*, II, 168–89.

4. Ibid.; Planning Department Memorandum, February 15, 1918, and response in Lord, "The History of Naval Aviation, 1898–1939," 453–54, 456–57.

5. Cunningham's report dated January 24, 1918, box 1, Misc. Records 1918–1920 (Entry 38), RG 72; also Malandrino, "Alfred Austell Cunningham," 363.

6. General Board Letter, February 25, 1918, box 3, Records of USNAFFS Belgian Bombing to France, Misc. (Entry 35), RG 72; Summary NBG Correspondence, box 910, ZGU, RG 45.

7. Incoming Cables, March 7 and 10, 1918, Summary NBG Correspondence; Cunningham received orders to create escort squadrons March 11, 1918, all box 910, ZGU, RG 45.

8. Lovett to Cone, March 19, 1918, box 1, Records USNAFFS, Belgian Bombing to France, Misc. (Entry 35), RG 72.

9. Outgoing Cable, March 18, 1918, ibid; Lord, "The History of Naval Aviation, 1898–1939," 175; Sims to OpNav, March 18 and 23, 1918, box 910, ZGU, RG 45; Memo of Conversation with Commandant Loubigniac by Guggenheim and Smith, March 22, 1918, and Craven to Loubigniac, March 26, 1918, both SS/Ga-144, SHM.

10. McDonnell, "Report on Observation of British Day and Night Bombing," March 29, 1918, Box 1, Records of USNAFFS, Belgian Bombing to France, Misc. (Entry 35), RG 72; Lovett's report reprinted in Paine, *The First Yale Unit*, II, 175–80.

11. Cable, OpNav to Sims, April 6, 1918, or OpNav to Sims, April 9, 1918, both box 910, ZGU, RG 45.

12. Cone's report reprinted in Paine, *The First Yale Unit*, II, 185–86; Lord, "The History of Naval Aviation, 1898–1939," 176; Weekly Report, April 13, 1918, box 133, GA-2 file, RG 45; Rossano, *The Price of Honor*, 215; Still, *Crisis at Sea*, 476.

13. Discussion of these estimates, AIR 1/70/15/9/122, NAUK; Cone to Sims, April 18, 1918, re: Dunkirk bombing project, AIR 1/70/15/9/122, NAUK; Edwards to Cone, April 24, 1918; Sims to OpNav, April 27, 1918; and CNO to all Bureaus, April 30, 1918, all box 910, ZGU; Sims to Wilson, May 2, 1918, box 461, PA. In early June the Department instructed Cone to reconsider basing squadrons and assembly/repair facility in France, see Cable, June 4, 1918, box 910, ZGU, all RG 45.

14. Outgoing Cables, April 17, 1918; Cone to Sims, May 11, 1918; Benson to Daniels, April 30, 1918; also CNO to SecNav, same date, all box 910, ZGU, RG 45.

15. The Daniels-Baker correspondence is found in ibid.

16. Concerning Air Service disputes, see Craven to Cone, May 30, 1918, Craven Papers, LC.

17. Benson to Sims; cable to Cone; Cone to Irwin, June 5, 1918; Benson to Sims, May 31, 1918, Sims to Cone, May 31, 1918; Cable, May 31, 1918; Cone to Sims, June 3, 1918; Cone to Sims, all box 910, ZGU, RG 45.

18. Complaints seem to have come from Army/RAF types, perhaps Trenchard; Cone received similar advice from General Lambe who suggested he formally notify Admiralty and Air Ministry, with Sims to carry the news. Lambe to Cone, May 24, 1918, AIR 1/70/15/9/122, NAUK; see Edwards to Cone, May 27, 1918, box 910, ZGU; Cone to Edwards June 26, 1918, ibid.; Edwards to Cone, June 29, 1918, box 145, GN; Cables 2471, 2124, both June 6, 1918, in NBG Summary. Placed under command of Vice-Admiral, Dover; C. L. Lambe to Cone, July 1, 1918, box 145, GN, all RG 45.

19. Irwin to Benson, June 5, 1918, quoted in Lord, "The History of Naval Aviation, 1898–1939," 521; NBG, Misc. Histories, box 910, ZGU, and Edwards to Cone, May 5, 1918, box 133, GA-2, RG 45; also Sims, *Victory at Sea*, 521.

20. Telegram, Paris Headquarters, April 10, 1918, SS/Ga-146, SHM. Ingalls to Davison, May 13, 1918, and Gates to Davison, May 24, 1918, both Davison Papers, YA; *Extracts from the Letters of George Clark Moseley*, 171–74.

21. Sheely, *Sailor of the Air*, 130–38.

22. *Extracts from the Letters of George Clark Moseley*, 174–86; Rossano, *The Price of Honor*, 166–79. "Machines are very different from sensitive little machines most of us have been driving." Beach in Paine, *The First Yale Unit*, II, 24–25; also Ingalls to Mother and Father, May 29, June 1, 5, 6, and 11, 1918, and Ingalls Diary, May 24–June 30, 1918, all IF.

23. Lambe to Cone, June 8, 1918, and Grey to Lambe, July 13, 1918, both AIR 1/70/15/9/122, NAUK; Sims to Paris HQ, June 6, 1918; Memo to London HQ re: Navy pilots at Stonehenge, June 17, 1918; and Weekly Reports, June 29, July 20 and 27, 1918, all box 133, GA-2, RG 45; Ramsey to Craven, Training Memo, June 9, 1918, box 2, Records of Naval Forces Operating in European Waters, Aviation Section (Entry 34), RG 72. Concerning assignment of Ensign Lee to Stonehenge, see Craven to Cone, May 17, 1918, Craven Papers, LC.

24. Weekly Reports, July 20 and 27, 1918, box 133, GA-2, RG 45.

25. Cable, Sims to Paris HQ, June 14, 1918; Sims to Cone, June 21, 1918; and Weekly Report, August 17, 1918, all box 133, GA-2, RG 45.

26. Letters of May 31 and September 30, 1918, Alvord Papers, NAM.

27. Beach in Paine, *The First Yale Unit*, II, 25; Rossano, *The Price of Honor*, 185.

28. Acquisition of the NBG fields through RAF in AIR 1/70/15/9/122, NAUK; also Lord, "The History of Naval Aviation, 1898–1939," 181–84.

29. Hanrahan to Craven, December 31, 1918, box 2, Records Relating to Demobilization Overseas, (Entry 44), RG 72.

30. Johnson relieved in August by Lovett, who also acted as Night Wing commander; Weekly Reports of June 29 and July 6, 1918, box 144, GN, RG 45.

31. "History of Construction NBG," 21, box 144, GN, RG 45.

32. Paine, *The First Yale Unit*, II, 216–17, 224, 232–41; McDonnell to Hanrahan, and Train to Cone, both August 12, 1918, and McDonnell to Cone, August 13, 1918. Complete

recapitulation of Navy Capronis in Memo, Hanrahan to Cone, August 24, 1918; Aviation Ministry to Turin, August 20, 1918, all box 156, GU, RG 45.

33. Ops. Officer to Group Commander (RAF), October 1, 1918, box 144, GN; Bulletin #20, October 5, 1918, box 910, ZGU, both RG 45.

34. Rossano, *The Price of Honor*, 185–91; Sheely, *Sailor of the Air*, 149–53; Ingalls Diary, July 8–22, 1918, IF; *Extracts from the Letters of George Clark Moseley*, 187–201; Toulon to Hanrahan, August 20 (30), 1918; Gates to Hanrahan, August 22, 1918, both box 144, GN, RG 45.

35. See especially Ingalls Diary, August 9–October 3, 1918, IF.

36. On September 1 General Lambe suggested that all surplus Marine pilots be assigned to the Audembert pool. Lambe to Cone, September 1, 1918, AIR 1/70/15/9/122, NAUK; Operations Officer to Group Commander, NBG, October 1, 1918, box 156, GU; Weekly Reports, October 12 and 18, 1918, box 133, GA-2 file, both RG 45.

37. Captain Francis Mulcahy and observer Thomas McCullough, flying with No. 218 Squadron, also received credit for destroying a Fokker D-VII over Coremarch. [*Sounds like same incident*]; see Bulletin #20, October 5, 1918, USNAF Operating in European Waters. Bulletin #25 says each pilot received the Distinguished Service Medal for this mission. Their observers—Gunnery Sergeants Archie Paschal and Amil Wiman—received the Navy Cross, box 910, ZGU file, RG 45.

38. Sims to Cone June 24, 1918, box 963, ZPA, RG 45; also Bludworth, *The Battle of Eastleigh*, 86–90.

39. Cone to Irwin July 25, 1918, box 132, GA-1 and Edwards to Cone, July 26, 1918, box 133, GA-2, both RG 45.

40. Chevalier to Cone, August 16, 1918; Paine, *The First Yale Unit*, II, 223; Coombe to Callan, July 28, 1918, box 156, GU, and ms. "History of Northern Bombing Group," box 910, ZGU, both RG 45; Bludworth, *The Battle of Eastleigh*, 10–13.

41. Rossano, *The Price of Honor*, 214; Ingalls Diary, October 4–November 18, 1918, IF.

42. Bulmer to Sims, September 27, 1918, box 962, ZPA, RG 45; Ingalls to Mother and Father, October 10, 1918, IF.

43. Bludworth, *The Battle of Eastleigh*, 96–98.

44. Bulmer to Sims, Inspection Form, October 10, 1918, box 963, ZPA, RG 45.

45. Mayo's report in box 1, Records USNAFFS, Belgian Bombing to France, Misc. (Entry 35), RG 72; Ingalls to Mother, October 10, 1918, IF; Bludworth, *The Battle of Eastleigh*, 143; Cable of February 2, 1919, says transfer "permitting you to dispose of Brest Air Station." Cable of February 9, 1919, both box 963, ZPA, RG 45.

46. Records of Proceedings of a Board of Inquiry, September 15, 1918, and Memo, Lovett to Hanrahan, September 15, 1918, both box 910, ZGU; unsigned, undated report, box 461, PA, all RG 45; and Coombe quoted in Paine, *The First Yale Unit*, II, 238–39.

47. Marines received their first DH-4 September 7; the first reached France September 23; Squadron D/10, Capt. R. A. Presley, reached La Fresne October 8. Cone to Craven, September 30, 1918, Craven Papers, LC; Lord, "The History of Naval Aviation, 1898–1939," 554.

48. Sims to Irwin, November 1, 1918, box 133, GA-2, RG 45; Medal of Honor citation.

49. Ten aircraft took part in raid, four reached the target; "News release from Committee on Public Information," undated; Cable, Hanrahan to Sims, October 26, 1918, both box 144, GN, RG 45.

50. Statement made by Gibbs, November 5, 1918, and statement by Nelms, same date; heavy rain in the fall caused all Marine flight operations to be concentrated at La Fresne field.

51. Ames to Davison, September 29, 1918, Davison Papers, YA.

CHAPTER 12. TILL IT'S OVER, OVER THERE: SEPTEMBER 1918–APRIL 1919

1. American plans projected a force of 510 aircraft, 12 dirigibles, and 18 kite balloons by January 1, 1919, operated by 1,880 officers (1,038 pilots) and 19,585 enlisted men; it would include 451 officers/4,583 ratings with NBG, 795/10,666 at French coastal stations, 287/2,467 in Ireland, 144/2,470 in Italy, and 106/1,100 in England. Cone, Memo, 8 August 1918, SS/Ga-144, SHM. Edwards to Cone, June 3, August 4 and 5, 1918, box 133, GA-1, RG 45.

2. Maxfield to Cone, August 17, 1918, in Lord, "The History of Naval Aviation, 1898–1939," 561.

3. Craven to Cone, August 6, 1918, box 131, GA-1, RG 45.

4. McCrary to Cone, August 9, 1918, in Lord, "The History of Naval Aviation, 1898–1939," 562; Memo, McCrary to Cone, box 156, GU, RG 45.

5. Callan to Cone, August 14 and September 6, 1918, in Lord, "The History of Naval Aviation, 1898–1939," 563–64.

6. Additional French participants included Capitaine de Vaisseau Chauvin, Chef du Service Militaire de l'Aeronautique et des Patrouilles Aeriennes, and Capitaine de Frigate Stotz, Chef des Sections Aviation et Aerostation. Cone to Minister of Marine, July 29, 1918, SS/Ga-144, SHM; proces Verbal de la Conference Franco-Americain du 29 Aout 1918, SS/Ga-144, SHM; Lord, "The History of Naval Aviation, 1898–1939," 565.

7. British Notes on Proposed Conference, September 11, 1918; unsigned Memo (Edwards?) to Cone, September 12, 1918; Guggenheim to Cone, September 11, 1918, all Lord, "The History of Naval Aviation, 1898–1939," 566–67.

8. American representatives were F. H. Schofield, Cone, McCrary, Whiting, W. A. Edwards, H. F. Guggenheim, and G. R. Fearing.

9. Sims, Highly Secret to CNO, September 25, 1918, and Cone to Irwin, September 24, 1918, both in Lord, "The History of Naval Aviation, 1898–1939," 568, 571; also Sims to SecNav, September 26, 1918, box 3, Records of USNAFFS, Belgian Bombing to France, Misc. (Entry 35), RG 72.

10. Cone to Craven, September 27 and 30, 1918, Craven Papers, LC

11. Edwards to Cone, August 5, 1918; "Notes on proposed agenda for American Conference," Sept 17, 1918; "Memo of September 17 Conference," all quoted in Lord, "The History of Naval Aviation, 1898–1939," 563–64, 566–72; also Cone to Craven September 30, 1918, Craven Papers, LC.

12. Edwards to Planning Section, October 17, 1918, in Lord, "The History of Naval Aviation, 1898–1939," 575; Train to Ministry of Marine, October 30, 1918, box 156, GU; "History of Headquarters U.S. Naval Aviation Forces in Italy," box 919, ZGU, both RG 45.

13. On shortages of supplies and equipment, see Memo, Engineering Officer (Ile Tudy) to Craven, October 12, 1918, box 156, GU; Sims to Daniels, Weekly Report, October 25, 1918, box 133, GA-2 file, both RG 45. Craven to Cone, October 2, 1918, Craven Papers, LC; Cone to Craven, October 4, 1918, Craven Papers, LC; Mayo to Daniels, October 13 and November 12, 1918, both box 460, PA, RG 45.

14. Minutes, Weekly Conference, August 21, 1918, box 1, Aviation Section Reports 1918–1919 (Entry 36), RG 72; Cone to Craven, September 5, 1918, Craven Papers, LC.

15. OpNav to Sims, August 29, 1918, box 446, Dispatches to/from Naval Forces Operating in European Waters (Entry 55), RG 72; The Board's tour described by Graham Brush in Paine, *The First Yale Unit*, I, 284–85; see also Cone to Craven, September 12, 1918, Craven Papers, LC.

16. Paine, *The First Yale Unit*, I, 138.

17. Progress Report October 1, 1918, to November 1, 1918, box 133, GA-1, RG 45; Memo to CNO, February 8, 1919, box 335, Requisitions and Shipping Orders from Air Squadrons Abroad (Entry 33), RG 72.

18. Sims to Daniels, Weekly Report, October 25, 1918, box 133, GA-2, RG 45; see also undated Memorandum for Director of Naval Aviation (extract of October 10 General Report) listing overseas strength on October 1 as 660 officers, 15,000 enlisted men, 97 H-16 aircraft, 167 HS types, 110 other aircraft. Box 133, GA-2, RG 45.

19. Miley Report, AIR 1/475/15/312, NAUK.

20. Craven to Cone, November 8, 11, 15, 1918; Cone to Craven, November 16, 1918. Craven discounted Irwin, he being "so many thousands of miles away and who cannot understand the difficulties we are laboring under." Craven to Cone, December 16, 1918, all Craven Papers, LC.

21. See previous recommendation by Cdr. Henry Dinger, July 15, 1918, box 1, Records USNAFFS, Belgian Bombing to France, Misc. (Entry 35), RG 72; Sims to Daniels, October 17, 1918, box 134, GA-2, RG 45.

22. Turnbull and Lord, *History of United States Naval Aviation*, 153–54; Train to Sims, December 17, 1918, box 13, Papers as Assistamt Secretary of the Navy, 1913–1920, FDRPLM.

23. "Brief Summary of U.S. Navy in France November 1918–October 1919," 65–71, ZO, RG 45.

24. Craven to Cone, November 8 and 11, 1918, Craven Papers, LC.

25. Aviation Section Bulletin #25, November 9, 1918, box 1, Aviation Section Reports 1918–1919 (Entry 36), RG 72; Craven to Minister of Marine, January 24, 1919, forwarding a photographic history "as an indication of a part of the Navy of the United States to be of assistance to the Naval Forces of the Allies during the great struggle which has just terminated," SS/Ga-144, SHM.

26. Letter, Craven to Cone, November 11, 1918, Craven Papers, LC. Sims to OpNav, November 22, 1918, box 446, Dispatches to/from Naval Forces Operating in European Waters (entry 54); Ramsey to Craven, April 17, 1919, box 2, Records of Naval Forces Operating in European Waters, Aviation Section (Entry 34), both RG 72. Naval Constructor Jerome Hunsaker, for example, served as part of the Allied Naval Armistice Commission dispatched to Germany in 1919 that gathered intelligence on aeronatutic technology. Trimble, *Jerome C. Hunsaker*, 60–62; see also F. L. Tottenham, "Report of Naval Armistice Commission Inspection," April 15, 1918, box 3, Records USNAFFS, Belgian Bombing to France, Misc. (Entry 35), RG 72.

27. "History, United States Naval Air Station Fromentine," box 963, ZPA. Demobilization discussed in "A Brief Summary of U.S. Navy in France November 1918–October 1919," 65–71, ZO, both RG 45; Aviation Circular No. 79, box 1, Records Relating to Demobilization Overseas (Entry 44), RG 72; Demobilization Circular Letter, No. 1, November

15, 1918, and Circular Letter No. 212–18, Demobilization of Enlisted Personnel of the Navy, November 21, 1918, both box 13, Papers as Assistant Secretary of the Navy, 1913–1920, FDRPLM.

28. Board of Appraisal to Wilson, December 4, 1918, SS/Ga-144, SHM.

29. Demobilization Order No. 3, November 25, 1918, box 1, Records of Naval Forces Operating in European Waters, Aviation Section (Entry 34), RG 72; Turnbull and Lord, *History of United States Naval Aviation*, 148–49; Robert Read to Hanrahan, November 24, 1918, box 144, GN, RG 45.

30. From Fromentine entry in "Report for the Assistant to the Secretary of the Navy," February 5, 1918, box 1, Records relating to NAS in France 1919 (Entry 41), RG 72.

31. CNO to Sims, December 4, 1918, box 1, Records relating to Demoblization Overseas (Entry 44), and Wilson to Ministry of Marine, December 16, 1918, box 1, Records Relating to NAS in France, 1919 (Entry 41), both RG 72; Craven to Cone, November 15, 1918, Craven Papers, LC.

32. Roosevelt to Sims, January 17, 1919; he filed his own extensive report on April 10, 1919, both box 13, Papers as Assistant Secretary of the Navy, 1913–1920, FDRPLM; see also Roosevelt cable, January 18, 1919, box 1, Records relating to NAS in France, 1919 (Entry 41), RG 72; Morgan, *FDR*, 212–13. Turnbull and Lord claimed that the French drove hard bargains, *History of United States Naval Aviation*, 148–49; Craven to Cone, November 28, 1918, and February 17, 1919, both Craven Papers, LC. The Paymaster Craven referred to was Commander John Hancock, who filed a lengthy report to Roosevelt on March 27, 1919, box 13, Papers as Assistant Secretary of the Navy, 1913–1920, FDRPLM.

33. For costs, see box 2, Records Relating to Demobilization Overseas (Entry 44), RG 72.

34. Daniels to Tobey and Daniels to Craven, both February 12, 1919, quoted in "Report of Franklin Roosevelt with Regard to Demobilization in Europe, 13–18, box 13, Papers as Assistant Secretary of the Navy, 1913–1920, FDRPLM; Sims to Wilson, November 11, 1918, box 1, and "Report for the Assistant to the Secretary of the Navy," February 5, 1918, boxes 1 and 2, Records relating to NAS in France 1919 (Entry 41), RG 72; Craven to Minister of Marine, November 23, 1918 SS/Ga-147, SHM; Turnbull and Lord, *History of United States Naval Aviation*, 148; a list of claims is included in "Report Submitted by Commander J. M. Hancock," March 27, 1919, 35–36, box 13, Papers as Assistant Secretary of the Navy, 1913–1920, FDRPLM.

35. Irish cost estimates in box 1, Records of European Forces Operating in European Waters, Aviation Section (Entry 34), RG 72; see also "Minutes of a Conference . . . Held in Dublin, February 17, 1919," and Letter, Jackson to Roosevelt, June 21, 1920, both box 13, Papers as Assistant Secretary of the Navy, 1913–1920, FDRPLM.

36. Capehart to Craven, January 6, 1919; Cabaniss to Craven, January 15, 1919; Cecil to Craven, February 16, 1919; Griffin to Craven, February 15, 1919, all Craven Papers, LC; also Roosevelt, "Attitude of the Navy Toward a United Air Service," June 14, 1919, Ramsey Papers, NHHC.

37. Craven to Cone, January 28 and February 17, 1919, Craven Papers, LC.

38. There is no agreement on these numbers among the various official and unofficial sources.

39. This was just a fraction of the flight activity carried out by the Navy in World War I. In the period August–October 1918, aviators in the United States compiled at least

5,000,000 miles of training flights and 1,300,000 miles of patrol. Ellington, "Naval Aviation Activities during the World War," box 910, ZGU, RG 45.

40. Craven to Cone, November 8, 1918, Craven Papers, LC

41. See Craven's c. 1946 memoir of this period in box 909, ZGN, RG 45.

42. Earle to Craven, November 22, 1918. Cone discounted the threat. Cone to Craven, December 19, 1918, both Craven Papers, LC; also Trimble, *Jerome C. Hunsaker*, 62, 69–70, and *Admiral William W. Moffett*, 64–80.

BIBLIOGRAPHY

ARCHIVES

David Ingalls and Louise Harkness Ingalls Foundation, Shaker Heights, Ohio (IF)

David Ingalls Papers

Library of Congress (LC)

Adm. William Benson Papers
Adm. John Callan Papers
Adm. Thomas Craven Papers
Adm. William Sims Papers

Marine Corps Historical Center (MCHC)

Lt. Col Alfred Cunningham Diary

Massachusetts Historical Society (MHS)

Robert Gilbert interview

National Archives of the United States (NA)

RG 45 Sub File 1911–1927 Naval Records Collection of the Office of Naval Records and Library
RG 72 Records of the Bureau of Aeronautics 1911–1946
RG 80 General Records of the Department of the Navy 1804–1958
General Board Hearings Microfilm 1493 Roll #11, #12, #13, Begins 1919 hearings #14

National Archives of the United Kingdom, Kew, England (NAUK)

Record Group AIR 1   Air Historical Branch: Papers (Series I)
Record Group AIR 2   Air Ministry and Ministry of Defense: Registered Files
Record Group AIR 27   Air Ministry and Successors: Operations Record Books, Squadrons, or inherited by the Air Ministry, the Royal Air Force, and related bodies

National Naval Aviation Museum (NAM), Emil Buehler Library (EBL)

Donald Alvord Papers
Herr W. Brady Papers
Joseph Cline Papers/Flight Log Books

Arden Dudley Andrew Papers
Wayne Duffet Papers
Joseph Eaton Papers
J. D. Jernigan Papers/Flight Log Books
D. L. Jolly Papers
Wellesley Laud-Brown Papers
William Townsley Papers

Navy History and Heritage Command (NHHC)

John Callan Scrapbooks
Cdr. Albert M. Cohen Collection
Carlton McKelvey Memoir
Adm. DeWitt Ramsey Papers

Franklin D. Roosevelt Presidential Library and Museum (FDRPLM)

Papers as Assistant Secretary of the Navy, 1913–1920

Service Historique de la Marine, Chateau de Vincennes, Paris (SHM)

Series SS, Sub-series Ga *Direction generale de la guerre sous-marine de l'aeronautique et les patrouilles aeriennes*
Ga-143   Liaison avec les Allies, Etats-Unis 1917–1919
Ga-144   Aviation Americaine en France, organisation generale, operations, 1917–1919
Ga-145   Aviation Americaine en France, personnel, materiel, colombophile 1917–1919
Ga-146   Aviation Americaine en France, dossiers de centers (Dunquerke, Tréguier, L'Aber-Wrach, Brest, Ile Tudy, Le Croisic), plans, photos, 1917–1919
Ga-147   Aviation Americaine en France, dossiers de centers (La Pallice, La Trinité, St. Trojan, Pauillac, Arcachon, Moutchic), plans, photos, 1917–1919
Ga-148   Brevets, Orders, Movement of Personnel
Ga-149   French Bases, dossiers de centers, plans, photos, 1917–1919

Yale University Library and Archives (YA)

F. Trubee Davison Papers

PUBLISHED BOOKS AND ARTICLES

Abbatiello, John. *Anti-Submarine Warfare in World War One: British Naval Aviation and the Defeat of the Submarine*. London: Routledge, 2006.
"An American Naval Air Base." *Sphere* (October 26, 1918): 66–67.
Arthur, Reginald Wright. *Contact! Careers of Naval Aviators Assigned Numbers 1–2000.* Washington, D.C.: Naval Aviation Register, 1967.
Bludworth, T. Francis. *The Battle of Eastleigh, England, USNAF.* New York: Thompson, 1919.
Christiansen, Friedrich. "Battle Flights over the Channel." *Over the Front* 15, No. 3 (Autumn 2000): 230–32.
Coletta, Paolo E., and K. Jack Bauer. *United States Navy and Marine Corps Bases, Overseas.* Westport, Conn.: Greenwood Press, 1985.

Congress, U.S. Subcommittee of the Committee on Naval Affairs, Hearings: Naval Investigation, 66th Congress, 2nd session, Washington, D.C.: GPO, 1921.
Cosmas, Graham A., and Edward C. Johnson. *Marine Corps Aviation: The Early Years 1912–1940*. Washington, D.C.: History and Museums Division, U.S. Marine Corps, 1977.
Cunningham, Alfred A. *A Marine Flyer in France*. Washington, D.C.: History and Museums Division, U.S. Marine Corps, 1974.
Davison, Daniel. "The First Yale Unit." *Over the Front* 12, No. 3 (Autumn 1997): 265–69.
Edwards, W. Atlee. "The U.S. Naval Air Force in Action, 1917–1918." *United States Naval Institute Proceedings* 48, No. 11 (November 1922): 1863–82.
Emons, Roger. "The First Marine Aviation Force." *Cross and Cockade* 6, No. 2 (1965): 173–86 and 6, No. 3 (1965): 272–92.
Extracts from the Letters of George Clark Moseley during the Period of the Great War. Privately printed, 1930.
Fitzgerald, Pat. *Down Paths of Gold*. Middleton, Ire.: Litho Press, 1992.
Flying Officers of the United States Navy. Washington, D.C.: Naval Aviation War Book Committee, 1919.
Friedel, Frank. *Franklin D. Roosevelt: The Apprenticeship*. Boston: Little, Brown, 1952.
Goodall, Michael. "Lighters." *Cross and Cockade International* 12, No. 20 (Summer 1981): 72–80.
Grant, Robert. "Aircraft against U-Boats." *United States Naval Institute Proceedings* 65, No. 6 (June 1939): 824–28.
Grossnick, Roy. *Kite Balloons to Airships . . . The Navy's Lighter-than-Air Experience*. Washington, D.C.: Deputy Chief of Naval Operations (Air Warfare) and the Commander, Naval Air Systems Command, n.d.
———. *United States Naval Aviation 1910–1995*. Washington, D.C.: Naval Historical Center, 1997.
Hallam, T. D. *The Spider Web: The Romance of a Flying-Boat War Flight*. Edinburgh: William Blackwood and Sons, 1919.
Hayes, Karl E. *The History of the Royal Air Force and the United States Naval Air Service in Ireland, 1913–1923*. Dublin: Irish Air Letter, 1988.
Hildreth, Alonzo. "Over There—World War I." *All Hands*, Bureau of Naval Personnel Information (June 1962): 56–63.
Hudson, James. *Hostile Skies*. Syracuse, N.Y.: Syracuse University Press, 1968.
Kennett, Lee. *The First Air War*. New York: Free Press, 1991.
Killingholme Yearbook. London: Hudson & Kearns, 1918.
Klachko, Mary, with David Trask. *Admiral William Shepherd Benson: First Chief of Naval Operations*. Annapolis, Md.: Naval Institute Press, 1987.
Knapp, Mary W. "Flying Boats over the North Sea—1918." *Over the Front* 9, No. 2 (Summer 1994): 120–33.
Knott, Richard C. *The American Flying Boat, an Illustrated History*. Annapolis, Md.: Naval Institute Press, 1979.
Lamberton, W. M. (edited by E. E. Cheeseman). *Reconnaissance and Bomber Aircraft of the First World War*. Letchworth, UK: Harrlyford, 1962.
———. *Fighter Aircraft of the First World War*. Letchworth, UK: Harrlyford, 1960.
Layman, R. D. *Naval Aviation in the First World War*. London: Chatham, 1996.

———. "Rubber Cows: U.S. Navy Shipboard Balloons in World War I." *Over the Front* 11, No. 2 (Summer 1996): 164–68.
Layman, R. D., and E. J. L. Halpern. "Allied Aircraft vs. German Submarines." *Cross and Cockade* 11, No. 4 (Winter 1970): 289–304.
Lord, Clifford L. "The History of Naval Aviation, 1898–1939." 1946. Office of the Deputy Chief of Naval Operations (Air). Naval Aviation History Unit Office, Washington, D.C.
MacLeish, Kenneth (edited by Martha MacLeish). *Kenneth: A Collection of Letters Written by Lt. Kenneth MacLeish*. Chicago: Privately printed, 1919.
Malandrino, Greg. "Alfred Austell Cunningham: Father of Marine Corps Aviation." *Over the Front* 14, No. 2 (Summer 1999): 358–67.
Melville, Phillips. "Piloti Americani in Italia." *AAHS Journal* 18, No. 4 (Winter 1973): 229–43.
———."Piloti Americani in Italia: An Addendum." *AAHS Journal* 19, No. 1 (Spring 1974): 58–65.
Mersky, Peter. "David S. Ingalls: Naval Air Reservist, First Navy Ace." *Foundation* (Spring 1991): 81–91.
Messimer, Dwight R. *Find and Destroy: Antisubmarine Warfare in World War I*. Annapolis, Md.: Naval Institute Press, 2001.
Miller, Nathan. *FDR: An Intimate History*. Garden City, N.Y.: Doubleday, 1983.
Miller, Thomas. "The Hornets of Zeebrugge." *Cross and Cockade* 11, No. 1 (Spring 1970): 9–30.
———. "Naval Aviation Overseas, 1917–1918: Early Planning and Organization." *Cross and Cockade* 4, No. 1 (Spring 1963): 52–83.
Molson, Kenneth. "The Felixstowe F5L." *Cross and Cockade* (Br) 9, No. 2 (Summer 1978): 49–67.
Morgan, Ted. *FDR: A Biography*. New York: Simon and Schuster, 1985.
Morris, Michael J. "Combat Effectiveness: United States Marine Corps Aviation in the First World War." *Over the Front* 12, No. 3 (Autumn 1997): 232–38.
Munson, Kenneth. *Bombers, Patrol, and Reconaissance Aircraft 1914–1919*. London: Blandford/MacMillan/Cassell PLC, 1968.
O'Neal, Michael. "First to Fall: George Herbert Manley, USN." *Over the Front* 17, No. 1 (Spring 2002): 37–48.
Owers, Colin. "The Curtiss HS Flying Boats," part 1. *Over the Front* 18, No. 2 (Summer 2003): 160–87.
———. "Handley Page Trainee Pilot." *Cross and Cockade International* 23, No. 3 (Autumn 1992): 113–19.
———. "Killingholme Diary," parts 1 and 2, *Cross and Cockade International* 35, Nos. 3, 4 (Autumn, Winter 2004): 169–95, 211–32.
———. *Curtiss H-12: Windsock Data File 125*. Berkhamsted: Albatross Productions, 2007.
Paine, Ralph. *The First Yale Unit: A Story of Naval Aviation 1916–1919*. Cambridge, Mass.: Riverside Press, 1925. 2 vols.
Perry, Lawrence. *Our Navy in the War*. New York: Charles Scribner's Sons, 1919.
Price, Alfred. *Aircraft vs. Submarine: The Evolution of Anti-Submarine Aircraft 1912 to 1972*. London: William Kimber, 1972.

Ramsey, DeWitt. "The Development of Aviation in the Fleet." *United States Naval Institute Proceedings* 49, No. 9 (September 1923): 1395–1418.

Reynolds, Clark. *Admiral John H. Towers: The Struggle for Naval Air Supremacy.* Annapolis, Md.: Naval Institute Press, 1991.

Roseler, Al, Michael O'Neal, and Frank Bailey, eds. "The Observer: The Memoirs of Valentine J. Burger, Part I." *Over the Front* 23, No. 1 (2008): 4–39.

Roskill, S. W., ed. *Documents Relating to the Naval Air Service*, Vol. 1, 1910–1918. London: Navy Records Society, 1969.

Rossano, Geoffrey. "Doing Their Duty Side by Side." *AAHS Journal* 28, Nos. 3/4 (Fall/Winter 1983): 181–89.

———. *The Price of Honor: The World War One Letters of Naval Aviator Kenneth MacLeish.* Annapolis, Md.: Naval Institute Press, 1991.

Russell, Sandy, et al., eds. *Naval Aviation 1911–1986: A Pictorial Study.* Washington, D.C.: Deputy Chief of Naval Operations (Warfare) and the Commander, Naval Air Systems Command, 1986.

Sheely, Lawrence. "Irving Edward Sheely–Naval Observer." *Over the Front* 3, No. 2 (Summer 1988): 99–133.

———, ed. *Sailor of the Air: The 1917–1919 Letters and Diary of USN CMM/A Irving Edward Sheely.* Tuscaloosa: University of Alabama Press, 1993.

Shirley, Noel. "A Brief History of U.S. Naval Dirigible Stations in France." *Over the Front* 2, No. 4 (Winter 1987): 356–70.

———. "Capt. LaGuardia, Caproni Bombers, and the U.S. Navy." *Cross and Cockade* 25, No. 2 (Summer 1984): 125–40.

———. "John Lansing Callan—Naval Aviation Pioneer." *Over the Front* 2, No. 4, (Winter 1987): 180–85.

———. *United States Naval Aviation 1910–1918.* Atglen, Pa.: Schiffer Military History, 2000.

———. "Wartime Memoirs of John Jay Schieffelin." *Over the Front* 9, No. 2 (Summer 1994): 99–119.

Sims, William. *The Victory at Sea.* New York: Doubleday, 1920.

Sitz, W. H. "A History of United States Naval Aviation." Technical Note #18, Series of 1930. Washington, D.C.: Bureau of Aeronautics, 1930.

Sloan, James J. *Wings of Honor: American Airmen in World War I.* Atglen, Pa.: Schieffer, 1994.

Sprague, G. E. "Flying Gobs." *Liberty Magazine* (January 7–21, 1939): 14–16, 24–27, 51–53.

Still, William N., Jr. *Crisis at Sea: The United States Navy in European Waters in World War I.* Gainesville: University Press of Florida, 2006.

Stock, James. *Zeebrugge, 23 April 1918.* New York: Ballantine Books, 1974.

Stratham, D. G. *The Gosport Diaries.* Privately published, 1981.

Swanborough, Gordon, and Peter Bowers. *United States Naval Aircraft since 1911.* New York: Putnam, 1968.

Trask, David. *Captains and Admirals; Anglo-American Naval Relations 1917–1918.* Columbia: University of Missouri Press, 1972.

Treadwell, Terry. *America's First Air War: The United States Army, Naval, and Marine Air Services in the First World War.* Osceola, Wis.: MBI Publishing, 2000.

———. *The First Naval Air War*. Stroud, UK: Tempus, 2002.

Trimble, William. *Admiral William W. Moffett: Architect of Naval Aviation*. Washington, D.C.: Smithsonian Institution Press, 1994.

———. *Jerome C. Hunsaker and the Rise of American Aeronautics*. Washington, D.C.: Smithsonian Institution Press, 2002.

———. *Wings for the Navy: A History of the Naval Aircraft Factory 1917–1956*. Annapolis, Md.: Naval Institute Press, 1990.

Turnbull, Archibald D., and Clifford L. Lord. *History of United States Naval Aviation*. New Haven, Conn.: Yale University Press, 1949.

United States Naval Air Station, Killingholme. Killingholme: The Station, 1918.

U. S. Naval Air Station Wexford Souvenir. London: Griggs & Sons, 1918.

United States Naval Aviation 1910–1980, 3rd ed. Washington, D.C.: Naval Historical Center, 1981.

van Deurs, George. *Wings for the Fleet*. Annapolis, Md.: Naval Institute Press, 1966.

Van Wyen, Adrian O. *Naval Aviation in World War I*. Washington, D.C.: Office of CNO, Navy Department, 1969.

Whistler, Richard T. "The Making of a Dunkirk Aviator: The War Experiences of Ensign James Henry O'Brien, USNRF," Parts I and II. *Over the Front* 14, No. 4 (Winter 2001): 347–61 and 17, No. 1 (Spring 2002): 4–25.

Wickes, Z. W. "Destruction of the Flanders Triangle." *United States Naval Institute Proceedings* 45, No. 7 (July 1919): 1093–116.

Woolbridge, E. T., ed. *The Golden Age Remembered*. Annapolis, Md.: Naval Institute Press, 1998.

Wortman, Marc. *The Millionaires' Unit*. New York: Public Affairs, 2006.

Wright, Peter. "Dunkerque Days and Nights." *Cross and Cockade International* 23, No. 2 (Summer 1992): 131–144.

INDEX

Accidents and crashes, 234, 242; at Dunkirk, 60, 61, 69–70, 97, 103; First Aeronautic Detachment and, 31, 34, 41; with French coastal unit, 91–92, 94–95, 97–98, 116–17; in Ireland, 218; in Italy, 291, 293, 300; at Moutchic, 87; with RNAS/RAF, 154, 158, 183, 184, 392n37; with NBG, 333–34, 335, 340–41, 342–43

Admiralty (British): 1919 plans and, 346; aviation proposals, 146–47; cooperation with U.S. naval aviation, 134–35, 167; Ireland, plans for, 50, 168, 208–11, 219, 224, 227; lighter program and, 168–69, 182, 391n19; Northern Bombing Group and, 319, 324–25, 403n18

Adriatic Mine Barrage, 349, 350

Adriatic Sea, 127, 285, 286, 287, 303, 305, 348–52 passim

AEF. *See* American Expeditionary Force

Aeronautical Detachment #1. *See* First Aeronautic Detachment

Aghada. *See* Queenstown

Aircraft, 373–75; acquisition, 45, 56, 81–82, 125, 169–70, 242, 264; Breguet, characteristics, 326; Caproni, defects, 297, 303–6, 307, 332–33, 340–41; characteristics, 17, 30, 39, 75, 79, 116, 234–35, 243, 334, 373–75; Curtiss H-16, 170, 218, 219; cost, 242; crashes of (*see* Accidents and crashes); decoration, 70–71, 300; DH-4, 132; DH-9, 334; defects, 96, 103, 109–10, 113, 144–45, 146, 166; enemy, 18, 66, 163–64, 299, 317; F2A "Large America," 158–60; Killingholme aircraft, defects, 174–75, 179–80; Lighter-than-Air craft, 261, 264, 274; Lovett's descriptions, 161–62; "Porte Superbaby," 157; shipping delays, 120, 143–44, 146, 212, 354–55; Short seaplanes, 165; Sopwith Camel, 151; Navy types, 373–75; Westervelt Board investigation, 354–55. *See also individual aircraft types*

Aircraft motors (engines), 30, 33, 166, 373–75; Clerget, 33, 39, 166; Fiat, 304, 305, 307, 311, 339; Hispano-Suiza, 33, 101, 135; Isotta-Fraschini, 304, 307, 311, 339; Liberty, 33, 101, 110, 113, 125, 127, 130, 138, 142–44, 179, 354–55, 358; Rolls-Royce, 1, 157, 161, 179, 374, 391; Sunbeam, 235

Air Ministry (British), 6, 134, 139, 337, 360, 403

Airships. *See* Lighter-than-Air (LTA) operations

Aldis signaling lamp, 110, 118, 166, 233

Alembon aerodrome, 330, 331

Alvord, Ens. Donald "Doc," 166, 328

Amalgamation controversy, 123, 133, 137–40, 145, 148, 167, 315; Hutch Cone views and, 139, 350; Edwards' views and, 138, 139, 389n28, 389n29; junior officers views and, 138–39; RAF role in, 135, 139

American Expeditionary Force (AEF), 89, 278, 288, 316, 341–42, 362; Navy relations with, 46, 133, 136–38, 306, 309, 319, 324, 326

Ancona, 312, 348, 349, 351

Anderson, Wilfred (radio operator), 223

Andrews, Lt.(jg) Edward, 276

Antisubmarine tactics: aircraft employed, 158–60, 165, 233, 242–43, 373–75; *Alerte/Allo* responses, 237–38; attacks on U-boats, 71–72, 83, 102–3, 155, 164, 177, 184, 216, 219, 238; convoy duty, 160, 237; intelligence, importance of, 239–40; patrol methods, 235–36; weapons, 155, 233–34

Arcachon naval air station, 22, 24, 82, 125, 347; construction, 119–20; operational history, 120–22; postwar disposition, 122, 363; selection and description, 119

Army General Purchasing Board, 264, 306

Arnold, Col. Henry "Hap," 325
Ash Can (newspaper, Lough Foyle), 256
Aster, Lt. M. J., 281
Astra-Torres airships, 264, 278
Athletics, 13, 220, 231, 249, 256–58
Atwater, Ens. William "Bull," 200, 250, 291, 400; commanding officer at Bolsena, 293–95, 302; early career of, 292
Austria-Hungary, 23, 227, 312, 348, 351, 352, 359
Autingues, 314, 330, 332
Avord (Avord-Cher), 32, 49, 59, 87, 124, 325, 327
Ayr School of Aerial Fighting: deaths of Navy pilots at, 32, 153, 379; training of Navy pilots at, 49, 59, 150–53

Babbitt, Lt. Leman L.: commanding officer at NAS Arcachon, 120; commanding officer at NAS Gujan, 257, 277–78
Baker, Claude (seaman), death of at Moutchic, 87
Baker, Capt. Hobey, 74
Baker, Newton (secretary of war), 323
Baldwin, Lt. Augustus, 104, 105
Bamrick, Ens. Edward, 71, 73
Banks, John (observer), 103
Bantry Bay station. *See* Whiddy Island naval air station
Barnes, Asst. Paymaster Douglas, 283
Barnes, Ens. Phillip, 270
Barnett, Commandant George, 319
Barr, Lt. Chapin, 336
Barr, Ens. W. M., 116
Barrett, LQM Thomas, death of, 31
Barry, Ens. Edmund, death of, 117
Bartlett, Lt. Harold "Cueless," 20, 21, 86, 87, 88
Bassett, Ens. Charles "Chet," 59, 60, 62, 335
Bastedo, Lt. Paul, 43
Bayly, Adm. Lewis, 208, 214, 229
Bay of Biscay, 24, 25, 32, 34, 41, 81, 99, 147, 169, 277, 349
Beach, Ens. Frederick, 85, 87, 327, 329, 335, 403n22
"Beef Trip," 160–61
Bell (ship), 268
Bella (ship), 91, 108, 112, 124, 272, 363
Benham (ship), 268, 281, 357
Benson, Adm. William S., 21, 26, 52, 54, 140, 317, 359; Craven offered position of director of naval aviation, 366; First Aeronautic Detachment and, 7; naval aviation, attitudes toward, 26, 27, 51, 52, 168, 169, 210, 285, 354–55; Northern Bombing Group, views of, 288, 319, 323, 324; postwar reorganization of naval aviation and, 369; Sims, relations with, 28, 51, 269; trips to Europe, 51, 85, 95, 141, 255, 363
Bergen, Ens. Louis, death of, 300
Bergues aerodrome, 64, 65
Bessaneau hangar, 37, 93, 100, 104, 115, 243, 244, 402
Billings, LCdr. A.W.K., 44, 48, 129, 322, 337, 352, 380
Blakely, Ens. Robert, 281
Blimps. *See* Lighter-than-Air (LTA) operations
Bluejackets. *See* Enlisted personnel
Bolles, LCdr. Frederick, 337, 338
Bolling, Maj. Raynal C., 20, 137; cooperation with naval aviation, 46, 136, 381
Bolling Commission, 20, 27, 112, 305, 353, 378
Bolsena, Lake, 123, 250, 256, 258, 353, 357; Calderara role at, 286, 290, 292, 293; Italian seaplane school at, 286, 292; Navy relations with Italians at, 290, 294–95; training Navy personnel at, 124, 292–94, 295, 297
Bone, Wing Cdr., 135
Boorse, Arthur, death of, 91
Bordeaux: First Aeronautic Detachment and, 12, 13, 15; LCdr. Callan in, 35, 36; liberty in, 37, 89, 93; possible headquarters evacuation to, 53–54; Whiting visits, 19
Boscombe Down, training of Navy personnel at, 124, 327, 328
Bowhill, Cdr. F. W., 171, 174
Boylan, QM1c Charles J., 9, 102
Brady, Frank (observer), 94, 95, 385
Brancker, Gen. Sefton, 139
Bray, CBM John, 108
Bregar, Asst. Paymaster J. M., 115
Brest: First Aeronautic Detachment and, 13, 14; naval operations there, 27, 84, 89–90, 213–14, 240–41, 267–68, 281–82; relocation of Paris headquarters to, 83, 127, 147
Brest kite balloon station, 265, 267, 268, 364; cruises with destroyers, 279–82; establishment, 279
Brest naval air station: assembly and repair facility development, 91, 92, 109, 123, 127, 132, 193; construction, 50, 90–91, 364; operational history, 91–92, 125, 242, 354,

371; postwar disposition, 92; selection and description, 89–90, 262
Brewer, Lt. Everett, 336
Bridgeport (ship), 279
Briscoe, LCdr. Benjamin, 44, 47, 59, 322, 323, 337; Italy, duties in, 312, 351; Pauillac, activities at, 129, 255
Bristol, Capt. Mark, 27, 261
Brown, Ens. J. N., 120
Brownell, Civil Engineer Ernest H., 44, 47, 48, 211
Bruges, 342; aerial bombardment of, 57, 67, 80, 320–21, 334; defenses, 66, 315; German submarine campaign, role in, 15, 55, 63, 67
Bulmer, Cdr. Bayard, 249, 257; background and early career of, 339; commanding officer at Eastleigh, 338, 339, 340
Bureau of Aeronautics, 138, 365, 368, 370
Burnham, Lt.(jg) Hubert, 129, 331–32
Bush, Ens. Rufus H., 93, 250

Cabaniss, LCdr. Robert, 10, 365; commanding officer at NAS Moutchic, 88–89
Cabot, Ens. Norman, 99
Calais, 62, 320, 330–36 passim, 343
Calderara, Lt. Mario: background and early career of, 286; as commanding officer at Bolsena, 286; relation with Americans at Bolsena, 290, 292, 293
Callan, LCdr. John L., 26, 35–36, 93, 99, 312, 328; background and early career of, 34–35, 285; Caproni aircraft issues and, 304–5, 306, 309, 311; Italian expansion proposals by, 312, 343, 348–49, 351; Italy, activities in, 124, 147, 250, 289–99 passim, 301–2, 311; Italy, mission to, 285–89; Capt. Fiorello LaGuardia and, 305, 309–10; NAS Moutchic, development of, 36–41, 380n52; Paris headquarters, duties at, 44, 49, 87
Calshot, 164, 167, 218, 235
Camaret, 14, 15, 32, 238
Campagne aerodrome, 323, 330, 331, 332
Capehart, Lt. Wadleigh, 126, 250, 365, 368; background and early career of, 112–13; as commanding officer at Fromentine, 113
Capel Royal Naval Air Station, Navy personnel at, 269–270
Capitaine Caussin (airship), 264, 272, 274, 276, 277, 282, 356, 397n6, 398n19
Caproni aircraft, 124, 288, 312, 313; attempts to fly aircraft to France, 291, 332–33; characteristics, 305; difficulties in acquiring, 305–7, 310, 311–12, 323; Eastleigh, attempts to refurbish at, 339; ferry operations to southern Italy, 310–11; Capt. LaGuardia controversy concerning, 305–7, 309–11; May 10 Agreement, 304; McDonnell role in selecting, 303–4; NBG operations with, 316, 322, 340–41, 355; training in, 307–9
Caproni, Giani, 304
Carson, Ens. Julian, 72, 74
Castletownbere (Berehaven) kite balloon station, 210; activities of Navy personnel at, 165–66; operational history, 213–14, 223–24, 228–30; postwar disposition, 230; selection, description, and construction, 212, 227–28
Cattewater Royal Naval Air Station, 147, 164, 165
Caudron aircraft, 19, 30, 31, 38
Cayley, Rear Adm. Cuthbert, 156, 158
Cazaux, 19, 32, 36, 37, 38, 42, 49, 86, 120, 380n53
Cazenave, Cdr., 14
Cecil, Lt. Henry B., 126, 129, 365; background and early career, 108; commanding officer at NAS L'Aber Vrach, 109–11
Chalais Meudon airships, 264
Chambers, Capt. Washington, 5
Chapin, QM2c(A) M. J., death of at NAS Dunkirk, 69
Chevalier, Lt. Godfrey DeC., 250; background and early career of, 9; commanding officer at NAS Dunkirk, 44, 53, 56, 57, 58, 59, 60, 61, 64, 68, 321, 325; commanding officer at Eastleigh, 337, 338, 340; First Aeronautic Detachment, duties with, 7, 11, 15, 19, 30, 31; postwar activities, 358; training at French aviation schools, 32
Chiesa, Eugenio (Commissioner of Aeronautics), 322–24, 329
Child, Lt. Warren "Gerry," 26, 262; Bolling Commission, service on, 20, 21, 23, 27; commanding officer at NAS Fromentine, 112; lighter-than-air experiences, 252
Christiansen, Capt. Friedrich, 66–67, 162
Clark, Ens. Ransom, 118
Clark, Ens. Robert, death of, 91, 242
Clayton, Capt. Henry, 310

Clermont-Ferrand, 77, 87, 91, 124, 138, 325, 334, 335; Army-Navy tensions at, 326; description of, 326; Northern Bombing Group pilots training at, 325–27
Cline, Joseph (pilot), 30, 40, 41, 93, 97, 197; Pensacola, early training at, 10
Coatsworth, Ens. Caleb, 301
Cobb, Chief Machinist's Mate, 272
Cohen, Cdr. Albert M., 147
Committee for Relief in Belgium (CRB), 361, 363, 364
Communications, 71, 126, 147, 226, 241
Compo, Ens. George, 164, 178
Cone, Capt. Hutchinson I. "Hutch," 13; Allies, conferences with, 346–52; amalgamation, views on, 137–40; Army, relations with, 136–37, 306–7, 310; early career of, 26; England and Ireland inspections tours in, 167–68, 169, 209–10; France, inspection trips in, 59, 64, 85, 95, 112, 113; injured in sinking of RMS *Leinster*, 215, 356; Irwin and, 358; Italy program and, 285–90 passim, 303–10 passim; lighter bombing project and, 169, 182; LTA and, 263–68 passim; naval aviation in Europe, commander of, 26–27, 244–45, 257, 278; Navy Department, relations with, 135, 140–41, 142–43, 145, 356; Northern Bombing Group and, 67, 74, 75, 316–26 passim, 337, 341; organizes Paris headquarters, 43–48, 128; relieves LCdr. Whiting, 43; Sims' Aide for Aviation, 83, 127, 147, 149; Sims' appreciation of, 28; Westervelt Board and, 353–55; Henry Wilson relations with, 52
Conger, Paymaster Omar, 7, 11, 13–20 passim, 28, 30, 44, 46, 47, 119, 136, 249, 264, 288, 352, 362
Conrad, Lt. C. P., 106–7, 275, 276
Construction, 37, 48, 212, 255, 276, 278; at Eastleigh, 338; difficulties encountered, 3, 50, 56, 57; France, difficulties in, 91, 107, 112, 115, 119–20, 388n3; at French stations, 85, 100, 109, 114; Ireland, difficulties in, 212–13, 220, 222–23, 225; Italy, difficulties in, 302–3; Mayo's views concerning, 353; at Pauillac, 129–31; record of achievement, 367; Westervelt's views concerning, 354
Cooke, Cdr. Henry, 225
Coombe, Lt. (jg) Reginald, 29; comments by, 157, 236; in Italy, 308; at Le Croisic, 42, 93, 95, 96, 97; with Northern Bombing Group, 323, 333, 339, 341
Copeland, D. Graham (civil engineer), 211–12
Corry, Lt. William, 20, 21, 37, 40, 90, 93, 94, 97, 257, 258
Couderkerque aerodrome, 18, 316, 335
Cowan, Gunner J. H., 277
Cranwell Royal Naval Air Station, 49, 150, 154, 262, 268
Craven, Capt. Thomas T., xviii, 40, 132, 220, 265, 271, 347, 349, 380n1, 388n2; demobilization, role in, 275, 358, 360, 362–63, 365; early career, 47; Irwin and, 357–58; naval aviation in France, head of, 127, 147; Naval Aviation, postwar director of, 52, 365–67, 369; Operations Division (Paris), head of, 43, 44, 83, 124; working with the French, 132, 362–63
CRB. *See* Committee for Relief in Belgium
Crowell, Benedict (asst. secretary of war), 138, 369
Culbert, Lt. Frederick, 262–63, 271–73, 275
Cunningham, Capt. Alfred A.: France and England, tour of aviation activities in, 58–59, 155; General Board report to, 317–18; Marine Corps, organization of aviation role in, 319, 329–30; Northern Bombing Group, activities with, 330, 332
Curran, Ens. Stanley, 180
Curtiss CB "Liberty Battler," 384n37
Curtiss H-4 "Small America," 158, 164, 168
Curtiss H-12 "Large America," 24, 392n37; operational use at British stations, 159, 161, 162, 163, 167, 168, 169–70; operational use at Killingholme, 173, 177
Curtiss H-16 aircraft, 91, 125, 130, 242; description of, 162, 169–70; mechanical problems of, 143, 174–75, 218, 230, 252; price of, 241; operational use of, 176–80, 211, 215–16, 223, 226
Curtiss HA "Dunkirk Fighter," 75, 383n37
Curtiss HS-1L/2L aircraft: accidents and, 91–92, 103, 109–10, 242; description of, 233, 374; first flight in Europe, 130; mechanical problems of, 101, 104, 117, 120, 121; operational use at French coastal stations, 82, 89, 91, 101, 105, 114, 121, 122; possible use in Italy, 301, 351; price of, 241

Curtiss N-9 aircraft, 44
Curtiss R-6 aircraft, 44
Cushing (ship), 134, 268, 279–81
Cuyama (ship), 218

Daniels, LCdr. J. F., 28
Daniels, Josephus (secretary of the navy), 6, 20, 21, 140, 143, 144, 145; Allies, calls for information from, 6–7; FDR and, 145–46, 353; Northern Bombing Group and, 318, 319, 322, 323; Westervelt Board and, 353–54, 355
Darden, Lt. Colgate, 342
Darien, Lt. de Vaisseau, 13
Dashiell, Lt.(jg) J. H., 284
Davis, LCdr. F.R.E., 209, 210
Davison, Lt. (jg) F. Trubee, 29, 343
Day Bombing Squadrons, 322, 324, 329, 330, 332, 342; independent operations by, 341–43
De Blanpré, Cdr. Bernard, 9
De Bon, Adm. Ferdinand, 14, 17, 53
DeCernea, Ens. Edward, 62, 70–71, 73, 79, 87, 193
De Filippi, Capt. Ludovici, 285–88, 290, 292
De Laborde, Capt. de Fregate, 14, 17, 19, 64, 92, 119
Delano, Lt.(jg) Merrill, 277
DeMitt, CCM Milton, 107
Demobilization, 359; Craven role in, 365–66; difficulties encountered with, 362–63, 365; early efforts towards, 359–69; England and Ireland, demobilization in, 365; equipment, disposition of, 361–62, 365; FDR activities concerning, 362–63; France, demobilization in, 363–65; at individual stations, 92, 98, 114, 118, 122, 224, 275, 282, 344, 361–62; Italy, demobilization in, 359
DeSonnier, Ens. Lawrence, 74
Dessez, LCdr. J. H., 228
DH-4 aircraft, 64–68 passim, 75, 76, 78, 132, 315, 320, 322, 326, 334–43 passim, 349–55 passim, 384n37, 388n12, 404n47
DH-6 aircraft, 328
DH-9 aircraft, 75, 328, 334–43 passim
Dichman, Lt. Grattan C., 250, 360; background and early career, 8; commanding officer at NAS Brest, 90, 108; commanding officer at NAS Moutchic, 41, 44; detachment from aviation service, 62; Europe, voyage to, 8, 12; First Aeronautic Detachment, activities with, 7, 15, 19, 28, 30–32, 36, 37
Dinger, Cdr. Henry, 249; British facilities inspection by, 134, 167; Intelligence and Planning Division activities with, 44, 47, 81, 105
Dirigibles. *See* Lighter-than-Air (LTA) operations
Discipline, 220, 222–23, 245, 246, 259
Disease, 31, 61, 229, 260; Herbster and efforts to prevent, 221, 246; influenza, 78, 113, 117, 246, 249, 260, 283, 295, 303, 311, 338, 343
Dolececk, Ens. Edward, 218
Donnelly, Lt. Bernard P., 134, 167, 234
Donnet-Denhaut aircraft, 17, 56, 57, 59, 60, 79
Dover-Dunkirk barrage, 18
Dundee Royal Naval Air Station, 164, 165–66, 183–84, 234
Dunkirk naval air station (Dunkerque), 15, 42, 55–80, 349, 357; bombardment of, 53, 61, 62–64, 74; Chevalier and, 32, 59, 64; construction at, 56–57; Cunningham visit to, 58–59; FDR visit to, 145, 255; Di Gates, capture of, 76–77; German Spring Offensive and, 62–64; living conditions at, 57, 58, 60, 62, 254; MacLeish, death of, 77–78; operational difficulties, 60, 69–70, 74, 315; operational history, 59, 69–70, 76, 78–79; plans to abandon discussed, 74–76; RAF, service with, 64–68; Read and Eichelberger, deaths at, 61, 73; rescue launch, loss of, 72–73; Whiting's inspection of, 17–18, 21–22, 55–56
Dunwoody, Col. Halsey, 306
Dunwoody Institute, 306

Eastchurch/Leysdown, 49, 150, 154, 155, 156, 328; Cunningham, visit by, 154–55
East Fortune Royal Naval Air Station, 269, 271
Eastleigh assembly and repair base, 125–26, 127, 244, 252–53, 260, 343, 365; Bulmer as commanding officer, 257, 338–39; Chevalier as commanding officer, 337–38; construction of, 337–38; Irwin visit, 340; operational history, 339–40; selection of, 337
Eaton, Ens. Joseph, 134, 164–65, 181

Edwards, Lt. (later LCdr.) Walter Atlee, 2, 16; aide for aviation to Sims, 47; amalgamation and, 135, 137–39; background, 43, 133–34; discipline issues concerning naval aviators in Britain, 153–54, 268–69; Italian expansion, attitudes about, 351, 352; liaison with British and, 134–35; Northern Bombing Group and, 324, 325, 328, 343, 346; postwar comments about naval aviation, 2, 16

Eichelberger, Edward (observer), death of at Dunkirk, 61, 73

Eldridge, Ens. Carleton, 229

Elliott, Ens. Harold, 70, 74, 103

Ely, Eugene, 5, 35

Ellsworth, Asst. Civil Engineer G. D., 112

Ellyson, Lt. Theodore G. "Spuds," 5

Enlisted personnel: athletics, 256–58; daily schedule, 254; descriptions of France, 13; discipline, 259; food, 255–56; liberty, 258–59; morale, 255; at Moutchic, 88–89; pets, 256; as pilots 153, 250–51; recreation, 258; station complement, 252–53. *See also* First Aeronautic Detachment

Ericsson (ship), 134, 268, 281–82

Escadrille St. Pol, 76–77

Evans, Capt. Frank Taylor, 130–31, 249, 354

Fahy, Ens. Charles, 340

Fairfax (ship), 268

Fallon, Ens. Nugent, 157, 162

Farwell, Ens. John, 41, 95, 117

F2A aircraft. *See* Felixstowe flying boats

FBA aircraft, 18, 33, 37, 39, 40, 41, 81, 87, 286, 292, 294, 295

Fearing, Ens. George R., 44, 136

Felixstowe flying boats, 156–57, 233; F2A flying boat, 157–82 passim, 241; F5 flying boat, 171, 161, 169

"Felixstowe Fury." *See* "Porte Superbaby"

Felixstowe Royal Naval Air Station, 156–64; descriptions of, 156, 157; Lovett report about, 161–62; Navy personnel there, 157–59; Philip Page, death of, 158; Stephen Potter, death of, 162–63; Spider Patrol, 159; Sturtevant, death of, 162; war activities there, 159–61, 162–64

Fiat motors, 304, 305, 307, 311, 339

Finch-Noyes, Squadron Cdr. C. R., 168, 245

First Aeronautic Detachment, 5–41; Baltimore and New York, journey to, 10–11; at Cazaux, 38; Europe, voyage to, 11–12; formation at NAS Pensacola, 7, 9–10; France, first days in, 12, 13–14; at Lac Hourtin, 39–40; officers of, 7–9; at Moutchic, 34–38, 41–42; St. Raphael, training at, 32–34; Tours, training at, 28–32; Whiting's planning activities, 12–13, 14–26

First Marine Aviation Force, 330, 336

First Yale Unit, 29, 31, 38–39, 122, 251, 301, 308, 328

Flanders U-boats, 24, 55, 66, 67, 72, 232, 314, 317–19, 395n1

Flying Fox (ship), 214, 228

Foulois, Brig. Gen. Benjamin, 136, 137, 138, 306, 307, 324, 369, 381n8

France, U.S. naval aviation in: Dunkirk, 55–80; First Aeronautic Detachment, 12–42; French Coastal Unit, 81–122; lighter-than-air activities, 261–68, 271–84; naval aviation stations (*see individual stations*); Paris headquarters, 43–45, 46–48; training at: Cazaux, 38; Clermont-Ferrand, 325–27; Hourtin, 39–40; Moutchic, 37–38, 41–42, 85–87, 87–89; St. Raphael, 32–34, 40–41; Tours, 28–32

Fretnum aerodrome, 334, 336

Fromentine naval air station, 17, 19, 22; selection and description, 111–12; construction, 50, 111–13; operational history, 113–14; postwar history, 114

Frotheringham, Ens. Phillip, death of at St. Inglevert, 340–41

Fuller, Ens. Charles, 134, 165–66, 234

Gadsden, Ens. Phillip, 218

Ganges (ship), 158

Ganster, QM John, 9, 69–70

Gardiner, LCdr., 283

Gardner, Ens. Alfred, 274

Gasbags. *See* Lighter-than-Air (LTA) operations

Gaston, Ens. William, 334

Gas Valve (newspaper, Paimboeuf), 256

Gates, Lt. Artemus "Di," 29, 30, 39, 79, 150, 238, 369; capture by Germans, 76–77; commanding officer at NAS Dunkirk, 74–75; at Lac Hourtin, 39; NAS Dunkirk, duties/activities at, 58–74 passim; at St. Raphael, 40–41

Geiger, Capt. Roy, 329, 336, 368

Index   421

General Board hearings concerning Northern Bombing Group, 317–18
George V (King of England), 72, 145, 154
German Spring Offensive (1918), 52–53, 61, 69, 97, 300, 355
Gibbs, Lt. John, 342
Gibson, Ens. John, 226
Gilbert, MM Robert, 116–17
Glendenning, Maj. Robert, 310, 311
Goggins, James (enlisted pilot), 293, 295, 300
Goodspeed, Ens. Harrison, 279
Goodyear, 262, 268, 284, 357
Gosport School of Special Flying, 49, 59, 150; origins and training methods, 150–52
Great Britain, U.S. naval aviation in, 149–84; at Cattewater, 164–65; at Dundee, 165–66; at Eastleigh, 337–40; at Felixstowe, 156–64; at Great Yarmouth, 166–67; at Killingholme, 168–84; training in, 150–56
Great Yarmouth Royal Naval Air Station, 9, 163–64, 391; Navy pilots at, 166–67, 181, 241, 328
Grey, Lt. Col. Spenser, 134, 288, 304, 316, 322, 352
Griffin, Lt. Virgil, 44, 45, 60, 93, 360, 368; background and early career, 8; First Aeronautic Detachment, duties with, 7, 11, 14, 15, 22, 33, 36; NAS St. Trojan, commanding officer at, 115, 126, 250; postwar recommendations, 365
Grosvenor, Ens. Theodore, 176
Guggenheim, Lt. Harry, 44, 47, 180, 290, 304, 343, 349, 352
Guines (RAF depot in France), 330, 332
Guipavas dirigible station, 125, 262, 265; construction, 275–76; operational history, 267, 271, 274, 275, 276–77; postwar history, 277; selection and description, 275–76
Gujan dirigible station, 119, 125, 257, 259, 260, 262, 264, 267; construction, 277–78; origins, 277

Hale, D. C. (gunlayer), 340
Hallam, Maj. Douglas, 157–58
Halstead, Harold, 31
Hammann, Ens. Charles "Haze," 9, 251, 256, 293, 298–99
Handley Page aircraft, 58, 238, 304, 358; operations, 64, 72, 234, 315, 320–21, 331, 334
Hanrahan, Capt. David C., 249; early career, 314, 322; Northern Bombing Group, role as head of, 68, 74, 75, 305, 330, 331, 337, 341
Hanriot-Dupont aircraft, 56, 57, 59, 60, 62, 70, 72, 73, 75, 361
Hardin, Lt. E. D., M.D., 260
Harrell, QM1c Robert, 101
Harvard (ship), 268
Harvard Unit, 29, 165, 251
Harvey, BM1c Leo, 100
Harwich, 156, 161, 181
Hasselman, G. H. (enlisted pilot), 116
Haviland, Willis (pilot), 59, 60, 64, 126, 251, 288; commanding officer at NAS Porto Corsini, 297–301 passim, 399n15; Callan and, 291–92
Hawkins, Ens. Ashton "Tex," 173, 177, 178, 181, 183; zeppelin patrol, 1
Hawkins, Ens. Clarence, 250
Heligoland Bight, 350–51
Henderson, Ens. Jesse, 333
Herbster, LCdr. Victor D., 5, 250, 257, 261, 268; commanding officer at NAS Wexford, 220, 239; discipline, ideas about, 220–21, 245–47; quarantine program enforced, 221
Hildreth, MM Alonzo, diaries excerpts, 57, 58, 59, 61, 63, 64, 65, 71, 72, 73, 255
Hispano-Suiza motor, 33, 101, 125, 373
Hitherington, Lt., rescue of, 72
Hodges, Ens. George, 173, 177, 178, 183
Hodges, Ens. Kenneth, 176, 184
Hofer, Ens. Myron, 167
Holliday, Thomas (observer), in accident at NAS Dunkirk, 70
Homer, Ens. Joseph, 270
Hough, Ens. Frederick, 153
Hourtin. *See* Lacanau-Hourtin
Howden Royal Air Force base, 270
Huddleston, Ens. Walter, 74
Hull (RNAS base), 168
Hull, Lt. Carl, 157, 171, 173, 211, 225

Île d'Oléron, 18, 114
Île Tudy naval air station, 16, 22, 24, 35, 81, 82, 83; construction, 99–100; operational history, 49, 84, 85, 100–4; postwar disposition, 104; selection and description, 98–99
Île Vierge lighthouse, 106

Influenza. *See* Disease
Ingalls, Lt. David S., 29, 157, 338, 340, 369, 380n57; Britain, training in, 150–53; Clermont-Ferrand, training at, 325–26; NAS Dunkirk, duty at, 53, 62, 64, 65, 69, 72; RAF, service with, 123, 334–35
Intelligence and Planning Division (Paris), 44, 47, 81, 134, 167, 346
Ireland, U.S. naval aviation in, 208–30; Cone's inspection tour of, 209–10; construction of stations, 212–14; decision to operate in, 208–9; McCrary and, 211, 213, 214; naval aviation stations in, 216–30; operations, 214–16; organization of, 210–12, 214. *See also individual stations*
Irwin, Capt. Noble, 48, 51, 52, 141, 144, 255, 303, 337, 353, 355, 366; Cone, relations with, 45, 46, 128, 136, 138, 139, 140, 143, 146; European inspection tour, 275, 350, 357–58
Isle of Grain, 164, 328
Issoudun, 40, 49, 59, 152, 341
Italy, U.S. naval aviation in, 285–313; Callan and, 285–88, 290–92; Caproni issues and, 303–12; decision to operate in, 285–89; expansion plans and, 312; headquarters in, 289–90, 311; LaGuardia and, 305–7, 309–10; naval aviation stations in, 296–303; Train and, 286, 288, 289; training in, 286, 292–96, 307–9. *See also individual stations*
Ives, Ens. Paul, 164, 178, 183–84

Jackson, Capt. Richard, 114, 145, 353; Paris, early activities in, 21, 26, 28, 35, 90, 95, 136; Sims and, 21, 26, 27, 28
Jarvis (ship), 134
Jason (ship), 173, 365
Jazz bands, 3, 258, 260
Jernigan, LQM Jefferson D., 32, 40
Johnson, Lt.(jg) Avmar, 108
Johnson, C. M. (gunner), 282
Johnson, Ens. C. R., 56, 331, 403
Joint Army-Navy Board, 303, 305
Jones, Lt. J. E., 354
Jupiter (ship), 7, 10, 11, 12, 13, 15, 32, 368

Kanawha (ship), 218
Kenly, Gen. William L., 325, 369
Kennedy, C. W. (observer), rescue of, 72
Kennedy, Lt. Stanley, 184

Keyes, Ens. Kenneth, 163–64
Keyes, Vice-Admiral Sir Roger, 67
Kiely, Lt.(jg) Ralph, 262, 268, 294
Killeen, George (mechanic), death of, 242, 300
Killingholme naval air station, 75, 123, 126, 168; aircraft mechanical problems at, 174–75, 179–80; Cdr. F. W. Bowhill and, 171–74; history and description, 168, 170–71; Lee, death of at, 183; lighter project development, 44, 48, 51, 168–70, 181–82; operational history, 174–78, 179–80, 182–84; service with British at, 159, 171–74; Whiting's role at, 47, 147, 174; wartime record, 184; zeppelin patrols at, 1, 178–79
Kindall, Ens. Nolan, 110, 368
Kite balloons. *See* Lighter-than-Air (LTA) operations
Knapp, E. C. (observer), death of at NAS Le Croisic, 98
Knowles, LQM Clarence, 299
Knox, Capt. Dudley, 51

L'Aber Vrach naval air station, 106–11; construction, 106–9; operational history, 109–11; postwar history, 111; selection and description, 106
Lacanau-Hourtin (Lac Hourtin): seaplane school, 15, 19, 32, 36, 38; American training and, 39–40, 380n57. *See also* Moutchic-Lacanau naval air station/school
Lacaze, Adm. Marie-Jean-Lucien, 14
Lafayette Flying Corps, 59, 60, 70, 85, 150
La Fresne aerodrome, 78, 323, 330, 331, 332, 342, 404, 405
LaGuardia, Capt. (later Maj.) Fiorello, 288, 305; Navy relations with, 137, 138, 305–6, 309–10, 369
Lake Michigan (ship), 213
Lambe, Capt./Brig. Gen. Charles, 18; RNAS units at Dunkirk, commander of, 64; Northern Bombing Group, support of, 134, 316, 319, 320, 403, 404; Whiting's meetings with, 18, 21
Lancto, Ens. Joseph, 218
Landon, Ens. Henry, 29, 40, 93, 95, 99, 100, 102–3
Lane, H. H. (surgeon), 44, 47, 48, 352
Langley (ship), 368
Langley Field, 299
Lansdowne, Lt. Zachary, 262, 268, 276

La Pallice kite balloon station, 19, 24, 84, 125, 269, 363; construction, 283–84; selection and description, 283

La Rochelle, 19, 22, 283

Lasher, Ens. Herbert, 70, 74

La Trinité-sur-Mer kite balloon station, 84, 125, 254, 265, 364; construction, 282–83; operational history, 283; selection and description, 282

Laven, Harry (observer), accident at NAS Dunkirk, 70

Lawrence, Lt.(jg) George, 171, 173, 174, 178, 179; zeppelin hunting by, 1, 178

Leading Edge (newspaper, Porto Cassini), 256, 297

Learned, Ens. Norman, 269, 270

Le Croisic naval air station, 15, 16, 19, 35, 42, 49, 51, 81–84 passim; William Corry, commanding officer at, 93; description, 92; operational history, 93–97; postwar disposition, 98; Tellier aircraft destroyed by explosion, 97

Lee, Ens. Benjamin "Benny," 180, 181; death of, 183

Lefebvre, Capt. de Vaisseau, 13

Leighton, LCdr. Bruce G., 174, 176, 184, 247, 250

Leinster (ship), 215, 356

Lemanski, Ens. John, 101

Leviathan (ship), 184, 367

Levy-LePen aircraft, 81, 125, 233, 242, 373

Leysdown, training of Navy enlisted personnel at, 49, 155, 328

Liaison activities, 14, 17, 48, 123, 133, 137; Edwards and, 134; Paris and, 120, 135, 136, 89n22

Liberty motors, 75, 125, 130, 138, 169, 216, 339, 388n2; characteristics of, 33, 170, 358; complaints about, 142–44, 354–55; problems with, 101, 109–10, 113, 127, 179, 218, 230

Lighters, 381n5; construction of, 170; design of, 168–69; and long-distance bombardment program, 52, 168–69; operations with, 181–82; termination of program with, 182

Lighter-than-Air (LTA) operations, 261–84; blimps, 110; blimps (nonrigid airships), description and use of, 261; dirigibles, description and use of, 261–62, 265–67; dirigibles, Navy acquisition of, 264; dirigible stations (*see* Naval air stations); Royal Navy/Royal Air Force and, 268–71; kite balloons, description and use of, 210, 227–28, 267–68; kite balloon stations (*see* Naval air stations); sludge, dangers and disposal of, 264–65; zeppelins, description and use of, 261. *See also individual dirigible and kite balloon station entries*

Loegenboom gun, 382n17. *See also* "Mournful Mary"

Londonderry, 212, 224, 225, 226, 227

Loomis, Ens. Ralph, 60

Lough Foyle naval air station, 50, 125, 167, 209–16 passim, 227, 240, 254, 258; construction, 224–25; description, 224; operational history, 225–27

Love, W. C. (observer), accident at NAS Dunkirk, 70

Lovett, LCdr. Robert, 29, 30, 145, 150, 369; combat missions, 64–65, 68, 320–21; Felixstowe, report on, 161–62; Moutchic, duties at, 37, 41; Northern Bombing Group, duties with, 69, 341; Paris headquarters, duties at, 47, 290, 315–16, 320

Low, Lt. Seth, 74

LTA. *See* Lighter-than-Air (LTA) operations

Ludlow, Ens. George, 298–99

Lusitania (ship), 208

Lynch, Ens. Frank, 78

Lytle, Capt. Robert, 336, 342

Macchi aircraft, 286, 292, 296, 297, 298, 300, 374

MacLeish, Lt. Kenneth, 29; amalgamation controversy and, 138–39; Britain, training in, 150–53; Clermont-Ferrand, training at, 325–27, 329; death of, 77–78; NAS Dunkirk, duty at, 53, 63, 69, 70; Eastleigh, duty at, 338, 340; Hourtin and Moutchic, training at, 39, 85; Pauillac, duty at, 131–32; RAF, service with, 64, 66, 67, 334–35

Magruder, Capt. Thomas, 274

Maguire, LCdr. O.H.K., 156

Maloney, Lt. John, 276

Malpensa, Navy personnel at, 124, 307, 308, 309, 325, 332, 333

Manley, LQM George, 9, 10; death of at Tours, 31

Marchand, Chief Boatswain's Mate, 31

Marine Aeronautic Company, 329

Marine Corps aviation, 3, 5, 315, 317, 318–19; formation and training, 58–60, 325, 329–30; Northern Bombing Group, duty with, 329, 323, 324, 332, 336, 339, 342–43, 404n47
Marshburn, Djalma (enlisted pilot), death of at NAS Dunkirk, 70
Masek, Lt. William, 97, 368
Mason, Lt. Charles P., 130, 259, 352, 368, 389
Matthews, Steven, 121–22
Maxfield, Cdr. Louis, 82, 126, 275, 360, 369; lighter-than-air service, 262–63, 264, 271, 272, 274, 278, 346, 347
Maxwell, Lt. Howard "Tiny," 310–11
May 10 Agreement. *See* Caproni aircraft
Mayo, Vice Adm. Henry, 141, 209; inspection tour and report of, 78, 114, 131, 180, 229, 255, 275, 278, 295, 301, 340, 352–53; naval aviation views of, 358–59
McAlpin, LCdr. Kenneth, 171
McCann, Lt.(jg) Richard, 183
McCormick, Ens. "Mac," 221
McCormick, Lt.(jg) Alexander, 252; death of while with RAF, 334
McCracken, Ens. Thomas, 269
McCrary, Cdr. Francis B. (Frank), 26, 380n2; commander of naval aviation in Ireland, 211–14 passim, 222–23, 227, 228, 229, 269, 348; lighter-than-air service and, 261–64, 348; Paris Headquarters, early activities at, 44, 47, 48
McDonnell, Lt. Edward, 29, 250; Caproni aircraft, role in acquisition of, 303–4; Flanders bombing raids participation in, 234, 320; Italy, duty in, 332–33; Washington, D.C., duties in, 322
McGee, R. I. (gunner), 111, 112
McGowan, Rear Adm. Samuel, 20, 314
McIlvain, Capt. William, 329, 339
McIlwaine, Archibald "Chip," 39, 84, 384
McKean, Capt. Josiah, 355, 369
McKelvey, Gunner (Temporary Radio) Carlton, 106–7, 108, 256
McKinnon, Ens. Thomas, death of, 335
McKitterick, Lt. Edward, 225
McNamara, Ens. John, 164, 178, 181
Mecknes (ship), 108, 124
Mediterranean Sea: Italian operations and, 285, 286; Navy disinterest in, 290; possible operations in, 16–17, 23, 24, 146, 348–51 passim

Melville (ship), 208
Mercury (ship), 118, 344
Meyer, Lt. Cord, 74
Michel, Asst. Paymaster Frederick, 7, 11, 15, 41, 259
Mickey, Ens., 281
Milan, 124, 304, 307, 308, 310, 333
Miley, Maj. A. J., 357
Miller, Vice Adm. F. S., 224, 225
Miller, MM William, 250, 339
Ministry of Marine (French), 28, 104, 378n19; liaison with, 21, 26, 48, 135; negotiations with, 7, 13, 14, 20, 320, 351, 362; relations with, 91, 149
Minotaur (ship), 158
Mitchell, Brig. Gen. William "Billy," 137, 138, 344; naval aviation, opposition to, 369, 370
Montgomery, Ens. George, 236
Moran, T. J., and Co., 217, 222
More, Capt. Gilbert, 135
Moseley, Ens. George C., 335; Clermont-Ferrand, training at, 325–27; duties at NAS Dunkirk, 53, 59, 62, 64, 69–71 passim, 254, 255; duties with Escadrille St. Pol, 76–77; French, training with, 29–32; Moutchic, training at, 85
"Mournful Mary," 57. *See also* Loegenboom gun
Moutchic-Lacanau naval air station/school, 22–25 passim, 49; accidents at, 87; Bartlett and, 86; Cabaniss and, 88–89; Callan and, 35–36; Grattan Dichman and, 41; early history and conditions, 34–38, 31–42; postwar disposition, 89; training programs, 85–87, 87–89. *See also* Lacanau-Hourtin (Lac Hourtin)
Mulcahy, Capt. Francis, 336, 404
Murphy, Thomas (gunner), 174, 250, 368, 392; death of, 300
Mustin, Cdr. Henry, 45, 369

Naval Affairs Committee, 141–42, 255, 353
Naval Aircraft Factory, 140, 170, 253
Naval air stations: athletics at, 220, 249, 256–58; Arcachon, 119–22; Bolsena, 292–96; Brest, 89–92; Castletownbere, 227–30; design of, 243–44; dignitaries, visits by, 254–55; discipline at, 246–47, 259; Dunkirk, 56–80; Eastleigh, 336–49; enlisted personnel at, 252–53, 255; entertainment and recreation at, 256, 258; food at, 62, 154, 171, 247, 255–56,

Index 425

326, 338; Fromentine, 111–14; Guivapas, 275–77; Gujan, 277–78; Île Tudy, 98–103; illness at, 260; Killingholme, 168–85; L'Aber Vrach, 106–11; La Pallice, 283–84; La Trinité-sur-Mer, 282–83: liberty, 258–59; Le Croisic, 92–98; living conditions at, 255; Lough Foyle, 224–27; Moutchic, 35–38, 41–42, 84–89; officers' duties at, 245–49; Paimboeuf, 271–75; Pauillac, 127–33; Pescara, 302–3; pets at, 256; Porto Corsini, 296–302; Queenstown, 216–19; Rochefort, 278–79; schedules of, 254; St. Trojan, 114–19; Tréguier, 104–6; Wexford, 219–22; Whiddy Island, 222–24; YMCA activities at, 225–26, 259, 294, 297

Naval Aviation (U.S.): Allied relations and, 132–36; assembly and repair facilities, 25, 44, 46, 49, 82, 90–91, 125–26, 127–32, 193, 216, 255, 264, 279, 312, 337–40; conferences with Allies concerning, 13–17, 209, 345–51; documenting activities of, 360, 406n25; early history of, 5–6; female employees and, 48; First Aeronautic Detachment and, 5–42; future of, 365–66; impact of, 367–69; intelligence officers, work and, 126, 177–78, 214–15, 239, 240–41, 247, 248; late war proposals for and Navy Department reactions, 345–52; postwar controversy, 369–70; progress in Europe of, 43–51, 52–54, 123–32, 146–48, 345–52, 356–57; wartime record of, 367–69

Naval Reserve Flying Corps, 6, 251
NBG. *See* Northern Bombing Group
Nelms, Lt. Frank, 336, 342–43, 405
Nelson, Clarence (enlisted pilot), death of at Bolsena, 293
Neptune (ship), 7, 10, 11, 12, 13, 15, 32
Nevada (ship), 214, 229–30
Nichols, Ens. Alan, death of in Italy, 333
Night bombing squadrons, 316, 323, 330, 331, 334
No. 7 Squadron, RNAS, 64, 316, 320
No. 202 Squadron, RAF, 68
No. 213 Squadron, RAF, 65, 67, 76, 205, 300, 336
No. 214 Squadron, RAF, 334
No. 217 Squadron, RAF, 67, 73, 334, 335, 357
No. 218 Squadron, RAF, 77, 329, 334, 335, 336, 404
Nokomis (ship), 133

Norman, Lt. Harvey, death of, 342
North Carolina (ship), 9, 35, 86
Northern Bombing Group (NBG), 314–44; aerodromes, selection and construction, 323, 330–31; Allied views concerning, 324–25; Caproni aircraft and, 332–33, 339, 340–41; conception of and planning for, 315–23; Eastleigh and, 336–40; Hanrahan as commanding officer, 68, 74, 75, 78, 315, 322, 331, 337, 341; David Ingalls and, 335–36; Marine Corps participation in, 329–30, 336, 341–43; operational history, 340–43; RAF, service with, 333–36; relations with U.S. Army concerning, 323, 324, 325; St. Inglevert aerodrome, 331–32, 340–41; training personnel for, 325–28
North Hinder Lightship, 156, 159, 162, 163
North Sea, 126, 165, 168, 173, 175, 181–83 passim, 235, 262, 346–49 passim; patrol activities over 156, 159–61, 162–64
North Sea Mine Barrage, 126, 175, 349, 350, 358
Nourse, Ens. Ralph, 128, 129

O'Brien, Ens. James, 73, 74, 86, 295
O'Brien (ship), 268, 281
O'Gorman, Yeoman Marlon, death of, 335
Oklahoma (ship), 214, 229, 230, 357
Old Sarum, training of Navy personnel at, 327, 328
Operations Division (Paris), 43, 44, 47, 49, 124, 126
Ostend, 55, 57, 63, 66, 67, 381n1; bombing of, 66, 67, 314–15, 321, 334, 335; postwar condition, 78
Otranto (ship), 226
Otranto mine barrage, 349
Owen, Ens. George, 223, 368
Owen, Ens. Knight, 172, 176, 177
Oye aerodrome, 330, 331, 332

Padgett, Rep. Lemuel (chair of House Committee on Naval Affairs), 141–42, 255, 353, 358
Page, Ens. Phillip, 157; death of at RNAS Felixstowe, 158, 242
Page, Schuyler (observer), 172
Paimboeuf dirigible station, 19, 22, 49, 125, 146, 262; disposition of, 275; Navy activities at, 263–64, 267, 271–75
Paine, Fifth Sea Lord Adm. Godfrey, 134, 209

Palmer, Ens. Clyde, death of at St. Inglevert, 341–42
Palmer, Rear Adm. Leigh, 9, 26, 140, 141
Paris, bombardment of, 53, 99
Paris headquarters: organization, 43–48, 128; possible evacuation, 53–54
Park, Ens. Charles, 86
Parker, Ens. Austin, 301
Parker, Ens. Erlon, 74
Parker, Lt. William, 289, 311
Patrick, Gen. Mason, 138, 307, 309, 344
Patterson, Lt.(jg) R. D., 282
Pattinson, Capt. T. C., 178–79, 181
Patton, Cdr. John, 130, 388n7
Pau, 32, 49, 59
Pauillac (Trompeloup), 12, 19, 36, 46, 51, 52, 82, 126, 131, 244, 255, 388n12; delays at, 130–32, 143, 354–55; demobilization and, 359, 361, 362, 364; dockside fire at, 254; early activities at, 127–30; naval aviation activities at, 132; origins of, 49–50; women employees at, 48
Peiffer, Lt.(jg) L. J., 284
Pennsylvania (ship), 229
Pensacola naval aeronautic/air station, 2, 5, 8, 9, 10, 87, 88, 93, 141, 250, 329; First Aeronautic Detachment at, 9–11
Perkins (ship), 12
Pershing, Gen. John J., 93, 136, 138, 306, 307, 341, 351, 389n31
Pescara, 244, 286; construction at, 244, 289, 291, 302–3; selection and description of, 287, 289, 302
Peterson, Ens. William, 171, 222, 223
Pets, 203, 231, 256
Peyton, LCdr. Paul J., 211, 217, 223
Phelan, Ens. James, 172
Pickering, LCdr. N. W., 354
Pigeons, 241, 387n59; care and training, 241; exploits, 71, 118, 235, 241; use, 160, 215, 233, 239, 240
Pilot (newspaper, Pauillac), 256
Piper, Ens. Robert, 269, 270
Plane Talk (newspaper, Fromentine), 256
Planning conferences, 290, 348–51
Planning Section (London), 48, 51, 316, 346, 349
Pola, 126, 285, 287, 296; bombing raids against, 298–300, 357
Ponta Delgada, 329

Portable (prefabricated) buildings, 21, 90, 100, 129, 244, 332, 361
Porte, Cdr. John C., 135; role at RNAS Felixstowe, 156–57, 159, 169
"Porte Superbaby"/"Felixstowe Fury" (aircraft), 157
Porto Corsini naval air station, 127, 231, 251, 286; demobilization, 301–2; operational history, 296–301; selection and description, 287–89, 296–97
Potter, Lt.(jg) Austin, 307
Potter, Ens. Stephen, activities and death of, 162–63
Pou, Ens. Edwin, 102–3, 236; death of at Île Tudy, 103
Pratt, Capt. William, 228
Presley, Capt. Russell, 329, 336, 404n47
Princeton unit, 251, 252, 341
Prometheus (ship), 143, 279, 281
Promotions controversy, 140, 355, 356
Provenzani, Lt., 302
Puleston, Lt. W. W., 280
Puller, Lt. H. G., 120
Pyrene fire extinguisher, 265, 266

Queenstown (Aghada) naval air station, 50; assembly and repair activities, 49, 127, 216, 218; construction, 50, 212, 213; demobilization and postwar history, 219; civilian relations with, 212, 218; naval activities, 208–9; operational history, 126, 211, 212, 214–16, 218–19; selection and description, 209, 217–18

Radios, 223, 244–45, 385n23
Rambler (ship), 268
Ramsey, Lt. DeWitt C., 52, 127, 141, 236, 250, 360, 368; flight across France, 357
Rations, 12, 28, 53, 95, 103, 113, 160, 172, 176
Raymond, Ens. A. G., 225
Read, Albert C. (Navy officer), 20, 21, 368
Read, Ens. Curtis, 86, 400; death of at NAS Dunkirk, 61
Read, Ens. Robert, 78
Read, Ens. Russell "Bart," 299, 301
Recreation, 109, 113, 220, 231, 247, 255, 256–58, 338; *Recreation Bulletin*, 256, 257
Redman, MM2c William, death of at NAS Brest, 91
RFC. *See* Royal Flying Corps

Richards, Lt. Samuel, 256
Richardson, Naval Constructor Holden, and airship specifications, 261
Richardson, Civil engineer O. H., 129
Richardson, Robert (radio operator), 180
RNAS. *See* Royal Naval Air Service
Roben, Sqdr. Cdr. Douglas, 329, 336
Robinson, G/Sgt. Robert, 336, 342
Robinson, Lt., 173
Rochambeau (ship), 260
Rochefort, 19, 35, 263, 271, 272, 273, 278, 398; dirigible station plans for, 22, 82, 125, 262, 267, 278, 348, 352
Rodgers, Lt.(jg) (later Commodore) John, 5
Roe, Ens. George T., 166
Roehampton balloon school, 150, 153, 228, 268; poor performance by Navy personnel at, 268–69
Rolls-Royce motors, 1, 157, 161, 179, 374, 391
Rome, naval aviation headquarters in, 126, 288, 289, 311
Romulus, Lt.(jg) George, 90
Roosevelt, Franklin D. (asst. secretary of the navy), 74, 113, 123, 142, 144–46, 255, 345, 353, 355, 358, 362–63, 364, 366, 369, 407n32; demobilization role, 362–63, 364, 366; illness of, 146; inspection tour in summer 1918, 74, 113, 123, 144–145, 255; recommendations, 145–46
Roptker, Harry (observer), 103
Round, Ens. Glenn, 276
Rowen, Harold (pilot), 102
Royal Air Force (RAF), 48, 65, 75; amalgamation and, 137, 139–40; late war planning with, 346, 349; Northern Bombing Group and, 315, 330, 333–34, 335–36, 343, 403n18
Royal Flying Corps (RFC), 40, 65, 150, 152, 153, 168, 209, 251, 379n45
Royal Naval Air Service (RNAS), 149; Americans serving with, 91, 154–67, 171–73; at Dunkirk, 18, 56, 64, 65, 134
Royal Navy (RN), 7, 149, 262, 391n15; aviation experiments and, 358; at Felixstowe/Harwich, 156, 161; in Ireland, 209, 214, 228, 229
Rumill, Ens. George, 171, 184

Sangatte aerodrome, 323, 330–31
Sargent, Ens. Howard, 116, 134
Sayles, LCdr. William N., 12–13, 14, 20, 26, 28, 35, 128, 135–36; Jackson and, 21

Scarlett, Capt. Francis, 134–35, 139, 389n28
Seattle (ship), 8, 34
Schieffelin, Ens. John, 136, 159, 174, 177, 241, 258
Schofield, Capt. Frank H., 51, 349, 405
Scroggs, Ens., 269, 270
Seaplanes. *See* Short seaplanes
Second Yale Unit, 29, 87, 162, 193, 251
Shaw, Ens. George, 172
Sheely, CMM(A) Irving: at Dunkirk, 63, 68, 71, 383n25; First Aeronautic Detachment, recruit with, 10–11, 13, 34, 37–38, 42; with Northern Bombing Group, 326, 334–35; training with RNAS, 154–55
Short seaplanes: problems with, 165, 172, 235; use at British bases, 157, 165, 167, 168, 171–72, 173, 176–77, 233, 235, 240, 391n14
Shumway, Ens. (later Lt.[jg]) Carl, 229; commanding officer at NAS Castletownbere, 223, 228, 229
Sigourney (ship), 268
Sims, Vice Adm. William S., 127; amalgamation controversy and, 137, 138, 140; aviation equipment problems and, 143–44, 145; Benson and, 51; Commander U.S. Naval Forces Operating in European Waters, 2, 6, 7, 13, 17; Capt. Hutch Cone appointed head of naval aviation in Europe, 26–27, 28; demobilization and, 359–63 passim; Edwards and, 47, 134, 356; future of naval aviation and, 358; inspection trips by, 37, 85, 95, 228; Italian program and, 287–88, 289, 303; Jackson and, 21, 26, 27–28; liaison with Allies attitudes concerning, 134; Northern Bombing Group and, 75, 319, 320, 322, 324, 325, 327, 337; planning for 1919 and, 350; promotions and, 140–41; reorganization of naval aviation and, 147, 214; U.S. Army and, 306, 310; Westervelt Board and, 354–55; Whiting and, 17, 28, 379n34; Rear Adm. Henry Wilson and, 52
Sinn Fein, 208, 211, 212, 213, 217, 220, 349, 394
Sinton, Asst. Surgeon Arthur, 7, 11, 15, 31, 40, 44
Skaggs, Andrew (observer), 100
Smead, Cdr. Walter, 354
Smith, Capt. Bernard "Barney," 5, 7, 14, 17, 19, 26, 75, 167, 250, 309

428 Index

Smith, Edward (observer), death of at NAS Dunkirk, 70
Smith, Lt. (jg) Edward "Shorty," 64, 150, 151, 152
Smith, CMM E. M., 301
Smith, Ens. G. A., 120, 135
Smith, Ens. Kenneth, 29, 42, 93, 95, 100, 101, 103; forced landing at sea, 94–95; submarine attacked by, 101–2
Smith-Barry, Lt. Col. Robert, as founder of RFC School of Special Flying at Gosport, 150
Solhaus, Asst. Surgeon Samuel, 289
Sopwith Camel aircraft, 65, 77, 151, 153, 320
Sopwith Pup aircraft, 157
South Dogger Bank light ship, 183
Spencer, Lt. Earl W. "Win," 20, 21
Spider Web antisubmarine patrol, 4, 235; description of, 159
Sprague, LQM(A) George, 13
Sprague, Ens. William, 102–103
St. Inglevert aerodrome, 145, 330–31, 334, 364; Northern Bombing Group activities at, 340–41
St. Nazaire, 12, 15, 20, 34, 93, 271
St. Pol aerodrome, 18, 21, 58, 382
St. Raphael, 8, 15, 22; First Aeronautic Detachment mechanics training at, 33–34; pilot training at, 40–41
St. Trojan naval air station, 8, 15, 16, 19, 22, 44, 82; bomb explosion at, 116–17; construction, 115–16; operational history, 116–18; selection and description, 115–16; postwar disposition and history, 118–19
Stanley, Ens. Henry, 118
Stevens, Lt.(jg) Albert "Doc," 33, 41, 58, 59, 211; capture of, 73, 249
Stevenson, A. H. (wireless operator), 162
Stockhausen, Asst. Paymaster Thomas, 56, 59
Stone, Ens. E. A., 235
Stone, LCdr. A. J., 135
Stonehenge, training Navy personnel at, 124, 325, 327–28, 334
Stoppel, Ens. Fred, 269
Stringham (ship), 268
Sturtevant, Ens. Albert, 29; death of, 162; RNAS Felixstowe service at, 157, 158, 162
Submarines (Allied), 17, 237, 239, 240
Sugden, Lt. Charles "Chick," 99–100, 103, 126, 250
Sultana (ship), 268

Sunbeam motor, 165, 235, 374
Swaythling, Lord and Lady, 338

Taber, Ens. Leslie "Tex," 340
Talbot, Lt. Ralph, 336, 342; death of, 342
Talieferro, Ens. Albert, 301
Tatulinski, Ens. Charles, death of at NAS Dunkirk, 73
Taylor, Lt. Caleb, death of, 342
Taylor, Lt. Mosely, 334
Taylor (ship), 268
Tellier aircraft, 17, 93, 94, 96, 125, 233
Terres, Ens. Hugh, death of in Italy, 333
"Timbertown," 217, 219
"Tintown," 217, 219
Tours, 8, 15, 18–19; First Aeronautic Detachment training at, 22, 28–32
Towers, LCdr. John, 5, 35, 51, 317, 368, 369; testimony before General Board, 317
Trail, Ens. Oscar, 110
Train, Cdr. (later Capt.) Charles R., 285, 287–88, 291–92, 301, 351–52; Callan, relations with, 289–90; LaGuardia, difficulties with, 305–6, 309–10
Training: at Ayr, 152–54; at Bolsena, 292–96; at Eastchurch-Leysdown, 154–56; at Cazaux, 38; at Clermont-Ferrand, 325–27; at Gosport, 150–52; at Cranwell, 54; at Hourtin, 39–40; at Malpensa, 308–9; at Moutchic, 37–38, 41–42, 85–87, 87–89; at St. Raphael, 32–34, 40–41; at Tours, 28–32; at Turnberry, 152
Tréguier naval air station, 16, 22, 50, 82; civilian population, relations with, 105; demobilization and postwar history, 106; description, 104; operational history, 104–5
Trenchard, Gen. Hugh, 344, 403
Trompeloup. *See* Pauillac
Turnberry gunnery school, 59, 150, 152, 209
Tuttle, QM2c F. H., 31
Twining, Capt. Nathan C., 27, 43, 147, 328, 346

U-boats: Allied plans concerning, 22, 24; antisubmarine operations and tactics, 15, 20, 67, 97, 224, 227, 231–34, 236–40, 251, 395n1; attacks on, 71–72, 83, 102–3, 155, 164, 177, 184, 216, 219, 238, 262; bases for, 15, 55, 66, 314–15, 320–21, 395n1; capabilities of, 67, 71, 83, 95–96, 106, 209, 215, 219, 232, 314, 318; Flexistowe patrols,

159–61; intelligence, importance of, 171, 214–15, 239–40, 248; Whiting's views concerning, 22, 24, 25
Underwood, A. M. (observer), 341
United Kingdom. *See* Great Britain
Utah, 214, 229, 230, 357
Uxbridge, training of Navy personnel at, 328

Van der Veer, Lt. Norman, 44
Van Fleet, Ens. William C., 59, 77
Vaschalde, LCdr., 35
Vath, Earl (observer/electrician), death of, 117
Velie, Ens. Harry C., death of at Ayr, 153
Venice, 126, 288–301 passim
Venice, Gulf of, 312, 348, 369
Very lights, 160, 172, 177, 218
Vogt, Ens. John, death of at NAS Dunkirk, 73, 401
Voorhees, Ens. Dudley, 298
Vorys, Ens. John, 29; RNAS Felixstowe, activities at, 157–58, 161, 162; Hourtin, training at, 39; St. Raphael, training at, 40–41

Walker, Lt.(jg) Samuel, 29, 42, 93, 95, 96; in Italy, 307–9, 333
Walton, Ens. Mark, 293
Wardwell, Ens. Charles, 70, 74, 79, 295
Weddell, Thomas (enlisted pilot), death of at NAS Le Croisic, 96, 97–98
Wershimer, Sgt. Harry, 336
Westervelt, Cdr. George 21, 23, 26, 27, 353; Bolling Commission, member of, 20
Westervelt Board, 131, 141, 146, 345, 353–56
Wexford naval air station, 50, 125, 209, 211, 212; construction, 219–21; demobilization and postwar history, 221–22; operational history, 213–18 passim, 221; selection and description, 219
Whiddy Island (Bantry Bay) naval air station, 50, 209, 211; conditions at, 212, 222; construction, 222–23; demobilization and postwar history, 216, 224; disciplinary problems, 222–23; operational history, 213, 215, 223–24

White, Ens. Lawrence, 288, 311
White, Ens. Walter, 289, 303
Whitehouse, Ens. Robert, 237
Whiting, LCdr. Kenneth, 3, 26–28 passim, 42, 122, 147, 149, 157, 317, 352, 360, 368; Dunkirk, inspection trips, 17–18, 21–22, 56–57, 90, 92, 99, 106, 119, 128; early career, 7–8; French coastal sites, inspection, 18–20; French officials negotiations with, 13–17; First Aeronautic Detachment, forming of, 7; initial proposals by, 20–21; NAS Killingholme and, 44, 47, 169, 168–69, 171, 173–84 passim, 328; orders regarding First Aeronautic Detachment, 9; organizing Paris headquarters, 22, 22–25
Wicks, Lt. Zeno, 120, 121
Wilcox, Ens. Harold, 159, 171, 180, 183, 400
Wilkinson, Homer (mechanic), 94, 95, 385
Williams, Lt. Al, 300
Wilson, Rear Adm. Henry B., 27, 52, 83, 90, 92; relations with Sims, 52
Wilson, Bsn. G. A., 121
Wilson, Woodrow (president), 83, 154, 277
Wimperis bombsights, 86, 234
Winslow (ship), 268
Women at headquarters, 48

Yarnell, Cdr. Harry, 51
Yeomanettes, 48, 253
YMCA. *See* Young Men's Christian Association
Young Men's Christian Association (YMCA): facilities, 37, 96, 108–9, 247; services provided by, 12, 34, 226, 258, 294, 297
Young, Ens. Franklin, 73, 74, 79
Young, MM2c John, 103

Zeebrugge, 15, 18, 55, 67, 162, 361, 381n1; bombing of, 57, 67, 68, 321, 334–35; defenses/fortifications at, 66, 315
Zeppelins (German rigid airships), 10, 39, 41, 150, 173, 261, 349; zeppelin patrols, 1, 178–79, 181. *See also* Lighter-than-Air (LTA) operations
Zodiac airship, 264, 278, 397

Geoffrey R. Rossano has studied early military aviation for four decades. He is the editor of *The Price of Honor: The World War One Letters of Naval Aviator Kenneth MacLeish*.

NEW PERSPECTIVES ON MARITIME HISTORY AND NAUTICAL ARCHAEOLOGY
Edited by James C. Bradford and Gene Allen Smith

The Maritime Heritage of the Cayman Islands, by Roger C. Smith (2000; first paperback edition, 2001; second paperback edition, 2019)
The Three German Navies: Dissolution, Transition, and New Beginnings, 1945–1960, by Douglas C. Peifer (2002)
The Rescue of the Gale Runner: Death, Heroism, and the U.S. Coast Guard, by Dennis L. Noble (2002; first paperback edition, 2008)
Brown Water Warfare: The U.S. Navy in Riverine Warfare and the Emergence of a Tactical Doctrine, 1775–1970, by R. Blake Dunnavent (2003)
Sea Power in the Medieval Mediterranean: The Catalan-Aragonese Fleet in the War of the Sicilian Vespers, by Lawrence V. Mott (2003)
An Admiral for America: Sir Peter Warren, Vice Admiral of the Red, 1703–1752, by Julian Gwyn (2004)
Maritime History as World History, edited by Daniel Finamore (2004; first paperback edition, 2004)
Counterpoint to Trafalgar: The Anglo-Russian Invasion of Naples, 1805–1806, by William Henry Flayhart III (paperback edition, 2004)
Life and Death on the Greenland Patrol, 1942, by Thaddeus D. Novak, edited by P.J. Capelotti (2005; first paperback edition, 2014)
X Marks the Spot: The Archaeology of Piracy, edited by Russell K. Skowronek and Charles R. Ewen (2006; first paperback edition, 2007)
Industrializing American Shipbuilding: The Transformation of Ship Design and Construction, 1820–1920, by William H. Thiesen (2006)
Admiral Lord Keith and the Naval War against Napoleon, by Kevin D. McCranie (2006)
Commodore John Rodgers: Paragon of the Early American Navy, by John H. Schroeder (2006)
Borderland Smuggling: Patriots, Loyalists, and Illicit Trade in the Northeast, 1783–1820, by Joshua M. Smith (2006; first paperback edition, 2019)
Brutality on Trial: "Hellfire" Pedersen, "Fighting" Hansen, and the Seamen's Act of 1915, by E. Kay Gibson (2006)
Uriah Levy: Reformer of the Antebellum Navy, by Ira Dye (2006)
Crisis at Sea: The United States Navy in European Waters in World War I, by William N. Still Jr. (2006)
Chinese Junks on the Pacific: Views from a Different Deck, by Hans K. Van Tilburg (2007; first paperback edition, 2013)
Eight Thousand Years of Maltese Maritime History: Trade, Piracy, and Naval Warfare in the Central Mediterranean, by Ayse Devrim Atauz (2008)
Merchant Mariners at War: An Oral History of World War II, by George J. Billy and Christine M. Billy (2008)
The Steamboat Montana and the Opening of the West: History, Excavation, and Architecture, by Annalies Corbin and Bradley A. Rodgers (2008)
Attack Transport: USS Charles Carroll in World War II, by Kenneth H. Goldman (2008)
Diplomats in Blue: U.S. Naval Officers in China, 1922–1933, by William Reynolds Braisted (2009)
Sir Samuel Hood and the Battle of the Chesapeake, by Colin Pengelly (2009)
Voyages, the Age of Sail: Documents in American Maritime History, Volume I, 1492–1865, edited by Joshua M. Smith and the National Maritime Historical Society (2009)
Voyages, the Age of Engines: Documents in American Maritime History, Volume II,

1865–Present, edited by Joshua M. Smith and the National Maritime Historical Society (2009)

HMS Fowey Lost and Found: Being the Discovery, Excavation, and Identification of a British Man-of-War Lost off the Cape of Florida in 1748, by Russell K. Skowronek and George R. Fischer (2009)

American Coastal Rescue Craft: A Design History of Coastal Rescue Craft Used by the United States Life-Saving Service and the United States Coast Guard, by William D. Wilkinson and Commander Timothy R. Dring, USNR (Retired) (2009)

The Spanish Convoy of 1750: Heaven's Hammer and International Diplomacy, by James A. Lewis (2009)

The Development of Mobile Logistic Support in Anglo-American Naval Policy, 1900–1953, by Peter V. Nash (2009)

Captain "Hell Roaring" Mike Healy: From American Slave to Arctic Hero, by Dennis L. Noble and Truman R. Strobridge (2009; first paperback edition, 2017)

Sovereignty at Sea: U.S. Merchant Ships and American Entry into World War I, by Rodney Carlisle (2009; first paperback edition, 2011)

Commodore Abraham Whipple of the Continental Navy: Privateer, Patriot, Pioneer, by Sheldon S. Cohen (2010; first paperback edition, 2011)

Lucky 73: USS Pampanito's Unlikely Rescue of Allied POWs in WWII, by Aldona Sendzikas (2010)

Cruise of the Dashing Wave: Rounding Cape Horn in 1860, by Philip Hichborn, edited by William H. Thiesen (2010)

Seated by the Sea: The Maritime History of Portland, Maine, and Its Irish Longshoremen, by Michael C. Connolly (2010; first paperback edition, 2011)

The Whaling Expedition of the Ulysses, 1937–38, by Lt. (j.g.) Quentin R. Walsh, U.S. Coast Guard, edited and with an introduction by P.J. Capelotti (2010)

Stalking the U-Boat: U.S. Naval Aviation in Europe during World War I, by Geoffrey L. Rossano (2010; first paperback edition, 2021)

In Katrina's Wake: The U.S. Coast Guard and the Gulf Coast Hurricanes of 2005, by Donald L. Canney (2010)

A Civil War Gunboat in Pacific Waters: Life on Board USS Saginaw, by Hans K. Van Tilburg (2010)

The U.S. Coast Guard's War on Human Smuggling, by Dennis L. Noble (2011)

The Sea Their Graves: An Archaeology of Death and Remembrance in Maritime Culture, by David J. Stewart (2011; first paperback edition, 2019)